HANDBOOK OF SEMICONDUCTOR AND BUBBLE MEMORIES

HANDBOOK OF SEMICONDUCTOR AND BUBBLE MEMORIES

WALTER A. TRIEBEL
Systems Engineer
Texas Instruments Incorporated

ALFRED E. CHU
Product Engineering Group Leader,
Circuits Development and Components
Monroe Systems for Business
Division Litton Industries

PRENTICE-HALL, INC., Englewood Cliffs, NJ 07632

Library of Congress Cataloging in Publication Data

Triebel, Walter A.
Handbook of semiconductor and bubble memories.

Bibliography: p.
Includes index.
1. Computer storage devices. 2. Semiconductor storage devices. 3. Magnetic bubble devices.
I. Chu, Alfred E. II. Title.
TK7895.M4T73 621.3819'5833 81-2468
ISBN 0-13-381251-0 AACR2

Editorial/production supervision and
interior design by Karen Skrable
Manufacturing buyer: Gordon Osbourne
Cover design by: Jayne Conte

Printed in the United States of America

10 9 8 7 6 5 4 3 2 1

Prentice-Hall International, Inc., *London*
Prentice-Hall of Australia Pty. Limited, *Sydney*
Prentice-Hall of Canada, Ltd., *Toronto*
Prentice-Hall of India Private Limited, *New Delhi*
Prentice-Hall of Japan, Inc., *Tokyo*
Prentice-Hall of Southeast Asia Pte. Ltd., *Singapore*
Whitehall Books Limited, *Wellington, New Zealand*

Walter A. Triebel:

To my wife, Frieda

Alfred E. Chu:

To my wife, Susan

CONTENTS

PREFACE

Today's electronic memory marketplace represents one of the most dynamic sectors of the digital electronics industry. The state of the art in memory design is changing every day. New devices such as the magnetic bubble memory are being introduced, higher-capacity devices such as the 128k-bit read-only memory and 64k-bit random-access memory are becoming available, and faster devices are being manufactured such that MOS memory devices are now rivaling bipolar memories for high-speed operation.

This book has been written to fill the gap that exists between books on basic digital electronics and those on the subject of microprocessors. These books have traditionally provided a brief introduction to semiconductor memories. Our book constitutes an extensive study of modern memory devices, including their architecture, operation, standard devices, and applications. The early chapters of the book are devoted to the most widely used semiconductor memory devices—the read-only memory, the random-access memory, and the shift register. Chapters that follow introduce special-purpose memory devices such as the content addressable memory and first-in first-out memory, as well as newer emerging devices such as the programmable logic array, charge-coupled-device memory, and magnetic bubble memory.

Handbook of Semiconductor and Bubble Memories is intended primarily as a reference book for practicing technicians and engineers. As a handbook, it can also serve as a valuable reference for computer science specialists, programmers, and hobbyists. Assignments are provided at the end of each chapter. This will permit its use as a supplementary textbook in courses on basic digital electronics or microprocessors.

The book assumes prior knowledge of basic digital electronic theory and circuitry: number systems, logic gates, Boolean algebra, digital codes, decoders, and multiplexers. The level required of this background is consistent with that of the material in the textbook *Integrated Digital Electronics* by Triebel.

Because individuals in industry have exposure to both new equipment designs and older existing equipment, we have chosen to present material on older memory devices as well as the newer state of the art devices. Every effort has been made to provide popular devices from a wide range of semiconductor manufacturers and to include up-to-date information on these products. However, before using a device for a new design, it is recommended to check with the manufacturer on availability and for the most recent data.

WALTER A. TRIEBEL
ALFRED E. CHU

HANDBOOK OF SEMICONDUCTOR AND BUBBLE MEMORIES

1

INTRODUCTION TO ELECTRONIC MEMORIES

1.1 INTRODUCTION

This book, *Handbook of Semiconductor and Bubble Memories*, is a study of solid-state electronic memories. It covers modern memory circuits, standard memory devices, and their applications.

In recent years, the field of electronic memories has been one of the most dynamic areas of electronics. Since the semiconductor memory was introduced in the early 1960s, continuous advancements have been made in memory technologies and manufacturing processes. The results are that today memories are larger in storage capacity, with faster operating speeds, and with lower prices.

During this period, large growth has been experienced in the marketplace for memory devices. New devices have emerged, new applications have been identified, and the introduction of the microprocessor has led to new types of equipment that require memory. With additional breakthroughs occurring every day, the potential of the memory market is not yet near its limit.

In this chapter, we begin our study of electronic memories by discussing the following topics:

1. The computer and other digital equipment
2. The digital computer system
3. Electronic memories
4. Semiconductor memory technologies
5. Bipolar technologies

6. MOS technologies
7. CCD technology
8. Bubble memories
9. Use of memories in the computer system

1.2 THE COMPUTER AND OTHER DIGITAL EQUIPMENT[1]

Before we start our study of electronic memories, let us begin by introducing the digital computer. A *computer* is an electronic data processing system. *Data* are input to the computer in one form, processed within the computer, and the *information* that results is output or stored for later use. Figure 1.1 shows a modern computer system.

A computer cannot think about how it is to process input data. The user must tell the computer exactly what to do. The procedure by which a computer is told how to work is called *programming.* When operating, the computer follows a set of instructions called the *program.* As the program is executed, these instructions guide the computer step by step through the solution of the problem.

For example, a large department store can use a computer to take care of its charge accounts. In this application, data about items purchased by the customer, such as price and department, are entered into the computer by an operator. This information is stored in the computer under the customer's account number. On the next billing date, a tabular record of each customer's account is output by the computer. This statement is mailed to the customer as a bill.

Electronic computers first became available in the 1940s. These early computers were built with vacuum-tube electronic circuits. In the 1950s, a second generation of computers was built. During this period, transistor

Fig. 1.1 Large-scale computer system (Courtesy of International Business Machines Corp.).

[1] Walter A. Triebel, Integrated Digital Electronics, © 1979, p. 2, courtesy of Prentice-Hall, Inc.

electronic circuitry, instead of tubes, was used to produce more compact and reliable systems.

When the *integrated circuit* came into the electronics market during the 1960s, a third generation of computers appeared. With the integrated circuit (IC), industry could manufacture very complex, high-speed, and reliable computers.

The Minicomputer and Microcomputer[2]

For many years, the computer industry has aimed at developing larger and more powerful systems. The introduction of *small-scale integrated circuits* (SSI), followed by *medium-scale integrated circuits* (MSI), and *large-scale integrated circuits* (LSI) has revolutionized the computer industry. These devices have led the way in expanding the capacity for the large computer system market, but at the same time have permitted the introduction of smaller-scale computer systems: *minicomputers* and *microcomputers.*

As computer use developed, it was found that the powerful computing capability of a large computer was not needed in many applications. Instead, easy access to a smaller-capacity machine was desired by many customers. It is for this requirement that the minicomputer was developed. The minicomputer is also a digital computer system and is capable of performing the same basic operations as the earlier, larger systems, but it has a smaller functional capacity. A modern minicomputer system is illustrated in Fig. 1.2.

Fig. 1.2 Minicomputer system (Digital Equipment Corp.).

[2] Ibid., p. 4.

Fig. 1.3 Microcomputer system (Texas Instruments, Incorporated).

The newest development in the computer industry is the microcomputer. It represents a computer that has been reduced in size and capabilities from that of a minicomputer. However, it still contains all the basic functions of a computer system, but now the system is formed from just a few large-scale integrated circuits. In fact, a small microcomputer can be built into a single electronic device. Figure 1.3 is a typical microcomputer system.

General-Purpose and Special-Purpose Computers[3]

The large-scale computer, minicomputer, and microcomputer are examples of *general-purpose computer systems.* That is, they are designed with the ability to run a large number of different programs. For this reason, they can solve a wide variety of problems.

For instance, one customer can use the computer in a scientific application where its primary function is the solution of complex mathematical problems. A second customer can use the same basic system to perform a business application such as accounting. The basic difference between the two systems is in the customer's application program. In fact, in many applications a single computer is used for both functions.

Today, the minicomputer and microcomputer are continuing the evolution of the computer world with the development of a wide selection of *special-purpose computer systems.* By special purpose, we mean a system that has been tailored to meet the needs of a specific application. Examples of such applications are cash registers and word processors. This tailoring is done by installing a fixed program. Some special-purpose computer systems are shown in Figs. 1.4 through 1.6.

[3] Ibid., p. 3 and 4.

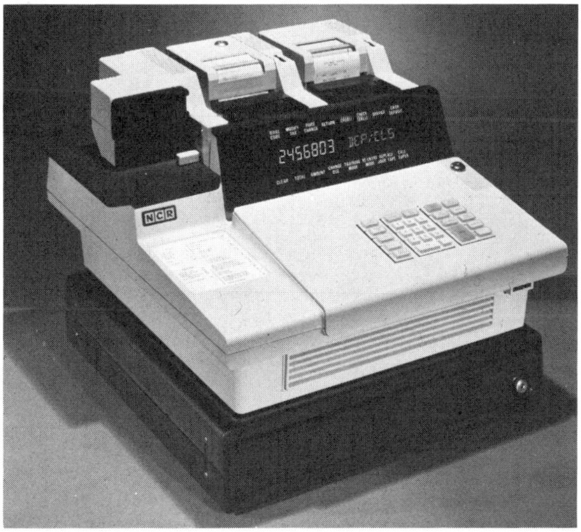

Fig. 1.4 Electronic cash register (NCR Corporation).

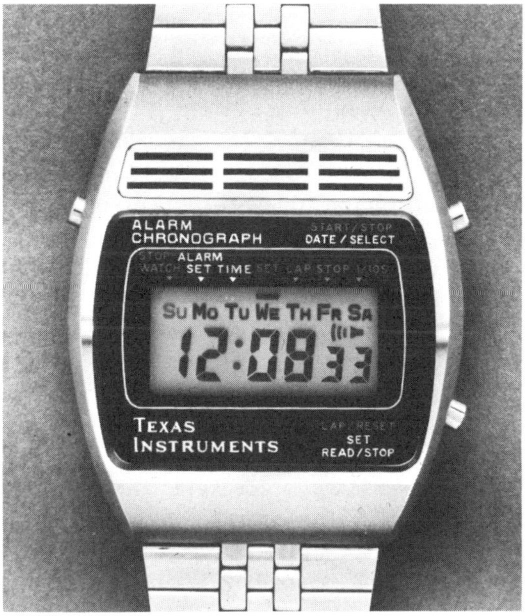

Fig. 1.5 Electronic watch (Texas Instruments, Incorporated).

Fig. 1.6 Electronic toy (Gabriel Industries, a division of CBS, Inc.).

1.3 THE DIGITAL COMPUTER SYSTEM

The computer system is divided into four functional sections. The block diagram of Fig. 1.7 shows the four basic units of a simplified digital computer: *input unit*, *central processing unit*, *memory unit*, and *output unit*. Each section has a special function in terms of overall computer operation.

The central processing unit is the heart of the computer system. It is responsible for performing all arithmetic operations and logic decisions initiated by the program. In addition to its arithmetic and logic functions, the *central processing unit* (CPU) controls overall system operation.

On the other hand, the input and output units permit the CPU to communicate with the outside world. The input unit is used to input information to the CPU for processing. For instance, a Teletype terminal can be used to input the program and data.

After processing, the information that results must be output. This output from the system is under the control of the output section. Examples of output information are printed pages produced by a high-speed printer or a display on a *cathode ray tube* (CRT) screen.

The memory is used to store information such as numbers, names, and addresses. By store, we mean that the memory holds information for pro-

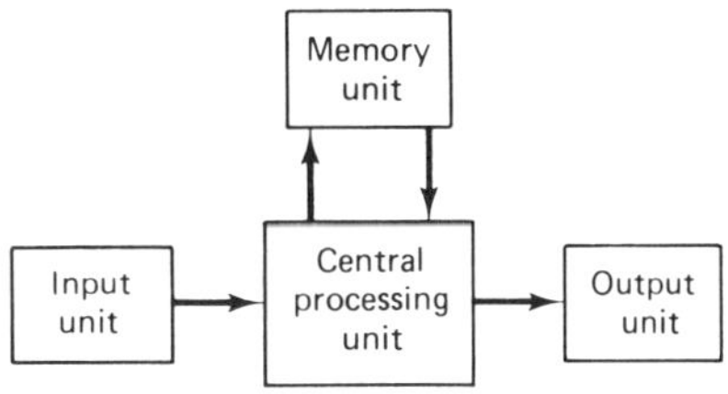

Fig. 1.7 Computer block diagram (Walter A. Triebel, Integrated Digital Electronics, © 1979. Adapted by Permission of Prentice-Hall, Inc., Englewood Cliffs, N.J.).

cessing or for output at a later time. The program that defines the processing to be performed by the computer also resides in the memory.

In computer systems, memory is divided into two sections, known as *primary storage* and *secondary storage.* They are also called *internal memory* and *external memory*, respectively.

The external memory is used for long-term storage of information such as programs, files of data, and files of information that are not in use. In most computers, this part of memory employs storage on magnetic media such as magnetic tapes, magnetic disks, and magnetic drums.

On the other hand, internal memory is used for temporary storage of program, data, and information. For instance, when a program is to be executed, the instructions are first brought in from the external memory together with the files of data and information that it will affect. After this, the program is executed and its files updated while held in the internal memory. When the processing defined by the program is complete, the updated files are returned to the external memory. Here, the program and files are retained for use at a later time.

The internal memory of a computer system usually uses electronic memory instead of storage on a magnetic medium. For example, semiconductor *random-access memory* (RAM) and magnetic core memory are widely used in this part of the computer's memory rather than tape or disk.

Neither electronic component memories nor magnetic-medium storage can satisfy all the requirements of a computer system. Because of this fact, both types are required in most larger computers. For instance, working storage may be provided by semiconductor RAM while long-term storage may be provided on magnetic tape. In many small computers, just electronic memory devices are used.

1.4 ELECTRONIC MEMORIES

In electronics, the term *memory* means the ability to store digital information. Memory is one of the key characteristics of computers and other digital equipment. That is, they have the ability to store and retrieve information. Depending upon the complexity of the system, the amount of storage can range from just a few pieces of information to many billions of pieces.

The ability to store information is made possible by the part of the computer system known as the memory unit. The devices used to build the memory section of a digital computer are called *memories* and can be divided into two main categories: *semiconductor memories* and *magnetic memories.*

Semiconductor Memories

Most modern memory devices are of the semiconductor type. In this type of memory, data are stored in electronic circuits as voltage or current levels. There are many different semiconductor memory devices available; however, the most widely used are the *read-only memory*, *random-access read/write memory*, and *shift register.* Figure 1.8(a) lists semiconductor memory devices in more detail.

Magnetic Memories

The second category includes a combination of memory devices and magnetic storage media. Examples of electronic devices that operate on the principle of magnetism are the *core memory* and *bubble memory. Magnetic tape*, *magnetic disks*, and *magnetic drums* are examples of magnetic memory media. They are listed in Fig. 1.8(b).

In all these devices, information is stored through magnetization instead of electrical signals. That is, data are coded as changes in magnetic flux.

Comparison of Semiconductor and Magnetic Memories

In earlier computer systems, the internal memory was constructed with core memory devices. However, since the introduction of semiconductor memories in the early 1960s, continuous improvements have been made in semiconductor technologies. Today, semiconductor memories are faster, denser, and less expensive than core magnetic memories for internal memory appli-

Read-only memory (ROM)
Programmable read-only memory (PROM)
Erasable programmable read-only memory (EPROM)
Random-access read/write memory (RAM)
Shift register
Programmable logic array (PLA)
First-in first-out memory (FIFO)
Content addressable memory (CAM)
Charge-coupled devices (CCD)

(a)

Core
Bubble memory
Magnetic tape
Magnetic disk
Magnetic drum

(b)

Fig. 1.8 (a) Types of semiconductor memories; (b) types of magnetic memories.

cations. For this reason, semiconductor memories are more widely used in modern digital equipment.

When comparing semiconductor and magnetic memory devices, RAM is normally compared to core. RAM offers the following advantages over magnetic core:

1. Smaller size
2. Higher operating speed
3. Requires less power
4. More versatility, resulting in a wider variety of storage devices
5. Greater compatibility with other electronic circuits in the system
6. Wider range of operating speeds
7. Lower cost

The *charge-coupled device* (CCD) is another semiconductor-type memory. It compares to the magnetic bubble memory, not core. Both of these devices offer substantially larger storage capacity than does RAM or core. That is, their capacity lies in the gap between that offered by RAM or core and the very large capacities of mass storage media such as tapes, disks, and drums. Both of these devices are relatively new; therefore, the state of the art of these types of memories is moving forward every day.

Figure 1.9 presents a comparison of the memory capacity of the most popular types of semiconductor and magnetic memories. In this book, we concentrate on semiconductor memories and the newest magnetic memory device, the bubble memory.

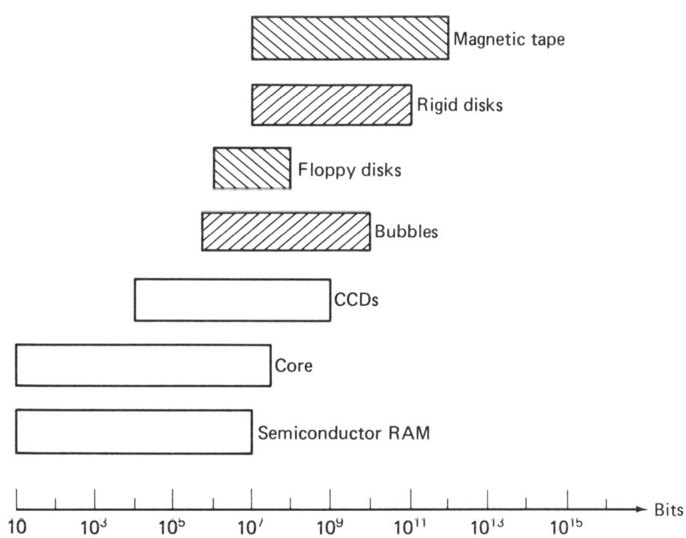

Fig. 1.9 Total memory storage capacity.

Memory Packaging[4]

The semiconductor memories that are available in the electronic marketplace are manufactured as integrated-circuit devices. The memory circuits themselves are known as large-scale integrated (LSI) circuits. To be called a large-scale integrated circuit, the device must have a complexity that is equivalent to more than 100 logic gates.

Some integrated memory devices are shown in Fig. 1.10(a). The chip that contains the circuitry is encased in a plastic or ceramic package. Ceramic material improves the operating-temperature characteristics of the device. The number of leads on the package can range from 8 to 24 pins, with the most common having 16 and 24 pins. Some of these leads provide dual functions: for example, one function during programming and another during normal operation.

Magnetic bubble memory devices are packaged in a similar way to semiconductor memories. However, they normally require larger packages. Figure 1.10(b) presents a typical magnetic bubble memory.

1.5 SEMICONDUCTOR MEMORY TECHNOLOGIES

The process by which a semiconductor memory is made is called a *technology*. All semiconductor technologies are grouped into two general cate-

(a) (b)

Fig. 1.10 (a) Typical semiconductor memory (Texas Instruments, Incorporated); (b) typical bubble memory (Texas Instruments, Incorporated).

[4] Ibid., p. 7, 8, and 11.

gories called *bipolar technologies* and *MOS technologies.* Figure 1.11 shows the technologies in each category.

Memory devices manufactured with these technologies differ in their electrical performance. The performance of semiconductor memories are compared in these ways:

1. Density
2. Speed
3. Power consumption
4. Cost
5. Noise immunity
6. Reliability

Before going any further, let us look into what each of these properties mean. The *density* of the circuitry produced by a technology is important because it determines the maximum amount of storage that can be provided on a single chip. On the other hand, characteristics such as *speed, power consumption*, and *cost* affect the whole system. Applications that require solution of complex equations will need to be implemented with high-speed memory devices whereas battery-operated systems must be implemented with low-power memories.

Noise immunity is a measure of how sensitive the memory is to environmental noise. This property must be considered if the circuitry is to be used in applications that require use in a noisy environment, such as in an automobile. Memories with low noise immunity cannot be used in this environment.

The last property, *reliability*, defines how long the memory is expected to work without failure. Reliability relates to the maturity of the technology. In general, technologies with high reliability are those that have been in use for the longest period of time. This is because the manufacturers have had time to refine their manufacturing techniques.

Both groups of technologies have their particular advantages and dis-

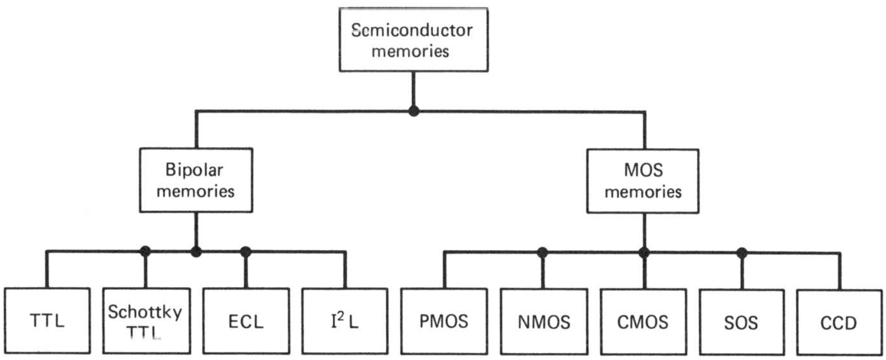

Fig. 1.11 Semiconductor memory technologies.

advantages. Basically, bipolar technology devices have the advantage in the area of speed, for they are high-speed devices. MOS memory technologies have the edge in most other areas.

Bipolar Technologies

Bipolar technology is the older and more mature of the two general memory categories. As shown in Fig. 1.11, there are four main bipolar technologies used to manufacture memory integrated circuits. They are *standard TTL technology*, *Schottky TTL technology*, *ECL technology*, and *I^2L technology*.

The one characteristic common to each of these technologies is that the memory circuitry within the IC is made from resistors, diodes, and bipolar transistors. Manufacturing of the chip that contains the circuitry begins with a doped silicon wafer. The circuit is built onto the wafer through a complex sequence of photolithographic and diffusion processes. The disadvantage of bipolar technologies is that the complexity of bipolar circuitry limits the density that can be obtained with bipolar memories.

Most of the bipolar memory devices in use today are made with the standard *transistor-transistor logic* (TTL) technology or the newer Schottky TTL technology. Using these technologies, the memory circuit is constructed with TTL logic gates or flip-flops. The storage element made with both technologies is essentially the same. One difference is that in Schottky TTL a *barrier diode* is added between the base and collector leads of each transistor. This diode acts as a clamp and prevents the transistors from saturating. The result is faster operating speed than standard TTL. A transistor with barrier diode connected is shown in Fig. 1.12(a). Figure 1.12(b) is a symbol used to represent this connection, which is known as a *Schottky transistor.*

The general operating characteristics of TTL technology memories are high operating speed, moderate density, high power consumption, relatively high cost, and relative sensitivity to noise. Schottky devices have the same basic characteristics; however, they operate at an even faster speed. TTL memories are widely used in applications that require high-speed operation, moderate storage capacity, and where power consumption is not critical.

The next bipolar technology is *emitter-coupled logic* (ECL) technology. The fastest memory devices available today are made with this technology. ECL is a current-mode logic rather than a voltage-mode logic as in TTL technologies. It uses nonsaturating circuitry which enables high-speed operation.

Even though ECL has the edge over other types of circuitry in speed,

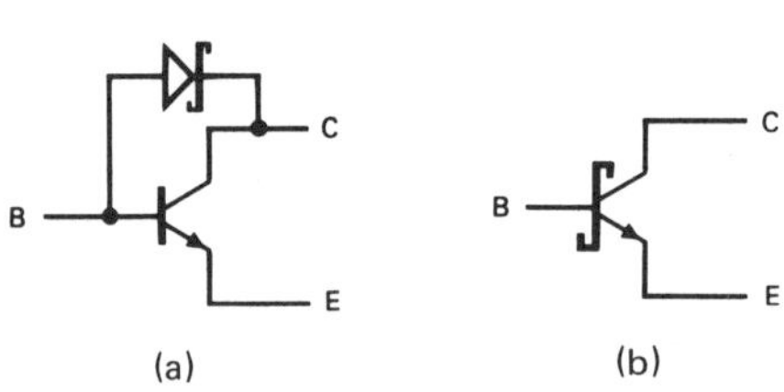

Fig. 1.12 (a) Transistor with barrier diode (Fairchild Camera and Instrument Corp.); (b) Schottky transistor symbol (Fairchild Camera and Instrument Corp.).

disadvantages are found in almost all other operating characteristics. They have the highest power consumption of all technologies; circuit density is very low, permitting only small-capacity devices to be manufactured; and they are the most expensive type of memory to produce. For this reason, ECL memories are used only in applications where very high-speed operation is the only concern.

Integrated-injection logic technology (I^2L) is the newest bipolar technology. It shows promise for use in manufacturing memory ICs. I^2L appears to offer opportunity for producing high-speed devices with high density, low power consumption, and good noise immunity.

Devices manufactured with I^2L technology have the unique property of adjustable speed/power operating characteristics. That is, the operation of the memory can be adjusted for high-speed operation or low power consumption by changing the value of an external resistor. This permits use of the memory device in a wide variety of applications.

Not all types of memory devices can be built with bipolar technologies. For example, erasable programmable read-only memories cannot be made with bipolar circuitry.

Metal-Oxide Semiconductor Technologies

The building blocks of *metal-oxide semiconductor* (MOS) technology memories are the *P-channel metal-oxide semiconductor field-effect transistor* (*MOSFET*) and the *N-channel MOSFET*. Figure 1.11 shows the five primary MOS technologies: *PMOS*, *NMOS*, *CMOS*, *SOS*, and *CCD*. Even though the CCD memories are made with MOS processes, they differ from other MOS technologies in that the storage elements are *channels* of integrated capacitors instead of MOSFETs.

MOS circuitry is formed on a wafer of silicon in a similar way to that used to manufacture bipolar devices. However, in this case the wafer is not initially doped. Moreover, the sequence of photolithographic operations and impurity diffusions used to produce the circuitry are somewhat simpler than for bipolar memories. The simplicity of MOS integrated circuitry results in much higher density memory devices than can be produced with bipolar technologies.

The first MOS technology used to manufacture memory devices was PMOS technology. In this technology, P-channel MOSFETs are used to make memory ICs. The results are high-density, low-cost memories, but with very slow operating speed and high power consumption. The slow speed and high power severely limit the range of applications for PMOS memories. Early MOS memories were made with this process; however, it is not widely used with newer ICs. This is because other MOS technologies have evolved that have overcome the limitations of PMOS.

For example, the next MOS technology, NMOS, results in faster operating speeds. Here N-channel MOSFETs instead of P-channel MOSFETs are employed as the memory element. Not only are high operating speeds achieved with NMOS, but it also results in higher-density circuitry than does PMOS. These devices are still much slower than bipolar memories and do not overcome the high power limitation.

NMOS technology presently produces the least expensive semiconductor memories. However, the state of the art in NMOS technology has not yet reached its limits in terms of speed and density. Today, NMOS devices are the primary ones used in new digital equipment.

The problem of high power consumption was overcome with CMOS technology. CMOS stands for *complementary symmetry metal-oxide semiconductor logic*. The circuit is built onto a silicon substrate called *bulk silicon*. Both P-channel and N-channel MOSFETs are used together to make a low-power storage circuit. In this circuit, one MOSFET acts as an electronic switch and the other as a load resistance. The complexity of this circuit leads to poor density and ICs with lower storage capacity.

The resulting memory device has very good power characteristics, but with slower operating speed. In fact, some CMOS memories are slower than those made with PMOS. However, memories made with CMOS technology have an added advantage in that they have higher noise immunity than do memories made with any other technology.

Improvements in the characteristics of CMOS memories are achieved by switching from a bulk silicon substrate to what is known as a *silicon-on-sapphire substrate*. The results are faster operating speed and higher circuit density.

CMOS and SOS memories find wide use in applications where power consumption is critical and in high-noise environments. For instance, equipment that operates from batteries requires CMOS memories.

CCD memory has resulted from research into methods of obtaining large storage capacity. It employs integrated capacitors as the storage element instead of P-channel or N-channel MOSFETs. Data are stored as charge on these capacitors. The simplicity of this storage element permits storage capacities far in excess of those available with NMOS technology.

The large capacity and slow operating characteristics of the CCD memory make it competitive with disk memory for use in small computer systems. For the future, the CCD technology appears to offer low-cost, large-capacity memories with slow operating speed. However, progress with this technology has been slow.

As for bipolar technologies, all types of memory devices are not manufactured using MOS circuitry. Examples are the *programmable logic array* (PLA) and *content addressable memory* (CAM). These two devices are known for their high-speed operation and are exclusively made with bipolar circuitry. Recent refinements of the MOS process known as *DMOS* (*double-diffusion MOS*), *VMOS* (*vertical MOS*), and *HMOS* (*high-performance MOS*) appear to bring MOS device capabilities to a point where its performance challenges that of bipolar technologies.

Comparison of Technologies

Each technology has a characteristic that makes it beneficial in specific categories of applications. For instance:

ECL—very high speed applications
TTL and Schottky TTL—high-speed applications
PMOS and NMOS—high-capacity applications
CMOS and SOS—low-power applications

The ideal memory would have very high speed with very low power consumption. These conditions are defined by what is known as the *speed/power product*. This is a figure of merit that indicates the efficiency of a technology.

We have found that no single technology completely satisfies both the high-speed and low-power conditions. Memories that are very fast require a large amount of power, and those that require very low power have a slow operating speed. Memories made with the SOS technology are the closest to an ideal memory. They have relatively high speed operation with very low power consumption. For these reasons, SOS has the best figure of merit of all memory technologies.

Figure 1.13 shows a comparison of the operating speeds for the various technologies.

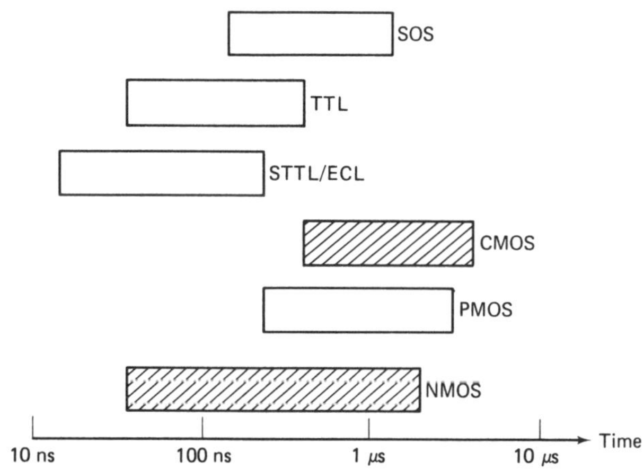

Fig. 1.13 Operating-speed comparison of various technologies.

1.6 MAGNETIC BUBBLE MEMORY TECHNOLOGY

The most recent developments in memory technology have been with a solid-state magnetic device known as *bubble memory*. Magnetic bubble memory (MBM) differs from semiconductor memory in that the logic states of data are represented by magnetic domains called *bubbles.*

The small size of the magnetic bubble results in the ability to manufacture memory devices with very large storage capacity. Presently, MBM devices are available with storage capacities more than 10 times higher than those made with semiconductor technologies. This large storage capacity is its primary advantage over semiconductor memory. Moreover, the MBM has the added advantage of *nonvolatility:* that is, the ability to retain stored data after the power supply has been removed.

Like the CCD, the MBM, with its high storage capacity and slow operating speed, competes for applications with magnetic devices such as the disk memory system.

1.7 USE OF MEMORY IN THE COMPUTER SYSTEM

From our earlier description of the computer, we found that the main function of memory in a system is storage of information. Moreover, we found that memory was divided into an internal and an external memory. The internal memory is used for working data. This section normally requires high-speed operation but does not normally require large storage capacity. Therefore, it is implemented with semiconductor or core memory. Figure 1.14 shows a typical memory circuit board from a minicomputer system.

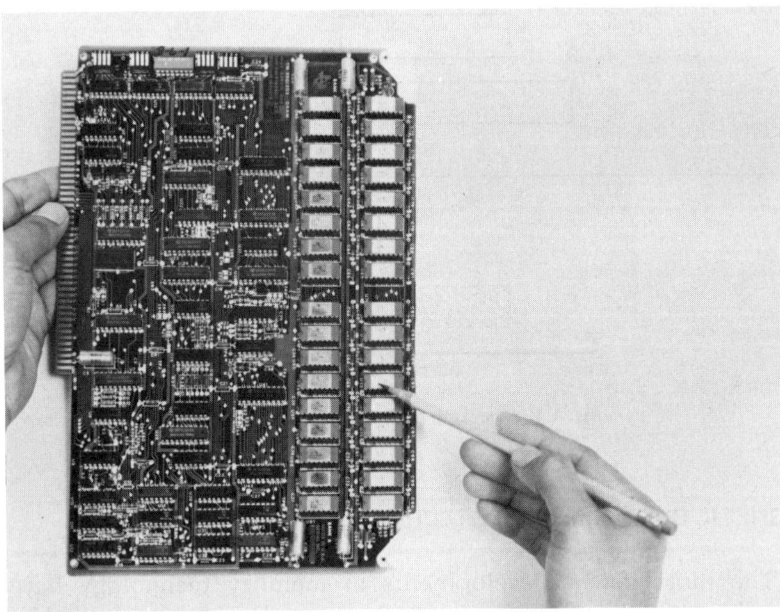

Fig. 1.14 Semiconductor memory circuit board (Texas Instruments, Incorporated).

The other part, the external memory, is used for storage of data, information, and programs that are not in use. External memory can be slow-speed but requires large storage capacity. In this area, magnetic-media memories such as disks, tapes, and drums are employed. These media are formed by putting a thin magnetic coating onto a flexible or rigid nonmagnetic surface. Examples are the floppy disk and rigid disk. A typical floppy disk is shown in Fig. 1.15(a).

A medium such as a disk must be inserted into a memory system that moves the medium and magnetic pickup, called the head, to the position where data are to be stored or from which data are to be retrieved. Figure 1.15(b) shows a floppy disk system.

But these are not the only applications of memory in the computer system. Memories serve many other important functions. Examples are mathematical look-up tables, code converters, character generators, data-rate buffers, implementing combinational logic, and sequential controllers.

For instance, in the input section of the computer a code-converter memory may be required to convert the coded information input from a Teletype terminal to a form that can be processed by the CPU.

At the output side of the system, memories find another function. Here a character generator may be required to code output information for presentation as 5×7 dot characters on a visual display unit.

These are just a few of the many ways in which memories can be applied in digital equipment. Memory devices play an important role in the design of modern digital systems.

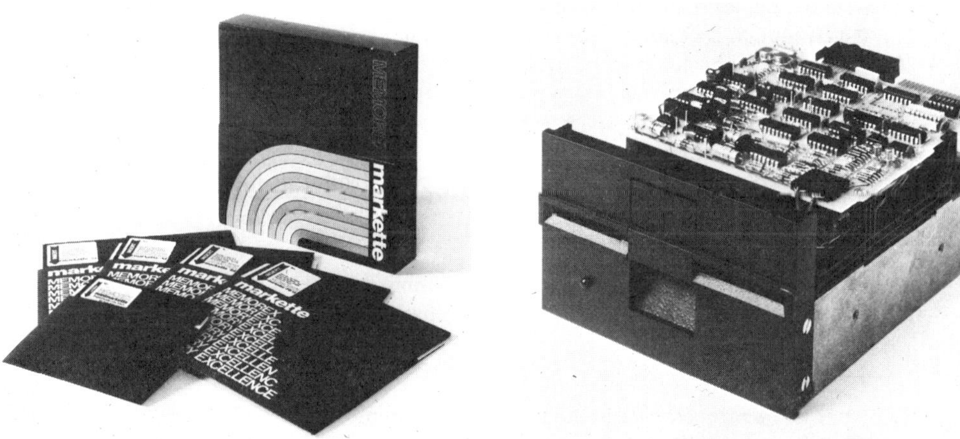

(a) (b)

Fig. 1.15 (a) Floppy disk (Memorex Corp.); (b) floppy disk memory system (Shugart Associates).

ASSIGNMENTS

Section 1.2

1. Name the three parts of the data processing cycle.
2. What guides the computer as to how to process data?
3. What type of device is the building block of third-generation computers?
4. What does "LSI" stand for?
5. What is the smallest-scale computer called?
6. Give three examples of special-purpose computers.

Section 1.3

7. List the four major parts of a computer system.
8. What does "CPU" stand for?
9. In which block of the computer system would a keyboard be used?
10. What is the other name for internal memory?
11. Name three magnetic storage units used in external memory.
12. What are the two most widely used memory devices for internal memory?

Section 1.4

13. What are the three most widely used semiconductor memory devices?
14. Give the names of two magnetic memory devices.
15. List three advantages of semiconductor RAM over core memory for internal memory applications.
16. To which semiconductor memory device is the magnetic bubble memory compared?

Section 1.5

17. Name the six performance characteristics used to compare semiconductor technologies.
18. Give the names of four bipolar technologies.
19. Which bipolar technologies are the most widely used?
20. Which bipolar technology produces the fastest operating circuitry?
21. What is the major disadvantage of bipolar technologies?
22. Give the names of three MOS technologies.
23. What is the primary advantage of NMOS technology over bipolar technologies?
24. Which MOS technologies have the capability of producing low-power circuitry?

Section 1.6

25. How are data represented in a magnetic bubble memory?
26. What is the major advantage of MBM compared to semiconductor memory?

Section 1.7

27. What is the primary requirement of internal memory in a computer system?
28. What is the primary requirement for external memory of a computer system?
29. List four uses of electronic memory other than primary storage and secondary storage.

2

READ-ONLY MEMORY

2.1 INTRODUCTION

In this chapter, we begin our study of semiconductor memories with read-only memory. The earlier part of the chapter concentrates on the theory of mask-programmable read-only memories: architecture, static operation, electrical characteristics, and standard ROM devices.

After the theory of mask-programmable ROMs has been developed, our interest for the rest of the chapter turns to additional members of the ROM family, such as the programmable read-only memory, erasable read-only memory, and dynamic read-only memories. Following are the topics discussed:

1. Read-only memory
2. ROM architecture
3. Mask programming
4. Static ROM operation and standard devices
5. Programmable read-only memory and standard PROM devices
6. Erasable programmable read-only memory and standard EPROM devices
7. Dynamic ROM operation and standard devices

2.2 READ-ONLY MEMORY

Read-only memory (ROM) is a type of semiconductor memory device. The information stored within a ROM integrated circuit is permanent in nature.

For some devices the data must be built in during manufacturing, and in others data must be electrically entered. The process of entering data into a ROM is called *programming*.

As the name implies, information stored within ROM can only be read out. ROM memories play an important role in modern digital system design. They are used primarily in applications where the data do not change frequently.

Types of Read-Only Memories

Two major semiconductor technologies are used in the manufacturing of ROM integrated circuits. These processes, called bipolar technology and MOS technology, are listed in Fig. 2.1. By using these technologies, we can make three basic types of read-only memories: *mask-programmable read-only memory*, *electrically programmable read-only memory*, and *erasable programmable read-only memory*.

Let us begin by looking more closely into the first type of read-only memory, mask programmable memory. A mask-programmable ROM is a device for which the memory data pattern must be programmed as part of the manufacturing process. Once the device has been programmed, the data pattern can never be changed. Because of this fact and the cost involved in making the programming masks used in the process, this type of read-only memory is mainly used in large-volume applications where the data do not change.

The second type of read-only memory, the electrically programmable device, is known as a PROM. PROMs differ from mask-programmable ROMs in that their data pattern must be electrically entered by the user instead of as a step in the manufacturing of the integrated circuit. Programming is usually done with automatic equipment. Once the data have been entered, they cannot be changed in any way. The PROM is used primarily in small-volume applications that do not warrant the costs involved in producing masks for programming.

Erasable read-only memory (EPROM) is more like PROM than is mask-programmable ROM. It is also electrically programmed with automatic

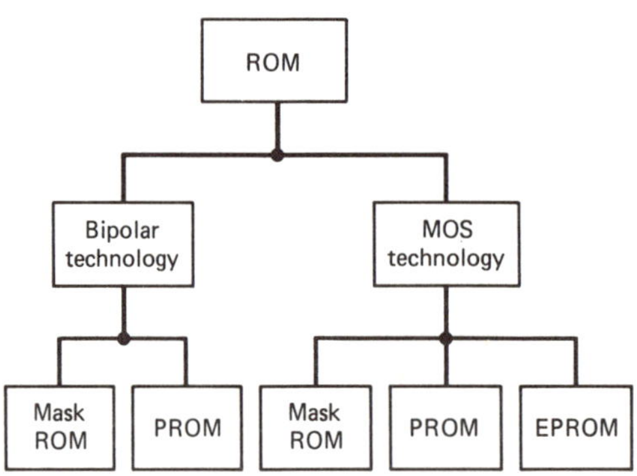

Fig. 2.1 ROM family devices.

equipment; however, its data pattern can be erased by exposing the device to ultraviolet light. This is the difference between the EPROM and PROM: the EPROM device can be programmed over and over again. EPROM devices find their widest use in the area of research and development and other situations in which the stored data may change.

By using bipolar technology processes, we can manufacture only ROM and PROM integrated circuit devices. On the other hand, MOS technology can be used to construct all three types of devices: ROMs, PROMs, and EPROMs.

Read-Only Memory Circuitry

A number of different device configurations can be used to build the electronic circuitry within a read-only memory. Figure 2.2 identifies the common types of circuitry used in bipolar and MOS technology devices. Here we see that bipolar devices are normally constructed with TTL or ECL circuitry. On the other hand, MOS ROMs can be built using any one of three basic circuit configurations: NMOS circuitry, PMOS circuitry, and CMOS circuitry.

Bipolar read-only memory devices are constructed with switching circuitry made from transistors, diodes, and resistors. ROMs made with this technology are high-speed devices; however, they require a large amount of power to operate. Moreover, this type of circuitry cannot be as compactly integrated as some of the MOS technology devices. For this reason, bipolar technology is restricted to smaller-memory-capacity devices. The maximum memory capacity of present-day bipolar ROMs is 16,384 bits, or 16*k* bits as it is also known.

The metal-oxide field-effect transistor (MOSFET) is the building block of NMOS, PMOS, and CMOS ROM integrated circuits. PMOS memories are made by using P-channel MOSFETs and NMOS memories with N-channel MOSFETs. NMOS and PMOS ROMs are slower than bipolar ROMs in operation, and like bipolar ICs, they consume a relatively large amount of power. The major advantage in NMOS and PMOS circuitry is their ability to be compactly integrated. Actually, we find that NMOS devices are both more

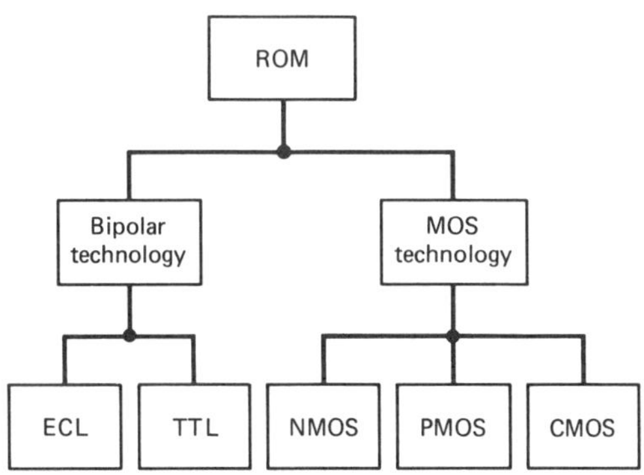

Fig. 2.2 ROM technologies.

dense and faster operating than are PMOS devices. Maximum memory capacities for NMOS devices are as large as 65,536 (64*k*) bits.

The circuitry within the last type of MOS ROM, the CMOS integrated circuit, is constructed from a low-power complementary symmetry circuit that uses both N-channel and P-channel MOSFETs. These ICs have a power consumption far below that of all other types of ROM circuitry, but their maximum storage capacities are not as high as for NMOS devices.

Because of their larger memory capacity, NMOS integrated circuits are the most popular type of ROM in use today. However, many applications exist wherein another type of device better meets the needs of the design. For example, we find that bipolar devices are required where high speed is the main consideration and power consumption is not a primary concern. On the other hand, CMOS devices are required when power consumption is very critical.

General ROM Block Diagram

A block diagram of a general read-only memory is shown in Fig. 2.3(a). Here we see that the device has three sets of signal leads: address inputs, data outputs, and control inputs. This block diagram is valid for mask ROMs, PROMs, and EPROMs. Figure 2.3(b) shows the ROM block diagram redrawn using *bus notation*. Now the signal lines are replaced by the address bus, data bus, and control bus. Each of these buses is shown to be *unidirectional*. That is, data will travel in just one direction.

The *address bus* is used to select data locations within the read-only memory. In Fig. 2.3(a) we find this bus consisting of address lines A_0 through A_4. The bits in the address word are arranged as $A_4A_3A_2A_1A_0$; therefore, A_4 is the MSB and A_0 the LSB. This gives a 5-bit address word length. When five address lines are provided, the memory can store 2^5 or

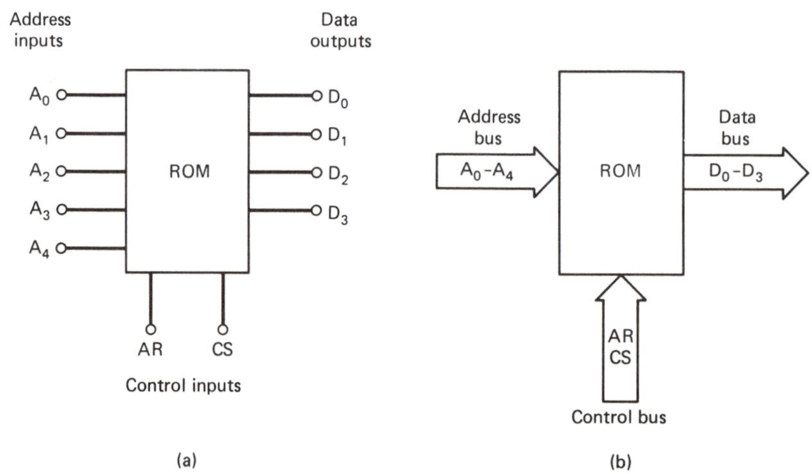

Fig. 2.3 (a) General ROM block diagram; (b) block diagram using bus notation.

32 words of data. These words are stored at consecutive addresses over the range 00000 through 11111. For convenience, ROM addresses are frequently written in hexadecimal form. In this way, our address range is expressed as 00_{16} to $1F_{16}$.

Standard memory devices are available with from 5 to 16 address lines. This results in storage capacities from $2^5 = 32$ data words to $2^{16} = 65{,}536$ data words.

EXAMPLE 2.1 What is the address location 11010 when written in hexadecimal form?

SOLUTION Expressing the address in hexadecimal form, we get

$$1\ 1010 = 1A_{16}$$

The binary word on the address bus selects one of the storage locations and the data word at this location is read out onto the data bus. In the block diagram of Fig. 2.3(a), we find that the *data bus* consists of four leads labeled D_0 through D_3. This tells us that each of the 32 data words stored in ROM has a word length of 4 bits. These data are stored in binary form within the memory; however, the output is frequently written using hexadecimal notation.

The most common output word lengths on standard ROM ICs are 4 bits and 8 bits. The outputs are usually either *open-collector* or *three-state*. This permits parallel output busing, which is required for memory expansion.

EXAMPLE 2.2 If the block diagram of Fig. 2.3(a) has 10 address lines, how many data words can be stored in the device?

SOLUTION The number of data words are found to be

$$2^{10} = 1024 \text{ words}$$

Now that address word length and data word length have been introduced, we are ready to determine the *organization* of the data stored within the ROM and to determine the *storage capacity* of the memory. By storage capacity, we mean the number of bits of storage available. Memory capacity is found by multiplying the number of data words by the word length.

For instance, the memory of Fig. 2.3(a) is organized into 32 4-bit words. Its capacity is found to be 32×4 or 128 bits. Other examples of standard ROM organization are 256 words by 8 bits, 1024 words by 4 bits, and 4096 words by 4 bits. These organizations correspond to memory capacities of $2k$, $4k$, and $16k$, respectively.

EXAMPLE 2.3 What is the memory capacity of a read-only memory organized as 256 words by 4 bits?

SOLUTION The memory capacity is obtained as

$$256 \times 4 = 1024 \text{ bits}$$

Since this device has a memory capacity of approximately 1000 bits, it is also known as a 1*k* ROM.

The control bus consists of control signals that are required to enable the address inputs and data outputs. In the block diagram of Fig. 2.3(a), the control leads are *AR* and *CS*. The *AR* line stands for *address ready* and it enables the address on lines A_0 through A_4 to enter the memory device. On the other hand, *CS* is a *chip select* signal that is normally used to enable outputs D_0 through D_3. The mnemonics used on these control leads vary from manufacturer to manufacturer. Some others are *CE* (chip enable), *OE* (output enable), and *OD* (output disable).

When a control signal is written without a bar over the top, such as *AR* or *CS*, it means that the operation described by the signal mnemonic (address ready, chip select) occurs when the signal is at the 1 logic level. Signals marked with a bar, such as $\overline{CS}$, perform the indicated operation when set to logic 0. For example, setting the *AR* line to logic 1 signals the device that the address is ready and initiates its input. Moreover, a 1 at *CS* enables the three-state outputs of the device. If *CS* is set to logic 0, the output lines are disabled or set to the *high impedance* (hi-Z) state.

The Program

The data stored within the read-only memory are called its *program*. One word of the program corresponds to each address location. The program may cause the ROM to implement a combinational logic function, sequential logic function, look-up table, code converter, or character generator. The data are stored within the integrated circuit device in binary form.

For instance, Fig. 2.4(a) shows a typical program for a 16-word by 4-bit ROM. Here we see that the data word stored at address $A_3A_2A_1A_0=0000_2$ is $D_3D_2D_1D_0=0010_2$. From top to bottom in the chart, each address is listed with its corresponding data word. The last address is $A_3A_2A_1A_0=1111_2$ and the data word held at this location is $D_3D_2D_1D_0=1110_2$.

For convenience, the address and data of the read-only memory are written using hexadecimal notation instead of binary. Figure 2.4(b) repeats the program in hexadecimal form. In this chart, the address 0000_2 is written as 0_{16} and the data word held at this storage location is 2_{16}. On the other hand, address 1111_2 is expressed as F_{16} and the data stored here is E_{16}.

EXAMPLE 2.4 In the program of Fig. 2.4(a), what data word is stored at address location $A_3A_2A_1A_0=1101$? Express the address and data word in hexadecimal form.

SOLUTION By locating the address 1101 in Fig. 2.4(a), we find that the data pro-

Word	$A_3A_2A_1A_0$	$D_3D_2D_1D_0$
0	0 0 0 0	0 0 1 0
1	0 0 0 1	1 0 0 0
2	0 0 1 0	1 0 1 0
3	0 0 1 1	0 0 0 1
4	0 1 0 0	0 0 0 0
5	0 1 0 1	1 1 1 1
6	0 1 1 0	0 1 1 1
7	0 1 1 1	0 1 0 1
8	1 0 0 0	0 1 1 0
9	1 0 0 1	0 1 0 0
10	1 0 1 0	0 1 0 0
11	1 0 1 1	1 0 0 0
12	1 1 0 0	0 0 0 0
13	1 1 0 1	1 1 0 0
14	1 1 1 0	1 1 0 1
15	1 1 1 1	1 1 1 0

(a)

Word	$A_3A_2A_1A_0$	$D_3D_2D_1D_0$
0	0	2
1	1	8
2	2	A
3	3	1
4	4	0
5	5	F
6	6	7
7	7	5
8	8	6
9	9	4
10	A	4
11	B	8
12	C	0
13	D	C
14	E	D
15	F	E

(b)

Fig. 2.4 (a) Typical program; (b) program written in hexadecimal notation.

grammed into this location are represented as 1100. The address and data word are expressed in hexadecimal form as D_{16} and C_{16}, respectively:

$$A_3A_2A_1A_0 = 1101_2 = \mathrm{D}_{16}$$

$$D_3D_2D_1D_0 = 1100_2 = \mathrm{C}_{16}$$

Input/Output Operation

Now that the block diagram and program of the read-only memory have been introduced, we are ready to study its operation from an input/output point of view. This is known as a *read operation.* Before a read operation can be performed, the address ready signal AR on the block in Fig. 2.5 must be set to the 1 logic level. This enables the address inputs. Moreover, the chip

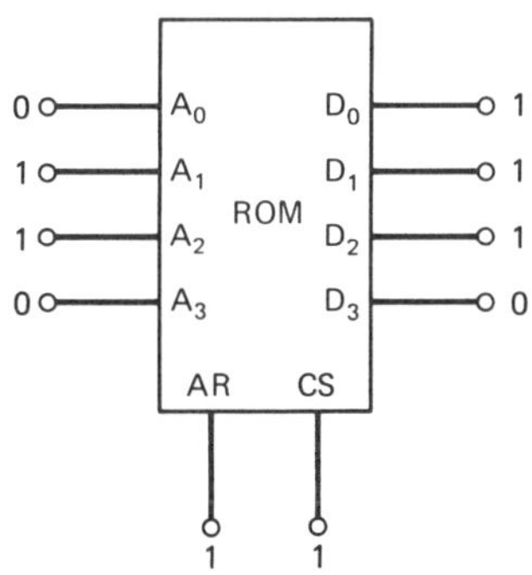

Fig. 2.5 ROM operation.

select lead CS must be switched to logic 1 to enable the outputs. In this state, the memory is ready to be read.

A binary address is now applied to the $A_3A_2A_1A_0$ inputs to access the desired memory location. This address is decoded within the device to select the appropriate data word, and the data word is read out on the $D_3D_2D_1D_0$ data lines.

EXAMPLE 2.5 Let us assume that the ROM in Fig. 2.5 has a 16-word by 4-bit organization and is programmed with the data shown in Fig. 2.4(a). What is the data output when the address word $A_3A_2A_1A_0$=0110 is applied to the inputs of the ROM?

SOLUTION Looking at the program in Fig. 2.4(a), we find that the data stored at address location 0110 are represented by the word 0111.

$$A_3A_2A_1A_0=0110$$

$$D_3D_2D_1D_0=0111$$

2.3 ROM ARCHITECTURE

Up to now we have introduced the read-only memory, its block diagram, and input/output operation. Next we turn our interest to its internal structure, or *architecture*.

Figure 2.6 shows a block diagram of general architecture for a ROM.

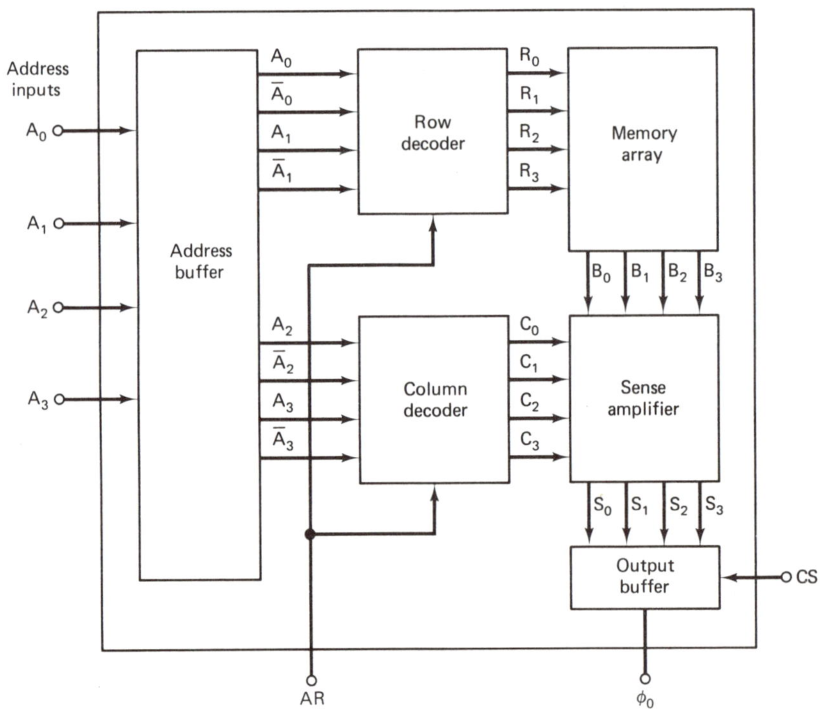

Fig. 2.6 ROM architecture.

Looking at this diagram, we find six fundamental parts: *address buffer*, *row decoder*, *memory array*, *column decoder*, *sense amplifier*, and *output buffer*. All these parts are built into a single integrated-circuit device.

In this section we describe the function of each part with respect to overall ROM operation and show the basic circuitry used in each part.

The Memory Array

The memory array is the section within the ROM that stores the data pattern of the program. This array consists of a number of memory cells. *Memory cell* is the name of the basic storage circuit. Each of these cells can store just one bit of data. A memory array consists of bipolar or MOS memory cells connected into a configuration called a *matrix*.

In a practical ROM device, the memory array contains a large number of cells. For example, some common bit capacities are 512 bits, 1k bits, 2k bits, and as high as 128k bits.

A general memory array is shown in Fig. 2.7. For simplicity, we have shown just 16 memory cells, represented with boxes, organized into a 4 × 4 matrix. The inputs to the array are the four *row lines* R_0, R_1, R_2, and R_3. These signals are produced by the row decoder circuit. The output lines of the memory array are *bit lines* B_0 through B_3.

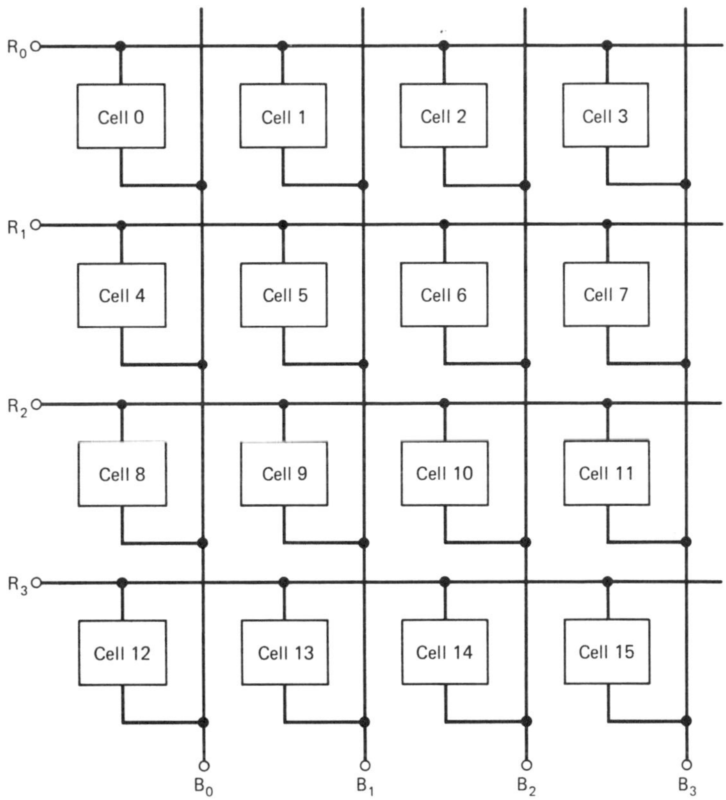

Fig. 2.7 General memory array.

Depending on the binary code applied to the address inputs of the ROM, the row decoder circuit selects one of the four rows in the memory array and the 4 bits of data stored in the cells attached to this line are output on the bit lines. For example, if row R_0 is selected, the data held in cell 0 through cell 3 are sent out of the array on bit lines B_0 through B_3, respectively.

The cells in a bipolar ROM array are constructed with either diodes or bipolar transistors. A single diode cell is shown in Fig. 2.8(a). In this circuit, the anode of the diode is attached to the row line R_0 and the cathode to the bit line B_0.

During programming, the cathode connection to the bit line can be connected or left open. When the connection is made, the cell is programmed with a logic 1. On the other hand, leaving the cathode open stores a logic 0.

The connection of 16 diode cells into a 4×4 diode matrix is shown in Fig. 2.8(b). Let us assume that the output of the row decoder has selected row R_0 by setting it to logic 1. In this row of the matrix, we find diodes connected to bit lines B_0 and B_1 while the diodes for lines B_2 and B_3 are left open. Therefore, the output word from the memory array is $B_3 B_2 B_1 B_0$ equals 0011.

Figure 2.9(a) gives the connection of an NPN transistor as a ROM memory cell. Here the base lead of the transistor is attached to the row line R_0 and its emitter lead to the bit line B_0. Moreover, the collector of the transistor is connected to the $+V_{CC}$ power supply voltage. The cell is programmed by making the emitter connection to the bit line or leaving out this connection. A 4×4 transistor matrix memory array is shown in Fig. 2.9(b).

EXAMPLE 2.6 Assume that in the memory array of Fig. 2.9(b) a connected emitter represents a logic 1 and an open emitter a logic 0. What is the output on the bit lines when the row decoder selects row R_1?

SOLUTION When row R_1 is selected, the contents of the transistor cells with their bases attached to this line are output. Emitters are attached to the B_0 and B_2 bit lines to give logic 1 stored in these cells. On the other hand, the emitters for the B_1 and B_3 lines are unattached and store a logic 0. This gives the output word

$$B_3 B_2 B_1 B_0 = 0101$$

The memory cell of a MOS ROM can be made with N-channel MOSFET, P-channel MOSFET, or CMOS circuit configurations. The basic MOSFET cell circuit used to construct a PMOS ROM is shown in Fig. 2.10(a). (See p. 31). The gate of the P-channel MOSFET is attached to the row input and the source to the bit line. The drain of the device is returned to ground.

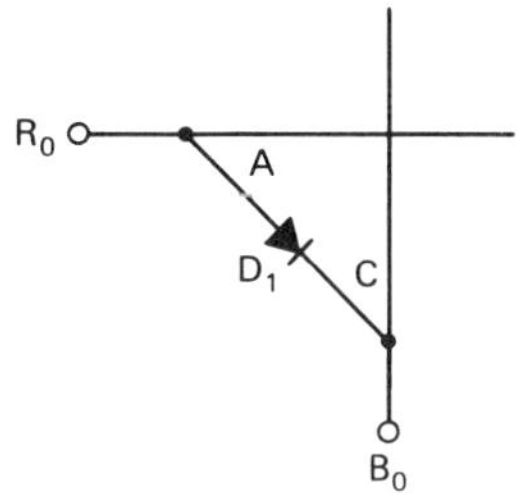

(a)

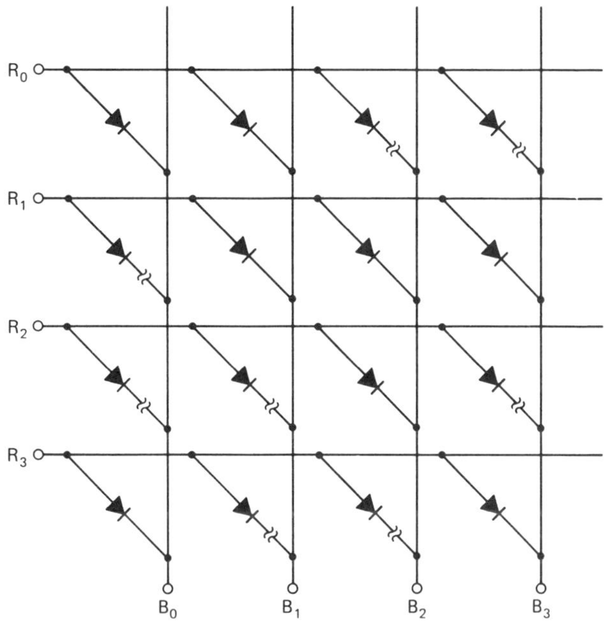

(b)

Fig. 2.8 (a) Diode cell; (b) diode matrix.

The circuit in Fig. 2.10(b) shows 16 MOSFETs connected into a 4×4 matrix. During programming, the data pattern of the program is formed by connecting gates or leaving them disconnected.

The Address Buffer

The address buffer is used to buffer the input signals for use within the read-only memory. A diagram of typical buffer circuitry for a 4-bit address is given in Fig. 2.11. (See p. 32). The address bits are labeled A_0, A_1, A_2, and A_3. Of these, A_3 is the MSB of the address and A_0 the LSB. For practical ROMs,

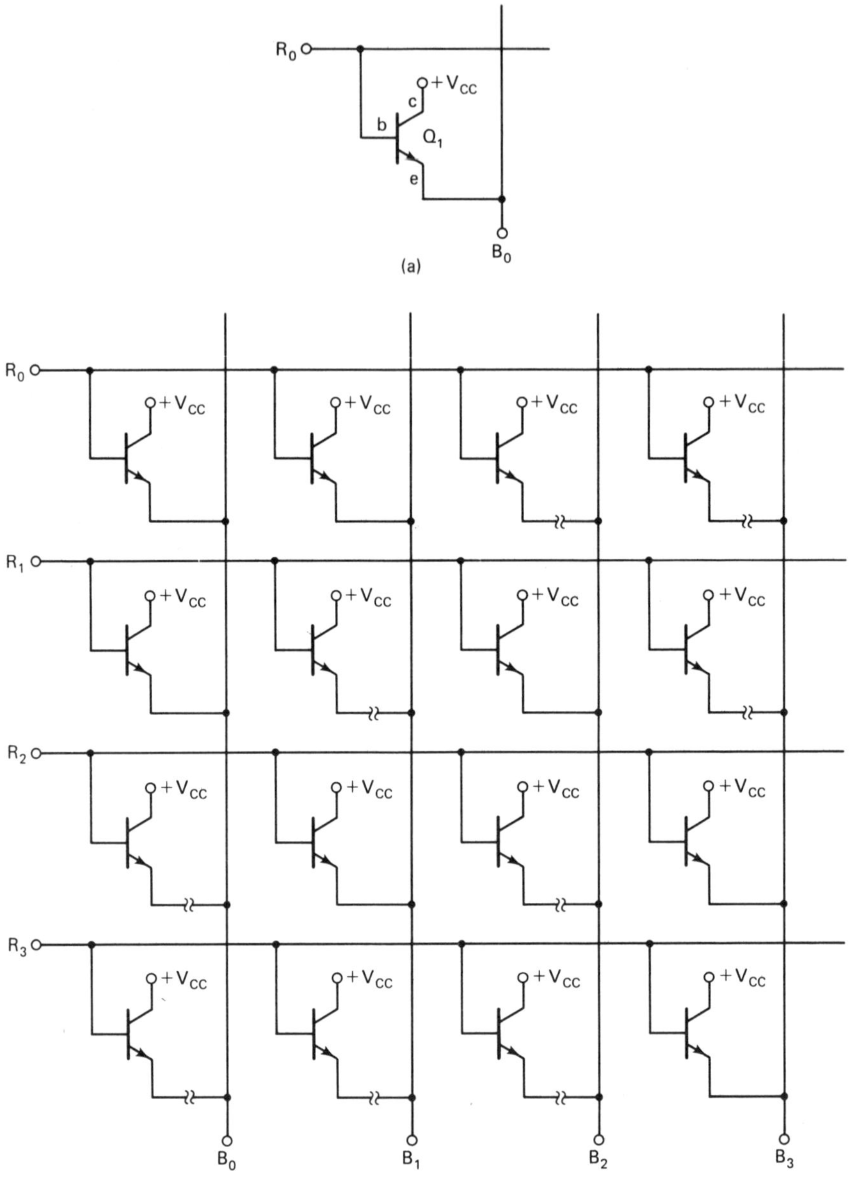

Fig. 2.9 (a) Bipolar transistor cell; (b) transistor matrix.

as many as 13 address inputs must be buffered.

In this circuit, the input buffer is constructed with eight inverter gates. Notice that the A_0, A_1, A_2, and A_3 address inputs are first inverted by gates 1 through 4, respectively, to give complemented inputs $\overline{A}_0$, $\overline{A}_1$, $\overline{A}_2$, and

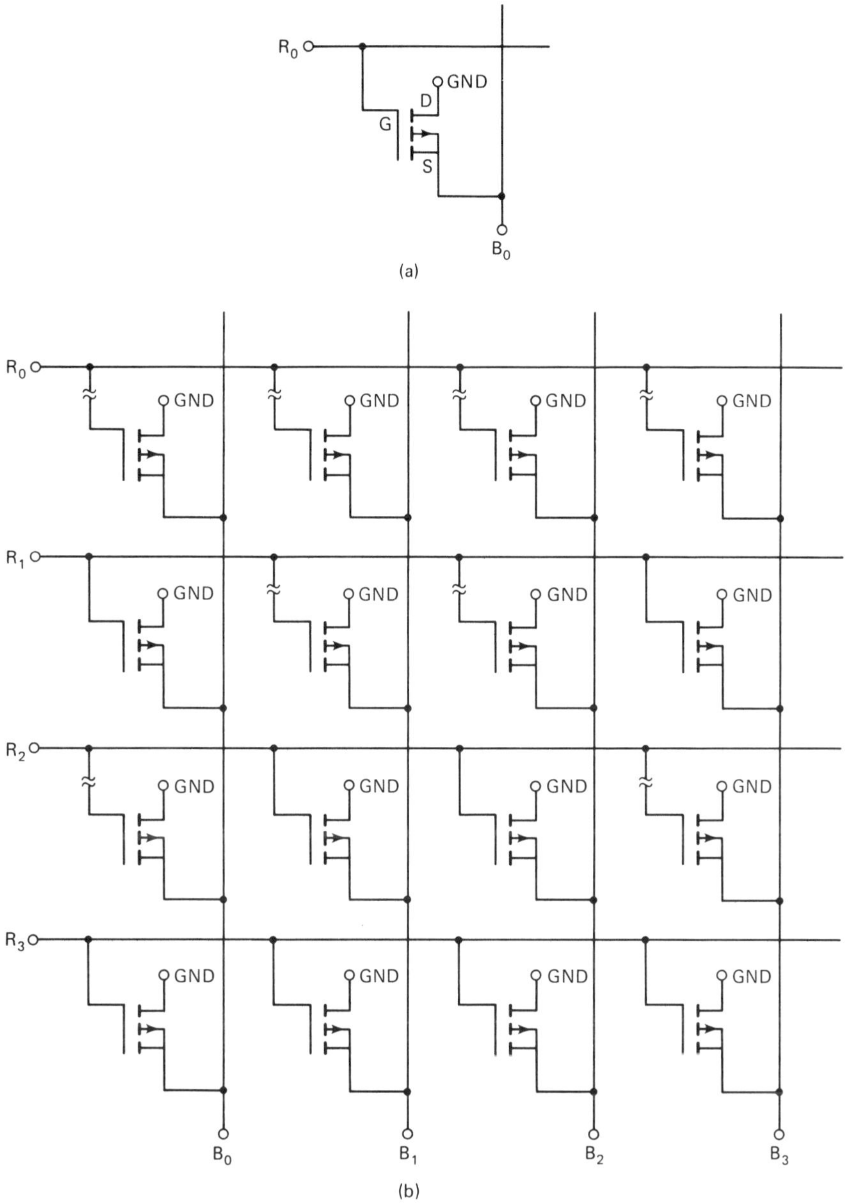

Fig. 2.10 (a) P-channel MOSFET cell; (b) MOSFET memory array.

$\bar{A}_3$. Then the inverted inputs are inverted once more to give the A_0, A_1, A_2, and A_3 buffered outputs. By buffering the address inputs in this way, external circuits that supply these inputs only experience one TTL or MOS load.

The two LSB A_0 and A_1 of the buffered address and their complements $\bar{A}_0$ and $\bar{A}_1$ are used as inputs to the row decoder section of the

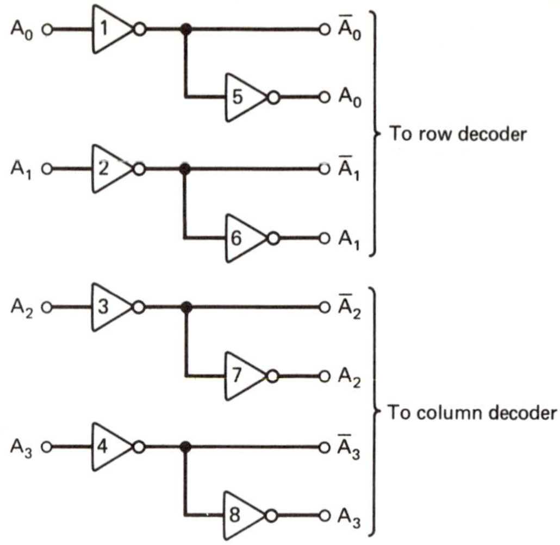

Fig. 2.11 Address buffer.

ROM. On the other hand, the two MSBs A_2 and A_3 with their complements $\bar{A}_2$ and $\bar{A}_3$ are inputs to the column decoder section.

The address buffer can also be used to match logic levels of the external circuitry to those required by the circuitry within the ROM. For instance, the buffer can provide compatibility of a PMOS ROM to TTL level signals at the address inputs.

The Row Decoder

Earlier in this section, we showed a 4 × 4 memory array that had four row lines; however, in practical ROM devices the array can require hundreds of rows. For this reason, the rows are not directly selected by address input signals. Instead, a small number of address inputs are decoded and the decoder outputs are used to select the rows of the array. For example, two address bits can select four rows and six address bits can select 64 rows. In some ROM devices, the row decoder is called the X decoder.

A typical row decoder circuit for a 4 × 4 memory matrix is shown in Fig. 2.12(a). Notice that the decoder is constructed from two-input AND gates and that there is one gate for each row in the matrix. Address buffer circuitry for address bits A_0 and A_1 are also included in this circuit drawing.

The truth table in Fig. 2.12(b) describes the operation of the decoder. When input address bits A_1 and A_0 are both equal to 0, the outputs of the address buffer inverters are A_1=0, A_0=0, $\bar{A}_1$=1, and $\bar{A}_0$=1. This makes both inputs on gate 5 logic 1 and its output R_0 switches to the 1 logic level. At the same time, at least one input on gates 6 through 8 is at the 0 logic level. Therefore, the R_1, R_2, and R_3 outputs stay at the 0 level. In this case, the input address has selected the R_0 row of the memory array.

Figure 2.13 is a row decoder with an address ready (AR) input. This input goes to a third input provided on each AND gate. When the AR signal

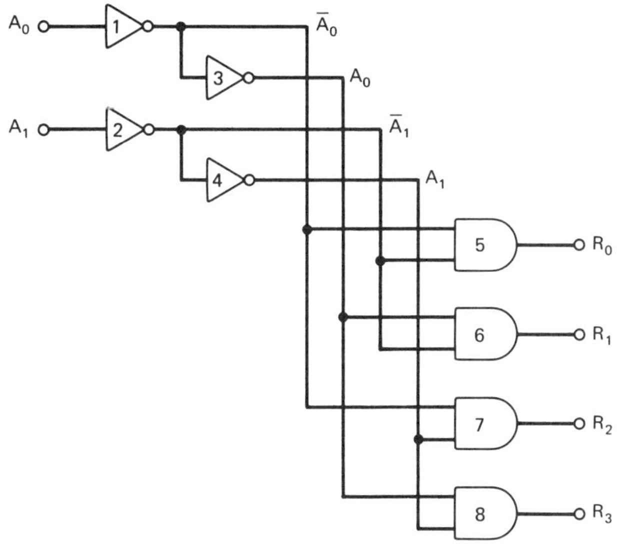

(a)

A_1	A_0	R_0	R_1	R_2	R_3
0	0	1	0	0	0
0	1	0	1	0	0
1	0	0	0	1	0
1	1	0	0	0	1

(b)

Fig. 2.12 (a) Row decoder circuit; (b) truth table.

is logic 1, the gates in the decoder are enabled. On the other hand, switching AR to logic 0 disables the address input by holding outputs R_0 through R_3 at the 0 logic level.

EXAMPLE 2.7 The inputs to the decoder circuit in Fig. 2.13 are AR=1, A_1=1, and A_0=1. What are the row outputs?

SOLUTION When the AR input is logic 1, the gates in the decoder are enabled. The address inputs and complemented inputs are

$$A_1=1, \quad \overline{A}_1=0$$

$$A_0=1, \quad \overline{A}_0=0$$

Gate 8 has as its inputs A_1, A_0, and AR, which are all logic 1. The output of gate 8, R_3, is logic 1. Each of the other AND gates has at least one input that is at the 0 logic level and their outputs are all logic 0.

$$R_0=R_1=R_2=0$$

$$R_3=1$$

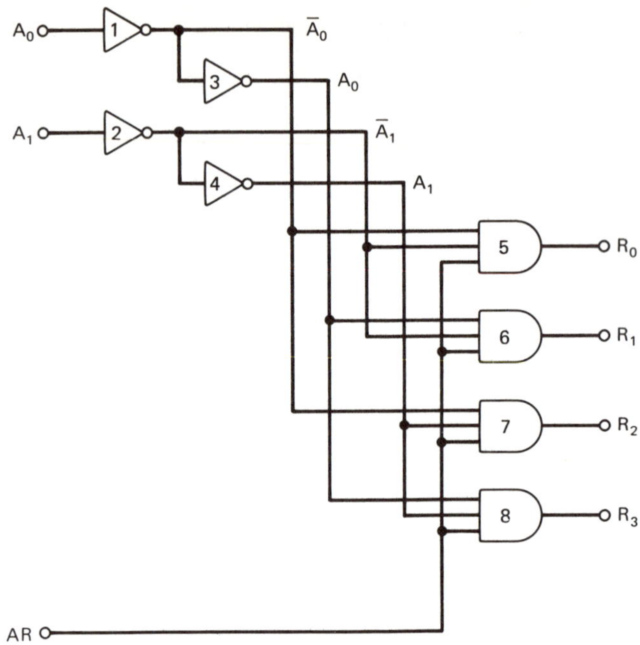

Fig. 2.13 Row decoder with address ready input.

The Sense Amplifier and Output Buffer

The output signals on the bit lines of the memory array in MOS ROMs are low-amplitude voltages or currents. For this reason, sense amplifiers are required at the bit outputs to detect the 0 or 1 logic states. The sense amplifiers act as loads on the outputs of the memory array and convert the small output signals to a level that can drive the output buffer circuitry. In bipolar ROMs, the sense amplifiers are replaced with logic gates.

Figure 2.14 shows how sense amplifiers and an output buffer are connected to a 4×4 memory array. Looking at this diagram, we see that there is one sense amplifier for each bit line of the memory array. The inputs to the sense amplifiers are bit lines B_0, B_1, B_2, and B_3. The outputs of the amplifiers, S_0, S_1, S_2, and S_3, go to the input of the output buffer.

The outputs of sense amplifiers 1 through 4 are controlled by the signals C_0, C_1, C_2, and C_3, respectively. These signals are produced by the column decoder circuitry of the ROM. Only one of the column select signals can be logic 1 at a time. For this reason, just one of the four memory array output bits can be passed through the sense amplifiers to the output buffer. For example, when C_0 is logic 1, the B_0 input to sense amplifier 1 is passed to its output S_0 and the input of the output buffer gate. This bit of data is output on the ϕ_0 data lead of the ROM.

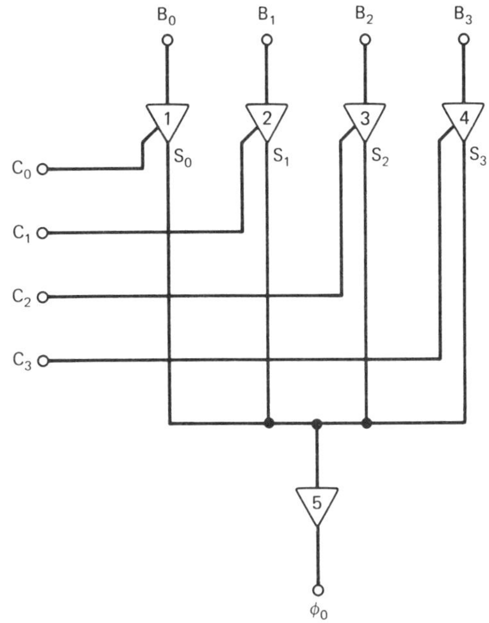

Fig. 2.14 Sense amplifiers and output buffer.

In this way, we see that the organization of a ROM using this output circuitry is actually 16 words by 1 bit instead of the 4 × 4 organization of the memory array.

The output buffer provides the drive required by external loads. For instance, the output of a PMOS ROM can be buffered to be TTL-compatible. In this case, the output voltage and current levels must be changed. ROM devices are available with open-collector (open-drain for MOS devices) or three-state output circuitry.

EXAMPLE 2.8 The bit line inputs to the sense amplifiers in the circuit of Fig. 2.14 are $B_3B_2B_1B_0$=1001. What is output ϕ_0 when column line C_2 is logic 1?

SOLUTION When C_2 is at the 1 logic level, sense amplifier 3 is enabled and the B_2 input is passed to the output buffer and output lead ϕ_0.

$$C_2 = 1$$

$$\phi_0 = B_2 = 0$$

The circuit in Fig. 2.15 includes a chip select (CS) lead to control the output buffer. When this input is logic 0, the three-state output is put in the hi-Z state and acts like an open circuit. However, making CS equal 1 enables the output buffer and the logic level of the data output ϕ_0 equals the output of the selected sense amplifier.

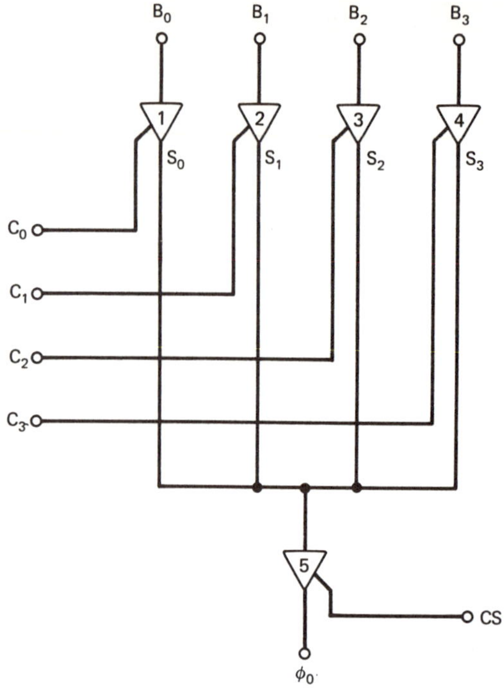

Fig. 2.15 Output circuitry with chip enable lead.

The Column Decoder

We have already shown how some of the address bits are decoded and used to select a single row of the memory array. Now we show how the remaining address bits are decoded by the column decoder and how the decoder output is used to organize the data at the bit lines of the memory array into words for output by the ROM. The column decoder is sometimes also called the Y decoder.

The circuit in Fig. 2.16(a) is a column decoder that can select for output the data at one of the four bit lines of a 4 X 4 memory array. The higher-order address bits A_3 and A_2 are the inputs to the decoder. There are four output signals, C_0, C_1, C_2, and C_3. The decoder is constructed by using one AND gate for each column output. Furthermore, the inverters required to buffer address inputs A_2 and A_3 are shown in the circuit.

When an address is input to the ROM device, the A_2 and A_3 bits cause one column output of the decoder to switch to the 1 logic level. At the same time, all other column outputs are logic 0. This operation is shown in the truth table of Fig. 2.16(b).

Each of the four column outputs controls a sense amplifier. The sense amplifier corresponding to the column output that is logic 1 is enabled and its bit line input is passed to the output buffer and on to the ROM output. As an example, let us make the address input A_3A_2 =10. The outputs of the address buffer are A_3=1, A_2=0, $\bar{A}_3$=0, and $\bar{A}_2$=1. Looking at the decoder

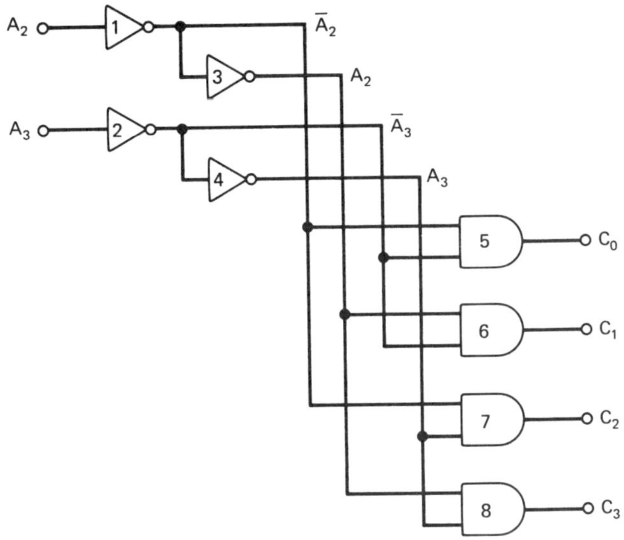

(a)

A_3	A_2	C_0	C_1	C_2	C_3
0	0	1	0	0	0
0	1	0	1	0	0
1	0	0	0	1	0
1	1	0	0	0	1

(b)

Fig. 2.16 (a) Column decoder circuit; (b) truth table.

gates, we find that gate 7 has as its inputs A_3 and $\bar{A}_2$. Since these inputs are both at the 1 logic level, column output C_2 switches to logic 1. The other outputs, C_0, C_1, and C_3, are held at the 0 logic level. In the sense amplifier circuit of Fig. 2.14, we saw that signal C_2 enables sense amplifier 3 and the data at bit line B_2 are output from the memory.

Circuitry external to the ROM does not recognize the internal organization of the memory array. Instead, the organization seen by the external circuitry is that of the output word. This output organization is determined by the connection of the column decoder circuit to the sense amplifiers.

Another output organization for a 4 × 4 memory array is shown in Fig. 2.17. In this circuit, the control leads of the sense amplifiers are arranged in 2-bit groups and an output buffer is supplied for each amplifier in the group. The control signal C_0 from the column decoder is used to select the group, including bits B_0 and B_2. Moreover, the C_1 column decoder output is used to enable the sense amplifiers for bits B_1 and B_3.

If the address input A_3A_2=00, the $\bar{A}_3$ and $\bar{A}_2$ signals are logic 1. Both inputs on gate 5 equal logic 1, and the C_0 output switches to the 1 level.

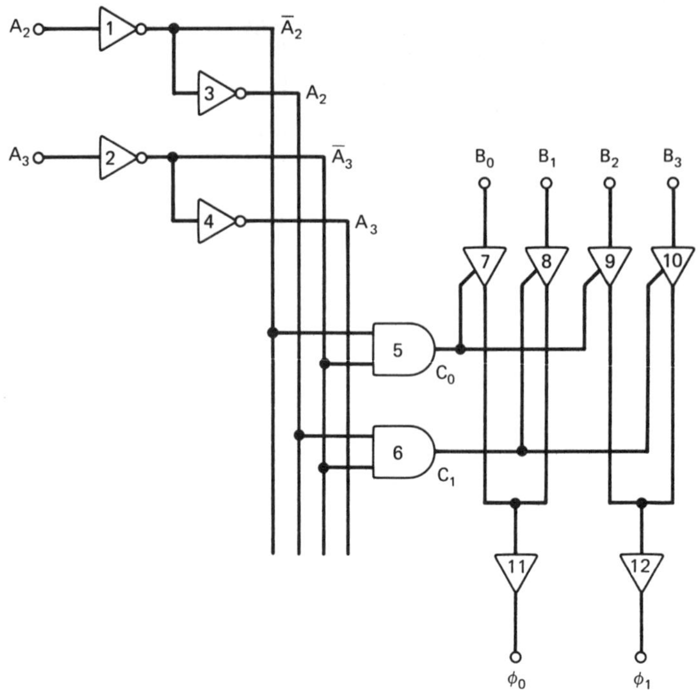

Fig. 2.17 Circuit configuration for eight 2-bit word organization.

Logic 1 at C_0 selects sense amplifiers 7 and 9 and data from B_0 and B_2 are sent to output buffers 11 and 12, respectively, to produce ROM outputs ϕ_0 and ϕ_1.

Here we see that two cells of the matrix are always read and the output from the 4×4 memory array has been reorganized into eight 2-bit words at the ROM data outputs.

Because of the small memory array, this circuit does not actually require a column decoder. The address bit A_2 and its complement $\bar{A}_2$ could directly select the sense amplifier groups. However, practical ROM devices have a large memory array and always require column decoder circuitry. For this reason, the decoder is included in Fig. 2.17.

EXAMPLE 2.9 The sense amplifiers in the circuit of Fig. 2.17 have inputs $B_3B_2B_1B_0$=1001. What are outputs ϕ_0 and ϕ_1 when the address inputs are A_3A_2=01?

SOLUTION When the address input is A_3A_2=01, the complemented inputs are $\bar{A}_3\bar{A}_2$=10. This makes both inputs to gate 6 logic 1 and its output switches to logic 1.

$$A_2=1$$

$$\bar{A}_3=1$$

$$C_1=1$$

With C_1 equal to logic 1, sense amplifiers 8 and 10 are enabled. Their inputs B_1 and B_3 are passed to the output buffers to produce the ROM outputs.

$$\phi_0 = B_1 = 0$$

$$\phi_1 = B_3 = 1$$

or

$$\phi_1 \phi_0 = 10$$

2.4 MASK PROGRAMMING

Read-only memory integrated circuits are built from a segment of silicon material by a multistep process that includes *photomasking*, *etching*, and *diffusion operations*. In this process, the data pattern of the program is created within the device with a *mask programming* step. The customer provides the manufacturer with the bit pattern to be programmed.

Bipolar ROMs are programmed by connecting the cathodes of the diodes in the memory array to the bit lines during the mask programming step. In the case of a bipolar array made with transistors, the emitter lines are connected to the bit lines through mask programming.

On the other hand, MOSFET memory arrays are mask-programmed by etching the surface of the gate lead connection to the row line away or by leaving the gate connection alone.

Since the data pattern is permanently programmed into the array of diode, transistor, or MOSFET memory cells, we say that ROM devices are nonvolatile. That is, a ROM device will not lose its data when the power supply is disconnected.

2.5 STATIC ROM OPERATION

The circuitry introduced up to this point in the chapter is that used for *static read-only memory* devices. By static ROM, we mean a circuit capable of dc operation. That is, the address and control signals can be applied without clock signals.

Figure 2.18 shows typical circuitry for a static ROM. This circuit has four address inputs, marked A_0, A_1, A_2, and A_3; four data outputs, indicated by ϕ_0, ϕ_1, ϕ_2, and ϕ_3; and the control inputs address ready (AR) and chip select (CS).

Now let us turn our interest to the memory array in the ROM circuit. Notice that the memory cells are arranged into eight rows represented by $\overline{R}_0$ through $\overline{R}_7$ and eight columns marked B_0 through B_7. The storage capacity of the array is 64 bits. However, through the use of column decoder circuitry the memory output is organized into 16 4-bit words.

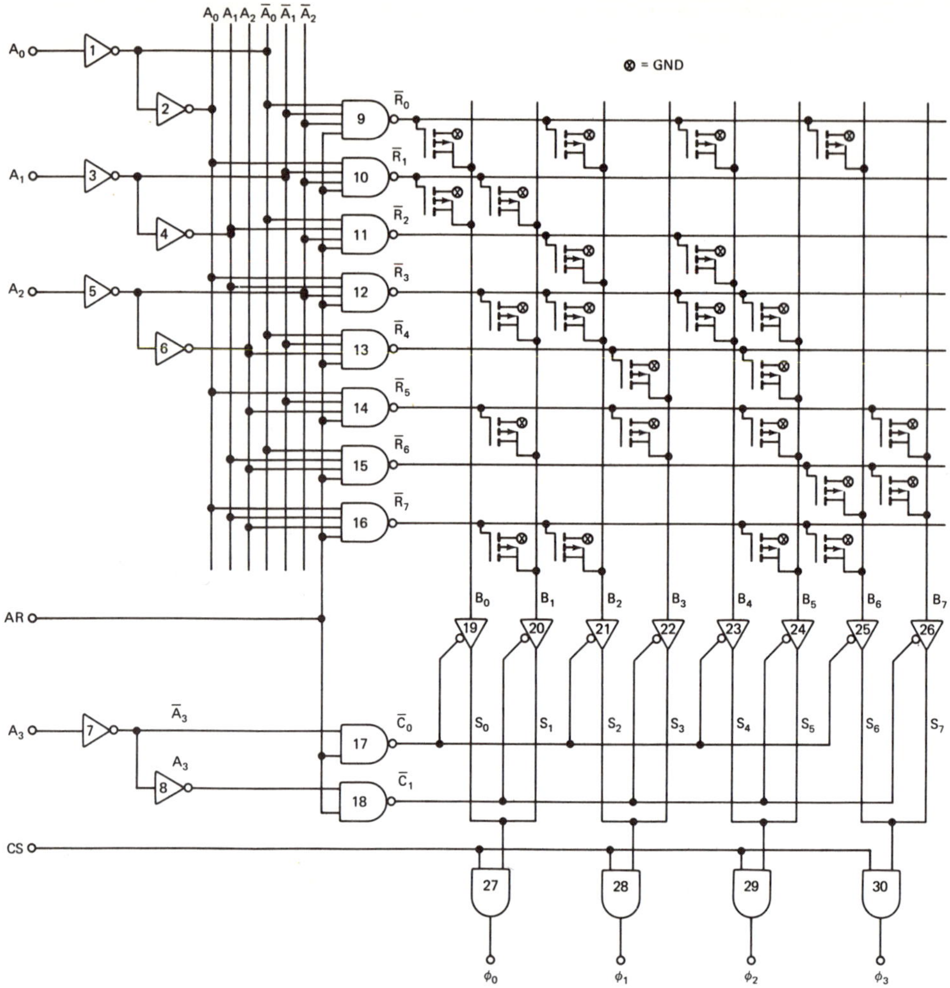

Fig. 2.18 Sixteen-word by 4-bit read-only memory.

Read Operation Cycle

Sixteen 4-bit words are stored in the memory array. A read operation must be performed to output any one of these words. As part of the read cycle, the *AR* input and *CS* input must be set to logic 1. In this way, the circuit is enabled for read operation.

The read operation starts when the address of the storage location to be accessed is applied to the A_0 through A_3 inputs. This code is buffered by inverter gates 1 through 8. The buffered address bits and their complements are passed to inputs of the row decoder and column decoder circuits. The row decoder consists of gates 9 through 16, and column decoder gates 17 and 18.

Based on the code at address bits A_0, A_1, and A_2, the row decoder selects one of the rows in the memory array by setting that row line ($\overline{R}_0$ through $\overline{R}_7$) to the 0 logic level. The 8 bits of data stored at this row are output on bit lines B_0 through B_7 to the sense amplifier inputs.

At the same time that the row decoder selects one row of the memory array, the buffered A_3 address is applied to the inputs of the column decoder. Depending upon the logic level of A_3, either column output $\overline{C}_0$ or $\overline{C}_1$ is set to logic 0. This selects one of the two sense amplifier groups. In this way, one of the two 4-bit words available on the bit lines is selected for output.

The sense amplifiers detect the 0 and 1 output signals on the bit lines of the memory array and convert them to levels appropriate to drive the output buffer. Sense amplifiers 19, 21, 23, and 25 are selected by the $\overline{C}_0$ line and amplifiers 20, 22, 24, and 26 by $\overline{C}_1$. When $\overline{C}_0$ is logic 0, data at bit inputs B_0, B_2, B_4, and B_6 are passed to sense lines S_0, S_2, S_4, and S_6, respectively. On the other hand, a 0 at $\overline{C}_1$ selects bits B_1, B_3, B_5, and B_7 and pass them to sense lines S_1, S_3, S_5, and S_7. In this way, one of the two 4-bit words on the bit lines of the memory array is passed to the inputs of the output buffer, which produces data outputs ϕ_0 through ϕ_3.

The data stored in the memory array can be randomly accessed. By *random access* we mean that storage locations in the memory array can be addressed in any order.

EXAMPLE 2.10 What are the data outputs of the memory in Fig. 2.18 when the address input is F_{16}? Assume that the *AR* and *CS* inputs are both logic 1.

SOLUTION The signal $AR=1$ enables the row and column decoders while $CS=1$ enables the output buffer. When the address input is F_{16}, the binary address is

$$A_3A_2A_1A_0=1111$$

These address bits are buffered by inverter gates 1 through 8 to produce

$$A_3A_2A_1A_0=1111$$

$$\overline{A}_3\overline{A}_2\overline{A}_1\overline{A}_0=0000$$

Bits A_0, A_1, and A_2 and their complements are inputs to the row decoder circuit. Inputs on AND gate 16 are A_0, A_1, A_2, and AR, which are all logic 1. This makes its output $\overline{R}_7$ switch to logic 0, and row 7 of the memory array is selected.

$$AR=1$$

$$A_2A_1A_0=111$$

$$\overline{R}_7=0$$

Looking at row 7 in the matrix, we see that MOSFETs are connected to the B_1, B_2,

B_5, and B_6 bit lines. For this reason, these four memory array outputs are logic 1 and the others are logic 0.

$$B_0=0,\quad B_1=1$$
$$B_2=1,\quad B_3=0$$
$$B_4=0,\quad B_5=1$$
$$B_6=1,\quad B_7=0$$

Address bit A_3 is in the 1 state and is buffered to $\overline{A}_3=0$ and $A_3=1$ at the output of inverter gates 7 and 8. Both inputs on AND gate 18 of the column decoder are logic 1 and its output $\overline{C}_1$ switches to the 0 logic level.

$$AR=1$$
$$A_3=1$$
$$\overline{C}_1=0$$

The logic 0 at $\overline{C}_1$ enables the group of sense amplifiers, including amplifiers 20, 22, 24, and 26. The sense amplifier outputs are

$$S_7S_5S_3S_1=B_7B_5B_3B_1=0101$$

These signals are inputs to buffer gates 27 through 30. Each of these AND gates are enabled by a 1 at *CS*.

$$CS=1$$
$$\phi_3\phi_2\phi_1\phi_0=S_3S_2S_1S_0=0101$$

Read-Cycle Timing

We have just traced the read operation of a ROM from address input to data output. In our description it was assumed that gate outputs appeared immediately after their inputs were set. However, in practice there are short propagation delays between input and output on all gates. This leads to a time delay between address input and data output during a read operation.

For this reason, there are three important timing properties defined for the read cycle of a ROM. These timing characteristics are called the *access time* (t_{ACC}), *chip select time* (t_S), and *chip deselect time* (t_D). These are only typical mnemonics used to identify the timing properties. Other notations are used from manufacturer to manufacturer.

The address input and data output waveforms in Fig. 2.19(a) show the access time (t_{ACC}) timing characteristic. Access time tells how long it takes to access data stored in a ROM location. In this diagram we see that a short period of time elapses between the instant the address is applied and the moment data appear at the output.

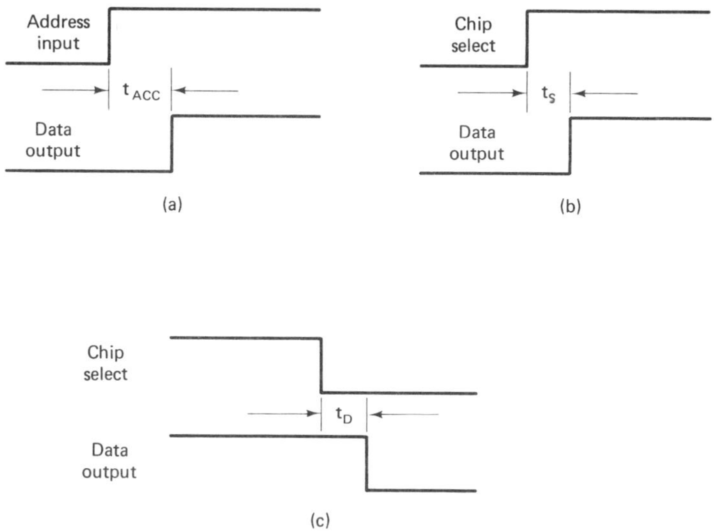

Fig. 2.19 (a) Access time; (b) chip select time; (c) chip deselect time.

Standard bipolar ROM integrated circuits have typical access times in the range 40 to 90 *nanoseconds* (ns). On the other hand, access times for MOS ROMs are about 10 times longer than those for bipolar devices. Their access times fall in the range 400 to 900 ns.

If the address has already been set but the output circuitry not yet enabled with the *CS* lead, the output will respond faster. In Fig. 2.19(b) we see that the chip select waveform is switched to logic 1 and then after a short delay, the output appears. This operation represents the chip select time t_S.

Chip deselect time (t_D), shown in Fig. 2.19(c), is the opposite of chip select time. It represents the amount of time it takes the outputs to turn OFF after the chip select lead is switched to logic 0 to disable the outputs.

Typical values of chip select and deselect times of standard bipolar ROM ICs are about 20 ns, and those for MOS ROMs are about 10 times longer, or 200 ns.

Input and Output Logic Levels

Another group of important electrical characteristics of a ROM comprises its input and output logic levels. Most ROM ICs are designed so that their inputs and outputs are compatible with TTL circuitry.

Input and output logic levels of a typical bipolar ROM are given in Fig. 2.20(a). Here we see that on the input side of the ROM, the maximum voltage value for a logic 0 (low logic level) is labeled $V_{IL\,max}$ and equals 0.8 V. If the voltage of a logic 0 rises above this value, the device will not necessarily read the input as a logic 0 state. Moreover, the minimum value of volt-

(a)	(b)
V_{ILmax} = 0.8 V	V_{ILmax} = 0.65 V
V_{IHmin} = 2 V	V_{IHmin} = 3 V
V_{OLmax} = 0.4 V	V_{OLmax} = 0.45 V
V_{OHmin} = 2.4 V	V_{OHmin} = 3.5 V

Fig. 2.20 (a) Bipolar ROM typical logic levels; (b) MOS ROM typical logic levels.

age that will be read as a logic 1 at the input of the ROM is written as V_{IHmin} and equals 2 V.

At the outputs of the bipolar ROM, the maximum 0 or low-level voltage is indicated with the notation V_{OLmax}. The value of this voltage is 0.4 V. If the output voltage exceeds this value, circuits tied at the output may not correctly read the signal as a logic 0. A logic 1 output is labeled V_{OHmin} and has a minimum value of 2.4 V. If the high-level voltage drops below 2.4 V, the output may not be read as a logic 1 by circuitry connected at the output.

Typical input and output logic levels for a MOS ROM integrated circuit are given in Fig. 2.20(b). Here we see that the maximum low-level voltage V_{ILmax} and minimum high-level voltage V_{IHmin} that can be applied to the inputs of a MOS ROM are rated at 0.65 and 3 V, respectively.

On the other hand, the maximum value of voltage that can be produced for a logic 0 at the data outputs of a MOS ROM is labeled V_{OLmax} and equals 0.45 V. For a logic 1 output, the minimum value that can be produced is V_{OHmin} equals 3.5 V.

These MOS outputs have current ratings sufficient to drive one standard TTL load. That is, each output can source 100 μA of current when in the 1 logic level and can sink 1.6 mA when in the 0 logic level.

2.6 STANDARD STATIC MASK ROMS

Having introduced the read-only memory, its architecture, mask programming, and static ROM operation, we are now ready to look into some of the standard static mask-programmable ROM integrated circuits. A number of the more popular bipolar and MOS devices are described in this section.

74187 Bipolar ROM

The 74187 mask programmable read-only memory device is a member of the 7400 family of TTL integrated circuits. A block diagram of the architecture inside the 74187 ROM is given in Fig. 2.21(a). Looking at this diagram, we find that its memory array is arranged into 32 rows by 32 columns. This gives a total storage capacity of 1024 ($1k$) bits. The memory cells used in the 74187 memory array are formed from bipolar transistors. The output is organized by on-chip decoders into 256 4-bit words. Figure 2.21(b) shows a pin layout of the 74187 IC.

This device has eight address inputs, labeled *A* through *H*. Of these address bits, *A* is the LSB and *H* the MSB. Bits *D* through *H* are inputs to the row decoder circuit, and *A* through *C* are inputs to the column decoder.

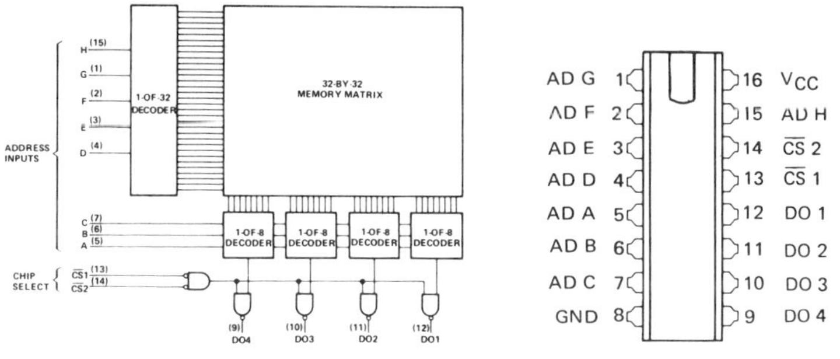

(a) (b)

Fig. 2.21 (a) 74187 block diagram (Texas Instruments, Incorporated); (b) 74187 ROM pin layout (Texas Instruments, Incorporated).

Besides the address inputs, we find four data outputs, DO_1 through DO_4. These outputs are open-collector and must be wired to a voltage supply through an external pull-up resistor to set the 1 level of output voltage. Each output can sink up to 16 mA of current.

There are also two chip select control leads, marked $\overline{CS}_1$ and $\overline{CS}_2$. These leads are used to control the data output bus. When both chip select inputs are logic 0, the output is enabled and the ROM is ready to perform a read operation. However, if either chip select lead is set to logic 1, the output buffer is disabled, and DO_1 through DO_4 are all held at the 1 logic level.

To operate, the 74187 requires a 5-V dc power supply which is connected between the $+V_{CC}$ lead at pin 16 and the ground (GND) at pin 8. The value of supply voltage can vary by about ±5% (±0.25 V) before the device will fail to work correctly. The 74187 is rated to dissipate 0.46 mW per bit. This gives a total power consumption of 0.471 W.

Let us assume that a 74187 is powered by a 5-V dc supply $+V_{CC}$ and its chip select leads are both at the 0 logic level. When an address is applied to the inputs, bits D through H are decoded to select one of the 32 rows of the memory array. Data bits stored in the cells attached to this row output their content on the 32 bit lines to the column decoder.

At the column decoder, address bits A through C select one of the eight 4-bit words on the bit lines and pass it to the output buffer NAND gates. The $\overline{CS}_1$ and $\overline{CS}_2$ signals are both logic 0 and are input to the output control gate. This produces a 1 at the gate output and enables the four buffer gates. The data word is passed through the output buffer to the data outputs DO_1 through DO_4.

Now that we have described the read operation of the 74187, let us look into its timing characteristics. The address to output access time t_{ACC} is 40 ns. Therefore, after setting $\overline{CS}_1$ and $\overline{CS}_2$ equal to logic 0 and applying the address to the inputs, a delay of 40 ns occurs before the data word appears at the outputs. Moreover, the devices chip select to output (t_S) and deselect output (t_D) times are both 20 ns.

The input and output logic levels specified for the 74187 are identical to other devices in the 7400 TTL family. The input logic level ratings are $V_{ILmax} = 0.8$ V and $V_{IHmin} = 2$V. On the other hand, its low-level output voltage rating is $V_{OLmax} = 0.4$ V; the high-level rating is not specified. No value is specified for V_{OHmin} because with an open-collector circuit this level is set by the external pull-up resistor and power supply.

74S271 Bipolar ROM

The 74S271 mask programmable ROM is a Schottky TTL IC that is similar to the 74187 just introduced. Its block diagram is shown in Fig. 2.22. Here we see that the memory array has been expanded to 32 rows by 64 columns. This size of matrix gives a total storage capacity of 2048 (2*k*) bits. The on-chip decoder circuitry organizes the output into 256 words each with 8 bits.

The circuit again has eight address inputs *A* through *H*, but in this case *A* through *E* are inputs to the row decoder and *F* through *H* are inputs to the column decoder. The 74S271 has eight data outputs (DO_1 through DO_8) instead of four outputs such as on the 74187 device. Again, the outputs are open-collector. The chip select inputs $\overline{CS}_1$ and $\overline{CS}_2$ operate in the same manner as on the 74187 and must both be logic 0 to enable the outputs.

The timing characteristics of a read operation are t_{ACC} equals 45 ns, t_S equals 15 ns, and t_D equals 15 ns. The input/output voltage levels are identical to those given for the 74187 IC.

3324A Bipolar ROM

The 3324A is another widely used bipolar mask-programmable ROM. As shown in the block diagram of Fig. 2.23(a), this device has a 4096 (4*k*)-bit storage capacity and its output is organized into 512 8-bit words. Figure 2.23(b) shows the pin layout of the 3324A.

This ROM has nine address bits, A_0 through A_8. Of these, A_0 is the LSB and A_8 the MSB. There are also eight three-state data outputs, $DATA\ OUT_1$ through $DATA\ OUT_8$. Moreover, four chip select leads are provided. These leads are labeled $\overline{CS}_1$, $\overline{CS}_2$, CS_3, and CS_4.

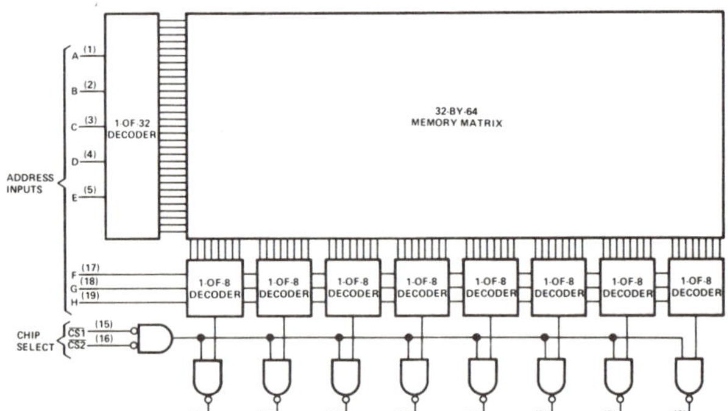

Fig. 2.22 74S271 block diagram (Texas Instruments, Incorporated).

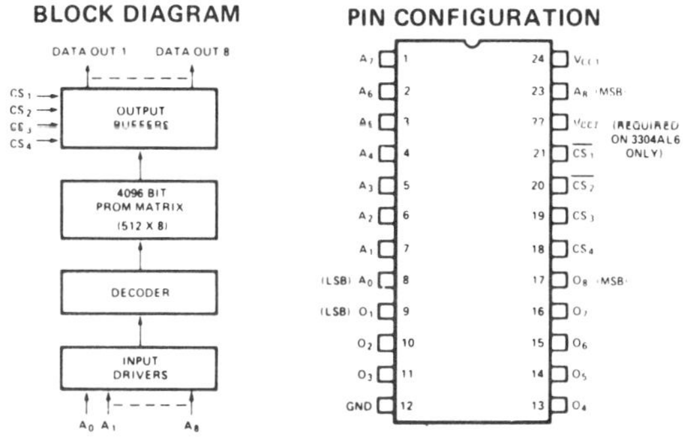

(a) (b)

Fig. 2.23 (a) 3324A block diagram (Intel Corp.); (b) 3324A pin layout (Intel Corp.).

For a read operation to be performed, the chip select leads must be set as follows:

$$\overline{CS}_1 = \overline{CS}_2 = 0$$

$$CS_3 = CS_4 = 1$$

If these conditions are not met, the outputs are held in the hi-Z third state.

The 3324A is somewhat slower than the earlier 7400 series devices. Its access time t_{ACC} is 70 ns and its chip select and deselect to output times are both 30 ns. Furthermore, small differences are found in the input/output logic-level ratings. The minimum high-level input and output voltage-level ratings are V_{IHmin} = 2 V and V_{OHmin} = 2.4 V, respectively. These ratings are identical to those for the earlier 7400 series ROMs. On the other hand, the maximum low-level voltages are slightly higher, V_{ILmax} = 0.85 V and V_{OLmax} = 0.45 V.

1302 MOS ROM

The 1302 integrated circuit is a static $2k$ MOS mask-programmable read-only memory. Figure 2.24(a) shows a block diagram of the circuitry within a 1302 device. The on chip decoders organize the output into 256 words, each with 8 bits. The pin layout of the 1302 is given in Fig. 2.24(b).

In the block diagram we find eight address inputs, A_0 through A_7; eight data outputs, $DATA\ OUT_1$ through $DATA\ OUT_8$; and a single chip select lead, $\overline{CS}$. When the logic level of $\overline{CS}$ is logic 0, the ROM is enabled for read operation. On the other hand, a 1 level at $\overline{CS}$ sets the three-state outputs into the hi-Z state.

There are three power-supply leads on the 1302: V_{CC}, V_{DD}, and V_{GG}. To operate the device, these three leads must be supplied with +5, -9, and -9 V, respectively. The device is rated to operate correctly with a ±5% variation in power-supply voltage. When operating, the 1302 requires 1 mW per bit, for a total of about 2 W per IC.

MOS devices like the 1302 have much slower switching speeds than do bipolar ROMs such as those just discussed. The typical address-to-output

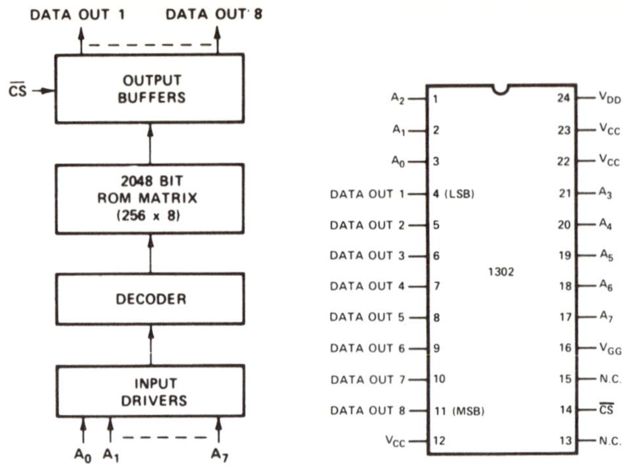

(a) (b)

Fig. 2.24 (a) 1302 block diagram (Intel Corp.); (b) 1302 pin layout (Intel Corp.).

access time is specified as 700 ns, which is more than 10 times longer than those experienced for bipolar ROMs. Similarly, the chip select-to-output time and deselect time, which are 500 and 300 ns, respectively, are more than 10 times longer than those for bipolar ROMs.

The input and output logic levels of the 1302 ROM are TTL-compatible. The input ratings are V_{IHmin} = 3V and V_{ILmax} = 0.65 V and the outputs are rated as V_{OHmin} = 3.5V and V_{OLmax} = 0.45 V.

2308 MOS ROM

The 2308 MOS read-only memory is similar to the 1302; however, it has an 8192 (8*k*) bit capacity instead of 2*k*. Moreover, its output is organized into 1*k* 8-bit words.

Looking at the block diagram of the 2308 in Fig. 2.25(a), we see that there are 10 address inputs, A_0 through A_9, as well as eight data outputs, ϕ_1 through ϕ_8. These inputs and outputs are TTL-compatible.

The two chip select leads are marked $\overline{CS}_1$ and $CS_2/\overline{CS}_2$. $\overline{CS}_1$ must be 0 to enable the ROM outputs. On the other hand, the enable level of the signal $CS_2/\overline{CS}_2$ can be defined as logic 0 or 1 as part of mask programming.

From the pin layout in Fig. 2.25(b), we find that there are four power-supply leads, V_{CC}, V_{DD}, V_{BB}, and V_{SS}. The dc voltages required at these pins are V_{CC} = +5 V, V_{DD} = +12 V, V_{BB} = -5 V, and V_{SS} = 0 V. The 2308 has a typical address-to-output time of 200 ns.

MCM14524 MOS ROM

The MCM14524 ROM shown in Fig. 2.26 is constructed using low-power CMOS circuitry. This device contains a 1*k*-bit memory array that is orga-

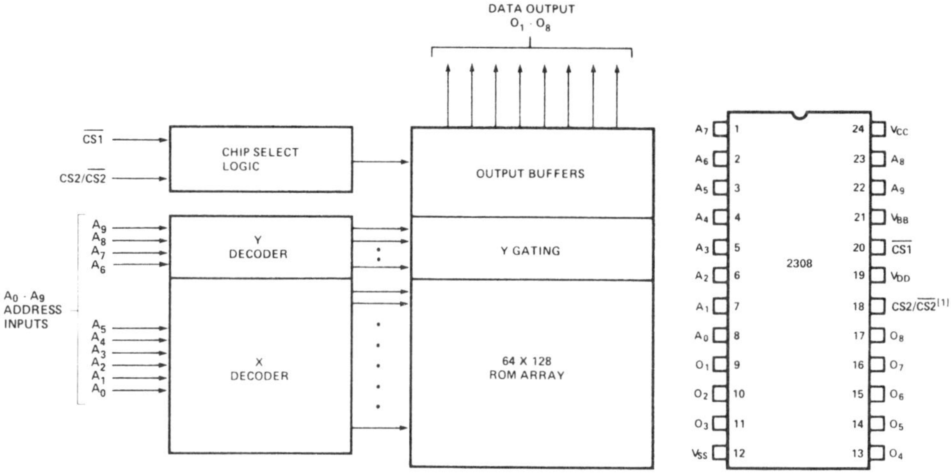

(a) (b)

Fig. 2.25 (a) 2308 block diagram (Intel Corp.); (b) 2308 pin layout (Intel Corp.).

nized into 256 4-bit output words by on-chip decoder circuitry. This CMOS ROM can be operated from any value of dc supply voltage V_{DD} from 3 to 18 V. With a 5-V supply, the typical quiescent power consumption is 50 nW. This is more than 1 million times lower than that required by a 1302 MOS ROM device.

The operation of the device is timed by a clock signal. On the negative

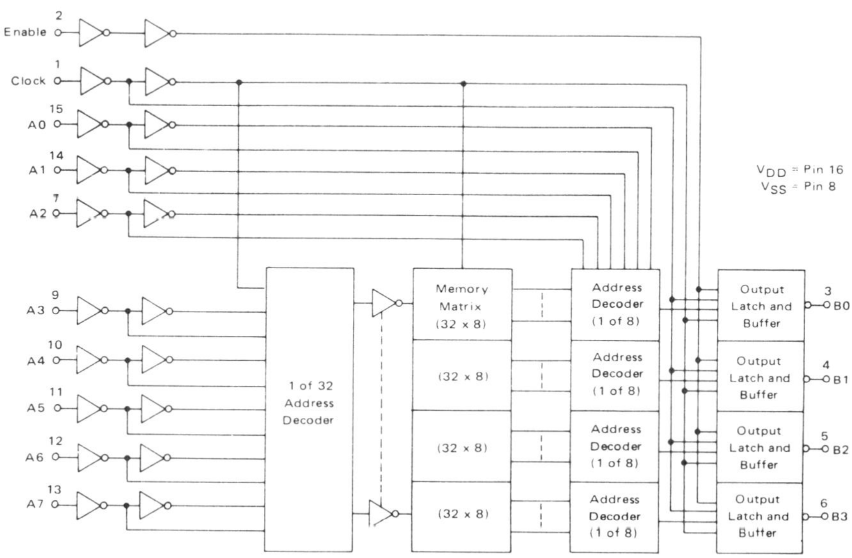

Fig. 2.26 MCM14524 256-word by 4-bit ROM (Motorola Semiconductor Products, Inc.).

edge of the pulse at the *CLOCK* lead, data stored at the addressed memory location are latched into the output buffer and appear on the four data output lines. When the device is powered from a 5-V power supply, the typical address-to-output access time is 1.35 μs. Notice that this device is relatively slow compared to other MOS devices, such as the 1302 ROM.

2.7 PROGRAMMABLE READ-ONLY MEMORIES

The read-only memories we have discussed so far in the chapter have all been mask-programmable. That is, the information of the program is built into the device as part of the manufacturing process. Now we shall continue with the programmable read-only memory (PROM). Unlike the mask ROM, PROMs are *field-programmable.* Therefore, the program information can be entered by the user.

The process of entering data into a PROM is called programming. After programming, the data pattern in the PROM is permanent and cannot be altered in any way.

Integrated PROM devices are manufactured by using both bipolar and MOS technologies. This type of memory device finds wide use in small-volume applications, in equipment where the program will frequently change, and for prototyping, where a mask ROM will replace the PROM after the program is finalized.

Programming a PROM

The data pattern is usually programmed into PROM ICs with automatic equipment. A typical PROM programmer is shown in Fig. 2.27. Program-

Fig. 2.27 PROM programming unit (Data I/O).

ming units like this usually have the ability to test the data pattern within a device to assure that it has been correctly programmed.

A number of different internal programming mechanisms are employed in PROM devices. Three of the most popular are the *fuse link process*, *avalanche-induced migration process*, and the *floating-gate avalanche injection MOS process.*

Fuse Link Process

Most bipolar PROM ICs use the fuse link process of programming. Figure 2.28 shows the architecture of a typical fuse link device. This architecture is essentially the same as that earlier given for mask ROMs. However, here a fuse link has been added between the emitter of each cell transistor and the corresponding bit line. Notice that the memory array is complete, all fuse links are in place, and the cells are all initially in the same logic state.

In a *Nichrome fuse link* PROM device, the fuses are made of a thin layer of nickel-chromium alloy. It is these fuses that are opened or left intact through the programming process to store the data pattern.

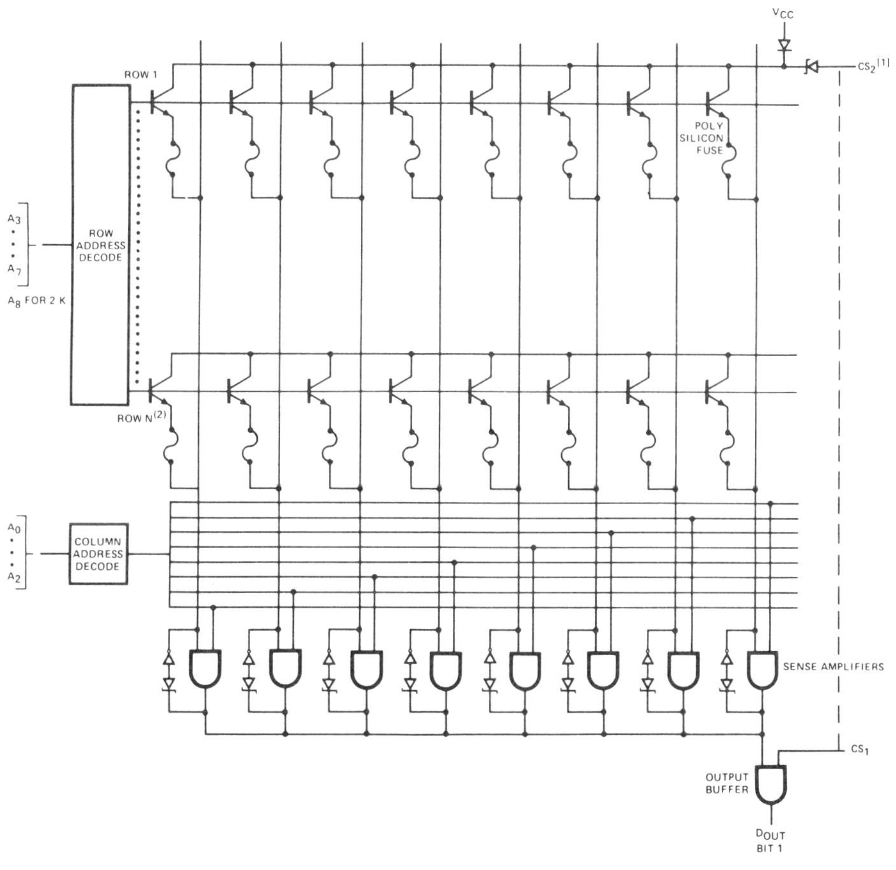

Fig. 2.28 Bipolar PROM architecture (Intel Corp.).

Programming is performed by selectively addressing the memory locations and injecting a current through those fuse links that are to be open-circuited. This current causes the link to open in a way similar to blowing a fuse.

Some manufacturers use *tungsten–titanium fuse links* or *polycrystalline silicon fuse links* in the memory array rather than nickel–chromium.

Avalanche-Induced Migration Process

Another method of programming PROMs is the avalanche-induced migration process. Using this method, the base-emitter junction of the transistor memory cell is electrically avalanched. This causes the base-to-emitter part of the transistor to short-circuit and permanently program the cell.

Floating-Gate Avalanche MOS Process

The third method, the most popular with MOS devices, is the *floating-gate avalanche MOS process* (FAMOS). A FAMOS storage cell consists of a MOSFET device with a floating gate such as that in Fig. 2.29.

This type of cell is programmed by applying a high voltage between the source and drain leads. This voltage causes electrons to be injected to the *floating gate.* The floating gate becomes charged. When the programming voltage is taken away, the charge is trapped at the floating gate and the cell is programmed. The charged gate causes a change in the drain-to-source conductance of the MOSFET, which is sensed to determine if the cell stores a logic 0 or 1.

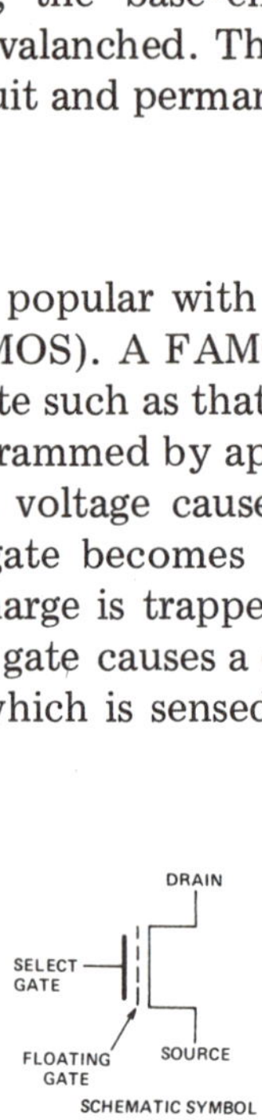

Fig. 2.29 Floating-gate MOSFET memory cell (Intel Corp.).

EXAMPLE 2.11 List the PROM program required to implement the seven-segment decoder required to form the numeric symbols in Fig. 2.30(a). Address input data are to be the *binary-coded decimal* (BCD) form of numbers 0 through 9 and the data outputs must be logic 0 to light segments.

SOLUTION Figure 2.30(b) shows the BCD values for numbers 0 through 9. These codes provide PROM address inputs A_0, A_1, A_2, and A_3. The seven-segment code for each number is listed under the output data columns D_0 through D_6. In this way, we see that a PROM must be programmed with 10 7-bit words to implement the seven-segment code.

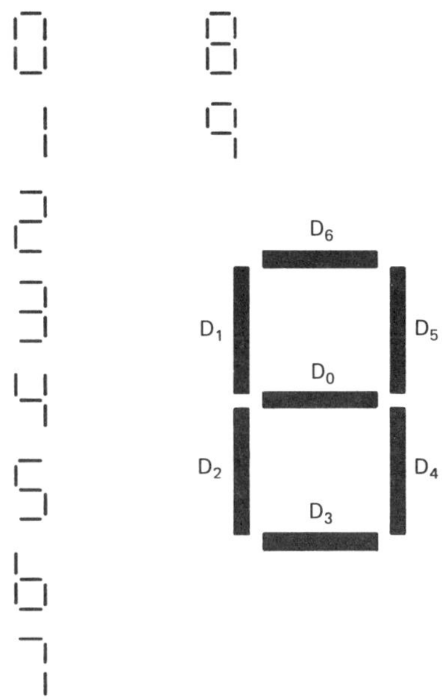

(a)

Address inputs				Data outputs						
A_3	A_2	A_1	A_0	D_6	D_5	D_4	D_3	D_2	D_1	D_0
0	0	0	0	0	0	0	0	0	0	1
0	0	0	1	1	0	0	1	1	1	1
0	0	1	0	0	0	1	0	0	1	0
0	0	1	1	0	0	0	0	1	1	0
0	1	0	0	1	0	0	1	1	0	0
0	1	0	1	0	1	0	0	1	0	0
0	1	1	0	1	1	0	0	0	0	0
0	1	1	1	0	0	0	1	1	1	1
1	0	0	0	0	0	0	0	0	0	0
1	0	0	1	0	0	0	1	1	0	0

(b)

Fig. 2.30 (a) Seven-segment coded numbers; (b) seven-segment decoder function PROM program.

2.8 STANDARD PROM DEVICES

Equivalent PROM integrated circuits are available for many of the standard static mask ROM devices we introduced earlier. The PROM device can be used during the prototype phase of product development so that changes in the program can be made easily and quickly. However, in the final production of the product, the PROMs can be replaced with mask ROMs.

For a PROM and ROM to be equivalent, they must be pin-for-pin interchangeable and have compatible switching speeds and equivalent input/output logic levels.

74S387/TBP14SA10 Bipolar PROM

The 74S387/TBP14SA10 static bipolar PROM is a Schottky TTL device. Comparing the pin layout in Fig. 2.31 to that in Fig. 2.21, we see that the 74S387/TBP14SA10 is a pin-for-pin replacement for the 74187 mask ROM device.

The 74S387/TBP14SA10 has eight address inputs labeled AD_A through AD_H and four open-collector outputs marked DO_1 through DO_4. The memory array consists of 1024 cells that use a tungsten–titanium fuse link programming mechanism and cells are all initially in the logic 1 state. The output of the PROM is organized into 256 4-bit words by on-chip decoders. Its two chip select leads $\overline{CS}_1$ and $\overline{CS}_2$ must both be logic 0 to enable the PROM for operation. The power supply $+V_{CC}$ is 5 V with respect to ground (*GND*).

The switching characteristics of the 74S387/TBP14SA10 are close to those of its equivalent mask ROM. Typical access time is 42 ns, compared to 40 ns for the 74187. Moreover, the 74S387/TBP14SA10 chip select to output and disable output times are typically 15 ns. The input and output logic levels are identical to other 7400 series TTL devices.

Figure 2.32 shows a circuit configuration that can be used for programming the 74S387/TBP14SA10 PROM. Here the address inputs are first set up with switches to select the storage location. After this, each output that is to be logic 0 is pulsed to blow the fuse. A fuse link programs in less than 1 ms. This procedure must be repeated for each of the 256 memory locations.

In this way we see that hand programming of a PROM would be very time consuming and that the only practical approach to programming is with automatic equipment.

3624 Bipolar PROM

The 3624 is another popular static bipolar PROM IC. It is equivalent to the 3324A mask ROM. A pin layout, block diagram, and logic symbol of this device are shown in Fig. 2.33. Like the 3324A, the 3624 has eight address inputs, A_0 through A_7; eight data outputs, O_1 through O_8; and four chip select leads, $\overline{CS}_1$, $\overline{CS}_2$, CS_3, and CS_4.

The memory array contains 4096 memory cells. This device is manufactured such that all cells produce logic 1 outputs in the initial state. Each cell within the 3624 contains a polycrystalline fuse that can be blown during programming to store logic 0 data. Individual cells can be programmed in less than 1 ms. The output is organized into 512 8-bit words.

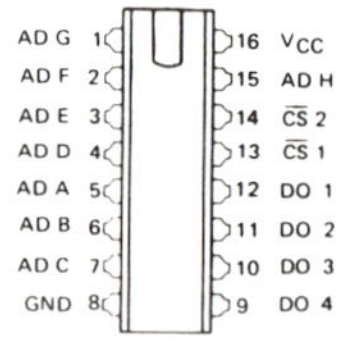

Fig. 2.31 74S387/TBP14SA10 pin layout (Texas Instruments, Incorporated).

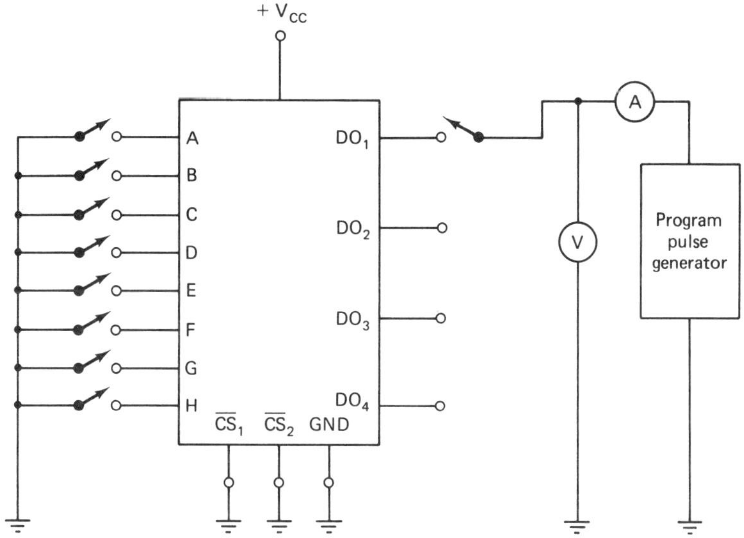

Fig. 2.32 PROM programming circuit configuration (Texas Instruments, Incorporated).

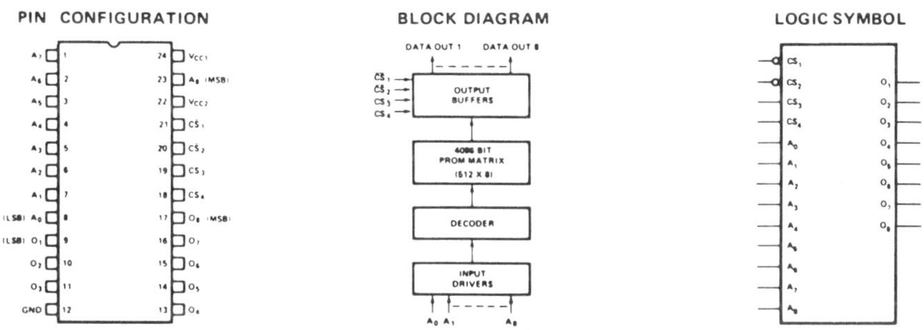

Fig. 2.33 3624 pin layout, block diagram, and logic symbol (Intel Corp.).

The switching times and input/output logic levels of the 3624 are identical to those earlier given for the 3324A IC.

1602A MOS PROM

The 1602A is a 2*k* static MOS PROM integrated circuit. This device is equivalent to the 1302 mask ROM in pin layout and electrical characteristics. FAMOS memory cells are used within the 1602A, and its output is organized into 256 words each with 8 bits by on-chip decoder circuitry. By using an automatic programmer, this device can be programmed at a rate of less than 1 ms per cell.

2.9 ERASABLE PROGRAMMABLE READ-ONLY MEMORY

The erasable programmable read-only memory (EPROM) is similar to the PROM in that it can be programmed by the user. However, the EPROM has an added advantage in that the programmed data pattern can be erased to restore its initial state.

EPROM IC devices are manufactured by using only MOS technology, and the most popular devices use the same FAMOS programming mechanism as that introduced for MOS PROMs. The ability to be programmed and erased makes the EPROM a valuable tool for product development work. As the program is updated, the EPROMs can be erased and reused instead of being discarded like standard PROMs.

Erasing an EPROM

The process of clearing out the programmed bit pattern is called *erasing.* For this purpose, EPROM ICs such as that shown in Fig. 2.34 are provided with a quartz lid. Exposing the device to ultraviolet light through the quartz lid causes the charged gates in the programmed FAMOS cells to discharge. In this way, the memory cells are returned to their initial state. An EPROM erasing unit such as that shown in Fig. 2.35 can be used to erase a number of ICs at a time.

1702A MOS EPROM

Figure 2.36 shows the pin layout of a widely used EPROM integrated circuit. This device, the 1702A, is a $2k$ static electrically programmable read-only

Fig. 2.34 EPROM IC (Texas Instruments, Incorporated).

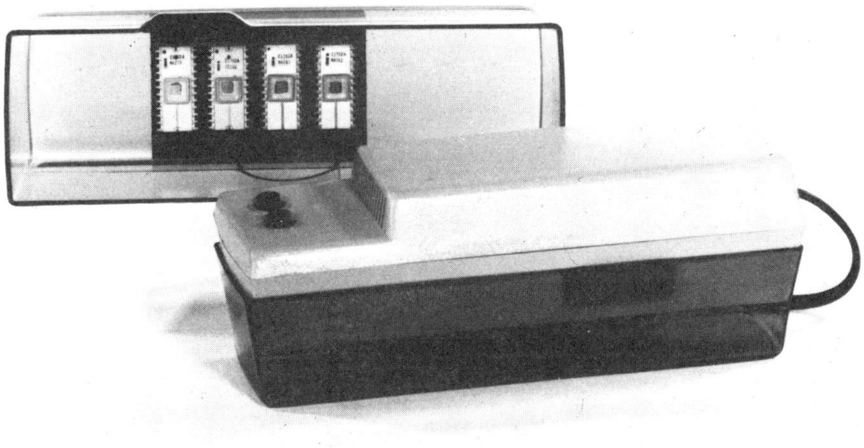

Fig. 2.35 EPROM erasing unit (Ultra-Violet Products, Inc.).

memory. The 1702A is pin-for-pin replaceable by the 1302 mask programmable ROM. Its address-to-output access time is 1 μs and its input/output logic levels are identical to those of the 1302 device.

A block diagram of the architecture of the 1702A is also given in Fig. 2.36. In this diagram we see that the device has eight address inputs, A_0 through A_7; and eight data outputs, $DATA\ OUT_1$ through $DATA\ OUT_8$. These data outputs are three-state and are controlled by the lead $\overline{CS}$. When $\overline{CS}$ is logic 1, the output is disabled and all data outputs are in the hi-Z third state. Setting $\overline{CS}$ to logic 0 enables the outputs.

To perform a read operation, the address corresponding to the memory location to be accessed must be applied to the A_0 through A_7 inputs and the $\overline{CS}$ control lead switched to logic 0. Within the 1702A device, the address

PIN CONFIGURATION

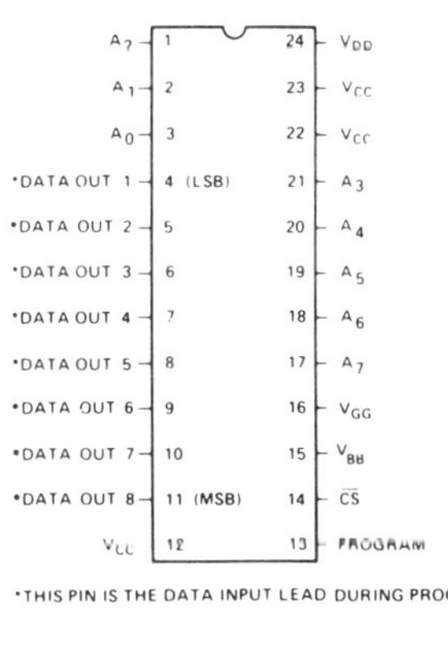

*THIS PIN IS THE DATA INPUT LEAD DURING PROGRAMMING

PIN NAMES

A_0–A_7	Address Inputs
$\overline{CS}$	Chip Select Input
D_{OUT1}–D_{OUT8}	Data Outputs

BLOCK DIAGRAM

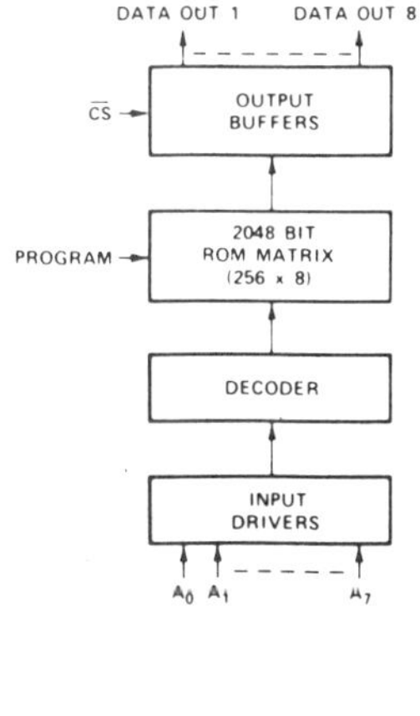

Fig. 2.36 1702A pin layout, pin names, and block diagram (Intel Corp.).

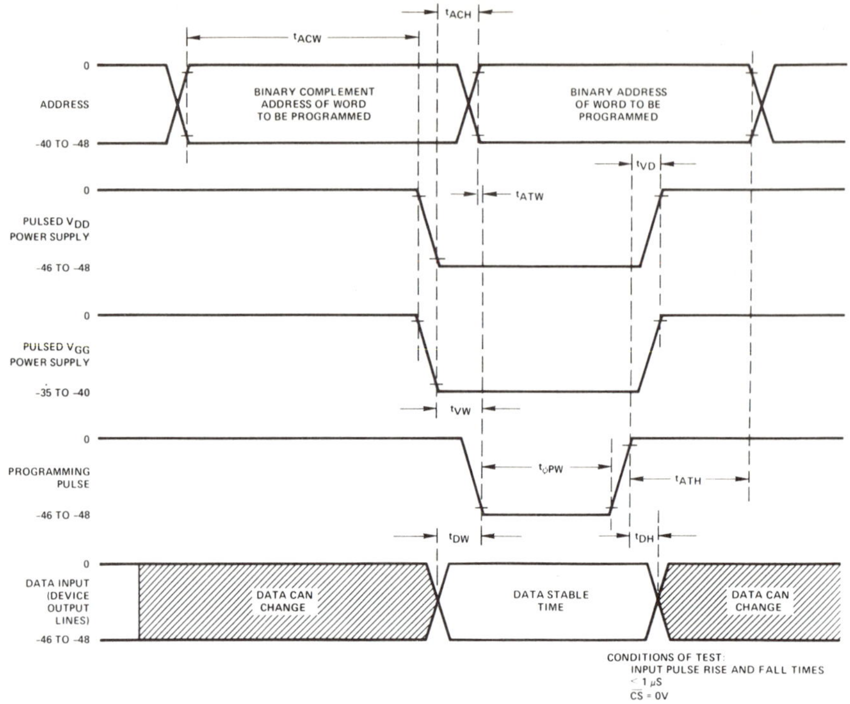

Fig. 2.37 1702A programming waveforms (Intel Corp.).

is decoded and applied to the memory array. This selects the row and column of the stored data. After a delay of about 1 μs, the data word is output on $DATA\ OUT_1$ through $DATA\ OUT_8$. The output is organized into 256 8-bit words. During read operation, the power supplies must be set to V_{CC} = +5 V, V_{DD} = -9 V, and V_{GG} = -9 V.

The memory cells in the array are initially set to logic 0. However, through programming they can be selectively reset to the 1 logic state. Waveforms of the signals involved in programming are shown in Fig. 2.37. Notice that the V_{DD} and V_{GG} power-supply leads must be pulsed, and a pulse must be applied to the *PROGRAM* lead (pin 13).

2708 MOS EPROM

The 2708 is another popular EPROM integrated circuit. It can be replaced by the 2308 mask ROM device in high-volume-production applications. A block diagram and pin layout are shown in Fig. 2.38. Looking at the block diagram, we find that there are ten address inputs, A_0 through A_9; eight data outputs, O_1 through O_8; and a chip select/write enable control lead, $\overline{CS}/WE$.

The memory array consists of 8192 FAMOS cells arranged into 64 rows and 128 columns. However, through the use of row and column decoder circuitry the output is organized into 1024 8-bit words.

During read operation, the power supplies must be set to V_{CC} = +5 V,

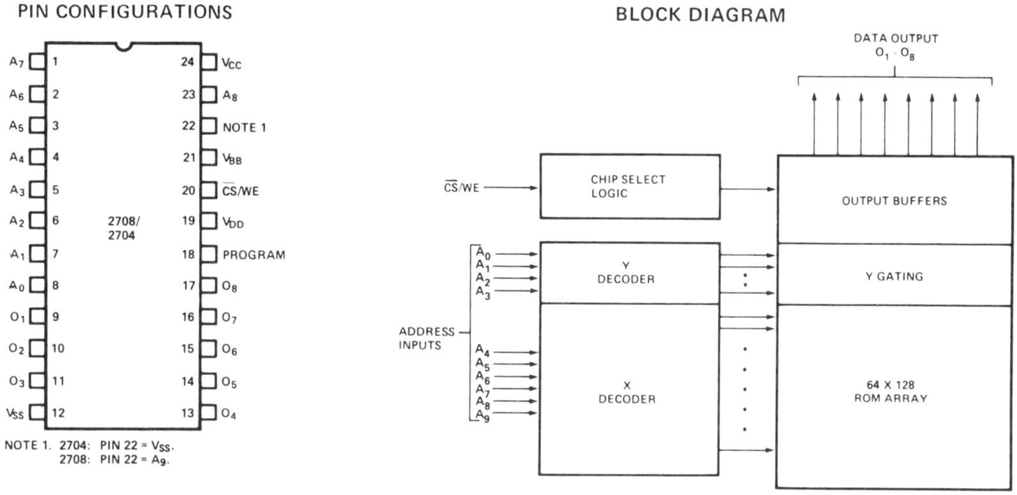

Fig. 2.38 2708 pin configuration and block diagram (Intel Corp.).

V_{DD} = +12 V, and V_{BB} = -5 V. Moreover, the chip select lead must be set to logic 0. After the address is applied to the inputs, there is an address to output delay of about 280 ns before data appear at the data outputs.

The memory cells in the 2708 device are all initially in the 1 logic state. Through programming, cells can be selectively set to logic 0. Like the 1702A, the 2708 device is programmed with pulse signals. EPROM devices can also be programmed with automatic equipment.

TMS 2516 MOS EPROM

The TMS 2516 is another widely used NMOS EPROM IC. This device has a bit storage capacity of 16,384 (16*k*) bits and its output is organized as 2*k* 8-bit words. Figure 2.39 shows a block diagram of the TMS 2516. Here we see that it has 11 address inputs, A_0 through A_{10}; and eight data outputs, Q_1 through Q_8. Moreover, we find two control inputs, $\overline{CS}$ (chip select) and *PD/PGM* (power down/program).

For the read mode of operation, both $\overline{CS}$ and *PD/PGM* must be set to the 0 logic level. The address applied at A_0 through A_{10} selects a location within the memory array and the data word stored at this location is output at Q_1 through Q_8. The maximum address-to-output access time for the read operation is 450 ns and its maximum chip select-to-output access time is 120 ns.

The cells in an erased TMS 2516 all hold the 1 logic level. To program data into the device, we must supply +25 V to the V_{PP} lead. After this, the address is applied at A_0 through A_{10}, $\overline{CS}$ is set to the 1 logic level, and the data are input at leads Q_1 through Q_8. When these signals are set up, the *PD/PGM* lead is pulsed to logic 1 to complete the programming operation. The programming pulse has a typical pulse width of 50 ms. Waveforms show-

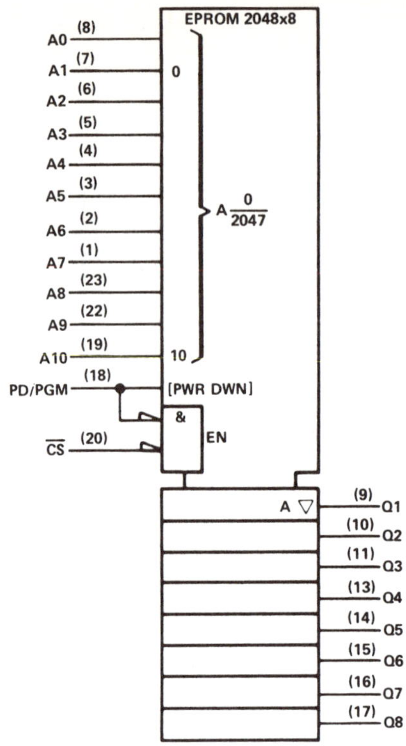

Fig. 2.39 TMS 2516 block diagram (Texas Instruments, Incorporated).

ing this sequence of events are given in Fig. 2.40. Notice that all signals other than V_{PP} are at TTL-compatible logic levels.

The TMS 2516 differs from the MOS devices mentioned earlier in that it can operate from a single +5 V ± 5% power supply $+V_{CC}$. This is because it has a built-in charge pump circuit that produces the other voltages required to operate an NMOS circuit. During read operation, typical power consumption is 285 mW. However, when not in use, the device can be put in a low-power standby mode, where it consumes just 50 mW. This is done by switching the *PD/PGM* input to the 1 level.

TMS 2532 MOS EPROM

The TMS 2532 NMOS EPROM is similar in architecture, operation, and pin layout to the TMS 2516. However, it has a 32*k*-bit storage capacity and 4*k* × 8 organization. A block diagram for the device is given in Fig. 2.41. Notice that the device has 12 address lines. The new address line, A_{11}, replaces the chip select lead of the TMS 2516. For this reason, on the TMS 2532, the $PD/\overline{PGM}$ lead also serves the chip select function and it must be switched to the 0 logic level for read operation. The address to output access time has a maximum value of 450 ns.

When operating in the read mode, the TMS 2532 consumes 840 mW from its +5 V power supply. However, a low-power version of the device,

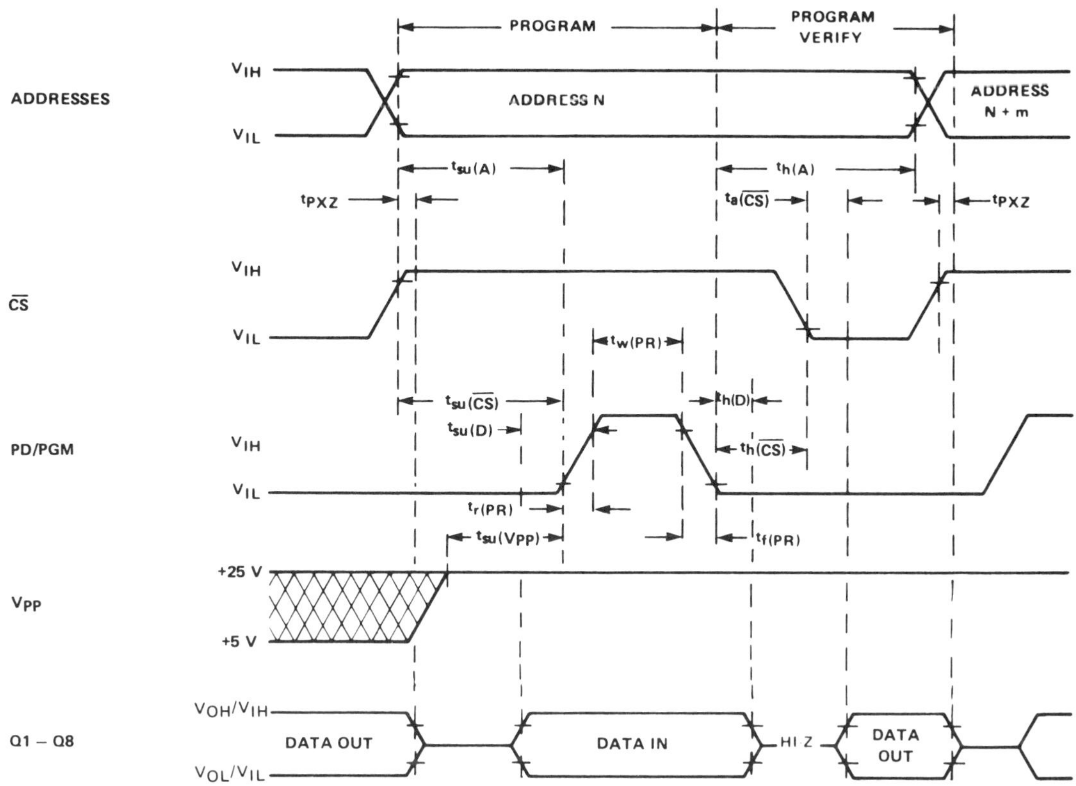

Fig. 2.40 TMS 2516 programming waveforms (Texas Instruments, Incorporated).

the TMS 25L32, is also available. This device requires just 500 mW to operate. Moreover, both devices can be set in a low-power mode when not in use.

TMS 2564 MOS EPROM

The TMS 2564 is one of the newest NMOS EPROMs. It is similar to both the TMS 2516 and TMS 2532, but its capacity has been increased to 64*k* bits, which is organized as 8*k* 8-bit words.

Figure 2.42 represents a block diagram of the device. Notice that the address has been expanded to 13 bits (A_0 through A_{12}), the outputs remain at eight (Q_1 through Q_8), and its larger package permits three control leads, $\overline{CS}_1$, $\overline{CS}_2$, and $PD/\overline{PGM}$. For the read mode of operation, both $\overline{CS}_1$ and $\overline{CS}_2$ must be logic 0. The maximum address-to-output access time is 450 ns and the typical read-mode power consumption is 400 mW.

2.10 DYNAMIC READ-ONLY MEMORIES

The read-only memory integrated-circuit devices introduced up to this point have all been static devices. A number of *dynamic read-only memory* devices

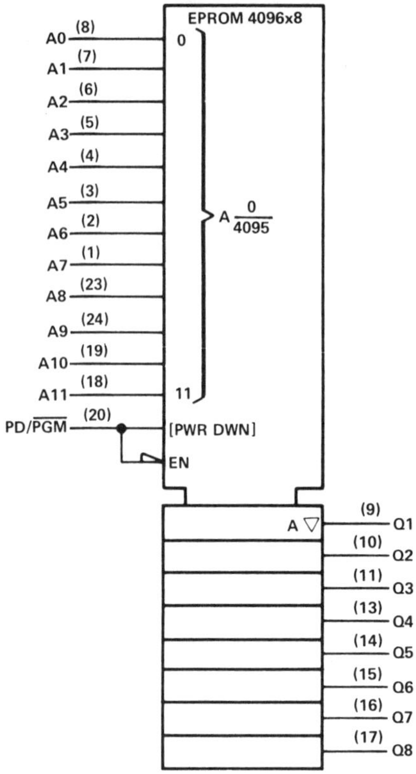

Fig. 2.41 TMS 2532 block diagram (Texas Instruments, Incorporated).

are also available. Dynamic ROMs do not have the capability for dc operation; instead, clock signals are required to control their operation. The most important advantage of dynamic operation is low-power operation while retaining a large storage capacity.

Data stored in the memory array of a dynamic ROM are static. However, some of the surrounding logic circuitry, such as the address decoder, address buffer, and output buffer, can be dynamic circuitry. That is, address data must be clocked in and data clocked out.

In some cases, the output data are held in an internal latch until the next address is clocked into the ROM. If the output data are not latched, care must be taken to assure that circuitry connected at the outputs read the data at the appropriate time. Otherwise, data can be lost.

1702AL MOS ROM

A popular dynamic EPROM is the 1702AL device. This integrated circuit is identical in block diagram and operation to the 1702A static EPROM shown in Fig. 2.36. However, its operation differs in that the -9 V V_{GG} power supply at pin 16 is clocked to reduce power dissipation. Read-operation waveforms are shown in Fig. 2.43.

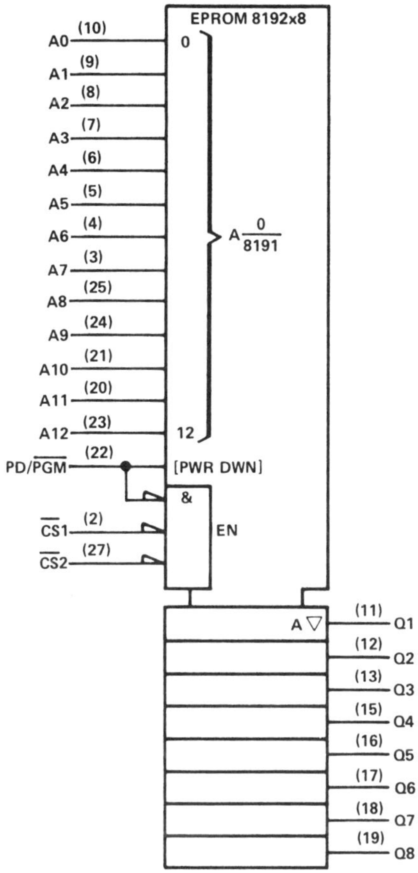

Fig. 2.42 TMS 2564 block diagram (Texas Instruments, Incorporated).

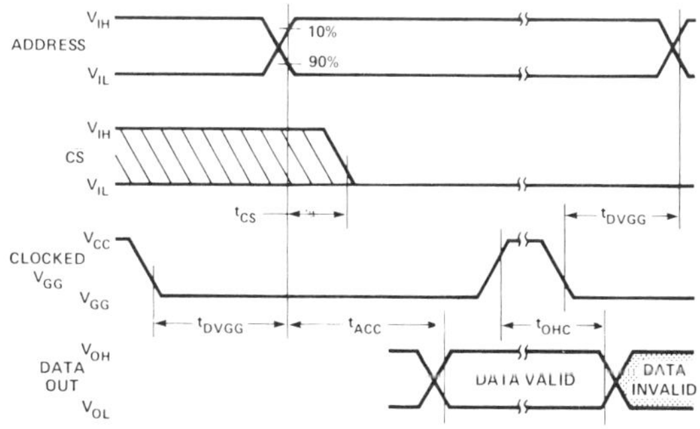

Fig. 2.43 1702AL read operation wave forms (Intel Corp.).

ASSIGNMENTS

Section 2.2

1. What does "ROM" stand for?
2. Describe what is meant by a mask-programmable ROM.
3. Write the address $A_7A_6A_5A_4A_3A_2A_1A_0$ to equal 11111111_2 in hexadecimal form.
4. How many data words can be stored in a ROM that has address lines A_0 through A_{12}?
5. What is the bit storage capacity of a ROM organized into $2k$ 8-bit words?
6. What data word is stored at address $A_3A_2A_1A_0$=0010 in a ROM that contains the program in Fig. 2.4(a)?
7. What data word is output by the ROM in Fig. 2.5 which contains the program in Fig. 2.4(a) when the address input is 0011? Express both the address and data word in hexadecimal form.

Section 2.3

8. What are the six fundamental parts of the ROM's internal architecture?
9. What are the outputs of the memory array in Fig. 2.9(b) when the R_3 input is selected?
10. Find the outputs of the address buffer in Fig. 2.11 for inputs $A_3A_2A_1A_0$=1100.
11. The inputs of the row decoder circuit in Fig. 2.12(a) are A_0=0 and A_1=1. What are the row decoder outputs?
12. The bit line inputs to the sense amplifiers and output buffer in Fig. 2.14 are $B_3B_2B_1B_0$=0101. What is output ϕ_0 when C_3 is logic 1?
13. Which column output of the circuit in Fig. 2.16 is logic 1 when A_3A_2=11?

Section 2.4

14. What is meant by "mask programming"?
15. Is ROM volatile or nonvolatile?

Section 2.5

16. In the circuit of Fig. 2.18, input *CS* is set to logic 1, *AR* is logic 1, and the address inputs are $A_3A_2A_1A_0$=0000. What are the data outputs?
17. Define "access time," "chip select time," and "chip deselect time."

Section 2.6

18. What are the bit storage capacity and output organization of the 74187 and 74S271 mask ROMs?
19. What is the difference between the memory arrays in the 74187 and 74S271 mask ROMs?
20. What are the storage capacities of the 1302 and 2308 ROMs?
21. How does the address-to-data output time of the 74S271 compare to that of the 1302 ROMs?
22. How does the power consumption of the MCM14524 CMOS ROM compare to that of the 74187?

Section 2.7

23. What does "PROM" stand for?
24. What is the main difference between a PROM and a mask ROM?

25. What is the fuse link process?
26. What is the floating-gate avalanche MOS process?

Section 2.8

27. What are the bit capacity, output organization, programming mechanism, and access time of the 74S387/TBP14SA10 PROM?
28. Which mask ROM can be used to replace the 3624 PROM in production equipment?

Section 2.9

29. What does "EPROM" stand for?
30. How does an EPROM differ from a PROM?
31. How is an EPROM erased?
32. Which mask ROM can be used to replace the 1702A MOS EPROM in production equipment?

Section 2.10

33. What is a dynamic ROM?
34. State the primary advantage of dynamic ROM.
35. What is the key difference between the 1702A and 1702AL EPROMs?

3

READ-ONLY MEMORY APPLICATIONS

3.1 INTRODUCTION

Chapter 2 introduced the read-only memory family of semiconductor memory devices: the ROM, PROM, and EPROM. Here we continue our study of read-only memories by introducing some of their most common applications in modern digital equipment and by presenting a number of integrated-circuit devices available with standard programs for use in these applications.

The chapter starts by showing how combinational and sequential logic circuitry can be implemented with read-only memories, how the ROM is used as a program controller for a microcomputer system, and how memory word length and word capacity are expanded by interconnecting memory devices. The balance of the chapter is devoted to common ROM applications such as mathematical look-up tables, code converters, and character generators, as well as standard integrated-circuit devices designed to implement these types of circuits. The following topics are discussed:

1. Implementing combinational and sequential logic
2. Microcomputer system control
3. Expanded word length and word capacity
4. Mathematical look-up tables
5. Code converters
6. Character generators

One important application of read-only memories is the *implementation of combinational logic functions.* Combinational logic means circuitry in which the logic level of the output depends only on the present state of the inputs. Instead of using a large number of logic gates to implement a complex truth table, a single ROM integrated circuit can be utilized to generate the output function.

A ROM can be thought of as a general combinational logic network. The number of combinational functions that can be implemented with a ROM equals the number of output leads. Each function can be described in terms of a number of variables equal to the inputs. The logic function is defined by programming appropriate data into each address location of the memory array.

For example, Fig. 3.1 shows a 1*k* ROM that is organized into 256 4-bit words. This circuit has four data outputs, D_0 through D_3; and eight address inputs, A_0 through A_7. Each of the four output leads can represent a separate logic function of the eight input variables.

When an address input is applied to the A_0 through A_7 lines, the data stored at the accessed location are read out on the data lines to produce the logic functions.

The use of ROM to replace combinational logic circuitry provides a powerful tool for the design of modern digital equipment. However, it should be used only where the approach is more economical than by implementing with standard logic gate circuitry.

Advantages of using ROM in combinational logic applications are reduced package count, size, cost, and improved reliability.[1]

An important electrical property that must be considered when designing combinational logic with ROMs is access time. During the access delay

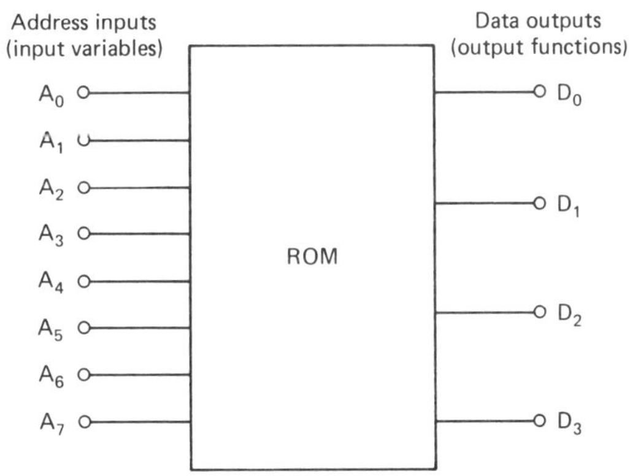

Fig. 3.1 Combinational logic connection of ROM.

[1] Jerry E. Prioste, "Replacing Sequential Logic with ROMs," AN 722 (Austin, TX: Motorola, Inc., 1974).

between address input and data output, the signals at the output leads are undefined and can change logic levels. For this reason, circuitry connected at the outputs should not read the data during this interval.[2]

BCD-to-Excess-3 Code Converter

Let us demonstrate how a ROM can be used to implement *numeric code-converter* circuitry. For instance, Fig. 3.2 shows a truth table with BCD coded input $A_3A_2A_1A_0$ and excess-3 (XS-3) coded output $D_3D_2D_1D_0$. The logic network must convert each word of the BCD code to its equivalent word expressed in XS-3 code.

One approach to implementing this table is to write a Boolean equation for each output. This gives

$$D_0 = \bar{A}_3\bar{A}_2\bar{A}_1\bar{A}_0 + \bar{A}_3\bar{A}_2A_1\bar{A}_0 + \bar{A}_3A_2\bar{A}_1\bar{A}_0 + \bar{A}_3A_2A_1\bar{A}_0 + A_3\bar{A}_2\bar{A}_1\bar{A}_0$$

$$D_1 = \bar{A}_3\bar{A}_2\bar{A}_1\bar{A}_0 + \bar{A}_3\bar{A}_2A_1A_0 + \bar{A}_3A_2\bar{A}_1\bar{A}_0 + \bar{A}_3A_2A_1A_0 + A_3\bar{A}_2\bar{A}_1\bar{A}_0$$

$$D_2 = \bar{A}_3\bar{A}_2\bar{A}_1A_0 + \bar{A}_3\bar{A}_2A_1\bar{A}_0 + \bar{A}_3\bar{A}_2A_1A_0 + \bar{A}_3A_2\bar{A}_1\bar{A}_0 + A_3\bar{A}_2\bar{A}_1A_0$$

$$D_3 = \bar{A}_3A_2\bar{A}_1A_0 + \bar{A}_3A_2A_1\bar{A}_0 + A_3\bar{A}_2\bar{A}_1\bar{A}_0 + A_3\bar{A}_2\bar{A}_1\bar{A}_0 + A_3\bar{A}_2\bar{A}_1A_0$$

These equations would next be simplified with Boolean algebra and the simplified expressions used to construct logic gate circuitry.

A simpler approach is to directly implement the truth table with ROM. To do this, the BCD codes are used as a 4-bit address input and the equivalent XS-3 code is programmed into each address location. For example, the data stored at address $A_3A_2A_1A_0$=0000 are $D_3D_2D_1D_0$=0011.

Implementing this function with ROM requires just 40 bits of ROM organized into 10 4-bit words. Therefore, a ROM or PROM device as small as 16 words by 4 bits could be used.

Decimal	BCD				XS-3			
	A_3	A_2	A_1	A_0	D_3	D_2	D_1	D_0
0	0	0	0	0	0	0	1	1
1	0	0	0	1	0	1	0	0
2	0	0	1	0	0	1	0	1
3	0	0	1	1	0	1	1	0
4	0	1	0	0	0	1	1	1
5	0	1	0	1	1	0	0	0
6	0	1	1	0	1	0	0	1
7	0	1	1	1	1	0	1	0
8	1	0	0	0	1	0	1	1
9	1	0	0	1	1	1	0	0

Fig. 3.2 BCD-to-XS-3 numeric code converter.

[2] Intel Corp., *Memory Handbook* (Santa Clara, CA: Intel Corp., 1978), p. 7-30.

EXAMPLE 3.1 A 16 × 4 bipolar PROM is programmed with the data in the table of Fig. 3.2. What XS-3 code is read out when the input is addressed with the BCD code 0111?

SOLUTION The address input is the BCD code

$$A_3A_2A_1A_0=0111_{\text{BCD}}$$

Looking in Fig. 3.2, we see that the XS-3 output is

$$D_3D_2D_1D_0=1010_{\text{XS-3}}$$

General Numeric Code Converter

In our application of the ROM as a BCD-to-XS-3 numeric code converter, we found that only a small-capacity device was required to implement the combinational logic function. In this way, we recognize the potential of practical devices with capacities of $8k$, $16k$, or even $32k$ in the area of implementing combinational functions.

As a second application, let us go just a little further by expanding the code-conversion capability to a larger number of numeric codes. Figure 3.3 gives a partial listing of addresses and data outputs of a ROM program for a *general numeric code converter.*

Looking at this table, we see that four address bits, A_4, A_5, A_6, and A_7, have been added. These address bits select the type of output code. For example, making these four bits 0000 selects BCD-to-XS-3 code conversion. On the other hand, changing the address to $A_7A_6A_5A_4A_3A_2A_1A_0$ $=00100011$ produces an XS-3 Gray code output instead of XS-3. The data read out of this location are $D_3D_2D_1D_0=0101$. In this way, up to 16 different output codes can be selected with address bits A_4 through A_7.

EXAMPLE 3.2 A read-only memory is programmed with the data of Fig. 3.3. What type of numeric code conversion takes place, and what is the output for address input 00011001?

SOLUTION The four MSBs select the type of code conversion and the four LSBs determine the output. Using the table in Fig. 3.3, we find that $A_7A_6A_5A_4$ $=0001$ sets the ROM for BCD-to-Gray code conversion.

$$A_7A_6A_5A_4=0001=\text{BCD to Gray code}$$

The Gray code word stored at address location $A_3A_2A_1A_0=1001$ is 1101 and it is output at data leads D_0 through D_3.

$$A_3A_2A_1A_0=1001$$

$$D_3D_2D_1D_0=1101$$

A_7	A_6	A_5	A_4	A_3	A_2	A_1	A_0	D_3	D_2	D_1	D_0	Output code
Address								Data output				
0	0	0	0	0	0	0	0	0	0	1	1	
0	0	0	0	0	0	0	1	0	1	0	0	
0	0	0	0	0	0	1	0	0	1	0	1	
0	0	0	0	0	0	1	1	0	1	1	0	
0	0	0	0	0	1	0	0	0	1	1	1	
0	0	0	0	0	1	0	1	1	0	0	0	XS-3 code
0	0	0	0	0	1	1	0	1	0	0	1	
0	0	0	0	0	1	1	1	1	0	1	0	
0	0	0	0	1	0	0	0	1	0	1	1	
0	0	0	0	1	0	0	1	1	1	0	0	
0	0	0	0	1	0	1	0	X	X	X	X	
.	.	.	.	.	.	.	.	.	.	.	.	
.	.	.	.	.	.	.	.	.	.	.	.	
.	.	.	.	.	.	.	.	.	.	.	.	
0	0	0	0	1	1	1	1	X	X	X	X	
0	0	0	1	0	0	0	0	0	0	0	0	
0	0	0	1	0	0	0	1	0	0	0	1	
0	0	0	1	0	0	1	0	0	0	1	1	
0	0	0	1	0	0	1	1	0	0	1	0	
0	0	0	1	0	1	0	0	0	1	1	0	Gray code
0	0	0	1	0	1	0	1	0	1	1	1	
0	0	0	1	0	1	1	0	0	1	0	1	
0	0	0	1	0	1	1	1	0	1	0	0	
0	0	0	1	1	0	0	0	1	1	0	0	
0	0	0	1	1	0	0	1	1	1	0	1	
0	0	0	1	1	0	1	0	X	X	X	X	
.	.	.	.	.	.	.	.	.	.	.	.	
.	.	.	.	.	.	.	.	.	.	.	.	
.	.	.	.	.	.	.	.	.	.	.	.	
0	0	0	1	1	1	1	1	X	X	X	X	
0	0	1	0	0	0	0	0	0	0	1	0	
0	0	1	0	0	0	0	1	0	1	1	0	
0	0	1	0	0	0	1	0	0	1	1	1	
0	0	1	0	0	0	1	1	0	1	0	1	
0	0	1	0	0	1	0	0	0	1	0	0	
0	0	1	0	0	1	0	1	1	1	0	0	XS-3 Gray code
0	0	1	0	0	1	1	0	1	1	0	1	
0	0	1	0	0	1	1	1	1	1	1	1	
0	0	1	0	1	0	0	0	1	1	1	0	
0	0	1	0	1	0	0	1	1	0	1	0	
0	0	1	0	1	0	1	0	X	X	X	X	
.	.	.	.	.	.	.	.	.	.	.	.	
.	.	.	.	.	.	.	.	.	.	.	.	
.	.	.	.	.	.	.	.	.	.	.	.	

Fig. 3.3 General numeric code-converter program.

3.3 IMPLEMENTING SEQUENTIAL LOGIC

In Section 3.2 we saw that the read-only memory could be used to implement combinational logic circuitry. Next, we see how ROMs can be used to *implement sequential logic functions.* Unlike a combinational circuit, the output of a sequential circuit depends on both the present inputs and the previous state of the outputs.

The block diagram of Fig. 3.4 shows the connection of a 256-word by 4-bit ROM into a sequential circuit configuration. Notice that the data outputs D_0 through D_3 are fed to inputs DI_1 through DI_4, respectively, of a

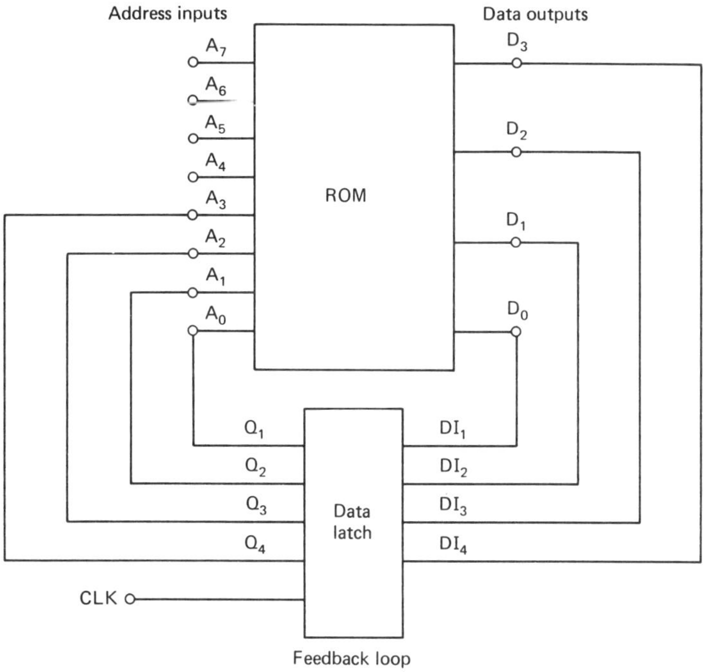

Fig. 3.4 Sequential logic connection of ROM.

data latch circuit. The latch outputs Q_1 through Q_4 are returned to address inputs A_0 through A_3, respectively, of the ROM.

Each time the *CLK* lead on the data latch is pulsed, the data at the outputs are loaded into the latch and applied to address inputs A_0 through A_3 of the ROM. These bits are combined with the code on lines A_4 through A_7 to produce an 8-bit address to access the new storage location. After a delay equal to the access time of the ROM, the read data appear at the output.

In this way, we see that the new address and data outputs depend upon the present state of inputs A_4, A_5, A_6, and A_7 as well as the previous state of outputs D_0, D_1, D_2, and D_3. This is consistent with sequential circuit operation.

Four independent sequential outputs are produced. These outputs can be taken directly from the ROM data outputs D_0 through D_3 or the Q_1 through Q_4 outputs of the latch. By appropriately programming the ROM, we can obtain the desired sequential operation at each output.

The data latch is used in the feedback loop to synchronize the address inputs. Recall from Section 3.2 that ROM outputs are undefined during the access-time interval. In fact, unwanted changes in the output logic levels can occur during this time. Moreover, all data outputs do not occur simultaneously. If the output latch was not used, but instead the data outputs were directly returned to the address inputs, this unsynchronized data output could produce a momentary false address input and error in the sequential output. Error pulses of this type produced in the output are called *glitches.*[3]

Gray Code Generator

Figure 3.5 gives a program that can be used to implement a Gray code counter with ROM. This *numeric code generator* is a simple sequential application for ROM. In the figure the address column lists each word in the Gray code. Notice that the data stored at each address location represent the next word in the code. For instance, the data stored at address $A_3A_2A_1A_0$=0000 are $D_3D_2D_1D_0$=0001.

To implement this table with the circuit in Fig. 3.4, the address inputs A_4, A_5, A_6, and A_7 are not used and can be wired to the 0 logic level. The sequential outputs are taken from the Q_1 through Q_4 outputs of the latch. For this application, we are using just 10 of the 256 4-bit storage locations available in the ROM.

The count sequence begins by clearing the output. This sets all latch outputs to logic 0 and the address input is $A_3A_2A_1A_0$=0000. Applying this address to the ROM inputs, causes the data output $D_3D_2D_1D_0$=0001.

$$A_3A_2A_1A_0=0000$$

$$D_3D_2D_1D_0=0001$$

The circuit stops in this stable state, with the first word of the Gray code held in the latch output and the second word at the ROM outputs, waiting for the next clock pulse.

Address input				Data output			
A_3	A_2	A_1	A_0	D_3	D_2	D_1	D_0
0	0	0	0	0	0	0	1
0	0	0	1	0	0	1	1
0	0	1	1	0	0	1	0
0	0	1	0	0	1	1	0
0	1	1	0	0	1	1	1
0	1	1	1	0	1	0	1
0	1	0	1	0	1	0	0
0	1	0	0	1	1	0	0
1	1	0	0	1	1	0	1
1	1	0	1	0	0	0	0

Fig. 3.5 Gray code counter program.

[3] Prioste, "Replacing Sequential Logic with ROMs," p. 8.

On the next clock pulse, D_0 through D_3 are loaded into the latch output. This causes the new address input

$$A_3 A_2 A_1 A_0 = 0001$$

This is the second word of the Gray code and the ROM output changes to

$$D_3 D_2 D_1 D_0 = 0011$$

With each new pulse at the *CLK* input, the output of the circuit increments through the Gray code count sequence. As the tenth clock pulse occurs, 0000 is reloaded into the latch, and the sequence starts over again.

EXAMPLE 3.3 The ROM in Fig. 3.4 is programmed for generation of the Gray code. What are the address input and data output after the fifth clock pulse following the clearing of the latch?

SOLUTION Clearing the latch starts the address input at

$$A_3 A_2 A_1 A_0 = 0000$$

Looking at the table in Fig. 3.5, we find that after the fifth pulse at the clock input, the address input and data output are

$$A_3 A_2 A_1 A_0 = 0111$$

$$D_3 D_2 D_1 D_0 = 0101$$

General Numeric Code Generator[4]

The sequential circuit in Fig. 3.4 had four unused address inputs when we used it to implement a simple numeric code generator. Using these address inputs, we can expand the code-generation capability of our circuit to include 16 different codes.

The program in Fig. 3.6 is a partial listing for a *general numeric code-generator* circuit. In this listing, we find that the address bits A_4, A_5, A_6, and A_7 are set to a static binary count to select the various code-generator routines. For instance, $A_7 A_6 A_5 A_4 = 0001$ picks the XS-3 code.

Storage locations indicated as XXXX are not used in the count sequence. The X's marked in these locations indicate don't-care states and can be programmed as logic 0 or 1. The complete 256 × 4 capacity of ROM or PROM is required to implement this sequential circuit.

EXAMPLE 3.4 The latch in Fig. 3.4 is cleared and the address inputs $A_7 A_6 A_5 A_4$ are set to 0010. What are the address inputs $A_3 A_2 A_1 A_0$ and data output produced

[4]Monolithic Memories, Inc., "ROM in Sequential and Combinational Logic," AN-102 (Sunnyvale, CA: Monolithic Memories, Inc., 1971). (Courtesy of Monolithic Memories, Incorporated.)

Address input								Data output				Code generated
A_7	A_6	A_5	A_4	A_3	A_2	A_1	A_0	D_3	D_2	D_1	D_0	
0	0	0	0	0	0	0	0	0	0	0	1	Gray code
0	0	0	0	0	0	0	1	0	0	1	1	
0	0	0	0	0	0	1	0	0	1	1	0	
0	0	0	0	0	0	1	1	0	0	1	0	
0	0	0	0	0	1	0	0	1	1	0	0	
0	0	0	0	0	1	0	1	0	1	0	0	
0	0	0	0	0	1	1	0	0	1	1	1	
0	0	0	0	0	1	1	1	0	1	0	1	
0	0	0	0	1	0	0	0	X	X	X	X	
0	0	0	0	1	0	0	1	X	X	X	X	
0	0	0	0	1	0	1	0	X	X	X	X	
0	0	0	0	1	0	1	1	X	X	X	X	
0	0	0	0	1	1	0	0	1	1	0	1	
0	0	0	0	1	1	0	1	0	0	0	0	
0	0	0	0	1	1	1	0	X	X	X	X	
0	0	0	0	1	1	1	1	X	X	X	X	
0	0	0	1	0	0	0	0	0	0	1	1	XS-3 code
0	0	0	1	0	0	0	1	X	X	X	X	
0	0	0	1	0	0	1	0	X	X	X	X	
0	0	0	1	0	0	1	1	0	1	0	0	
0	0	0	1	0	1	0	0	0	1	0	1	
0	0	0	1	0	1	0	1	0	1	1	0	
0	0	0	1	0	1	1	0	0	1	1	1	
0	0	0	1	0	1	1	1	1	0	0	0	
0	0	0	1	1	0	0	0	1	0	0	1	
0	0	0	1	1	0	0	1	1	0	1	0	
0	0	0	1	1	0	1	0	1	0	1	1	
0	0	0	1	1	0	1	1	1	1	0	0	
0	0	0	1	1	1	0	0	0	0	1	1	
0	0	0	1	1	1	0	1	X	X	X	X	
0	0	0	1	1	1	1	0	X	X	X	X	
0	0	0	1	1	1	1	1	X	X	X	X	
0	0	1	0	0	0	0	0	0	0	1	0	XS-3 Gray code
0	0	1	0	0	0	0	1	X	X	X	X	
0	0	1	0	0	0	1	0	0	1	1	0	
0	0	1	0	0	0	1	1	X	X	X	X	
0	0	1	0	0	1	0	0	1	1	0	0	
0	0	1	0	0	1	0	1	0	1	0	0	
0	0	1	0	0	1	1	0	0	1	1	1	
0	0	1	0	0	1	1	1	0	1	0	1	
0	0	1	0	1	0	0	0	X	X	X	X	
0	0	1	0	1	0	0	1	X	X	X	X	
0	0	1	0	1	0	1	0	0	0	1	0	
0	0	1	0	1	0	1	1	X	X	X	X	
0	0	1	0	1	1	0	0	1	1	0	1	
0	0	1	0	1	1	0	1	1	1	1	1	
0	0	1	0	1	1	1	0	1	0	1	0	
0	0	1	0	1	1	1	1	1	1	1	0	

Fig. 3.6 General numeric counter program.

by the circuit after the fourth clock pulse if the ROM contains the program shown in Fig. 3.6?

SOLUTION When address bits $A_7A_6A_5A_4$=0010, the XS-3 Gray code-generator routine in ROM is selected. Clearing the latch output makes the address input

$$A_3A_2A_1A_0=0000$$

This reads the first word in the XS-3 Gray code out of the ROM:

$$D_3D_2D_1D_0=0010$$

After the fourth clock pulse, the latch output holds the XS-3 Gray code word

$$A_3A_2A_1A_0=0101$$

The data produced at the ROM output are

$$D_3D_2D_1D_0=0100$$

This is the next count in the XS-3 Gray code sequence.

3.4 MICROCOMPUTER CONTROL

At present, ROMs, PROMs, and EPROMs are most widely used for storage of microprograms for microcomputer systems. A microcomputer is a small digital computer data processing system. It contains all the elements of a larger computer: central processing unit (CPU), memory unit, input unit, and output unit. However, each of these basic units is provided with a smaller working capacity. The central processing unit is also known as a *microprocessor* unit (MPU).

Unlike larger general-purpose computers, microcomputer systems are frequently customized for a specific application. Some examples are electronic calculators, cash registers, scales, and electronic games.

The Central Processing Unit and Its Microprogram

The heart of the microcomputer system is the central processing unit. It has the capability of performing many different operations, such as adding numbers, subtracting numbers, and making logical decisions. Each of these operations is represented as an instruction that can be coded in binary form.

The overall operation of the central processing unit (CPU) is controlled by a sequence of instructions called the *program*. To obtain the desired system performance, the designer must specify the instructions and the sequence in which they are to be performed. A typical program can consist of thousands of instructions.

It is this program that is stored in read-only memory. The program in ROM is called the *firmware*, while that in RAM or on magnetic disk or tape is called *software*. Remember that ROMs are nonvolatile. For this reason, the microprogram is not lost when power is removed.

PROMs and EPROMs play an important role in the development of the program. For initial development EPROM devices can be used so that the large number of changes required can be rapidly implemented. After the program has been developed, equipment can be made using PROMs instead of EPROMs. The equipment can be tested to assure that the program functions correctly. If satisfactory results are obtained from the test, a commitment can be made to produce mask-programmable ROMs.

In this way, we see one of the versatile features of microcomputer systems. In many applications, system operation can be easily modified by just replacing the program within the ROM devices instead of modifying the electronic circuitry.

Read-Only Memory/Microcomputer Interface

The connection of a read-only memory to the central processing unit of a microcomputer is illustrated in Fig. 3.7. The contents of the *program counter* and *address register* within the CPU are used to address the read-only memory over address bus lines A/B_1 through A/B_{12}. The address is input to the ROM on leads A_0 through A_{11}. With this 12-bit address, the CPU can select one of the $4k$ memory locations over the address range 000_{16} to FFF_{16}.

The 8-bit instruction word held at this location within ROM is output at data leads D_0 through D_7 of the ROM and fetched to the CPU over its *instruction/data* bus (I/D_1 through I/D_8). Within the CPU, the instruction is loaded into the *data register* and supplied as an input to the *instruction decoder.* This decoder controls the operation of the CPU during the execution of the instruction.

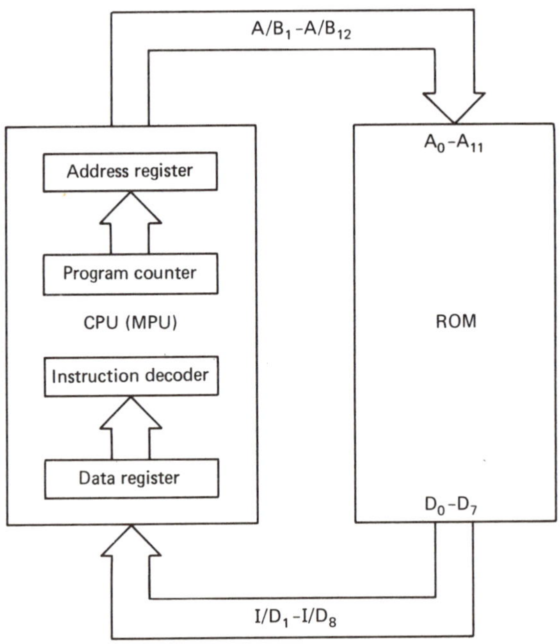

Fig. 3.7 ROM cycle block diagram.

Instruction Cycle

The ROM operating cycle of a microcomputer can be divided into two parts, called the *fetch phase* and the *execute phase*. During the fetch phase, an instruction is taken from the read-only memory and loaded into the CPU, where it is decoded by the instruction decoder.

The program counter always contains the address of the next instruction to be executed. As the fetch phase begins, the CPU loads the address held in the program counter into the address register that outputs onto address bus A/B_1 through A/B_{12}. The program counter is then incremented by 1, so that it contains the address of the next instruction.

Within the ROM, the address is decoded by the row and column decoders to select the storage location of the instruction. The ROM outputs the instruction on the instruction/data bus I/D_1 through I/D_8 for transfer to the data register within the CPU.

Inside the CPU, the instruction held at the data register output is used as an input to the instruction decoder. It is this decoder that controls the CPU during the execution phase. The decoder determines from the bits of the instruction word which type of instruction is to be performed and sets up the sequence of events that must occur for the CPU to execute the instruction. This completes the fetch phase.

The execution phase begins, and the CPU, under the control of the instruction decoder outputs, goes about performing the operation defined by the instruction.

The operating sequence just described represents the fetch and execution phase of just one instruction from ROM. This cycle repeats as the CPU fetches and executes one instruction after the other of the program. ROMs have *nondestructive readout;* therefore, the program can be read over and over again.

3.5 EXPANDING WORD LENGTH AND WORD CAPACITY

In many applications, the system requirement for read-only memory is greater than that available in a single device. There are basically two reasons for expanding the memory: first, the word length is not large enough; and second, the memory capacity does not provide enough data words.

Both of these expansion requirements can be satisfied by interconnecting a number of ROM, PROM, or EPROM devices. Here we will show how ROM devices can be connected to increase word length and memory capacity.

Word-Length Expansion[5]

Applications in which the output of a single ROM does not have enough bits require word-length expansion. For example, let us take a microcomputer

[5] Intel Corp., *Memory Handbook*, p. 7-22. (Courtesy of Intel Corp.)

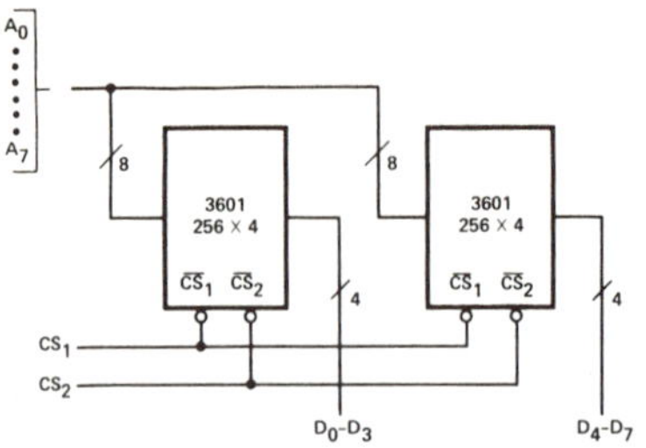

Fig. 3.8 Expanding word length (Intel Corp.).

that employs 8-bit instruction words but is to have its program stored in PROM devices such as the 3601 bipolar device. This device has a storage capacity of 256 4-bit rather than 8-bit words.

Figure 3.8 shows how two 3601 PROMs are interconnected to provide 256 8-bit words. Notice that the individual address inputs and chip select leads on the two devices are connected in parallel. On the other hand, the 4-bit outputs on the two devices are each used to provide 4 bits of the 8-bit output word. This PROM configuration doubles word length but does not affect word capacity.

If the $\overline{CS}_1$ and $\overline{CS}_2$ signals are switched to logic 0, both 3601 PROMs are enabled for operation. Applying an 8-bit address to A_0 through A_7 causes the data stored at this location in each ROM to be read out on the corresponding output lines. One PROM provides the four LSBs D_0 through D_3 and the other the MSBs D_4 through D_7 of the 8-bit data word.

This same device configuration can be used with larger-capacity ROMs, PROMs, and EPROMs.

EXAMPLE 3.5 How many 3601 ROMs must be connected in the configuration of Fig. 3.8 to form 256 16-bit words?

SOLUTION To expand the 4-bit word length of the 3601 PROM to 16 bits, four devices must be connected as in Fig. 3.8. This connection is shown in Fig. 3.9.

Word-Capacity Expansion[6]

The other limitation with respect to the application of a single read-only memory device was word capacity. For instance, the system may require 1*k* 4-bit words of PROM. However, the devices to be used have a 256-word by 4-bit organization. In this case, a single ROM device has the correct word length but not enough memory locations can be addressed.

The word-capacity limitation can also be overcome by interconnecting separate ROM, PROM, or EPROM ICs. The case just mentioned required 1*k* or 1024 words, which is four times the capacity of a single 3601 device. Connecting four of these devices together as shown in Fig. 3.10 produces our 1024-word by 4-bit PROM memory. With this connection, we have expanded the word capacity without affecting word length.

[6] Ibid., p. 7-23.

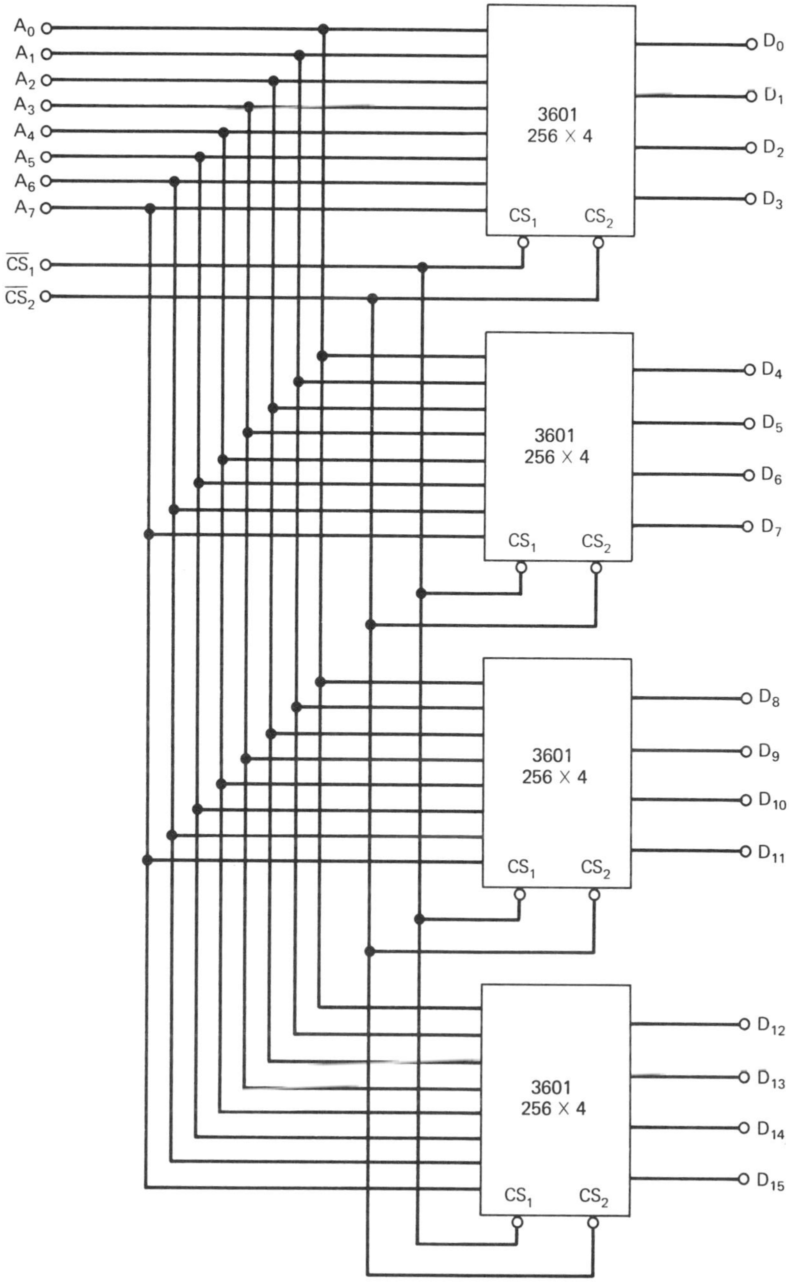

Fig. 3.9 Expanding word length to 16 bits.

Looking at this circuit configuration, we see that it differs from that used to expand word length. Here the address inputs A_0 through A_7 on the separate devices are again paralleled. Moreover, the $\overline{CS}_1$ chip select signal leads are also paralleled, and in this circuit they are supplied by a control sig-

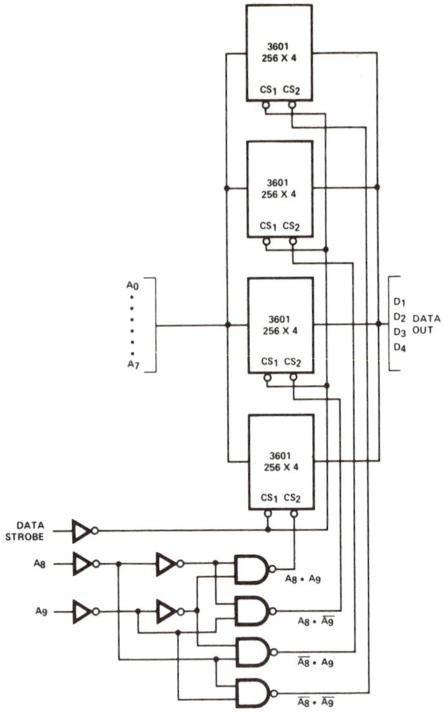

Fig. 3.10 Word-capacity expansion (Intel Corp.).

nal called *DATA STROBE.* A first change in the circuit is found with the connection of the chip select input $\overline{CS}_2$. The $\overline{CS}_2$ lead on each ROM is controlled by a separate output of a logic gate address decoder circuit. The inputs to the decoder are two additional address lines A_8 and A_9.

The other change is identified at the output leads D_1 through D_4. Notice that the outputs on all four PROM devices are tied in parallel. This connection is possible only for devices with open-collector or three-state outputs. The 3601 is equipped with open-collector outputs.

During memory operation, a 10-bit address is supplied to the input. Address bits A_0 through A_7 go to all ROMs in parallel and access a storage location. Different data can be programmed into this storage location in each ROM. At the same time, bits A_8 and A_9 go to inputs of the address decoder logic circuitry. This makes the output of one NAND gate in the decoder switch to logic 0. The other three NAND gate outputs stay at the 1 logic level. Assuming that the *DATA STROBE* signal is logic 1 at this time, the $\overline{CS}_1$ and $\overline{CS}_2$ leads are both logic 0 on one of the four ROMs. It is this device that outputs data stored at the addressed location on the data lines D_1 through D_4. When this occurs, the outputs of the other three ROMs are held disabled by the address decoder circuit.

Before going on, let us take an example to illustrate more clearly how the address decoder circuit enables one of the four ROMs for operation.

The *DATA STROBE* input is switched to logic 1 and makes the $\overline{CS}_1$ input on all ROMs logic 0. The address input is

$$A_9 A_8 A_7 A_6 A_5 A_4 A_3 A_2 A_1 A_0 = 1100000000$$

Bits A_8 and A_9 are input to the decoder:

$$A_9 A_8 = 11$$

When both of these signals are logic 1, the output of the upper NAND gate $A_8 \cdot A_9$ switches to logic 0. This signal goes to the $\overline{CS}_2$ input on the lowest ROM. Therefore, the lowest ROM has both $\overline{CS}_1$ and $\overline{CS}_2$ equal logic 0 and it reads out the content of address location $A_7 A_6 A_5 A_4 A_3 A_2 A_1 A_0 = 00000000$ onto data lines D_1 through D_4.

EXAMPLE 3.6 Which PROM in Fig. 3.10 is enabled, and what storage location is accessed, when the address input is 0000000000 and *DATA STROBE* is logic 1?

SOLUTION The PROM is selected by address bits A_8 and A_9.

$$A_9 A_8 = 00$$

When both A_8 and A_9 are logic 0, the $\overline{A}_8 \cdot \overline{A}_9$ NAND gate output switches to logic 0. The 1 at *DATA STROBE* makes all $\overline{CS}_1$ leads logic 0.

$$\overline{A}_8 \cdot \overline{A}_9 = 0$$

$$\overline{CS}_1 = 0$$

This enables the uppermost of the four ROMs for operation and the content of address location 00_{16} is output on the data lines.

$$A_7 A_6 A_5 A_4 A_3 A_2 A_1 A_0 = 00000000 = 00_{16}$$

Expanding Both Word Length and Word Capacity[7]

In many practical read-only memory designs, both word length and word capacity must be expanded. The circuit in Fig. 3.11 demonstrates this type of memory. Here a number of ROM devices are connected into rows and columns. Notice that the address inputs A_0 through A_7 on all devices are connected in parallel. Moreover, the most significant bits of the address A_8 through A_m are inputs to the address decoder circuit which is used to expand memory capacity. The outputs of ROMs in a column are paralleled to expand capacity but those of the rows are not; instead, they are used as separate 4-bit groups to expand the length of the output word.

When an address is applied to the input of the circuit, the decoder en-

[7] Ibid.

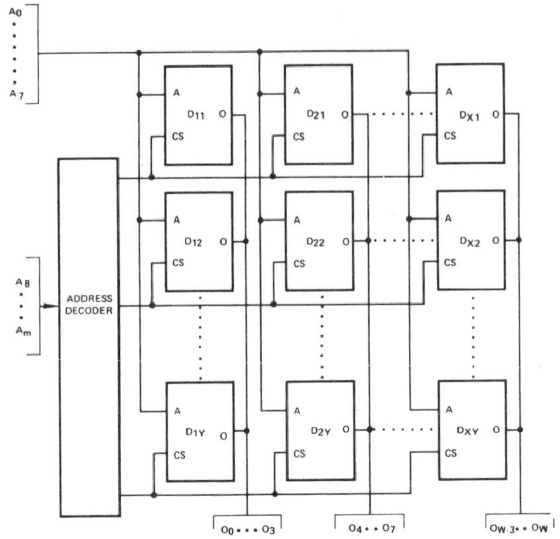

Fig. 3.11 General word-length and word-capacity expansion (Intel Corp.).

ables all ROMs in one row of the array. Each ROM outputs the 4 bits of data stored at the location defined by bits A_0 through A_7. The resulting output is data word O_0 through O_w.

Figure 3.12 shows two standard TTL IC devices that can be employed as an *address decoder* circuit. The 7442 device in Fig. 3.12(a) is a BCD-to-decimal decoder. The BCD code at input DCBA makes one of the 10 outputs 0 through 9 switch to logic 0. In this way, it can be used to enable one of 10 rows of ROMs.

The 74LS138 in Fig. 3.12(b) is a TTL demultiplexer device. It has just three inputs *CBA* and can be used to select one of eight rows of ROMs when used as an address decoder.

The output selected by the binary code at *CBA* has a logic level defined by the equation

$$D_0=\overline{G_1\cdot\overline{G_{2A}+G_{2B}}}$$

On the device in Fig. 3.12(b), the inputs are at fixed logic levels $G_1=1$, $G_{2A}=0$, and $G_{2B}=0$. These inputs produce the output that follows:

$$D_0=\overline{1\cdot\overline{0+0}}=\overline{1\cdot 1}=\overline{1}$$

$$D_0=0$$

For example, an input of $CBA=111$ causes output lead 7 to switch to logic 0.

Outputs 0 through 7 of the demultiplexer are used as control inputs for the chip select leads in the rows of ROMs.

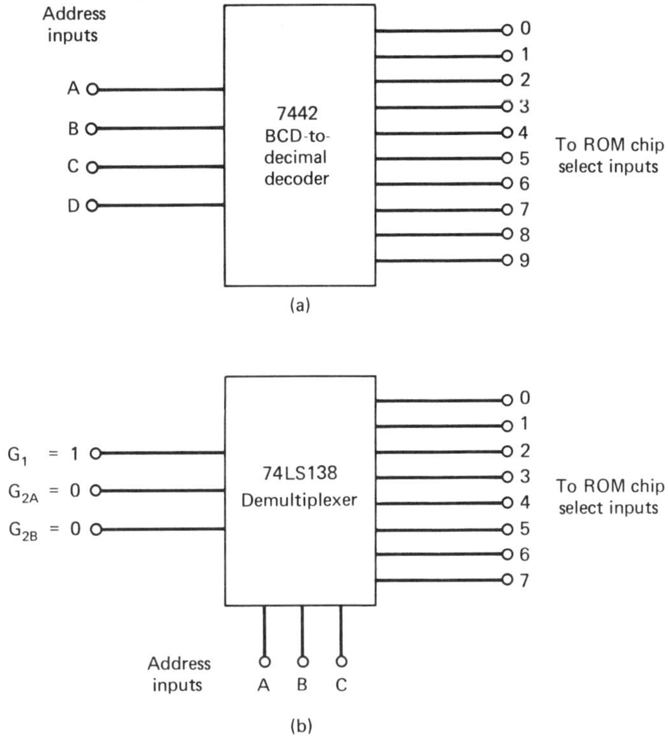

Fig. 3.12 (a) 7442 address decoder; (b) 74LS138 address decoder.

3.6 MATHEMATICAL LOOK-UP TABLES

Read-only memories can be used to store mathematical function look-up tables. A *look-up table* is used to store tabular information. Two examples are the trigonometric sine-function table and arctangent table. In this section, we look into standard ROM look-up table devices and how they can be cascaded to improve accuracy.

MM4220BN/5220BN Arctangent Look-up Table[8]

The MM4220BN/MM5220BN is a standard look-up table device. It is a 1*k* ROM programmed with the trigonometric arctangent table. Using this device, we can look up the angle for specific values of the tangent function.

Figure 3.13(a) shows the connection of the MM4220BN/MM5220BN for look-up table operation. In this circuit diagram, we see that the ROM has eight address inputs, A_1 through A_8. A_8 is the MSB of the address word. Moreover, we find eight data outputs, B_1 through B_8.

[8] National Semiconductor Corp., *Memory Data Book* (Santa Clara, CA: National Semiconductor Corp., 1976), p. 6-32. (Courtesy of National Semiconductor Corp.)

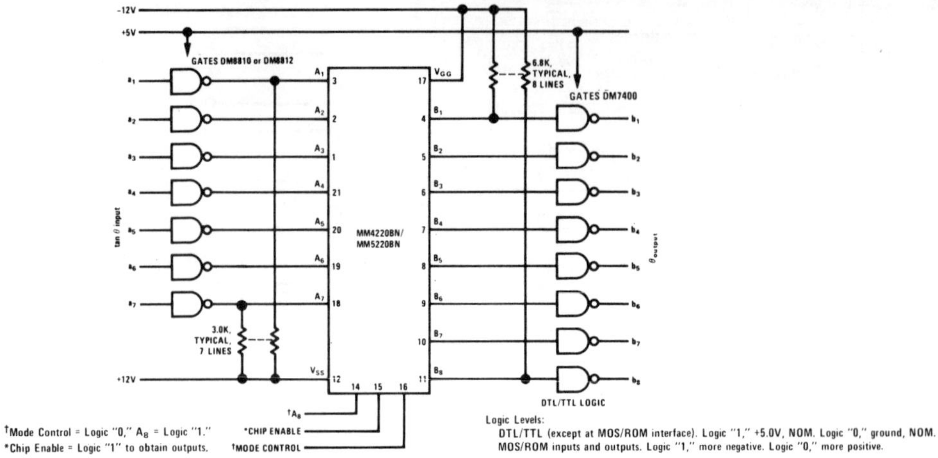

(a)

ADDRESS 128 (x)	OUTPUT CODE (θ_{OUTPUT}) B8	B7	B6	B5	B4	B3	B2	B1
0	0	0	0	0	0	0	0	0
1	0	1	0	0	0	0	0	0
2	1	0	1	0	0	0	0	0
3	1	1	1	0	0	0	0	0
4	0	1	0	1	0	0	0	0
5	0	0	1	1	0	0	0	0
6	1	1	1	1	0	0	0	0
7	0	1	0	0	1	0	0	0
8	0	0	1	0	1	0	0	0
9	1	1	1	0	1	0	0	0
10	1	0	0	1	1	0	0	0
11	0	0	1	1	1	0	0	0
12	0	1	1	1	1	0	0	0
13	1	0	0	0	0	1	0	0
14	1	1	0	0	0	1	0	0
15	0	1	1	0	0	1	0	0
16	0	0	0	1	0	1	0	0
17	1	1	0	1	0	1	0	0
18	1	0	1	1	0	1	0	0
19	0	0	0	0	1	1	0	0
20	0	1	0	0	1	1	0	0
21	1	0	1	0	1	1	0	0
22	1	1	1	0	1	1	0	0
23	0	1	0	1	1	1	0	0
24	0	0	1	1	1	1	0	0
25	1	1	1	1	1	1	0	0
26	1	0	0	0	0	0	1	0
27	0	0	1	0	0	0	1	0
28	0	1	1	0	0	0	1	0
29	0	0	0	1	0	0	1	0
30	1	1	0	1	0	0	1	0
31	1	0	1	1	0	0	1	0
32	0	0	0	0	1	0	1	0
33	0	1	0	0	1	0	1	0
34	0	0	1	0	1	0	1	0
35	1	1	1	0	1	0	1	0
36	1	0	0	1	1	0	1	0
37	1	1	0	1	1	0	1	0
38	0	1	1	1	1	0	1	0
39	0	0	0	0	0	1	1	0
40	0	1	0	0	0	1	1	0
41	1	0	1	0	0	1	1	0
42	1	1	1	0	0	1	1	0
43	1	0	0	1	0	1	1	0
44	0	0	1	1	0	1	1	0
45	0	1	1	1	0	1	1	0
46	0	0	0	0	1	1	1	0
47	0	1	0	0	1	1	1	0
48	1	0	1	0	1	1	1	0
49	1	1	1	0	1	1	1	0
50	1	0	0	1	1	1	1	0
51	1	1	0	1	1	1	1	0
52	0	1	1	1	1	1	1	0
53	0	0	0	0	0	0	0	1
54	0	1	0	0	0	0	0	1
55	0	0	1	0	0	0	0	1
56	0	1	1	0	0	0	0	1
57	0	0	0	1	0	0	0	1
58	0	1	0	1	0	0	0	1
59	1	0	1	1	0	0	0	1
60	1	1	1	1	0	0	0	1
61	1	0	0	0	1	0	0	1
62	1	1	0	0	1	0	0	1
63	1	0	1	0	1	0	0	1
64	1	1	1	0	1	0	0	1
65	1	0	0	1	1	0	0	1
66	1	1	0	1	1	0	0	1
67	1	0	1	1	1	0	0	1
68	1	1	1	1	1	0	0	1
69	1	0	0	0	0	1	0	1
70	1	1	0	0	0	1	0	1
71	1	0	1	0	0	1	0	1
72	1	1	1	0	0	1	0	1
73	1	0	0	1	0	1	0	1
74	1	1	0	1	0	1	0	1
75	1	0	1	1	0	1	0	1
76	0	1	1	1	0	1	0	1
77	0	0	0	0	1	1	0	1
78	0	1	0	0	1	1	0	1
79	0	0	1	0	1	1	0	1
80	0	1	1	0	1	1	0	1
81	0	0	0	1	1	1	0	1
82	1	0	0	1	1	1	0	1
83	1	1	0	1	1	1	0	1
84	1	0	1	1	1	1	0	1
85	1	1	1	1	1	1	0	1
86	1	0	0	0	0	0	1	1
87	0	1	0	0	0	0	1	1
88	0	0	1	0	0	0	1	1
89	0	1	1	0	0	0	1	1
90	1	1	1	0	0	0	1	1
91	1	0	0	1	0	0	1	1
92	1	1	0	1	0	0	1	1
93	1	0	1	1	0	0	1	1
94	0	1	1	1	0	0	1	1
95	0	0	0	0	1	0	1	1
96	1	0	0	0	1	0	1	1
97	1	1	0	0	1	0	1	1
98	1	0	1	0	1	0	1	1
99	0	1	1	0	1	0	1	1
100	0	0	0	1	1	0	1	1
101	1	0	0	1	1	0	1	1
102	1	1	0	1	1	0	1	1
103	1	0	1	1	1	0	1	1
104	0	1	1	1	1	0	1	1
105	0	0	0	0	0	1	1	1
106	1	0	0	0	0	1	1	1
107	1	1	0	0	0	1	1	1
108	0	0	1	0	0	1	1	1
109	0	1	1	0	0	1	1	1
110	1	1	1	0	0	1	1	1
111	1	0	0	1	0	1	1	1
112	0	1	0	1	0	1	1	1
113	1	1	0	1	0	1	1	1
114	1	0	1	1	0	1	1	1
115	0	1	1	1	0	1	1	1
116	0	0	0	0	1	1	1	1
117	1	0	0	0	1	1	1	1
118	1	1	0	0	1	1	1	1
119	0	0	1	0	1	1	1	1
120	1	0	1	0	1	1	1	1
121	1	1	1	0	1	1	1	1
122	0	0	0	1	1	1	1	1
123	1	0	0	1	1	1	1	1
124	1	1	0	1	1	1	1	1
125	0	0	1	1	1	1	1	1
126	1	0	1	1	1	1	1	1
127	0	1	1	1	1	1	1	1

Note: 1 more negative output.
0 more positive output.

MM522BN

(b)

Fig. 3.13 (a) MM4220BN/MM5220BN connected as a look-up table (National Semiconductor Corp.); (b) MM4220BN/MM5220BN program (National Semiconductor Corp.).

The ROM inputs and outputs are represented with negative logic. Therefore, the 0 logic level is more positive than logic 1. The ROM IC operates from a +12-V dc power supply called V_{SS} and a -12-V supply V_{GG}. Buffers are added at the inputs and outputs to produce TTL-compatible logic levels.

The *CHIP ENABLE*, *MODE CONTROL*, and A_8 leads are used as control inputs for the look-up table ROM. A logic 1 at *CHIP ENABLE* enables the outputs of the ROM for operation. Moreover, the signal *MODE CONTROL* must be logic 0 with A_8 equal to logic 1.

The data stored within the ROM define the trigonometric function

$$\theta = \tan^{-1} X$$

This equation reads "theta equals the arctangent of X." For instance, we could use the ROM to find the angle θ that has a tangent value equal to 0.258. That is,

$$\theta = \text{arctangent } 0.258$$

In the circuit of Fig. 3.13(a), the address inputs A_1 through A_7 represent the tangent value X and data outputs B_1 through B_8 represent angle θ.

Actually, the look-up table in the MM4220BN/MM5220BN just describes the arctangent function over the range of X from 0 to 1. This corresponds to θ from 0° to 45°.

$$0 \leqslant X \leqslant 1 \qquad 0^\circ \leqslant \theta \leqslant 45^\circ$$

A table showing the program of this ROM is given in Fig. 3.13(b). Notice that the table contains 128 values of X, one value for each address from 0 to 127 in binary form.

The tangent value X must be converted into a binary address for input to the ROM. Since the memory represents the angle θ for 128 values of X, the address code is obtained by multiplying X by 128 and then converting the integer part of the result to binary form:

$$A_7 A_6 A_5 A_4 A_3 A_2 A_1 = 128(X) \text{ expressed in binary form}$$

As an example, let us convert the value of X we used in our earlier example into a binary address. This value was $X = 0.258$.

$$A_7 A_6 A_5 A_4 A_3 A_2 A_1 = 128(X) = 128(0.258) = 33$$

Expressing 33 in binary form, we get

$$
\begin{array}{c|c}
2 & 33 \longrightarrow 1 \\ \hline
2 & 16 \longrightarrow 0 \\ \hline
2 & 8 \longrightarrow 0 \\ \hline
2 & 4 \longrightarrow 0 \\ \hline
2 & 2 \longrightarrow 0 \\ \hline
2 & 1 \longrightarrow 1 \\ \hline
 & 0
\end{array}
$$

$$A_7A_6A_5A_4A_3A_2A_1 = 0100001$$

It is this address that must be applied to the buffer inputs. The conversion of X to this form must be done in circuitry external to the look-up table.

The data stored at the selected address location is read out on the ROM outputs. Output bits B_1 through B_8 represent fractional binary weights $1/2$ through $1/256$, respectively. This code represents the angle in binary form and *normalized* to 45°. To obtain the actual value of θ, we must convert the binary output to decimal form and multiply by 45°.

When the address applied to the input of the ROM is

$$A_7A_6A_5A_4A_3A_2A_1 = 0100001 = 33$$

the table in Fig. 3.13(b) tells us that the output is

$$B_1B_2B_3B_4B_5B_6B_7B_8 = 0.01010010$$

Converting to decimal form results with

$$
\begin{aligned}
0.01010010 &= 0\left(\frac{1}{2}\right) + 1\left(\frac{1}{4}\right) + 0\left(\frac{1}{8}\right) + 1\left(\frac{1}{16}\right) \\
&\quad + 0\left(\frac{1}{32}\right) + 0\left(\frac{1}{64}\right) + 1\left(\frac{1}{128}\right) + 0\left(\frac{1}{256}\right) \\
&= 0.3203125
\end{aligned}
$$

To find the angle θ, we must multiply by 45°:

$$
\begin{aligned}
\theta &= 45^\circ(0.3203125) \\
&= 14.4^\circ
\end{aligned}
$$

This conversion of the normalized binary output to the angle θ must also be done with circuitry external to the look-up table.

Although the table within the MM4220BN/MM5220BN only represents X from 0 to 1, the device can be used to find angles for X greater than 1. This is done by applying the address for the decimal reciprocal of X to the inputs. The output produced by this address is the complementary angle rather than the angle to be found. Therefore, the value of the complementary angle θ_c must be subtracted from 90° to obtain θ.

$$\theta = 90^\circ - \theta_c$$

EXAMPLE 3.7 Use the look-up table in Fig. 3.13(b) to find the angle θ for $\tan^{-1} 1.506$.

SOLUTION Since the value of X is greater than 1, we must find the address from its reciprocal.

$$X = 1.506$$

$$\frac{1}{X} = \frac{1}{1.506} = 0.664$$

$$A_7A_6A_5A_4A_3A_2A_1 = 128\left(\frac{1}{X}\right) = 128(0.664) = 85$$

The data stored at address 85 in the table are

$$B_1B_2B_3B_4B_5B_6B_7B_8 = 0.10111111$$

Converting to decimal form, we get

$$\begin{aligned} 0.10111111 &= 1\left(\frac{1}{2}\right) + 0\left(\frac{1}{4}\right) + 1\left(\frac{1}{8}\right) + 1\left(\frac{1}{16}\right) \\ &\quad + 1\left(\frac{1}{32}\right) + 1\left(\frac{1}{64}\right) + 1\left(\frac{1}{128}\right) + 1\left(\frac{1}{256}\right) \\ &= 0.746 \end{aligned}$$

The complementary angle is

$$\theta_c = 45^\circ(0.746) = 33.6^\circ$$

and θ is found to be

$$\begin{aligned} \theta &= 90^\circ - \theta_c = 90^\circ - 33.6^\circ \\ &= 56.4^\circ \end{aligned}$$

MM4220BM/MM5220BM Sine Look-up Table[9]

Another standard ROM look-up table is the MM4220BM/MM5220BM device. The table stored within this ROM describes the solution to the equation

$$X = \sin\theta$$

[9] Ibid., p. 6-28. (Courtesy of National Semiconductor Corp.)

ADDRESS REFERENCE	FUNCTION		CODE							
	INPUT		OUTPUT							
	DEGREES	RADIANS	B_8	B_7	B_6	B_5	B_4	B_3	B_2	B_1
0	.00	.000	0	0	0	0	0	0	0	0
1	.70	.012	1	1	0	0	0	0	0	0
2	1.41	.025	0	1	1	0	0	0	0	0
3	2.11	.037	1	0	0	1	0	0	0	0
4	2.81	.049	0	0	1	1	0	0	0	0
5	3.52	.061	1	1	1	1	0	0	0	0
6	4.22	.074	1	1	0	0	1	0	0	0
7	4.92	.086	0	1	1	0	1	0	0	0
8	5.63	.098	1	0	0	1	1	0	0	0
9	6.33	.110	0	0	1	1	1	0	0	0
10	7.03	.123	1	1	1	1	1	0	0	0
11	7.73	.135	0	1	0	0	0	1	0	0
12	8.44	.147	1	0	1	0	0	1	0	0
13	9.14	.160	0	0	0	1	0	1	0	0
14	9.84	.172	0	0	1	1	0	1	0	0
15	10.55	.184	1	1	1	1	0	1	0	0
16	11.25	.196	0	1	0	0	1	1	0	0
17	11.95	.209	1	0	1	0	1	1	0	0
18	12.66	.221	0	0	0	1	1	1	0	0
19	13.36	.233	1	1	0	1	1	1	0	0
20	14.06	.245	0	1	1	1	1	1	0	0
21	14.77	.258	1	0	0	0	0	0	1	0
22	15.47	.270	0	0	1	0	0	0	1	0
23	16.17	.282	1	1	1	0	0	0	1	0
24	16.88	.295	0	1	0	1	0	0	1	0
25	17.58	.307	1	0	1	1	0	0	1	0
26	18.28	.319	0	0	0	0	1	0	1	0
27	18.98	.331	1	1	0	0	1	0	1	0
28	19.69	.344	0	1	1	0	1	0	1	0
29	20.39	.356	1	0	0	1	1	0	1	0
30	21.09	.368	0	0	1	1	1	0	1	0
31	21.80	.380	1	1	1	1	1	0	1	0
32	22.50	.393	0	1	0	0	0	1	1	0
33	23.20	.405	1	1	1	0	0	1	1	0
34	23.91	.417	1	1	1	0	0	1	1	0
35	24.61	.430	0	1	0	1	0	1	1	0
36	25.31	.442	1	0	1	1	0	1	1	0
37	26.02	.454	0	0	0	0	1	1	1	0
38	26.72	.466	1	1	0	0	1	1	1	0
39	27.42	.479	0	1	1	0	1	1	1	0
40	28.13	.491	0	0	0	1	1	1	1	0
41	28.83	.503	1	1	0	1	1	1	1	0
42	29.53	.515	0	1	1	1	1	1	1	0
43	30.23	.528	0	0	0	0	0	0	0	1
44	30.94	.540	1	1	0	0	0	0	0	1
45	31.64	.552	0	1	1	0	0	0	0	1
46	32.34	.565	1	0	0	1	0	0	0	1
47	33.05	.577	1	1	0	1	0	0	0	1
48	33.75	.589	0	1	1	1	0	0	0	1
49	34.45	.601	1	0	0	0	1	0	0	1
50	35.16	.614	1	1	0	0	1	0	0	1
51	35.86	.626	0	1	1	0	1	0	0	1
52	36.56	.638	0	0	0	1	1	0	0	1
53	37.27	.650	1	1	0	1	1	0	0	1
54	37.97	.663	1	0	1	1	1	0	0	1
55	38.67	.675	0	0	0	0	0	1	0	1
56	39.37	.687	0	1	0	0	0	1	0	1
57	40.08	.699	1	0	1	0	0	1	0	1
58	40.78	.712	1	1	1	0	0	1	0	1
59	41.48	.724	1	0	0	1	0	1	0	1
60	42.19	.736	0	0	1	1	0	1	0	1
61	42.89	.749	0	1	1	1	0	1	0	1
62	43.59	.761	0	0	0	0	1	1	0	1
63	44.30	.773	1	1	0	0	1	1	0	1

Fig. 3.14 MM4220BM/MM5220BM program (National Semiconductor Corp.).

ADDRESS REFERENCE	FUNCTION		CODE							
	INPUT		OUTPUT							
	DEGREES	RADIANS	B_8	B_7	B_6	B_5	B_4	B_3	B_2	B_1
64	45.00	.785	1	0	1	0	1	1	0	1
65	45.70	.798	1	1	1	0	1	1	0	1
66	46.41	.810	1	0	0	1	1	1	0	1
67	47.11	.822	1	1	0	1	1	1	0	1
68	47.81	.834	1	0	1	1	1	1	0	1
69	48.52	.847	0	0	0	0	0	0	1	1
70	49.22	.859	0	1	0	0	0	0	1	1
71	49.92	.871	0	0	1	0	0	0	1	1
72	50.62	.884	0	1	1	0	0	0	1	1
73	51.33	.896	0	0	0	1	0	0	1	1
74	52.03	.908	0	1	0	1	0	0	1	1
75	52.73	.920	1	1	0	1	0	0	1	1
76	53.44	.933	1	0	1	1	0	0	1	1
77	54.14	.945	1	1	1	1	0	0	1	1
78	54.84	.957	1	0	0	0	1	0	1	1
79	55.55	.969	1	1	0	0	1	0	1	1
80	56.25	.982	1	0	1	0	1	0	1	1
81	56.95	.994	0	1	1	0	1	0	1	1
82	57.66	1.006	0	0	0	1	1	0	1	1
83	58.36	1.019	0	1	0	1	1	0	1	1
84	59.06	1.031	1	1	0	1	1	0	1	1
85	59.77	1.043	1	0	1	1	1	0	1	1
86	60.47	1.055	0	1	1	1	1	0	1	1
87	61.17	1.068	0	0	0	0	0	1	1	1
88	61.87	1.080	0	1	0	0	0	1	1	1
89	62.58	1.092	1	1	0	0	0	1	1	1
90	63.28	1.104	0	0	1	0	0	1	1	1
91	63.98	1.117	0	1	1	0	0	1	1	1
92	64.69	1.129	1	1	1	0	0	1	1	1
93	65.39	1.141	0	0	0	1	0	1	1	1
94	66.09	1.154	0	1	0	1	0	1	1	1
95	66.80	1.166	1	1	0	1	0	1	1	1
96	67.50	1.178	0	0	1	1	0	1	1	1
97	68.20	1.190	1	0	1	1	0	1	1	1
98	68.91	1.203	1	1	1	1	0	1	1	1
99	69.61	1.215	0	0	0	0	1	1	1	1
100	70.31	1.227	1	0	0	0	1	1	1	1
101	71.02	1.239	0	1	0	0	1	1	1	1
102	71.72	1.252	1	1	0	0	1	1	1	1
103	72.42	1.264	0	0	1	0	1	1	1	1
104	73.12	1.276	1	0	1	0	1	1	1	1
105	73.83	1.289	0	1	1	0	1	1	1	1
106	74.53	1.301	0	1	1	0	1	1	1	1
107	75.23	1.313	1	1	1	0	1	1	1	1
108	75.94	1.325	0	0	0	1	1	1	1	1
109	76.64	1.338	1	0	0	1	1	1	1	1
110	77.34	1.350	0	1	0	1	1	1	1	1
111	78.05	1.362	0	1	0	1	1	1	1	1
112	78.75	1.374	1	1	0	1	1	1	1	1
113	79.45	1.387	1	1	0	1	1	1	1	1
114	80.16	1.399	0	0	1	1	1	1	1	1
115	80.86	1.411	0	0	1	1	1	1	1	1
116	81.56	1.424	1	0	1	1	1	1	1	1
117	82.27	1.436	1	0	1	1	1	1	1	1
118	82.97	1.448	0	1	1	1	1	1	1	1
119	83.67	1.460	0	1	1	1	1	1	1	1
120	84.38	1.473	1	1	1	1	1	1	1	1
121	85.08	1.485	1	1	1	1	1	1	1	1
122	85.78	1.497	1	1	1	1	1	1	1	1
123	86.48	1.509	1	1	1	1	1	1	1	1
124	87.19	1.522	1	1	1	1	1	1	1	1
125	87.89	1.534	1	1	1	1	1	1	1	1
126	88.59	1.546	1	1	1	1	1	1	1	1
127	89.30	1.559	1	1	1	1	1	1	1	1

Fig. 3.14 Continued

That is, it is programmed to produce the trigonometric sine-function value X for angle θ.

This device has the same pin layout as the MM4220BN/MM5220BN IC and must also be connected for operation as shown in the circuit configuration of Fig. 3.13(a).

The program within the device is specified by the table in Fig. 3.14. Looking at this table, we find that it stores 128 codes representing the value of X over the range of θ from 0° to 90°. The actual angle θ must be converted to binary address A_7 through A_1 for input to the ROM. Moreover, the value of sin θ supplied at the output is in binary form. The output bits B_1 through B_8 represent binary weights ½ through 1⁄256, respectively.

The input address is found by normalizing the angle θ to 90°, multiplying by 128, and then converting to binary form.

$$A_7A_6A_5A_4A_3A_2A_1 = \frac{\theta}{90^\circ}(128) \quad \text{expressed in binary form}$$

As an example, let us convert the angle 45° into its equivalent address:

$$A_7A_6A_5A_4A_3A_2A_1 = \frac{\theta}{90^\circ}(128) = \frac{45^\circ}{90^\circ}(128) = 64$$

Divisor	Quotient	Remainder
2	64 →	0
2	32 →	0
2	16 →	0
2	8 →	0
2	4 →	0
2	2 →	0
2	1 →	1
	0	

$$A_7A_6A_5A_4A_3A_2A_1 = 01000000$$

The binary value of sin θ for each of the 128 angle values is stored at the corresponding address location. For address 64, which we just found, the data read out onto data lines B_1 through B_8 are given in the table as

$$B_1B_2B_3B_4B_5B_6B_7B_8 = 0.10110101$$

The decimal value of sin θ is found to be

$$X = 1\left(\frac{1}{2}\right) + 0\left(\frac{1}{4}\right) + 1\left(\frac{1}{8}\right) + 1\left(\frac{1}{16}\right) + 0\left(\frac{1}{32}\right) + 1\left(\frac{1}{64}\right) + 0\left(\frac{1}{128}\right) + 1\left(\frac{1}{256}\right)$$
$$= 0.7070$$

Increasing the Accuracy and Resolution of Look-up Tables[10]

The *accuracy* of the sine function look-up table we just introduced is quite good. For instance, the ROM produced the X value for sin 45° as 0.7070, but looking the value up in a handbook of trigonometric tables we find a value of 0.7071. The value produced by the ROM is approximately 0.01% lower than the value found in the handbook.

On the other hand, the *resolution* of the sine look-up table is very low. We saw that angle θ was broken up into 128 values over the range 0° to 90°. This resulted in an angular increment of 90°/128, which equals approximately 0.7°. All input angles are rounded to the nearest table value. For this reason, larger errors are produced.

Both accuracy and resolution can be vastly improved by interconnecting look-up table ROMs into a system configuration such as that shown in Fig. 3.15. Here we see that four ROM ICs are interconnected with three TTL adder devices. The look-up table system has an 11-bit address input and 13-bit data output.

Expanding the address input causes improved resolution. For instance, the 11-bit address in this system provides 2048 storage locations. The new angular increment is 90°/2048, or approximately 0.044°. Comparing this

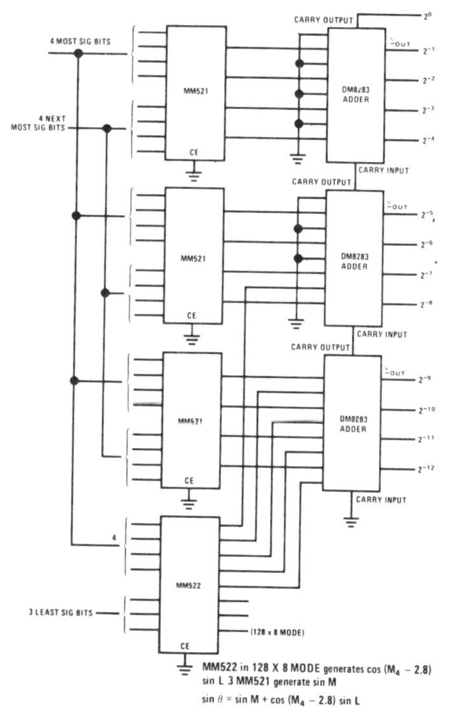

Fig. 3.15 Four ROM look-up table system (National Semiconductor Corp.).

[10] National Semiconductor Corp., "Trig Function Generators," MOS Brief 10 (Santa Clara, CA: National Semiconductor Corp., 1976). (Courtesy of National Semiconductor Corp.)

value to that for a single ROM IC, we find that resolution has been improved by a factor greater than 10.

Moreover, the expansion of the output word from 8 bits to 13 bits results in increased accuracy. The values in the look-up table are now within 0.002% of equivalent handbook values.

This system does not directly implement the sine function $X = \sin \theta$. Instead, the angle θ is divided into two parts, M and L, and the form of the expression modified using trigonometric identities. This gives

$$\begin{aligned} X &= \sin(M + L) \\ &= \sin M \cos L + \cos M \sin L \end{aligned}$$

In this expression, the value of $\cos L$ is approximately 1. Therefore, the equation simplifies to

$$X = \sin M + \cos M \sin L$$

It is this equation that is implemented with the circuit in Fig. 3.15. The upper three ROMs represent the $\sin M$ term. On the other hand, the term $\cos M \sin L$ is produced by the lowest of the four ROMs.

The angle θ must be converted into an 11-bit address for input to the system. The eight most significant bits of the address are input to the upper three ROMs and determine the value of $\sin M$. The four MSBs and three LSBs of the address are applied to the lowest ROM to produce $\cos M \sin L$. The ROM outputs for the two terms are combined with adder circuits to produce the sine-function value X.

3.7 CODE CONVERTERS

A code converter is a circuit that takes data expressed in one code as its input and produces as its output the equivalent data expressed in another code. For instance, in one type of application it may be necessary to convert binary data produced by a microprocessing unit to BCD code for driving a seven-segment display. In this case, a binary-to-BCD code converter is needed.

Moreover, in many digital systems, data are coded for communication using different alphanumeric codes. Some examples are the *Binary Coded Decimal Interchange Code* (*BCDIC*), *American Standard Code for Information Interchange* (*ASCII*), and the *Extended Binary Coded Decimal Interchange Code* (*EBCDIC*). In communication between systems, it may be necessary to convert among these standard codes.

One of the simplest ways of implementing code-converter circuitry is with read-only memories. The ROM is programmed with each word of the new code stored at the address defined by the equivalent word in the original code.

Many code converters are available as preprogrammed ROMs. Furthermore, PROMs and EPROMs can be programmed to make custom code converters. In this section, we introduce a number of the more popular standard devices.

The 74184 BCD-to-Binary Code Converter

The most widely used ROM numeric code converters are those designed to convert between the binary and BCD codes. For example, a BCD-to-binary converter accepts BCD words at the address inputs and produces equivalent binary words at the output.

A standard bipolar ROM programmed to operate as a BCD-to-binary code converter, the 74184 device, is shown in Fig. 3.16(a). Looking at this pin layout, we see that the IC operates from a standard +5-V TTL power supply labeled $+V_{CC}$.

Input/output organization of the 74184 is shown in Fig. 3.16(b). Here we see that the device accepts 6-bit BCD code at the inputs labeled *BADCBA* and produces a 6-bit binary output marked $2^5\,2^4\,2^3\,2^2\,2^1\,2^0$. The inputs actually represent two digits of BCD code. The rightmost inputs, which are marked *DCBA*, are for the least significant digit and the *BA* inputs on the left are for the most significant digit. At the output, the 2^5 lead represents the MSB and 2^0 the LSB.

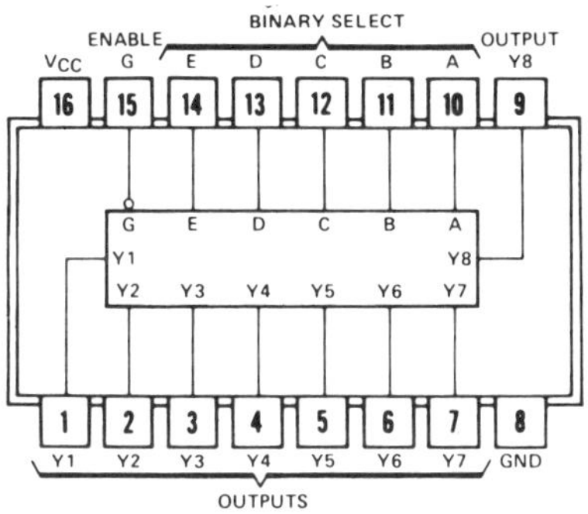

(a)

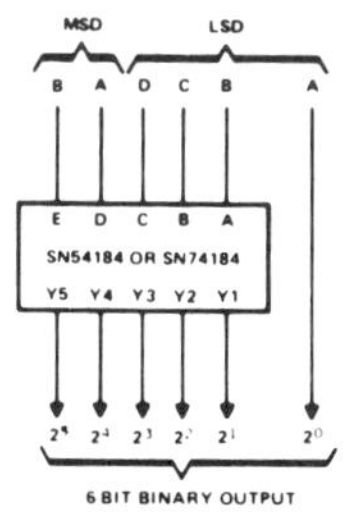

(b)

FUNCTION TABLE
BCD-TO-BINARY
CONVERTER

BCD WORDS	INPUTS (See Note A)						OUTPUTS (See Note B)				
	E	D	C	B	A	G	Y5	Y4	Y3	Y2	Y1
0-1	L	L	L	L	L	L	L	L	L	L	L
2-3	L	L	L	L	H	L	L	L	L	L	H
4-5	L	L	L	H	L	L	L	L	L	H	L
6-7	L	L	L	H	H	L	L	L	L	H	H
8-9	L	L	H	L	L	L	L	L	H	L	L
10-11	L	H	L	L	L	L	L	L	H	L	H
12-13	L	H	L	L	H	L	L	L	H	H	L
14-15	L	H	L	H	L	L	L	L	H	H	H
16-17	L	H	L	H	H	L	L	H	L	L	L
18-19	L	H	H	L	L	L	L	H	L	L	H
20-21	H	L	L	L	L	L	L	H	L	H	L
22-23	H	L	L	L	H	L	L	H	L	H	H
24-25	H	L	L	H	L	L	L	H	H	L	L
26-27	H	L	L	H	H	L	L	H	H	L	H
28-29	H	L	H	L	L	L	L	H	H	H	L
30-31	H	H	L	L	L	L	L	H	H	H	H
32-33	H	H	L	L	H	L	H	L	L	L	L
34-35	H	H	L	H	L	L	H	L	L	L	H
36-37	H	H	L	H	H	L	H	L	L	H	L
38-39	H	H	H	L	L	L	H	L	L	H	H
ANY	X	X	X	X	X	H	H	H	H	H	H

(c)

Fig. 3.16 (a) 74184 pin layout (Texas Instruments, Incorporated); (b) BCD-to-binary code-converter connection (Texas Instruments, Incorporated); (c) input/output operation (Texas Instruments, Incorporated).

The A bit of the LSD input is passed directly to the 2^0 output and is not actually involved with the code-converter circuitry. This is because the LSB of BCD and binary numbers are always the same. When A is logic 0, the 2^0 output is also 0 and a 1 at A makes the 2^0 output logic 1.

In the block diagram of the 74184 device, the input leads to the ROM are labeled A through E. However, the A input on the ROM does not correspond to the A input bit of the LSD of BCD code. Instead, it is supplied by the B input. The code-converter output leads, labeled Y_1 through Y_5, produce the 2^1 through 2^5 binary bits, respectively.

These two facts are important to an understanding of how the program in Fig. 3.16(c) relates to BCD-to-binary code converter operation. In the table, the inputs and outputs are labeled based upon the ROM input and output leads rather than the BCD inputs and binary outputs. Therefore, this table does not describe the input/output operation of the code-converter circuit in Fig. 3.16(b). It just describes the bits that are processed within the ROM IC.

The column marked "BCD WORDS" represents the address inputs. Notice that groups of two addresses are listed together: 0–1, 2–3, and so on. This is because the BDC and binary words for these groups differ only in the LSB, and this bit is not produced by the ROM. Remember that this LSB does not address the ROM; therefore, both BCD inputs address the same storage location and produce the same output.

This idea is illustrated by the following example. Assume that the BCD data $BADCBA$=000000 is applied to the input of the code converter in Fig. 3.169B). The LSB of this input is passed directly to the 2^0 output. In this way, we get 2^0 equals logic 0:

$$2^0 = 0$$

The other five bits, $BADCB$, go to address leads $EDCBA$ on the ROM. This gives an address input of

$$EDCBA = 00000$$

From the program table in Fig. 3.16(c), we find that the data output for this address is

$$Y_5\, Y_4\, Y_3\, Y_2\, Y_1 = 00000$$

These outputs are combined with the 2^0 bit to produce the binary number

$$2^5\, 2^4\, 2^3\, 2^2\, 2^1\, 2^0 = 000000$$

Let us change the BCD input to $BADCBA$=000001. This makes the 2^0 output logic 1 while the address inputs on the ROM stay at logic 0.

$$EDCBA = 00000$$

The Y outputs are again all at the 0 logic level.

$$Y_5\,Y_4\,Y_3\,Y_2\,Y_1 = 00000$$

This gives the binary output:

$$2^5\,2^4\,2^3\,2^2\,2^1\,2^0 = 000001$$

In this way, we see that consecutive BCD numbers address the same memory location as indicated in the table of Fig. 3.16(c).

There is one more lead on the 74184 that must be mentioned. It is labeled G and is a chip enable input. G must be set to the 0 logic level to enable the ROM for operation. If G is logic 1, the outputs are all held at the 1 logic level.

The outputs on the 74184 are open-collector and require external pull-up circuitry to set the output logic levels. On the other hand, all inputs are TTL-compatible.

EXAMPLE 3.8 The input to the circuit in Fig. 3.16(b) is number 12 expressed in BCD code. What is the binary output?

SOLUTION Expressing 12 in BCD code, we get

$$BADCBA = 010010$$

The least significant A bit, which is logic 0, is used as the 2^0 output:

$$2^0 = 0$$

The rest of the input bits are applied to the address leads of the ROM.

$$EDCBA = 01001$$

From the program in Fig. 3.16(c), we find that the ROM output is

$$Y_5\,Y_4\,Y_3\,Y_2\,Y_1 = 00110$$

These outputs are combined with 2^0 to give

$$2^5\,2^4\,2^3\,2^2\,2^1\,2^0 = 001100$$

This result can be checked by converting to decimal form.

$$\begin{aligned} 001100 &= 0(2^5) + 0(2^4) + 1(2^3) + 1(2^2) + 0(2^1) + 0(2^0) \\ &= 12 \end{aligned}$$

In practical applications, the BCD-to-binary code converter will have to

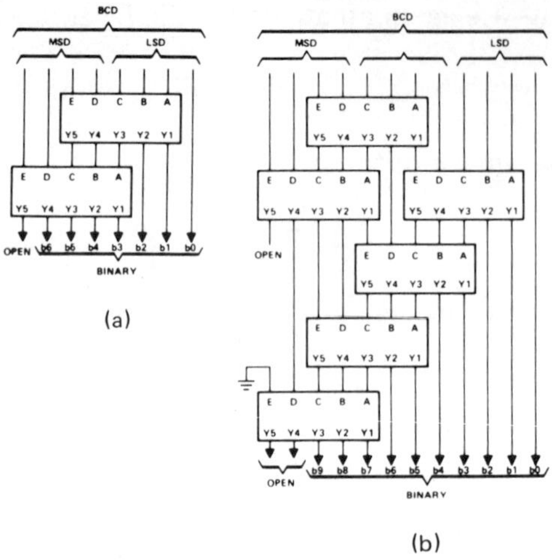

Fig. 3.17 (a) Two-decade BCD-to-binary code converter (Texas Instruments, Incorporated); (b) three-decade BCD-to-binary code converter (Texas Instruments, Incorporated).

convert larger words: for example, words of 8, 12, 16, or even 32 bits. In these cases, a number of 74184 devices must be connected to expand the input and output word lengths.

Figure 3.17(a) shows the connection of two 74184 ROMs to implement a two-decade (8-bit) BCD-to-binary converter, and Fig. 3.17(b) shows how six 74184 devices are used to make a three-decade (12-bit) converter.

The 74185A Binary-to-BCD Code Converter

The 74185A ROM is similar to the 74184 device just introduced. However, it is programmed to convert binary data to BCD code. The pin layout of the 74185A is identical to that shown in Fig. 3.16(a).

The diagram in Fig. 3.18(a) shows the connection of the 74185A as a code converter. Notice that the 2^0 input passes through to the output. It is used as bit A in the LSD of the BCD output. The remaining inputs are used to address the ROM and select the Y output corresponding to the rest of the BCD bits.

The table in Fig. 3.18(b) shows the input and output words for the ROM. The Y_7 and Y_8 outputs in this table are not used in our code converter. Moreover, the Y_6 output is required as the MSB for all binary inputs greater than 39.

As an example, let us make the input to the code-converter circuit

$$2^5\ 2^4\ 2^3\ 2^2\ 2^1\ 2^0 = 010111$$

6-BIT CONVERTER

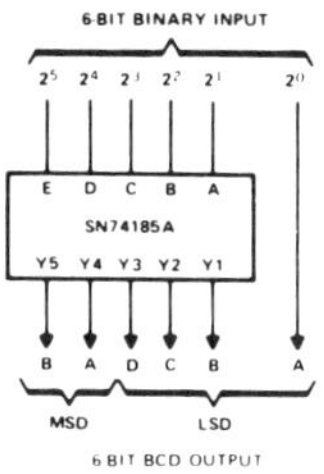

(a)

FUNCTION TABLE

BINARY WORDS	INPUTS						OUTPUTS							
	BINARY SELECT					ENABLE								
	E	D	C	B	A	G	Y8	Y7	Y8	Y5	Y4	Y3	Y2	Y1
0 1	L	L	L	L	L	L	H	H	L	L	L	L	L	L
2 3	L	L	L	L	H	L	H	H	L	L	L	L	L	H
4 5	L	L	L	H	L	L	H	H	L	L	L	L	H	L
6 7	L	L	L	H	H	L	H	H	L	L	L	L	H	H
8 9	L	L	H	L	L	L	H	H	L	L	L	H	L	L
10 11	L	L	H	L	H	L	H	H	L	L	H	L	L	L
12 13	L	L	H	H	L	L	H	H	L	L	H	L	L	H
14 15	L	L	H	H	H	L	H	H	L	L	H	L	H	L
16 17	L	H	L	L	L	L	H	H	L	L	H	L	H	H
18 19	L	H	L	L	H	L	H	H	L	L	H	H	L	L
20 21	L	H	L	H	L	L	H	H	L	H	L	L	L	L
22 23	L	H	L	H	H	L	H	H	L	H	L	L	L	H
24 25	L	H	H	L	L	L	H	H	L	H	L	L	H	L
26 27	L	H	H	L	H	L	H	H	L	H	L	L	H	H
28 29	L	H	H	H	L	L	H	H	L	H	L	H	L	L
30 31	L	H	H	H	H	L	H	H	L	H	H	L	L	L
32 33	H	L	L	L	L	L	H	H	L	H	H	L	L	H
34 35	H	L	L	L	H	L	H	H	L	H	H	L	H	L
36 37	H	L	L	H	L	L	H	H	L	H	H	L	H	H
38 39	H	L	L	H	H	L	H	H	L	H	H	H	L	L
40 41	H	L	H	L	L	L	H	H	H	L	L	L	L	L
42 43	H	L	H	L	H	L	H	H	H	L	L	L	L	H
44 45	H	L	H	H	L	L	H	H	H	L	L	L	H	L
46 47	H	L	H	H	H	L	H	H	H	L	L	L	H	H
48 49	H	H	L	L	L	L	H	H	H	L	L	H	L	L
50 51	H	H	L	L	H	L	H	H	H	L	H	L	L	L
52 53	H	H	L	H	L	L	H	H	H	L	H	L	L	H
54 55	H	H	L	H	H	L	H	H	H	L	H	L	H	L
56 57	H	H	H	L	L	L	H	H	H	L	H	L	H	H
58 59	H	H	H	L	H	L	H	H	H	L	H	H	L	L
60 61	H	H	H	H	L	L	H	H	H	H	L	L	L	L
62 63	H	H	H	H	H	L	H	H	H	H	L	L	L	H
ALL	X	X	X	X	X	H	H	H	H	H	H	H	H	H

H high level, L low level, X irrelevant

(b)

Fig. 3.18 (a) Binary-to-BCD code-converter connection (Texas Instruments, Incorporated); (b) input/output operation (Texas Instruments, Incorporated).

This input represents the decimal number 23. The LSB 2^0 which equals 1 is sent directly to the A output in the LSD.

$$A_{LSD}=1$$

The rest of the inputs are applied to the address leads of the ROM.

$$EDCBA=2^5\ 2^4\ 2^3\ 2^2\ 2^1=01011$$

Looking at the program, we see that the ROM outputs for this address are

$$Y_5\ Y_4\ Y_3\ Y_2\ Y_1=10001$$

The complete BCD output is written as

$$BADCBA=100011$$

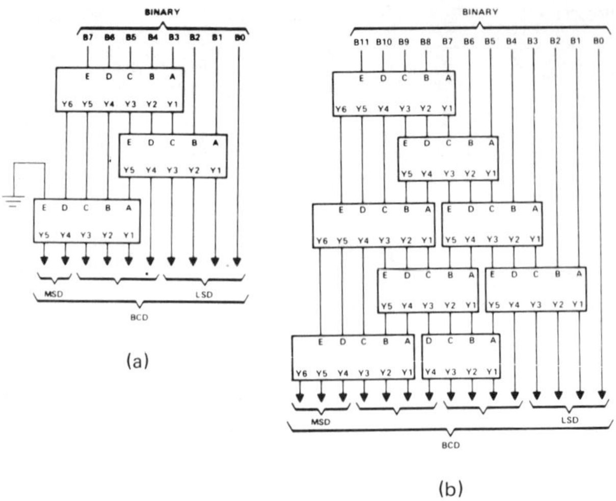

Fig. 3.19 (a) Eight-bit binary-to-BCD code converter (Texas Instruments, Incorporated); (b) 12-bit binary-to-BCD code converter (Texas Instruments, Incorporated).

We can check this output by converting the BCD digits to decimal form.

$$BA_{MSD}DCBA_{LSD} = 10\,0011 = 23$$

The interconnections of 74185A devices to make 8-bit and 12-bit binary-to-BCD converters are shown in Fig. 3.19(a) and (b), respectively.

The MM4220EK/MM5220EK BCDIC-to-EBCDIC and ASCII-to-EBCDIC Code Converter

The MM4220EK/MM5220EK is a widely used alphanumeric code-converter ROM. It is programmed with the capability to convert either the Binary Coded Decimal Interchange Code (BCDIC) or American Standard Code for Information Interchange (ASCII) to the Extended Binary Coded Decimal Interchange Code (EBCDIC).

Figure 3.20 shows the connection of the device for code-converter operation. Notice that the seven address inputs A_1 through A_7 and eight outputs B_1 through B_8 are buffered for TTL compatibility.

The input to the buffer for address bit A_7 is marked "*CODE*." It is the logic level of this input that signals to the ROM which type of code is applied at the input.

The input/output operation for the ASCII-to-EBCDIC code-converter function of the MM4220EK/MM5220EK is shown in Fig. 3.21. This mode of operation is selected when *CODE* equals 1. The ASCII conversion data are

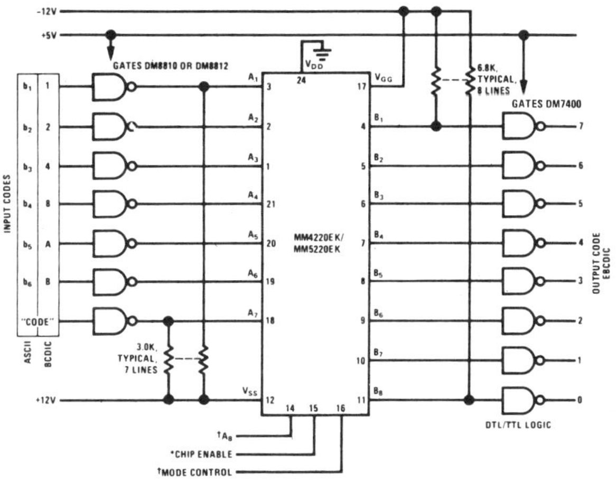

†Mode Control = Logic "0," A_8 = Logic "1."
*Chip Enable = Logic "1" to obtain outputs.
Logic Levels:
DTL/TTL (except at MOS/ROM interface). Logic "1," +5.0V, NOM. Logic "0," ground, NOM.
MOS/ROM inputs and outputs. Logic "1," more negative. Logic "0," more positive.

Fig. 3.20 MM4220EK/MM5220EK code-converter connection (National Semiconductor Corp.).

stored at the 64 most significant address locations within the ROM. The table includes codes for numbers, letters, and control characters. For example, the letter A expressed as an ASCII address input is

$$b_6 b_5 b_4 b_3 b_2 b_1 = 000001$$

The EBCDIC code produced at the output is

$$01234567 = 11000001$$

Figure 3.22 shows the input/output operation of the code converter when BCDIC-to-EBCDIC operation is selected by a logic 0 at the *CODE* input.

EXAMPLE 3.9 What are the input and output of the circuit in Fig. 3.20 when the symbol $ is input in ASCII code?

SOLUTION In the table of Fig. 3.21, the input and output for symbol $ are

$$b_6 b_5 b_4 b_3 b_2 b_1 = 100100$$

$$01234567 = 01011011$$

ROM ADDRESS	FUNCTION		CODE														
	INPUT	OUTPUT	INPUT							OUTPUT							
	ASCII SYMBOL	EBCDIC SYMBOL	CODE	ASCII b_6	b_5	b_4	b_3	b_2	b_1	EBCDIC 0	1	2	3	4	5	6	7
64	@	@	1	0	0	0	0	0	0	0	1	1	1	1	1	0	0
65	A	A	1	0	0	0	0	0	1	1	1	0	0	0	0	0	1
66	B	B	1	0	0	0	0	1	0	1	1	0	0	0	0	1	0
67	C	C	1	0	0	0	0	1	1	1	1	0	0	0	0	1	1
68	D	D	1	0	0	0	1	0	0	1	1	0	0	0	1	0	0
69	E	E	1	0	0	0	1	0	1	1	1	0	0	0	1	0	1
70	F	F	1	0	0	0	1	1	0	1	1	0	0	0	1	1	0
71	G	G	1	0	0	0	1	1	1	1	1	0	0	0	1	1	1
72	H	H	1	0	0	1	0	0	0	1	1	0	0	1	0	0	0
73	I	I	1	0	0	1	0	0	1	1	1	0	0	1	0	0	1
74	J	J	1	0	0	1	0	1	0	1	1	0	1	0	0	0	1
75	K	K	1	0	0	1	0	1	1	1	1	0	1	0	0	1	0
76	L	L	1	0	0	1	1	0	0	1	1	0	1	0	0	1	1
77	M	M	1	0	0	1	1	0	1	1	1	0	1	0	1	0	0
78	N	N	1	0	0	1	1	1	0	1	1	0	1	0	1	0	1
79	O	O	1	0	0	1	1	1	1	1	1	0	1	0	1	1	0
80	P	P	1	0	1	0	0	0	0	1	1	0	1	0	1	1	1
81	Q	Q	1	0	1	0	0	0	1	1	1	0	1	1	0	0	0
82	R	R	1	0	1	0	0	1	0	1	1	0	1	1	0	0	1
83	S	S	1	0	1	0	0	1	1	1	1	1	0	0	0	1	0
84	T	T	1	0	1	0	1	0	0	1	1	1	0	0	0	1	1
85	U	U	1	0	1	0	1	0	1	1	1	1	0	0	1	0	0
86	V	V	1	0	1	0	1	1	0	1	1	1	0	0	1	0	1
87	W	W	1	0	1	0	1	1	1	1	1	1	0	0	1	1	0
88	X	X	1	0	1	1	0	0	0	1	1	1	0	0	1	1	1
89	Y	Y	1	0	1	1	0	0	1	1	1	1	0	1	0	0	0
90	Z	Z	1	0	1	1	0	1	0	1	1	1	0	1	0	0	1
91	[	(	1	0	1	1	0	1	1	0	1	0	0	1	1	0	1
92	\	\	1	0	1	1	1	0	0	0	1	0	0	0	0	0	0
93	]	)	1	0	1	1	1	0	1	0	1	0	1	1	1	0	1
94	⌒ or ^	¬	1	0	1	1	1	1	0	0	1	0	1	1	1	1	1
95	—	—	1	0	1	1	1	1	1	0	1	1	0	1	1	0	1
96	Space	Space	1	1	0	0	0	0	0	0	1	0	0	0	0	0	0
97	!	!	1	1	0	0	0	0	1	0	1	0	1	1	0	1	0
98	"	"	1	1	0	0	0	1	0	0	1	1	1	1	1	1	1
99	#	#	1	1	0	0	0	1	1	0	1	1	1	1	0	1	1
100	$	$	1	1	0	0	1	0	0	0	1	0	1	1	0	1	1
101	%	%	1	1	0	0	1	0	1	0	1	1	0	1	1	0	0
102	&	&	1	1	0	0	1	1	0	0	1	0	1	0	0	0	0
103	'	'	1	1	0	0	1	1	1	0	1	1	1	1	1	0	1
104	(	(	1	1	0	1	0	0	0	0	1	0	0	1	1	0	1
105	)	)	1	1	0	1	0	0	1	0	1	0	1	1	1	0	1
106	•	•	1	1	0	1	0	1	0	0	1	0	1	1	1	0	0
107	+	+	1	1	0	1	0	1	1	0	1	0	0	1	1	1	0
108	,	,	1	1	0	1	1	0	0	0	1	1	0	1	0	1	1
109	-	-	1	1	0	1	1	0	1	0	1	1	0	0	0	0	0
110	.	.	1	1	0	1	1	1	0	0	1	0	0	1	0	1	1
111	/	/	1	1	0	1	1	1	1	0	1	1	0	0	0	0	1
112	0	0	1	1	1	0	0	0	0	1	1	1	1	0	0	0	0
113	1	1	1	1	1	0	0	0	1	1	1	1	1	0	0	0	1
114	2	2	1	1	1	0	0	1	0	1	1	1	1	0	0	1	0
115	3	3	1	1	1	0	0	1	1	1	1	1	1	0	0	1	1
116	4	4	1	1	1	0	1	0	0	1	1	1	1	0	1	0	0
117	5	5	1	1	1	0	1	0	1	1	1	1	1	0	1	0	1
118	6	6	1	1	1	0	1	1	0	1	1	1	1	0	1	1	0
119	7	7	1	1	1	0	1	1	1	1	1	1	1	0	1	1	1
120	8	8	1	1	1	1	0	0	0	1	1	1	1	1	0	0	0
121	9	9	1	1	1	1	0	0	1	1	1	1	1	1	0	0	1
122	:	:	1	1	1	1	0	1	0	0	1	1	1	1	0	1	0
123	;	;	1	1	1	1	0	1	1	0	1	0	1	1	1	1	0
124	<	<	1	1	1	1	1	0	0	0	1	0	0	1	1	0	0
125	=	=	1	1	1	1	1	0	1	0	1	1	1	1	1	1	0
126	>	>	1	1	1	1	1	1	0	0	1	1	0	1	1	1	0
127	?	?	1	1	1	1	1	1	1	0	1	1	0	1	1	1	1

Fig. 3.21 MM4220EK/MM5220EK ASCII-to-EBCDIC conversion (National Semiconductor Corp.).

ROM ADDRESS	FUNCTION		CODE														
	INPUT	OUTPUT	INPUT							OUTPUT							
	BCDIC SYMBOL	EBCDIC SYMBOL	CODE	BCDIC B	A	8	4	2	1	EBCDIC 0	1	2	3	4	5	6	7
0	Space	Space	0	0	0	0	0	0	0	0	1	0	0	0	0	0	0
1	1	1	0	0	0	0	0	0	1	1	1	1	1	0	0	0	1
2	2	2	0	0	0	0	0	1	0	1	1	1	1	0	0	1	0
3	3	3	0	0	0	0	0	1	1	1	1	1	1	0	0	1	1
4	4	4	0	0	0	0	1	0	0	1	1	1	1	0	1	0	0
5	5	5	0	0	0	0	1	0	1	1	1	1	1	0	1	0	1
6	6	6	0	0	0	0	1	1	0	1	1	1	1	0	1	1	0
7	7	7	0	0	0	0	1	1	1	1	1	1	1	0	1	1	1
8	8	8	0	0	0	1	0	0	0	1	1	1	1	1	0	0	0
9	9	9	0	0	0	1	0	0	1	1	1	1	1	1	0	0	1
10	0	0	0	0	0	1	0	1	0	1	1	1	1	0	0	0	0
11	# or =	#	0	0	0	1	0	1	1	0	1	1	1	1	0	1	1
12	@ or '	@	0	0	0	1	1	0	0	0	1	1	1	1	1	0	0
13	:	:	0	0	0	1	1	0	1	0	1	1	1	1	0	1	0
14	>	>	0	0	0	1	1	1	0	0	1	1	0	1	1	1	0
15	√(TM)	TM	0	0	0	1	1	1	1	0	0	0	1	0	0	1	1
16	Space	Space	0	0	1	0	0	0	0	0	1	0	0	0	0	0	0
17	/	/	0	0	1	0	0	0	1	0	1	1	0	0	0	0	1
18	S	S	0	0	1	0	0	1	0	1	1	1	0	0	0	1	0
19	T	T	0	0	1	0	0	1	1	1	1	1	0	0	0	1	1
20	U	U	0	0	1	0	1	0	0	1	1	1	0	0	1	0	0
21	V	V	0	0	1	0	1	0	1	1	1	1	0	0	1	0	1
22	W	W	0	0	1	0	1	1	0	1	1	1	0	0	1	1	0
23	X	X	0	0	1	0	1	1	1	1	1	1	0	0	1	1	1
24	Y	Y	0	0	1	1	0	0	0	1	1	1	0	1	0	0	0
25	Z	Z	0	0	1	1	0	0	1	1	1	1	0	1	0	0	1
26	‡(RM)	RM	0	0	1	1	0	1	0	1	1	1	0	0	0	0	0
27	,	,	0	0	1	1	0	1	1	0	1	1	0	1	0	1	1
28	% or (	%	0	0	1	1	1	0	0	0	1	1	0	1	1	0	0
29	v	+	0	0	1	1	1	0	1	0	1	0	0	1	1	1	0
30	\	¢	0	0	1	1	1	1	0	0	1	0	0	1	0	1	0
31	⧻	=	0	0	1	1	1	1	1	0	1	1	1	1	1	1	0
32	-	-	0	1	0	0	0	0	0	0	1	1	0	0	0	0	0
33	J	J	0	1	0	0	0	0	1	1	1	0	1	0	0	0	1
34	K	K	0	1	0	0	0	1	0	1	1	0	1	0	0	1	0
35	L	L	0	1	0	0	0	1	1	1	1	0	1	0	0	1	1
36	M	M	0	1	0	0	1	0	0	1	1	0	1	0	1	0	0
37	N	N	0	1	0	0	1	0	1	1	1	0	1	0	1	0	1
38	O	O	0	1	0	0	1	1	0	1	1	0	1	0	1	1	0
39	P	P	0	1	0	0	1	1	1	1	1	0	1	0	1	1	1
40	Q	Q	0	1	0	1	0	0	0	1	1	0	1	1	0	0	0
41	R	R	0	1	0	1	0	0	1	1	1	0	1	1	0	0	1
42	!	!	0	1	0	1	0	1	0	0	1	0	1	1	0	1	0
43	$	$	0	1	0	1	0	1	1	0	1	0	1	1	0	1	1
44	•	•	0	1	0	1	1	0	0	0	1	0	1	1	1	0	0
45	]	)	0	1	0	1	1	0	1	0	1	0	1	1	1	0	1
46	;	;	0	1	0	1	1	1	0	0	1	0	1	1	1	1	0
47	∧	''	0	1	0	1	1	1	1	0	1	1	1	1	1	1	1
48	& or +	&	0	1	1	0	0	0	0	0	1	0	1	0	0	0	0
49	A	A	0	1	1	0	0	0	1	1	1	0	0	0	0	0	1
50	B	B	0	1	1	0	0	1	0	1	1	0	0	0	0	1	0
51	C	C	0	1	1	0	0	1	1	1	1	0	0	0	0	1	1
52	D	D	0	1	1	0	1	0	0	1	1	0	0	0	1	0	0
53	E	E	0	1	1	0	1	0	1	1	1	0	0	0	1	0	1
54	F	F	0	1	1	0	1	1	0	1	1	0	0	0	1	1	0
55	G	G	0	1	1	0	1	1	1	1	1	0	0	0	1	1	1
56	H	H	0	1	1	1	0	0	0	1	1	0	0	1	0	0	0
57	I	I	0	1	1	1	0	0	1	1	1	0	0	1	0	0	1
58	?	?	0	1	1	1	0	1	0	0	1	1	0	1	1	1	1
59	.	.	0	1	1	1	0	1	1	0	1	0	0	1	0	1	1
60	⌑ or)	⌑	0	1	1	1	1	0	0	0	1	1	0	1	0	1	0
61	[	(	0	1	1	1	1	0	1	0	1	0	0	1	1	0	1
62	<	<	0	1	1	1	1	1	0	0	1	0	0	1	1	0	0
63	‡	'	0	1	1	1	1	1	1	0	1	1	1	1	1	0	1

Fig. 3.22 MM4220EK/MM5220EK BCDIC to EBCDIC conversion (National Semiconductor Corp.).

The MM4220LR/MM5220LR BCDIC-to-ASCII-7/ASCII-7-to-BCDIC Code Converter

The MM4220LR code-converter circuit shown in Fig. 3.23 is used to convert between the 7-bit ASCII and 6-bit BCDIC alphanumeric codes. This circuit can be set to convert either way between the two codes by changing the logic level of address bit A_7. A_7 is set to logic 0 in Fig. 3.23 to select conversion from ASCII-7 to BCDIC code. A table of the circuits input/output operation is shown in Fig. 3.24.

ASCII to BCDIC

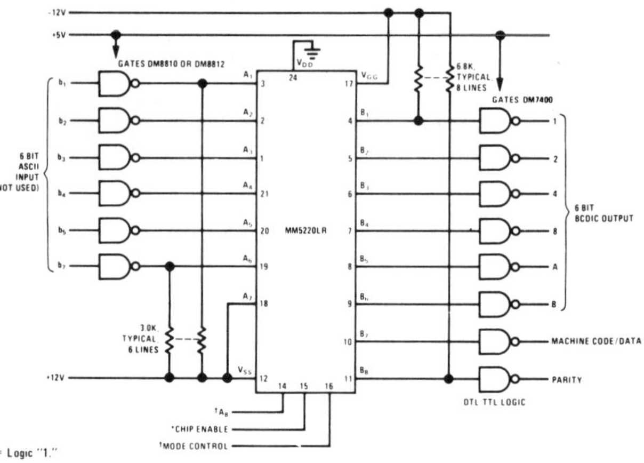

†Mode Control = Logic "0," A_8 = Logic "1."
*Chip Enable = Logic "1" to obtain outputs.
Logic Levels:
DTL/TTL (except at MOS/ROM interface). Logic "1," +5.0V, NOM. Logic "0," ground, NOM.
MOS/ROM inputs and outputs. Logic "1," more negative. Logic "0," more positive.

Fig. 3.23 MM4220LR/MM5220LR connection as an ASCII-7-to-BCDIC code converter (National Semiconductor Corp.).

EXAMPLE 3.10 The ASCII-7 input to the circuit in Fig. 3.23 is

$$b_7 b_5 b_4 b_3 b_2 b_1 = 111010$$

Find the character being converted and the BCDIC output of the circuit.

SOLUTION Under the input columns in the table, we find that the ASCII input represents the letter Z. The BCDIC code produced at the output is

$$BA8421 = 011001$$

3.8 CHARACTER GENERATORS

Another important application for read-only memories is its use as a *character generator*. In this type of application, a ROM is used to convert data expressed in a standard alphanumeric code such as the ASCII, BCDIC, or EBCDIC code to a form capable of driving a dot matrix display, dot matrix

ASCII to BCDIC

	FUNCTION		CODE															
	INPUT	OUTPUT		INPUT						OUTPUT								
ROM ADDRESS	ASCII SYMBOL	BCDIC SYMBOL	CODE	ASCII b7	b5	b4	b3	b2	b1	MC/ DATA	E P	BCDIC B	A	8	4	2	1
0	SP	SP	0	0	0	0	0	0	0	0	0	0	0	0	0	0	0
1	!	!	0	0	0	0	0	0	1	0	1	1	0	1	0	1	0
2	″	+++	0	0	0	0	0	1	0	0	1	0	1	1	1	1	1
3	#	#	0	0	0	0	0	1	1	0	1	0	0	1	0	1	1
4	$	$	0	0	0	0	1	0	0	0	0	1	0	1	0	1	1
5	%	%	0	0	0	0	1	0	1	0	1	0	1	1	1	0	0
6	&	&	0	0	0	0	1	1	0	0	0	1	1	0	0	0	0
7	'	V	0	0	0	0	1	1	1	0	0	0	1	1	1	0	1
8	(	Blank	0	0	0	1	0	0	0	0	1	0	1	0	0	0	0
9	)	Δ	0	0	0	1	0	0	1	0	1	1	0	1	1	1	1
10	•	•	0	0	0	1	0	1	0	0	1	1	0	1	1	0	0
11	VT	†	0	0	0	1	0	1	1	1	0	0	1	1	0	1	0
12	,	,	0	0	0	1	1	0	0	0	0	0	1	1	0	1	1
13	CR	‡	0	0	0	1	1	0	1	1	1	1	1	1	1	1	1
14	.	.	0	0	0	1	1	1	0	0	1	1	1	1	0	1	1
15	/	/	0	0	0	1	1	1	1	0	0	0	1	0	0	0	1
16	0	0	0	0	1	0	0	0	0	0	0	0	0	1	0	1	0
17	1	1	0	0	1	0	0	0	1	0	1	0	0	0	0	0	1
18	2	2	0	0	1	0	0	1	0	0	1	0	0	0	0	1	0
19	3	3	0	0	1	0	0	1	1	0	0	0	0	0	0	1	1
20	4	4	0	0	1	0	1	0	0	0	1	0	0	0	1	0	0
21	5	5	0	0	1	0	1	0	1	0	0	0	0	0	1	0	1
22	6	6	0	0	1	0	1	1	0	0	0	0	0	0	1	1	0
23	7	7	0	0	1	0	1	1	1	0	1	0	0	0	1	1	1
24	8	8	0	0	1	1	0	0	0	0	1	0	0	1	0	0	0
25	9	9	0	0	1	1	0	0	1	0	0	0	0	1	0	0	1
26	:	:	0	0	1	1	0	1	0	0	1	0	0	1	1	0	1
27	;	;	0	0	1	1	0	1	1	0	0	1	0	1	1	1	0
28	<	<	0	0	1	1	1	0	0	0	1	1	1	1	1	1	0
29	=	√	0	0	1	1	1	0	1	0	0	0	0	1	1	1	1
30	>	>	0	0	1	1	1	1	0	0	1	0	0	1	1	1	0
31	?	?	0	0	1	1	1	1	1	0	0	1	1	1	0	1	0
32	@	@	0	1	0	0	0	0	0	0	0	0	0	1	1	0	0
33	A	A	0	1	0	0	0	0	1	0	1	1	1	0	0	0	1
34	B	B	0	1	0	0	0	1	0	0	1	1	1	0	0	1	0
35	C	C	0	1	0	0	0	1	1	0	0	1	1	0	0	1	1
36	D	D	0	1	0	0	1	0	0	0	1	1	1	0	1	0	0
37	E	E	0	1	0	0	1	0	1	0	0	1	1	0	1	0	1
38	F	F	0	1	0	0	1	1	0	0	0	1	1	0	1	1	0
39	G	G	0	1	0	0	1	1	1	0	1	1	1	0	1	1	1
40	H	H	0	1	0	1	0	0	0	0	1	1	1	1	0	0	0
41	I	I	0	1	0	1	0	0	1	0	0	1	1	1	0	0	1
42	J	J	0	1	0	1	0	1	0	0	0	1	0	0	0	0	1
43	K	K	0	1	0	1	0	1	1	0	0	1	0	0	0	1	0
44	L	L	0	1	0	1	1	0	0	0	1	1	0	0	0	1	1
45	M	M	0	1	0	1	1	0	1	0	0	1	0	0	1	0	0
46	N	N	0	1	0	1	1	1	0	0	1	1	0	0	1	0	1
47	O	O	0	1	0	1	1	1	1	0	1	1	0	0	1	1	0
48	P	P	0	1	1	0	0	0	0	0	0	1	0	0	1	1	1
49	Q	Q	0	1	1	0	0	0	1	0	0	1	0	1	0	0	0
50	R	R	0	1	1	0	0	1	0	0	1	1	0	1	0	0	1
51	S	S	0	1	1	0	0	1	1	0	0	0	1	0	0	1	0
52	T	T	0	1	1	0	1	0	0	0	1	0	1	0	0	1	1
53	U	U	0	1	1	0	1	0	1	0	0	0	1	0	1	0	0
54	V	V	0	1	1	0	1	1	0	0	1	0	1	0	1	0	1
55	W	W	0	1	1	0	1	1	1	0	1	0	1	0	1	1	0
56	X	X	0	1	1	1	0	0	0	0	0	0	1	0	1	1	1
57	Y	Y	0	1	1	1	0	0	1	0	0	0	1	1	0	0	0
58	Z	Z	0	1	1	1	0	1	0	0	1	0	1	1	0	0	1
59	[	[	0	1	1	1	0	1	1	0	1	1	1	1	1	0	1
60	\	\	0	1	1	1	1	0	0	0	0	0	1	1	1	1	0
61	]	|	0	1	1	1	1	0	1	0	0	1	0	1	1	0	1
62	^	¤	0	1	1	1	1	1	0	0	0	1	1	1	1	0	0
63	—	-	0	1	1	1	1	1	1	0	1	1	0	0	0	0	0
			A_7	A_6	A_5	A_4	A_3	A_2	A_1	B_8	B_7	B_6	B_5	B_4	B_3	B_2	B_1

Fig. 3.24 MM4220LR/MM5220LR ASCII-7-to-BCDIC conversion (National Semiconductor Corp.).

printer, or other character display device. A number of standard ROM character generators are presently available.

The MM4240AA/MM5240AA Horizontal-Scan Character Generator[11]

The MM4240AA/MM5240AA ROM in Fig. 3.25(a) is a standard character-generator device. It is used to convert data expressed in ASCII code to a form capable of generating *5 × 7 dot characters.* This means that each alphanumeric character is formed from an array of dots arranged into 5 columns by 7 rows.

This device is capable of generating the set of 64 characters shown in Fig. 3.25(b). Notice that each character is listed with its octal and binary address. For example, letter N is stored at 16_8 or 001110_2.

From the input side of the block in Fig. 3.25(a), we see that the ROM has a 6-bit character address input. These address leads are labeled b_1 through b_6. Of these bits, $b_6\, b_5\, b_4$ represent the MSD of the octal address and $b_3\, b_2\, b_1$ represent the LSD. The code at these leads selects the character to be displayed.

Besides this, there are three row address inputs, marked L_0, L_1, and L_2. The code on these lines determine which row of the pattern is to be output. The remaining input is the control lead *CHIP ENABLE,* which is used to enable the ROM outputs.

On the output side of the block, we find five open-collector row outputs B_1 through B_5. These outputs produce a parallel word that is used to drive the five columns of the dot character display. In some applications, the output must be converted to serial form with external circuitry.

Let us assume that the outputs of the ROM are enabled by connecting *CHIP ENABLE* to the voltage V_{DD} and the address applied at the input is

$$b_6\, b_5\, b_4\, b_3\, b_2\, b_1 = 16_8 = 001110$$

This address represents the letter N, which is illustrated in Fig. 3.25(a).

The row address $L_2\, L_1\, L_0$ is started at 000 and incremented toward 111 to output the data words required to produce the character. When the row address is 000, the outputs B_1 through B_5 are set for a blank row representing the horizontal space between lines of characters. As $L_2\, L_1\, L_0$ changes to 001, the second-row output causes the dots in columns B_1 and B_5 to form. As it increments to 010, a new output is produced and dots form in columns B_1, B_2, and B_5 of the third row. This continues until the data for $L_2\, L_1\, L_0 = 111$ are output to complete the character. After this, the character generation sequence starts again with a row count of 000.

The MM4240AA/MM5240AA is said to be a *horizontal-scan* character generator. This is because its output data words generate a character by scanning the horizontal rows of the array.

[11] National Semiconductor Corp., "American and European Fonts in Standard Character Generators," AN-57 (Santa Clara, CA: National Semiconductor Corp., 1976). (Courtesy of National Semiconductor Corp.)

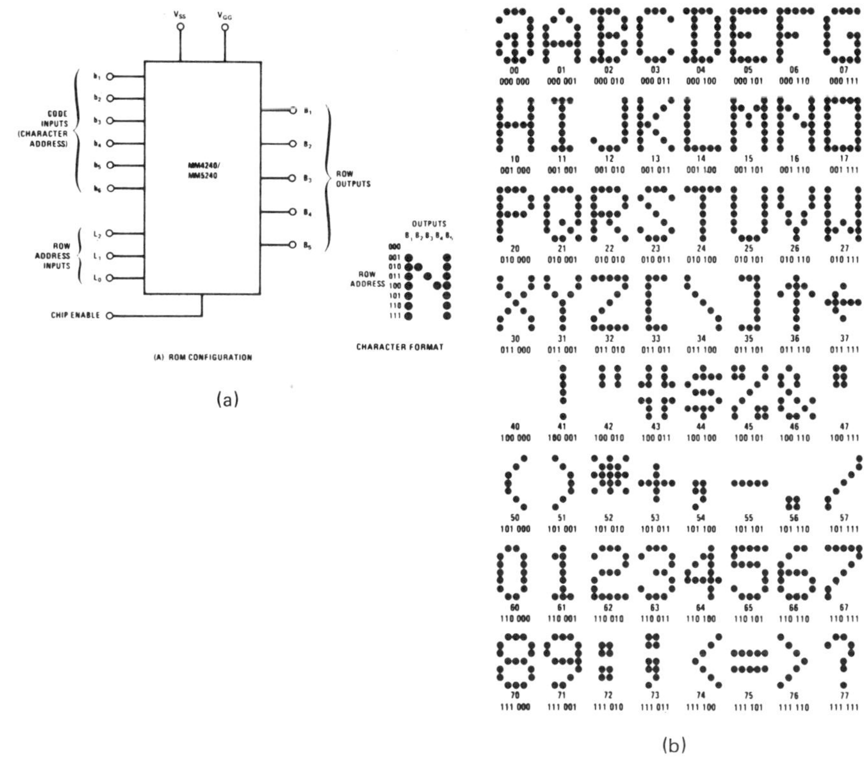

Fig. 3.25 (a) MM4240AA/MM5240AA block diagram (National Semiconductor Corp.); (b) MM4240AA/MM5240AA character set (National Semiconductor Corp.).

EXAMPLE 3.11 What is the address for the storage location of letter S in the MM4240AA/MM5240AA ROM?

SOLUTION From the chart in Fig. 3.25(b), we find that the character S is located at address 23_8.

$$b_6 b_5 b_4 b_3 b_2 b_1 = 23_8 = 010011$$

The MM4241ABL/MM5241ABL Vertical-Scan Character Generator[12]

Figure 3.26(a) shows another popular character-generator device, the MM4241ABL/MM5241ABL. Like the MM4240AA/MM5240AA IC, this device takes ASCII coded data at its input and produces output codes to generate a 5 × 7 character.

The characters generated by this device are illustrated in Fig. 3.26(b). Here we see that they are similar to those produced by the MM4240AA/MM5240AA. However, these characters are generated by a *vertical-scan* method instead of by horizontal scan.

[12] Ibid.

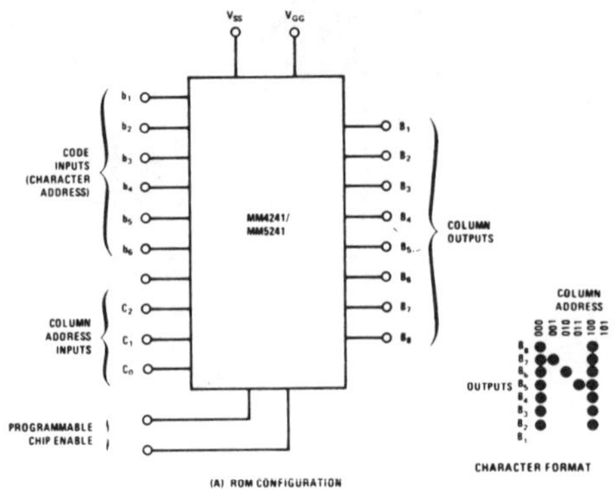

(a)

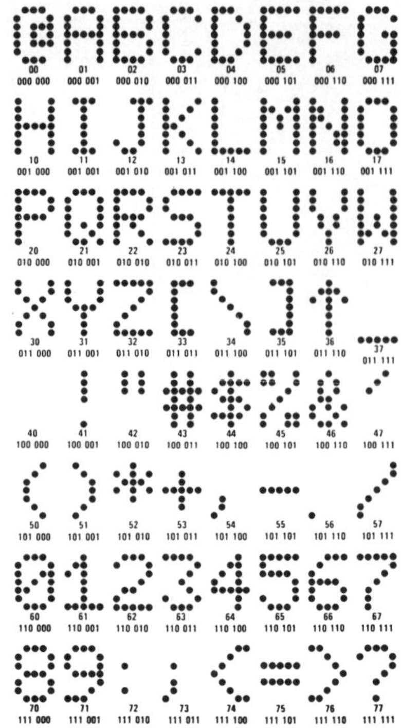

(b)

Fig. 3.26 (a) MM4241ABL/MM5241ABL block diagram (National Semiconductor Corp.); (b) MM4241ABL/MM5241ABL character set (National Semiconductor Corp.).

Looking at the block diagram in Fig. 3.26(a), we see that the ROM has six character address inputs, b_1 through b_6; three column address inputs, C_0, C_1 and C_2; and eight column outputs, B_1 through B_8. The ASCII code for the characters to be displayed is applied to the character address inputs. After this, the column address $C_2 C_1 C_0$ is incremented from 000 toward 111. For each new column address, an 8-bit word representing the dots to be formed in the columns of the array is output on B_1 through B_8. Actually, bit B_1 is used to produce a blank line between lines of characters and the outputs for $C_2 C_1 C_0$, equal to 101, 110, and 111, produce blank spaces between adjacent characters.

In this way we see that the ROM generates a character with five vertical sets of seven dots corresponding to its columns rather than seven rows of five dots. This vertical-scan method is required for dot matrix printing mechanisms.

EXAMPLE 3.12 What is the range of address corresponding to letter A within the MM4241ABL/MM5241ABL device?

SOLUTION Looking at the character set chart in Fig. 3.26(b), we find that the character address for A is 01_8=000001. These bits are combined with $C_2C_1C_0$=000 through 111 to define the address range.

$$b_6b_5b_4b_3b_2b_1C_2C_1C_0=000001000=010_8$$

$$b_6b_5b_4b_3b_2b_1C_2C_1C_0=000001111=017_8$$

CRT Display System[13]

One of the most common uses of the dot matrix character generator is to display data on a cathode ray tube (CRT) terminal. A simplified block diagram of a typical CRT display system is shown in Fig. 3.27. It contains four basic sections: M-N character register, N-character register, character generator ROM, and parallel-to-serial converter.

ASCII-coded characters are input to the M-N character register. This register is used to store the ASCII codes for a complete page of characters. A *page* on the screen consists of M lines, each line having N characters. One line of N 6-bit character codes are loaded from the M-N register output into the N-character register for display on the screen. The N-character register sends out one ASCII code after the other to the address inputs of the character generator ROM. The 5-bit parallel output produced by the ROM is the first row code for each character in the line. This output is converted to serial form for use in modulating the CRT beam as it sweeps across the screen.

During the first scan across the screen, the line code is set to 000 and left at this value as the complete line of character codes is circulated through the register. The N-character register is a recirculating-type register, and each time it outputs an ASCII character, the code is reloaded at the input. This is indicated by the arrow from its output back to its input. In this way, only the uppermost row of dots for all characters in the line are displayed during the first scan across the screen, but the line of character codes is still held in the N-character register.

After the first scan is complete, the line select count is incremented to 001. Now the characters are circulated through the N-character register

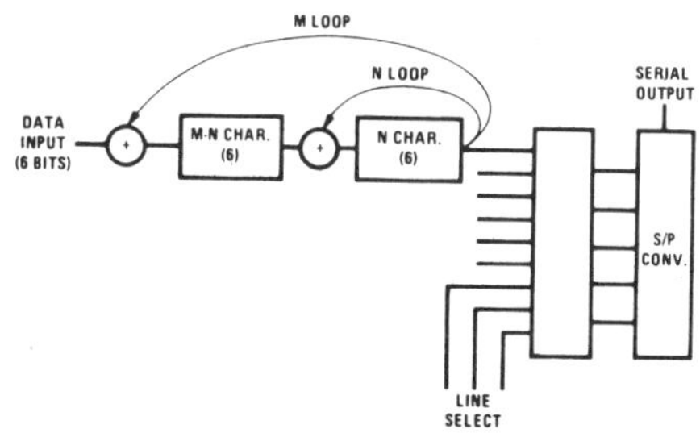

Fig. 3.27 CRT display system block diagram (National Semiconductor Corp.).

[13] National Semiconductor Corp., "The Systems Approach to Character Generators," AN-40 (Santa Clara, CA: National Semiconductor Corp., 1976). (Courtesy of National Semiconductor Corp.)

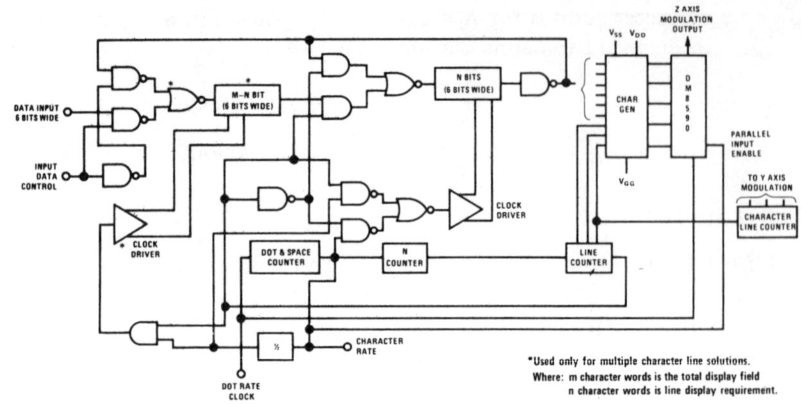

Fig. 3.28 CRT display system circuitry (National Semiconductor Corp.).

a second time and the second row of dots for each character is displayed. This sequence is repeated for each line count up through 111 to produce the first line of characters on the screen.

During the eighth circulation of the N-character register, output data are returned to the input of the M-N character register, to be stored for later use. At the same time, the next line of characters is loaded into the N-character register. This sequence of events repeats until all M lines of data held in the M-N register are displayed on the screen. Then the sequence starts over with the first line on the display.

A display that operates in this way is called a *raster scan system.* Figure 3.28 shows the circuitry required to implement this type of raster display system.

High-Resolution Dot Matrix Characters[14]

All the dot matrix characters we have introduced up to this point were formed from a 5 × 7 array of dots. However, to reduce eyestrain and improve definition of lowercase characters, the array can be expanded to 7 × 9, or 7 × 12, or even to larger sizes.

Figure 3.29(a) shows the representation of a number of characters using a 5 × 7 array which are then repeated with a high-resolution 7 × 12 array. Notice that capital letters are formed using a 7 × 9 array of dots, and lower-case letters are permitted to go below the line by expanding to the full 7 × 12 array.

High-resolution characters can be obtained by interconnecting character-generator ROMS. Figure 3.29(b) shows the parallel connection of two MM4240/MM5240 ROMs to produce 7 × 9 to 7 × 12 characters.

[14] National Semiconductor Corp., "Saving ROMs in High-Resolution Dot-Matrix Displays and Printers," AN-85 (Santa Clara, CA: National Semiconductor Corp., 1976). (Courtesy of National Semiconductor Corp.)

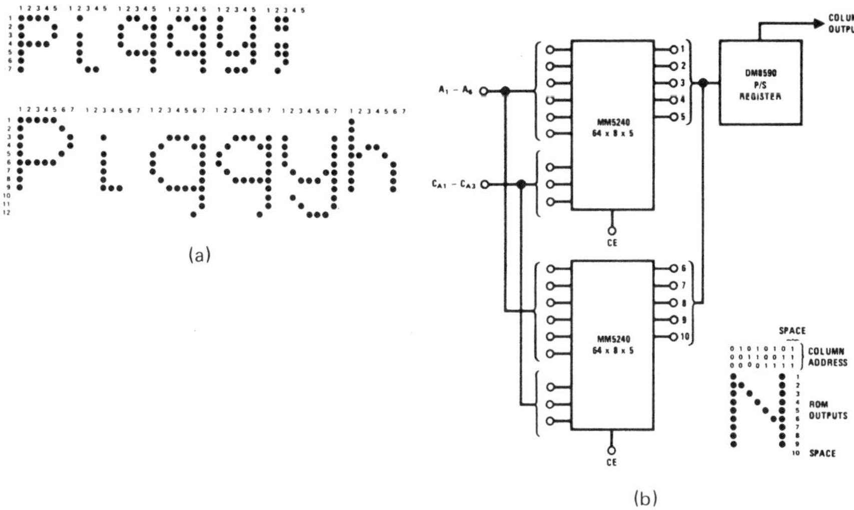

Fig. 3.29 (a) 5 X 7 and 7 X 12 characters (National Semiconductor Corp.); (b) expanded MM4240/MM5240 circuit for 7 X 9 to 7 X 12 character generation (National Semiconductor Corp.).

ASSIGNMENTS

Section 3.2

1. What is meant by implementing combinational logic with ROM?
2. Make a truth table like that shown in Fig. 3.2 to show the program required to implement a combinational logic function that converts BCD to Gray code.
3. A ROM programmed with the data in the table of Fig. 3.3 has as its address inputs A_7 through A_0 the word 00100000. What type of code conversion is taking place?

Section 3.3

4. How is a sequential logic function implemented with ROM?
5. Make a chart such as that in Fig. 3.5 showing the program of an XS-3 code counter.
6. The ROM in the sequential logic connection of Fig. 3.4 is programmed with the information of Fig. 3.6. If the most significant address bits are $A_7A_6A_5A_4$=0000, draw the output waveforms generated at Q_1 through Q_4 as the outputs are clocked into the latch to address the ROM through its count sequence.

Section 3.4

7. What is the function of ROM in a microcomputer system?
8. Describe the instruction cycle of a microcomputer system.

Section 3.5

9. Show how to connect two 74S271 ROMs to give a memory organization of 256 16-bit words.
10. The address input to the circuit in Fig. 3.10 is A_9 through A_0 equals 0111111111.

Which PROM is enabled, and what storage location is read? Assume that *DATA STROBE* is logic 1.

11. Show how a 74LS138 decoder can be connected with two banks of 74S271 ROMs to make a memory organized as 512 16-bit words.

Section 3.6

12. What is a mathematical look-up table ROM?
13. The input for the ROM shown in the table of Fig. 3.13(a) is the value $X = 0.7$. Find the address input, data output, and angle θ.
14. Determine the address that must be input to an MM4220BM/MM5220BM ROM to look up the sine of 60°. What is the output produced by the ROM?

Section 3.7

15. What is a code-converter ROM?
16. The BCD input to the two-decade BCD-to-binary converter in Fig. 3.17(a) is 10011001. What are the outputs of the code converter?
17. What are the inputs and outputs of the circuit in Fig. 3.23 if the symbol to be converted from ASCII-7 to BCDIC is $?

Section 3.8

18. What is a character-generator ROM?
19. What is the range of addresses associated with the character X in the MM4240AA/MM5240AA ROM of Fig. 3.25?
20. What is the difference between a horizontal-scan character generator and vertical-scan character generator?

4

RANDOM-ACCESS READ/WRITE MEMORY

4.1 INTRODUCTION

In this chapter, we continue our study of semiconductor memories with a second important element: the random-access read/write memory. This type of memory can be implemented with semiconductor or magnetic devices. However, this chapter deals only with the semiconductor variety.

The chapter begins by introducing the architecture, static RAM operation, electrical characteristics, and some standard static RAM ICs. This material is followed by the topics of dynamic RAM operation and devices, expanding RAM storage capacity, and RAM applications.

1. Random-access read/write memory
2. RAM architecture
3. Static RAM operation and standard IC devices
4. Dynamic RAM operation and standard IC devices
5. Expanded word length and word capacity
6. Applications of RAM

4.2 RANDOM-ACCESS READ/WRITE MEMORY

In the electronics industry, *random-access read/write memory* devices are referred to as *RAMs*. The storage locations in RAM, as in ROM, can be accessed in a random order. But unlike ROM, the data stored in RAM are not permanent in nature; that is, they can be altered. We are able to both write new data into a location in RAM for storage and read data back out for use in processing. Because of its versatile read and write features, RAM finds wide use in applications where data change frequently.

A second important way in which RAM differs from ROM is that it is *volatile* memory. If we remove the power supply from the IC, the data are lost or otherwise changed.

Types of RAM Memories

The types of RAM devices that can be manufactured with the bipolar and MOS technologies are shown in Fig. 4.1. Here we find that there are two basic categories: static RAM and dynamic RAM. In static RAM data, once entered, remain valid as long as the power supply on the device is not turned OFF. Standard static RAM ICs are made by using all the bipolar and MOS technologies described in Chapter 1.

On the other hand, it is not sufficient to maintain just the power supply on a dynamic RAM. To retain data in this kind of device, we must both keep the power supply turned on and periodically rewrite the data into the storage array. This added requirement is necessary because the storage elements are capacitors. If the storage capacitors were not recharged by rewriting the data, they would discharge and the data would be lost. This recharging process is known as *refreshing* the RAM. Dynamic RAMs are manufactured using only MOS technologies.

RAM Circuitry

Figure 4.2 lists the various bipolar and MOS technologies used to implement random-access memories. The bipolar technologies, which include ECL, TTL, and I^2L, are employed to construct RAM circuits with resistors, diodes, and bipolar transistors. The primary characteristics of bipolar RAMs are high speed, high power consumption, and low density. The present-day maximum storage capacity of a single bipolar RAM IC is 16,384 (16k) bits. Bipolar memories play an important role in the design of modern digital systems when high-speed operation is essential.

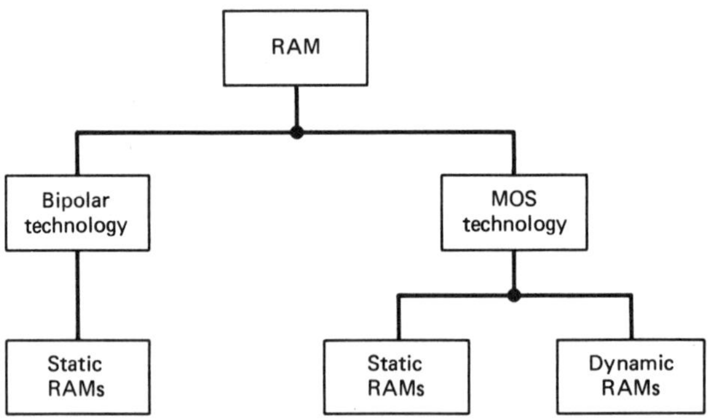

Fig. 4.1 RAM family devices.

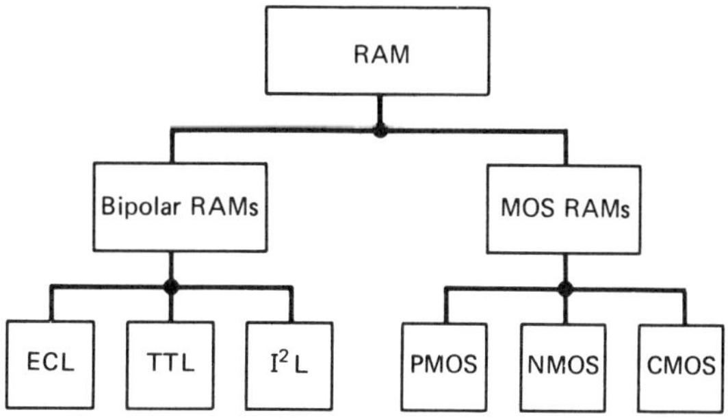

Fig. 4.2 RAM circuitry.

Utilizing N-channel and P-channel MOSFET circuitry, we can manufacture MOS RAM ICs. The three technologies widely used are PMOS, NMOS, and CMOS. These technologies produce RAMs with improved density and power characteristics compared with bipolar technologies. For instance, NMOS and PMOS circuitry can be more compactly integrated than bipolar circuitry and results in higher-density devices. With NMOS, we have already increased maximum storage capacity to 65,536 (64*k*) bits.

CMOS RAMs offer another advantage over bipolar RAMs. They need very low power to operate. For this reason, they are used in equipment where low power consumption is of primary concern. An example of this type of application is the battery-operated calculator. The prime disadvantage of MOS technology RAMs is their slower operating speed.

General RAM Block Diagram

A general block diagram of a RAM is shown in Fig. 4.3(a). By comparing this diagram to the one introduced in Chapter 2 for ROM, we find that they are similar; both devices have *address inputs*, *data outputs*, and *control inputs*. However, the RAM has a new set of leads called the *data inputs*.

Figure 4.3(b) shows the RAM block diagram using bus notation. Here the individual signal lines are grouped to form the *address bus*, *data input bus*, *control input bus*, and *data output bus*. Each of these buses is unidirectional; that is, they carry data in only onc direction in or out.

Some RAM ICs have a single bus that is used to input and output data. This is called a *bidirectional data bus* and is illustrated in Fig. 4.3(c). RAMs using the configuration with separate data-in and data-out buses generally operate faster than do those with a single data bus.

The address bus on the RAM in Fig. 4.3(a) consists of address lines A_0 through A_3. The binary word input over these lines select the storage location within RAM to which data are to be written or from which data are to be read. Four-bit data words can be stored at each of the 16 address locations over the range $A_3A_2A_1A_0 = 0000_2 = 0_{16}$ through $A_3A_2A_1A_0 = 1111_2 = F_{16}$.

RAM devices are available with bit storage capacities from 16 data words to 65,536 data words. Depending on the storage capacity, RAM ICs require from 4 through 16 address bits to select the storage locations. Because of the limited number of pins available on an IC package, the address

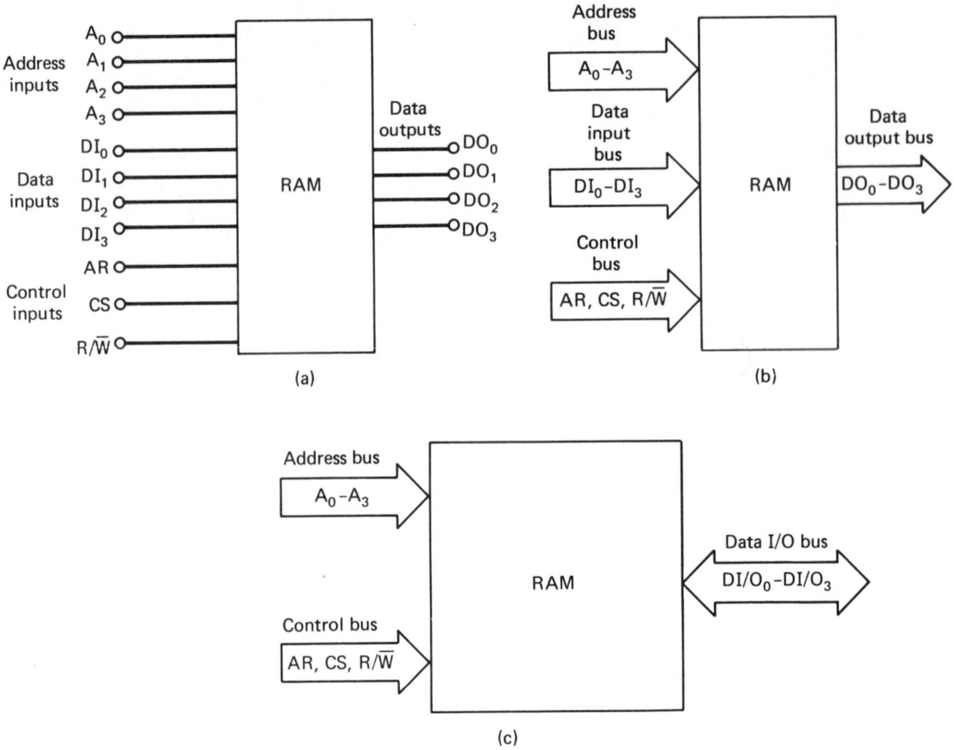

Fig. 4.3 (a) General RAM block diagram; (b) RAM block diagram using bus notation; (c) RAM block with bidirectional bus.

word for large-capacity RAMs is divided into two parts. For instance, the address for a 64*k* RAM is divided into two 8-bit bytes. These two parts are time-multiplexed into the device over a single set of eight address lines.

Earlier, we pointed out that data can be written into RAM for storage or read out for further processing. When data are written into the RAM in Fig. 4.3(a), they enter on the four data input leads marked DI_0 through DI_3. On the other hand, data are read out at output leads DO_0 through DO_3.

Input and output word length are always the same. The most common word lengths available with standard RAMs are 1, 4, and 8 bits. For this reason, 8*k*-bit RAM ICs are produced with 8*k* by 1-bit, 2*k* by 4-bit, and 1*k* by 8-bit organizations.

The outputs of the RAM IC are usually open-collector or three-state. This allows the parallel busing required for memory expansion.

In addition to the address and data buses, the RAM in Fig. 4.3(a) has a three-line control bus. From the diagram we find that the control inputs are *AR*, *CS*, and $R/\overline{W}$. As with ROM, *AR* stands for *address ready* and is used to enable the address on lines A_0 through A_3 to enter the memory device. Moreover, *CS* stands for *chip select*, which is again used to activate the outputs. The new lead is the *read/write control* $R/\overline{W}$. This input is used to signal the device whether a read or write operation is to be performed.

Control signals written with a bar over the top indicate that the operation described by the mnemonic occurs when the signal is at the 0 logic level. For instance, $R/\overline{W}$ means that a write operation is to be performed by the RAM when the input is logic 0. If $R/\overline{W}$ is changed to logic 1, it signals for a read operation.

Input/Output Operation

The input/output operation of the RAM in Fig. 4.3(a) is similar to that of the ROM in that we can read data output from its storage locations. However, RAM has the additional capability of entering new data into the device. The process of entering data into a RAM is called a *write operation.*

The sequence of events that must take place to write a word of data into RAM is called a *write cycle*. The write cycle begins with the switching of the *address ready* (AR) control line to logic 1. This enables the address inputs. Next, the address is applied at leads A_0 through A_3 and input data at DI_0 through DI_3. After the address and data have had a chance to stabilize, the *read/write* control ($R/\overline{W}$) is set to logic 0. This signals that a write operation is in progress.

All of the input signals are held stable for a short time. This permits the address, control signals, and data inputs to propagate through the circuits within the RAM. After this interval, the word is stored at the address location.

The read operation of the RAM is similar to the read operation of the ROM. The sequence of events that must occur to output a word is called a *read cycle*. As with the ROM, it also starts by setting AR to logic 1 and by inputting the address over lines A_0 through A_3. But this time, no data are applied to inputs DI_0 through DI_3. Instead, $R/\overline{W}$ is left at logic 1 to indicate that a read operation is to be performed, and CS is set at logic 1 to enable the output buffers.

The address, control, and data signals propagate through the internal circuitry of the RAM. After a short delay, the data word at the location specified by the address appears at outputs DO_0 through DO_3.

4.3 RAM ARCHITECTURE

Now that we have introduced the RAM, let us turn our attention to its internal structure. The block diagram of a typical RAM is given in Fig. 4.4. The architecture shown has eight basic parts: *address buffer, row decoder, memory array, column decoder, write and sense amplifier, control buffer, data input buffer,* and *data output buffer.*

The Memory Array

The memory array, or storage array, is a special group of circuits that store the data within RAM. This array consists of one storage element (cell) for each bit of data the memory must store. These cells are organized in an

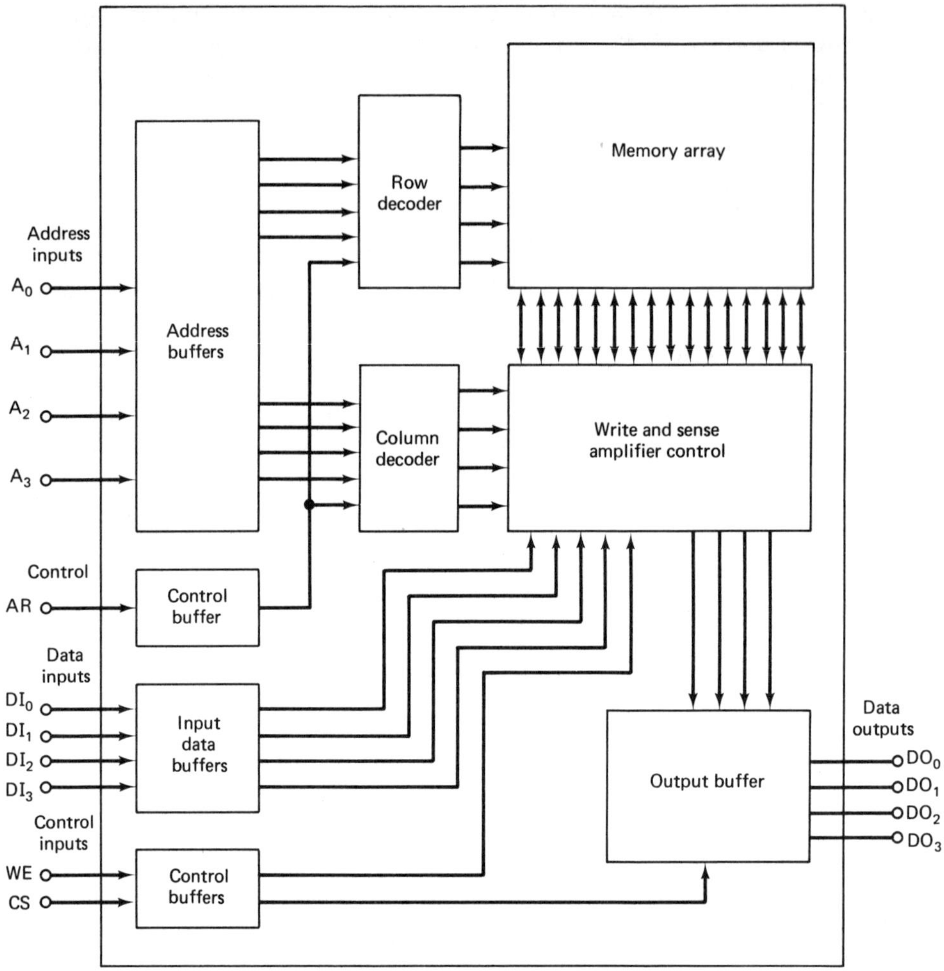

Fig. 4.4 Typical RAM architecture.

orderly matrix pattern. As with ROM, RAM cells can be made with bipolar or MOS circuitry.

The number of bits of data that a memory array can store is said to be its capacity or size. A practical RAM must be able to store many bits of data. RAM ICs are available in which the size of the memory array ranges from 16 bits to 65,536 ($64k$) bits.

A simplified memory array is shown in Fig. 4.5(a). This array consists of 16 cells arranged 4 rows by 4 columns. The select inputs to the array are row signals R_0, R_1, R_2, and R_3. There are also data input/output lines designated B_0, B_1, B_2, and B_3 and their complements $\overline{B}_0$, $\overline{B}_1$, $\overline{B}_2$, and $\overline{B}_3$. These are known as the *bit lines.*

Based on the address input to the RAM, one of the four row inputs

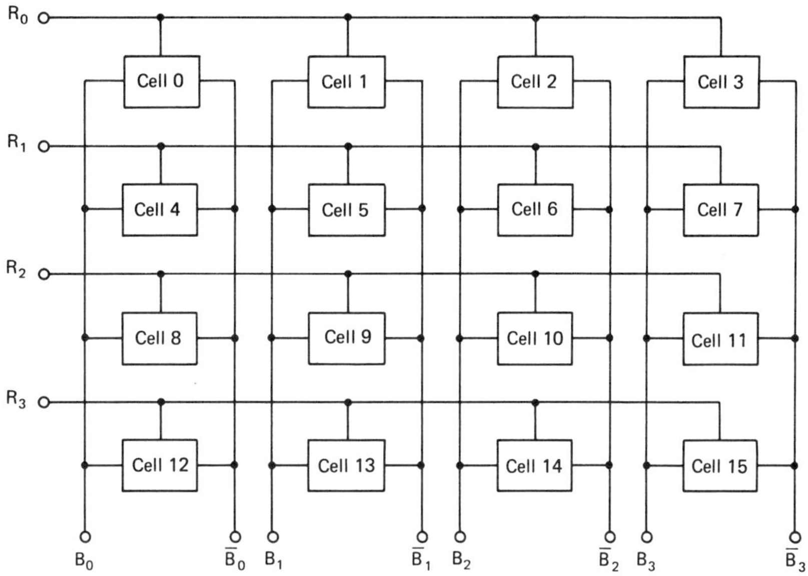

(a)

R	B_3	B_2	B_1	B_0
0	1	1	1	0
1	0	1	1	0
2	0	0	1	1
3	0	0	1	0

(b)

Fig. 4.5 (a) Simplified RAM array; (b) data content of the memory array.

switches logic levels to select that row of the memory array. The selected row line is attached to four cells. It is these four cells into which data are written in or from which data are read out. The data are input or output over the bit lines.

EXAMPLE 4.1 Suppose that the memory array shown in Fig. 4.5(a) contains the data in the table of Fig. 4.5(b). Assume that row R_2 is selected. What data appear on bit lines B_0, B_1, B_2, and B_3 when a read operation is performed?

SOLUTION Row R_2 connects to cells 8, 9, 10, and 11 of the memory array. During a read operation, the data from these cells appear on the bit lines. Looking at Fig. 4.5(b), we find that these data are

$$B_3B_2B_1B_0=0011$$

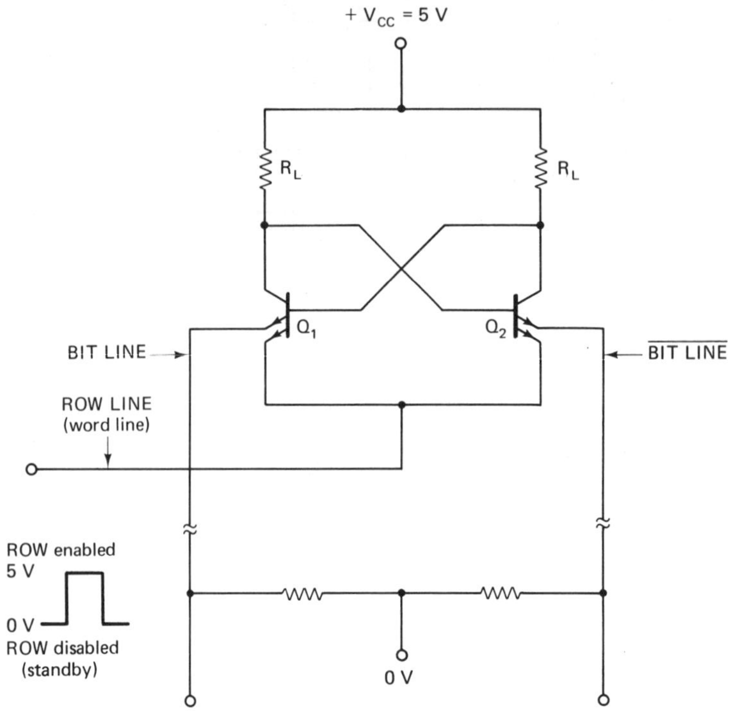

Fig. 4.6 Typical bipolar RAM cell (Texas Instruments, Incorporated).

Bipolar RAM Cell[1]

The cells in a bipolar RAM are constructed by using transistors, resistors, and in some cases diodes. A typical bipolar cell circuit is shown in Fig. 4.6, where two multiemitter transistors Q_1 and Q_2 connect with load resistors to form a flip-flop circuit. One emitter from each transistor is connected together to form the *ROW LINE* input. The other emitter on Q_1 is the *BIT LINE* output, and the other emitter on Q_2 is its complement $\overline{BIT\ LINE}$.

Let us look at the operation of the multiemitter flip-flop. We will start with *ROW LINE* at logic 0 or 0 V. This is because the cell is not yet selected for a read or write operation. Assuming that Q_1 begins turned ON, the collector of Q_1 is at 0 V, which is the 0 logic level. This action cuts off Q_2. With Q_2 OFF, its collector is pulled toward the 5-V supply V_{CC} through its load resistor. This voltage supplies base current to Q_1, holding it ON. The cell is latched in this state with Q_1 ON and Q_2 OFF. This condition defines a logic 1 held in the cell.

With the circuit in this state, no current flows in the bit lines. Therefore, the sense amplifiers they feed do not detect a data bit.

[1] Gerald Luecke, Jack P. Mize, and William N. Carr, *Semiconductor Memory Design and Application*, (Texas Instruments Incorporated) Electronics Series (New York: McGraw-Hill Book Company, 1973), p. 95. (Courtesy of Texas Instruments, Incorporated).

To read the data in the cell, we must switch *ROW LINE* to logic 1 (5 V). This causes current to flow through the bit line of Q_1 instead of *ROW LINE*. Now the sense amplifier detects the current through *BIT LINE* and produces logic 1 at its output.

To write new data into the cell, we again begin by setting *ROW LINE* to logic 1 (5 V). However, this time the input data make one bit line logic 1 and the other logic 0. For instance, let us make $\overline{BIT\ LINE}$=0 and *BIT LINE*=1. Now Q_2 has 0 V on its emitter and it turns ON. At the same moment, Q_1 has 5 V on its emitter and turns OFF. The cell latches into this new state with Q_1 OFF and Q_2 ON. Returning *ROW LINE* to logic 0, the cell maintains these data, which represents storage of logic 0.

MOS RAM Cell[2]

The cells in a MOS RAM storage array are constructed with N-channel or P-channel MOSFETs. Figure 4.7 shows the circuit of a typical MOS cell.

In this circuit, MOSFETs Q_1, Q_2, Q_3, and Q_4 form the flip-flop. Here Q_1 and Q_2 are the active switching elements while Q_3 and Q_4 work as load resistors for Q_1 and Q_2, respectively. MOSFETs Q_5 and Q_6 act as *transmission gates* which serve to isolate or connect the outputs of the cell with the bit lines. These two gates are turned ON and OFF by the row line. Q_7 and Q_8 are two more transmission gates. These devices are controlled by the column select line. When turned OFF, they isolate the bit lines from the sense amplifier inputs. Turning Q_7 and Q_8 ON connects the bit lines to the sense amplifier inputs.

The operation of this MOS flip-flop is essentially the same as that of the bipolar flip-flop. Let us assume we are using N-channel enhancement-mode transistors in the cell.

To write data into the cell, the gate leads of MOSFETs Q_5, Q_6, Q_7, and Q_8 must be held positive. This is done by selecting the cell with its row and column line. In this way, the drain lead of MOSFET Q_1 connects to *BIT LINE* and the drain of Q_2 to $\overline{BIT\ LINE}$. By forcing *BIT LINE* to logic 1 and $\overline{BIT\ LINE}$ to logic 0, Q_2 is turned ON and Q_1 OFF. When transmission gates Q_5, Q_6, Q_7, and Q_8 are turned back OFF, the flip-flop stays in this state. The cell now holds new data.

The cell is read in a similar way. Q_5 through Q_8 are again turned ON. But this time data are not applied to the bit lines. Instead, the sense amplifier is enabled to read the status of *BIT LINE* and $\overline{BIT\ LINE}$. A logic level representing the data held in the cell is produced at the output of the sense amplifier.

The Address Buffer

The address buffer is used to limit loading on the circuitry driving the address inputs of the RAM. Figure 4.8 is a 4-bit address buffer circuit. This circuit consists of eight inverters. As with ROM, the address $A_3A_2A_1A_0$ passes

[2] Ibid., p. 117.

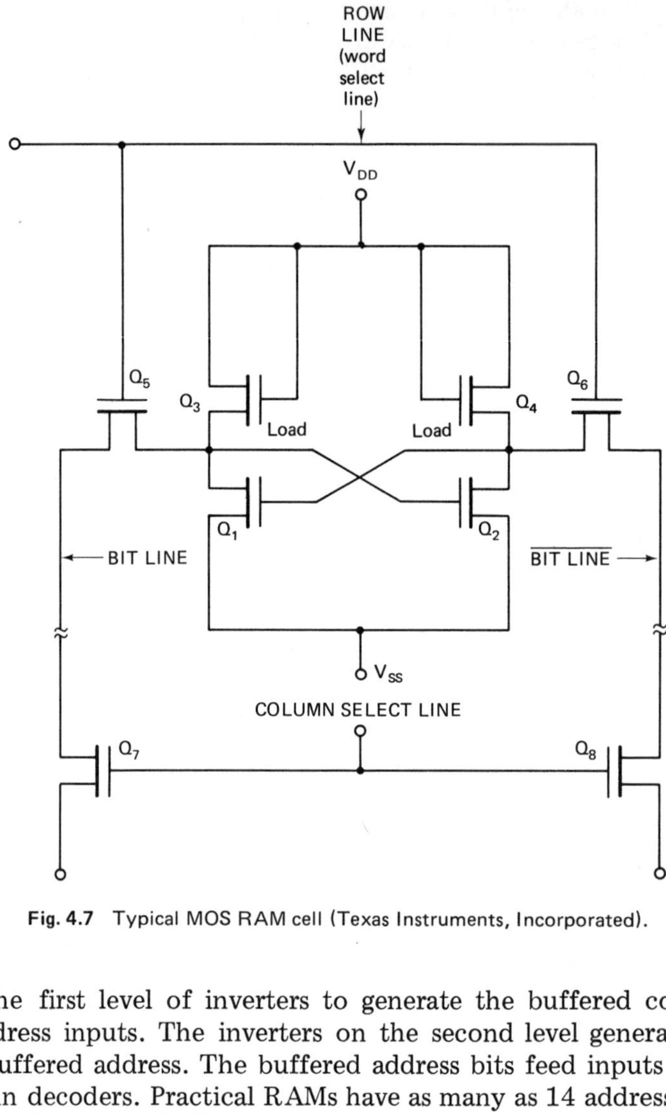

Fig. 4.7 Typical MOS RAM cell (Texas Instruments, Incorporated).

through the first level of inverters to generate the buffered complements of the address inputs. The inverters on the second level generate the non-inverted buffered address. The buffered address bits feed inputs of the row and column decoders. Practical RAMs have as many as 14 address lines, each equipped with separate buffer gates.

The Row Decoder

This part of the RAM is used to select one of the rows in the memory array. A row decoder for a 4 × 4 array is shown in Fig. 4.9(a). The inputs of the circuit are fed by the buffered address signals derived from the two least significant bits of the input addresses, A_0 and A_1. The outputs of the decoder are $\overline{R}_0$, $\overline{R}_1$, $\overline{R}_2$, and $\overline{R}_3$. These signals supply the row inputs of the memory array.

The truth table in Fig. 4.9(b) describes the operation of the row decoder circuit. Notice that the R output corresponding to the binary input

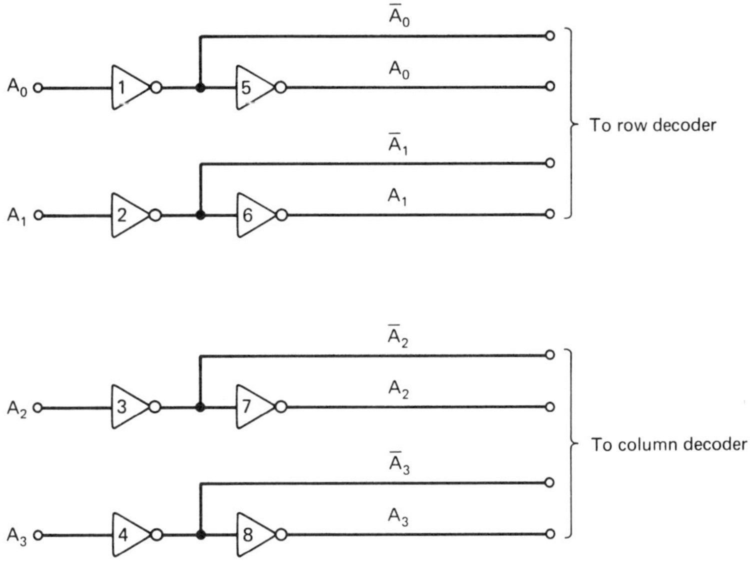

Fig. 4.8 Address buffer.

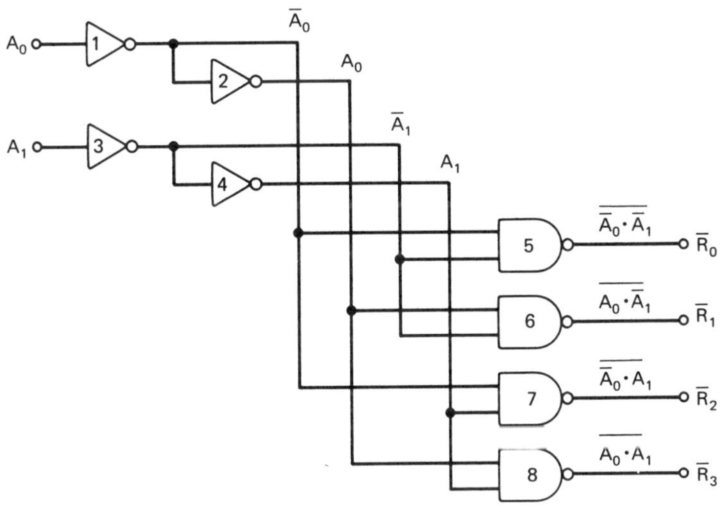

(a)

A_1	A_0	$\bar{R}_0$	$\bar{R}_1$	$\bar{R}_2$	$\bar{R}_3$
0	0	0	1	1	1
0	1	1	0	1	1
1	0	1	1	0	1
1	1	1	1	1	0

(b)

Fig. 4.9 (a) Row decoder; (b) truth table.

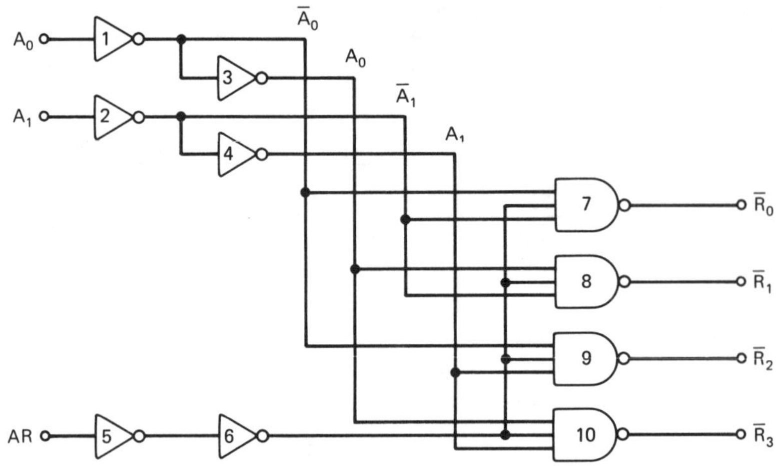

Fig. 4.10 Row decoder with address ready input.

switches to logic 0. For example, an input of $A_1 A_0$=00 makes output $\bar{R}_0$ logic 0 while all other outputs stay at the 1 level.

This decoder is suitable for activating row lines of RAM cells constructed with P-channel MOSFETs. This type of MOSFET requires logic 0 at its gate leads to turn ON and logic 1 to turn OFF.

The address ready feature can be implemented by adding another input to the gates that form the decoder. This input is supplied by the signal *AR*. Such a circuit is shown in Fig. 4.10. If *AR* is set to logic 0, all outputs of the decoder are held at logic 1 and the input of an address is disabled.

Sense Amplifier and Data Output Buffer

The outputs of the memory array require some amplifiers and output buffers to interface properly with external circuitry. The outputs of the cells in a RAM are low-amplitude voltages and currents. Sense amplifiers provide detection and amplification for these signals.

Figure 4.11 shows the connection of sense amplifiers and an output buffer required to organize the output of a 4 × 4 memory array into 16 1-bit words. The sense amplifiers are labeled 1 through 4 and are connected to detect outputs on bit lines BO_0 through BO_3. The logic outputs of the sense amplifiers are S_0 through S_3. By making one of the column inputs C_0 through C_3 logic 1, the corresponding sense amplifier is enabled and its logic output sent on to the input of the data output buffer. The output buffer is enabled by the chip select signal *CS*=1 and $R/\overline{W}$=1 and the data passes through to *DATA OUT*.

RAMs are available with open-collector and three-state outputs to permit parallel busing of the outputs from many RAM ICs. RAMs with open-collector outputs require external pull-up resistors.

The other output configuration widely used in both bipolar and MOS RAMs is the three-state output. It permits switching of the outputs into a

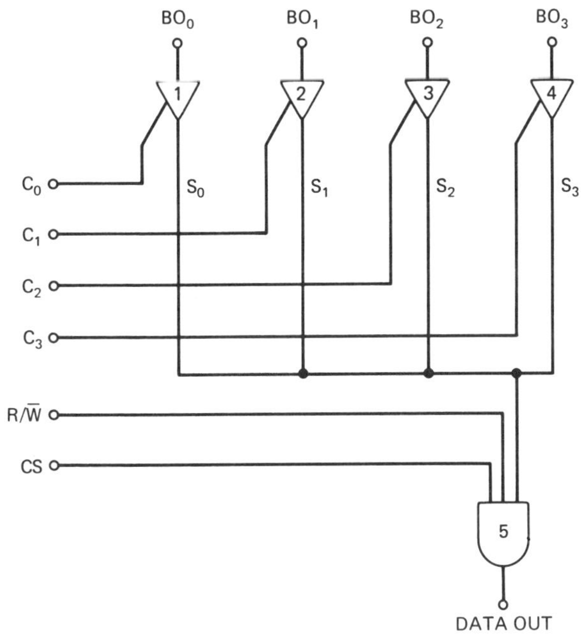

Fig. 4.11 Sense amplifiers and output buffer.

high impedance third state called the hi-Z state. The three-state output is made with internal active pull-up circuitry. The high-impedance output state is obtained by turning OFF both pull-up and pull-down output transistors.

One advantage of the three-state output over the open-collector output is that it can pull faster to the 1 logic level. This is because it contains active pull-up circuitry as opposed to a passive device such as a resistor.

The Column Decoder

In addition to the row decoder, a column decoder such as that shown in Fig. 4.12(a) is included in the RAM. This decoder selects data from specific columns of the memory array for output. This column decoder operates in a way similar to the row decoder; however, it controls the data input/output logic in bipolar RAMs or the transmission gates for input/output of data in MOS RAMs.

The circuit in Fig. 4.12(a) accepts the two MSBs of the address A_2 and A_3 as its inputs. These inputs are first buffered by gates 1 through 4 of the address buffer. The decoder that is formed from AND gates 5 through 8 produces column signals C_0 through C_3.

Figure 4.12(b) is a truth table of column decoder operation. Notice that for each binary combination at the address inputs just one of the column outputs is logic 1. During a read operation, it is these outputs that enable the output logic or sense amplifiers to pass data at the corresponding bit line of the memory array to the output.

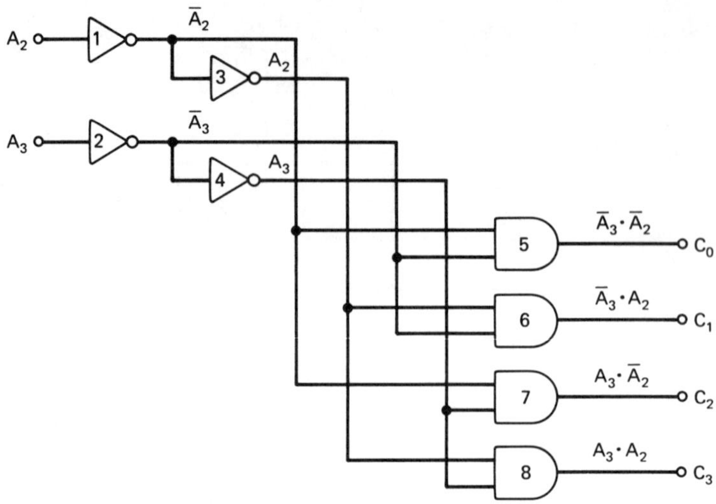

(a)

A_3	A_2	C_0	C_1	C_2	C_3
0	0	1	0	0	0
0	1	0	1	0	0
1	0	0	0	1	0
1	1	0	0	0	1

(b)

Fig. 4.12 (a) Column decoder; (b) truth table.

If the RAM is set up to perform a write of new data into the memory array, the column decoder outputs control the input of data to the selected cell.

Data Input Buffers and Gating

The circuitry needed to write a single bit of data into a cell is shown in Fig. 4.13. The data bit is applied to input DI_0. It is inverted by gates 1 and 2 to give buffered inputs DI_0 and $\overline{DI}_0$. These signals are passed to inputs of the three-state buffers, gates 3 and 4, respectively. The outputs of the buffers drive bit lines BO_0 and $\overline{BO}_0$ of the cell. These bit lines act as both inputs and outputs of the cell. As we saw earlier, they also supply data to inputs of the sense amplifiers used to read out data.

The control inputs of the three-state buffers are wired together and operate by the output of the AND gate marked 5. Inputs to these gates are read/write control ($R/\overline{W}$), output C_0 from the column decoder, and chip select (CS). When all three inputs are logic 1, the output of the AND gate switches to the 1 level. This enables the buffer gates and passes inputs DI_0

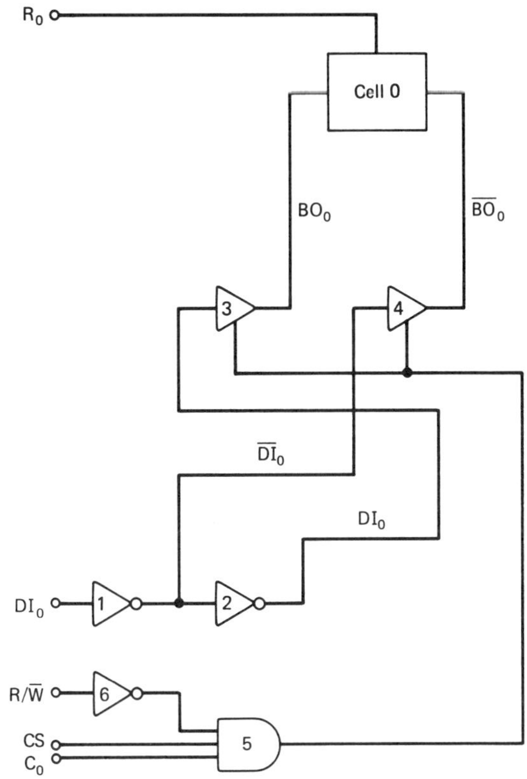

Fig. 4.13 Data input buffering and gating.

and $\overline{DI}_0$ to bit lines BO_0 and $\overline{BO}_0$, respectively. During a read operation, $R/\overline{W}$ holds the outputs of the buffer in the hi-Z third state.

To write new data into the cell, we begin by applying logic 0 or 1 to input DI_0. The address selects the appropriate row and column line. In this case, we assume that row R_0 and column C_0 have been selected. Chip select is to be logic 1 and $R/\overline{W}$ 0, indicating that a write operation is to occur. The data from DI_0 are applied to bit lines and the cell sets or resets.

4.4 STATIC RAM OPERATION

The circuit configurations introduced up to this point in the chapter are those used to make a static RAM. By static RAM, we mean one that can store data indefinitely as long as power is supplied to the device. That is, the memory array is composed of cells that retain data once they are written in.

The word "static" is used in a different way when applied to RAMs than when applied to ROMs. When "static" is used in describing a RAM, the term refers to the type of storage element used in the memory array. On the other hand, when "static" is applied to ROM, it refers to the ability of

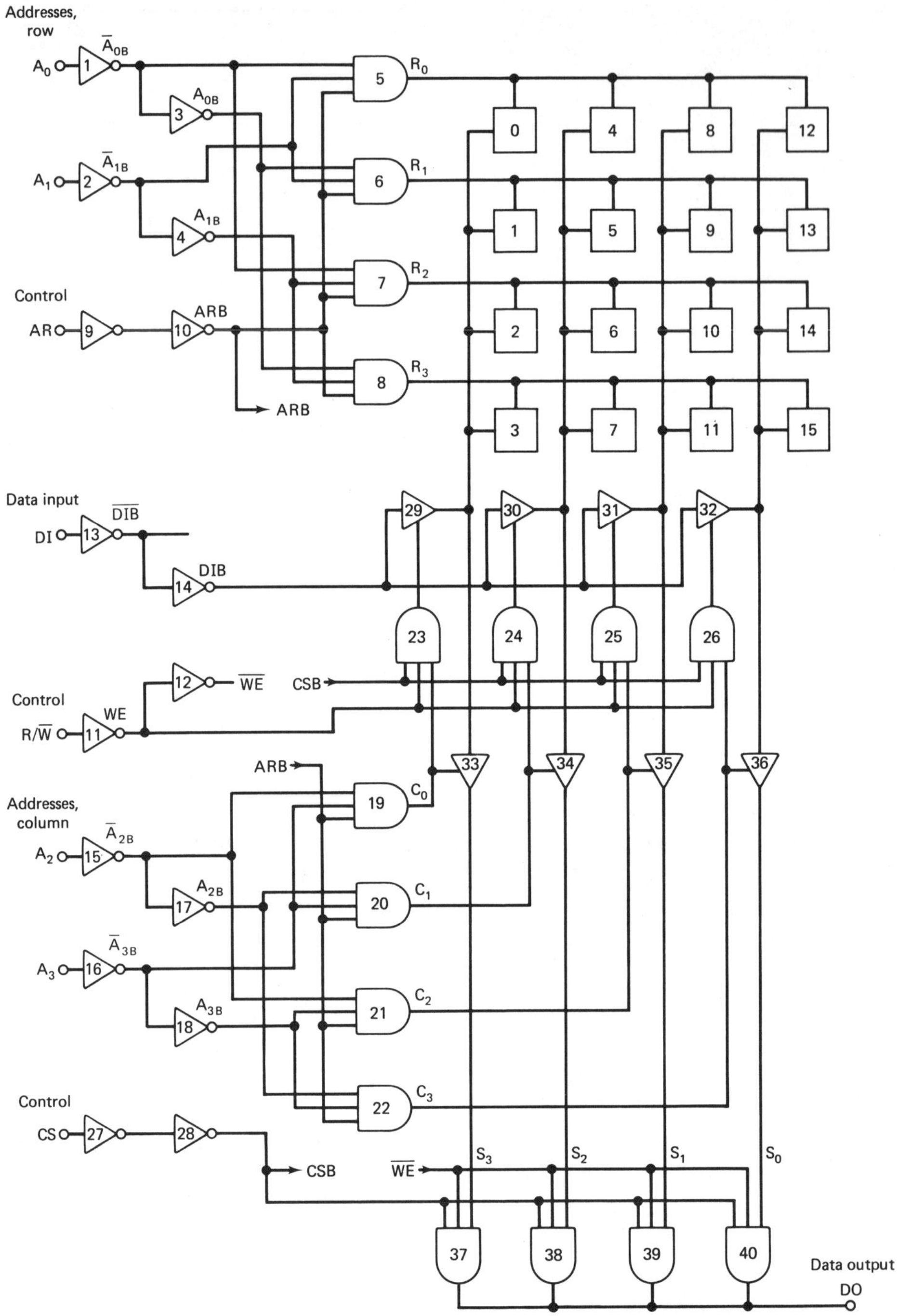

(a)

Fig. 4.14 (a) RAM architecture; (b) address and associated cell.

Data word address	Data word cell
0	0
1	1
2	2
3	3
4	4
5	5
6	6
7	7
8	8
9	9
A	10
B	11
C	12
D	13
E	14
F	15

Fig. 4.14 Continued (b)

the address and control signals to operate without the need of an external clock.

Figure 4.14(a) shows the complete circuit of a static RAM. This configuration is not typical for a RAM with such a small capacity. However, it represents the type of architecture employed in devices with larger storage capacity.

Looking at the circuit diagram, we find four address inputs, A_0, A_1, A_2, and A_3; a single data input, DI; a single data output, DO; and control inputs address ready (AR), chip select (CS), and read/write ($R/\overline{W}$). The memory array has 16 cells, which gives a total storage capacity of 16 bits.

If we examine the array more closely, we notice that the memory cells are horizontally arranged into four rows. The row inputs are labeled R_0, R_1, R_2 and R_3. Vertically, it consists of four columns, each with four cells. Each column produces one of the bit line outputs BO_0 through BO_3 of the memory array. Through the use of row and column decoders, the output of the memory array is organized into 16 1-bit words. Each word is stored at a unique address location. Hexadecimal addresses for the 16 words and the associated cell in the memory array are indicated in the table of Fig. 4.14(b).

Write Operation Cycle

When using a RAM in an electronic system, one operation we want to perform is to enter data into the device for storage. To do this, we must perform a write operation. The write cycle starts with the application of the address of the storage location to input leads A_0 through A_3. Gates 1 through 4 buffer and invert bits A_0 and A_1 to give buffered signals $\bar{A}_{0B}$, $\bar{A}_{1B}$, A_{0B}, and A_{1B}. These signals are fed to inputs of AND gates 5 through 8, which form the row decoder. After this, *AR* is set to logic 1. This enables the row decoder and the row output, R_0 through R_3, which corresponds to the binary input switches to logic 1. This selects one of the four rows of cells in the memory array.

Notice that the row line actually selects four cell locations, one in each column. But we want to write data into just one cell. This is achieved through the column address and column decoder. At the same moment, bits A_2 and A_3 of the address are passed through inverting buffer gates 15 through 18 to inputs of the column decoder. Based on bits A_2 and A_3, one of the column outputs C_0 through C_3 produced by decoder gates 19 through 22 switches to logic 1.

These column outputs are combined with write signal *WE* and chip select *CSB* by the control AND gates 23 through 26. It is these gates that select one of the four columns of cells in the selected row for input of data. For a write operation to occur, $R/\overline{W}$ must be set to logic 0 and *CS* to logic 1. These conditions, combined with the column line that is logic 1, make all inputs on one of the four AND gates logic 1. The output of the enabled gate switches to logic 1. In this way, the three-state buffer for one of the four columns in the memory array is enabled for input of data.

Input data at *DI* are fed through buffer gates 13 and 14 to inputs of all four three-state buffers, 29 through 32, that supply the bit lines of the cells. However, the buffers do not permit data to pass to bit lines of the cells until their outputs are enabled. The buffer selected by the column decoder and control gate causes the data to be passed onto the bit line. The bit line is pulled to logic 1 or 0 based upon the logic level of the input data. This causes the cell to set or reset. The data have now been written into the memory array; therefore, control lines $R/\overline{W}$ can be returned to logic 1 and *AR* and *CS* to logic 0.

EXAMPLE 4.2 Into what cell in the circuit of Fig. 4.14(a) is data *DI*=0 written when the input address is B_{16}? Assume that control lines *AR*, $R/\overline{W}$, and *CS* have been set to their proper logic levels to perform the write operation.

SOLUTION If the address input to the RAM is B_{16}, the levels applied to the address leads are 1011_2. Since A_0 is the LSB and A_3 the MSB, we have

$$\left.\begin{aligned} A_0 &= 1 \\ A_1 &= 1 \end{aligned}\right\} \text{row decoder inputs}$$

$$\left.\begin{aligned} A_2 &= 0 \\ A_3 &= 1 \end{aligned}\right\} \text{column decoder inputs}$$

The inputs to the row decoder make output R_3 switch to logic 1, and the column decoder inputs switch output C_2 to the 1 level. In this way, we see that data are written into column 2 of row 3. This represents cell 11.

Read Operation Cycle

At other times, we may want to retrieve data that are stored in RAM. This is done with a read operation. The sequence of events that occurs during a read cycle is similar to the one just introduced for the write cycle. Again we begin by applying the address of the storage location to inputs A_0 through A_3 of the circuit in Fig. 4.14(a). Just as in the write operation, A_0 and A_1 are buffered by gates 1 through 4 and combined with AR in the row decoder, gates 5 through 8, to select one row of the memory array. The column address bits A_2 and A_3 are buffered and decoded in the same way by gates 15 through 18 to select one of the columns in the memory array.

At this point in the sequence, a change occurs between the write operation and the read operation. This time we set CS to logic 1 but leave $R/\overline{W}$ at logic 1 instead of switching it to logic 0. This means that the outputs of the three-state drivers from the data input are in the hi-Z third state. Therefore, data at input DI cannot enter into the memory array. At the same time, the output of one of the four sense amplifiers 33 through 36 is enabled by the output of the column decoder.

The enabled sense amplifier detects the logic level of the bit line for the selected cell and produces the corresponding 0 or 1 at its outputs. The sense amplifier outputs are input to the output buffers, gates 37 through 40. During a read operation, the output buffers are enabled by control signals CS=1 and $R/\overline{W}$=1. We have now read data out of the cell and it appears at output DO.

EXAMPLE 4.3 The RAM shown in Fig. 4.14(a) stores the data shown in the table of Fig. 4.15. What is the logic level of the data at output DO if a read operation is performed for address D_{16}? Assume that the control inputs are correctly set to perform a read operation.

SOLUTION This address input is $A_3A_2A_1A_0=D_{16}=1101_2$. Therefore, the row decoder input is $A_1A_0=01$ and the column decoder input $A_3A_2=11$. This selects row 1 and column 3 of the array.

$$A_1A_0=01 \quad \text{row 1}$$

$$A_3A_2=11 \quad \text{column 3}$$

In Fig. 4.15, we find that this corresponds to cell 13. This cell stores logic 0. The output of the RAM is

$$DO = 0$$

Row \ Column	0	1	2	3
0	0	0	0	0
1	1	0	0	0
2	0	1	0	0
3	1	1	0	0

Fig. 4.15 Data stored in a memory array.

Switching Characteristics

The operation of the RAM circuit has been traced as data are written in and read out. During our study, we introduced the address, data, and control signals, but the timing of these signals that is critical to the correct operation of the RAM was not considered. If signals are not switched at the appropriate instants or held for long enough intervals, the internal logic levels of the memory cannot be guaranteed, and the device will not operate correctly.

There are five types of switching characteristics defined for the write and read operations of the RAM. They are *cycle time*, *setup time*, *hold time*, *access time*, and *disable time*.

It is interesting to note that the time that influences overall speed of a computer is cycle time. On the other hand, when designing interface circuitry for RAM, one must take into account all the switching times.

Write-Cycle Timing

Let us examine Fig. 4.16(a), which shows typical waveforms for a write operation. The first switching characteristic found is the write-cycle time, labeled t_{CYW}. It represents the minimum amount of time that must be allowed for writing data into RAM. This means that if all other timing of the write cycle is performed at maximum speed, it will take an interval equal to t_{CYW} to enter data into the memory. Write-cycle time is simply the sum of the switching delays of the internal circuitry involved in the write operation.

The other important timing characteristics of the write cycle are its setup and hold times. Setup time indicates how long the specified signal must be held stable before the transition of the reference signal. For instance, in Fig. 4.16(a) the address setup time, t_{SA}, represents the minimum amount of time the address input must be stable before $\overline{W}$ can be switched to logic 0. There are two other setup times for the write operation. They are the chip select setup time, $t_{S\overline{CS}}$, and data setup time, t_{SD}.

On the other hand, hold time tells how long the specified signal must be maintained stable after the transition of the reference signal. An example of a hold time is t_{HA} in Fig. 4.16(a). This is the address hold time and represents the minimum amount of time the address must be maintained after $\overline{W}$ is returned to logic 1. The other hold time identified for the write cycle is data hold time, t_{HD}.

Signals can be set up or held for intervals longer than the minimum values specified for their setup and hold times, respectively. However, this results in a longer value of write-cycle time.

Read-Cycle Timing

Waveforms for the read cycle of a RAM are shown in Fig. 4.16(b). Notice the read-cycle time, t_{CYR}. This represents the minimum amount of time required to read data out of RAM.

There are two other timing characteristics identified for reading data from RAM. They are its access time and disable time. Access time represents

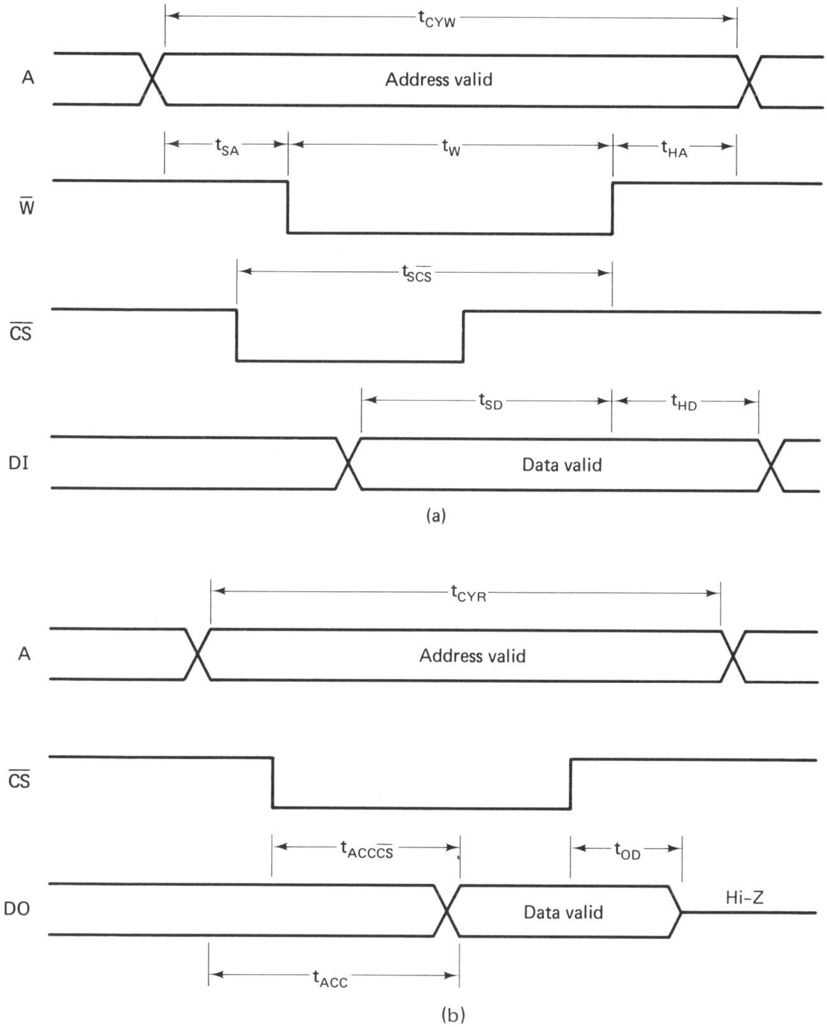

Fig. 4.16 (a) Write-cycle timing; (b) read-cycle timing.

the delay from a specified input signal until the moment that valid data exist at the output. As for ROM, two different access times are specified: chip select-to-data output access time ($t_{ACC\overline{CS}}$) and address-to-output access time (t_{ACC}).

The address-to-output access time assumes that the RAM is already selected. In this case, t_{ACC} represents the maximum delay experienced between the moment the address is stable and the instant valid data appear at the outputs. This time corresponds to the delays of signals propagating through the buffers, decoders, memory array, sense amplifiers, and output buffer.

On the other hand, chip select-to-data output access time assumes that the address has been stable for a period of time. When $\overline{CS}$ is switched to logic 0, data at the output of the memory array only have to propagate through the output circuitry to the data outputs. For this reason, the maximum value of $t_{ACC\overline{CS}}$ is shorter than that of t_{ACC}.

The remaining characteristic specified for the read operation is labeled t_{OD}. This is the output disable time and represents the maximum delay that occurs between the instant $\overline{CS}$ is switched to logic 1 and the moment the output is turned OFF or switches into the hi-Z state.

Input and Output Logic Levels

As with ROM, the input and output logic levels of RAM ICs are usually TTL-compatible. Even though the outputs of the devices are TTL-compatible, they are generally capable of driving just one or two TTL loads. For this reason, external buffering is often required at the data outputs.

4.5 STANDARD STATIC RAMS

The static read/write random-access memory, its architecture, operation, and timing have just been discussed. We continue by introducing some of the standard static RAM integrated circuits.

74S189A and 74S289 Bipolar RAMs

The 74S189A and the 74S289 are RAM ICs that are part of the 74S00 family of Schottky TTL devices. Figure 4.17(a) shows a block diagram of an architecture that is representative of both devices. These devices have a total

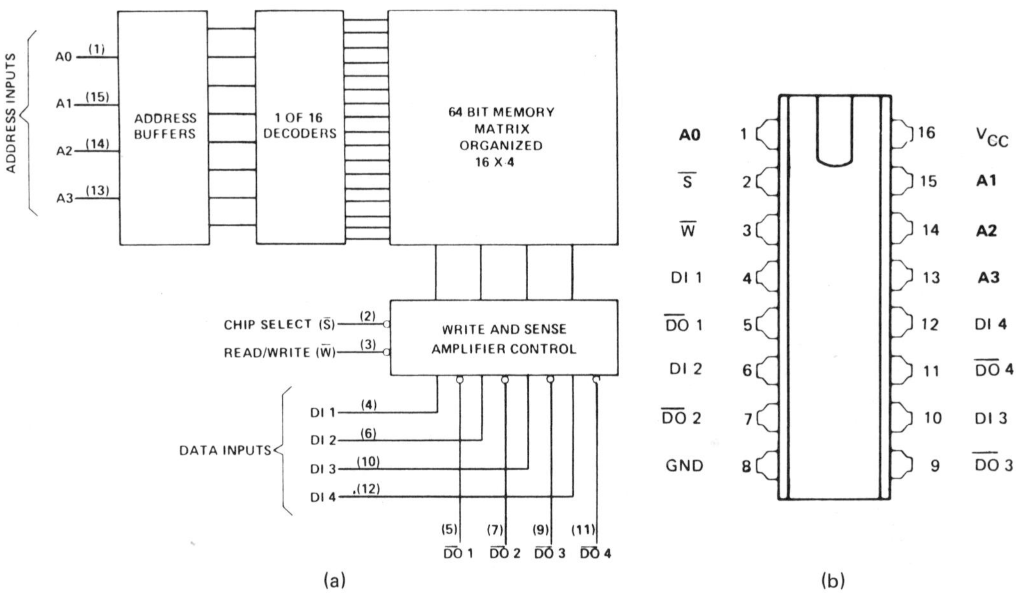

Fig. 4.17 (a) 74S189A block diagram (Texas Instruments, Incorporated); (b) pin layout (Texas Instruments, Incorporated).

storage capacity of 64 bits. The memory array is constructed with bipolar RAM cells made with Schottky-clamped transistors.

The two devices differ in their output circuitry. The 74S189A has three-state outputs, whereas the 74S289 has open-collector outputs. A pin layout for the devices is shown in Fig. 4.17(b).

Referring to the block diagram, we see that the memory array is organized into 16 4-bit words. Because the storage capacity is so small, the devices employ a simplified internal architecture. Notice that they have no column decoder circuit. There are four address inputs, labeled A_0 through A_3. Of these address inputs, A_3 is the MSB and A_0 the LSB. The address bits are buffered and then fed to inputs of a 16-line decoder, which is the row decoder. Each output of the decoder selects one of the rows in the memory array.

On the block diagram, we also find data inputs called DI_1 through DI_4 and four data outputs labeled $\overline{DO}_1$ through $\overline{DO}_4$. Notice that the data bits produced at the outputs of the RAM are the complements of the data bits that were entered. With RAMs, complemented output data are a characteristic that we will have to watch.

The control signals chip select marked $\overline{S}$ and read/write marked $\overline{W}$ are also inputs to the device. Chip select is used to control the output buffers and data inputs. It must be set to logic 0 for the RAM to operate. On the other hand, read/write is used to control whether data are to be input or output. Logic 0 at $\overline{W}$ sets the RAM for write operation and logic 1 sets it for a read operation.

Both the 74S189A and the 74S289 require a 5-V dc power supply. The positive terminal of the supply is called V_{CC} and is connected at pin 16. The negative terminal or return of the supply is called ground, *GND*, and is connected to pin 8. The power supply is rated to vary by ±5%. This means that they will correctly operate with variations of the input power line, changes in load, and noise as long as they do not cause the voltage between $+V_{CC}$ and *GND* to go below 4.75 V or above 5.25 V. They need about 110 mA and 0.55 W to operate. This corresponds to 8.5 mW per bit, which is a relatively high value.

To write data into a storage location in a 74S189A RAM, the address at which we want to write data is applied to inputs A_0 through A_3. The address bits are buffered and fed to the row decoder. The output produced by the row decoder selects one of the 16 possible rows of the memory array. At the same time that the address is fed to these leads, data are applied to leads DI_1 through DI_4. Chip select, $\overline{S}$, is set to logic 0, and $\overline{W}$ is pulsed to logic 0. The data word is written into the specified storage location. $\overline{W}$ is now returned to logic 1 followed by $\overline{S}$ to logic 1. After this, the data and address can be changed.

Reading data from RAM follows the same sequence as writing data into RAM. The primary difference is that $\overline{W}$ is not set to logic 0; instead, it is held at logic 1. The address is applied to A_0 through A_3. When $\overline{S}$ is set to logic 0 and $\overline{W}$ is held at logic 1, the address passes through the buffer and decoder to select one of the rows in the memory array. This row contains four cells. The data in these cells are output on the bit lines for detection by the sense amplifiers. The logic outputs of the sense amplifiers are fed through the output gates and buffered. The complement of the 4-bit data word appears at output pins $\overline{DO}_1$ through $\overline{DO}_4$.

Having traced a write and a read operation through the 74S189A, let us look at its timing characteristics. The address setup time $t_{SU(ad)}$ and chip select setup time $t_{SU(\overline{S})}$ before the $\overline{W}$ control can switch to logic 0 is 0 ns. This means that the address, chip select, and write inputs can all occur simultaneously. On the other hand, the data setup time $t_{SU(da)}$ is 25 ns. Therefore, the data must be valid for 25 ns before $\overline{W}$ is switched to logic 0. After $\overline{W}$ is switched to logic 0, the hold times for address, data, and chip select are all 0 ns. So they can all be removed at the same moment that $\overline{W}$ returns to logic 1. Therefore, the fastest write-cycle time can be 25 ns.

For the read cycle, the access time from valid address to data output is 50 ns for the 74S189A and 35 ns for the 74S289. The sense amplifier recovery time is 40 ns for the 74S189A and 35 ns for the 74S289. The fastest read-cycle time is 50 ns for the 74S189A and 35 ns for the 74S289.

3101 and 3101A Bipolar RAMs

The 3101 and the 3101A are two more 64-bit Schottky-clamped bipolar RAMs. These devices are essentially the same as the 74S289. Figure 4.18 shows a single block diagram representing the 3101 and 3101A. Pin numbers are marked in the block diagram. There are some small differences between the specifications of these devices and the 74S289; however, they are what is known in the industry as "pin-for-pin" equivalents. This means that it is possible to substitute one device for the other in most applications.

2101A MOS RAM

The 2101A integrated circuit is a 1024-bit static RAM implemented with the NMOS technology. Its output is organized into 256 4-bit words. Figure 4.19 shows a block diagram of the circuitry within the 2101A. Notice that this architecture is consistent with the general architecture introduced in the preceding section.

From the block diagram, we find that the RAM has eight address lines,

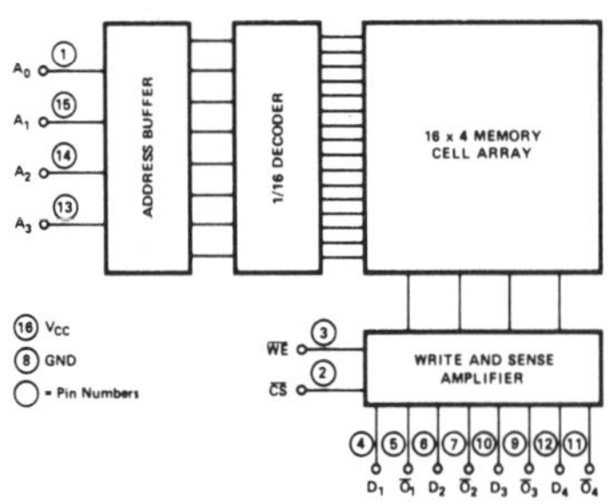

Fig. 4.18 3101 block diagram (Intel Corp.).

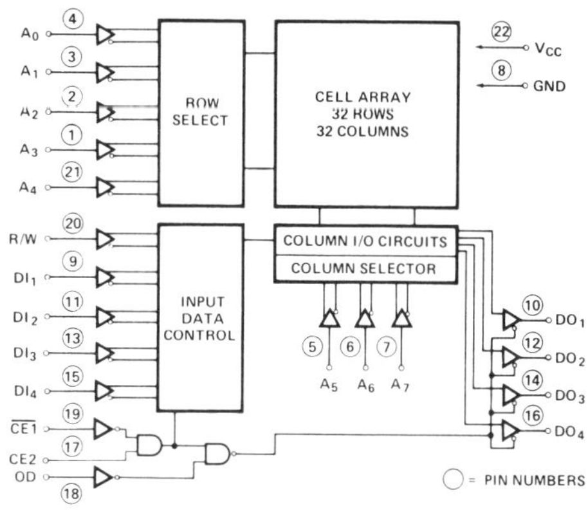

Fig. 4.19 2101A block diagram (Intel Corp.).

A_0 through A_7. Of these bits, A_0 through A_4 enter the row select circuit while bits A_5 through A_7 enter the column select circuit. Moreover, there are four data inputs, labeled DI_1 through DI_4, and four data outputs, DO_1 through DO_4. Finally, there are four control inputs: read/write control $R/\overline{W}$, two chip enable controls $\overline{CE}_1$ and CE_2, and the output disable control OD.

To perform a write operation, the address at A_0 through A_7 must first be stable. The chip is enabled by making $\overline{CE}_1$ equal logic 0 and CE_2 logic 1. As $R/\overline{W}$ is pulsed to logic 0, the data word at DI_1 through DI_4 is written into the storage location.

The read operation again requires a stable address. But this time $\overline{CE}_1$ and OD are set to logic 0, while CE_2 and $R/\overline{W}$ are held at logic 1. Data stored at the addressed location appear at output pins DO_1 through DO_4 of the RAM.

For some applications, the data output and data input leads are tied together to form a common I/O data bus.

The 2101A operates from a single +5-V power supply with ±5% tolerance. It requires 60 mA of current for a power consumption of 300 mW. This corresponds to about 0.3 mW per bit. This value compares favorably with the 8.5 mW per bit of the 74S189A.

As we found with ROMs, MOS devices are slower than bipolar devices. This speed difference is more evident when this MOS RAM is compared with a Schottky TTL RAM. Remember that Schottky devices are among the fastest of bipolar memories. The read cycle of the 2101A has a maximum address-to-output access time of 250 ns. This value is five times slower than the 50 ns maximum access time of the 74S189A. Moreover, its maximum chip enable access time t_{CO} equals 180 ns, about seven times longer than the chip select access time for the 74S189A. During write operations, the minimum data setup time t_{DW} is 150 ns and minimum data hold time D_{DH} equals 0 ns.

The input and output logic levels of the 2101A are TTL-compatible. Its inputs represent $^1/_{160}$ the logic 0 input requirement of a standard TTL device. This low current is expected with MOS devices since it represents the

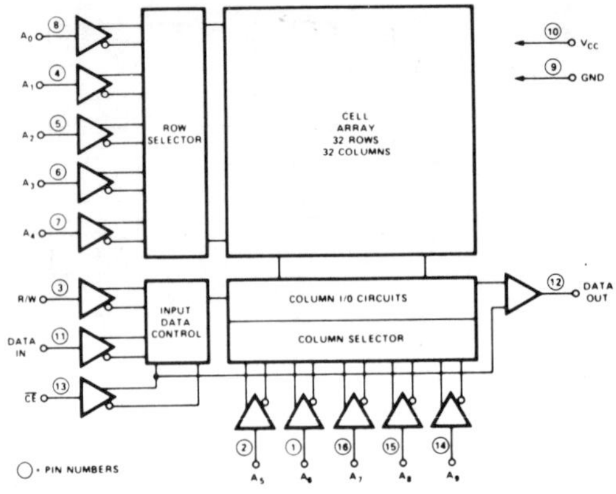

Fig. 4.20 2102A block diagram (Intel Corp.).

leakage of the gate of a MOSFET. The outputs are capable of driving one TTL load.

2102A MOS RAM

The 2102A MOS RAM is similar to the 2101A just described. Its capacity is also 1024 bits. But this time the output is organized into 1024 1-bit words instead of 256 4-bit words.

A block diagram of the internal circuitry of the 2102A is shown in Fig. 4.20. Here, there are 10 address inputs A_0 through A_9. However, there is just one data input labeled *DATA IN* and one data output marked *DATA OUT*. The control leads on the 2102A are $R/\overline{W}$ and $\overline{CE}$.

To perform a write, the address and data must be stable, and $\overline{CE}$ and $R/\overline{W}$ set to logic 0. The data at *DATA IN* are written into the storage location defined by the address at A_0 through A_9.

To read from the 2102A, the address must be applied and $\overline{CE}$ set to logic 0. This time $R/\overline{W}$ is left at the 1 logic level. Data held at the addressed storage location appear at *DATA OUT*. The 2102A consumes about 289 mW and has a maximum access time of 350 ns.

5101L CMOS RAM

The 5101L RAM shown in Fig. 4.21 is constructed with low-power CMOS circuitry. This is another 1024-bit RAM device which is organized to store 256 4-bit words.

The block diagram of Fig. 4.21 shows that the architecture of the 5101L is similar to that of the 2101A. There are eight address lines, A_0 through A_7; four data input lines, DI_1 through DI_4; four data outputs, DO_1 through DO_4; and four control lines, RW, OD, $\overline{CE}_1$, and CE_2.

A feature of this device is that when CE_2 is logic 0, its row address buffer, column address buffer, and output buffer are all disabled. When these peripheral circuits are disabled, the RAM is in a low-power mode. In this

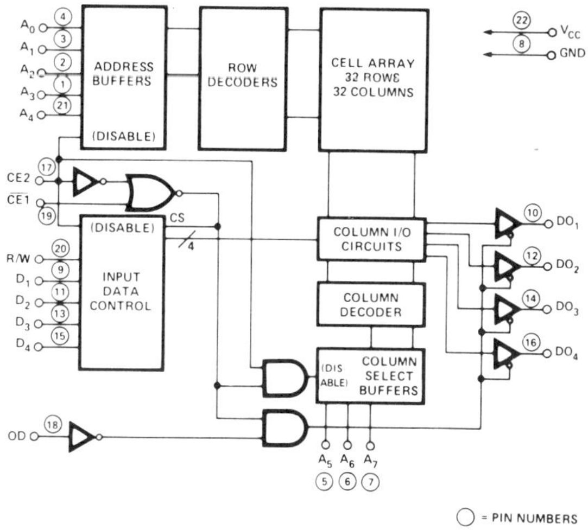

Fig. 4.21 5101L block diagram (Intel Corp.).

deselected state, the RAM draws a maximum of 10 μA, which corresponds to a standby power of about 10 nW per bit. The operating 5101L draws a maximum of about 135 mW or 0.132 mW per bit. Maximum access time is 650 ns.

MM2114 MOS RAM

The MM2114 is a 4k NMOS static RAM device. Its output is organized into 1024 words each with 4 bits. A block diagram of the MM2114's architecture is shown in Fig. 4.22.

In the block diagram, the device has 10 address lines, A_0 through A_9; one chip select line, $\overline{CS}$; a read/write control, $\overline{WE}$; and four bidirectional data lines, I/O_1 through I/O_4. These lines carry data during both read and write operations. If control line $\overline{CS}$ is logic 1, the data lines are in the hi-Z third state.

To perform a write operation, the address is applied to A_0 through A_9 and data are applied to I/O_1 through I/O_4 of the device. After the required setup time has elapsed, the control lines CS and WE are switched to logic 0. This sets the I/O bus for input operation, and data are next written into the selected storage location. After the hold time has elapsed, $\overline{CS}$ and $\overline{WE}$ are pulled to logic 1, completing the write operation.

A read cycle is similar to the write cycle; however, $\overline{WE}$ is set to logic 1 and $\overline{CS}$ is set to logic 0. Actually, $\overline{CS}$ can be set prior to the application of the address. The I/O bus now works in the output mode. After the address-to-output access time interval, valid data are available on the I/O lines.

The MM2114 also has a low-power standby mode like that of the 5101L. To go to the power-down mode, $\overline{CS}$ must be brought to 2 V before the power supply drops below +4.75 V. Data will be retained if the correct power-down sequence is followed. The V_{CC} supply can go as low as +1.5 V during standby. In this state, the device draws 70 mA and consumes 105 mW.

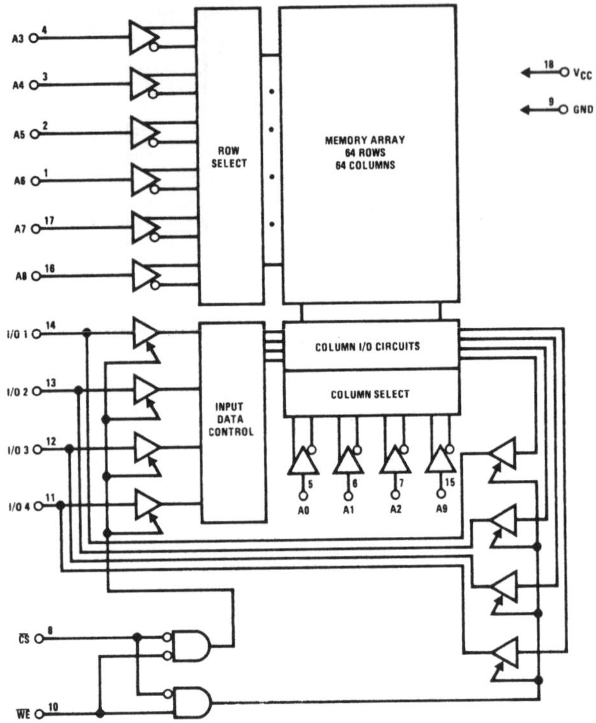

Fig. 4.22 MM2114 block diagram (National Semiconductor Corp.).

TMS 4046 MOS RAM

The TMS 4046 is another 4*k* NMOS RAM IC. This device is organized to store 4096 words each with 1 bit instead of 1*k* of 4-bit words like the MM2114. Figure 4.23 is a block diagram of the device.

To accommodate addressing of 4096 storage locations, the TMS 4046 has a 12-bit address bus. These are lines A_0 through A_{11}. Data are input at D and output at Q under control of the read/write control $\overline{W}$. Output Q is in the hi-Z state if $\overline{S}$ is logic 1.

The TMS 4046 has two power-supply leads. One set is V_{CC1} to V_{SS}, which is the 5-V supply required to operate the peripheral circuits. This supply voltage is rated with a ±10% tolerance. The additional lead V_{CC2} only supplies power to the memory array. For normal operations it is also 5V ± 10%. However, during power down the memory array voltage supply can be decreased to as low as 2.4 V. At this voltage, data will be maintained. This voltage can be supplied by batteries in some applications to obtain non-volatile operation.

The package size of the TMS 4046 is noteworthy. It is just 0.3 inch wide. This gives a long, thin, high-density package configuration.

The TMS 4046 is available with different access times over the range from 150 to 450 ns. The faster access devices require more power, with the

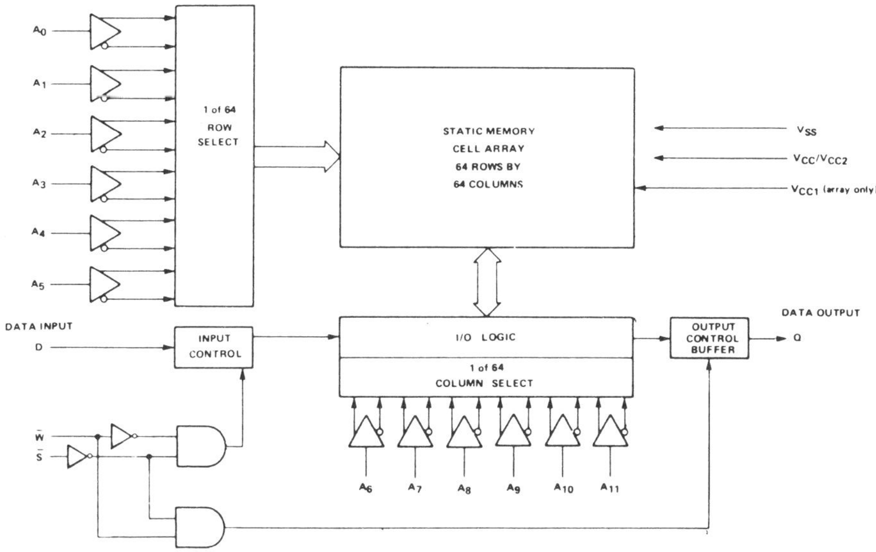

(a)

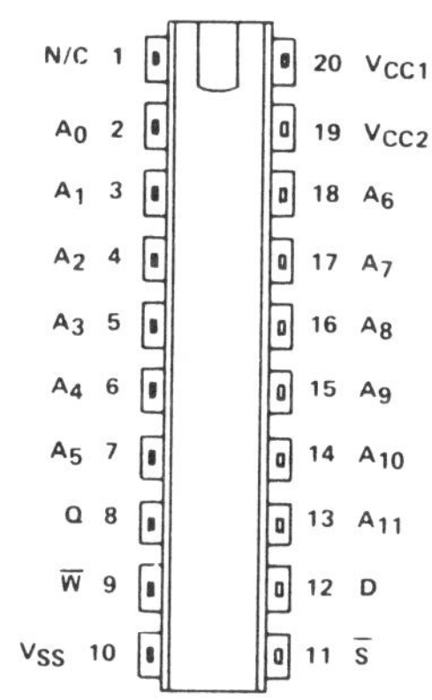

(b)

Fig. 4.23 (a) TMS 4046 block diagram (Texas Instruments, Incorporated); (b) pin layout (Texas Instruments Incorporated).

maximum consumption equal to 440 mW. This corresponds to 0.108 mW per bit. During standby, the maximum power is just 13 mW or 6 μW per bit.

4.6 DYNAMIC RAM

This section examines the structure and operation of the second type of random-access read/write memory, the *dynamic RAM*. In Section 4.5 we saw how resistors, diodes, bipolar transistors, and MOSFETs could be connected to form static RAM cells. RAMs are also made with cells that store data as charge on capacitors. These types of devices are known as dynamic RAMs.

Because of the relatively low leakage currents that are characteristic of MOS transistors, they are more suitable for the fabrication of dynamic RAMs. Charge representing the 0 or 1 logic levels at the gate leads of MOS devices tends to leak off the capacitive nodes in the cells. If this were permitted to occur, the data would be lost. However, if the charge is periodically replaced, the data would be retained. The process of restoring charge to the cells in a dynamic RAM is called *refreshing*.

To refresh a dynamic RAM, a sequence of address and control operations must be periodically performed. This can be achieved with circuits that are added externally to the RAM IC. However, RAMs have been proposed that would contain internal circuitry for generating the refresh signals. Such dynamic RAMs are said to have transparent refresh. They are also said to be pseudostatic RAMs; however, they are still dynamic because their memory array employs cells that need refreshing.

It should be noted that the memory array in a dynamic RAM is always made with dynamic cells, but the circuits of the address decoder and sense amplifiers can be dynamic or static. For this reason, RAMs are classified in several ways. For example, there are dynamic RAMs with static address decoders and sense amplifiers. In this type of device, the decoders and amplifiers are always operating; however, the cells are only periodically turned ON.

On the other hand, in a fully dynamic RAM, the address decoders and sense amplifiers are also operated synchronously with the clock. Since the circuitry in dynamic RAM is not continuously operating, its power consumption is lower. This is a primary advantage of dynamic RAM over static RAM.

Typical Dynamic MOS RAM Cells

Before going into the architecture of the dynamic RAM system, let us look at the dynamic storage cell circuit. There are a number of different circuit configurations that can be used to implement a dynamic storage element. Two of these circuits are known as the *four-transistor cell* and the *one-transistor cell.*

As the number of transistors per cell decreases, so does the area used per cell. Since small size is essential for high-density integrated circuits, the less area occupied by the cell, the better. This is the second main advantage of dynamic RAM—larger storage capacity. In fact, the largest-capacity RAMs, which today have 64*k* bits, are of the dynamic type.

The Four-Transistor Dynamic Cell[3]

As a starting point, let us take the circuit shown in Fig. 4.24. This is the four-transistor dynamic cell. Looking closely at the circuit, we see that it is similar to that of the static RAM cell of Fig. 4.7. However, in this circuit the

[3] Ibid., p. 120.

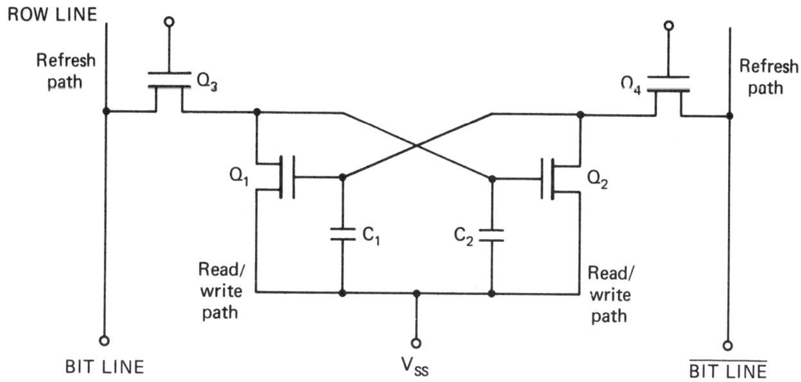

Fig. 4.24 Four-transistor dynamic RAM cell (Texas Instruments, Incorporated).

cell is formed with just two MOSFETs, Q_1 and Q_2. Notice that the load MOSFETs have been removed. C_1 and C_2 represent the gate capacitances of Q_1 and Q_2, respectively.

In the four-transistor cell, the transmission gates Q_3 and Q_4 serve two purposes. First, they are used to switch in the refresh power-supply voltages during refresh operations; and second, they are used to connect the cell to the bit lines for input/output of data during write and read operations.

The operation of the transmission gates is controlled by the *ROW LINE* signal. Q_3 and Q_4 are normally OFF. In this way, they isolate the cell elements Q_1 and Q_2 from *BIT LINE* and $\overline{\textit{BIT LINE}}$. When the row line of the cell is selected, the transmission gates are turned on. Now the drains of Q_1 and Q_2 are connected to *BIT LINE* and $\overline{\textit{BIT LINE}}$, respectively.

Data to be written into the cell are represented by logic levels on *BIT LINE* and $\overline{\textit{BIT LINE}}$. As transmission gates Q_3 and Q_4 are turned ON, the bit lines are connected to the cell, and it sets or resets. The write operation is completed by turning the transmission gates OFF. The new data are retained within the cell.

The ON and OFF states of Q_1 and Q_2 are maintained by the charge on C_1 and C_2, respectively. For instance, if Q_1 is ON, C_2 is charged to the 0 logic level. This holds Q_2 OFF. Since Q_2 is OFF, C_1 charges to the 1 logic level. This keeps Q_1 ON. However, the circuit will not remain in this state indefinitely. This is because the charge slowly leaks off the capacitors. To overcome this, the charge on C_1 and C_2 must be periodically refreshed to replenish the charge.

Performing a refresh operation on the four-transistor cell is straightforward. Transmission gates Q_3 and Q_4 are again turned ON by selecting *ROW LINE*. The memory cell is connected to the bit lines. But this time *BIT LINE* and $\overline{\textit{BIT LINE}}$ are supplied with a refresh voltage instead of data. This voltage replenishes the charge on C_1 and C_2. In this way, cell transistors Q_1 and Q_2 are kept in the set or reset state.

The data stored in the cell are read out in a similar way. *ROW LINE* is

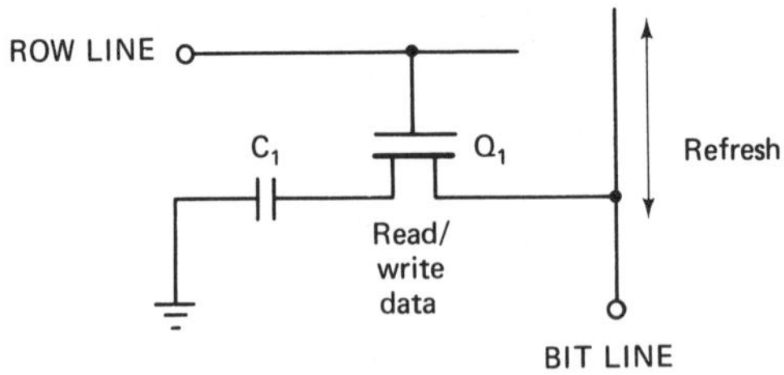

Fig. 4.25 One-transistor dynamic RAM cell (Texas Instruments, Incorporated).

selected to turn transmission gates Q_3 and Q_4 ON. This puts the data stored in the cell on *BIT LINE* and $\overline{BIT\ LINE}$. They must be detected by sense amplifiers to produce output logic levels.

The One-Transistor Dynamic Cell[4]

Since one of the major advantages of dynamic circuitry is small size, the ideal dynamic cell would have just one capacitor and one transistor. Such a circuit is shown in Fig. 4.25. Here data are stored as charge on capacitor C_1 and isolated from *BIT LINE* by transmission gate Q_1.

To read data from the cell, *ROW LINE* is set to select the cell. This turns ON the transmission gate, and the logic level represented by the charge on C_1 is put on *BIT LINE*. The charge causes a current to flow on *BIT LINE*, which is detected as logic 0 to 1 by a sense amplifier. The data must be restored in the cell after reading.

Writing is accomplished by driving *BIT LINE* to the level of the data and selecting the cell with *ROW LINE*. This causes C_1 to be recharged or changed to the new state. As *ROW LINE* is deselected, Q_1 turns OFF trapping the charge on C_1.

Refreshing of the data in the cell is achieved by applying a refresh voltage, representing the stored logic level, to *BIT LINE*. By turning ON the transmission gate, capacitor C_1 is recharged.

The Refresh Cycle

We have already found that the key difference between static RAMs and dynamic RAMs lies in the type of cell circuit used for storage of data. Moreover, dynamic cells will not retain data indefinitely. The stored charge that represents the data leaks off the capacitors with time. Because of this characteristic, the cells in a dynamic RAM must be refreshed on a cyclic basis.

Generally, extra circuitry is required to perform the refresh operation. This circuitry includes a counter for generating refresh addresses for the rows of the memory array, a multiplexer to switch between the refresh address and system address, and control logic to disable the outputs of the RAM so that unwanted data do not appear on the data bus during refresh operations. These refresh circuits can be external or internal to the RAM IC.

Figure 4.26 shows a dynamic RAM circuit configuration that employs

[4] Ibid., p. 123.

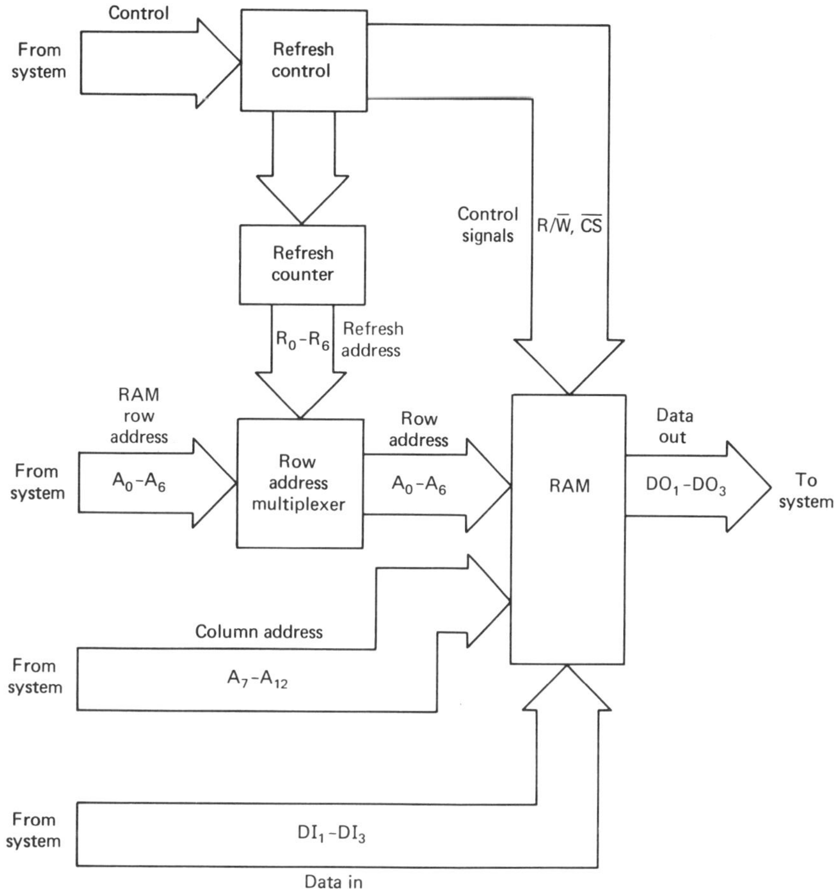

Fig. 4.26 Block diagram of a dynamic RAM with typical external refresh circuitry.

external refresh circuitry. Notice that we have added blocks called *refresh control*, *refresh counter*, and *row address multiplexer*. In this case, the internal architecture of the RAM is essentially the same as that of a static RAM. However, it contains dynamic cells in the memory array that are designed to permit external refreshing.

Recall that in our study of the dynamic RAM cell, we found that the *ROW LINE* was selected and a voltage was supplied to refresh the cell. Similarly, to refresh the whole memory array, we just have to cycle through the row addresses. This must be done before the storage capacitors in the RAM cells discharge.

The refresh counter is a binary counter. It is used to drive the row address inputs of the dynamic RAM during the refresh cycle. This counter must have one output for each bit of the address that is used to select the rows of the memory array. In Fig. 4.26, the row address inputs are A_0 through A_6; therefore, the refresh counter must have seven outputs.

These outputs are labeled R_0 through R_6. The output of the counter is incremented from 0000000 toward 1111111. This row address is kept independent of the system address input at A_0 through A_6.

Both the system and refresh addresses are applied to inputs of the row address multiplexer. The refresh address must be switched to the address inputs of the RAM before its refresh time has elapsed. Refresh time represents the maximum amount of time permitted between refreshes of a particular row in a dynamic RAM. If a row is not refreshed before this interval elapses, the data held in its cells are lost.

One of the more popular methods of refreshing RAM is to have the memory system signal the refresh control that it is ready to have a refresh operation occur. The multiplexer is set so that refresh address bits R_0 through R_6 are applied to address inputs A_0 through A_6 of the RAM. At the same instant, the refresh control circuit sets the control inputs of the RAM for a refresh operation. The counter proceeds to increment from 0000000 to 1111111. In this way, the 128 rows of the memory array are selected and refreshed one after the other. This refresh sequence is known as a *burst refresh*. After the refresh cycle is completed, the system address is switched back to the RAM and normal read or write operation can occur.

In another scheme, the memory has an additional line that tells the rest of the digital system whether it is busy performing a refresh, or ready to perform read/write operations. If the memory is in the process of refreshing its cells, the system cannot initiate a read or write to memory.

Some dynamic RAM ICs have these refresh circuits built within the device. Figure 4.27 shows a block diagram of the architecture of a dynamic RAM with built-in refresh circuitry. Every time a row is to be refreshed, the *REFRESH* input is activated. This causes the internal circuitry to take care of the refresh addresses, multiplexing, and control required during the refresh cycle. An external timer is needed to activate the refresh input. This type of device can still be operated with external refresh circuitry.

4.7 STANDARD DYNAMIC RAM DEVICES

Having been introduced to the dynamic read/write random access memory, dynamic cells, and refreshing, here are some of the standard dynamic RAM integrated circuits available in the electronics marketplace.

1103A Dynamic RAM

The 1103A is one of the earlier dynamic RAM ICs that found wide use in electronic equipment. Its circuitry is implemented with the PMOS technology. Figure 4.28(a) shows a block diagram of the internal architecture of the device and its pin layout is given in Fig. 4.28(b).

Referring to the block diagram in Fig. 4.28(a), we see that the memory array is organized into 32 rows by 32 columns. This size of memory array gives a total storage capacity of 1*k* bits. The five row address lines A_0

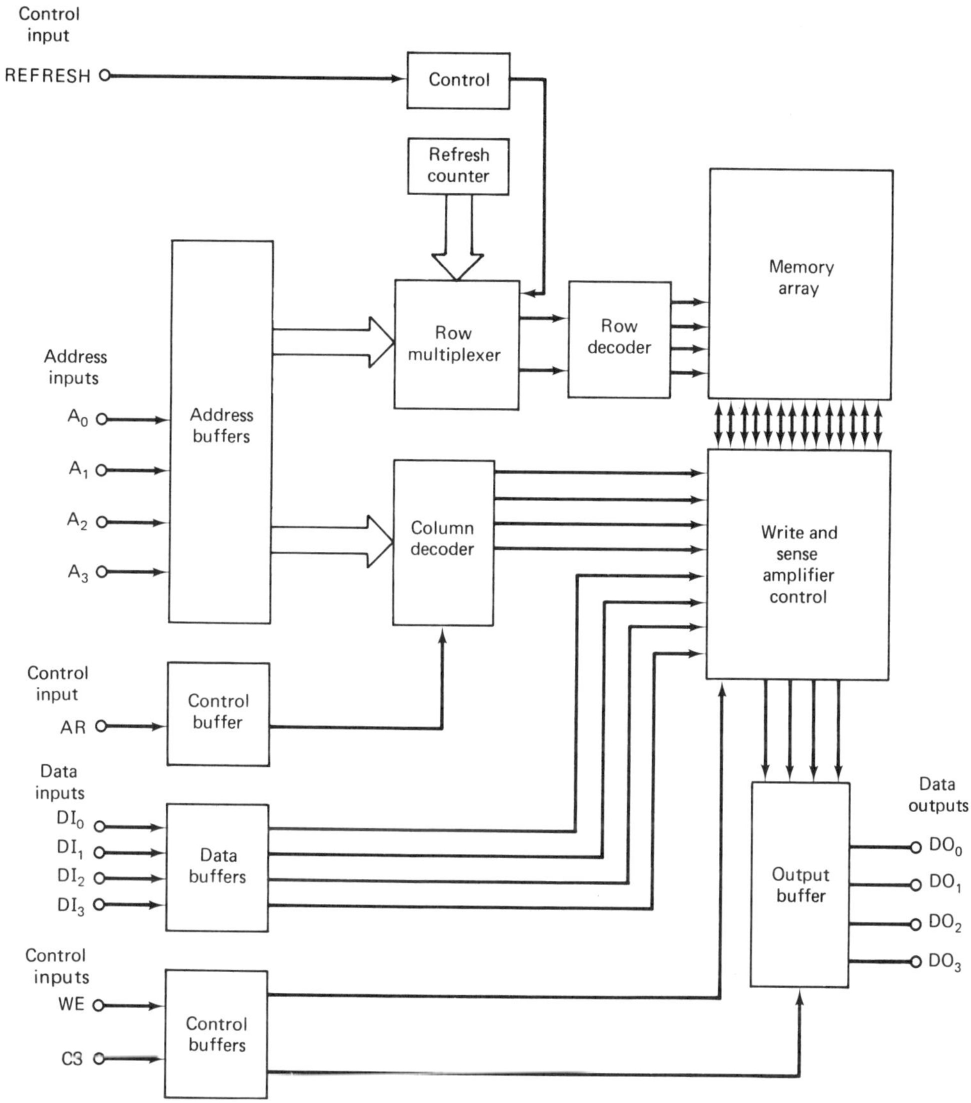

Fig. 4.27 Architecture of a dynamic RAM with internal refresh circuitry.

through A_4 feed the row decoder. The binary combination at these inputs is decoded to select one of the 32 rows in the RAM array. The row selected contains 32 cells.

At the same instant, the five column address lines A_5 through A_9 feed the column decoder. The outputs of this decoder are input to the enable logic that selects one of the 32 cells of the selected row.

In this way, the memory array is organized for reading and writing of data into 1024 1-bit words. Data are written into the cell from data input D_{IN} and read out from data output $\bar{D}_{OUT}$. Notice that the complement of the input data is supplied at the output.

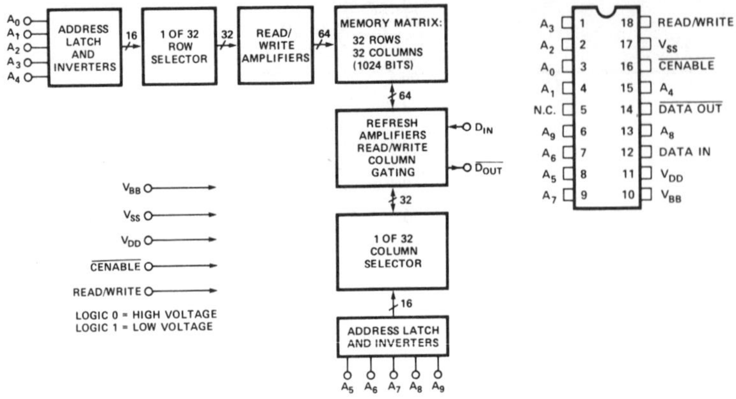

(a) (b)

Fig. 4.28 (a) 1103A block diagram (Intel Corp.); (b) pin layout (Intel Corp.).

The control signals that are input to the IC are $\overline{CENABLE}$ and *READ/WRITE.* Chip enable, $\overline{CENABLE}$, is a clock input that is active low. It must be switched to logic 0 to activate the RAM for any memory operation, including refresh, to occur. On the other hand, *READ/WRITE* is used to indicate whether a read or write operation is to take place during the memory cycle.

In this integrated circuit, a storage location is refreshed whenever a read operation is performed to its address. To refresh the dynamic cells in the 1103A RAM, we must perform a read operation to each of the 32 row addresses. The *refresh period* of the device is 2 ms. Therefore, the row addresses must be scanned once every 2 ms. If this requirement is not met, the storage capacitors will discharge and the data will be lost.

The easiest way to ensure that each of the 32 row addresses has the read operation performed on it is to use an external refresh circuit configuration such as that shown in Fig. 4.26. The control leads must be set up for a read operation. The counter applies row addresses over the range 00000 to 11111 to the five lines A_0 through A_4 of the RAM in the sequence shown in Fig. 4.29. This whole address cycle must be repeated at a minimum of every 2 ms.

Burst refresh, as mentioned earlier, is the technique of performing all of the required refresh operations in one continuous sequence, that is, as a burst. For the 1103A, this means that 32 read operations must be performed one after the other. Since the RAM cannot be used during the refresh cycle, the read-cycle timing for the refresh operations should be kept at a minimum. The read-cycle time of the 1103A is 480 ns. Therefore, the RAM is tied up for a minimum of 32 times 480 ns equals 15.36 μs for a burst refresh.

A second method of refreshing the 1103A is known as a *distributed refresh.* With this technique, the RAM is controlled so that the rows are read one at a time at even intervals of time. The requirement is that all

Address A_9-A_5	16 A_4	8 A_3	4 A_2	2 A_1	1 A_0	Address
	0	0	0	0	0	0
	0	0	0	0	1	1
	0	0	0	1	0	2
	0	0	0	1	1	3
	0	0	1	0	0	4
	0	0	1	0	1	5
	0	0	1	1	0	6
	0	0	1	1	1	7
	0	1	0	0	0	8
	0	1	0	0	1	9
	0	1	0	1	0	10
	0	1	0	1	1	11
	0	1	1	0	0	12
	0	1	1	0	1	13
Don't-	0	1	1	1	0	14
care	0	1	1	1	1	15
states	1	0	0	0	0	16
	1	0	0	0	1	17
	1	0	0	1	0	18
	1	0	0	1	1	19
	1	0	1	0	0	20
	1	0	1	0	1	21
	1	0	1	1	0	22
	1	0	1	1	1	23
	1	1	0	0	0	24
	1	1	0	0	1	25
	1	1	0	1	0	26
	1	1	0	1	1	27
	1	1	1	0	0	28
	1	1	1	0	1	29
	1	1	1	1	0	30
	1	1	1	1	1	31

Fig. 4.29 Refresh sequence for the 1103A dynamic RAM.

rows must be refreshed during an interval shorter than the refresh time. Within the intervals between these single row refreshes, read and write operations can be performed.

For the 1103A, this means that 32 single row refresh operations must be performed over the 2-ms refresh interval. As a maximum figure, one row must be read to refresh the cells attached to it every 62.5 μs.

A third approach is to combine the burst and distributed refresh methods. In this case, the rows are still refreshed in a distributed fashion; but more than one row is refreshed at a time. For instance, for the 1103A, eight distributed refresh operations may be performed equally spaced over the 2-ms refresh interval. Within each time slot, four rows must be addressed and read to refresh the data. This gives a total of 32 row refreshes. In this way, one distributed burst refresh can occur every 250 μs.

Some systems in which dynamic RAMs are used may require repeated reading of the data in all locations. If the refresh requirement is satisfied by this repeated reading, the RAM may not need to be refreshed with a separate operation.

The 1103A requires two power supplies to operate. These supplies are V_{SS} to V_{DD}, which is 16 V, and V_{BB} to V_{DD}, which is 19 V.

All the input signals to the 1103A are 16 V. Moreover, the data output is a current that must be detected by an external sense amplifier. This means that in addition to external refresh circuitry, the 1103A must have an external level shifting input circuit and current sensing output circuit. However, there are IC devices such as the 3207A quadruple TTL-to-MOS level shifter and the 3208A or 3408A hex sense amplifier readily available to perform these functions.

MCM6605A Dynamic RAM

The MCM6605A is an NMOS dynamic RAM IC. It has 4*k* of storage capacity and its output is organized to produce 4096 1-bit words. Figure 4.30 shows a block diagram of the internal circuitry of the MCM6605A. Numbers for its 22 leads are marked in this diagram.

In the block diagram, there are a few unusual features. Notice that the cells are organized into four blocks of 32 rows by 32 columns. This gives a total capacity of 4 × 32 × 32 equals 4096 bits. The binary input at the five lower-order address lines A_0 through A_4 are decoded to select one column in each of the four blocks of cells. Since four groups of 32 cells are selected, a total of 128 storage locations have been selected. The input to the seven higher-order address lines A_5 through A_{11} are decoded by the row decoder to select one of the 128 cells. Data can be read out of the cell or new data written in.

In addition to the address, the other input signals to the device are *CHIP ENABLE*, *READ/WRITE*, *DATA IN*, *CHIP SELECT*, and *PRESET*. The data output at $\overline{DATA\ OUT}$ is the complement of that input at *DATA IN*.

To perform a refresh of the cells in a MCM6605A, a write cycle must be performed to each row address. This is done with $\overline{CHIP\ SELECT}$ at logic 1 to put the outputs in the hi-Z state. Notice that the refresh operation is different from most dynamic RAMs in that it is performed with a write operation instead of a read.

As we saw earlier, the five low-order address bits feed the column decoder. The outputs of the column decoder select one column in each of the four blocks of the memory array. Selecting a column causes all cells along the column to be refreshed. Therefore, to refresh the complete array, just set $\overline{CHIP\ SELECT}$ to logic 1, *READ/WRITE* to logic 0, and apply binary codes 00000 through 11111 to the low-order address inputs. Its minimum refresh time is 2 ms.

Logic levels for inputs A_0 through A_{11}, *DATA IN*, $\overline{CHIP\ SELECT}$, and *READ/WRITE* of the MCM6605A are TTL-compatible. The minimum high logic threshold is 3 V. This value is slightly above the usual 2-V high threshold of TTL signals. The maximum low logic threshold is 0.8 V.

The output signals are also directly TTL-compatible. The logic 0 level is rated from 0 to 0.45 V at 2 mA. This means that 2 mA of current can flow into the device when the output is logic 0, and the output voltage will remain below 0.45 V. The logic 1 rating is 2.4 V at –100 μA. This means that 100 μA can flow from the output of the device when it is logic 1.

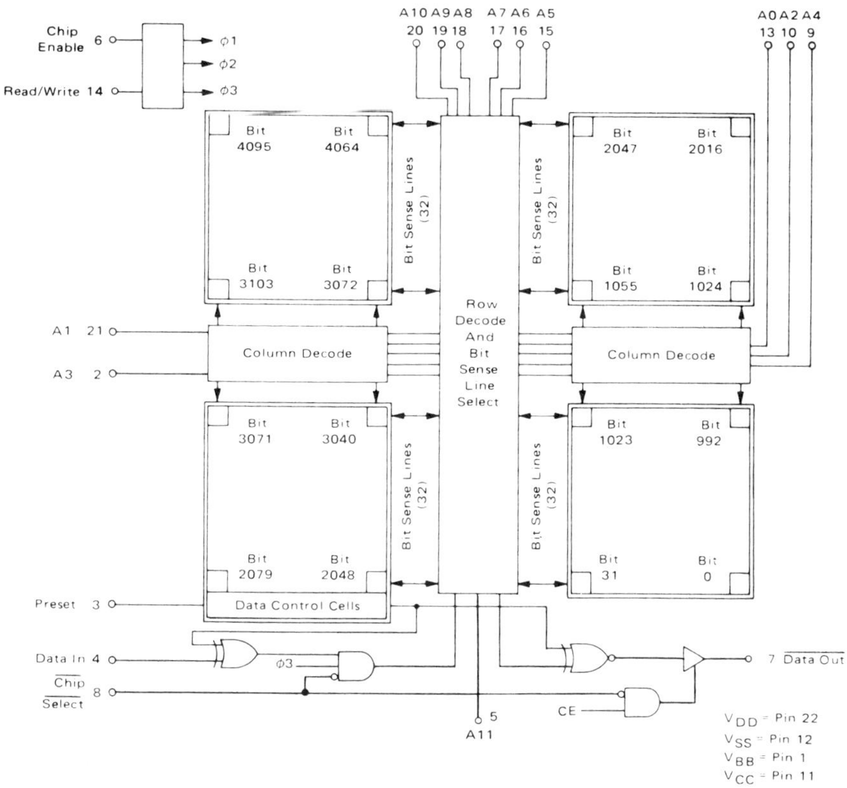

Fig. 4.30 MCM6605A block diagram (Motorola Semiconductor Products, Inc.).

The MCM6605A operates from three power-supply voltages. They are V_{DD} to V_{SS} equals +12 V, V_{CC} to V_{SS} equals +5 V, and V_{BB} to V_{SS} equals -5 V.

MK4096 Dynamic RAM

The MK4096 is another NMOS dynamic RAM IC. The storage capacity of the MK4096 is $4k$ and its output is organized into 4096 words by 1 bit per word. A block diagram of the circuitry within the device is shown in Fig. 4.31(a), and the layout of its 16-pin package is shown in Fig. 4.31(b).

In the block diagram shown in Fig. 4.31(a), input signals to the chip are the six address bits A_0 through A_5, the *row address strobe RAS*, the *column address strobe* $\overline{CAS}$, read/write $\overline{WRITE}$, chip select $\overline{CS}$, and data in D_{IN}. There is a single output lead, data out D_{OUT}.

The addressing of the MK4096 is different from that of the devices we have considered up to this point. It utilizes *address pin sharing*. Notice that there are just six address lines. Therefore, the complete address must be multiplexed into the device as two separate pieces. A 6-bit row address

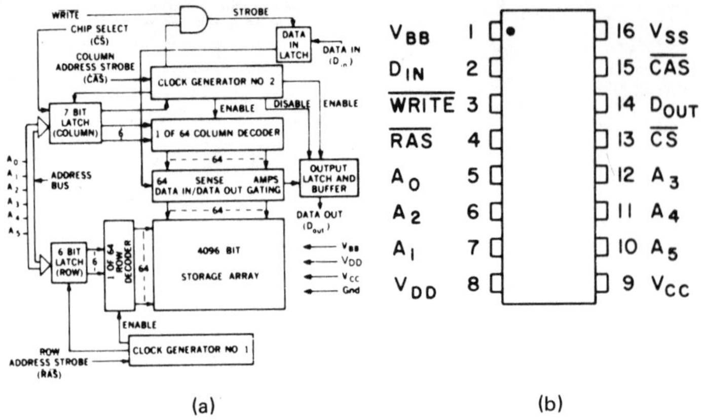

Fig. 4.31 (a) MK4096 block diagram (copyright Mostek 1980); (b) pin layout (copyright Mostek 1980).

is applied to A_0 through A_5 and then $\overline{RAS}$ is strobed to logic 0 to enter the bits into the device. After this, the six column bits are supplied to the same lines and entered by switching $\overline{CAS}$ to logic 0. This enters a 12-bit address which is latched within the device.

This addressing technique is used in all larger capacity dynamic RAMs. It is important because shared address lines reduce the number of pins needed on the IC package. With less pins, the package is more compact, thus allowing more devices to be placed on a circuit board. Therefore, smaller package size leads to increased packing density in memory systems.

The row address bits feed the row decoder, and the column address bits feed the column decoder. These decoders produce outputs that select one row and one column in the 64-row by 64-column dynamic memory array. It is this location that is to be accessed.

If a write is to be performed to this cell, the data at D_{IN} are latched within the device with the falling edge of $\overline{WRITE}$ and $\overline{CAS}$ while $\overline{RAS}$ is logic 0. When reading data from the storage location, the bit is latched at D_{OUT} with the falling edge of $\overline{CAS}$.

Refresh is accomplished by performing a read or write memory cycle for each of the 64 row addresses. $\overline{CS}$ need not be set to logic 0 to refresh the RAM with read operations. However, to refresh the device with write operations, $\overline{CS}$ must be set to the 1 logic level. In fact, refresh operations can be performed by entering the row part of the address alone.

Before a read or write operation can be performed with the MK4096, a dummy read or write operation to both a row and a column address must be done. This operation is required to recharge the output circuitry.

MK4116 Dynamic RAM

The MK4116 is a 16*k* dynamic RAM integrated circuit. It is organized to output 16,384 words each with 1 bit. A block diagram for the device is shown in Fig. 4.32(a) and its package layout in Fig. 4.32(b).

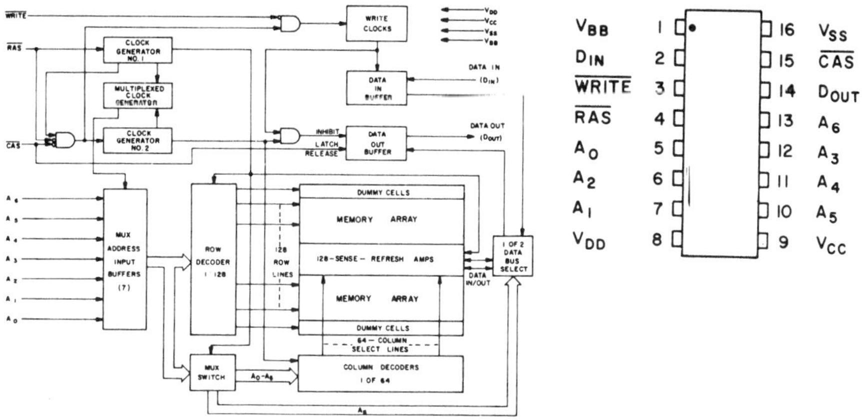

(a) (b)

Fig. 4.32 (a) MK4116 block diagram (copyright Mostek 1980); (b) pin layout (copyright Mostek 1980).

The block diagram shows the 11 input signals to the RAM and its one output. The inputs are the seven address lines, A_0 through A_6; row address strobe, $\overline{RAS}$; column address strobe, $\overline{CAS}$; read/write, $\overline{WRITE}$; and data input, D_{IN}. The output line is data out, D_{OUT}.

On the MK4116, the seven address lines are shared for input of a 7-bit row address and 7-bit column address. After the row address is applied to A_0 through A_6, it is latched within the device by setting $\overline{RAS}$ to logic 0. The column address is next put on the address lines and $\overline{CAS}$ is set to logic 0 to latch it within the IC. Now the complete 14-bit address that selects the storage location to be accessed has been entered.

The seven bits of the row address are input to the row decoder. Here they are decoded to select one row in each of the two 128-row by 64-column dynamic memory arrays. At the same time, six of the seven bits of the column address are fed to the column decoder. The output of this decoder selects one column out of the 64 columns in each of the memory arrays. There are now just two cells selected, one in each of the memory arrays. The final bit of the column address is used to select one of these two cells.

Since there is no separate chip select input, the states of the data in and data out ports are determined by the logic level and timing of control signals $\overline{RAS}$, $\overline{CAS}$, and $\overline{WRITE}$. For example, a write operation is performed when $\overline{RAS}$, $\overline{WRITE}$, and $\overline{CAS}$ are all logic 0. However, if the timing is such that $\overline{WRITE}$ occurs before $\overline{CAS}$ goes to logic 0, the output D_{OUT} is in the hi-Z state as data at D_{IN} are written into the cell. But if $\overline{WRITE}$ occurs after $\overline{CAS}$ is already logic 0, the data held in the addressed cell are first latched at D_{OUT} and then the data at D_{IN} are written into the cell.

When $\overline{WRITE}$ is held at logic 1 after $\overline{RAS}$ and $\overline{CAS}$ are logic 0, a read operation takes place. In this case, data stored in the addressed location are latched at output D_{OUT}.

To refresh the MK4116 RAM, we must read from or write to all 128 row addresses. The simplest way to perform the refresh operation is to periodically apply externally generated row addresses to the address lines. $\overline{RAS}$ must be strobed to logic 0 as each new address word is available. Column addresses do not have to be entered. Therefore, $\overline{CAS}$ can be left at logic 1 during the refresh cycle. All 128 rows must be refreshed every 2 ms.

Increased speed can be obtained by using *page mode operation.* With page mode, a single row address is latched within the RAM. Then consecutive column addresses are applied to the address inputs together with the appropriately timed $\overline{CAS}$. In this way, we can read from or write to consecutive columns of a single row in the memory array.

TMS 4164 Dynamic RAM

The TMS 4164 is one of the newer dynamic RAM devices. It contains a $64k$ NMOS storage array which is organized into 65,536 1-bit words. A block diagram of the internal architecture of the TMS 4164 is shown in Fig. 4.33(a) and the pin designations of its 16-pin package are shown in Fig. 4.33(b).

Looking at the block diagram, we find eight address input lines, A_0 through A_7; and control signals row address strobe ($\overline{RAS}$), column address strobe ($\overline{CAS}$), and read/write ($\overline{W}$). The data input and data output are marked D and Q, respectively.

One of the nicer features of the TMS 4164 is that it operates from a single +5-V supply. This voltage is applied between V_{DD} at pin 8 and V_{SS} at pin 16. The other supply voltages required by NMOS circuitry are generated within the device with *charge pump circuits.*

For the TMS 4164, the 8-bit row address is first applied to A_0 through A_7. When $\overline{RAS}$ goes to logic 0, the row address is latched into the RAM. Next, the column address is applied and $\overline{CAS}$ strobed to logic 0 to enter it into the device. Each of the arrays of memory cells are organized into 128 rows each with 256 columns. The 8-bit row address feeds inputs of the two row decoders. The outputs of the decoders select one row of their respective memory array.

The six column address bits are fed to the column decoder. Here they select the column of two of the 256 cells in the row selected in each array. At this point, four cell locations have been selected. The two remaining bits of the column address are used to select one of these four cells.

Once a row address has been latched into the chip, page mode access is possible. This is done by addressing consecutive cells in the columns along the row.

Since there is no separate chip select control on the TMS 4164, the input and output of data from D and Q, respectively, are controlled by the logic levels and timing of control signals $\overline{RAS}$, $\overline{CAS}$, and $\overline{W}$. During a write operation, input data at D are latched at the falling edge of $\overline{CAS}$ or $\overline{W}$. On the other hand, data are read into the output latch at Q after the falling edge

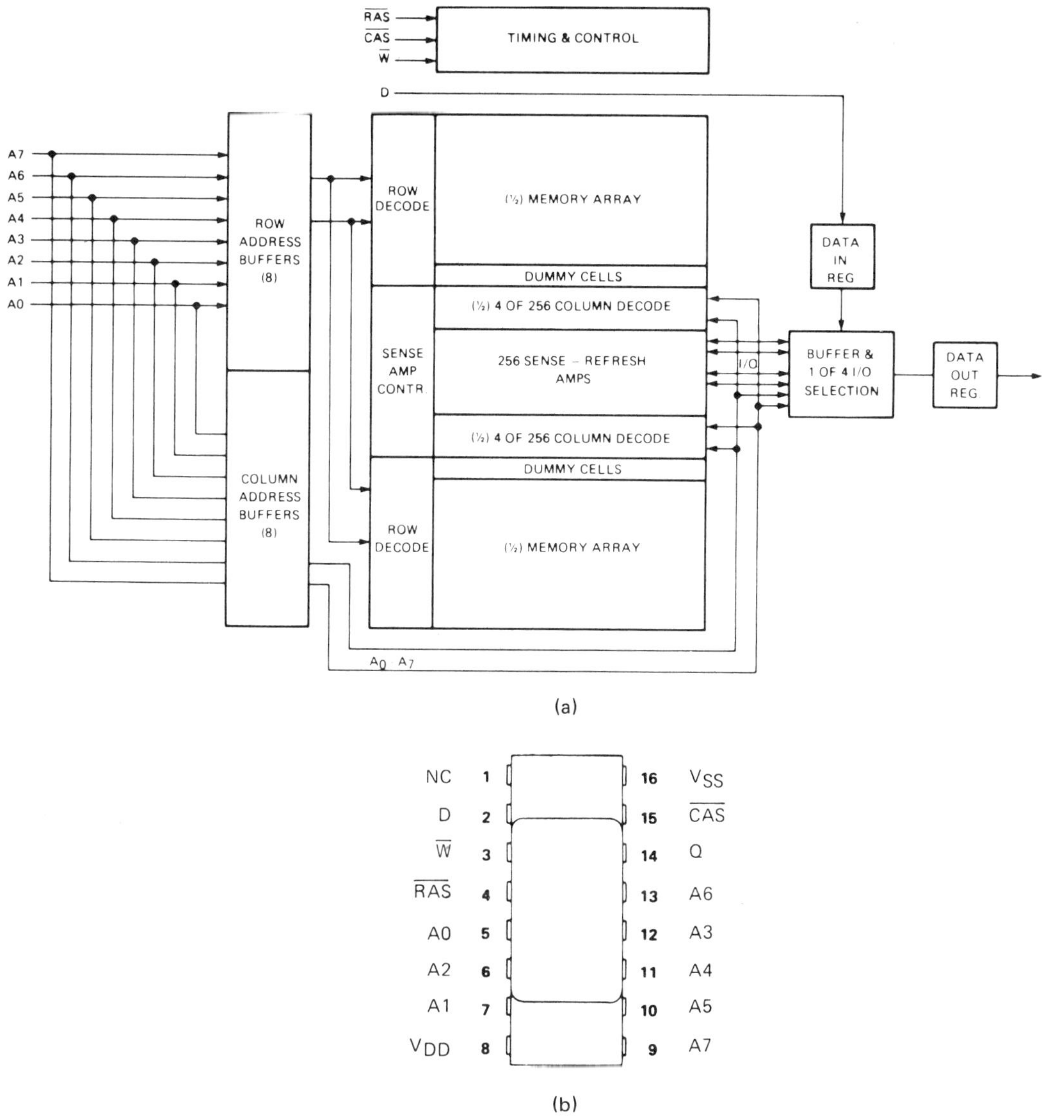

Fig. 4.33 (a) TMS 4164 block diagram (Texas Instruments, Incorporated); (b) pin layout (Texas Instruments, Incorporated).

of $\overline{CAS}$. The output Q is in the high-impedance state whenever $\overline{CAS}$ is logic 1.

Refresh of the TMS 4164 is accomplished in the same way as for earlier dynamic RAM ICs. We must apply each of the 256 row addresses and strobe $\overline{RAS}$ as each new address is applied. $\overline{CAS}$ can be logic 1 during the refresh cycle. If $\overline{CAS}$ is 1, the outputs are in hi-Z third state, and no data output lines are divided into two 4-bit groups. In this way, each RAM

4.8 EXPANDING WORD LENGTH AND WORD CAPACITY

Random access read/write memories are manufactured with many different word organizations and capacities. Sometimes it is possible to use a RAM device without any further memory subsystem design. However, many applications require longer word length or larger capacity of data words than can be provided by a single IC. As for ROM, these expansion requirements can be met by interconnecting a number of RAM ICs.

Word-Length Expansion

Let us take the case where the RAM does not have enough data input or output bits for the system requirements. For instance, we can use 5101L static RAMs in an 8-bit microcomputer system. Assume that the system requires 256 8-bit words, but the 256 words provided by the 5101L are just 4 bits wide. This limitation can be overcome by connecting two ICs together in such a way as to expand word length to 8 bits.

Figure 4.34 shows the circuit connections needed to configure two 5101L RAMs into a 256-word by 8-bit memory. Notice that address inputs A_0 through A_7 and control inputs $R/\overline{W}$, $\overline{CE}_1$, CE_2, and OD of the two devices are connected in parallel. Moreover, the eight data input lines and eight data output lines are divided into two 4-bit groups. In this way, each RAM provides 4 bits of the 8-bit word.

Expansion of word length in this way increases word size and the total number of bits but does not increase word capacity. This technique can be used for any type of RAM device.

EXAMPLE 4.4 How many 5101L RAMs must be connected in the configuration of Fig. 4.34 to form 256 words, each with 16 bits?

SOLUTION To expand word length to 16 bits, four 5101L devices must be connected in a configuration similar to that of Fig. 4.34.

Word-Capacity Expansion

As with the ROM, RAM ICs can be connected to expand the storage capacity. For example, we could have a system that requires $1k$ 4-bit words for storage of data. But the devices to be used are 5101L RAMs organized as 256 4-bit words. The key to expanding word capacity is to use extra higher-order address bits. These bits are decoded to select separate RAM ICs. Figure 4.35 shows such a circuit configuration.

By examining this circuit, we find that lower-order address lines A_0 through A_7 of all devices are connected in parallel. On the other hand, the two higher-order bits A_8 and A_9 are decoded and the decoder outputs applied to chip enable inputs of the four RAMs. CE_2 was selected because switching it to logic 0 puts the 5101L IC into the low-power mode.

This circuit connection differs from that of word-length expansion in

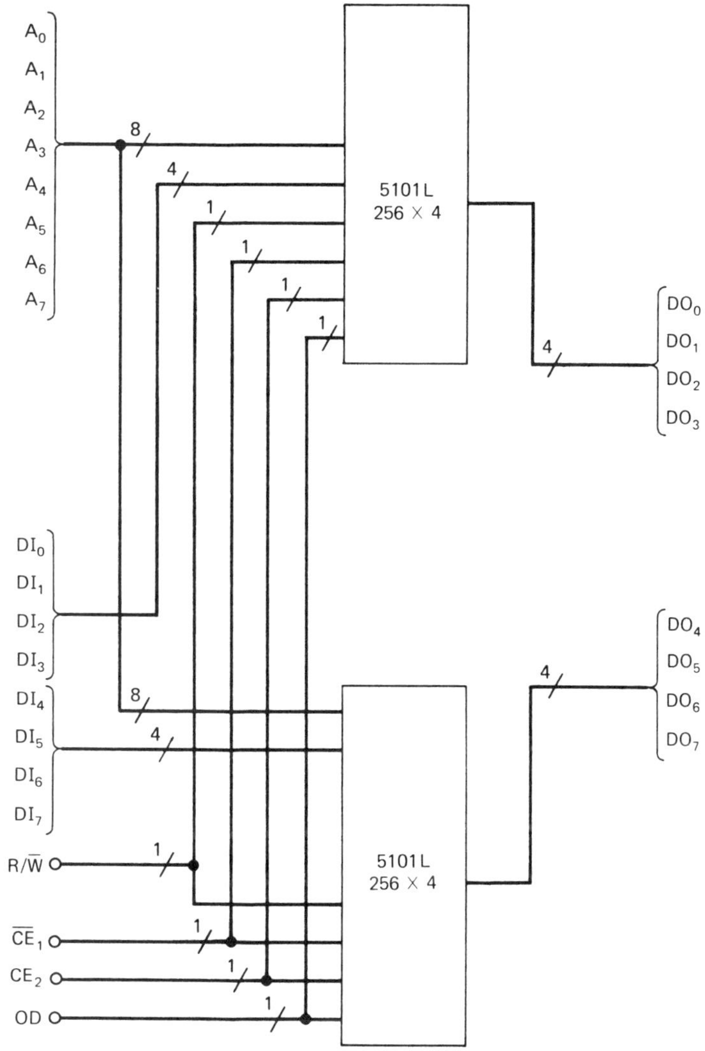

Fig. 4.34 Expanding word length.

that the separate data input leads DI_0 through DI_3 of all devices are paralleled. The data output leads DO_0 through DO_3 are connected in the same way. The parallel connection at the outputs is possible only if the devices in use have open-collector or three-state outputs. The 5101L shown in the diagram has three-state outputs. Control inputs $R/\overline{W}$, $\overline{CE}_1$, and OD are again tied in parallel.

When an address is supplied to the inputs of the circuit, bits A_0 through A_7 go to all devices. However, bits A_8 and A_9 go only to the decoder. The decoder output corresponding to the code at A_9A_8 causes one decoder output to switch to logic 1. This selects one of the four RAMs for operation.

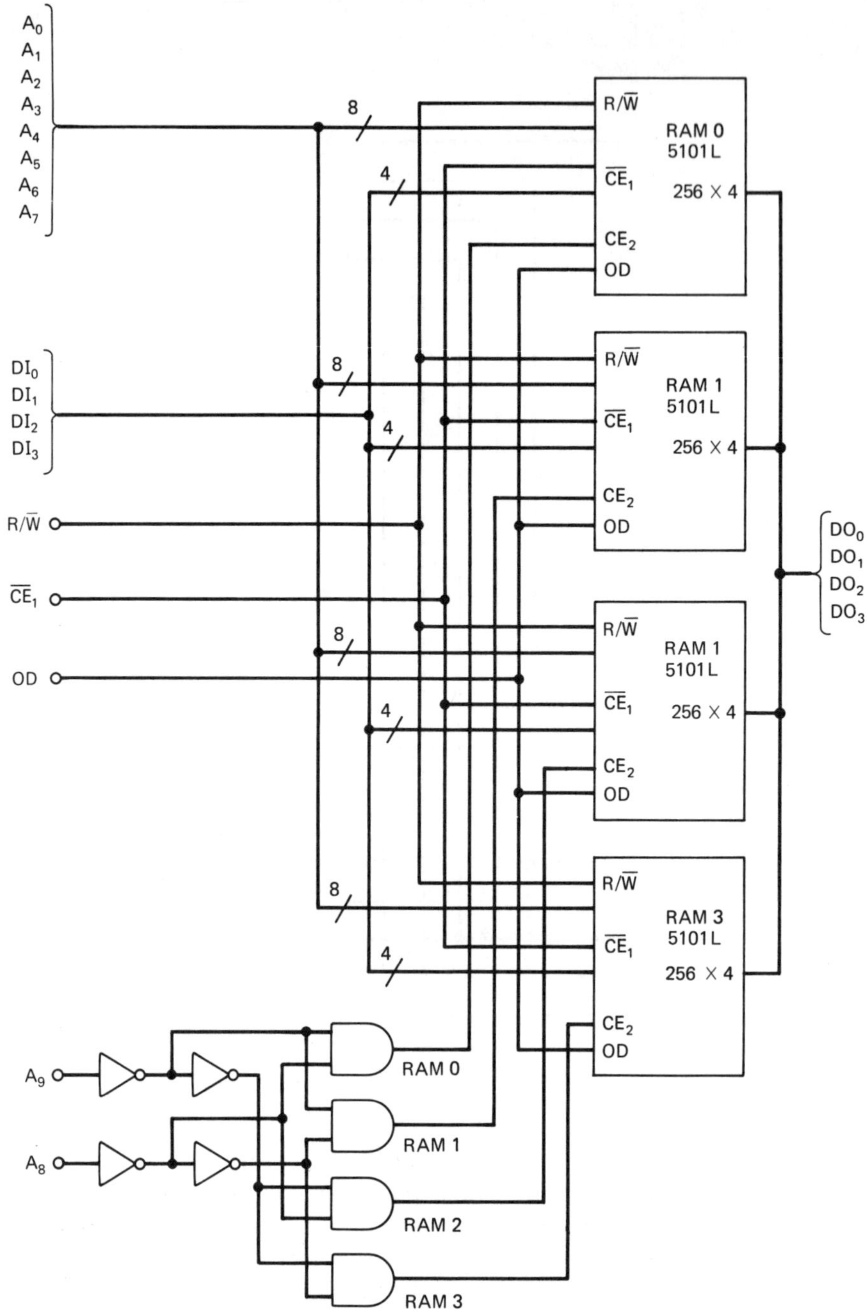

Fig. 4.35 Expanding word capacity.

Data can be read out or written into this device at the storage location defined by A_0 through A_7.

EXAMPLE 4.5 Which RAM in Fig. 4.35 is selected when the address input A_9 through A_0 is 1010100110? What is the address of the storage location within this device that is accessed for read/write operation?

SOLUTION The two most significant bits of the address determine which of the four RAMs is selected:

$$A_9A_8 = 10_2 = 2_{16}$$

This input makes the RAM 2 output of the decoder switch to logic 1.

The address location accesses in RAM 2 is given by the eight lower-order bits:

$$A_7A_6A_5A_4A_3A_2A_1A_0 = 10100110_2 = A6_{16}$$

Expanding Word Length and Word Capacity[5]

In practical digital systems, RAM frequently requires expansion of both word length and word capacity. The circuit configuration in Fig. 4.36 demonstrates how this is done. Here we find 24 2102A 1*k* by 1-bit RAMs connected with appropriate input, output, and control circuitry to make a 2*k* by 12-bit memory system. Notice that the RAMs are arranged in two 1*k* by 12-bit rows.

Data are input and output from a common *I/O* bus. Input data are latched in 3404 high-speed bipolar latches. On the other hand, the data outputs are buffered with 7438 open-collector NAND gates. In the circuit diagram, the NAND gates are drawn as OR gates with inverted inputs.

An 11-bit address is needed to select the 2048 storage locations available in memory. The 10 lower-order bits of the address are held in 3404 latches. This part of the address is applied to the address inputs of all RAMs in parallel. It selects the storage location to be accessed. At the same instant, the MSB of the address A_{10} is used to select one of the two rows of RAMs for operation.

To perform a write operation to the RAM system in Fig. 4.36, the address of the storage location to be accessed is applied to the inputs of the address latch. The data outputs are disabled by making *MEM 0* equal logic 1, or *MEM 1* equal logic 1, or *MEM 2* equal logic 0. Next, the data are put on the data bus. Setting $R/\overline{W}$ to logic 0 while *CYREQ* is pulsed to logic 1 latches the address and data inputs. At the same time, the 0 at $R/\overline{W}$ triggers the first stage of the 9602 one-shot. After the monostable times-out, the $\overline{WRITE}$ pulse occurs. This causes the data held in the input data latches to be written into the storage location defined by the address. $R/\overline{W}$ is set back to logic 1 to complete the write cycle.

[5]Intel Corp., *Memory Handbook* (Santa Clara, Calif.: Intel Corp., 1978), p. 6-16. (Courtesy of Intel Corp.)

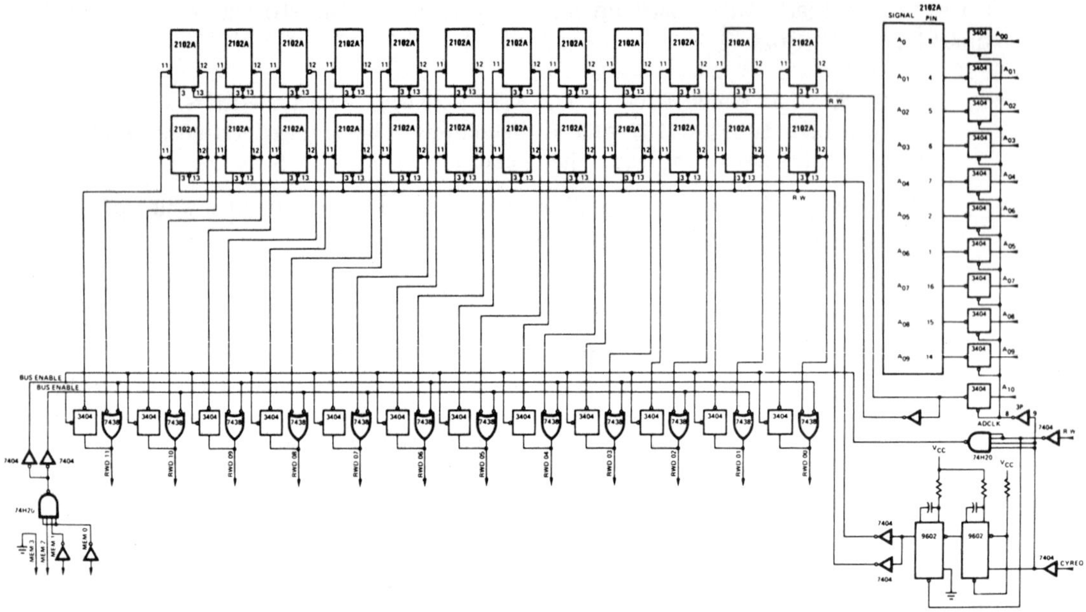

Fig. 4.36 Expanding both word length and word capacity (Intel Corp.).

For a read operation, the address is applied to the inputs of the address latch. Then *MEM 0* and *MEM 1* are set to logic 0 while *MEM 2* is set to logic 1. These control inputs enable the output data buffers. *CYREQ* is pulsed to logic 1 to latch the address. Since the second stage of the 9602 one-shot is held reset by $R/\overline{W}$ equal logic 1, no pulse is produced at $\overline{WRITE}$. The data at the addressed location appear on the data bus. Setting *MEM 0* or *MEM 1* to logic 1 or *MEM 2* to logic 0 disables the output buffer and completes the read operation.

4.9 RAM AND THE MICROCOMPUTER SYSTEM

As pointed out in Chapter 3, the microcomputer is a small digital computer data processing system. Remember that it contains all the elements of a larger computer system: central processing unit, memory unit, input unit, and output unit. However, each unit of the microcomputer is limited to fewer operating capabilities than those of larger computer systems.

Use of Memory in a Microcomputer

The memory part of the microcomputer system is one of the most common applications of semiconductor memory. It is normally formed from both ROM and RAM devices. Figure 4.37 shows how ROM and RAM are connected to the CPU in a microcomputer. Data, whether they are to be interpreted as numbers, characters, or instructions, can be stored in either ROM or RAM. But in most microcomputer systems, information such as

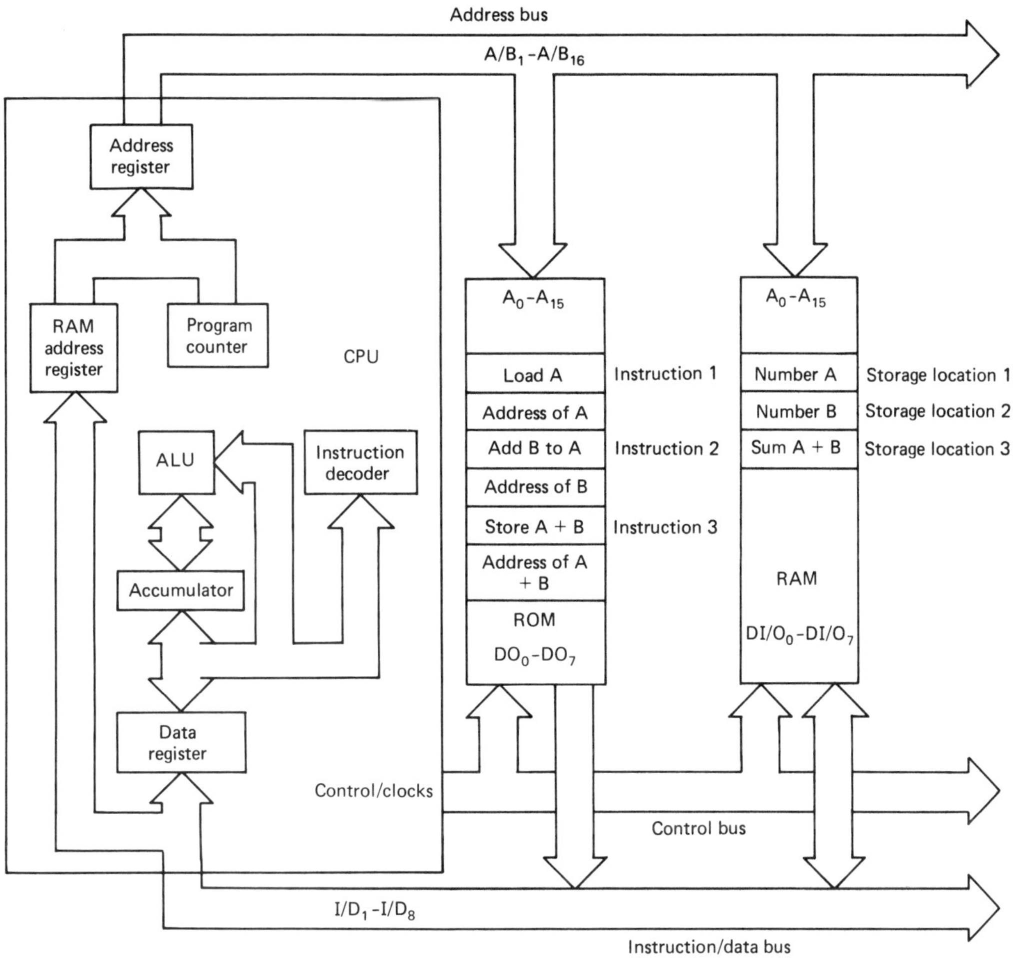

Fig. 4.37 Microprocessor connection with ROM and RAM memory.

instructions of its program or look-up tables are stored in ROM. This is because this type of information does not normally change. By using ROM, its storage is made nonvolatile.

On the other hand, the data to be processed by the CPU can change values repeatedly. For this reason, it is stored in RAM instead of ROM.

Looking at Fig. 4.37, we find that ROM and RAM share the same address bus and data bus. Notice that the address word can originate in one of two places: the *program counter* or the *RAM address register.* The program counter holds the address of the next instruction to be fetched from ROM for execution. On the other hand, the RAM address register is loaded with the address of the data to be processed by the instruction. For some CPUs, the RAM address register is actually an index register.

The address in either the RAM address register or program counter is loaded into the address register for output to memory. This 16-bit address,

A/B_1 through A/B_{16}, is capable of selecting one of up to $64k$ of 8-bit bytes. These bytes are stored at addresses in ROM or RAM over the range 0000_{16} to $FFFF_{16}$. The fact that a storage location in RAM or ROM is accessed is decided by the address assignments of the two parts of memory.

One way of assigning address locations to ROM and RAM is by using one bit of the address and its complement to chip select ROM and RAM, respectively. For example, RAM can be set up to respond to only addresses for which the MSB of the address A/B_{16} is logic 1 and ROM to respond to all addresses for which A/B_{16} is logic 0. This is done by supplying $\overline{A/B_{16}}$ to the $\overline{CS}$ input of the RAM and A/B_{16} to $\overline{CS}$ on ROM. For all addresses from 0000_{16} to $7FFF_{16}$, A/B_{16} is logic 0 and storage locations in ROM are selected. However, for those addresses in the range 8000_{16} to $FFFF_{16}$, A/B_{16} is logic 1 and the selected storage locations are in RAM.

An alternate approach is to use several bits of the address as a memory *bank select code.* For example, the four most significant bits, A/B_{16} A/B_{15} A/B_{14} A/B_{13}, could be used for bank selection. The binary combination at these bits can be decoded and the outputs of the decoder device used to select one of 16 banks of ROM or RAM ICs. This allows partitioning of the $64k$ address range into 16 equal blocks of $4k$ addresses. Each of these blocks can be assigned to ROM ICs, RAM ICs, or even remain unused. Figure 4.38 shows a map of memory organized in this way.

EXAMPLE 4.6 How many address locations are allotted to ROM in Fig. 4.38?

SOLUTION The address range of ROM is from

$$0000_{16} = 0000000000000000_2 = 0_{10}$$

through

$$3FFF_{16} = 0011111111111111_2 = 16{,}383_{10}$$

This gives a total of $16k$ storage locations for ROM.

The data bus carries data and instructions between ROM or RAM and the CPU. Information can only be read out of ROM. When the content of the program counter is put on the address bus, the instruction held at the address location in ROM is output at DO_0 through DO_7. It is carried over the data bus, lines I/D_1 through I/D_8, and loaded into the data register within the CPU. From here, the instruction is channeled to the instruction decoder, where it is interpreted for execution. Transfer between ROM and CPU over the data bus is unidirectional.

If RAM is addressed instead of ROM, data can be written into or read out of the selected location. The content of the RAM address register is output on the address bus under control of the CPU. Then the CPU sets its control lines for a read or write operation. After this, data are transferred between RAM and CPU over the bidirectional data bus.

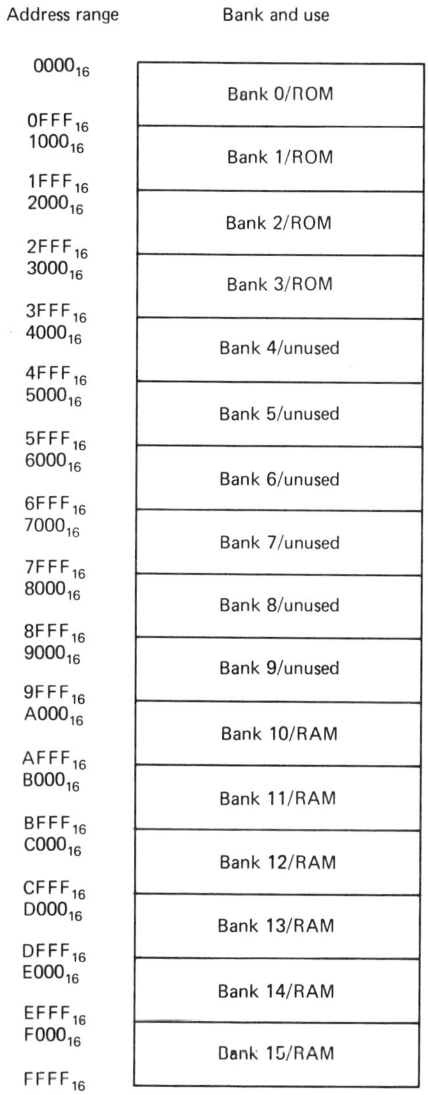

Fig. 4.38 Microcomputer memory map.

Executing a Simple Addition Program

The CPU or MPU, as it is also known, can perform operations such as additions and subtractions on data. In the microcomputer system, the instructions that tell the CPU to add are held in ROM, but the numbers to be added are normally held in RAM. These numbers are stored in RAM because their values frequently change. In fact, the result of the addition or subtraction may replace one of the original numbers in memory. Therefore, the same location may be used over and over again, each time being loaded with different data. This is possible with RAM because of its *destructive write-in* characteristics.

Let us now demonstrate how ROM and RAM are used during the execution of a microcomputer program. In Fig. 4.37, we have indicated a sequence of instructions in the ROM block. This represents a short program that when executed will read two numbers identified as A and B from locations in RAM, add them together, and write their sum to another location in RAM called sum $A+B$.

The first instruction which is indicated by load A, is needed to load number A into the *accumulator* of the CPU. The address of this instruction is output from the program counter through the address register and over the address bus to ROM. The program counter is then incremented by 1 to point to the next instruction. The load instruction is read out of ROM and is carried over the data bus to the data register of the CPU. From here it is transferred to the instruction decoder for execution. It causes the next address in the program counter to be output. This address in ROM holds the RAM address of the location of number A. This address is put into the RAM address register.

During the execution phase of instruction 1, the outputs of the instruction decoder cause the RAM address to be output on the address bus. The content of this location is read out at DI/O_0 through DI/O_7 and carried over the I/D bus to the CPU. Within the CPU, it is channeled through the data register to the accumulator. Number A is now held in the accumulator of the CPU.

The program counter now points to the second instruction. This instruction causes number B to be added to A and their sum put in the accumulator. Putting the program counter content on the address bus fetches the add instruction from ROM and puts it in the instruction decoder. The second byte of the instruction, which is the address of number B, is fetched from RAM and put into the RAM address register.

As the execution phase of instruction 2 begins, the address for number B is put on the address bus. The value of B is read out of RAM and stored in the data register. The output of the data register is applied to the input of the *arithmetic logic unit* (ALU). Now the ALU has two sets of inputs: number B from the output of the data register and number A from the output of the accumulator. As the execution phase continues under instruction decoder control, the two numbers are added within the ALU and the resulting sum loaded into the accumulator.

Now the sum of A and B is held in the accumulator, but it still remains to output the result to RAM for storage at the location for $A+B$. This is achieved with instruction 3. The program counter now points to instruction 3. It is output to ROM. This causes the store accumulator instruction to read into the instruction decoder. The next value of the program counter is output to ROM and it returns the address of sum $A+B$ to the RAM address register.

As the execution phase starts, the address of sum $A+B$ is put on the address bus and the data held in the accumulator are passed through the data register to the I/D bus. Then the CPU sets up its control lines for a

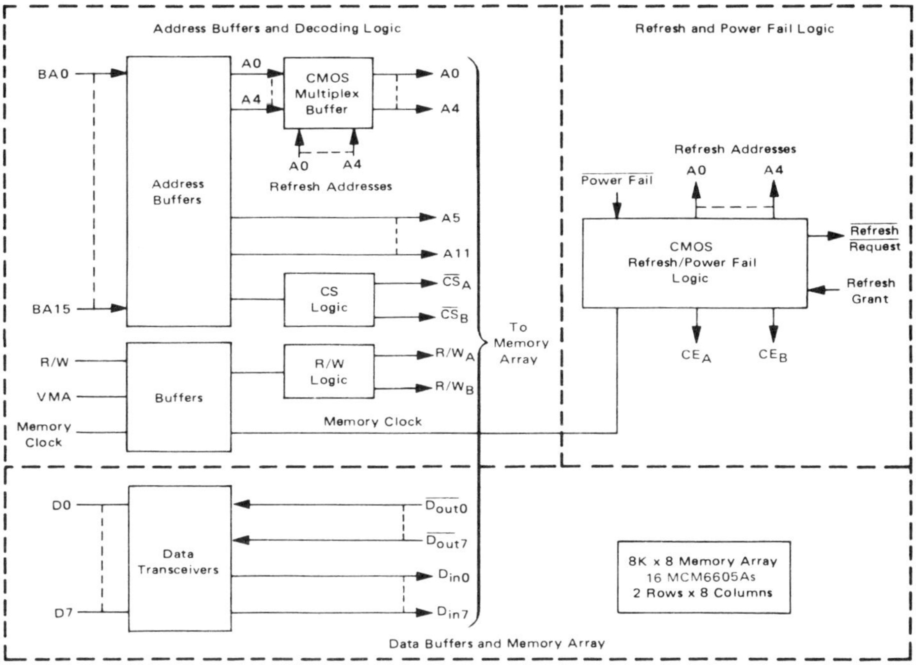

Fig. 4.39 Nonvolatile RAM subsystem block diagram (Motorola Semiconductor Products, Inc.).

write operation and the data at DI/O_0 through DI/O_7 of the RAM are written into the storage location.

Nonvolatile Dynamic RAM Subsystem[6]

Earlier in this chapter, we pointed out that the RAM ICs are volatile. That is, if their power-supply voltage is removed, the data stored in the memory are lost. This characteristic is not acceptable in many applications. An example is a business machine where irreplaceable information about the operation of a business could be lost. To satisfy the nonvolatile requirement, additional circuitry can be included in the RAM subsystem. These circuits can sense the occurrence of a power failure and automatically switch the system over to a backup battery. In this way, the system can be made at least temporarily nonvolatile.

A block diagram of such a RAM subsystem is shown in Fig. 4.39. It represents an 8*k*-byte dynamic RAM subsystem designed for use along with an MC6800 8-bit microcomputer. Dynamic RAMs are used in this application because of the higher storage capacity at reduced power consumption. Moreover, CMOS ICs are utilized wherever possible to further

[6]Motorola Semiconductor Products, Inc., *Semiconductor Data Library, MOS Memories*, Vol. 7, Series A Austin, TX: Motorola, Inc., pp. 225–238. (Courtesy of Motorola Semiconductor Products, Inc.)

reduce power consumption. Power consumption is critical because a battery is used to retain data when power is down.

Looking at the block diagram, we see that the system is composed of eight functional parts. They are the address buffer, control buffer, data transceiver, multiplex buffer, *CS* logic, *R/W* logic, refresh/power fail logic, and an 8*k* by 8-bit memory array. The memory array is not shown in the block diagram.

The memory array contains two independently addressable blocks of 4*k* by 8-bit words. These blocks are called A and B. Each block is formed with eight MCM6605L-1 RAM ICs. The output of this type of RAM is organized 4*k* by 1 bit. Therefore, each of the eight ICs in a block produces one bit of the storage byte.

The microcomputer inputs a 16-bit address word to the RAM subsystem. The address word is input at lines BA_0 through BA_{15}. These address bits are buffered as they enter the subsystem. The five LSBs of the address, A_0 through A_4, are buffered and then applied to inputs of the multiplex buffer. Here they are combined with refresh address A_0 through A_4. This refresh address is generated in the refresh logic section of the subsystem. Bits BA_5 through BA_{11} of the address are buffered and then applied directly to address inputs of the RAM array. The four most significant bits of the address BA_{12} through BA_{15} are buffered and then decoded to produce the block chip select signals $\overline{CS}_A$ and $\overline{CS}_B$.

The bidirectional data bus of the microcomputer is interfaced to the separate data input lines and data output lines of the RAM array by the data transceiver section. The direction of data transfer through this bidirectional buffer section is set up by control signals derived on the memory subsystem from the microcomputer's read/write control signal *R/W*. During a write operation, the transceiver is set up to pass data at D_0 through D_7 onto input lines D_{IN0} through D_{IN7} and store them in the addressed location. But when *R/W* indicates that data are to be read from the RAM subsystem, the direction of the buffers in the transceiver section are set up to pass data held in the addressed memory location from $\overline{D}_{OUT0}$ through $\overline{D}_{OUT7}$ onto the microcomputer's data bus D_0 through D_7.

The dynamic memory array is designed to be refreshed on a distributed basis. Periodically, the clock in the refresh control logic section produces a pulse. This pulse increments the refresh address and initiates the $\overline{REFRESH}$ $\overline{REQUEST}$ signal. The microprocessor responds to $\overline{REFRESH}$ $\overline{REQUEST}$ with the *REFRESH GRANT* signal. It is this signal that initiates a refresh operation for one row of the RAM array at a time. At the same time, it resets the $\overline{REFRESH}$ $\overline{REQUEST}$ line. This sequence of events repeats every 64 μs. Therefore, all 32 row addresses are refreshed every 2 ms.

An orderly switch over to battery back up during power failure is achieved through the power-fail logic circuitry. $\overline{POWER}$ $\overline{FAIL}$ signals this section that a power failure has occurred; however, the logic is designed so that a RAM refresh cycle or RAM access cycle that is in progress will not be interrupted. When the subsystem is complete with the cycle in progress, the

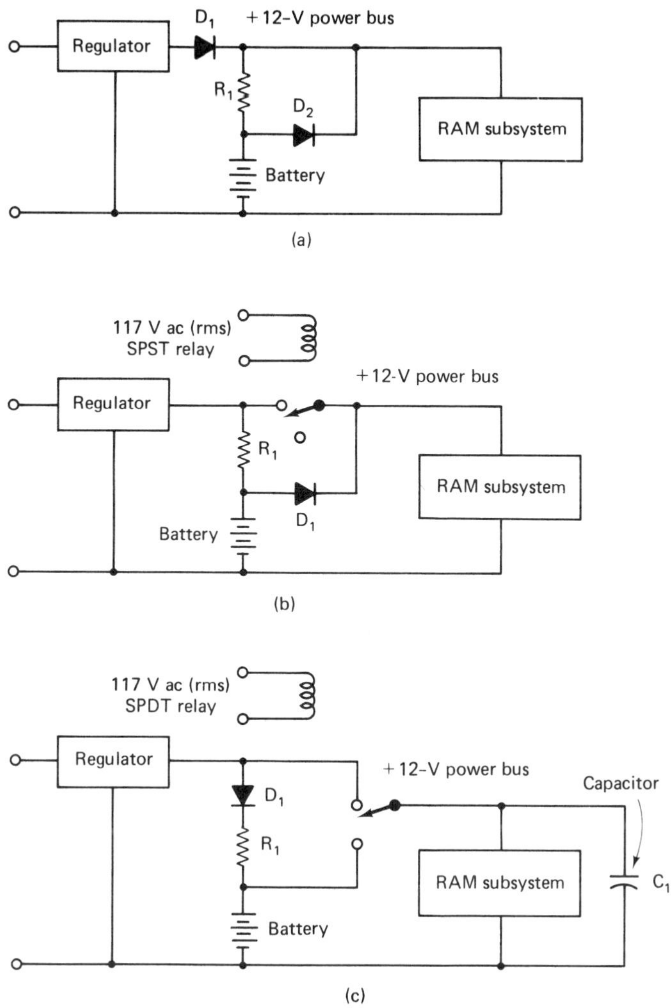

Fig. 4.40 Battery connections to the RAM subsystem (Intel Corp.).

power-fail logic takes over and locks the memory system in the refresh mode. Moreover, it switches in the memory clock signals generated from the refresh clock to the CE_A and CE_B outputs of the power-fail logic. The battery has taken over as the power source. The circuit remains in this state with the RAM array being continuously refreshed until power returns.

The backup battery can be attached to the RAM subsystem by means of an isolation diode or by an ac line dropout sensing relay. Some of the common circuit configurations are shown in Fig. 4.40[7]. If diode isolation is used, the 12-V power supply produced by the system cannot be permitted

[7] Intel Corp., *Memory Handbook*, pp. 5-7 to 5-15. (Courtesy of Intel Corp.)

to go below the battery voltage. When this happens, battery current would flow into the 12-V power supply.

If a relay is used to switch in the battery supply, enough capacitor storage must be provided on the RAM subsystem to overcome its switching delay. The charge on the capacitor decays slowly. This assures that the voltage of the system does not fall below the retention level of the memory ICs before the relay completes the switchover to the backup battery.

ASSIGNMENTS

Section 4.2

1. What does "RAM" stand for?
2. Is RAM volatile or nonvolatile?
3. What are the two basic categories of RAM?
4. Which technology is used to manufacture the highest-storage-capacity RAMs?
5. How does the RAM block diagram in Fig. 4.3(a) differ from that introduced in Chapter 2 for the ROM?
6. Describe the write operation of a RAM.

Section 4.3

7. What are the eight key parts of the RAM's architecture?
8. What is the output of the memory array in Fig. 4.5(a) and (b) when row 3 is selected?
9. Find the logic levels at the output of the circuit in Fig. 4.10 when its inputs are A_0=1, A_1=1, and AR=1.
10. In Fig. 4.11, which data bit is output at *DATA OUT* when CS=1, $R/\overline{W}$=1, and $C_0C_1C_2C_3$=0100?
11. Which column output is logic 1 in Fig. 4.12(a) when the inputs are A_2=0 and A_3=1?
12. For the circuit in Fig. 4.13, what logic levels must be applied at R_0, C_0, $R/\overline{W}$, and CS to select cell 0 for input of data from DI_0?

Section 4.4

13. The control inputs of the circuit in Fig. 4.14(a) are set up for write operation. If the address inputs are $A_3A_2A_1A_0$=0011, which cell is selected for input of data?
14. The RAM in Fig. 4.14(a) is set for a read operation. It already contains the data shown in Fig. 4.15. What is *DO* if the address input is 1100?

Section 4.5

15. What is the bit capacity and output organization of the 74S189A bipolar RAM?
16. How does the 74S289 RAM differ from the 74S189A RAM?
17. Which device is similar to the 3101 and 3101A bipolar RAMs?
18. How do the 2101A and 2102A RAMs differ?
19. What is the primary advantage of the 5101L RAM over the 2101A device?
20. What are the total storage capacity and output organization of the MM2114 NMOS RAM?

Section 4.6

21. What is the storage element of the dynamic RAM?
22. What is one advantage of using dynamic cells instead of static cells?
23. What is the process of restoring charge to dynamic cells called?
24. Describe the write operation of the four-transistor dynamic cell in Fig. 4.24.
25. Describe the refresh cycle of a dynamic RAM such as that in Fig. 4.26.

Section 4.7

26. What is the total storage capacity and input/output organization of the 1103A dynamic RAM?
27. How frequently must the 1103A be refreshed?
28. What is the key difference between the MCM6605A and MK4096 RAMs?
29. What are the total storage capacity and input/output organization of the TMS 4164 RAM?

Section 4.8

30. In the circuit of Fig. 4.35, which RAM and storage location are selected when the address inputs are A_9 through A_0 equal 0011111111?
31. Make a drawing showing how eight 5101L RAMs can be connected to give a memory organized as 1k words, each with 8 bits.

Section 4.9

32. What are the functions of the ROM and RAM in the microcomputer system of Fig. 4.37?
33. In Fig. 4.39, what is the total byte capacity of RAM?

5

SHIFT REGISTER

5.1 INTRODUCTION

The chapters up to this point introduced random-access memories. In this chapter, we introduce the most widely used serial-accessed memory device, the shift register.

The chapter begins with an introduction to the shift register circuit and its basic configurations. After this, it concentrates on the operation of static shift register circuits and standard IC devices. This material is followed by a study of dynamic shift registers. The chapter closes with memory applications on the shift register. The following topics are discussed:

1. The shift register circuit
2. The serial-in, serial-out shift register
3. The serial-in, parallel-out shift register
4. The parallel-in, serial-out shift register
5. Recirculating shift registers
6. Shift-right, shift-left registers
7. The universal shift register
8. The dynamic shift register
9. Serial memory
10. Pseudo-random-access memory

5.2 THE SHIFT REGISTER CIRCUIT

The shift register is an electronic circuit that is widely used for temporary storage of digital information. Memory devices such as the ROM and RAM introduced in earlier chapters operated with *parallel data*; however, shift register memories involve *serial data*. That is, the input of data, output of data, or search for data in a shift register are performed in sequence, one bit after the other.

Serial and Parallel Data

This section defines the difference between serial data and parallel data. When data are expressed in serial form, one bit of the data word is made available after the other in time.

Figure 5.1(a) shows the ASCII code for letter B expressed in serial form. Notice that the MSB b_7, which is logic 1, is available during the first interval of time, 0 to 1. The next time interval, 1 to 2, represents bit b_6 of the code and it is logic 0. Bit b_6 is followed by bits b_5 through b_3 over the

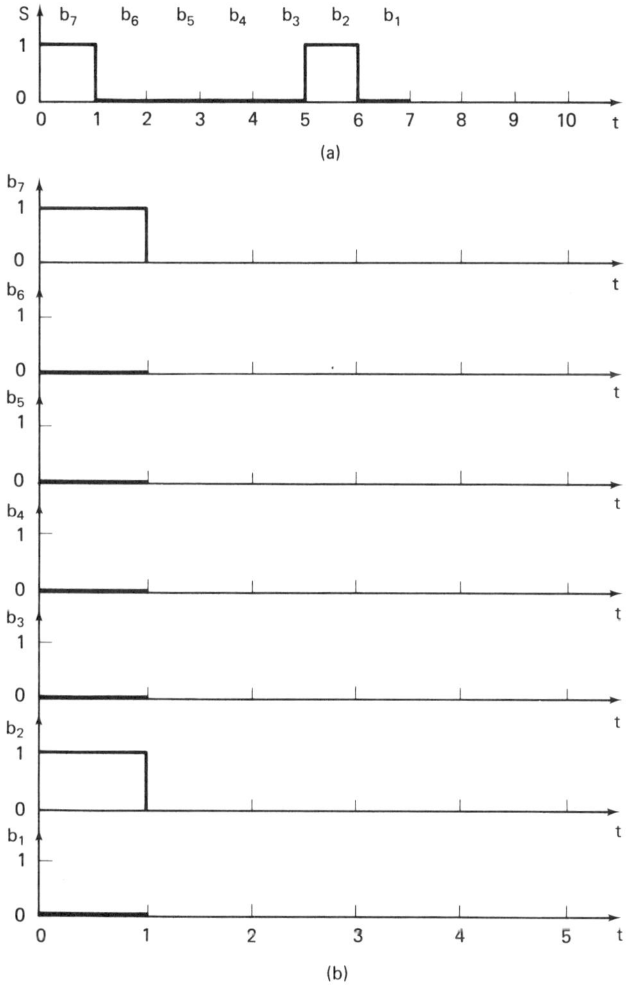

Fig. 5.1 (a) Serial-form data; (b) parallel-form data.

time interval from 2 through 5. The signal stays at logic 0 for each of these bits.

After this, bit b_2 causes the signal to switch back to logic 1 and the LSB b_1 returns the logic level to 0. Serial data are also referred to as *bit-serial data.*

The ASCII letter B is expressed in parallel form in Fig. 5.1(b). Here we find that all bits of the word are produced as separate signals during the same interval of time instead of one after the other in time. Data expressed in parallel form are also known as *bit-parallel data.*

Serial Access

Shift registers are *serial-accessed* storage devices. By "serial-accessed" we mean that the data held at a storage location cannot be directly accessed; instead, it must be shifted bit by bit through the register to the output.

The amount of time required to access data stored in a cell in a shift register is called *access time.* In *random-accessed* memory, the maximum access time is the same, independent of the cell to be read. However, in serial-accessed memories such as the shift register, the maximum time required to read data from a cell depends on its location within the register. In general, serial memories have slower data-access rates than random-accessed memories.

Shift Register Configurations

Four basic shift register circuit configurations are in wide use. They are called the *serial-in, serial-out shift register*; the *serial-in, parallel-out shift register*; the *parallel-in, serial-out shift register*; and *parallel-in, parallel-out shift register.*

The names of these configurations are derived from the form of input and output data. For example, a serial-in, serial-out register accepts serial data at its input, delays the data by a fixed number of clock cycles, and then outputs the data which are still in serial form.

On the other hand, a serial-in, parallel-out register also accepts input data in serial form, but it converts the data to parallel form for output.

Bipolar and MOS Technology ICs

Integrated circuits that contain shift registers can be manufactured with bipolar technology circuitry or MOS technology circuitry. Each of these technologies can be used to manufacture devices with their own unique advantages and disadvantages.

The most popular types of bipolar shift register devices are those constructed with standard TTL and Schottky TTL circuitry. This kind of circuitry produces high-speed registers with typical data propagation delays in the range 20 to 40 ns.

Together with this important advantage of high-speed operation, bipolar devices have other characteristics that prove to be disadvantageous in some applications. For instance, they consume a large amount of power. Typical power consumption is in the 100-mW range.

Moreover, the integration of TTL circuitry requires a large amount of area. This severely limits the maximum storage capacity of bipolar devices. Standard devices are manufactured with 4-, 5-, 8-, and 16-bit storage capacities.

Three types of circuitry are used in the manufacture of MOS shift register ICs: CMOS circuitry, PMOS circuitry, and NMOS circuitry. Shift registers produced with complementary symmetry metal-oxide semiconductor (CMOS) circuitry have much slower operating characteristics than those made with bipolar circuitry. For example, the propagation delay of data between input and output is as long as several hundred nanoseconds. This amount of delay is about 10 times longer than for an equivalent bipolar device.

However, another electrical characteristic, its low power consumption, proves to be an important advantage offered by CMOS circuitry. The operation of a CMOS register requires several microwatts. By comparing this amount of power to the hundreds of milliwatts required by a TTL circuit, we see how little power is required to operate a CMOS device.

As with bipolar circuitry, integration of CMOS requires a lot of area. Maximum storage capacities are also small, with typical values of 4, 8, 18, and 32 bits.

The advantage of using PMOS and NMOS circuitry to manufacture shift register ICs lies in their ability to produce compact circuitry. Earlier we said the bipolar registers are limited to about 16-bit capacities and CMOS registers to 32 bits; however, with PMOS and NMOS, storage capacities as large as 1*k* bits can be obtained.

PMOS and NMOS registers require about the same amount of power as TTL registers, but they are much slower than TTL, with propagation delays in the same range as CMOS registers.

The Shift Register Storage Cell[1,2]

The storage cells used in shift registers are flip-flop circuits. Figure 5.2 shows the connection of four flip-flops to form a serial-in, serial-out register. Each flip-flop in the circuit is capable of storing 1 bit of data. Therefore, the register has a 4-bit storage capacity.

In this circuit, we used *set-reset flip-flops*. Equivalent register circuits can be constructed with *D-type* or *J-K flip-flops*. Circuits having the other basic shift register configurations can also be constructed with all three types of flip-flops.

[1] R. Heuner, J. Litus, Jr., and A. Havasy, "COS/MOS MSI Counter and Register Design and Applications," ICAN-6166 (Sommerville, NJ: RCA Solid State Division, June 1978). (Courtesy of RCA Solid State Division)

[2] Gerald Luecke, Jack P. Mize, and William N. Carr, *Semiconductor Memory Design and Application*, Texas Instruments Electronics Series (New York: McGraw-Hill Book Company, 1973), p. 66. (Courtesy of Texas Instruments, Incorporated)

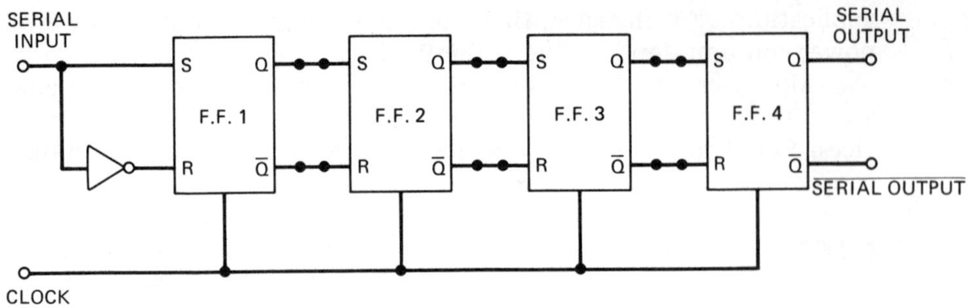

Fig. 5.2 Typical shift register circuit.

Master-slave-type flip-flop circuits are employed in shift registers. The structure of this kind of flip-flop is shown in Fig. 5.3. Looking at this circuit, we find that it uses two clocked set-reset flip-flops. The flip-flop on the input side is called the master and the one on the output side is called the slave. The data inputs to the circuit are the set S_1 and reset R_1 leads on the master flip-flop. Outputs Q_1 and $\overline{Q}_1$ of the master flip-flop are used as set S_2 and reset R_2 inputs to the slave. The outputs of the circuit are Q_2 and $\overline{Q}_2$ from the slave flip-flop.

Input data at S_1 and R_1 cause the output of the master flip-flop to set or reset on the 0-to-1 edge of the clock pulse at CLK. These data are available at the Q_1 and $\overline{Q}_1$ outputs of the master flip-flop.

On the negative edge of the clock pulse, data are transferred from the master outputs into the slave. This produces the circuit outputs Q_2 and $\overline{Q}_2$.

By using master-slave flip-flops, the shift register is able to transfer data at its outputs into the master section of the flip-flop in the next stage of the register before changing its outputs to the new state.

A master-slave set-reset flip-flop made with TTL circuitry uses a circuit such as that shown in Fig. 5.4. In this circuit, the master and slave flip-flops are constructed from a set of cross-coupled NAND gates with the data inputs controlled by NAND gates.

On the leading edge of the clock pulse, CLK switches to logic 1. This

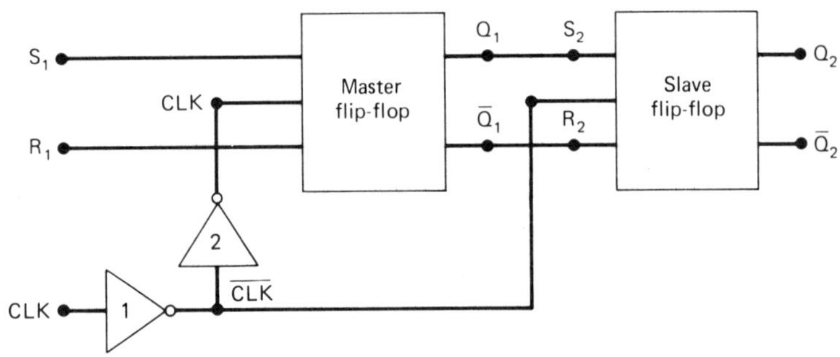

Fig. 5.3 Master-slave flip-flop (Walter A. Triebel, Integrated Digital Electronics, © 1979. Adapted by permission of Prentice-Hall, Inc., Englewood Cliffs, N.J.).

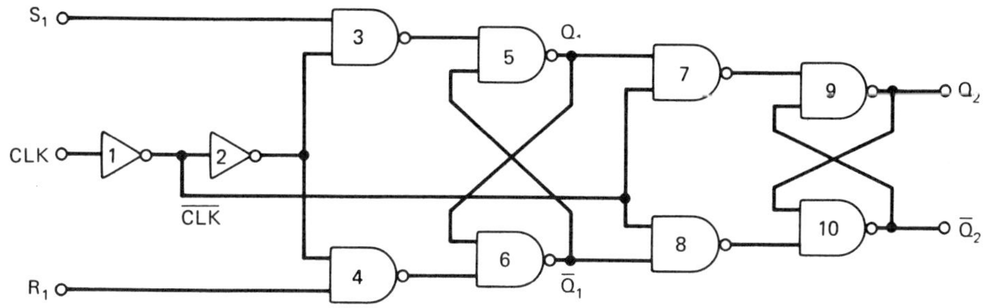

Fig. 5.4 TTL master-slave set-reset flip-flop logic diagram.

makes $\overline{CLK}$ at the output of gate 1 equal to logic 0 and CLK from gate 2 equal to logic 1.

When set in this way, gates 3 and 4 are enabled and the master flip-flop is ready to read data inputs S_1 and R_1. In response to these inputs, outputs Q_1 and $\bar{Q}_1$ from gates 5 and 6, respectively, switch to the set or reset state. At this moment, the logic 0 at $\overline{CLK}$ disables the inputs of the slave flip-flop.

As the trailing edge of the clock occurs, $\overline{CLK}$ from gate 1 switches to logic 1 and CLK from gate 2 switches to the 0 level. This disables the inputs through gates 3 and 4 to the master flip-flop and enables input gates 7 and 8 to the slave. In turn, the Q_2 and $\bar{Q}_2$ outputs are set or reset, depending on the logic levels held at the master flip-flop outputs.

The storage cells in CMOS shift registers are normally D-type flip-flops. A logic diagram of a CMOS flip-flop circuit is given in Fig. 5.5(a). Here we find that the master and slave flip-flops are each formed from two NOR gates and two transmission gates. The transmission gates are marked TG in the diagram.

As the clock input CL switches from logic 0 to 1, the transmission gate at the D input is enabled. Data from the D input are loaded into the output of the master flip-flop. When CL returns from 1 to 0, the transmission gate to the input of the slave is enabled and the data held at the master outputs are passed to the buffer and Q output. At the same time, data are loaded into the slave flip-flop to produce complemented output $\bar{Q}$.

The complementary MOSFET circuitry in Fig. 5.5(b) is used to implement a D-type flip-flop circuit such as that shown in Fig. 5.5(a).

Figure 5.6 shows a MOS D-type flip-flop circuit. Arrows are not shown to identify P-channel or N-channel MOSFETs. This is because it is a general circuit structure and is valid for either type of MOSFET device. The master part of the flip-flop circuit consists of devices T_1, T_2, and T_3 together with the intrinsic device capacitance C_1. Moreover, T_4, T_5, T_6, and C_2 provide the slave section of the flip-flop.

This circuit operates off a three-phase clock. Its phases are labeled ϕ_1, ϕ_2, and ϕ_3. During phase ϕ_1, data are input to the master flip-flop and held at node B. On the other hand, during ϕ_2 the new data in the master flip-flop are transferred to the slave input at node C and produces the output at node

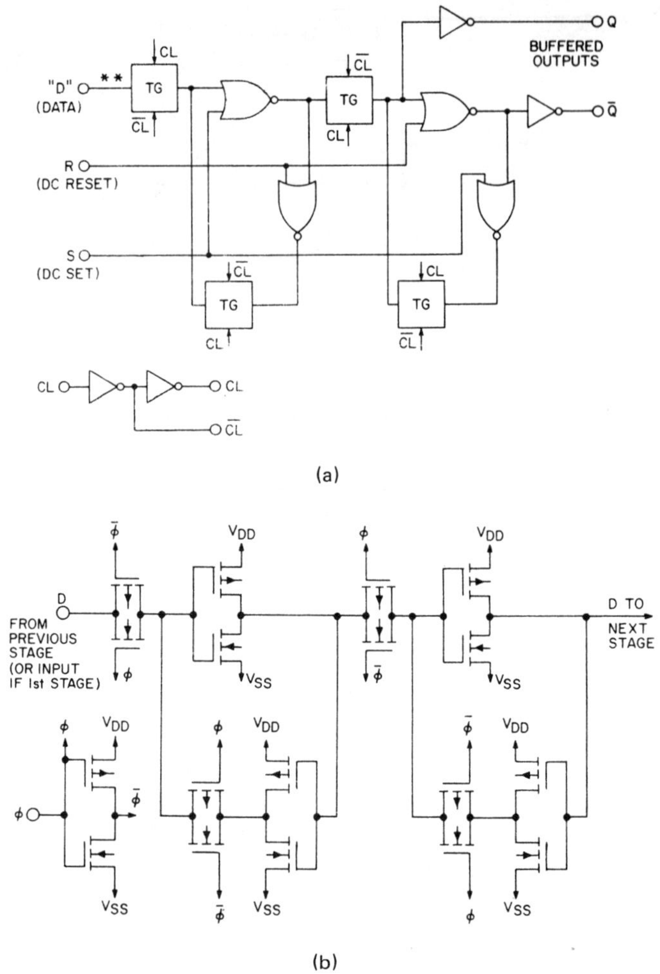

Fig. 5.5 (a) CMOS D-type flip-flop logic diagram (RCA Solid State Division); (b) CMOS D-type flip-flop circuit (RCA Solid State Division).

D. MOSFET T_7 is used to feed back the output of the slave to node A during phase ϕ_3. This locks the output in the new state.

C_1 and C_2 are the capacitive nodes of the circuit. Data are stored in the master and slave flip-flops as charge on capacitive nodes C_1 and C_2, respectively.

Static and Dynamic Operation

In our earlier study of ROMs and RAMs, we found that both of these devices could be manufactured with static and dynamic circuitry. Both types of shift registers are also in use.

A static shift register stores data as 0 or 1 logic levels in active flip-flop circuits. If the clock input of a static register is set to the appropriate logic

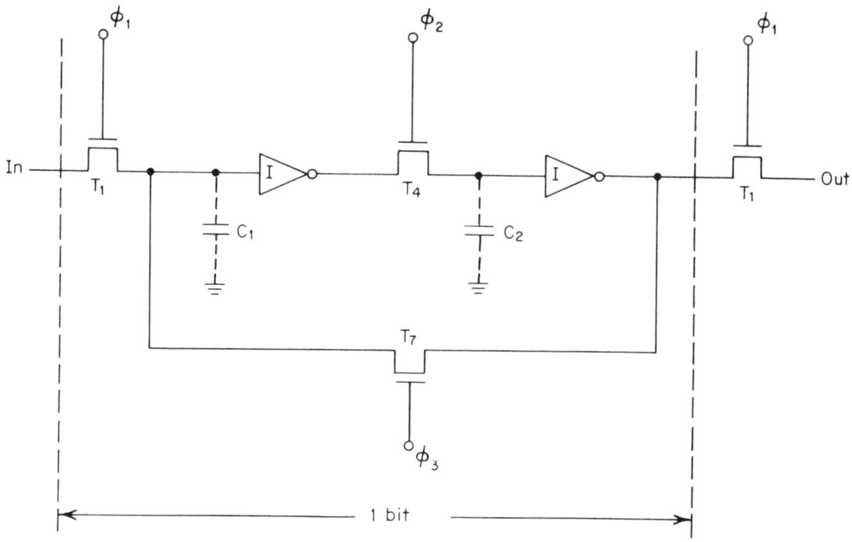

Fig. 5.6 MOS D-type flip-flop circuit (Texas Instruments, Incorporated).

level, operation of the device is switched to a temporary storage state. Data are maintained in the flip-flops until the clock is again pulsed.

This does not mean that a static shift register is a nonvolatile memory device. If the power supply is removed from the register, all data are lost.

On the other hand, in a dynamic shift register data are stored in flip-flops that are only active during certain clock phases. During these active intervals, the capacitive nodes that hold the data are recharged. Between clock phases, charge on the capacitive nodes begins to leak off. For this reason, dynamic shift registers must be continuously clocked at a minimum rate; otherwise, data would be lost. The process of clocking a dynamic shift register to maintain its data is called *refreshing*.

Static shift register devices that are manufactured with both bipolar and MOS technology circuitry are available. However, all dynamic devices are made with MOS technology.

5.3 THE SERIAL-IN, SERIAL-OUT SHIFT REGISTER[3]

In Section 5.2 we introduced the shift register and its storage cells. Here the first configuration, the serial-in, serial-out shift register, is discussed in detail.

Figure 5.7(a) shows a block diagram of a 4-bit serial-in, serial-out shift register. On this block, the *serial input* lead is marked with the symbol S_i and the *serial output* S_o. The input and output of data are synchronized by the signal at the *clock input CLK*. This type of register can be used for temporary storage when both input and output data are in serial form.

[3] Walter A. Triebel, *Integrated Digital Electronics*, © 1979. Adapted by permission of Prentice-Hall, Inc., Englewood Cliffs, N.J.

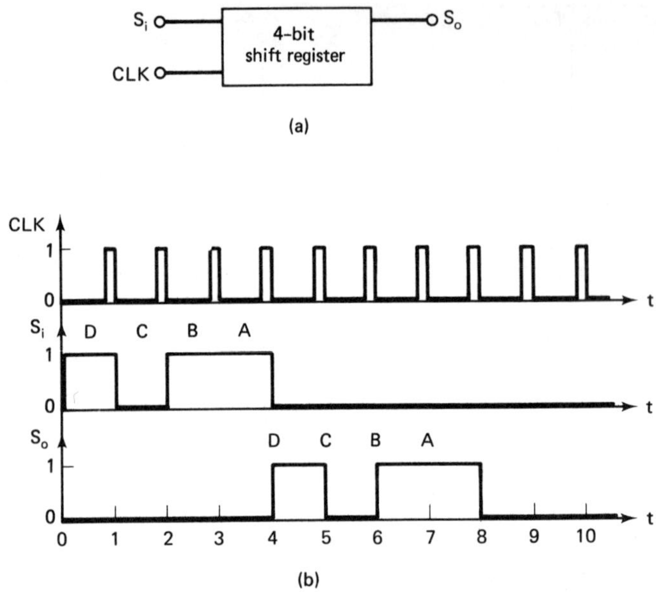

Fig. 5.7 (a) Four-bit serial-in, serial-out shift register block (Walter A. Triebel, Integrated Digital Electronics, © 1979. Adapted by permission of Prentice-Hall, Inc., Englewood Cliffs, N.J.); (b) input/output waveforms (Walter A. Triebel, Integrated Digital Electronics, © 1979. Adapted by permission of Prentice-Hall, Inc., Englewood Cliffs, N.J.).

Waveforms of the circuit's operation are given in Fig. 5.7(b). As the 0-to-1 transition occurs for the first clock pulse at the *CLK* input, a logic 1 representing bit *D* of the 4-bit input data word is written into the shift register from S_i.

For each clock pulse that follows, another bit of data is loaded into the register. At the same time, the data held in all flip-flops within the register shift 1 cell toward the S_o output. After the fourth clock pulse, bit *D* of the input data word is written out at S_o.

In this example, the serial data at the input is binary code $DCBA$=1011, and it is delayed by four clock cycles between input and output of the register. In this way we see that the shift register delays the serial data by a number of clock cycles equal to the number of flip-flops in the register.

The amount of time delay experienced between input of a data bit and the instant at which it appears at the output is determined by the frequency of the clock. Its period can be found as the reciprocal of frequency. For instance, for a 100-kHz clock the period of a cycle is found to be

$$T = \frac{1}{f} = \frac{1}{100 \text{ kHz}} = 10 \ \mu\text{s}$$

For serial data to pass from input to output, four clock cycles must elapse. This gives a time delay t_d between serial input and serial output equal to 40 μs:

$$t_d = 4T = 4(10\ \mu s) = 40\ \mu s$$

7491 8-Bit Shift Register

The 7491 device is an MSI circuit that contains an 8-bit static serial-in, serial-out shift register. It is a member of the 7400 family of TTL devices. In Fig. 5.8(a), the circuitry within the 7491 is shown and the IC pin layout is given in Fig. 5.8(b). Here we see the register is formed by cascading eight set-reset flip-flops.

The circuit has two serial data inputs that are labeled A and B. The signal sent to the set input S of the first S-R flip-flop is the AND function of logic signals A and B. On the other hand, the logic level of reset input R is the complement of the S data:

$$S=AB$$

$$R=\overline{S}=\overline{AB}$$

The clock input to the register is first inverted and then applied to all eight flip-flops in parallel. This inverter is used to buffer the clock input so that it acts like one TTL load to circuits supplying the input.

Let us assume that both the A and B inputs are logic 1. This makes the set input of flip-flop 1 logic 1 and its reset input logic 0. On the positive edge of the first clock pulse, the Q output on flip-flop 1 switches to logic 1 and $\overline{Q}$ to logic 0. The outputs of flip-flop 1 are used as inputs to flip-flop 2.

At the next clock pulse, the set input on flip-flop 2 is 1 and reset is 0. These data cause the Q output to set to 1, and $\overline{Q}$ switches to 0. At the same moment, a logic 0 or 1 due to a new A and B input is loaded into flip-flop 1. As the clock input is pulsed one more time, data shift another flip-flop toward the S_o output and another data bit enters flip-flop 1.

On the eighth clock pulse, the data bit entered at the serial input on the first clock pulse appears at serial output S_o. The complement of the serial input is produced at the $\overline{S}_o$ output.

To operate, the 7491 requires a 5-V dc power supply. This voltage is applied between $+V_{CC}$ at pin 5 and GND at pin 10. The value of supply voltage is rated to vary by ±5% before the device will fail to operate correctly. Typical power consumption of the 7491 register is 175 mW.

In our earlier description of operation for the 7491, we neglected its *propagation-delay* characteristic. Actually, a short interval of time is required for data to pass through the flip-flops in the register. A maximum propagation delay of 40 ns can be experienced between the write in of data at the S_i input and the transition of the output logic level at S_o. Waveforms showing the clock to output propagation delays t_{pHL} or t_{pLH} are given in Fig. 5.9(a). Their maximum values are both 40 ns.

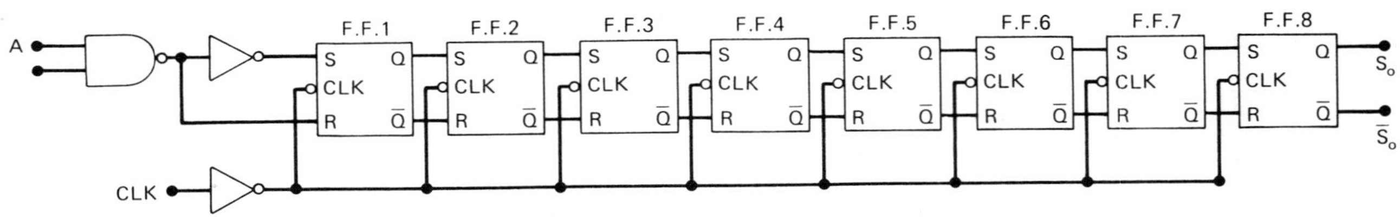

(a)

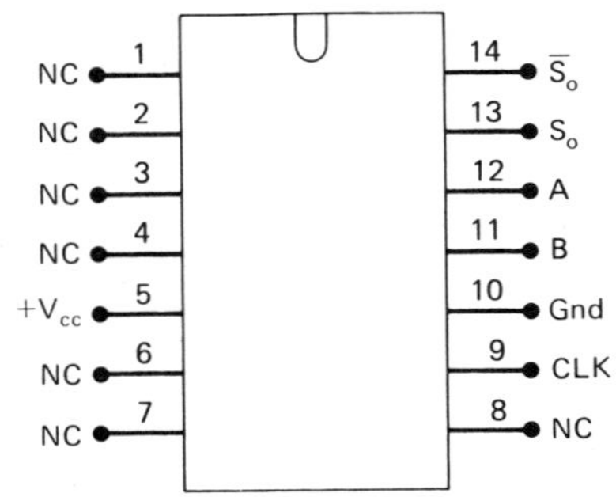

(b)

Fig. 5.8 (a) 7491 8-bit shift register circuit (Walter A. Triebel, Integrated Digital Electronics, © 1979. Adapted by permission of Prentice-Hall, Inc., Englewood Cliffs, N.J.); (b) 7491 pin layout (Walter A. Triebel, Integrated Digital Electronics, © 1979. Adapted by permission of Prentice-Hall, Inc., Englewood Cliffs, N.J.).

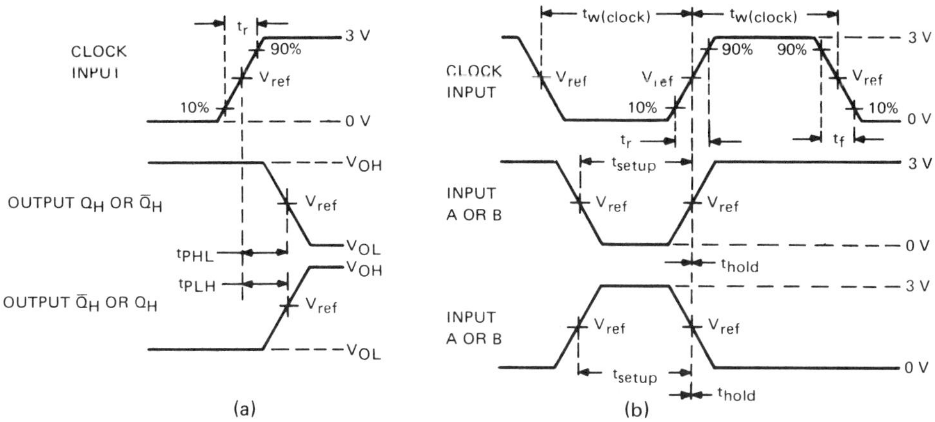

Fig. 5.9 (a) Propagation delay time characteristics (Texas Instruments, Incorporated); (b) setup and hold time switching characteristics (Texas Instruments, Incorporated).

Another important switching property of a shift register is its *maximum clock frequency*, f_{max}. This tells the maximum repetition rate of the signal that can be applied to the clock input. For the 7491, its value is 10 MHz.

The last switching characteristics we shall introduce for the shift register are *setup time* and *hold time*. Setup time tells how long input data must be present at the data input before the clock edge occurs that loads the data into the master section of the input flip-flop. This property is labeled t_{SETUP} for the 7491 register and has a value of 25 ns. On the other hand, hold time indicates how long data must be held at the input after it is loaded with a clock edge. The hold time of the 7491 is zero. Therefore, data do not have to be maintained at the input after the loading edge of the clock pulse has occurred. Figure 5.9(b) shows waveforms with the setup and hold times for data at the *A* and *B* inputs.

Input and output logic levels are the same as for all other devices in the 7400 family of TTL integrated circuits. The maximum low level at the input V_{ILmax} is rated at 0.8 V and the minimum high level V_{IHmin} is rated at 2 V. Furthermore, its low-level output voltage rating is V_{OLmax} = 0.4 V and high-level output voltage rating is V_{OHmin} = 2.4 V.

EXAMPLE 5.1 Find the S_o output waveform for the 7491 shift register of Fig. 5.10(a). It has the *A* input and *CLK* signals shown in Fig. 5.10(b).

SOLUTION When the *B* input is logic 1, the *A* data are entered to S-R flip-flop 1 in the register. On the eighth clock pulse, the *A* data bit appears at the S_o output. This occurs at time t = 8 μs. For the ninth clock pulse and on, data bits B through H are provided at the output.

In applications where more than 8 bits of serial data storage are required, 7491 devices can be cascaded to obtain larger capacity. For instance, Fig. 5.11 shows how two 7491 devices are connected to form a 16-bit

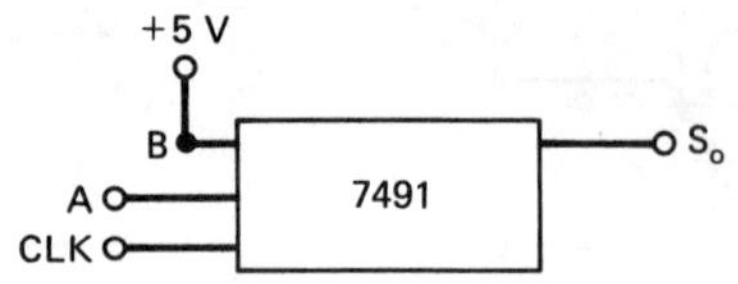

(a)

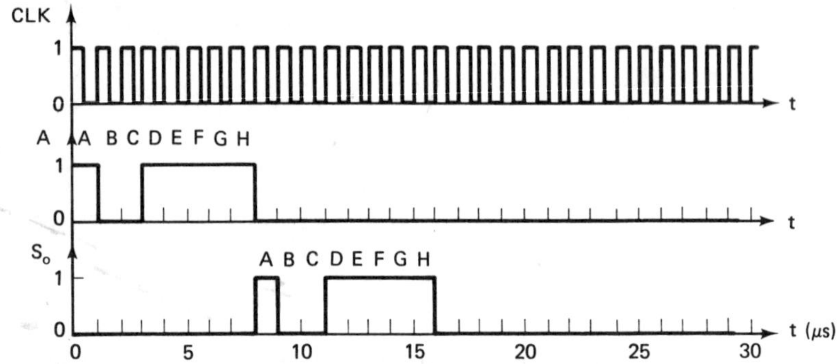

(b)

Fig. 5.10 (a) 7491 serial-in, serial-out shift register (Walter A. Triebel, Integrated Digital Electronics, © 1979. Adapted by permission of Prentice-Hall, Inc., Englewood Cliffs, N.J.); (b) input/output waveforms (Walter A. Triebel, Integrated Digital Electronics, © 1979. Adapted by permission of Prentice-Hall, Inc., Englewood, Cliffs, N.J.).

serial-in, serial-out register. Notice that the two registers are *cascaded* by feeding the serial output of the left register to the A input of the register on the right. The clock inputs are wired in parallel and the B inputs wired to the 1 logic level. Now a 16-bit data word can be written into the register from the A input of the left register and read out from S_o on the right device.

9328 Dual 8-Bit Shift Register

Another popular bipolar shift register IC is the 9328. This device contains two static 8-bit serial-in, serial-out shift register circuits. A block diagram of its registers is shown in Fig. 5.12(a) and its pin layout in Fig. 5.12(b).

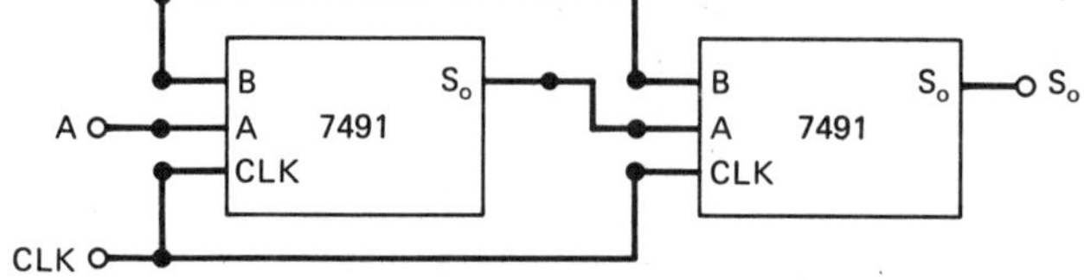

Fig. 5.11 Sixteen-bit serial-in, serial-out shift register.

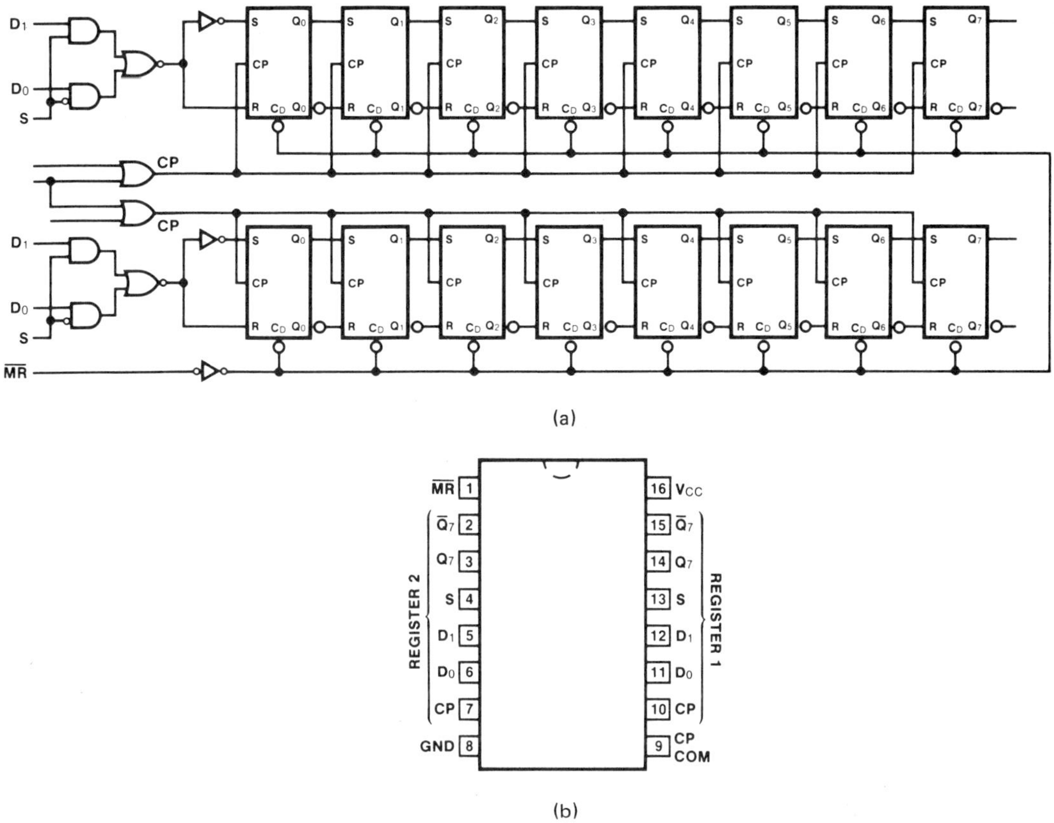

Fig. 5.12 (a) 9328 block diagram (Fairchild Camera and Instrument Corp.); (b) 9328 pin layout (Fairchild Camera and Instrument Corp.).

Looking at the block diagram, we see that the shift registers are formed by connecting eight set-reset flip-flops in cascade. Each register has a pair of data inputs which are labeled D_0 and D_1. The logic level at the data select input S decides which of the input signals is supplied to the input of the first flip-flop in the register. When S is at the 0 logic level, the logic 0 or 1 at D_0 is used as the data input. On the other hand, a logic 1 at S selects the data at D_1.

As the *CP* input is switched from logic 0 to logic 1, data are loaded into the first flip-flop. At the eighth clock pulse, this bit of data enters the last flip-flop in the register and appears at the Q_7 output. The complement of the data at Q_7 is presented at the $\overline{Q}_7$ output.

Notice that there are two types of clock inputs on the 9328. They are the separate clock leads labeled *CP* and the *common clock* denoted *CP COMM*. When data are to be entered independently into the two registers, the circuits must be clocked at their respective *CP* leads. However, if the two registers are to be used together, for instance in cascade to make a 16-bit register, both registers are clocked at the same time from the *CP COMM* lead. If the clocks are held at the 0 logic level, data are stored within the register.

The master reset input can be used to clear the data held in the register. When $\overline{MR}$ is pulsed to the logic 0 level, the outputs of the flip-flops in both registers are cleared to Q=0 and $\overline{Q}$=1. Reset occurs independent of the state of the other input signals.

The minimum data setup time t_s for the 9328 is 20 ns, its maximum propagation delay t_p is 35 ns, and its maximum clock frequency is 20 MHz.

CD4006B 18-Bit Shift Register

The CD4006B is a widely used static CMOS shift register device. It contains two 4-bit registers and two 5-bit registers. A block diagram of this circuitry is shown in Fig. 5.13. These register sections can be interconnected to form serial-in, serial-out registers with capacities from 8 to 18 bits. All four sections of the CD4006B are clocked from a common clock input and data enter on the negative edge of the clock pulse.

The dc power supply for the CD4006B, $+V_{DD}$ measured with respect to V_{SS}, can range from 3 to 18 V. With the supply set to +5 V, the quiescent power dissipation of the device is just 1.5 μW. This is more than 1 million times lower than the power required to operate an 8-bit bipolar register. When working from a +5-V supply, the input and output logic levels are rated as V_{ILmax} = 1.5 V, V_{IHmin} = 3.5 V, V_{OLmax} = 0.05 V, and V_{OHmin} = 4.95 V.

The timing properties of CMOS shift registers also differ from those of bipolar devices. CMOS circuitry is much slower than bipolar. When the CD4006B is operating at +5 V, the propagation delay t_p between input and output is 200 ns. This amount of time is about five times longer than for a similar TTL device. The typical value of data setup time t_s is 50 ns, which is also longer than for a TTL device, and its typical value of maximum clock frequency is 5 MHz.

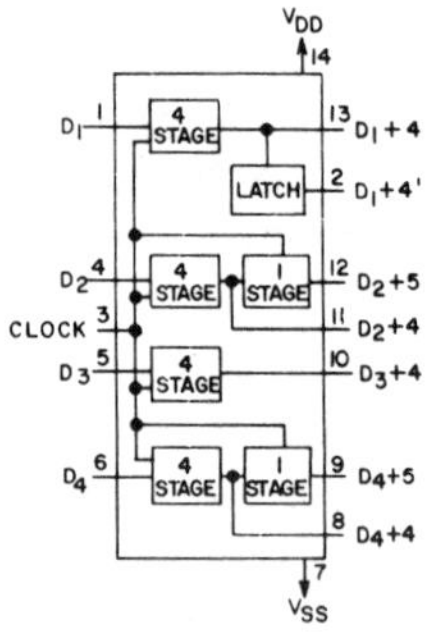

Fig. 5.13 CD4006B block diagram (RCA Solid State Division).

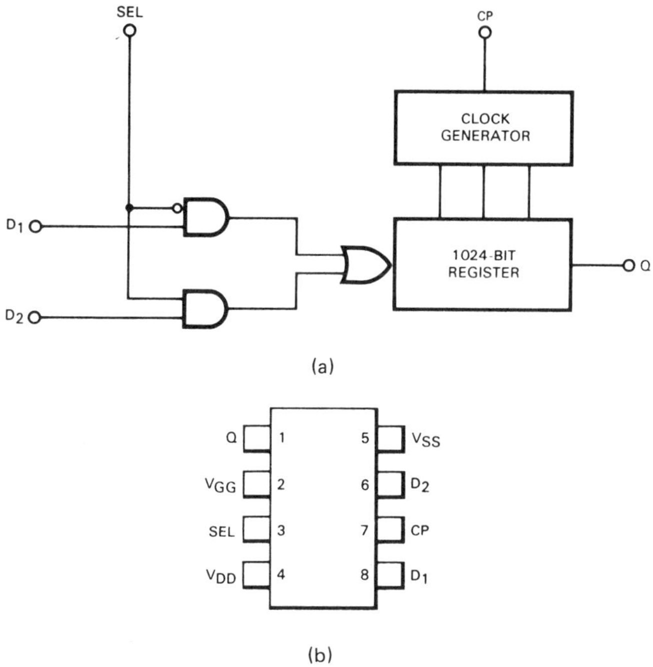

Fig. 5.14 (a) 2533 block diagram (Fairchild Camera and Instrument Corp); (b) 2533 pin layout (Fairchild Camera and Instrument Corp.).

2533 1024-Bit Shift Register

The 2533 integrated circuit contains a single 1024-bit static serial-in, serial-out register. The device is made with PMOS circuitry which permits construction of a register with such a large storage capacity.

A block diagram of the 2533 register is given in Fig. 5.14(a) and its pin layout in Fig. 5.14(b). In the block diagram there are two serial data inputs marked D_1 and D_2. When the *data select input SEL* is logic 0, data applied to D_1 are passed to the input of the 1*k*-bit register. However, a 1 at *SEL* inputs data from D_2. Data are written into the register on the 1-to-0 transition of clock pulse *CP*. The serial output is produced at the *Q* lead.

The 2533 device requires three dc power-supply voltages. These voltages are V_{SS} = +5 V, V_{DD} = 0 V, and V_{GG} = -12 V. Power dissipation on a per bit of storage basis is lower than for a bipolar register but still much higher than for CMOS. The maximum power dissipation of the device is 398 mW.

The data input, clock input, and data output of the 2533 are TTL-compatible. Its inputs are rated at V_{IHmin} = 4 V and V_{ILmax} = 0.8 V. An external load resistor is required from the input lead to the V_{SS} supply for each input that is driven from the output of a TTL circuit. Furthermore, the serial output is capable of driving one TTL load. Output logic levels are rated at V_{OHmin} = 4 V and V_{OLmax} = 0.4 V.

The propagation delay of the 2533 is 300 ns. This time is much longer than for bipolar registers and close to that of a CMOS register. Its minimum setup time t_{DS} is 70 ns and its maximum clock frequency is 1.5 MHz.

5.4 THE SERIAL-IN, PARALLEL-OUT SHIFT REGISTER

One of the most important features of shift registers is their ability to convert data between the serial and parallel forms. For example, data are normally communicated between digital systems in serial form over transmission lines. But after the data are received by the system, it is faster to process the data in parallel form. Shift registers play an important role in this area of electronic applications.

Serial-to-parallel data conversion can be performed with a serial-in, parallel-out shift register. A block diagram of this type of register is shown in Fig. 5.15(a). Here we see that the circuit has a single data input, labeled S_i. Entry of data at this lead is synchronized to pulses at the *CLK* input. Four *parallel data outputs*, A_o, B_o, C_o, and D_o, are provided on the circuit. Of these, D_o usually represents the MSB and A_o the LSB.

During normal serial-in, parallel-out operation, one bit of data after the other is clocked into the register from serial input S_i. At the same time that a new bit of data enters, the bits already stored within the register shift one flip-flop toward the D_o output.

As an example, let us assume that the flip-flop storage cells within the register have already been cleared. This makes all outputs initially zero.

$$D_oC_oB_oA_o=0000$$

The serial data that are to be applied to the input is shown in Fig. 5.15(b). It represents $DCBA$=1011.

At the 0-to-1 transition of the first pulse at *CLK*, the *D* bit of data is written into the *A* flip-flop. This makes output A_o equal 1. All other outputs stay at the 0 logic level.

$$D_oC_oB_oA_o=0001$$

These outputs are shown in the waveforms of Fig. 5.15(b).

Before the second clock pulse occurs, the logic level of S_i changes to binary 0. As the positive edge of the clock pulse occurs, the 1 stored in flip-flop *A* shifts into the output of the *B* flip-flop and the 0 at S_i is loaded into flip-flop *A*. This gives the new output state:

$$D_oC_oB_oA_o=0010$$

After this, the data at S_i switches back to binary 1. The third clock pulse causes the data in flip-flops *A* and *B* to shift into the *B* and *C* flip-flops,

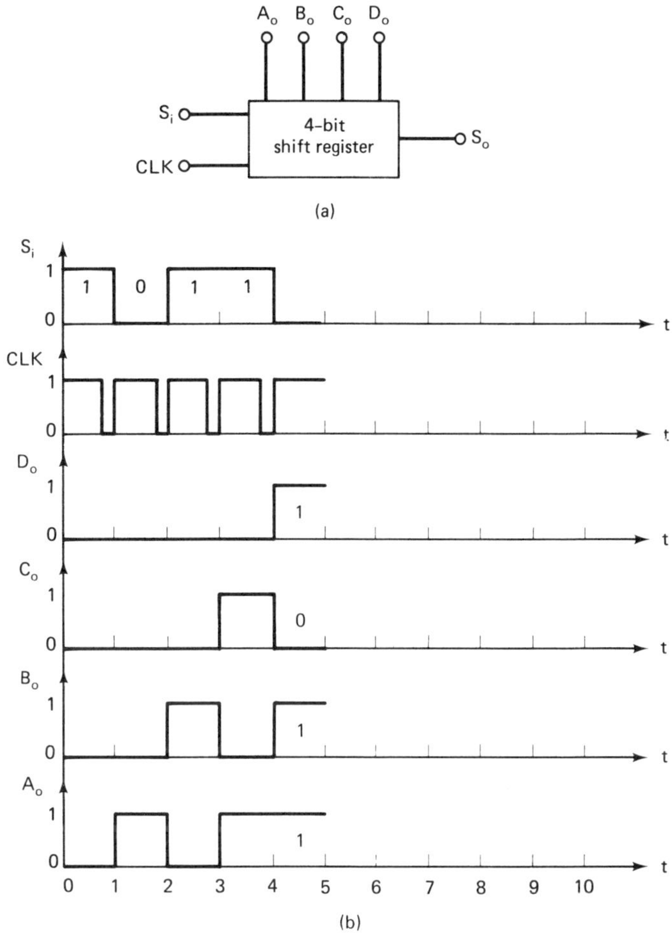

Fig. 5.15 (a) Serial-in, parallel-out shift register block; (b) input/output waveforms.

respectively. At the same moment, a 1 is written into the A flip-flop:

$$D_oC_oB_oA_o=0101$$

The fourth clock pulse shifts the data stored in each flip-flop through the register and writes a 1 into the A flip-flop. Now the four data bits are all held in the register and the parallel output is

$$D_oC_oB_oA_o=1011$$

As long as no more clock pulses are applied to the circuit, the data are stored in the register. The outputs provide the parallel code 1011 and the serial-to-parallel data conversion is complete.

74164 8-Bit Shift Register

The 74164 is a widely used bipolar integrated circuit that contains a static 8-bit serial-in, parallel-out register. The circuit within the 74164 is shown in Fig. 5.16.

The operation of this circuit is similar to that just described for the block diagram in Fig. 5.15(a); however, a *clear input* is included on the circuit. When *CLEAR* is set to logic 0, its inverter output switches the clear inputs on all flip-flops to logic 1. This clears outputs Q_A through Q_H to logic 0.

Moreover, the circuit has two serial data inputs labeled *A* and *B*. These inputs are gated together with a NAND gate to produce set and reset inputs for flip-flop *A*. If both *A* and *B* are at the 1 logic level, the data bit clocked into the register is logic 1. However, if either *A* or *B* is logic 0, the data input is 0 instead of 1. Data enter the register on the 0-to-1 clock transition.

The pin assignments of the 74164 are marked in Fig. 5.16. A power supply is connected between $+V_{CC}$ at pin 14 and *GND* at pin 7. The device requires 170 mW to operate. Its input and output logic levels are identical to those indicated for other devices in the 7400 series.

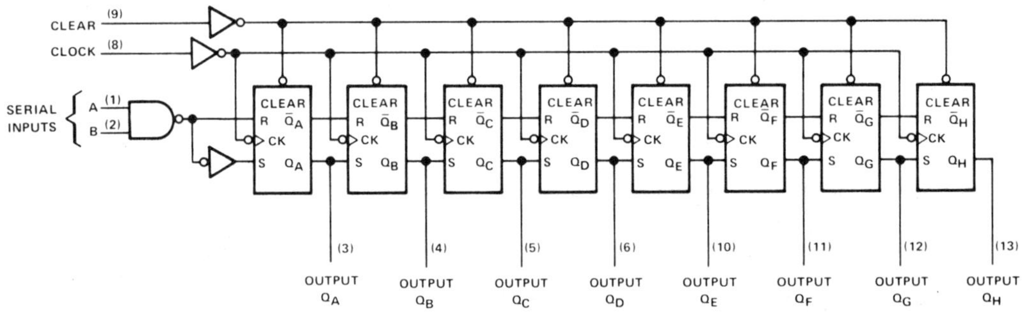

Fig. 5.16 74164 8-bit shift register circuit (Texas Instruments, Incorporated).

EXAMPLE 5.2 The *CLEAR*, *A*, *B*, and *CLOCK* waveforms of a 74164 shift register are given in Fig. 5.17. What is the output of the register after the sixth clock pulse?

SOLUTION The pulse to logic 0 at the *CLEAR* input resets the outputs of the register to logic 0.

$$Q_H Q_G Q_F Q_E Q_D Q_C Q_B Q_A = 00000000$$

At the 0-to-1 transition of the first clock pulse, the *A* input is logic 1 and *B* is logic 0. This makes the inputs to flip-flop *A*

$$S = AB = 10 = 0$$

$$R = \overline{AB} = \overline{10} = 1$$

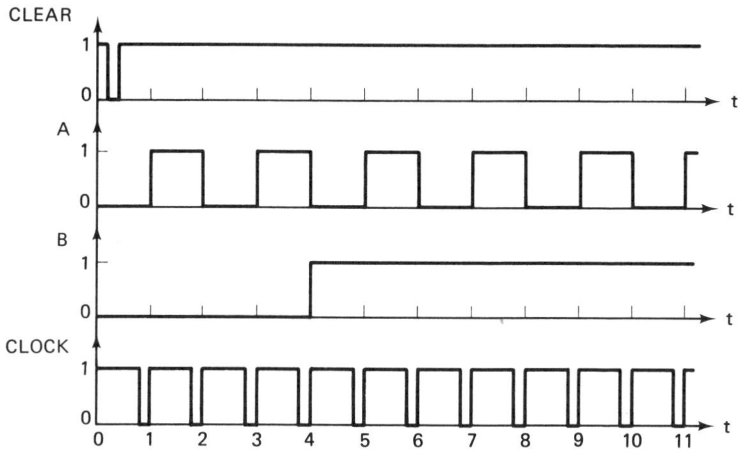

Fig. 5.17 Input waveforms.

Therefore, the A flip-flop resets and A_o switches to logic 0. At the positive edge of the next three clock pulses, the B input is still at logic 0, and logic 0 is loaded into the register for all three cases.

As the 0-to-1 edge of the fifth clock pulse occurs, both the A and B inputs are logic 1. This produces the inputs

$$S=AB=11=1$$

$$R=\overline{AB}=\overline{11}=0$$

For these inputs, flip-flop A sets and A_o switches to logic 1. This makes the output

$$Q_H Q_G Q_F Q_E Q_D Q_C Q_B Q_A=00000001$$

At the positive edge of the sixth clock pulse, input A is logic 0 and B is still at logic 1. This causes the 1 held at A_o to shift to B_o and 0 to be loaded into flip-flop A. The output after the sixth clock pulse is

$$Q_H Q_G Q_F Q_E Q_D Q_C Q_B Q_A=00000010$$

Several 74164 devices can be cascaded to form a larger-capacity register. The circuit in Fig. 5.18 combines two ICs to make a 16-bit serial-in, parallel-out register. Notice that the *CLEAR* leads of the two devices are paralleled to make a single clear input. The same connection is made for the *CLOCK* leads. Moreover, the Q_H output of the left register is used as the serial input to the register on the right.

CD4015B Dual 4-Bit Shift Register

Serial-in, parallel-out registers are also available in the CD4000 family of CMOS IC devices. The CD4015B is such a device. It has a total storage capacity of 8 bits; however, the circuitry is organized into two 4-bit shift registers.

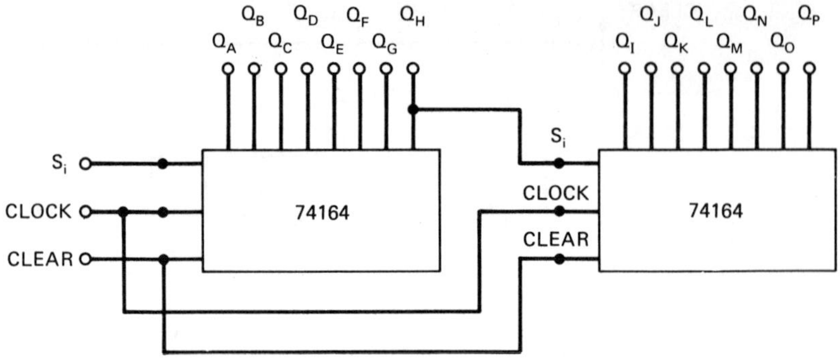

Fig. 5.18 Sixteen-bit serial-in, parallel-out shift register.

Each circuit has a structure such as that shown in Fig. 5.19. Looking at this circuit diagram, we see that the inputs to the circuit are the serial data input marked *DATA*, the *CLOCK* input, and the *RESET* input. Data at the serial input are written into the register synchronously with the positive edge of the clock pulse. The data held in the register are available at parallel outputs Q_1 through Q_4. Pulsing the *RESET* lead to logic 1 clears the output to $Q_4\,Q_3\,Q_2\,Q_1 = 0000$.

The input and output logic level ratings are the same as for other CD4000 series devices. They depend on the value of power-supply voltage. For a +5-V dc supply, the input logic levels are $V_{ILmax} = 1.5$ V and $V_{IHmin} = 3.5$ V. At the output, the logic levels are $V_{OLmax} = 0.05$ V and $V_{OHmin} = 4.95$ V.

The timing characteristics of the CD4015B are also dependent on the value of supply voltage. Let us again consider the ratings when working from a +5-V supply. The propagation delay, data setup time, and maximum clock frequency are 200 ns, 50 ns, and 5 MHz, respectively.

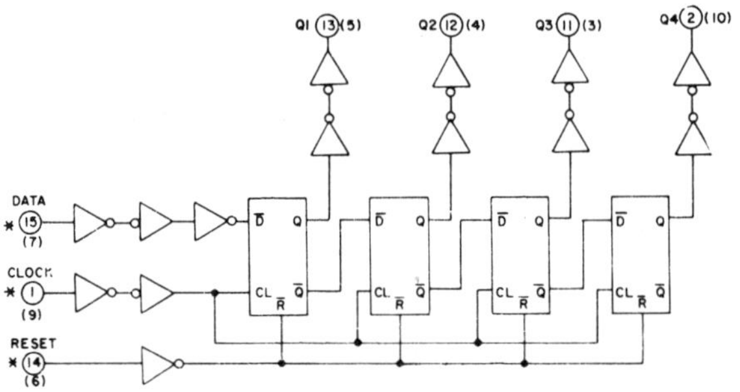

Fig. 5.19 CD4015B dual 4-bit shift register (RCA Solid State Division).

5.5 THE PARALLEL-IN, SERIAL-OUT SHIFT REGISTER[4]

In many digital systems, it is necessary to convert parallel-coded information to serial form. For instance, parallel data must be converted to serial form

[4] Ibid., p. 286–289.

for transmission over communication lines. For this application, we use a parallel-in, serial-out shift register circuit. It works the opposite of the serial-in, parallel-out circuit we studied in Section 5.4. That is, it takes binary information available on parallel data lines and converts it to an equivalent serial pattern.

A block diagram of a parallel-in, serial-out register is shown in Fig. 5.20(a). Here, we find a clock input *CLK*, load control input *LD*, serial output S_o, and four *parallel data inputs* A_i, B_i, C_i, and D_i.

During normal operation, a 4-bit code at parallel inputs $D_iC_iB_iA_i$ is written into the register by applying a pulse to the load (*LD*) control lead. After loading, the data word can be temporarily stored within the register or clocked out at the S_o lead in serial form.

The register operation just described represents what is known as *asynchronous parallel input* of data. We said that data at inputs D_i through A_i are directly loaded into the register by pulsing the *LD* control input. In this case, entry of data is independent of the clock.

Another type of parallel entry is called *synchronous data input*. Reg-

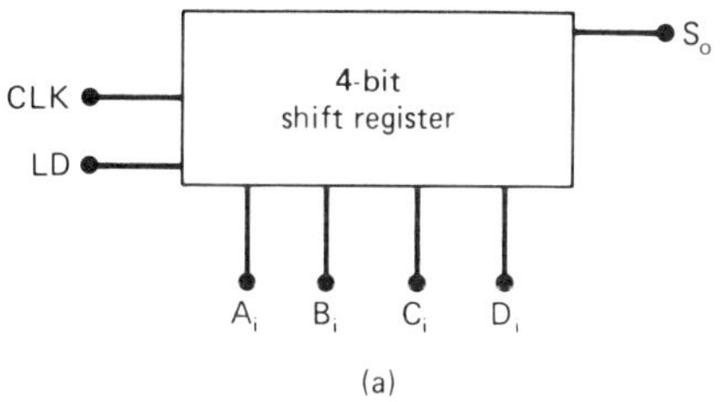

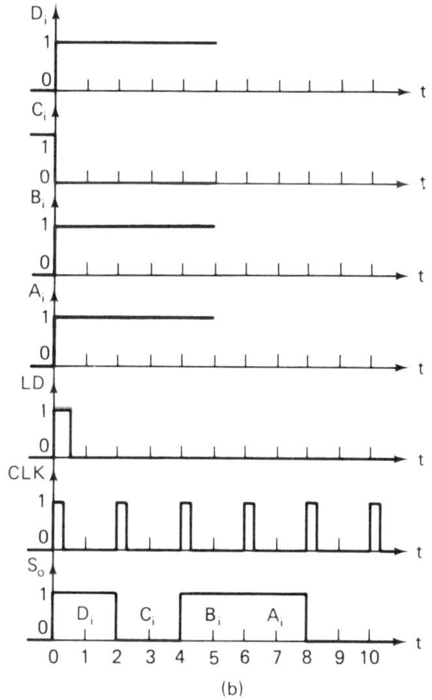

Fig. 5.20 (a) Parallel-in, serial-out shift register block (Walter A. Triebel, Integrated Digital Electronics, © 1979. Adapted by permission of Prentice-Hall, Inc., Englewood Cliffs, N.J.); (b) input/output waveforms (Walter A. Triebel, Integrated Digital Electronics, © 1979. Adapted by permission of Prentice-Hall, Inc., Englewood Cliffs, N.J.).

isters that have synchronous parallel inputs also require a load signal to be set, but data are not written into the flip-flops until the next clock pulse occurs.

Figure 5.20(b) shows input/output waveforms for a parallel-in, serial-out shift register. Looking at these signals, we see that a pulse at the *LD* lead at time $t = 0$ causes the data word $D_iC_iB_iA_i$=1011 to enter the flip-flops of the register. The logic 1 at D_i makes output S_o switch to the 1 level. The clock pulse at time $t = 2$ causes all data to shift one flip-flop toward the output and S_o switches to logic 0. As the third clock pulse occurs, the serial output switches back to 1 and stays at the 1 level for the fourth clock cycle.

If we compare the 4-bit input word 1011 to the waveform at the output lead, it is found that both are the same. However, the input is expressed in bit-parallel form, and the output is in bit-serial form.

7494 4-Bit Shift Register

The 7494 is a bipolar integrated shift register device. It contains a 4-bit static register circuit that can perform both serial-in, serial-out operation and parallel-in, serial-out operation. This circuit is shown in Fig. 5.21(a) and its pin layout in Fig. 5.21(b).

The parallel-in, serial-out operation of this circuit is similar to that described for the block diagram in Fig. 5.20(a). However, the 7494 has two sets of asynchronous parallel inputs instead of one. Notice that parallel inputs $D_1C_1B_1A_1$ are gated to the preset inputs of the flip-flops by control input PE_1. The other set of parallel inputs $D_2C_2B_2A_2$ are selected by PE_2.

Figure 5.22 shows the connection of the 7494 for operation as a parallel-in, serial-out shift register. The *parallel enable inputs* PE_1 and PE_2 load data into the register when made logic 1. In this circuit PE_2 is wired to logic 0; therefore, parallel inputs $D_2C_2B_2A_2$ are not in use.

To load data from the $D_1C_1B_1A_1$ inputs, the flip-flops in the register must first be reset by pulsing the *CLR* lead to logic 1. Clearing is necessary because the parallel data inputs drive the preset leads of the flip-flops and can only set a flip-flop. Now PE_1 is pulsed to the 1 logic level to preset those flip-flops corresponding to data inputs that are logic 1.

The clock input is positive-edge-triggered. Therefore, pulsing the *CLK* lead to logic 1 causes the data to shift toward serial output S_o. Data are stored in the register if the clock input is set to logic 0.

The 7494 device contains TTL circuitry which uses a +5-V dc supply $+V_{CC}$. Its input and output logic levels are identical to those of the other devices in the 7400 TTL family. Moreover, its timing characteristics are similar to those of other bipolar shift register devices. The maximum setup time for clocking in data is 35 ns, the maximum propagation delay between input and output is 40 ns, and the maximum clock frequency is 10 MHz.

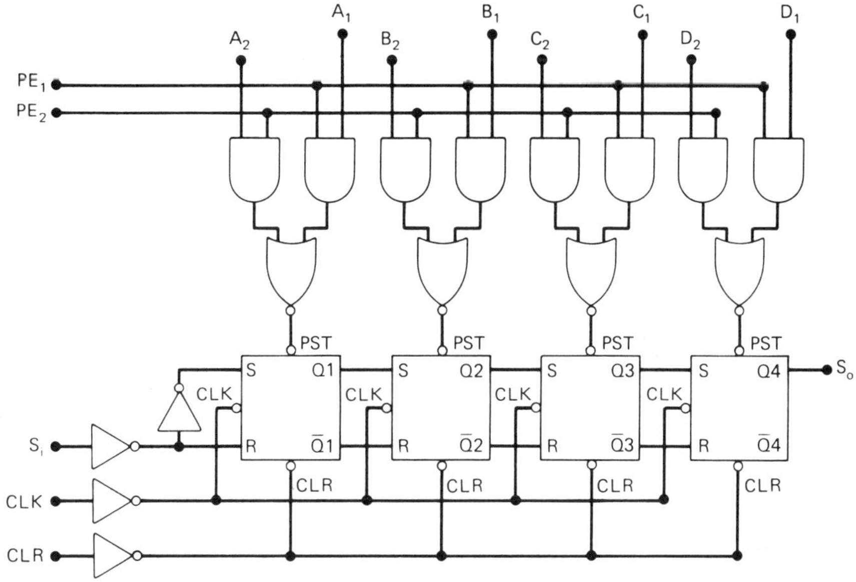

(a)

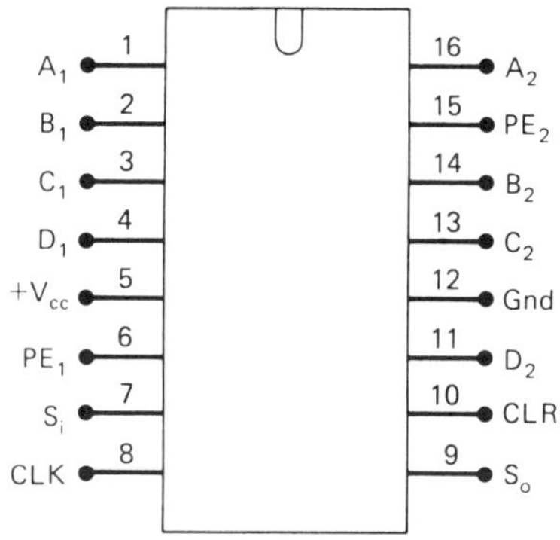

(b)

Fig. 5.21 (a) 7494 4-bit shift register circuit (Walter A. Triebel, Integrated Digital Electronics, © 1979. Adapted by permission of Prentice-Hall, Inc., Englewood Cliffs, N.J.); (b) 7494 pin layout (Walter A. Triebel, Integrated Digital Electronics, © 1979. Adapted by permission of Prentice-Hall, Inc., Englewood Cliffs, N.J.).

EXAMPLE 5.3 The input $D_2C_2B_2A_2$=1001 is applied to the parallel inputs of a 7494 register. The *CLR* lead is first pulsed to logic 1 to reset the register, and then PE_2 is pulsed to logic 1 to write in the data. Draw the serial output waveform produced at S_O.

SOLUTION When the *CLR* input goes to logic 1, flip-flops *A* through *D* are reset. As PE_2 is pulsed to 1, the *A* and *D* flip-flops are set, while the other two stay reset. This makes the register content

$$Q_4Q_3Q_2Q_1=1001$$

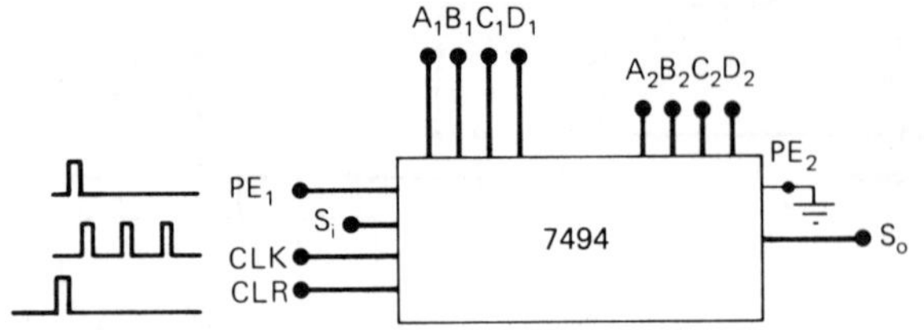

Fig. 5.22 7494 parallel-in, serial-out connection (Walter A. Triebel, Integrated Digital Electronics, © 1979. Adapted by permission of Prentice-Hall, Inc., Englewood Cliffs, N.J.).

Since Q_4 is logic 1, the S_o output is logic 1:

$$S_o = 1$$

The output waveform is shown in Fig. 5.23. At the first clock pulse, the data content of all flip-flops shift one bit toward the output. This causes the serial output to switch to logic 0. For the second pulse at *CLK*, output S_o remains at logic 0, and on the third clock pulse it switches back to logic 1.

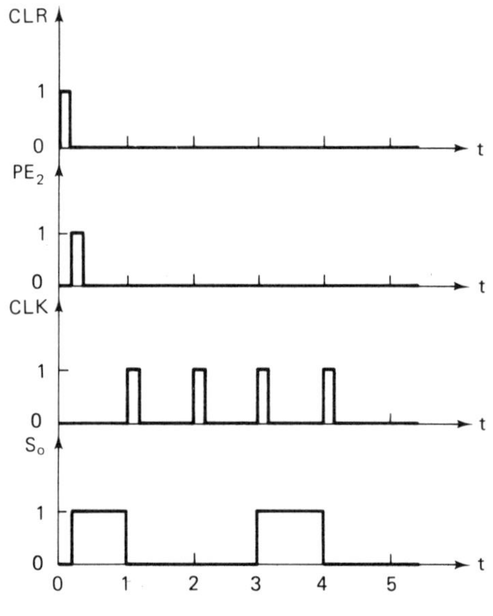

Fig. 5.23 Waveforms (Walter A. Triebel, Integrated Digital Electronics, © 1979. Adapted by permission of Prentice-Hall, Inc., Englewood Cliffs, N.J.).

Parallel-in, serial-out shift register devices can be cascaded to form large-capacity registers. For instance, Fig. 5.24 shows two 7494 devices connected to make an 8-bit register circuit. Here, group 1 parallel inputs on both devices are in use. The PE_1, *CLR*, and *CLK* leads are paralleled, and the serial output of the register on the left is input to the serial input of the register on the right.

With this circuit, an 8-bit data word can be loaded at the H_1 through A_1 inputs by clearing the register and then pulsing the PE_1 lead. Serial data are clocked out of the register at the S_o lead of the register on the right.

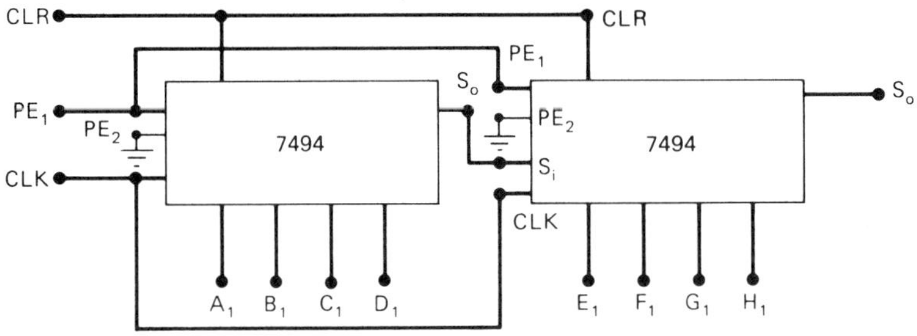

Fig. 5.24 Eight-bit parallel-in, serial-out shift register (Walter A. Triebel, Integrated Digital Electronics, © 1979. Adapted by permission of Prentice-Hall, Inc., Englewood Cliffs, N.J.).

CD4014B 8-Bit Shift Register

The CD4014B device contains a static 8-bit parallel-in, serial-out shift register. Figure 5.25 shows the circuitry within the device. This register is made with low-power CMOS circuitry and requires about 5 μW of power when operating from a +10-V supply. Actually, the CD4014B can operate from any supply voltage $+V_{DD}$ over the range 3 to 18 V.

The register circuit in the CD4014B is formed from D-type flip-flop memory cells. The eight parallel inputs P_1 through P_8 are inverted and then supplied to the preset inputs of the individual flip-flops. These are synchronous parallel inputs not asynchronous. For synchronous parallel loading of data, the *PARALLEL/SERIES* control input must first be set to the 1 logic level. At the positive edge of the next clock pulse, data at P_1 through P_8 are written into the register.

Notice that there are three serial output leads on the circuit, not just one. They are Q_6 from the output of the sixth flip-flop, Q_7 from the seventh flip-flop, and Q_8 from the eighth flip-flop. When the *PARALLEL/SERIES* control is set to logic 0 and the clock input pulsed, data are shifted through the register.

Serial data can also be entered into the CD4014B from the *SERIAL IN* lead. This is required when devices are cascaded to expand storage capacity.

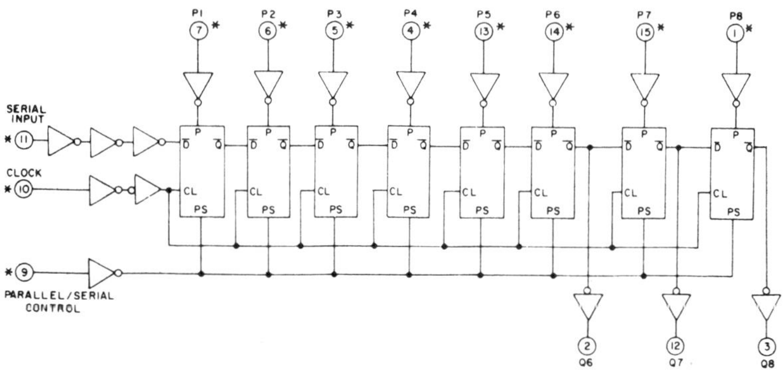

Fig. 5.25 CD4014B 8-bit shift register circuit (RCA Solid State Division).

5.6 RECIRCULATING SHIFT REGISTERS

A widely used variation on the standard serial-in, serial-out shift register is shown in Fig. 5.26. This circuit is known as a *recirculating shift register.*

Although this circuit appears to contain a standard serial-in, serial-out register, control logic has been added at the serial input. These logic gates permit two modes of operation. The first mode is where data enter from serial input D_i and shifts through the register toward serial output S_o. The circuit can be switched to a second mode, called *recirculation operation.* D_i is no longer the source of input data; instead, the logic gates switch data from serial output S_o back into the input S_i of the register. Now data can be clocked out of the register at S_o and at the same time reloaded at the front end of the register. In this way, the data stored in the register can be output but still retained for use at a later time.

Before we demonstrate the operation of the recirculating register with an example, let us look more closely at the operation of the control gates added at the serial input. From the circuit diagram in Fig. 5.26, we notice that serial data D_i are input to one AND gate while there is a feedback loop from the serial output to one input on the other AND gate. These are the two sources of data for the serial input S_i of the register. The other input on each of these gates are supplied by the *recirculation input REC* and its complement $\overline{REC}$, respectively.

The logic level at REC determines if D_i or S_o is the source of data for serial input S_i. When REC is logic 1, the lower AND gate is enabled to pass data from D_i to the input of the OR gate and through to S_i. This path is used to load the register with new data.

On the other hand, logic 0 at REC causes the $\overline{REC}$ output of the inverter to switch to logic 1. This enables the upper AND gate and allows data shifted out of the register at S_o to return through the AND gate and OR gate to the serial input. Here it is reloaded into the first flip-flop stage of the register.

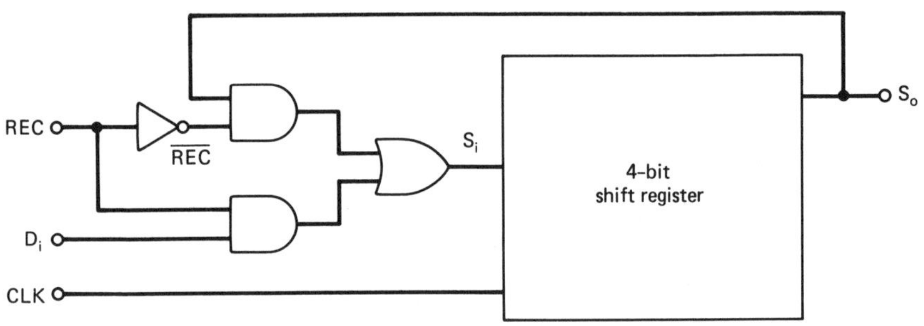

Fig. 5.26 Recirculating shift register block diagram.

EXAMPLE 5.4 The waveforms in Fig. 5.27 show the data, clock, and recirculate signals of a shift register like that shown in Fig. 5.26. Assume that the register was initially reset so that all flip-flop stages store logic 0. What is the logic level at S_o

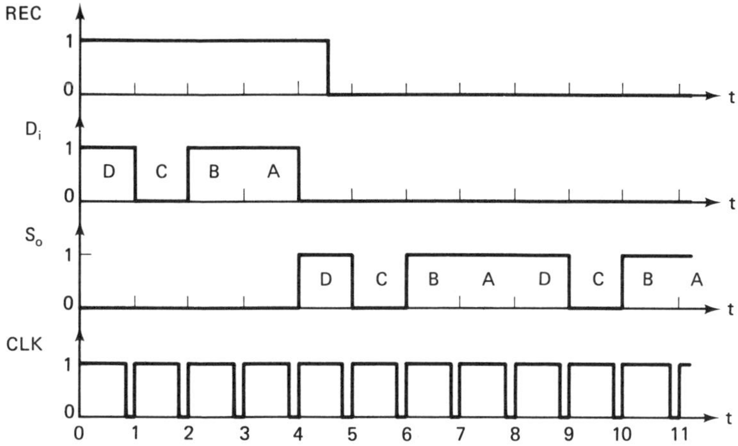

Fig. 5.27 Input/output waveforms.

after the sixth clock pulse, and what is the data word stored within the register at that moment?

SOLUTION Looking at the waveforms in Fig. 5.27, we find that the recirculation input is logic 1 during the first four clock cycles. This selects serial data input operation.

$$REC=1 \qquad \text{data input from } D_i$$

During this interval, one bit of data after the other is clocked into the register from the D_i input.

After the fourth pulse, the register holds the data word

$$DCBA=1011$$

This makes the serial output logic 1.

$$S_o=1$$

Before the fifth clock pulse occurs, the *REC* input switches to logic 0. This disables data input from D_i and sets the register for recirculation operation.

$$REC=0 \qquad \text{recirculation of data from } S_o$$

The logic 1 from S_o is applied to serial input S_i. As the fifth pulse occurs, the logic 1 from S_o is written into the first flip-flop and all data shift one flip-flop toward the output. The new data held in the register and serial output are

$$DCBA=0111$$

$$S_o=0$$

As the sixth clock pulse occurs, the register is still set up for recirculation. The 0 at

S_o is reloaded at the serial input and all data held in the register move one more cell toward S_o. The output and stored data after the sixth clock pulse are

$$DCBA = 1110$$

$$S_o = 1$$

The waveform produced at S_o is shown in Fig. 5.27.

Recirculating shift registers are required in many storage applications. For instance, they are a building block of character-generator drive circuitry in CRT terminals as well as serial memory subsystems.

AM2809 Dual 128-Bit Shift Register

The AM2809 integrated circuit is a recirculating shift register that is organized into two 128-bit recirculating register circuits. The device has a total storage capacity of 256 bits. This large storage capacity is permitted because the register circuit is constructed with PMOS circuitry.

The block diagram of Fig. 5.28(a) shows us that each register within the AM2809 is similar to that shown in the block diagram of Fig. 5.26. The one change made is that a noninverting buffer has been added at the output of each register. This buffer enables the output to directly drive one TTL load.

Both registers operate from a common clock input marked *CP* and *common recirculate input* $\overline{RC}$. When $\overline{RC}$ equals logic 1, the register is set for normal serial-in, serial-out operation. As a pulse is applied to the *CP* input, bits of data are written into the *A* and *B* registers from serial inputs *IN A* and *IN B*, respectively. At the same time, data shifted into the 128th flip-flop of the *A* and *B* registers are output at *OUT A* and *OUT B*.

If $\overline{RC}$ is switched to logic 0, the operation of the registers is changed to the recirculate mode. Now data at *IN A* and *IN B* are locked out. Each time the *CP* input is clocked, data bits are shifted to *OUT A* and *OUT B*. At the same moment, these outputs are fed back to the serial inputs, where they are reloaded into the first flip-flop of their respective register.

The clock input is positive-edge-triggered. Therefore, data are entered into the register or recirculated back to the input on the 0-to-1 transition of the clock. If *CP* is held at the 1 logic level, operation of the register is halted and data stored.

A pin layout of the AM2809 is shown in Fig. 5.28(b). Looking at the layout, we see that two power supplies are required to operate the circuitry. The $+V_{CC}$ supply at pin 8 is rated at +5V ± 5%, and the $-V_{GG}$ supply at pin 4 is rated at −12V ± 5%.

All input and output leads on the AM2809 are TTL-compatible. The logic levels of the *CP*, $\overline{REC}$, *IN A*, and *IN B* inputs are rated at V_{IHmin} = 3.3 V and V_{ILmax} = 1.05 V. Its serial outputs, *OUT A* and *OUT B*, are rated at V_{OHmin} = 3.5 V and V_{OLmax} = 0.4 V.

The data input to PMOS registers have both setup-time and hold-time requirements. For the AM2809, the setup-time t_s is 75 ns and the hold time

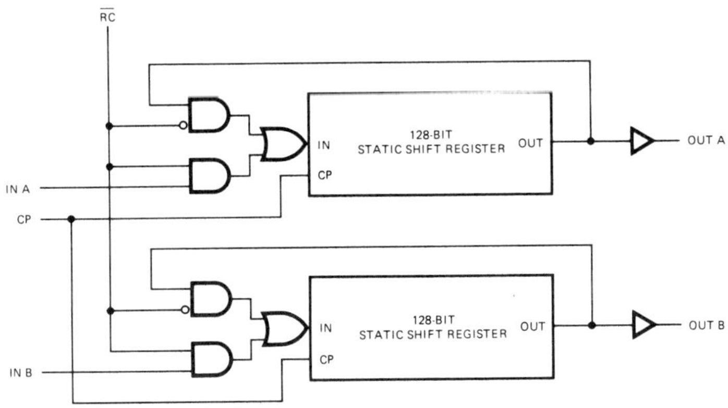

(a)

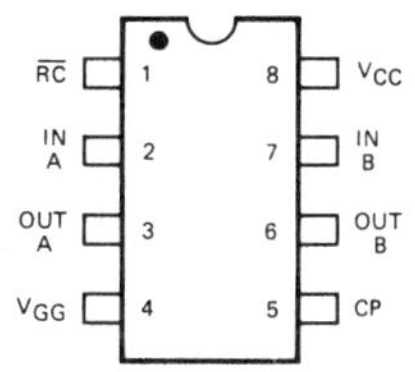

(b)

Fig. 5.28 (a) AM2809 dual 128-bit shift register circuit (copyright © 1974 Advanced Micro Devices, Inc. Reproduced with permission of copyright owner.); (b) AM2809 pin layout (copyright © 1974 Advanced Micro Devices, Inc. Reproduced with permission of copyright owner.).

is 50 ns. To assure correct data input, the logic levels of *IN A* and *IN B* must be steady for at least 75 ns before the 0-to-1 clock transition and held at these voltage values for at least 50 ns after this edge of the clock.

AM2810 Dual 128-Bit Shift Register

The AM2810 shown in Fig. 5.29(a) and (b) contains dual 128-bit recirculating shift registers that operate in a similar way to those in the AM2809. The main difference between the registers in the AM2810 and AM2809 is that the register circuits in the AM2810 do not include an internal recirculation loop. Instead, separate recirculating inputs are provided to allow external connection of the feedback loop. To do this, the output lead *OUT* must be connected with a wire to the recirculating input R_{IN}. Moreover, each register has a separate $\overline{RC}$ input. This permits the registers to be individually switched between the serial data input and recirculate modes of operation.

The AM2810 has three voltage reference leads, labeled V_{RA}, V_{RB}, and $V_{R\phi}$. These inputs are wired to the $-V_{GG}$ supply (−12V) to set the inputs for MOS compatibility or to $+V_{SS}$ (+5 V) for TTL compatibility. The V_{RA} and V_{RB} leads control the TTL/MOS compatibility of the $\overline{RC}$ and D_{IN} inputs, respectively. $V_{R\phi}$ sets the clock input for TTL/MOS compatibility.

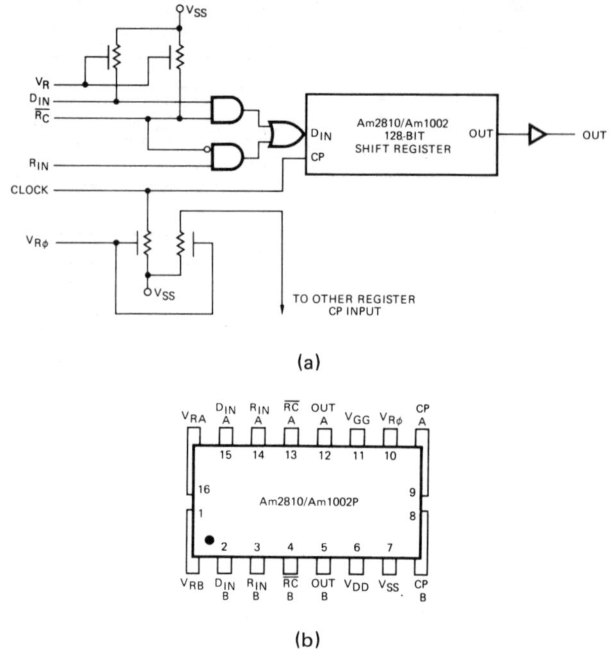

Fig. 5.29 (a) AM2810 dual 128-bit shift register circuit (copyright © 1974 Advanced Micro Devices, Inc. Reproduced with permission of copyright owner.); (b) AM2810 pin layout (copyright © 1974 Advanced Micro Devices, Inc. Reproduced with permission of copyright owner.).

3347 Quad 80-Bit Shift Register

Another popular recirculating shift register is the 3347 IC. This device has a total storage capacity of 320 bits and is internally organized into four 80-bit registers. These registers are made with PMOS circuitry.

The register circuits within the device are shown in Fig. 5.30(a). Here we find that the feedback loop from output to recirculation input is built into the IC. The inputs of the 3347 are TTL-compatible, and its output can drive one TTL load.

Looking at the pin layout in Fig. 5.30(b), we see that two power supplies are required to work the device: $+V_{SS}$ at pin 16 is +5 V and $-V_{GG}$ at pin 12 is -12 V. Both voltages are measured with respect to V_{DD} at pin 8.

The setup and hold times for input of data from the serial input are 200 ns and 100 ns, respectively.

5.7 SHIFT-RIGHT, SHIFT-LEFT REGISTERS[5]

In each of the shift register circuits discussed up to this point, data are shifted from the A flip-flop toward the D flip-flop. When data shift in this

[5] Ibid., p. 290-293.

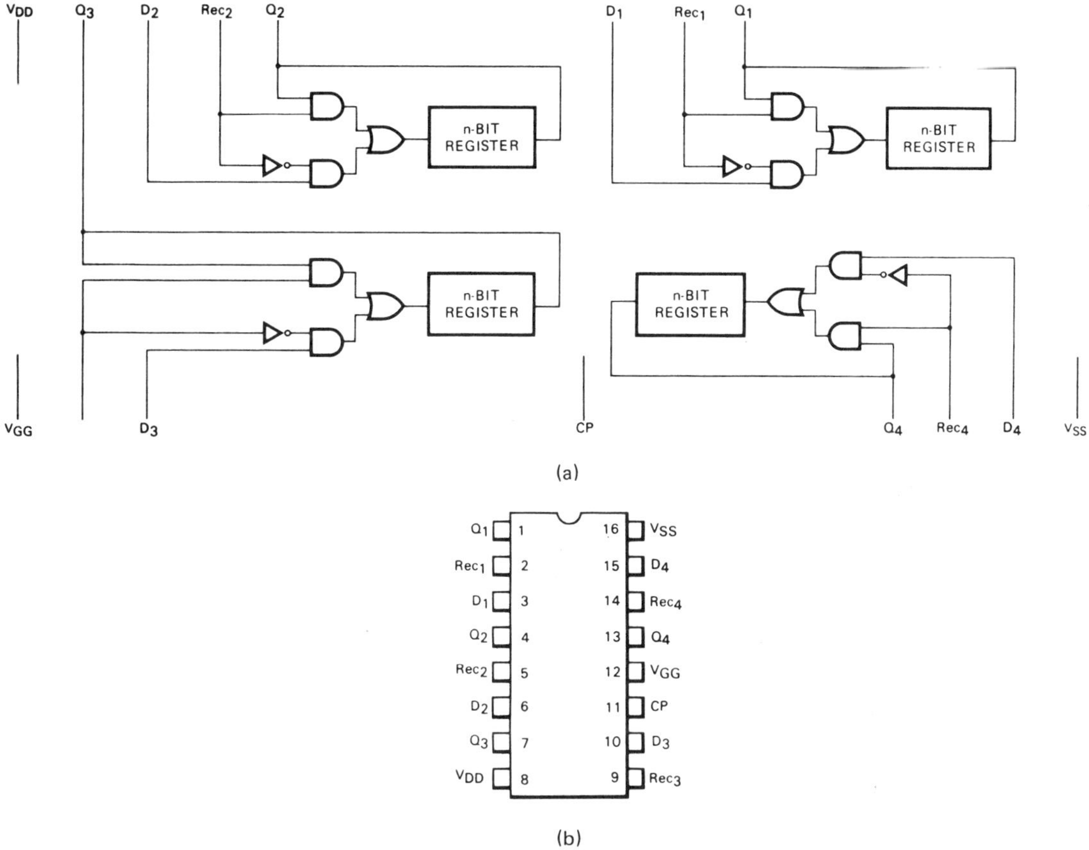

Fig. 5.30 (a) 3347 quad 80-bit shift register circuit (Fairchild Camera and Instrument Corp.); (b) 3347 pin layout (Fairchild Camera and Instrument Corp.).

direction, the circuit is known as a *shift right register.* A variation on the standard shift-right register circuit can be made which allows transfer of data in both directions. This is called a *shift-right, shift-left register.*

Looking at the shift-right, shift-left register in Fig. 5.31, we find that the register has two serial inputs. The input labeled S_{iR} is used to enter serial data during shift-right operation. On the other hand, the S_{iL} input is for entry of data during shift-left operation. Besides this, there are separate shift-right and shift-left outputs marked S_{oR} and S_{oL}, respectively. Shift-left or shift-right mode of operation are selected by the logic level of the *LEFT/ RIGHT* control input. Data are input and output synchronously with pulses at the clock input.

Shift-Right Operation

For *shift-right operation,* data are entered at the S_{iR} serial input and shifted toward the S_{oR} serial output. In this case, the *LEFT/RIGHT* control must

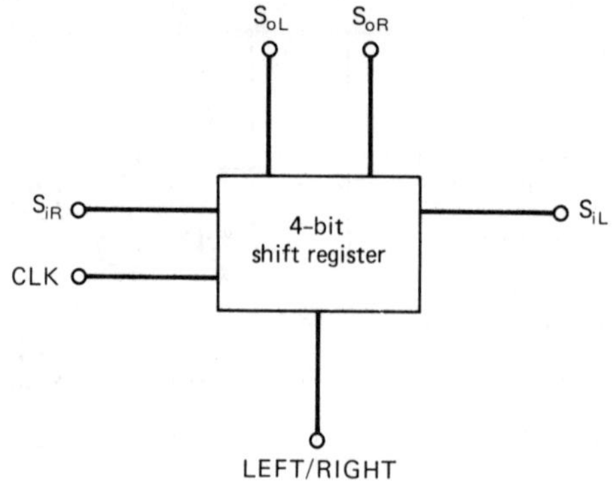

Fig. 5.31 Shift-right, shift-left register block.

first be set to the correct logic level for shift-right operation. After this, data are clocked into the register by pulses applied to the *CLK* lead.

For example, the binary word $DCBA$=0110 could be entered into the register with four clock pulses. Now the register stores the data 0110 and the logic level of the shift right output S_{oR} is 0. On the next pulse at *CLK*, the data word shifts one flip-flop toward the S_{oR} output. The new data word held in the register is $DCBA$=1100 and S_{oR} equals 1.

The original word entered into the register corresponds to decimal number 6, and after it is shifted 1 cell to the right the number is 12. In this way, we notice that a shift right of 1 cell causes the register content to be multiplied by 2.

Shift-Left Operation

If the *LEFT/RIGHT* control is set to the logic level for *shift-left operation*, data are clocked into the register at the S_{iL} input and shifts through the flip-flops toward the S_{oL} output. Let us assume that the contents of the register are again $D_o C_o B_o A_o$ equals 0110 or decimal 6. This makes the S_{oL} output logic 0. As the *CLK* input is pulsed once, data shift one flip-flop toward output S_{oL}. This makes the output S_{oL}=1 and the register now stores 0011 or decimal 3. This shows that shift left by 1 bit divides the register content by 2 instead of multiplying by 2.

7495 4-Bit Shift-Right, Shift-Left Register

The 7495 MSI device contains a static shift-right, shift-left register that can be operated in a similar way to the register shown in Fig. 5.31. Its block diagram is shown in Fig. 5.32(a) and pin layout in Fig. 5.32(b).

This register differs somewhat from the earlier block diagram. Notice that it has a serial input S_i, parallel inputs A_i through D_i, and parallel outputs A_o through D_o instead of separate shift-left and shift-right serial inputs. Moreover, the single clock input is replaced with separate CLK_R and CLK_L leads. These clock inputs are negative-edge-triggered.

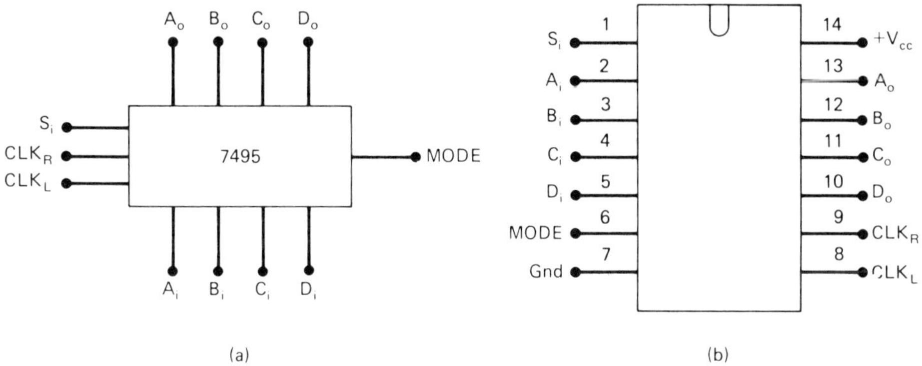

Fig. 5.32 (a) 7495 block diagram (Walter A. Triebel, Integrated Digital Electronics, © 1979. Adapted by permission of Prentice-Hall, Inc., Englewood Cliffs, N.J.); (b) 7495 pin layout (Walter A. Triebel, Integrated Digital Electronics, © 1979. Adapted by permission of Prentice-Hall, Inc., Englewood Cliffs, N.J.).

Connecting the 7495 as shown in Fig. 5.33 produces a shift-right, shift-left register circuit that operates similarly to the block shown in Fig. 5.31. Here the S_i input is used to enter data during shift-right operation and the shift-right serial output is provided at D_o. To select shift-right operation, the *MODE* control must be set to logic 0. Data are synchronously entered on the 1-to-0 transition of CLK_R.

On the other hand, logic 1 at *MODE* sets the register for shift-left operation. In this case, the D_i input serves as the serial input, and A_o is the shift-left output. As pulses are applied to CLK_L, serial data are synchronously shifted from input D_i toward output A_o.

The CLK_R and CLK_L inputs of the 7495 can be connected together to obtain a single clock input such as that shown on the block diagram in Fig. 5.31.

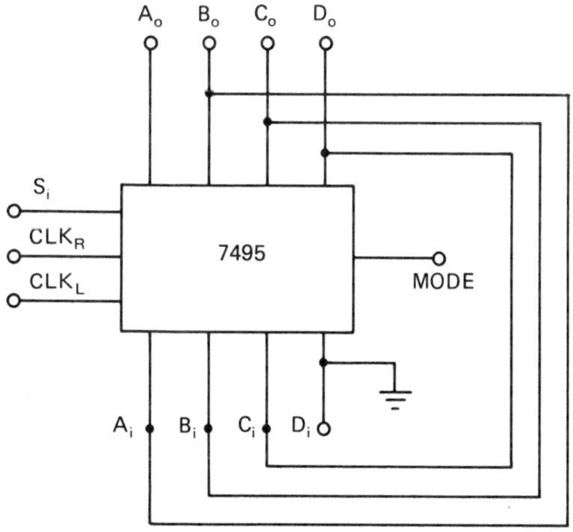

Fig. 5.33 7495 shift-right, shift-left register connection (Walter A. Triebel, Integrated Digital Electronics, © 1979. Adapted by permission of Prentice-Hall, Inc., Englewood Cliffs, N.J.).

EXAMPLE 5.5 The 7495 shift register in Fig. 5.33 has been serial-loaded with the word $DCBA$=1000 and the MODE control is set to logic 1. Find the serial output at the A_o lead as the shift-left clock input CLK_L is pulsed.

SOLUTION After the register is loaded, the parallel output is

$$D_oC_oB_oA_o=1000$$

This makes the serial output at A_o start at logic 0. For the first and second clock pulses the register contents are

$$D_oC_oB_oA_o=0100$$

and

$$D_oC_oB_oA_o=0010$$

So we see that the serial output at the A_o lead stays at the 0 logic level during both clock cycles. However, on the third clock pulse at CLK_L logic 1 is loaded into the A flip-flop, and A_o changes to the 1 logic level:

$$D_oC_oB_oA_o=0001$$

The clock and serial output waveforms are shown in Fig. 5.34.

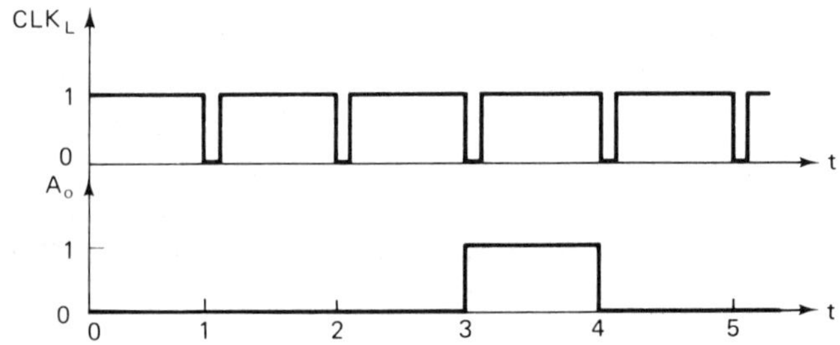

Fig. 5.34 Waveforms (Walter A. Triebel, Integrated Digital Electronics, ©1979. Adapted by permission of Prentice-Hall, Inc., Englewood Cliffs, N.J.).

CD40100B 32-Bit Shift-Right, Shift-Left Register

This device contains a 32-bit static shift-right, shift-left register circuit. Figure 5.35 is a diagram of the internal architecture of the CD40100B IC. This register is constructed with low-power CMOS circuitry.

The *LEFT/RIGHT* control input determines if the register will work in the shift-left mode or shift-right mode. A logic 0 at this input selects shift-right operation. In this case, serial data presented at the *SHIFT RIGHT IN* lead are shifted to the right. It takes 32 clock pulses to shift data from the input to the *SHIFT RIGHT OUT* output. The register operates off the positive edge of the clock pulse.

Shift-left operation is obtained by switching the *LEFT/RIGHT* control

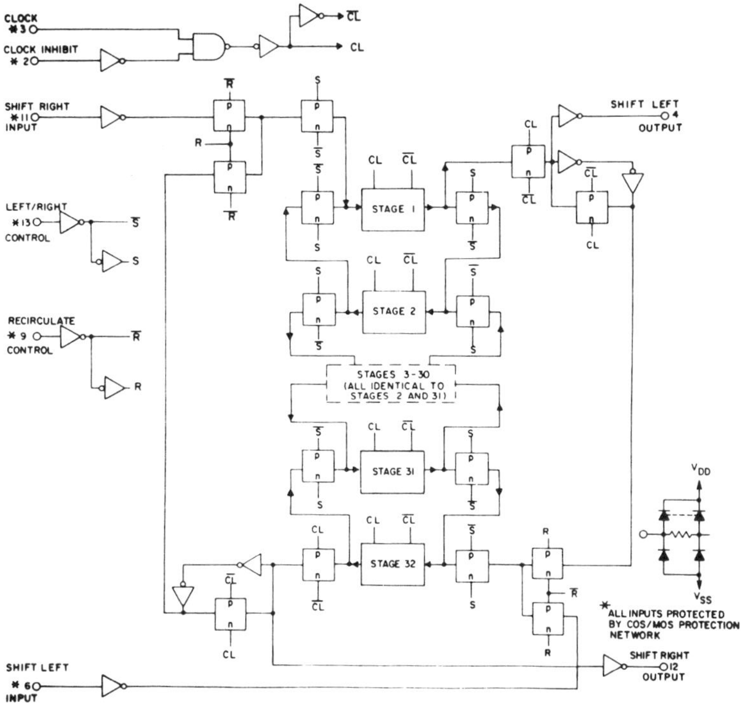

Fig. 5.35 CD40100B 32-bit shift register circuit (RCA Solid State Division).

input to the 1 logic level. Now data are clocked into the register at the *SHIFT LEFT IN* lead and output at *SHIFT LEFT OUT*.

The *RECIRCULATE CONTROL* input must be held at logic 1 during both shift-left and shift-right operation. When this input is switched to logic 0, data cannot enter from the shift-right or shift-left inputs. Instead, the internal control logic is set up to recirculate the data stored in the register. During recirculation with the *LEFT/RIGHT* control set at logic 0, data are clocked from the output of the thirty-second stage of the register back into the first stage.

On the other hand, setting the register for shift-left operation and recirculation causes the output of the first stage in the register to be reloaded at the thirty-second stage.

The CD40100B also has a *CLOCK INHIBIT* lead. If this input is held at logic 1, the operation of the register is inhibited. *CLOCK INHIBIT* must be held at logic 0 during shift-left, shift-right, or recirculation operation.

5.8 THE UNIVERSAL SHIFT REGISTER

The shift register ICs covered up to this point could be connected to form one or, at the most, two of the four basic shift register configurations. Devices are available with the capability to perform all four types of input/output: serial input, parallel input, serial output, and parallel output. These devices are known as *universal shift registers.* In this section we introduce three such devices.

8270 4-Bit Universal Shift Register

The 8270 integrated circuit is a 4-bit universal shift register device. The register circuit within the 8270 is shown in Fig. 5.36. These flip-flops and control gates are made with TTL circuitry.

From the circuit in Fig. 5.36, we find that the serial data input is labeled D_s and the parallel inputs are D_A, D_B, D_C, and D_D. Moreover, the parallel outputs of the circuit are marked A_o, B_o, C_o, and D_o. Output D_o also serves as the serial output. By selectively using these inputs and outputs, the 8270 can be set up to work as a serial-in, serial-out register, serial-in, parallel-out register, parallel-in, serial-out register, or parallel-in, parallel-out register.

The overall operation of the register is determined by the logic levels of control inputs *LOAD* and *SHIFT*. When both *LOAD* and *SHIFT* are at logic 0, the register is in the hold mode. In this case, data are stored within the register and new data cannot be entered from the serial or parallel inputs.

Changing the logic levels at the control inputs to *LOAD* equals 1 and *SHIFT* equals 0, the register is set for synchronous parallel loading of data. On the next clock pulse, data applied at parallel inputs D_A through D_D are entered into the flip-flops of the register. These data appear at parallel outputs A_o through D_o, respectively.

As the *SHIFT* input is switched to logic 1, the register goes into shift-right operation. Now data shift to the right with each pulse at the *CLOCK* input. The clock is negative-edge-triggered. Therefore, data input and output occur synchronously with 1-to-0 transitions at the clock input.

9300 4-Bit Universal Shift Register

Another popular universal shift register IC is the 9300. It also contains a 4-bit register constructed with TTL circuitry.

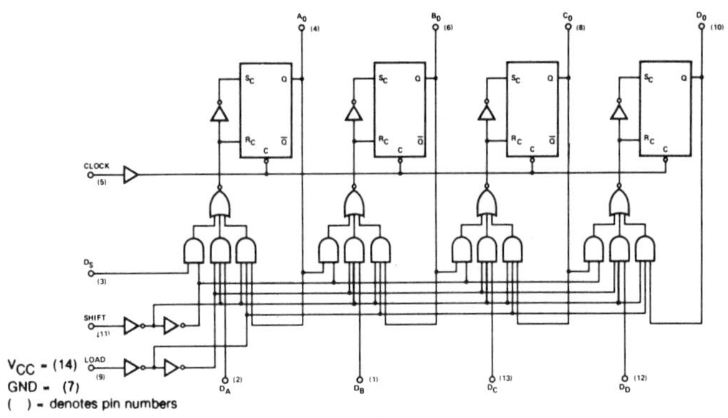

Fig. 5.36 8270 4-bit universal shift register (Permission to reprint granted by Signetics Corporation, a subsidiary of U.S. Philips Corp., 811 East Arques Avenue, Sunnyvale, CA 94806).

As shown in Fig. 5.37(a), the register is formed from four D-type flip-flops with additional logic gate circuitry to control the serial and parallel input of data. The $\overline{PE}$ input is used to select between serial and parallel input. When $\overline{PE}$ is logic 1, serial data are input from the J and $\overline{K}$ leads to the D input of the first flip-flop. However, if $\overline{PE}$ is logic 0, the parallel data bits input at P_0 through P_3 enter into their corresponding flip-flops. Loading of serial and parallel data occurs synchronously with the 0-to-1 transition of the clock.

During serial input operation, the new output state Q_0 of the first flip-flop in the register depends on the logic level of both the J and $\overline{K}$ input signals. If both J and $\overline{K}$ are logic 0, the Q_0 output switches to logic 0 on the next clock pulse. On the other hand, making J and $\overline{K}$ both 1 causes Q_0 to switch to logic 1. A logic 0 at J and logic 1 at $\overline{K}$ causes Q_0 to remain in its previous state while 1 at J and 0 at $\overline{K}$ causes Q_0 to toggle to the opposite logic level of its previous state.

To operate in the shift-right mode, input $\overline{PE}$ must be held at the 1 logic level. Then data held within the register are shifted toward the Q_3 output as the CP input is pulsed. During shift-right operation, parallel data are available at outputs Q_0 through Q_3. A serial output is provided by output Q_3 or its complement by $\overline{Q}_3$.

The 9300 device is provided with a master reset lead $\overline{MR}$. Pulsing this input to logic 0 asynchronously clears the flip-flops and initializes the output to $Q_3 Q_2 Q_1 Q_0$=0000.

A pin layout of the 9300 IC is shown in Fig. 5.37(b).

CD40104B 4-Bit Universal Shift Register

The CD40104B is another 4-bit universal shift register IC; however, it differs from the 8270 and 9300 devices in three important ways. First, its circuitry is CMOS for low-power consumption instead of TTL for high-speed operation. Second, it is bidirectional as well as having serial-in, parallel-in, serial-out, and parallel-out capability. Bidirectional means that it has the ability to shift data to the right or to the left on command. Third, the circuit is equipped with three-state outputs.

A block diagram of the CD40104B is shown in Fig. 5.38(a). Here serial data are entered at the *SHIFT RIGHT IN* or *SHIFT LEFT IN* leads while parallel inputs are applied to D_0 through D_3. The three-state outputs are marked Q_0 through Q_3. A logic 0 at the *OUTPUT ENABLE* input puts the outputs into the hi-Z third state. When the register is to be used for serial output operation, Q_3 is the shift-right serial output and Q_0 is the shift-left serial output.

The CD40104B register can be set for four different modes of operation. This is done by applying a binary code to *mode select inputs* S_0 and S_1. Codes for reset, shift-right, shift-left, and parallel-load operations are listed in Fig. 5.38(b). The selected mode changes synchronously with the positive edge of the clock.

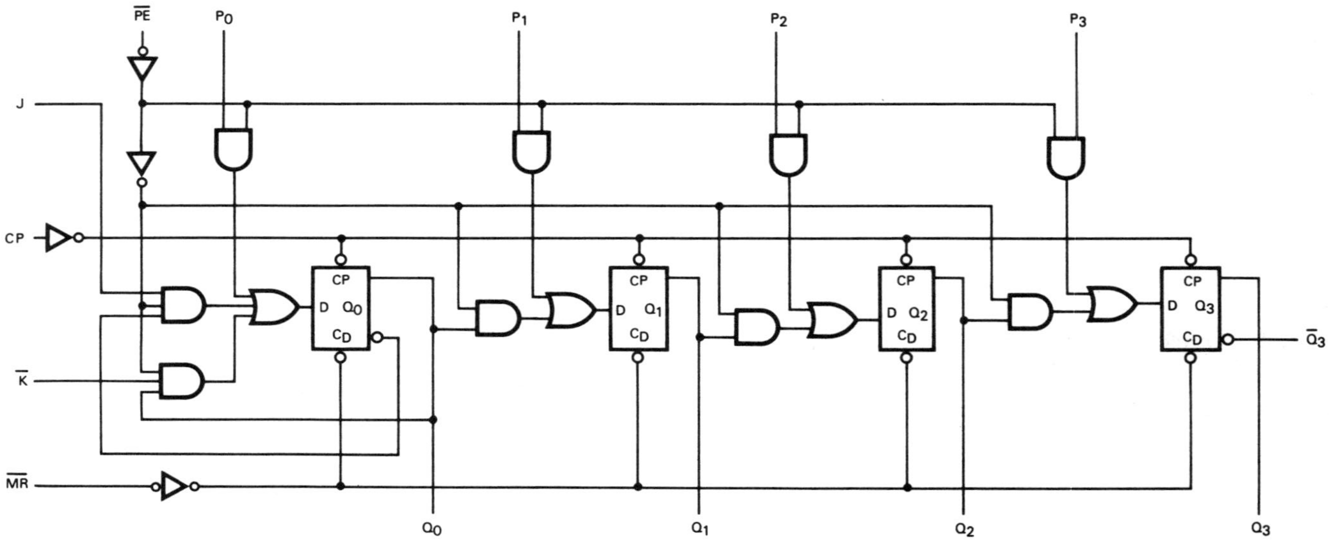

(a)

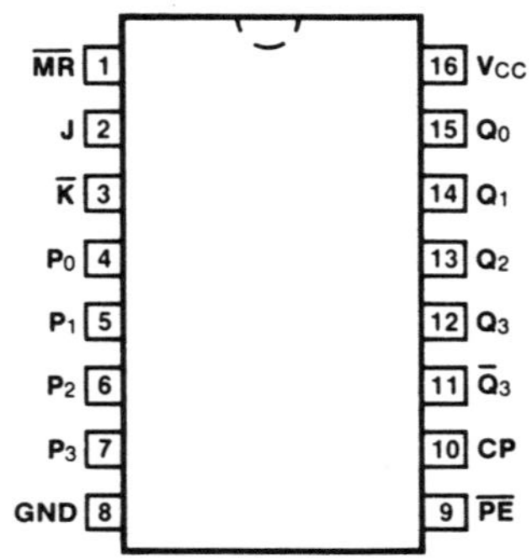

(b)

Fig. 5.37 (a) 9300 4-bit universal shift register (Fairchild Camera and Instrument Corp.); (b) 9300 pin layout (Fairchild Camera and Instrument Corp.).

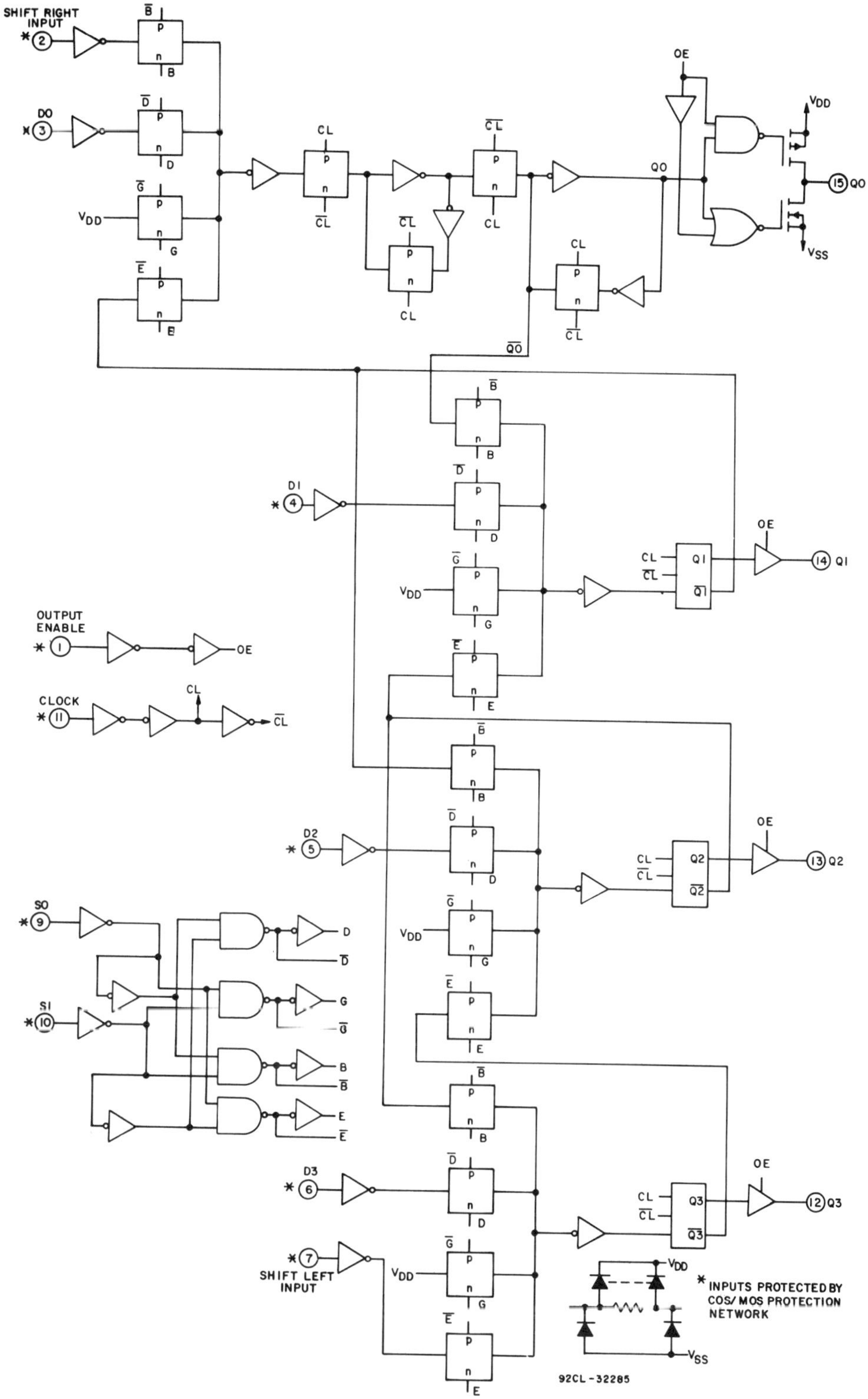

(a)

Fig. 5.38 (a) CD40104B block diagram (RCA Solid State Division); (b) CD40104B operation truth table (RCA Solid State Division).

CONTROL TRUTH TABLE FOR CD40104B SERIES

CLOCK▲	MODE SELECT		OUTPUT ENABLE	ACTION
	S_0	S_1		
↑	0	0	1	Reset
↑	1	0	1	Shift right (Q_0 toward Q_3)
↑	0	1	1	Shift left (Q_3 toward Q_0)
↑	1	1	1	Parallel load
X	X	X	0	Operations occur as shown above, but outputs assume high impedance

1 = High level
0 = Low level
X = Don't care
▲ = Level change

(b)

Fig. 5.38 Continued

5.9 THE DYNAMIC SHIFT REGISTER

As with ROM and RAM memories, shift register devices are available that use dynamic circuitry as well as static circuitry. In a *dynamic register,* data are stored as charge on capacitive nodes instead of voltage levels in an active flip-flop circuit. These capacitive nodes are actually internal capacitances of the device.

Dynamic shift registers cannot be dc-operated. If this were done, data would be lost because the capacitive nodes would quickly discharge. To prevent loss of data, dynamic registers require continuous refreshing of the charge stored on its capacitors. During the refresh operation, charge that has leaked off is restored.

Dynamic shift registers are refreshed by simply recirculating the data held within the register. For this reason, dynamic registers must be continuously operated at a minimum operating frequency and cannot be used in applications that require dc operation. The value of the minimum operating frequency is determined by the maximum amount of time that can elapse between refresh operations.

Shift registers made with dynamic circuitry have the serial-in, serial-out configuration. Moreover, they are manufactured with MOS technology circuitry. An advantage of using dynamic CMOS, PMOS, or NMOS circuitry is that more dense registers can be manufactured than with static circuitry. Dynamic circuitry results in registers with storage capacities as high as 2048 bits.

Another advantage of dynamic register circuitry is its lower power requirements. For instance, dynamic registers made with PMOS or NMOS circuitry consume less power than an equivalent register made with static circuitry. This is because the input is sampled only during one of the clock phases and that the output is due to charge stored on a capacitor instead of a constant voltage level. The amount of power consumed by a dynamic register varies with operating frequency of the clock: the lower the operating frequency, the less power dissipated.

Dynamic Storage Cell Circuits[6]

There are two basic storage cell circuits used to construct dynamic shift registers. These circuits are called the *ratioless cell* and the *ratio cell.*

Figure 5.39 shows a ratioless cell circuit. In this circuit, the master section is formed from MOSFETs Q_1, Q_2, and Q_3. Furthermore, the slave section contains MOSFETs Q_4, Q_5, and Q_6. The capacitors represent the intrinsic capacitances of the MOSFET devices. This circuit is also known as a *two-phase dynamic shift register cell.* That is, it requires synchronization by a two-phase clock. The clock phases are denoted by ϕ_{IN} and ϕ_{OUT}.

During the first clock phase, data are loaded into the master section. As ϕ_{IN} is pulsed, MOSFET Q_3 turns ON and C_2 at capacitive node *B* charges toward the $-V_{GG}$ supply voltage. At the same moment, data applied to the *INPUT* lead are passed through transfer MOSFET Q_1, which is also turned ON by ϕ_{IN}. The input data charge capacitance C_1. Let us assume that the *INPUT* is logic 0. Then the charge on C_1 keeps Q_2 OFF and C_2 is permitted to continue to charge. After ϕ_{IN} is complete, Q_3 turns back OFF and charge is isolated at capacitive node *B*. This condition is known as *precharge.*

As the next clock phase occurs with a pulse at ϕ_{OUT}, Q_4 switches ON and the charge stored at node *B* is redistributed between the capacitances at nodes *B* and *C*. The negative voltage produced across C_3 gives a 1 logic level at the gate lead of Q_5. Q_5 turns ON and *OUTPUT* switches to logic 0. When ϕ_{OUT} is complete, the charge isolated at node *C* holds Q_5 ON and maintains the 0 level at *OUTPUT*.

If the data at *INPUT* are logic 0 instead of 1, MOSFET Q_2 turns on during phase ϕ_{IN}. This drains the charge off of C_2 at node *B*. The output switches to logic 1 during phase ϕ_{OUT}.

In both cases, the output logic level is maintained just by charge stored at node *C*. This is the reason the clock cannot be set to a dc level to store data. Charge on node *C* would quickly drain off C_3 and the data would be

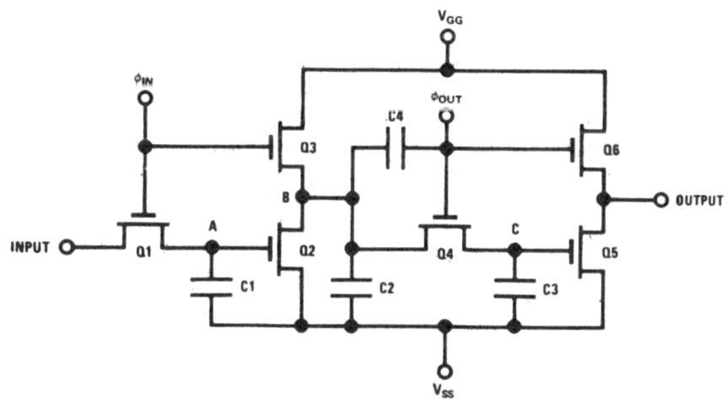

Fig. 5.39 Ratioless dynamic shift register cell (National Semiconductor Corp.).

[6] National Semiconductor Corp., "Low Frequency Operation with Dynamic Shift Registers," AN-55 (Santa Clara, CA: National Semiconductor Corp., 1976). (Courtesy of National Semiconductor Corp.)

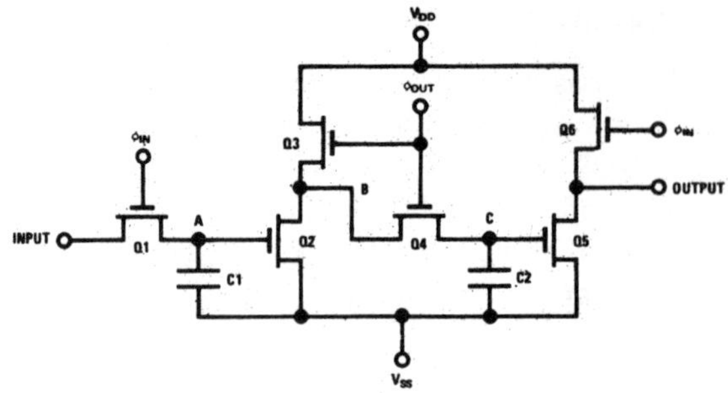

Fig. 5.40 Ratio-type dynamic shift register cell (National Semiconductor Corp.).

lost. Clocking the cell at a minimum rate causes capacitor C_3 to maintain its charge.

A ratio-type dynamic register cell is given in Fig. 5.40. This circuit is similar to that used in a static MOS register. However, in this dynamic cell, the feedback MOSFET that is used to return the slave section output back to the master section input is left out.

AM2805 512-Bit Shift Register

The AM2805 is a widely used dynamic shift register device. This IC contains a 512-bit PMOS serial-in, serial-out register circuit. A diagram of the circuitry within this IC is given in Fig. 5.41(a).

From this diagram we see that the circuit is that of a standard recirculating shift register. Serial data are input at the *IN* lead and output in serial form at *OUTPUT.* The logic level of the write control *W* selects between data input and recirculation operation. Logic 1 at *W* selects data input and 0 at *W* selects recirculation of data.

The serial output of data is controlled by the read control *R* on the output AND gate. *R* must be logic 1 to enable read out of stored data. The chip select inputs, which are both labeled *CS*, must both be logic 1 to enable the device for read/write operation. If either *CS* input is logic 0, the register is set for recirculation.

Dynamic operation is synchronized by the two clock inputs ϕ_1 and ϕ_2. The timing diagram of a read/write operation is shown in Fig. 5.41(b). Looking at this diagram, we see that data must be available at *IN* during phase ϕ_2. The maximum set up time t_s for input data is 150 ns and the data do not have to be held after the clock edge. Data appear at the output during phase ϕ_1 of the clock. The propagation delay between the 1-to-0 edge of ϕ_1 and the appearance of data at the output is rated at 150 ns. The *maximum clock frequency* and *data rate* are 3 MHz.

A pin layout of the device is shown in Fig. 5.41(c). Here we see that two power-supply voltages are needed to operate the AM2805. These voltages are V_{CC} = +5 V and V_{DD} = -5 V. Both voltages are permitted to vary by ±5%.

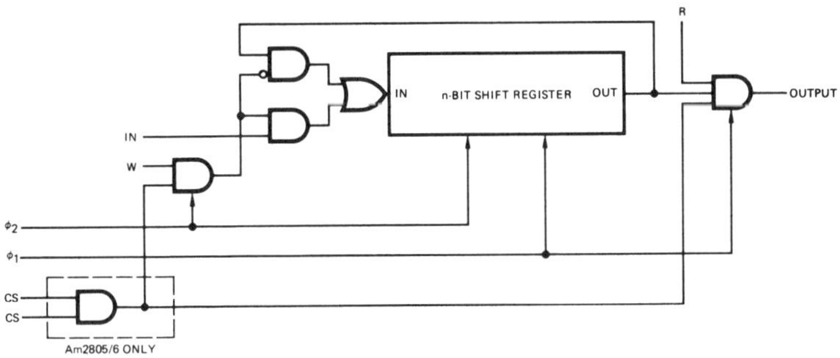

(a)

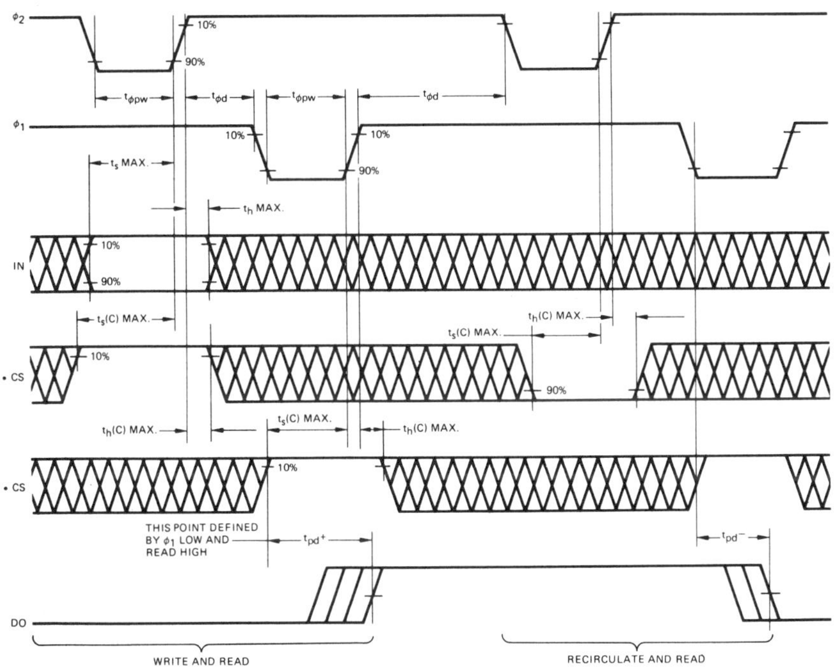

(b)

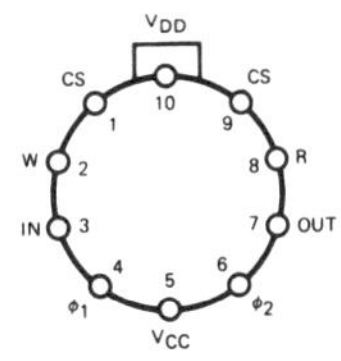

(c)

Fig. 5.41 (a) AM2805 dynamic shift register circuit (copyright © 1974 Advanced Micro Devices, Inc. Reproduced with permission of copyright owner.); (b) input/output waveforms (copyright © 1974 Advanced Micro Devices, Inc. Reproduced with permission of copyright owner.); (c) AM2805 pin layout (copyright © 1974 Advanced Micro Devices, Inc. Reproduced with permission of copyright owner.).

All inputs except ϕ_1 and ϕ_2 are TTL-compatible. The open drain outputs can drive a TTL load if it is pulled down to the $-V_{DD}$ supply with a 3-kΩ resistor. The clock inputs must be driven by MOS level signals.

AM1402A Quad 256-Bit Shift Register

Another popular dynamic shift register IC is the AM1402A. This device has 1024 bits (1*k* bits) of storage capacity and is organized into four 256-bit serial-in, serial-out registers.

The register configuration used in the AM1402A device is shown in Fig. 5.42(a). Notice that each register circuit has a separate *INPUT* lead and *OUTPUT* lead. Their locations on the IC package are given in the pin layout of Fig. 5.42(b). This dynamic shift register architecture differs from that in the AM2805 IC. Here the cells in the register are divided into two parallel groups. Moreover, the master and slave parts of the memory cells in each group are driven with opposite phases of the clock. In this way, one bit of data is written into the register on each phase of the clock.

Control logic is provided so that alternate bits of data are multiplexed into opposite sides of the register. That is, odd-numbered bits are stored in one group of cells and even-numbered bits in the other. The result of this multiplexed operation is that the data rate is twice that of a normal circuit. The AM1402A is rated to operate over a frequency range from 400 Hz to 10 MHz.

The power supplies of the AM1402A are V_{CC} = +5 V and V_{DD} = -4.75 to -9.45 V. Its dynamic circuit requires only 0.1 mW per bit when operating at 1 MHz.

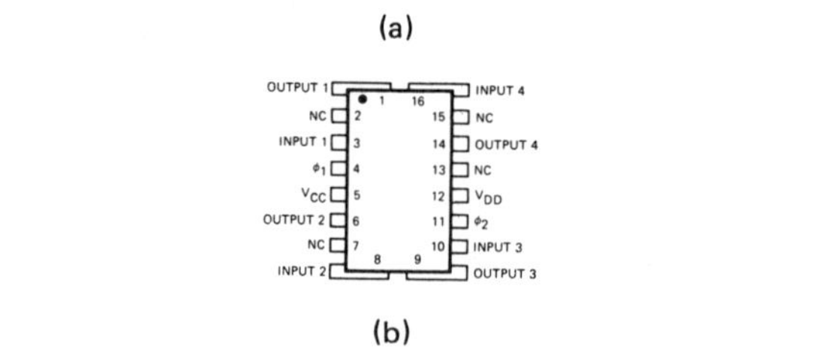

Fig. 5.42 (a) AM1402A dynamic shift register (copyright © 1974 Advanced Micro Devices, Inc. Reproduced with permission of copyright owner.); (b) AM1402A pin layout (copyright © 1974 Advanced Micro Devices, Inc. Reproduced with permission of copyright owner.).

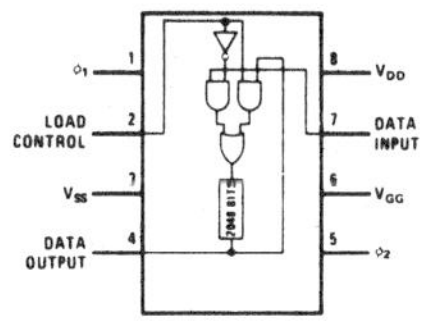

Fig. 5.43 MM5027 block diagram and pin layout (National Semiconductor Corp.).

MM5027 2048-Bit Shift Register

The MM5027 IC is another PMOS shift register device. It contains a 2048-bit serial-in, serial-out register circuit that has built-in recirculation logic. Figure 5.43 shows a block diagram of the register and pin numbering of its leads on the IC.

Here we see that data are entered into the register from the *DATA INPUT* lead and output from *DATA OUTPUT*. Moreover, the mode of register operation can be switched between recirculation operation and data input by changing the logic level at the *LOAD CONTROL* lead. Logic 0 at this input selects recirculation and logic 1 selects data input.

Looking at the diagram in Fig. 5.43, we also find that the circuit operates from a two-phase clock. The clock inputs are called ϕ_1 and ϕ_2. Internal multiplexing similar to that in the AM1402A is used in the MM5027, so that one bit of data is input and output on each phase of the clock. Again the result is a maximum data rate equal to twice the maximum clock frequency. This maximum data rate is 6 MHz.

The MM5027 works from dc power supplies V_{SS} = +5 V and V_{GG} = -12 V. Both supplies are referenced to the V_{DD} pin, which is used as ground. Because of its low-power dynamic circuitry, the register needs just 120 μW per bit to operate at a 1-MHz clock rate.

The *DATA INPUT*, *DATA OUTPUT*, and *LOAD CONTROL* leads are TTL-compatible. However, the clock inputs ϕ_1 and ϕ_2 must be at MOS logic levels.

5.10 SERIAL MEMORY[7]

Static and dynamic shift register devices can be used to form a large-capacity *serial read/write memory*. The circuit in Fig. 5.44 shows how 16 AM2810 128-bit serial-in, serial-out shift registers can be connected to make a static memory with 2*k* bits of storage capacity.

The memory array in this circuit consists of eight groups of AM2810 shift registers. Each group contains two 128-bit registers cascaded to make a 256-bit recirculating register. Recirculation operation is obtained by returning the serial output from the *OUT* lead of the register on the right to the recirculation input R_{IN} on the left register. Serial data are applied to the

[7] Advanced Micro Devices, *Data Book* (Sunnyvale, CA: Advanced Micro Devices, 1974), p. 5-40. (Copyright © 1974 Advanced Micro Devices, Inc. Reproduced with permission of the copyright owner)

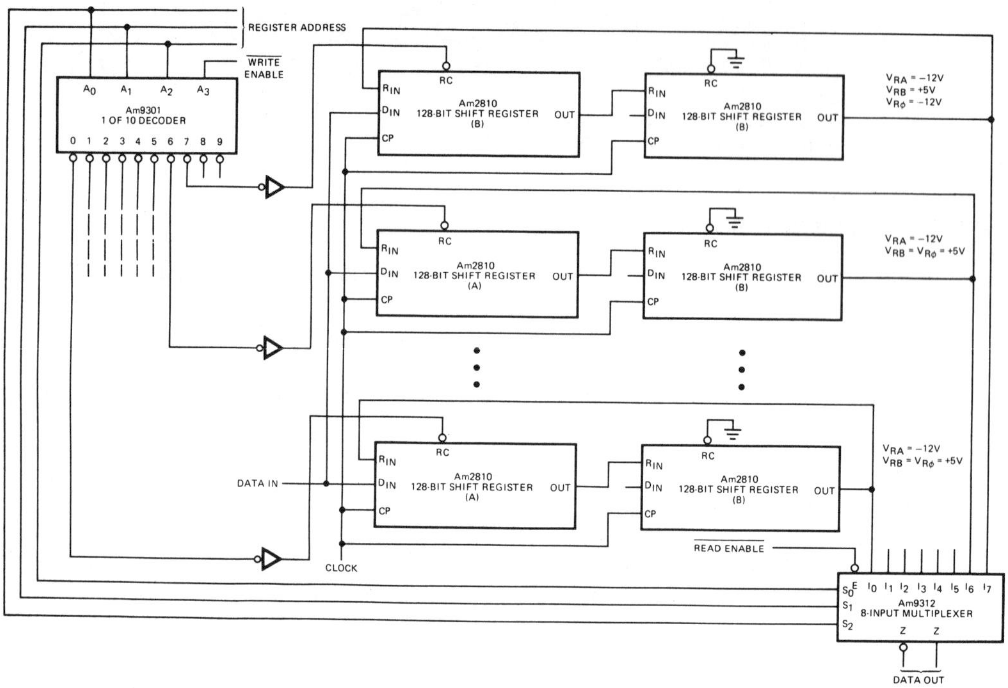

Fig. 5.44 2K-bit serial memory (copyright © 1974 Advanced Micro Devices, Inc. Reproduced with permission of copyright owner.).

DATA IN terminal of the circuit. From *DATA IN*, it is supplied to the D_{IN} lead of the left register in each group.

An AM9301 BCD-to-decimal decoder and AM9312 8 line-to-1 line multiplexer have been added to the circuit to organize its memory array into eight 256-bit words. Address inputs $A_3 A_2 A_1 A_0$ are applied to the decoder. Here a logic 0 at A_3 ($\overline{WRITE\ ENABLE}$) signals that a write operation is to be performed to the register group indicated by $A_2 A_1 A_0$. The decoder output corresponding to $A_2 A_1 A_0$ switches to logic 0 and all other outputs stay at logic 1.

The decoder outputs are inverted and then passed to the *RC* input of the left-shift register in one of the eight groups. Notice that the 0 decoder output goes to the lowest group of registers and output 7 to the uppermost group of registers. The decoder output that is logic 0 is first inverted to logic 1 and then applied to the *RC* input of a register. It is this 1 that selects the register into which new data will be written. The *RC* inputs on all other registers are at logic 0. Therefore, they are set for recirculation operation.

On the next 256 clock pulses, data are loaded from *DATA IN* into the enabled register. At the same time, data are recirculated from output to input for the other seven registers.

The logic level of the $\overline{READ\ ENABLE}$ input determines if data are to be read out of the memory. The serial outputs of the register groups are used as inputs to the multiplexer. Notice that the output of the lowest register group is supplied to I_0 on the multiplexer and the output of the uppermost register group goes to the I_7 input. Address inputs A_2, A_1, and A_0 go to select inputs S_0, S_1, and S_2, respectively. The code at $S_0 S_1 S_2$ selects the output from one of the eight registers for multiplexing to serial data output Z.

For example, setting $\overline{READ\ ENABLE}$ to logic 0 enables the multiplexer for operation. Then a code of $A_2 A_1 A_0$=000 sets the multiplexer to pass data from input I_0 to the Z output. With $\overline{WRITE\ ENABLE}$ set to logic 1, data are recirculated through the registers by the next 256 clock pulses. Data at the *OUT* lead of the lowest group of registers are multiplexed from I_0 to the Z output.

Actually, data can be written into and read out of the serial memory at the same time. This is done by setting both $\overline{WRITE\ ENABLE}$ and $\overline{READ\ ENABLE}$ to logic 0. For this reason, the circuit can also be called a *read-while-write memory*.

EXAMPLE 5.6 The $\overline{WRITE\ ENABLE}$ input of the memory in Fig. 5.44 is set to logic 0 and its $\overline{READ\ ENABLE}$ input is at logic 1. The remaining address inputs are $A_2 A_1 A_0$=111. Which type of memory operation is to be performed by the register, and for which register group will it be performed?

SOLUTION Since $\overline{WRITE\ ENABLE}$ is logic 0 and $\overline{READ\ ENABLE}$ logic 1, the circuit is set for a write operation. The other address bits $A_2 A_1 A_0$=111 cause output 7 of the decoder to switch to logic 0. This output is inverted to logic 1 and applied to the *RC* input of the uppermost register group. As the *CLOCK* input is pulsed, data at *DATA IN* are written into the uppermost register group.

5.11 PSEUDO-RANDOM-ACCESS MEMORY[8]

The equivalent of a random-access read/write memory can be constructed using shift registers as the storage device. This type of circuit is known as a *pseudo-RAM*.

The circuit in Fig. 5.45 is a 128-word by 8-bit pseudo-random-access memory. The storage array, which is located on the right side of the circuit, is formed from four AM2809 dual 128-bit serial-in, serial-out recirculating shift registers. These devices are clocked in parallel with serial data entering at their *IN A* and *IN B* leads and serial data output at their *OUT A* and *OUT B* leads.

Above the shift registers in the circuit diagram, we find two AM93L16 ICs. These devices are used to latch the 8-bit data words that are to be written into the memory. Parallel words are applied to data inputs D_0 through D_7 and are synchronously loaded into the latch outputs when the *LOAD DATA* input is set to logic 0. Data held in outputs Q_0 through Q_3 of the two latches supply the serial inputs of the register memory array.

A similar circuit connection exists at the output of the memory array.

[8] Ibid., p. 5-36.

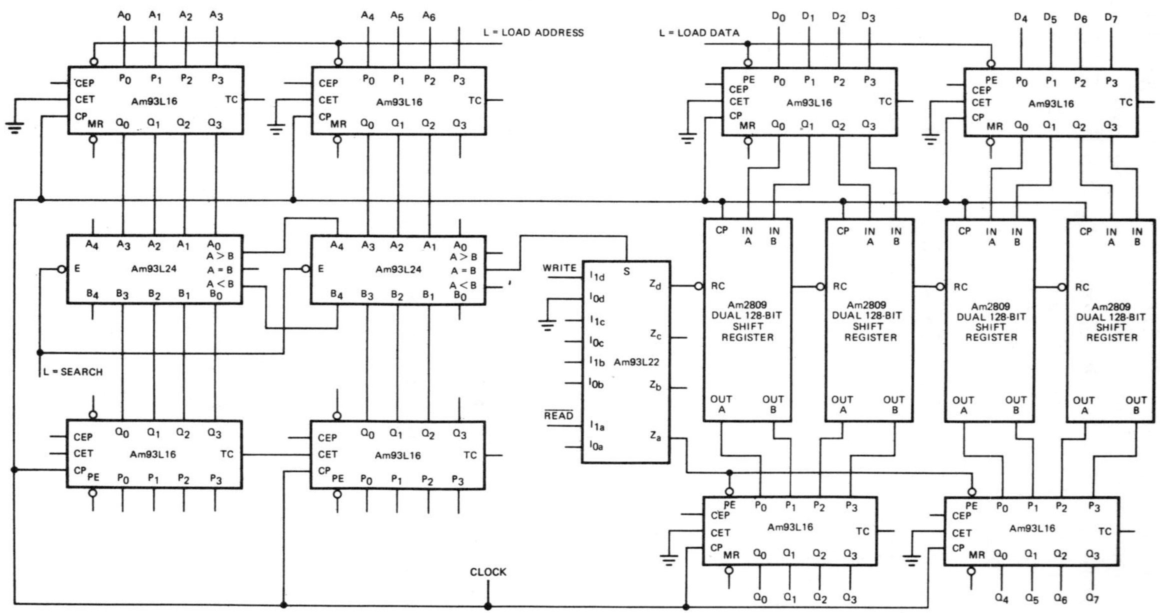

Fig. 5.45 128-word × 8-bit pseudo-random-access memory (copyright © 1974 Advanced Micro Devices, Inc. Reproduced with permission of copyright owner.).

Here two AM93L16 devices are used as a holding register for the memory array output. The read outputs of the memory are O_0 through O_7 from these two devices.

At the left side of Fig. 5.45 is the address circuitry. Here the upper two AM93L16 devices are used to latch the 7-bit input address A_0 through A_6 of the storage location to be accessed. By setting the *LOAD ADDRESS* input to logic 0, the address word at A_0 through A_6 is synchronously loaded with the next clock pulse.

At the bottom of this section, there are two more AM93L16 ICs. However, these devices are connected to operate as an 8-bit ripple counter. The output of the circuit increments with each pulse at the *CLOCK* input. In this way, it tracks the addresses of the storage locations within the memory array as data are continuously recirculated through the shift registers.

The latched input address and that produced by the counter are inputs to the two AM93L24 magnitude comparator ICs. This 8-bit comparator compares the two addresses and outputs a 1 at $A=B$ when the two addresses are equal in every bit position.

If the two addresses are not the same, the $A=B$ output of the comparator is logic 0. This 0 logic level goes to the select input S on the AM93L22 data selector and causes the logic 0 at input I_{0d} to be output at Z_d to the *RC* input of all shift registers. This keeps the shift registers in the recirculate mode of operation and the address counter continues to increment as data circulate through the registers.

As the counter becomes equal to the latched address, the data location to be accessed has been found. The comparator output switches to logic 1. Now the data selector passes *WRITE* to output Z_d and $\overline{READ}$ to output Z_a. Logic 1 at Z_d sets the registers for a write of new data from D_0 through D_7 into the memory and 0 at Z_a enables a read of the output data by causing it to be parallel-loaded into outputs O_0 through O_7 of the holding register.

EXAMPLE 5.7 Trace the write operation of data word $D_7D_6D_5D_4D_3D_2D_1D_0=10011100$ into address location $A_6A_5A_4A_3A_2A_1A_0=0000111$ of the pseudo-RAM of Fig. 5.45. The *WRITE* input is set to logic 1.

SOLUTION The write operation begins as the 7-bit address is applied to inputs A_0 through A_6 and an 8-bit data word is applied to data inputs D_0 through D_7. When *LOAD ADDRESS* and *LOAD DATA* are set to logic 0, the address and data latches are loaded with the next clock pulse.

The magnitude comparator compares the address counter output to the address 0000111 held in the latch outputs. Let us assume that the address counter starts at 0000000. Since both addresses are not the same, the $A=B$ output is logic 0 and the data selector passes the logic 0 at I_{0d} to the Z_d output and *RC* inputs of the registers. Therefore, the registers remain in the recirculate mode of operation.

As the circuit is clocked, the data in the register are recirculated and the counter increments toward 0000111. On the seventh clock pulse, the two addresses match and the $A=B$ output of the comparator switches to logic 1. Now the 1 at *WRITE* is switched to the Z_d output of the data selector. This 1 at *RC* sets the register for serial input operation and on the next clock pulse the data 10011100 held at the latch outputs are loaded into the shift registers from their serial inputs.

ASSIGNMENTS

Section 5.2

1. Draw the EBCDIC code for letter A as a serial waveform.
2. What is meant by "serial access"?
3. Describe the operation of the TTL flip-flop circuit in Fig. 5.4 for inputs $S_1=1$ and $R_1=0$ and the CLK input pulsed to logic 1. Assume that the flip-flop outputs were initially reset with $Q_1=0$, $\overline{Q}_1=1$, $Q_2=0$, and $\overline{Q}_2=1$.
4. Is the shift register a volatile or a nonvolatile memory device?

Section 5.3

5. Figure 5.46 shows the B input and clock input waveforms of a 7491 shift register. The A input is held at the 1 logic level. If the flip-flops are all initially reset, draw the waveforms at outputs S_0 and $\overline{S}_0$.

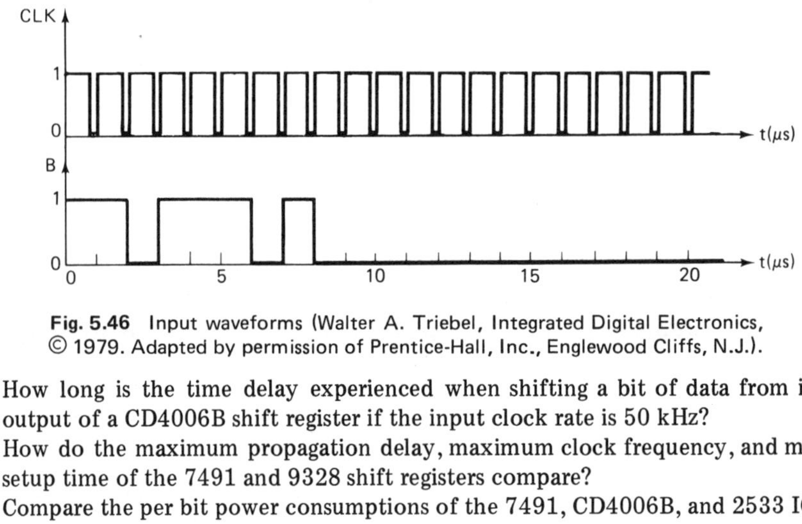

Fig. 5.46 Input waveforms (Walter A. Triebel, Integrated Digital Electronics, © 1979. Adapted by permission of Prentice-Hall, Inc., Englewood Cliffs, N.J.).

6. How long is the time delay experienced when shifting a bit of data from input to output of a CD4006B shift register if the input clock rate is 50 kHz?
7. How do the maximum propagation delay, maximum clock frequency, and minimum setup time of the 7491 and 9328 shift registers compare?
8. Compare the per bit power consumptions of the 7491, CD4006B, and 2533 ICs.

Section 5.4

9. A 74164 shift register has its $CLEAR$ and B inputs fixed at the 1 logic level. Show the Q_A through Q_H output waveforms for the synchronous loading of the EBCDIC code for letter A into the register with pulses at the $CLOCK$ input.
10. Make a block diagram showing how the two 4-bit shift registers in the CD4015B device can be cascaded to form an 8-bit serial-in, parallel-out register.

Section 5.5

11. The binary data word 1101 is parallel-loaded into the 7494 shift register of Fig. 5.22. After this, it is clocked through the register with a 100-kHz square wave. Draw the serial output waveform.

12. The 8-bit word *HGFEDCBA*=10101110 is parallel-loaded into the cascaded 7494 register of Fig. 5.24. Draw the serial output waveform if data are clocked through the register with a 200-kHz signal at the *CLK* lead.
13. Make a block diagram showing how the CD4014B should be set up for parallel loading of data words.

Section 5.6

14. Repeat Example 5.4; however, this time assume that the *REC* input is held at logic 1 for the first five clock cycles and switched to logic 0 before the sixth clock pulse occurs.
15. Draw a block diagram showing how the two shift registers in an AM2810 can be cascaded to form a 256-bit recirculating register.

Section 5.7

16. A 7495 register is parallel-loaded with the code *DCBA*=1110. When the *MODE* control is set to logic 0, draw the serial output. The clock is a 1-MHz square wave.
17. The data word $D_iC_iB_iA_i$=1110 is parallel-loaded into a 7495 register set for shift-left operation. Find the parallel output of the register after the first clock pulse, second clock pulse, and third clock pulse.
18. Use a block diagram to show how the CD40100B is set up for shift-left operation.

Section 5.8

19. Make a block drawing to show how the 9300 universal register can be set up as a 4-bit serial-in, serial-out shift register that can be initially set with all outputs logic 1.
20. What are the three primary differences of the CD40104B universal shift register device from the 8270 and 9300 ICs?

Section 5.9

21. How does a dynamic shift register differ from a static shift register?
22. The ratio-type dynamic shift register cell in Fig. 5.40 initially has capacitive node C_1 discharged. Describe the operation of the circuit during clock phase ϕ_{IN} and ϕ_{OUT} if the input is at the 0 logic level.

Section 5.10

23. The address input to the serial memory in Fig. 5.44 is $A_3A_2A_1A_0$=1111 and the $\overline{READ\ ENABLE}$ input is logic 0. What type of operation is to be performed by the memory, and for which register group will it be performed?

Section 5.11

24. The data word $D_7D_6D_5D_4D_3D_2D_1D_0$=10011100 is stored at address $A_6A_5A_4$-$A_3A_2A_1A_0$=0000111 in the pseudo-RAM circuit of Fig. 5.45. Describe how the word is read out of the storage location.

6

PROGRAMMABLE LOGIC ARRAY

6.1 INTRODUCTION

In previous chapters, the most widely used random-accessed and serial-accessed memory devices were introduced. This chapter continues the study of memory devices, circuits, and applications with another random-accessed storage device, the programmable logic array. We begin by introducing the architecture and operation of the programmable logic array. After this, standard IC devices and applications are described. The following topics are presented:

1. Programmable logic array
2. Internal architecture of the PLA
3. Programming PLAs
4. Internal operation of the PLA
5. Standard PLA and FPLA integrated circuits
6. Programmable logic arrays in random logic and ROM applications
7. Expanding PLA capacity
8. Alphanumeric display controller

6.2 PROGRAMMABLE LOGIC ARRAY

Programmable logic array (PLA) is another type of nonvolatile storage device. It is suitable for implementing random logic circuitry and for replacing ROMs in some applications. The PLA is similar to a ROM in that stored data can only be read out. However, it has certain distinct differences from the standard ROM IC. For example, the PLA has more inputs than a ROM, has faster access time, and employs a totally different internal architecture.

Technology

PLAs are manufactured with static bipolar circuitry. By using this technology, both *mask-programmable PLA*s and *field-programmable PLA*s can be made. The mask-programmable device must have the data pattern of the program built in by the manufacturer. On the other hand, the data pattern can be entered into a field-programmable device by the user. Field-programmable logic arrays are called FPLAs.

Electrical Characteristics

The electrical characteristics of the PLA are similar to those of other bipolar memory devices. In general, they require a lot of power to operate. Standard PLA ICs consume about 500 mW. However, owing to the changes in the internal architecture of the PLA, it is faster than ROM. Maximum address to output data access times are in the range 80 to 150 ns and maximum chip enable-to-output times are as low as 50 ns.

Capacity

The large size of integrated bipolar transistors, diodes, and resistors limit PLA ICs to low storage capacity. For a ROM, we talk about its total bits of storage. For instance, ROM ICs have storage capacities of up to 64*k* bits. Storage capacity of a PLA is defined differently than for ROM. Capacity of a PLA is described in terms of the *number of inputs*, the *number of outputs*, and the *number of product terms*. Presently, standard PLA ICs are available with a maximum of 16 inputs, 8 outputs, and 96 product terms.

Block Diagram of a PLA

The block diagram in Fig. 6.1 represents a typical PLA. Looking at the diagram, we see that it has 16 *input leads*, marked I_0 through I_{15}. Moreover, there are eight *output leads*. These leads are labeled F_0 through F_7. This PLA is equipped with three-state outputs. For this reason, it has a *chip enable control lead*. In the block diagram, this input is marked $\overline{CE}$. The logic level of $\overline{CE}$ determines if the outputs are enabled or disabled.

When a PLA is used to implement a random logic network, the inputs represent Boolean variables, and the outputs can be used to provide eight separate random logic functions. The logic levels at inputs I_0 through I_{15} and the program determine what logic levels are produced at outputs F_0 through F_7. In this type of application, all the inputs and outputs need not be in use.

When the PLA is programmed to operate as a ROM, inputs I_0 through I_{15} are used as a 16-bit address input and the eight outputs are grouped together to produce an 8-bit output data word. The 16-bit address defines

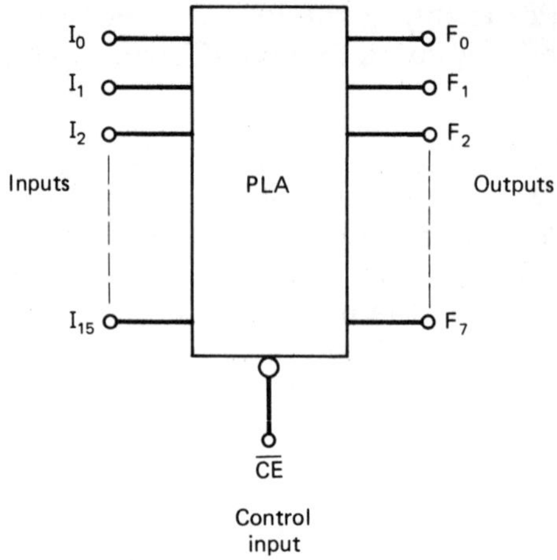

Fig. 6.1 Block diagram of a PLA.

2^{16} or 65,536 input states. When an address is applied to I_0 through I_{15}, the PLA responds by generating an 8-bit word at F_0 through F_7.

6.3 INTERNAL ARCHITECTURE OF THE PLA

The internal architecture of a PLA is different than that of a ROM. It does not contain a rectangular storage array, row decoder, nor column decoder

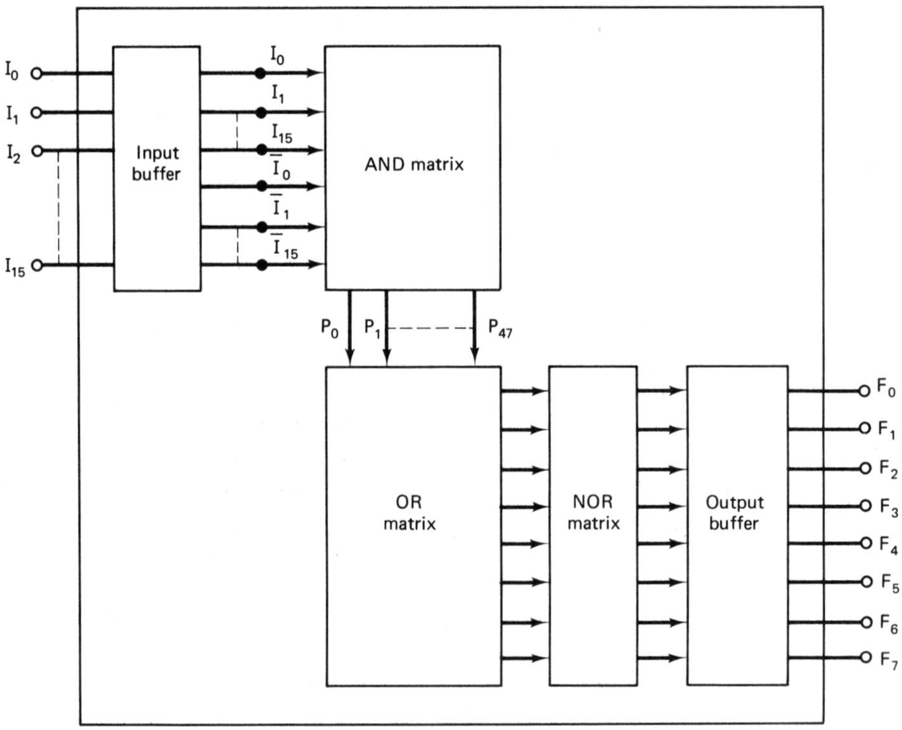

Fig. 6.2 PLA internal architecture.

like the ROM. Instead, the PLA is formed from arrays of logic gates. These gate arrays can be interconnected through programming to produce specific outputs for given input conditions.

Architecture of a PLA is shown in Fig. 6.2. Here we see that it contains five functional sections: *input buffer*, *AND matrix*, *OR matrix*, *NOR matrix*, and *output buffer*. Logic circuitry for the PLA is shown in Fig. 6.3. This circuit has a capacity of 16 inputs I_0 through I_{15}, 8 outputs F_0 through F_7, and 48 product terms P_0 through P_{47}.

Through programming, we determine how the outputs of the PLA will respond to each input condition. In a ROM, each storage location corresponds to an address that is programmed with data. On the other hand, the data stored in a PLA are defined by programming connections in the AND matrix, OR matrix, and NOR matrix.

The PLA must be programmed in three ways: first, the inputs are decoded by making connections from the input buffer outputs I_0 through I_{15} and their complements $\bar{I}_0$ through $\bar{I}_{15}$ to inputs of the AND gates in the AND matrix; next, select product terms from P_0 through P_{47} are combined by connections in the OR matrix to produce sum outputs S_0 through S_7; finally, the inputs of the exclusive-OR gates in the NOR matrix are programmed to set the active logic level for outputs F_0 through F_7. In this way, we see that the PLA is actually a programmable two-level AND/OR logic element.

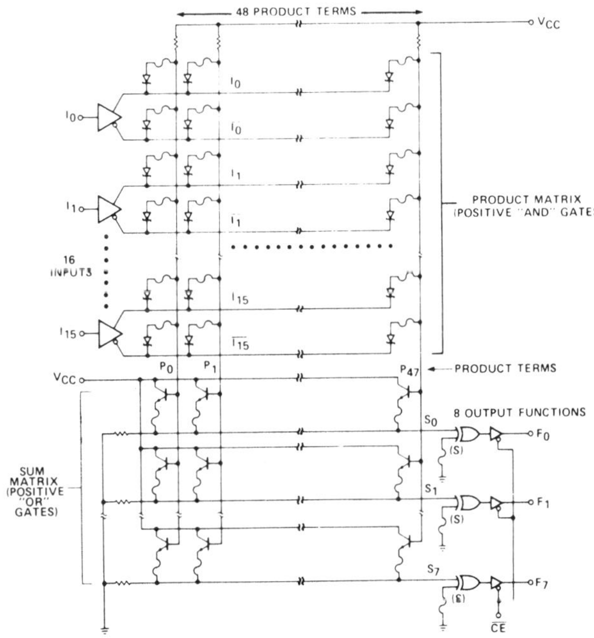

Fig. 6.3 Typical PLA circuitry (Permission to reprint granted by Signetics Corporation, a subsidiary of U.S. Philips Corp., 811 East Arques Avenue, Sunnyvale, CA 94806).

Input Buffer

The buffer circuitry at the inputs are included to limit loading on circuitry that drives the inputs. A simplified input buffer circuit is shown in Fig. 6.4. Here we find one inverting buffer for each of the four inputs. These gates are labeled 1 through 4 and produce complemented input signals $\overline{I}_0$ through $\overline{I}_3$. These outputs are inverted once more by gates 5 through 8 to produce buffered input signals I_0 through I_3. Address words or logic signals at the inputs are passed through the buffer to the inputs of the AND matrix.

EXAMPLE 6.1 What are the output logic levels of the input buffer in Fig. 6.4 when the input address word is $I_3I_2I_1I_0$=1000?

SOLUTION The input signals are first inverted by gates 1 through 4 to produce complemented inputs. These outputs are

$$\overline{I}_3\overline{I}_2\overline{I}_1\overline{I}_0=0111$$

These inverter outputs are complemented once more to produce the buffered inputs.

$$I_3I_2I_1I_0=1000$$

AND Matrix

The AND matrix section of the PLA is used to form product terms. A simplified AND matrix circuit is shown in Fig. 6.5(a). It is an array of four diode logic AND gates. Each gate circuit is formed from a pull-up resistor and eight diodes. One diode is included for each input I_0 through I_3 and their complements $\overline{I}_0$ through $\overline{I}_3$. In the circuit of Fig. 6.5(a), each AND gate generates one product term. The four product term outputs are denoted P_0 through P_3.

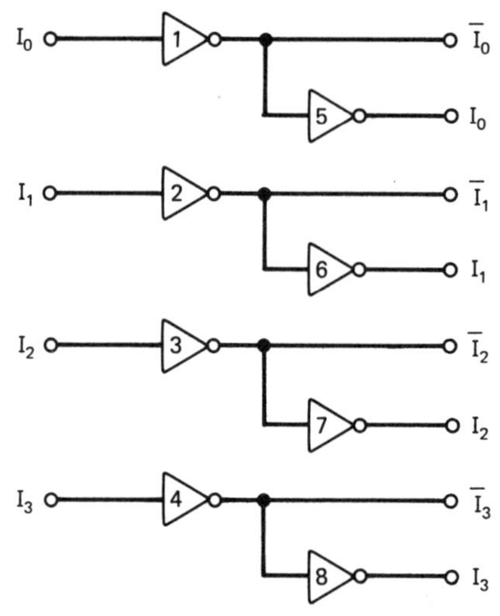

Fig. 6.4 Simplified input buffer.

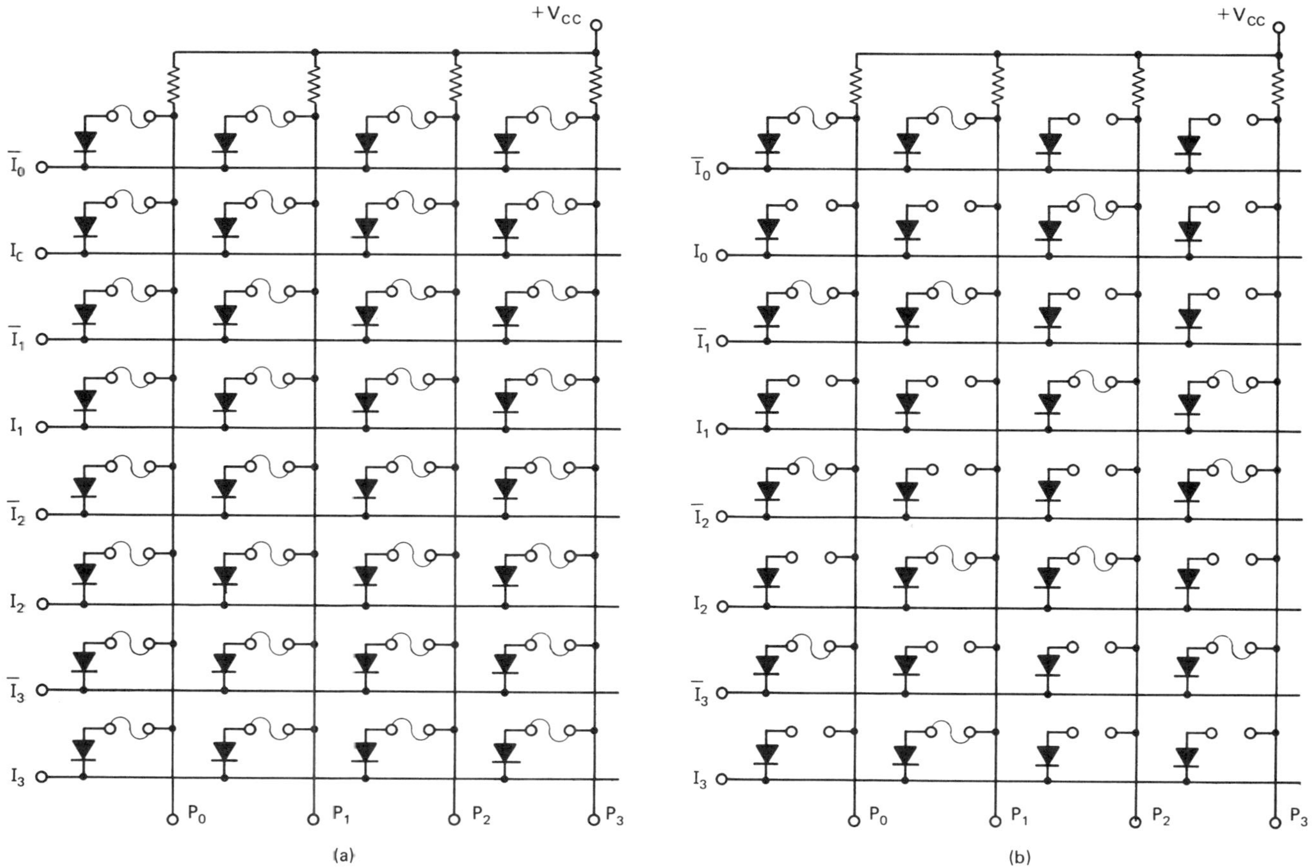

Fig. 6.5 (a) Simplified AND matrix; (b) programmed AND matrix.

The product terms are formed by connecting the inputs of the AND gates to appropriate input buffer outputs. These connections are formed as part of the programming procedure. In the FPLA of Fig. 6.5(a), these connections are provided with Nichrome fuse links. All links are intact in an unprogrammed matrix. Product terms are formed by opening unwanted inputs.

Each product term can be a function of any combination of inputs I_3, I_2, I_1, and I_0. If each input is used in the product term, the P output will respond to just one input combination. On the other hand, if both an input and its complement are opened, the input does not have any effect on AND gate operation. Therefore, the input represents a don't-care state and the output will respond to more than one input condition.

Here are some examples of product terms:

$$P_0 = \bar{I}_3 \bar{I}_2 \bar{I}_1 \bar{I}_0$$

$$P_1 = I_3 I_2 \bar{I}_1 \bar{I}_0$$

$$P_2 = I_2 I_1 I_0$$

$$P_3 = \bar{I}_3 \bar{I}_2 I_1$$

The first product term is programmed into the AND matrix by leaving the fuse links for complemented inputs $\bar{I}_0, \bar{I}_1, \bar{I}_2$, and $\bar{I}_3$ intact on the AND gate for P_0. Links for inputs I_0, I_1, I_2, and I_3 are open-circuited. These connections are shown in the AND matrix of Fig. 6.5(b).

The P_0 output responds with logic 1 for just one input condition. This is when inputs I_0 through I_3 are all at the 0 level. For all other input states, the output stays at logic 0.

Product term P_1 is formed in a similar way to P_0; however, the I_2 and I_3 inputs are connected to the AND gate inputs instead of $\bar{I}_2$ and $\bar{I}_3$. The P_1 output is logic 1 when the input is $I_3 I_2 I_1 I_0 = 1100$.

The other two product terms have a don't-care input. The product term for P_2 does not include input I_3. In the matrix of Fig. 6.5(b), I_3 is made a don't-care state by opening the fuse links for both I_3 and $\bar{I}_3$. This product term output is logic 1 for two input states. P_2 is logic 1 for $I_2 I_1 I_0 = 111$ with I_3 equal to either logic 0 or logic 1. Notice that output P_2 is independent of the logic level at input I_3.

EXAMPLE 6.2 For what input conditions is product term P_3 in Fig. 6.5(b) logic 1?

SOLUTION The product term for AND matrix output P_3 is

$$P_3 = \bar{I}_3 \bar{I}_2 I_1$$

Here we see that I_0 is a don't-care state and that to produce a logic 1 output the inputs of the gate must be $I_3 = 0$, $I_2 = 0$, and $I_1 = 1$. Therefore, the two input states that produce a logic 1 output are

$$I_3 I_2 I_1 I_0 = 0010$$

and

$$I_3 I_2 I_1 I_0 = 0011$$

OR Matrix

The OR matrix in the PLA is used to sum the product term outputs of the AND matrix into Boolean equations. In the circuit of Fig. 6.6(a), we find one OR gate for each of the four S outputs. These OR gates are formed with *resistor transistor logic* (RTL) circuitry. An OR gate consists of four parallel-connected transistors driving a common load resistor at the emitter lead. Each transistor base represents the input for one of the four product terms P_0, P_1, P_2, and P_3. The output of the OR gate is from the connection of the transistor emitters to the load resistor. These outputs are identified by S_0 through S_3.

Through programming, any combination of product terms can be selected as inputs to an OR gate. This is done by leaving their fuse links intact. The gate combines the selected product terms with the OR operator to give a sum-of-products equation for the output. For instance, the sum output S_0 could be formed from product terms P_0 and P_1. For the FPLA OR matrix in Fig. 6.6(b), this is done by opening the P_2 and P_3 fuse links and leaving those for P_0 and P_1 in place. The resulting output is

$$S_0 = P_0 + P_1$$

By using the earlier defined product terms for P_0 and P_1, the OR gate output equation becomes

$$S_0 = \overline{I}_3 \overline{I}_2 \overline{I}_1 \overline{I}_0 + I_3 I_2 \overline{I}_1 \overline{I}_0$$

The S_0 output of the OR gate switches to logic 1 if at least one of its input product terms is at the 1 logic level. These product terms, P_0 and P_1, are logic 1 for the input states $I_3 I_2 I_1 I_0 = 0000$ and $I_3 I_2 I_1 I_0 = 1100$, respectively.

Sum outputs do not have to correspond to more than one product term. For example, output S_1 in Fig. 6.6(b) is formed from just product term P_2:

$$S_1 = P_2 = I_2 I_1 I_0$$

In this case, all fuse links to the S_1 output except that from P_2 are open-circuited.

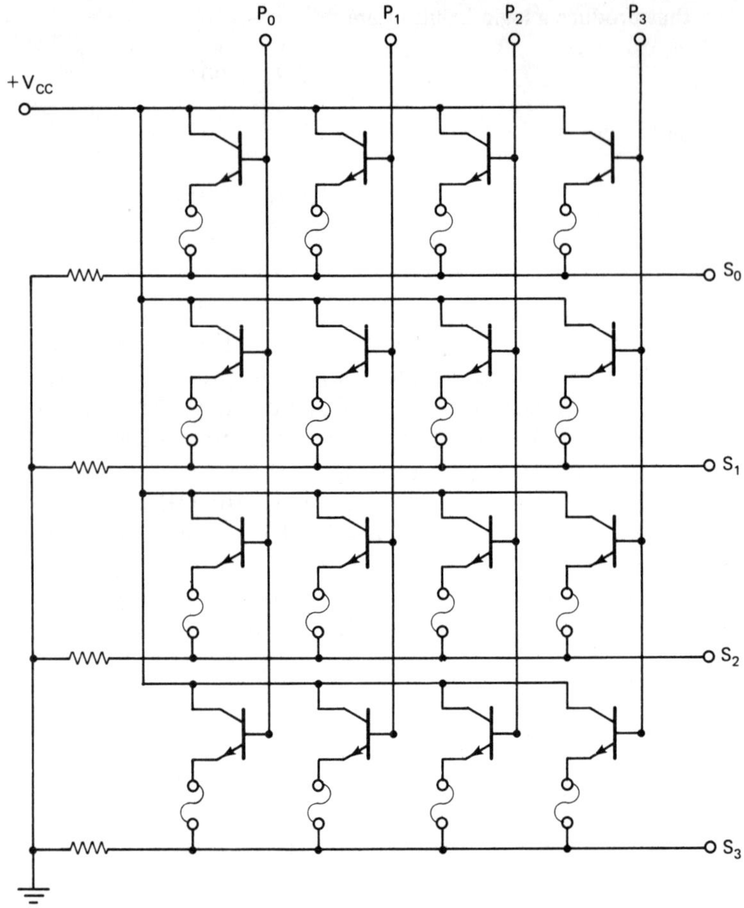

(a)

Fig. 6.6 (a) Simplified OR matrix; (b) programmed OR matrix.

Even though S_1 is formed with just one product term, it is at the 1 logic level for two input conditions. These states are $I_3 I_2 I_1 I_0$ =0111 and $I_3 I_2 I_1 I_0$ =1111. This is because input I_3 is a don't care state and can be logic 0 or 1.

EXAMPLE 6.3 What is the output equation for S_2 and for which input states is it logic 1? Assume that the product terms are those set up in the AND matrix of Fig. 6.5(b).

SOLUTION Looking at the circuit in Fig. 6.6(b), we see that the fuse links for product terms P_0 and P_3 are in place for the S_2 OR gate. Therefore, its sum-of-products equation is

$$S_2 = P_0 + P_3$$

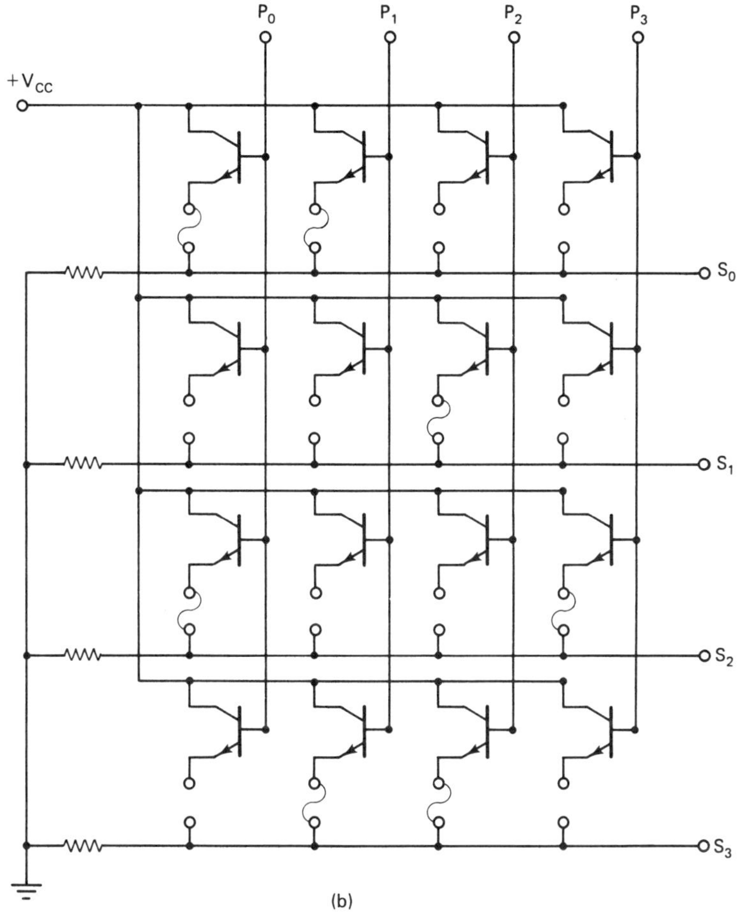

(b)

Fig. 6.6 Continued

Replacing the product terms with those defined by the AND matrix in Fig. 6.5(b), we get

$$S_0 = \bar{I}_3\bar{I}_2\bar{I}_1\bar{I}_0 + \bar{I}_3\bar{I}_2 I_1$$

The S_0 output is logic 1 if either or both of its product terms is logic 1. The first term is logic 1 when all inputs are logic 0:

$$I_3 I_2 I_1 I_0 = 0000$$

The other term is 1 when $I_1 = 1$, $I_2 = 0$, and $I_3 = 0$. This occurs for two input states because I_0 is a don't-care state. The states are

$$I_3 I_2 I_1 I_0 = 0010$$

and

$$I_3 I_2 I_1 I_0 = 0011$$

NOR Matrix

The NOR matrix is a programmable buffer that can be set for inverting or noninverting operation. With it the PLA outputs can be set for active 1 or active 0 logic levels.

Although it is called the NOR matrix, this part of the PLA circuit does not contain NOR gates. Instead, it uses one exclusive-OR gate for each output of the OR matrix. NOR-matrix circuitry for four outputs of a PLA is shown in Fig. 6.7. In some PLA devices the NOR matrix is formed with inverters instead of exclusive-OR gates.

The name of this matrix comes from the way in which it affects PLA operation, not from the type of circuitry. Through programming, the NOR matrix can be set to work as an inverter at the output of the OR matrix. In this way, it converts the OR matrix into a NOR matrix.

In the circuit of Fig. 6.7, we find that one input on each exclusive-OR gate is a sum signal supplied by the output of the OR matrix. The other input on all gates is connected to ground through a programmable fuse link.

Let us look into the operation of the NOR matrix when the fuse links are left intact. With ground supplied through the fuse link, one input on each exclusive-OR gate is logic 0. If a 0 logic level is applied to the S input, both inputs are logic 0. The output switches to logic 0 for this input condition. On the other hand, changing S to logic 1 makes the inputs of the gate 0 and 1. Now the output switches to logic 1. In this way, we see that with the fuse links in place, NOR-matrix operation is noninverting. The NOR-matrix outputs follow the inputs from the OR matrix and the active output levels are logic 1.

Now that we have determined how the NOR matrix operates with the fuse links left intact, let us look at what happens if the fuse links are opened

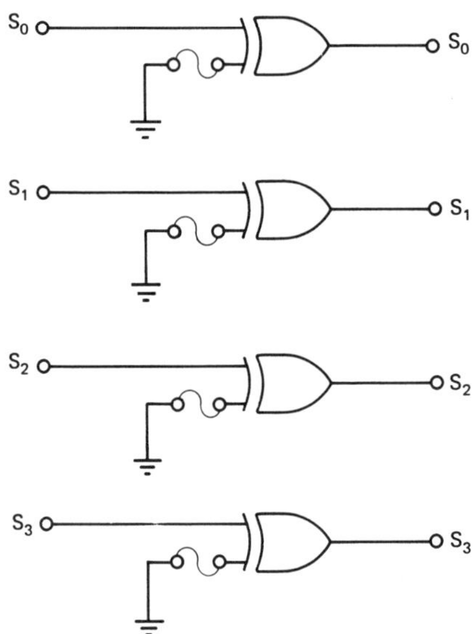

Fig. 6.7 Simplified NOR matrix.

through programming. The open link makes the programmable input on the exclusive-OR gate logic 1. Applying logic 0 at the S input, we get a logic 1 output. Moreover, applying logic 1 at S produces a logic 0 output. This time the exclusive-OR gate output is the opposite logic level of the sum input. Therefore, the NOR matrix is set for inverting operation and the active output logic level is 0. In actual applications, the gates in the NOR matrix can be individually set for inverting and noninverting operation.

EXAMPLE 6.4 Assume that the NOR matrix in Fig. 6.7 is to be programmed so that the links for the gates corresponding to S_0 and S_1 are left intact and those for S_2 and S_3 are opened. What is the output of the NOR matrix when its inputs are $S_3S_2S_1S_0$=0101?

SOLUTION The exclusive-OR gates for the S_0 and S_1 inputs are set up to be noninverting. Therefore, their outputs are logic 1 and 0, respectively. The other two exclusive-OR gates are programmed to be inverting. For this reason, the S_2 and S_3 inputs are inverted to the 0 and 1 logic levels, respectively.

Output Buffer

The output buffer takes the outputs from the NOR matrix and produces TTL-compatible output signals F_0 through F_7. IC devices are available with standard TTL output circuitry, open-collector output circuitry, and three-state output circuitry. The circuit in Fig. 6.8 shows four three-state output buffers.

The $\overline{CE}$ control lead sets the mode of output buffer operation. A logic 0 at $\overline{CE}$ enables the output for operation. If $\overline{CE}$ is set to logic 1, the outputs are switched to the hi-Z third state. Now the outputs electrically operate as open circuits. Open-collector and three-state outputs are necessary for applications that require parallel busing at the output leads.

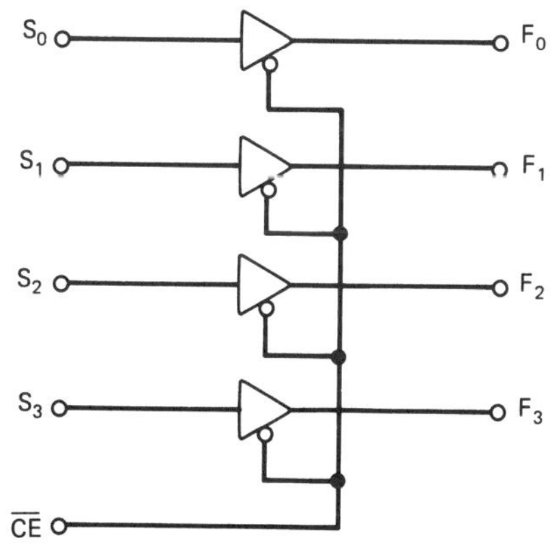

Fig. 6.8 Simplified output buffer.

6.4 PROGRAMMING THE PLA

Programming of PLAs is similar to the programming of ROMs. Through programming, the device is told which output will be produced for which input condition. In a ROM, data are programmed at the storage locations for all addresses; however, in a PLA only the active output states need to be programmed. Outputs default to the inactive logic levels; therefore, inactive states do not have to be programmed.

For a mask-programmable PLA device, the required program connections for the AND, OR, and NOR matrix are written as a specification and sent to the manufacturer of the device. The appropriate mask connections specified for the data pattern are built in during a mask-programming step of the manufacturing process.

If shorter turnaround time is required for devices, FPLAs can be obtained and programmed by the user. FPLAs are more difficult to program than PROMs, because they need three separate programming steps: one for the AND matrix, one for the OR matrix, and one for the NOR matrix.

In the initial state, an FPLA has all its Nichrome fuse links intact. During programming, unwanted links are electrically open-circuited. The user is able to access the fuse links that are to be opened by applying addresses to the inputs and outputs of the device. Once a fuse is addressed, a current is injected through the fuse to blow it open and program the connection. The links left intact determine the storage pattern.

Editing of a FPLA is possible if all unused P terms in the matrix have been left with their input and output links intact. With all inputs still connected, the input condition cannot be satisfied. Therefore, the product term output stays at the 0 logic level. This term will not affect the OR-matrix outputs. Using these extra product terms, we can make postprogramming changes in the data pattern.

For example, to add a product term to an output function that already exists, just program the inputs of an unused AND gate to form the product term and then disable the product term from all sum outputs, other than the one corresponding to the function to which it is to be added.

Another common edit is to remove an existing product term. This can be done by simply opening the fuse link connection to the OR matrix. A third type of edit permits the changing of an active 1 logic level to an active 0 logic level by opening the fuse link in the NOR matrix.

6.5 INTERNAL OPERATION OF THE PLA

The PLA, its input/output operation, internal architecture, and programming have just been introduced. Let us now trace the operation of the PLA circuit from input to output. For this purpose, we shall use the simplified circuit in Fig. 6.9.

PLA operation begins when an address or group of logic signals is applied to inputs I_0 through I_3. Let us make the input 1000. These inputs go through the inverter gates to produce buffered inputs:

$$I_3 I_2 I_1 I_0 = 1000$$

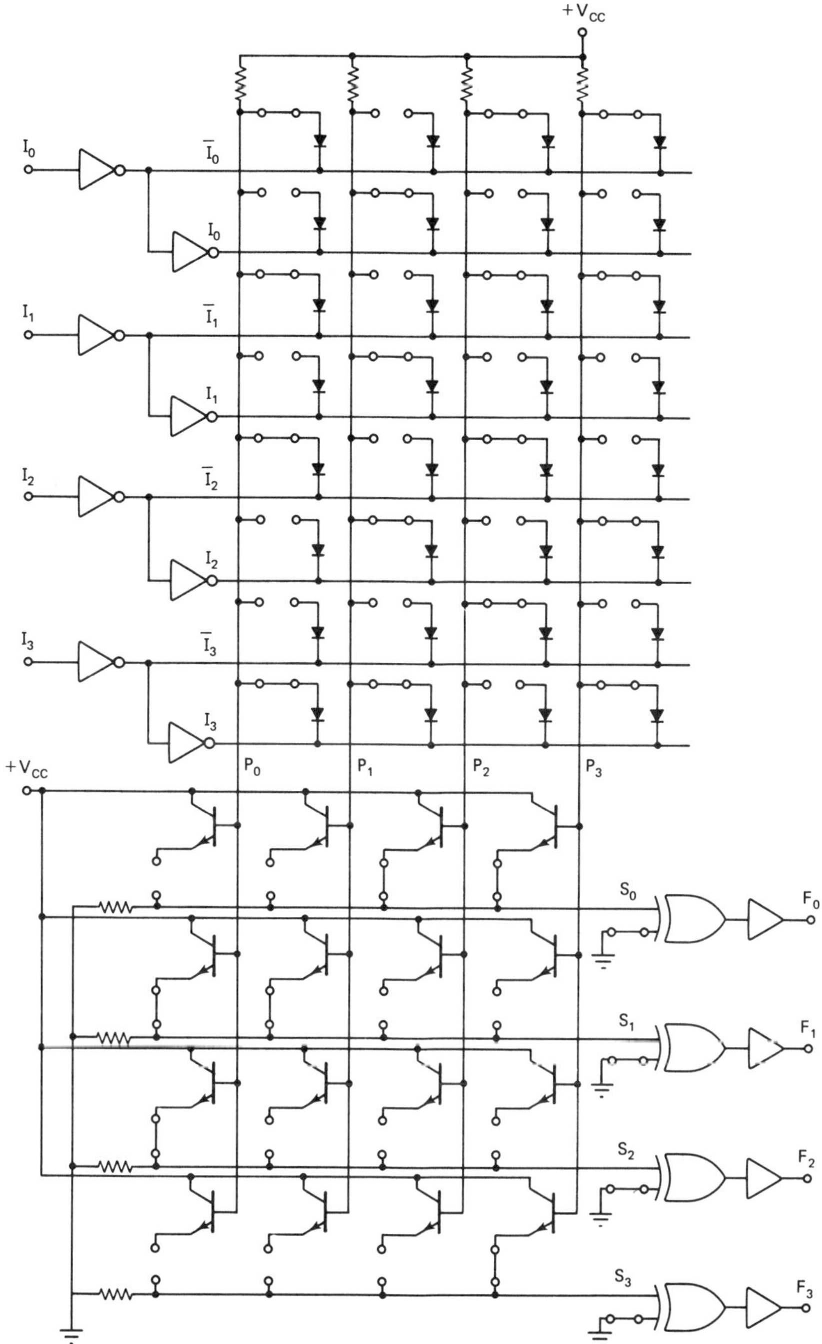

Fig. 6.9 Simplified PLA circuit.

and

$$\bar{I}_3 \bar{I}_2 \bar{I}_1 \bar{I}_0 = 0111$$

These buffered signals supply inputs to the AND matrix. The AND gates decode these inputs to produce product term outputs P_0 through P_3. The outputs of the gates which have all inputs at logic 1 switch to the 1 level and all other outputs stay at logic 0. In the AND matrix of Fig. 6.9, we see that P_0 represents the product term $I_3 \bar{I}_2 \bar{I}_1 \bar{I}_0$. Because we applied 1000 to the address inputs, these signals are all logic 1; therefore, P_0 switches to the 1 level. All other AND gates have at least one input that is logic 0. For this reason, outputs P_2, P_3, and P_4 are logic 0.

$$P_0 = 1$$

$$P_1 = P_2 = P_3 = 0$$

The product term outputs are used as inputs to the OR matrix. Here they are combined to produce the sum outputs. Each OR gate must have at least one input at logic 1 to produce a 1 level at its sum output. We have already determined that $P_0 = 1$ and $P_1 = P_2 = P_3 = 0$. The OR gates for outputs S_1 and S_2 have P_0 as an input. Therefore, both of these outputs switch to logic 1, while the other two sum outputs default to logic 0.

$$S_0 = S_3 = 0$$

$$S_1 = S_2 = 1$$

The NOR matrix in the circuit is set for noninverting operation, so the sum outputs of the OR matrix are passed through the exclusive-OR gates and output buffer without inverting logic levels.

$$F_3 F_2 F_1 F_0 = S_3 S_2 S_1 S_0 = 0110$$

EXAMPLE 6.5 Write the Boolean equation for the F_0 output of the PLA in Fig. 6.9.

SOLUTION To write the Boolean equation for output F_0, we begin by recognizing that it is the same as that for the S_0 output of the OR matrix.

$$F_0 = S_0$$

Next, the product terms that produce S_0 must be determined. Looking at the circuit in Fig. 6.9, we find that just P_2 and P_3 are programmed as inputs to the S_0 OR gate.

$$S_0 = P_2 + P_3$$

Product terms for P_2 and P_3 are formed by identifying which inputs are connected to their respective gate in the AND matrix. The AND gate for P_2 has inputs $\bar{I}_0, \bar{I}_1, \bar{I}_2$, and $\bar{I}_3$; therefore, its product term is

$$P_2 = \bar{I}_3 \bar{I}_2 \bar{I}_1 \bar{I}_0$$

The P_3 AND gate has inputs $\bar{I}_0, \bar{I}_1, I_2$, and I_3. This gives the product term

$$P_3 = I_3 I_2 \bar{I}_1 \bar{I}_0$$

Substituting into the output equation results with

$$F_0 = S_0 = \bar{I}_3 \bar{I}_2 \bar{I}_1 \bar{I}_0 + I_3 I_2 \bar{I}_1 \bar{I}_0$$

EXAMPLE 6.6 What are the outputs of the PLA in Fig. 6.9 when the input is $I_3 I_2 I_1 I_0 = 1100$?

SOLUTION The inputs to the buffer produce the outputs

$$I_3 I_2 I_1 I_0 = 1100$$

$$\bar{I}_3 \bar{I}_2 \bar{I}_1 \bar{I}_0 = 0011$$

All inputs to the AND gate for product terms P_3 are logic 1. This produces a 1 logic level at its output.

$$P_3 = I_3 I_2 \bar{I}_1 \bar{I}_0 = 1111 = 1$$

The other three AND gates have at least one input at the 0 level and their outputs are logic 0.

$$P_0 = P_1 = P_2 = 0$$

In the OR matrix, P_3 is connected to outputs S_0 and S_3. These outputs switch to logic 1 while the other two remain at the inactive 0 logic level.

$$S_0 = S_3 = 1$$

$$S_1 = S_2 = 0$$

The sum signals are passed through the noninverting NOR matrix and output buffer. This gives the output

$$F_3 F_2 F_1 F_0 = 1001$$

6.6 STANDARD PLA AND FPLA INTEGRATED CIRCUITS

In previous sections, we introduced the PLA and FPLA devices, their internal architecture, programming, and operation. Now we are ready to look into some of the PLA and FPLA ICs presently available.

The 82S200 integrated circuit is a mask-programmable PLA device. Figure 6.10(a) shows its internal architecture. From the diagram we see that the architecture of the circuit in the 82S200 is identical to the architecture introduced earlier. A pin layout of the 82S200 is given in Fig. 6.10(b).

From the circuit diagram of Fig. 6.10(a), we find that the 82S200 has a capacity of 16 inputs, 8 outputs, and 48 product terms. The inputs are denoted I_0 through I_{15}. If this PLA is used as a ROM, the 16-bit input has an address range from 0 to 65,535. Moreover, the outputs which are labeled F_0 through F_7 can produce an 8-bit output word. Each of these outputs can be individually set for active 1 of active 0 logic levels. Besides this, the outputs can be enabled or disabled with the $\overline{CE}$ control input.

The address or logic signals applied to the PLA inputs are first buffered to produce signals I_0 through I_{15} and $\bar{I}_0$ through $\bar{I}_{15}$. These buffered input signals are used as inputs for the AND gate matrix. The AND-gate matrix decodes this input to produce product terms. It contains 48 32-input diode logic AND gates. The inputs of these AND gates must be connected to the appropriate input signals by mask programming to generate the appropriate product terms P_0 through P_{47}.

The product term outputs of the AND matrix go to inputs of the OR matrix. Here they are combined to form Boolean equations describing the sum outputs. The OR matrix is formed from eight 48-input RTL OR gates. Transistors for the appropriate product terms must be connected into the OR gate by mask programming. In this way, each OR gate generates an equation for one of the sum outputs S_0 through S_7.

The sum outputs go to inputs of the NOR matrix. This matrix sets the active logic level of the outputs. In this matrix, we find eight programmable exclusive-OR gates. If the programmable input is connected to ground, the gate operates as a noninverting buffer and the active state of the output is logic 1. On the other hand, leaving the programming input disconnected makes the gate inverting. This results in an active 0 output level.

The outputs of the NOR matrix are applied to the inputs of the three-state output buffers. The operation of these noninverting buffer gates are controlled by the $\overline{CE}$ input. When $\overline{CE}$ is logic 1, the outputs are in the hi-Z state, while logic 0 at $\overline{CE}$ enables the outputs for operation.

The 82S200 requires a +5-V dc power supply. Looking at the pin layout in Fig. 6.10(b), we see that this voltage is applied between $+V_{CC}$ at pin 28 and *GND* at pin 14. This device is rated to operate correctly with up to ±0.5 V variation in supply voltage. Typical power consumption is 600 mW.

Moreover, the input and output logic levels of the 82S200 are TTL-compatible. The input logic levels are rated at V_{ILmax} = 0.8 V and V_{IHmin} = 2 V and the outputs are rated at V_{OLmax} = 0.5 V and V_{OHmin} = 2.4 V.

Up to this point, we have not yet considered the switching characteristics involved in PLA operation. Just like the ROM device, a short amount of time delay is experienced between address input and data output. This

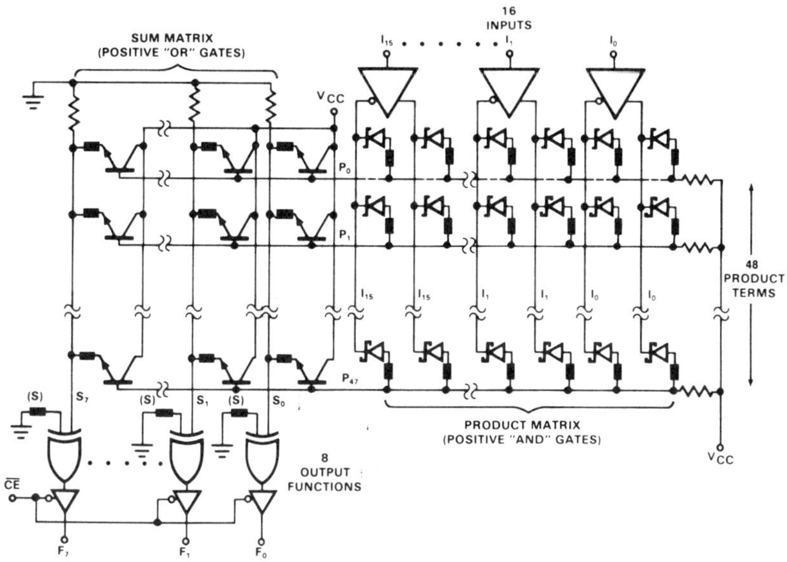

(a)

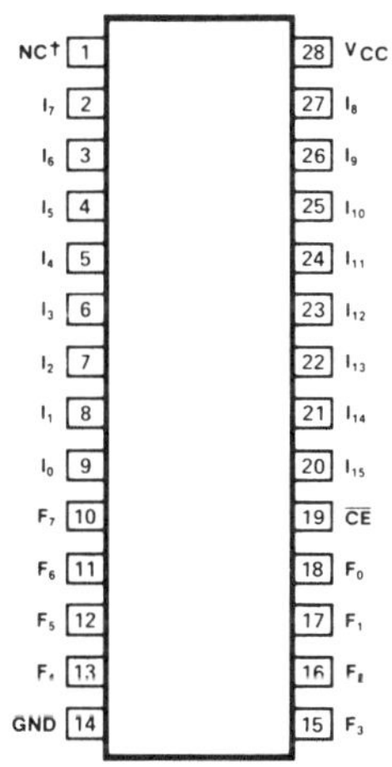

(b)

Fig. 6.10 (a) 82S200 circuit diagram (Permission to reprint granted by Signetics Corporation, a subsidiary of U.S. Philips Corp., 811 East Arques Avenue, Sunnyvale, CA 94806); (b) 82S200 pin layout (Permission to reprint granted by Signetics Corporation, a subsidiary of U.S. Philips Corp., 811 East Arques Avenue, Sunnyvale, CA 94806).

time is known as *input to output access time* t_{ACC}. For the 82S200 the maximum value of t_{ACC} is 80 ns. A second access time is also specified for the 82S200. It is called the *chip enable to output access time.* This time represents the delay between the instant at which the output circuitry is enabled with logic 0 at $\overline{CE}$ and the occurrence of stable data at the outputs.

For this operation, the input address is assumed to already be set up and stable. The maximum value of chip enable to output delay is 50 ns.

The 82S201 is a mask-programmable device with the same capacity as the 82S200. Their internal circuitry and operation are also identical. The only difference between the two devices lies in their output circuitry. The 82S201 is equipped with open-collector outputs instead of three-state outputs.

82S100 and 82S101 FPLAs

The 82S100 is a widely used field-programmable logic array IC. Its circuit diagram and pin layout are shown in Fig. 6.11(a) and (b), respectively.

Looking at this circuit diagram, we see that the architecture of the 82S100 is similar to that just described for the 82S200. Both devices have 16 inputs, 8 three-state outputs, and an AND matrix that can produce 48 product terms. The only difference between the two devices is that the 82S100 contains Nichrome fuse links that permit programming by the user. These fuse links come intact and are selectively opened through programming to make the data pattern within the device.

The 82S100 can be used in the design phase of a product. In this way, modifications can be quickly made to the program. For production equipment, the 82S200 can be used instead of the 82S100. The 82S200 in a pin-for-pin mask-programmable replacement for the 82S100.

The 82S101 is identical to the 82S100 except that it has open-collector outputs instead of three-state outputs. The 82S201 PLA is a mask-programmable replacement for the 82S101.

DM7575 and DM7576 PLAs

Another popular mask-programmable PLA device is the DM7575. This PLA has a different capacity than the ICs introduced so far. It has 14 inputs, 8 outputs, and the capability of 96 product terms. Notice that the DM7575 has two less inputs than the 82S200 and 82S201 devices, but has the ability to produce twice as many product terms.

The internal architecture of the DM7575 is shown in Fig. 6.12(a). Here we see the inputs are marked I_1 through I_{14}. The input buffer, AND matrix, and OR matrix are essentially the same as those found in the earlier devices. The only difference here is that the AND matrix has been expanded to accommodate 96 product terms.

On the other hand, the exclusive-OR gates and output buffers found in earlier ICs are replaced with eight programmable inverting buffers in the DM7575. When the programming link is left out during the mask-programming step of production, the buffer is inverting. This gives active 0 output logic levels. In this case, the outputs are denoted $\overline{F}_1$ through $\overline{F}_8$.

Installing the link during programming shorts out the inverter. This time the output of the OR matrix is not inverted, and logic 1 is the active output level. Now the outputs are identified as F_1 through F_8.

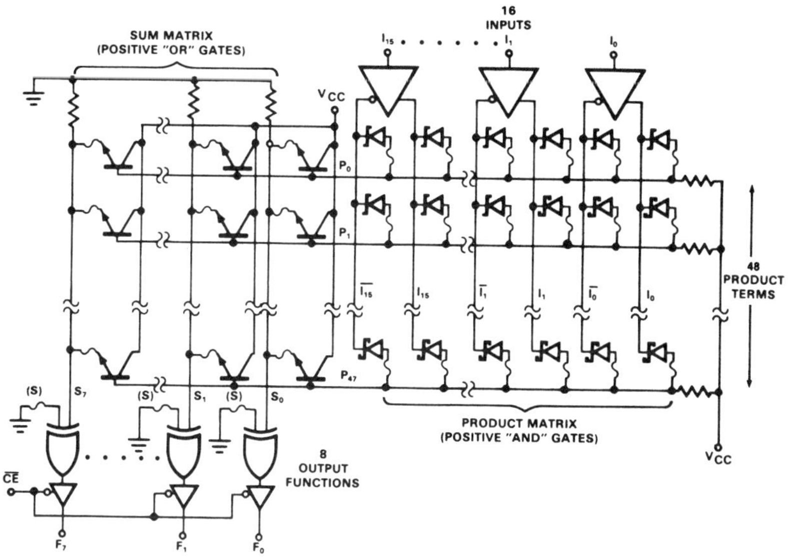

(a)

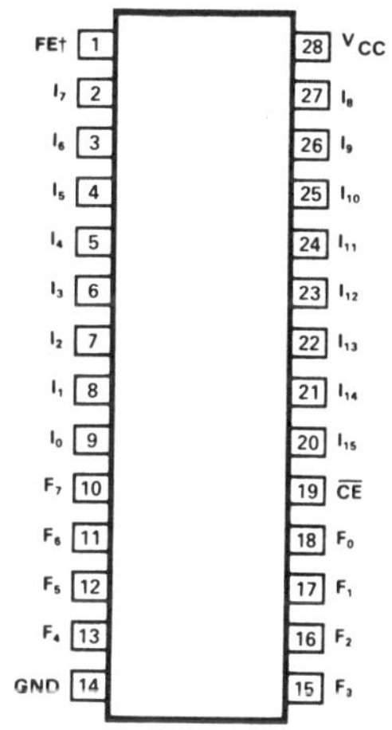

(b)

Fig. 6.11 (a) 82S100 circuit diagram (Permission to reprint granted by Signetics Corporation, a subsidiary of U.S. Philips Corp., 811 East Arques Avenue, Sunnyvale, CA 94806); (b) 82S100 pin layout (Permission to reprint granted by Signetics Corporation, a subsidiary of U.S. Philips Corp., 811 East Arques Avenue, Sunnyvale, CA 94806).

The DM7575 also operates from a 5V ± 0.5V dc power supply. As shown in Fig. 6.12(b), this voltage is applied between $+V_{CC}$ at pin 24 and *GND* at pin 12. This device requires 550 mW of power to operate. Moreover, the input and output logic levels of the DM7575 are TTL-compatible and its maximum input to output access time is 150 ns.

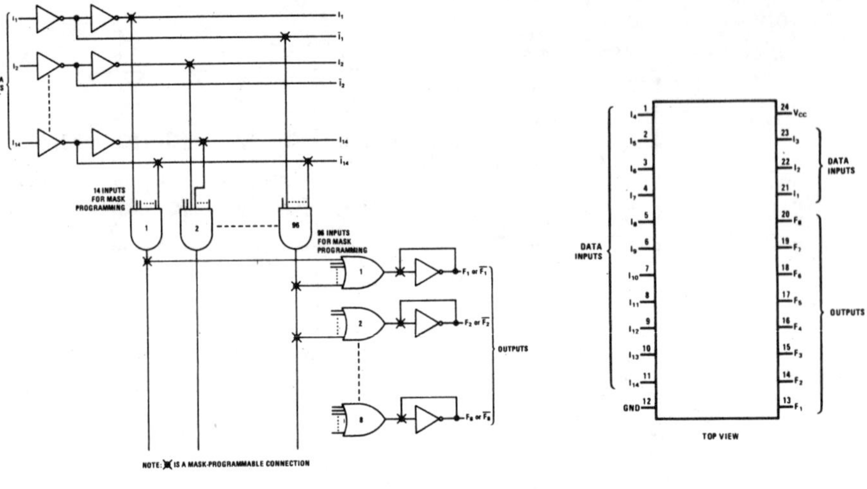

(a) (b)

Fig. 6.12 (a) DM7575 circuit diagram (National Semiconductor Corp.); (b) DM7575 pin layout (National Semiconductor Corp.).

The DM7576 is identical in capacity, architecture, and operation to the DM7575 PLA; however, it has open-collector output circuitry.

6.7 PROGRAMMABLE LOGIC ARRAYS IN RANDOM LOGIC AND ROM APPLICATIONS

In modern digital equipment, programmable logic array ICs can be used in many of the same basic applications as read-only memories. Next we show how PLAs can be used to implement random logic circuitry and a code-converter ROM.

Implementing Random Logic Circuitry

PLAs can be used in a wide variety of combinational and sequential logic applications. A single PLA IC can be programmed to implement any combinational logic network that can be represented with 16 or fewer inputs, 8 or fewer outputs, and 96 or fewer product terms.

When a PLA is used to implement a logic network, each output can represent an independent Boolean function. The AND matrix is programmed with all product terms required to form the output equations. This is done by connecting the appropriate input signals to the AND gates.

The product terms required by each output equation are combined by programming the OR matrix. The selected product terms are ORed together by the OR gates to produce sum-of-product equations. If a product term is to be used in more than one output equation, it should exist only once in the AND matrix. The corresponding P output is connected to the OR-gate input for each output in which it is used. In this way, product terms available in the IC are conserved.

The procedure used to implement combinational logic functions with a PLA can be broken down into the following steps:

1. Tabulate the I/O operation required of the logic network.
2. Write sum-of-product Boolean equations for the output functions.
3. Simplify the equations to obtain the minimum sum-of-products form.
4. Determine the AND-matrix input connections required to form the unique product terms.
5. Determine the OR-matrix connections required to sum the product terms into the output equations.
6. Determine the NOR-matrix connections required to set the active logic levels of the outputs.
7. Program the PLA.

The main advantage of PLAs over random logic circuitry in combinational logic network applications is their ability to compact circuitry. A network that requires many SSI and MSI devices can be implemented with a single PLA device. In an earlier chapter, we saw that read-only memory devices could also be used to implement combinational and sequential circuitry. However, the PLA with its faster access time is better suited than ROM for these high-speed switching circuits.

EXAMPLE 6.7 Demonstrate how a PLA should be programmed to produce the combinational functions defined by the equations $F_1 = I_1 + \overline{I}_3 I_2$ and $F_2 = \overline{I}_2 I_1 + I_3 \overline{I}_2 \overline{I}_1$. Show only the part of the PLA circuit that is required to implement the equations.

SOLUTION From the equations we see that the PLA requires three inputs, I_1, I_2, and I_3; two outputs, F_1 and F_2; and four six-input AND gates for product terms. Figure 6.13 shows this segment of circuitry for a mask-programmable PLA.

First the AND-gate inputs must be connected to the input buffer outputs to produce the product terms. The first product terms for function F_1 is simply input I_1. This term is formed with the leftmost AND gate by providing a mask-programmable link for the I_1 input. All other inputs to the gate are left disconnected.

The second product term of F_1 is $\overline{I}_3 I_2$. It is formed with the second AND gate from the left. Here links are provided for the $\overline{I}_3$ and I_2 inputs.

The two product terms required for function F_2 are $\overline{I}_2 I_1$ and $I_3 \overline{I}_2 \overline{I}_1$. These terms are formed with the next two AND gates in the matrix. The third AND gate from the left has I_1 and $\overline{I}_2$ mask-programmed with link connections. The rightmost gate has $\overline{I}_1$, $\overline{I}_2$, and I_3 connected.

Now we are ready to program the OR matrix by connecting the appropriate product terms through the OR gates to the sum outputs. Output S_1 produces function F_1, and S_2 produces F_2. The S_1 output is the sum of product terms P_1 and P_2. Therefore, the transistors for these two terms are connected with links in the upper OR gate. The links for P_3 and P_4 are left open.

The S_2 output is the sum of product terms P_3 and P_4. In the lower OR gate, transistors for these two terms are connected with links to the S_2 output.

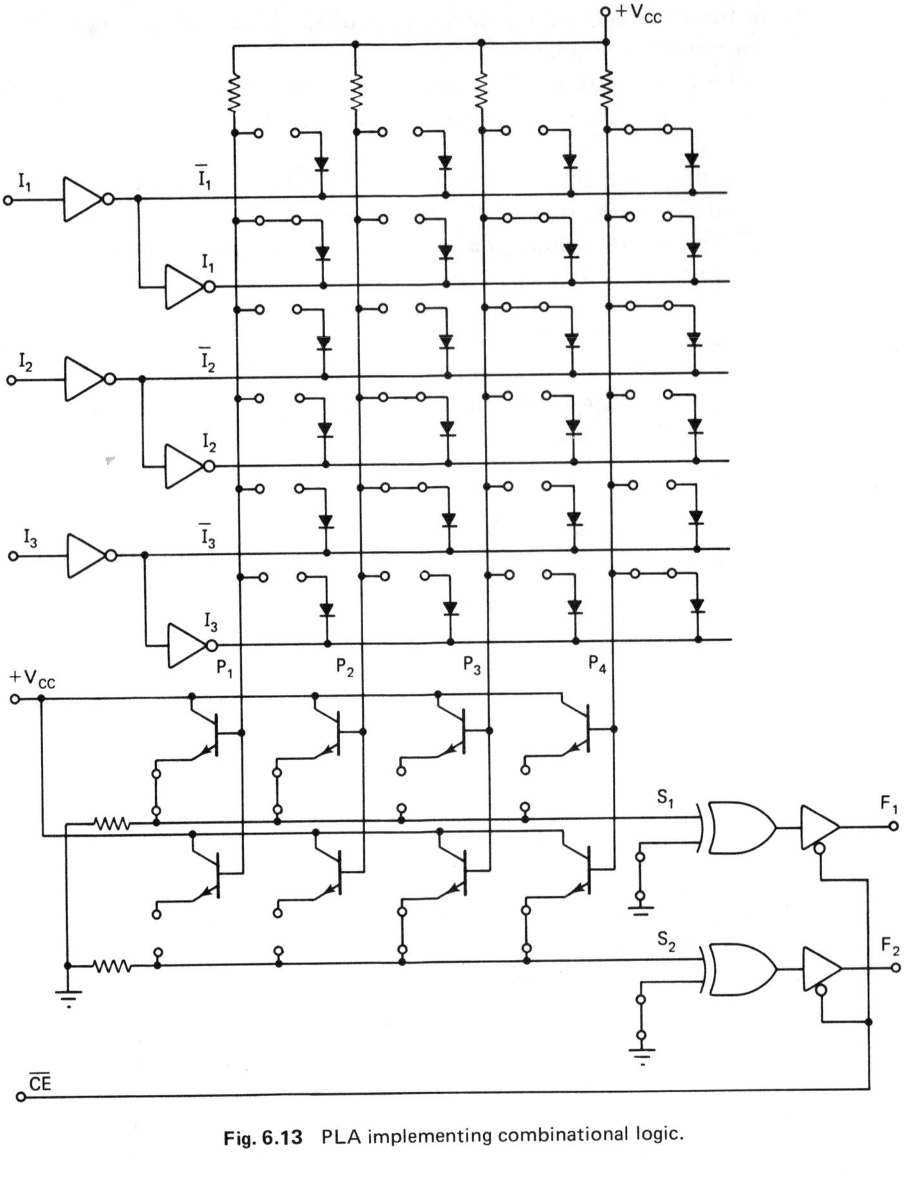

Fig. 6.13 PLA implementing combinational logic.

All the programmable inputs of the exclusive-OR gates in the NOR matrix are connected with links to ground. This sets outputs F_1 and F_2 to produce active 1 logic levels.

EXAMPLE 6.8 What are outputs F_1 and F_2 of the PLA in Fig. 6.13 for input $I_3I_2I_1$=101? Assume that $\overline{CE}$ is at the 0 logic level.

SOLUTION The input signals I_1, I_2, and I_3 are buffered to produce inputs for the AND matrix.

$$I_3 I_2 I_1 = 101$$

$$\bar{I}_3 \bar{I}_2 \bar{I}_1 = 010$$

Using these AND-matrix inputs, we find the product-term outputs to be

$$P_1 = I_1 = 1$$

$$P_2 = \bar{I}_3 I_2 = 0 \cdot 0 = 0$$

$$P_3 = \bar{I}_2 I_1 = 1 \cdot 1 = 1$$

$$P_4 = I_3 \bar{I}_2 \bar{I}_1 = 1 \cdot 1 \cdot 0 = 0$$

The product-term outputs are input to the OR matrix, where they produce the sum outputs.

$$S_1 = P_1 + P_2 = 1 + 0 = 1$$

$$S_2 = P_3 + P_4 = 1 + 0 = 1$$

The exclusive-OR gates in the NOR matrix are programmed not to invert logic levels. Therefore, the F_1 and F_2 outputs are equal to S_1 and S_2, respectively.

$$F_1 = S_1 = 1$$

$$F_2 = S_2 = 1$$

The PLA as a ROM

PLAs can also be programmed to operate as a *conditionally addressable ROM*. By conditionally addressable, we mean that all possible addresses cannot be programmed with data words. Some address words will not be programmed and will not read out data words. For unprogrammed address states, the outputs default to the inactive logic level, which can be logic 0 or logic 1. The PLA can be used in applications similar to those implemented with ROMs. For example, it can be programmed to operate as a code converter, character generator, or look-up table. The advantage of using the PLA instead of ROM in these applications is again its faster access time.

To use the PLA as a ROM, we begin by tabulating the input address words and their corresponding output words. Let us assume that the DM7575 PLA is to be programmed as a ROM. It provides capacity for 14-bit address words, 8-bit data words, and 96 product terms.

When the PLA is set up to work as a ROM, the AND matrix operates as an address decoder. The address words in the table of input/output operation are used to program the AND matrix. In a PLA, one AND gate is required to decode each address. This is done by connecting each AND gate input to the normal or complemented input produced by the input buffer.

For instance, Fig. 6.14 shows a simplified input buffer and AND gate connected to decode the 4-bit address word $I_3 I_2 I_1 I_0 = 1100$. The product

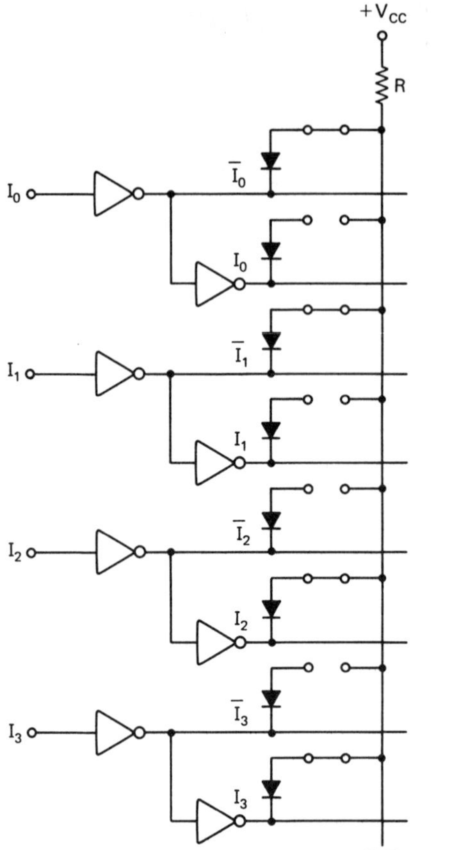

Fig. 6.14 Decoding an address.

term for this address is $I_3 I_2 \overline{I}_1 \overline{I}_0$. To program the AND gate to decode this input, we see that mask-programming links are connected to the $\overline{I}_0$, $\overline{I}_1$, I_2, and I_3 buffered inputs.

If we are using the DM7575 in this way, its 14-bit address word provides 16*k* of addresses. However, just 96 of these addresses can be uniquely decoded by the PLA. When one of the programmed addresses is applied to inputs I_1 through I_{14}, the corresponding product-term output switches to logic 1. At the same time, all other *P* outputs stay at logic 0. On the other hand, applying an unprogrammed address to the inputs would result in all *P* outputs staying at logic 0.

For example, if the address 1100 is applied to the circuit in Fig. 6.14, the input buffer outputs I_3, I_2, $\overline{I}_1$, and $\overline{I}_0$ are all logic 1. This makes all inputs of the AND-gate logic 1 and the P_3 product term output switches to the 1 level.

The OR gates in the OR matrix serve as the storage elements in a PLA set up to operate as a ROM. Data words are programmed into the OR-gate array by going down the *P*-term line for the address and connecting the OR-gate transistor to the sum line for each output that is to be logic 1. In this way, only 96 data words can be stored in the OR matrix of a DM7575 PLA. When an address that is not programmed into the address decoder is applied to the input of the PLA, we find that all P-term outputs stay at logic 0. Therefore, all OR-matrix outputs also remain at logic 0 and the data outputs are at the inactive logic level.

Figure 6.15 shows how the P_3 product-term output is programmed to produce the data word $S_3 S_2 S_1 S_0$=0110. Notice that transistors for P_3 have their emitters connected to the S_1 and S_2 outputs. These sum outputs are to be logic 1 in the output word. The transistors for the other two sum lines are left disconnected, because they are to produce logic 0.

If the address $I_3 I_2 I_1 I_0$=1100 is applied to the inputs, P_3 switches to logic 1. At the same time, all other P outputs in the AND matrix are at logic 0. The 1 at P_3 makes the S_1 and S_2 outputs switch to logic 1, while S_0 and S_3 remain at logic 0. The data word produced at the OR-matrix output is $S_3 S_2 S_1 S_0$=0110.

The sum outputs are input to the NOR matrix. This matrix, in a PLA set up for ROM operation, normally produces active 1 logic levels. In a DM7575 PLA, this type of operation is obtained by installing programming links for each inverter bypass. In this way, the data outputs of the PLA are made the same as the sum outputs of the OR matrix. Therefore, the data word is $F_3 F_2 F_1 F_0$=$S_3 S_2 S_1 S_0$.

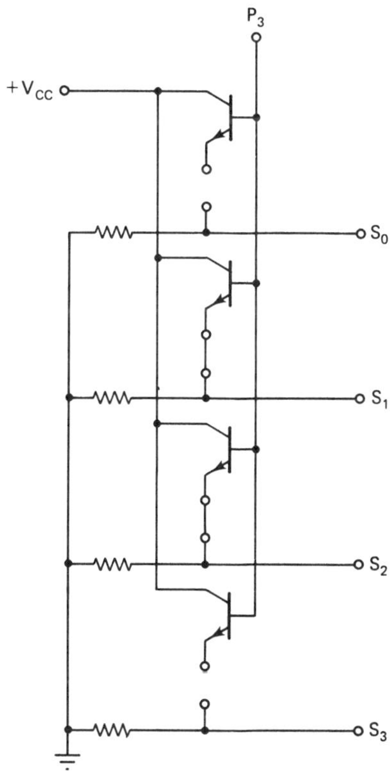

Fig. 6.15 Storing a data word.

BCD				XS-3			
I_3	I_2	I_1	I_0	F_3	F_2	F_1	F_0
0	0	0	0	0	0	1	1
0	0	0	1	0	1	0	0
0	0	1	0	0	1	0	1
0	0	1	1	0	1	1	0
0	1	0	0	0	1	1	1
0	1	0	1	1	0	0	0
0	1	1	0	1	0	0	1
0	1	1	1	1	0	1	0
1	0	0	0	1	0	1	1
1	0	0	1	1	1	0	0

Fig. 6.16 Input/output table of BCD-to-XS-3 code-converter operation.

EXAMPLE 6.9 Demonstrate how a PLA can be programmed to implement the BCD-to-XS-3 code-converter circuit described by the truth table in Fig. 6.16. Show only that part of the PLA circuit required to implement the code converter.

SOLUTION To implement the BCD-to-XS-3 code converter in Fig. 6.16, the PLA must have four-inputs, four-outputs, and 10 product terms. A section of PLA with this capacity is shown in Fig. 6.17.

The address inputs are programmed into the AND matrix. The first address word is 0000. This word is programmed into the leftmost AND gate as product term $P_0=\overline{I}_3\overline{I}_2\overline{I}_1\overline{I}_0$. The next address word down the table is 0001. It is programmed into the second AND gate from the left and produces product term $P_1=\overline{I}_3\overline{I}_2\overline{I}_1 I_0$.

The next eight AND gates implement the rest of the address words in the order in which they appear when going down the table. These product terms are

$$P_2=\overline{I}_3\overline{I}_2 I_1\overline{I}_0$$

$$P_3=\overline{I}_3\overline{I}_2 I_1 I_0$$

$$P_4=\overline{I}_3 I_2\overline{I}_1\overline{I}_0$$

$$P_5=\overline{I}_3 I_2\overline{I}_1 I_0$$

$$P_6=\overline{I}_3 I_2 I_1\overline{I}_0$$

$$P_7=\overline{I}_3 I_2 I_1 I_0$$

$$P_8=I_3\overline{I}_2\overline{I}_1\overline{I}_0$$

$$P_9=I_3\overline{I}_2\overline{I}_1 I_0$$

The OR matrix is next set up to store the data words. Address 0000 corresponds to product term P_0 and its data in the table are 0011. This data word is stored in the OR matrix by connecting the transistors from P_0 to output S_0 and P_0 to S_1.

The next address in the table of Fig. 6.16 corresponds to product term P_1. This address requires the data word 0100 and it is stored in the OR matrix by connecting the transistor for P_1 to the S_2 output. The remaining eight data words are formed in the same way.

In our use of the PLA as a ROM, we have used general product terms at the AND-matrix inputs. That is, each input or its complement is connected.

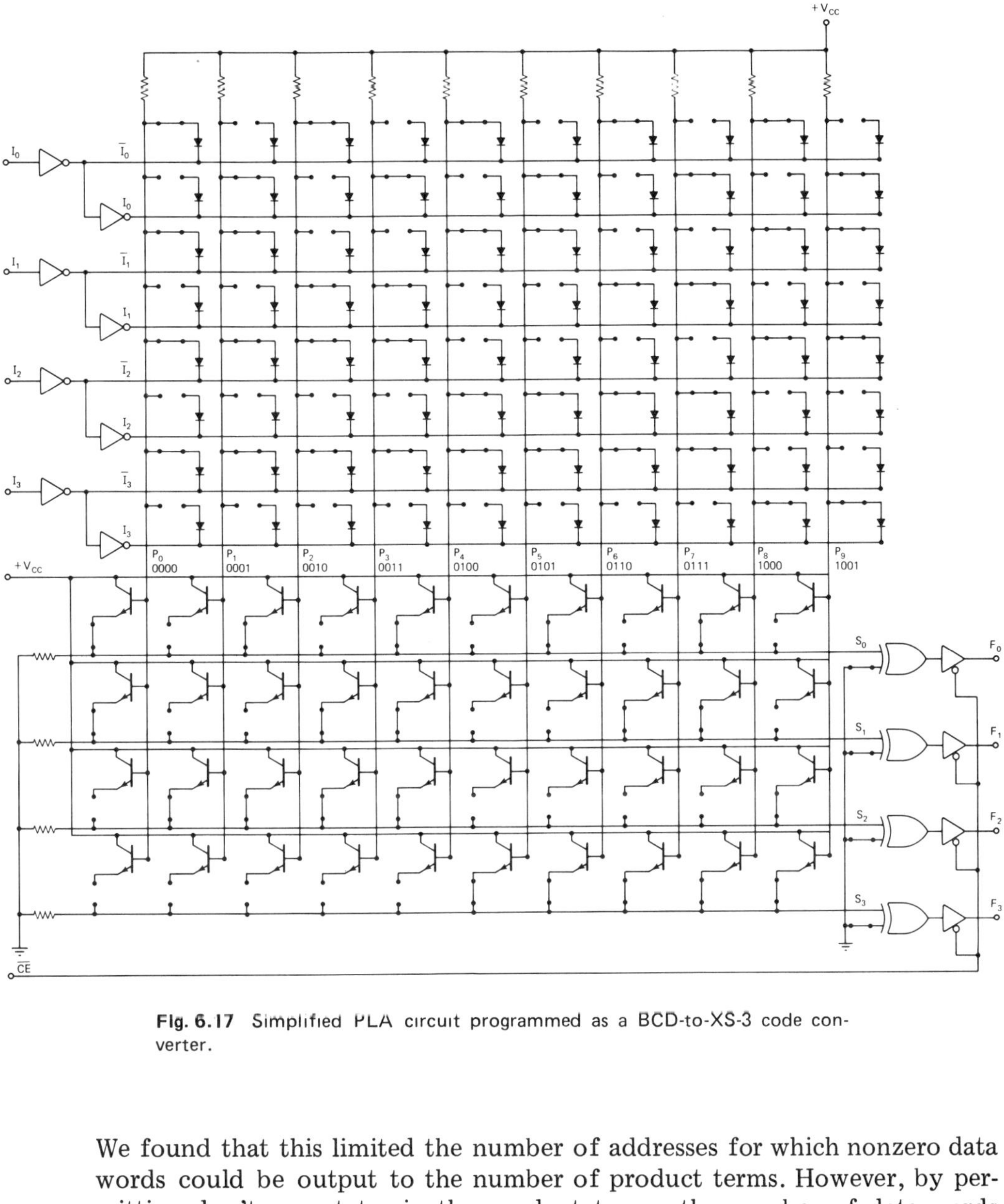

Fig. 6.17 Simplified PLA circuit programmed as a BCD-to-XS-3 code converter.

We found that this limited the number of addresses for which nonzero data words could be output to the number of product terms. However, by permitting don't-care states in the product terms, the number of data words stored in the PLA remains the same, but some of the words will now be output for more than one address. Therefore, the number of addresses that produce nonzero data words is now greater than the number of product terms.

For example, the addresses $I_3 I_2 I_1 I_0$=0000 and $I_3 I_2 I_1 I_0$=1000 in a PLA are to produce the data word 1100. One approach would be to program the addresses into the AND matrix as $P_0=\overline{I}_3\overline{I}_2\overline{I}_1\overline{I}_0$ and $P_1=I_3\overline{I}_2\overline{I}_1\overline{I}_0$, respectively. The data word is then programmed for each P term into the OR matrix. Figure 6.18(a) shows these connections.

However, when creating P terms it is more efficient to recognize that the two addresses are the same except for bit I_3. Independent of the logic level of I_3, the output of the PLA is to be 1100. Therefore, I_3 is actually a don't-care state and the two terms can be represented with a single product term of $P_0 = \overline{I}_2 \overline{I}_1 \overline{I}_0$. This connection is given in Fig. 6.18(b). Notice that one product term has been saved.

6.8 EXPANDING PLA CAPACITY

Some applications have requirements that exceed the capacity of a single PLA IC. It may require more than 8 outputs, more than 16 inputs, or more than 96 product terms. As we found for ROMs, capacity can be expanded by interconnecting several devices together.

Increasing the Number of Outputs

If a single PLA does not have enough outputs, two or more devices can be connected into the configuration of Fig. 6.19(a). Here we see that the address inputs I_0 through I_{15} on the two devices are individually connected in parallel. This connection does not change the address range. It is still 16 bits and can address 64*k* storage locations.

On the other hand, the 8-bit outputs of the two PLAs are separately used to form the upper and lower bytes of a 16-bit output word. The bits of this word are denoted F_0 through F_{15}. So with this connection, we have doubled output word length.

When an address is applied to the inputs, PLA 1 outputs the eight least significant bits of the data word. At the same instant, PLA 2 outputs the eight most significant bits.

Increasing the Number of Product Terms

In other applications, the number of inputs and outputs can be correct, but more product terms are needed. The circuit connection in Fig. 6.19(b) can be used to satisfy this requirement. Looking at the circuit, we find that the inputs and outputs of the two PLAs are individually connected in parallel. The number of inputs and outputs are unchanged; however, the product term capacity has doubled. For instance, if two DM7576 ICs are connected in this way, the 96-product-term capacity is expanded to 192 product terms.

Increasing the Number of Inputs

Another limitation on the application of PLAs is the number of input variables. The maximum number of inputs on a single 82S200 PLA is 16. However, additional ICs can be connected to expand the capacity of inputs. Figure 6.19(c) shows how one additional input is added. This permits a 17-

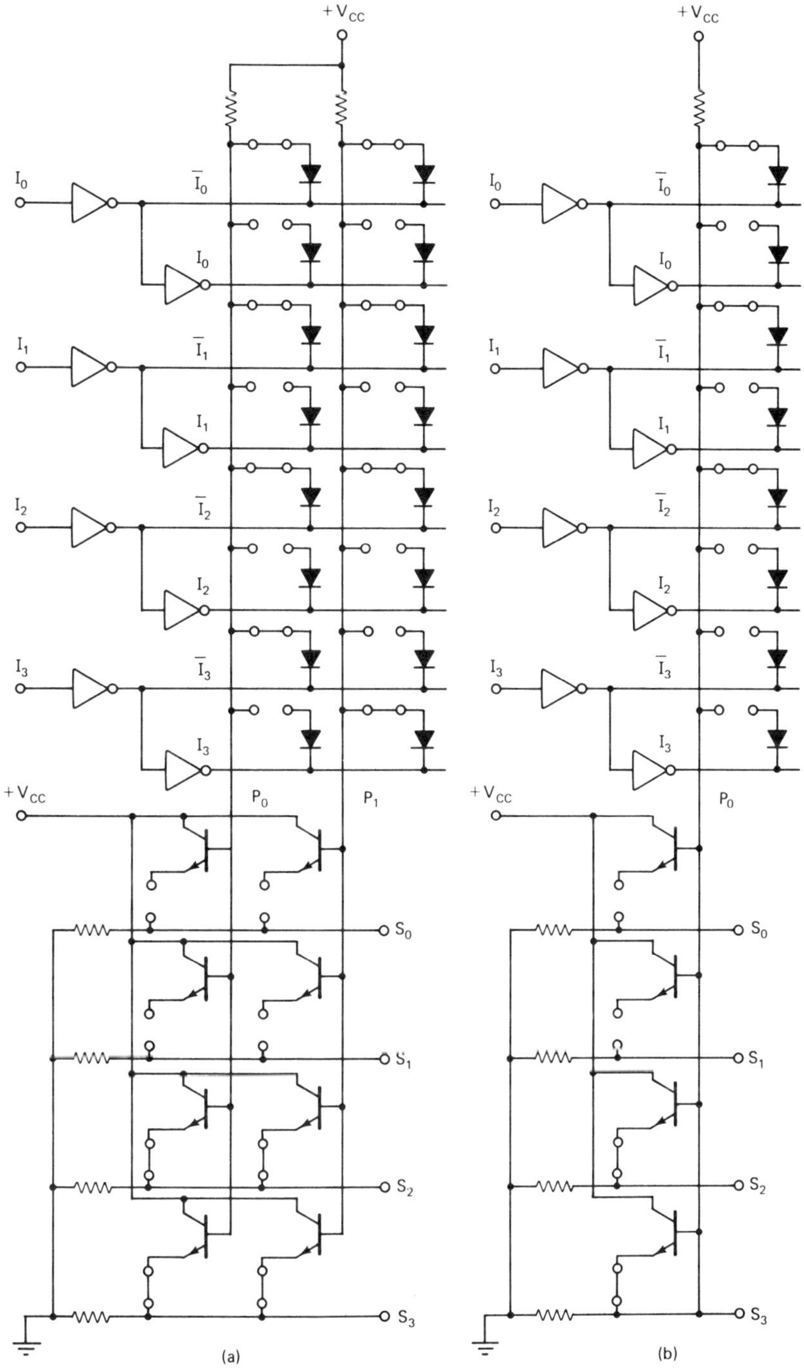

Fig. 6.18 (a) Implementing two data words; (b) implementing with a don't-care state.

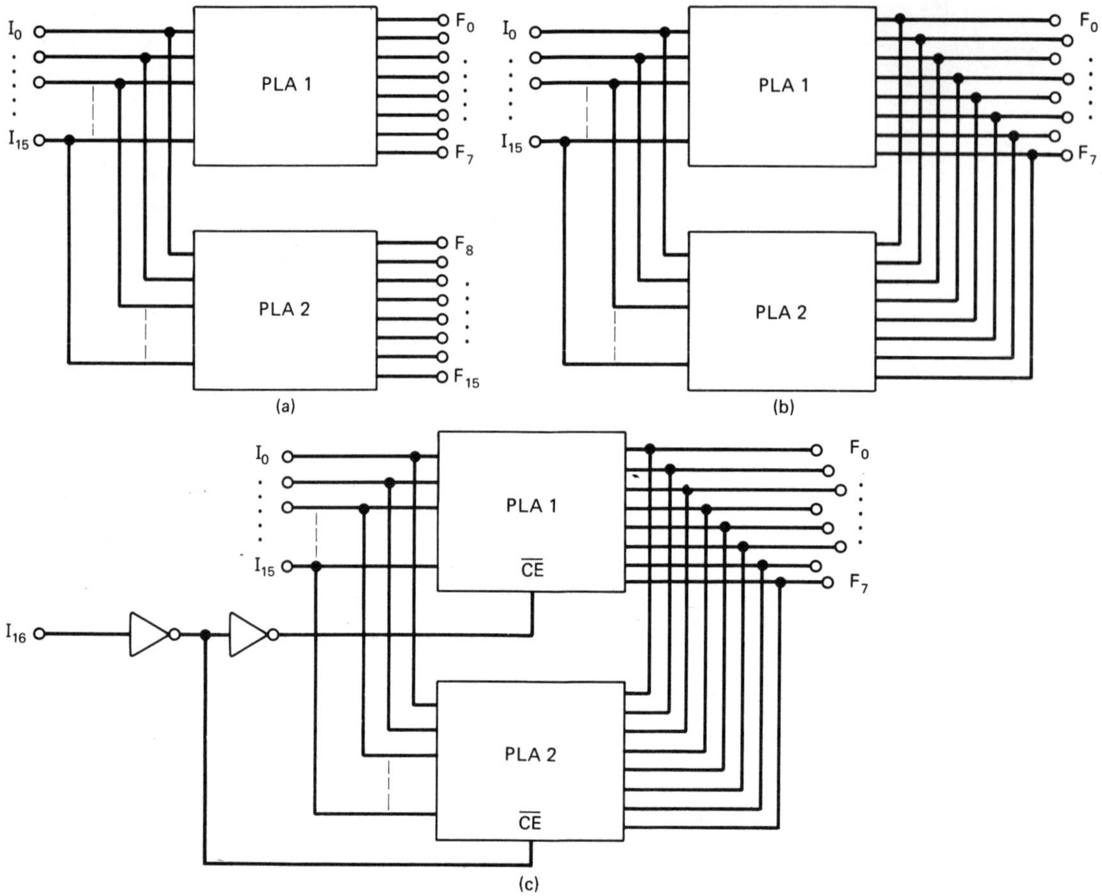

Fig. 6.19 (a) Expanding output word length; (b) increasing the number of product terms; (c) expanding input word length.

bit address word denoted I_0 through I_{16}. The new address bit I_{16} is supplied through inverters to the $\overline{CE}$ inputs on the two PLAs.

At the output side of the PLAs, outputs F_0 through F_7 of the two devices are individually connected in parallel. To use this connection, PLA devices with open-collector or three-state outputs must be used.

When I_{16} is logic 0, $\overline{CE}$ on PLA 1 is logic 0. This enables the device for operation, and the data stored for the address applied to I_0 through I_{15} are output at F_0 through F_7. At the same instant, $\overline{CE}$ on PLA 2 is logic 1 and it remains disabled.

Making the logic level of I_{16} equal 1 disables PLA 1 and enables PLA 2. Now the address at I_0 through I_{15} causes a data word stored in PLA 2 to be output at F_0 through F_7. Actually, this connection doubles the number of product terms as well as increases the address word length.

The address can be further expanded by connecting more PLA devices

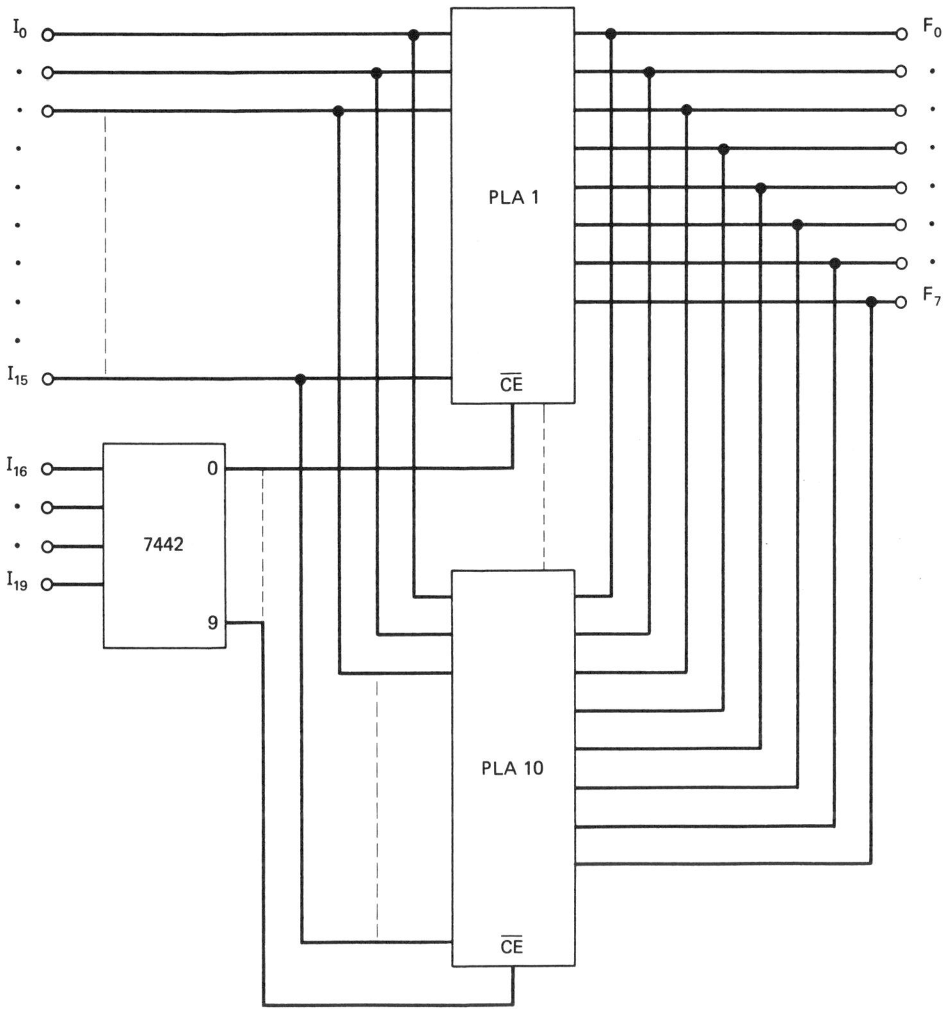

Fig. 6.20 Expanding input word length with a decoder.

in this way. Figure 6.20 shows how a 7442 BCD-to-decimal decoder can be used with 10 PLAs to expand the address word to 20 bits.

6.9 ALPHANUMERIC DISPLAY CONTROLLER[1]

A practical application using the FPLA is shown in Fig. 6.21. Here an 82S100 FPLA IC is combined with additional control circuitry to form an *alphanumeric display controller.*

[1] Signetics Corp., "FPLA Simplifies Alphanumeric Display Operation," *Field Programmable Logic Arrays—An Applications Manual* (Sunnyvale, CA: Signetics Corp., July 1978), pp. 70–73. (Permission to reprint granted by Signetics Corporation, a subsidiary of U.S. Philips Corp., 811 E. Argues Avenue, Sunnyvale, CA 94086)

ALPHA-NUMERIC DISPLAY CONTROLLER

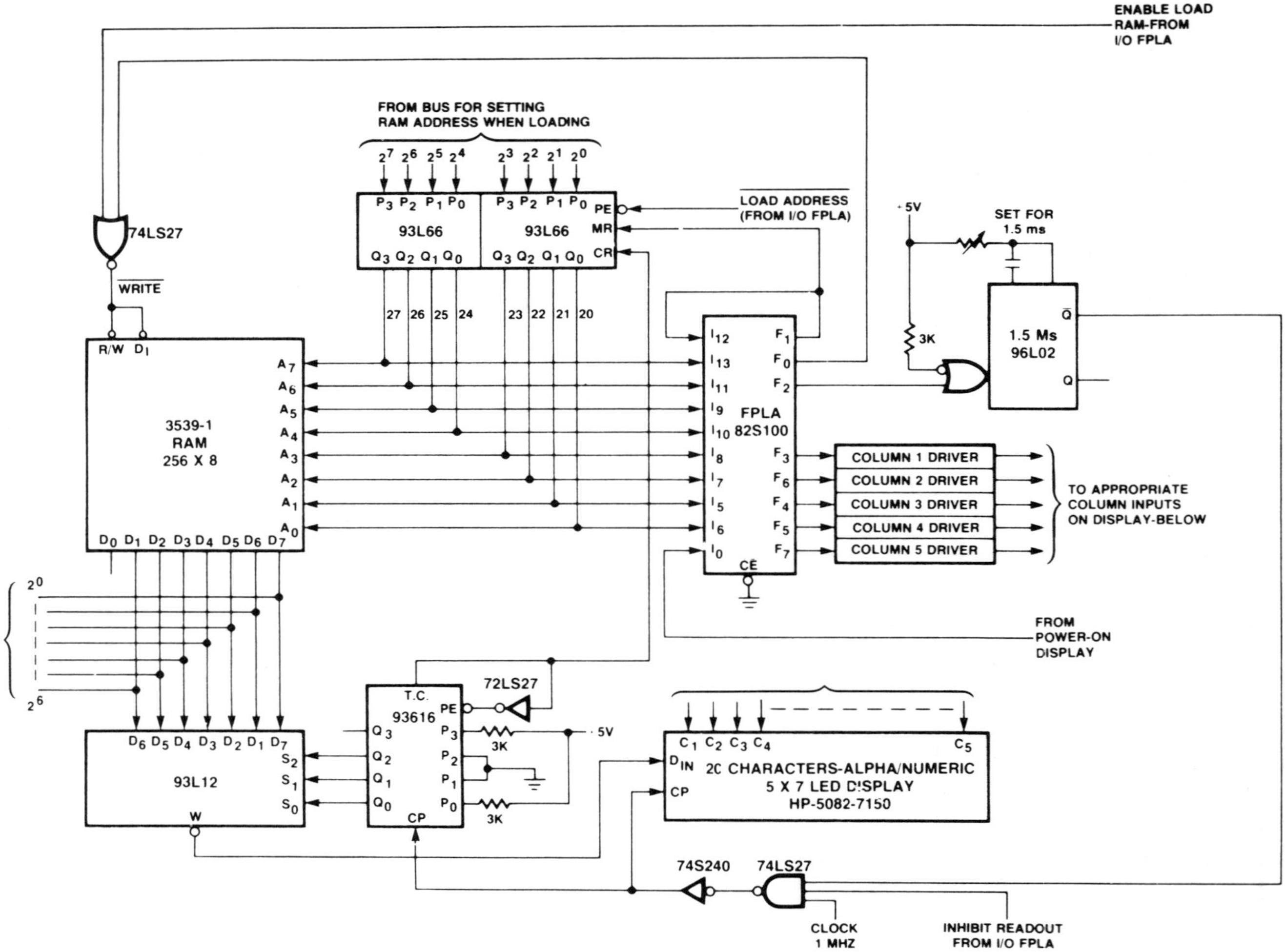

Fig. 6.21 Alphanumeric display controller (Permission to reprint granted by Signetics Corporation, a subsidiary of U.S. Philips Corp., 811 East Arques Avenue, Sunnyvale, CA 94806).

This circuit uses a HP5082-7150 20-digit 5 × 7 dot matrix display. The display has a built-in holding register with a 140-bit storage capacity. It is loaded with 20 7-bit codes representing the dots to be lit in one column of each of the 20 digits of the display. Data are entered into the holding register from the D_{IN} serial input synchronously with pulses at the *CP* clock input.

During display operation, the 140 bits of data for column 1 on all digits of the display are first loaded into the holding register in the display. When the register is full, the corresponding column input C_1 is pulsed. This lights the dots in the display. After this, the 140 bits of data for column 2 of all digits are clocked into the register from the serial input and column input C_2 is pulsed to light these dots. This is followed by data for columns C_3, C_4, and C_5 to complete one scan of the display. The display scan is repeated over and over again to refresh the data on the display.

The 7-bit column codes used to identify the dots that are to light on the display are stored in the RAM. This device has a total storage capacity of 256 8-bit data words. Each of the 20 digits on the display requires five 7-bit codes to define its character. This gives a total storage requirement of 100 7-bit words, which is well within the capacity of the RAM IC.

Data words are parallel-loaded into the RAM from the input lines marked 2^0 through 2^6. Words available on these lines are applied to data inputs D_1 through D_7 of the RAM and written into the storage location defined by the word at address inputs A_0 through A_7. The writing of data into RAM is controlled by the logic level at the *ENABLE LOAD* RAM input.

The chart in Fig. 6.22 shows how stored data are organized in the RAM. In this diagram, the 7-bit code for column 1 of the character to be displayed in digit 1 is stored at address location 000_8. It is followed by data words for column 1 of the characters for digits 2 through 20 of the display. These words are stored at consecutive addresses from 001_8 to 023_8. Data for columns 2 through 5 of the 20 character digits follow at addresses from 024_8 through 143_8.

Toward the top of the circuit in Fig. 6.21, we find an 8-bit counter made from 93L66 ICs. The binary output of this counter is used in addressing the RAM and FPLA devices in parallel. Moreover, the circuit contains a 93L12 multiplexer and 93L16 counter. These two devices are used to convert the parallel output of RAM to serial form for input to the display.

The 82S100 FPLA IC in this circuit is not used as a character generator. Data loaded into RAM are already coded for driving the dot matrix display. Instead, the FPLA stores a control program for sequencing the operation of the circuitry. This program is listed in Fig. 6.23.

At the upper right corner of the circuit in Fig. 6.21, we find a 96L02 monostable multivibrator IC. This circuit is used to generate a 1.5-ms pulse that determines how long each column of dots are lit on the display.

Let us assume that the 93L66 address counter starts at 000_8. This input to the FPLA causes the first output state in the program table of Fig. 6.23. Notice that outputs F_7 and F_2 switch to their active logic levels while

RAM MEMORY MAP

RAM ADR	Data Used For
00	Column 1 of character 1
↓	↓ ↓
23	Column 1 of character 20
24	Column 2 of character 1
↓	↓ ↓
47	Column 2 of character 20
50	Column 3 of character 1
↓	↓ ↓
73	Column 3 of character 20
74	Column 4 of character 1
↓	↓ ↓
117	Column 4 of character 20
120	Column 5 of character 1
↓	↓ ↓
143	Column 5 of character 20

Fig. 6.22 RAM map (Permission to reprint granted by Signetics Corporation, a subsidiary of U.S. Philips Corp., 811 East Arques Avenue, Sunnyvale, CA 94806).

the other outputs stay at their inactive levels. The active L (logic 0) level at F_7 produces a drive signal for column 5 of each digit in the display.

At the same moment, the active H (logic 1) at output F_2 triggers the 96L02 monostable circuit. It produces a 1.5-ms pulse to logic 0 at output $\overline{Q}$. $\overline{Q}$ goes to one input on the 74LS27 NAND gate. A logic 0 at this input stops the 1-MHz clock signal from passing to the 93L16 counter and dot matrix display. This time interval corresponds to the display of data in the fifth column of each digit in the display.

After the pulse elapses, $\overline{Q}$ returns to logic 1 and the 1-MHz clock is enabled through the NAND gate. At this time, the address applied to A_0 through A_7 of the RAM is still 000_8. This causes the 7-bit data word at that storage location to be available at parallel outputs D_1 through D_7.

The 93L16 counter has its outputs preset to $Q_3 Q_2 Q_1 Q_0 = 1001_2$. The three LSBs of this count are applied to the select inputs S_0 through S_2 of the 93L12 multiplexer. This select code causes the first bit of the 7-bit column code at the D_1 through D_7 outputs of RAM to pass to the W output of the multiplexer. On the next pulse at CP, the data bit at W is loaded into the holding register of the display from data input D_{IN}.

At the trailing edge of the clock pulse, the output of the 93L16 counter is incremented by 1. Its output is now 1010_2. This selects the next bit of the column code from the RAM output and sends it to W for loading into the

PROGRAM TABLE OF DISPLAY CONTROL FPLA

RAM ADDRESS ASSIGNMENT IS IN OCTAL, WHERE:
177 = MASTER CLEAR ADDRESS
XXX = POWER-ON OR CLEAR-MEMORY LOOP
200 = TERMINATE CLEAR-MEMORY LOOP

RAM $ADDR_8$	PRODUCT TERM NO.	INPUT VARIABLE 15	14	13	12	11	10	9	8	7	6	5	4	3	2	1	0	OUTPUT FUNCTION 7	6	5	4	3	2	1	0
ACTIVE LEVEL																		L	L	L	L	L	H	H	H
000	0	–	–	L	L	L	L	L	L	L	L	L	–	–	–	–	L	A	•	•	•	•	A	•	•
024	1	–	–	L	L	L	H	L	L	H	L	L	–	–	–	–	L	•	•	•	•	A	A	•	•
050	2	–	–	L	L	L	L	H	H	L	L	L	–	–	–	–	L	•	A	•	•	•	A	•	•
074	3	–	–	L	L	L	H	H	H	H	L	L	–	–	–	–	L	•	•	•	A	•	A	•	•
120	4	–	–	L	L	H	H	L	L	L	L	L	–	–	–	–	L	•	•	A	•	•	A	•	•
144	5	–	–	L	L	H	L	H	L	H	L	L	–	–	–	–	L	•	•	•	•	•	•	A	•
177	6	–	–	L	L	H	H	H	H	H	H	H	–	–	–	–	L	•	•	•	•	•	•	A	A
XXX	7	–	–	–	–	–	–	–	–	–	–	–	–	–	–	–	H	•	•	•	•	•	•	A	A
XXX	8	–	–	L	H	–	–	–	–	–	–	–	–	–	–	–	L	•	•	•	•	•	•	•	A
200	9	–	–	H	H	L	L	L	L	L	L	L	–	–	–	–	L	•	•	•	•	•	•	A	•
I/O ASSIGNMENT		UNUSED	UNUSED	2^7	F_1	2^6	2^4	2^5	2^3	2^2	2^0	2^1	UNUSED	UNUSED	UNUSED	UNUSED	Power-on	COL. 5	COL. 2	COL. 4	COL. 3	COL. 1	REFRESH	RESET CNTR	ENABLE RAM WE

Fig. 6.23 Display controller program (Permission to reprint granted by Signetics Corporation, a subsidiary of U.S. Philips Corp., 811 East Arques Avenue, Sunnyvale, CA 94806).

holding register. The sequence of events just described repeats until the seventh clock pulse. In this way, the complete 7-bit word is loaded into the register in the display.

The seventh clock pulse makes the count held in the 93L16 equal 1111 and the *TC* output switches to logic 1. This logic 1 at *TC* causes the output of the 93L66 address counter to increment to 001_8. With this address applied to the inputs of the RAM, the data word for column 1 of the character in digit 2 is output at D_1 through D_7.

At the same instant, the 1 at *TC* enables parallel loading of the 93L16 counter. On the next clock pulse, the output of the counter is again set to $Q_3 Q_2 Q_1 Q_0$=1001. The first bit of the second column code is now available at *W* and the parallel to serial conversion is repeated. This sequence of events repeats for all addresses up through 023_8. Over this address range, the program in Fig. 6.23 shows that the FPLA outputs are unchanged and the control sequence is maintained.

After the loading of the data word for column 1 of character 20 which is stored at address 023_8, the holding register is full. It holds 140 bits of code representing the dots to be lit in column 1 of all 20 digits of the display.

As the last bit of data is clocked into the holding register, the address counter increments to 024_8. This address causes the control outputs of the FPLA to change. In the program of Fig. 6.23, we see that output F_3 is set to its active L level and F_2 is again set to its active H level. The L at F_3 enables column drive for C_1 on the display. Moreover, the H at F_2 initiates another pulse at the $\overline{Q}$ output of the monostable. This pulse disables the NAND gate and shuts off the 1.5-MHz clock for 1.5 ms. During this 1.5-ms interval, the code stored in the holding register of the display unit causes the appropriate dots to light in column 1 of each digit in the display.

As the 1.5-ms pulse elapses, the clock is once more enabled. Now the data for column 2 of the 20 digits in the display begin to be loaded into the holding register. During this loading cycle, the address is incremented from 024_8 toward 050_8. At address 050_8, FPLA output F_6 is set L to light dots in column 2 of each digit of the display. This sequence is repeated up through address 144_8 to complete one scan of the display.

ASSIGNMENTS

Section 6.2

1. What are the main differences between a PLA and ROM?
2. What is the difference between a PLA and FPLA?
3. Are PLAs and FPLAs volatile or nonvolatile?
4. How is the capacity of a PLA described?

Section 6.3

5. What are the five fundamental parts of a PLA's internal architecture?
6. In the AND matrix of Fig. 6.5(a), which fuse links must be opened to make product term $P_0=\overline{I}_2\overline{I}_1\overline{I}_0$?

7. What are the outputs of the AND matrix in Fig. 6.5(b) when the inputs are $I_3I_2I_1I_0=$ 0100?
8. Which links in the OR matrix of Fig. 6.6(a) must be opened to form sum equation $S_0 - P_2 + P_3$?
9. Write an equation for sum output S_3 of the OR matrix in Fig. 6.6(b). Assume that the product terms are those set up in the AND matrix of Fig. 6.5(b). For which input states is S_3 logic 1?

Section 6.4

10. How does programming of a PLA differ from programming of a PROM?

Section 6.5

11. Write an equation for output F_1 of the PLA in Fig. 6.9.
12. What are the outputs of the PLA in Fig. 6.9 for input $I_3I_2I_1I_0=0100$?

Section 6.6

13. What is the storage capacity of the 82S200 PLA?
14. What is the difference between the 82S200 PLA and 82S201 PLA?
15. What device is the mask-programmable replacement for the 82S101 FPLA?

Section 6.7

16. Show the segment of PLA circuitry required to implement the equation $F_3 = P_4 + P_5 = I_2I_1 + \bar{I}_3I_2\bar{I}_1$.
17. Show how the address $I_3I_2I_1I_0=0000$ to a PLA can be decoded to produce output word $S_3S_2S_1S_0=1111$.

Section 6.8

18. Make a block diagram showing how two 82S200 PLAs can be connected to give 16-bit output words.
19. In the circuit of Fig. 6.20, which PLA is enabled and which word is output when inputs I_0 through I_{15} are all logic 0 and inputs $I_{19}I_{18}I_{17}I_{16}=1001$?

Section 6.9

20. Describe the function of each major part of the alphanumeric display controller in Fig. 6.21.

7

FIRST-IN FIRST-OUT MEMORY

7.1 INTRODUCTION

In Chapter 6, we began our study of additional memory devices with the programmed logic array. Here we continue by introducing another memory device: the first-in first-out memory. Unlike the general-purpose devices introduced in earlier chapters, this device is a special-purpose memory element. That is, it is designed for use in a specific type of application.

The earlier part of the chapter is devoted to a study of first-in first-out memory architecture and operation. The balance of the chapter covers integrated-circuit devices, how to expand their capacity, and their application as a data-rate buffer and keyboard buffer.

1. First-in first-out memory
2. Internal architecture of the FIFO
3. Write and read operations
4. Standard FIFO integrated circuits
5. Expanding FIFO capacity
6. FIFO applications

7.2 THE FIRST-IN FIRST-OUT MEMORY

The *first-in first-out memory* (FIFO) is another standard LSI building block. The FIFO is a serially accessed storage device with independent write-in and readout capability. In digital equipment, it is widely used as a *buffer memory* which is used to store input and output data words.

As its name implies, data words are stacked within the FIFO in the order in which they are written into the memory. Words are read out of the stack in the same order that they are put in. That is, the first word written in is the first word read out.

Technology and Storage Capacity

As with most of the earlier memory devices, the circuitry in FIFO ICs can be manufactured with either the bipolar or MOS technology. High-speed FIFOs are made with TTL circuitry, large-storage-capacity devices with PMOS circuitry, and low-power devices with CMOS circuitry.

The storage capacity of a FIFO is defined by two properties. They are the number of words that can be stored in the stack and the word length of each word. Standard devices are available with the capability of storing as many as 64 words and with word lengths as long as 9 bits.

Block Diagram of a FIFO

A block diagram of a general FIFO element is given in Fig. 7.1. Here we see that the device accepts 8-bit data words at inputs D_0 through D_7 and outputs the words at data outputs Q_0 through Q_7.

Write-in operations from the data inputs are controlled by signals *input ready* (*IR*) and *shift-in* (*SI*). *IR* is a control output of the FIFO. Its logic level indicates to circuits supplying the data and clock inputs whether the FIFO is ready to accept a data word. The other control signal *SI* is a clock input that is pulsed to synchronously load words from data inputs D_0 through D_7. One more input control lead is provided on most FIFOs. This input, labeled *IE*, is an *input enable* lead. Its logic level enables or disables the input circuitry.

At the output of the FIFO, we find the same type of control leads. The

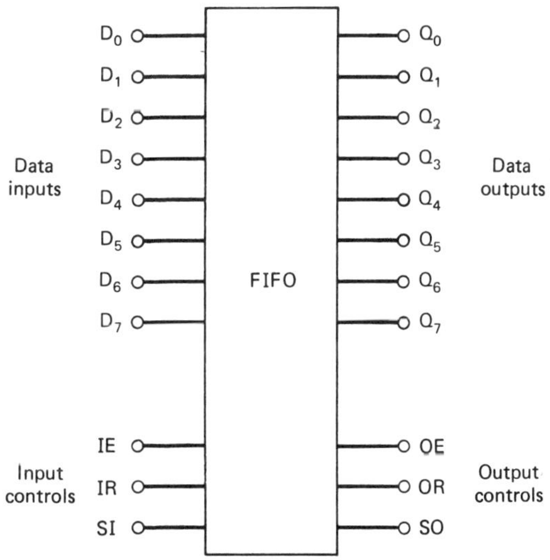

Fig. 7.1 FIFO block diagram.

operation of the output circuitry is enabled or disabled with the *output enable* lead (*OE*). When the output is enabled, data words are read out at data outputs Q_0 through Q_7 under control of the *output ready* (*OR*) signal and *shift-out* (*SO*) signal. The *OR* output indicates to circuits reading the outputs whether a valid data word is available. The *SO* clock input is pulsed to bring the next word in the stack to the output.

Input/Output Operation of the FIFO

The circuit connection in Fig. 7.2 shows how the FIFO is used as a *data-rate buffer*. In this circuit, the FIFO interfaces the transfer of data from high-speed system 1 to low-speed system 2.

Notice that the *IE* and *OE* enable leads of the FIFO are wired to ground. This fixes these inputs at logic 0 and permanently enables the input and output circuitry. Data words are written into the FIFO at the high clock rate *SI* of system 1. After transferring data into the FIFO, system 1 is free to do other processing. The data words are stacked in the FIFO for temporary storage until requested by system 2. System 2 reads out the words at its slower clock rate *SO*.

When the FIFO sets *IR* to logic 1, it indicates to system 1 that its input is ready to accept a data word. In response, system 1 puts an 8-bit data word on parallel data bus lines D_0 through D_7 and then generates a clock pulse at the *SI* input of the FIFO. The data word at D_0 through D_7 is written into the first storage stage of the FIFO synchronously with the leading edge of the clock pulse at *SI*.

As soon as the first stage inside the FIFO is filled with the data word, the FIFO sets *IR* to logic 0. This logic level tells system 1 that the FIFO input is busy and cannot yet accept another data word.

The FIFO does not remain in this state indefinitely. On the trailing edge of the clock pulse, the word held in the first stage automatically shifts up through the storage stack toward parallel outputs Q_0 through Q_7. As the word moves out of the first stage and into the second stage, the *IR* control line returns to the 1 level. This signals system 1 that the input is ready to accept the next word.

The word does not necessarily shift all the way through the stack to the FIFO outputs. Instead, it only propagates through the stack until it reaches the empty stage closest to the output. The word stops in this storage location.

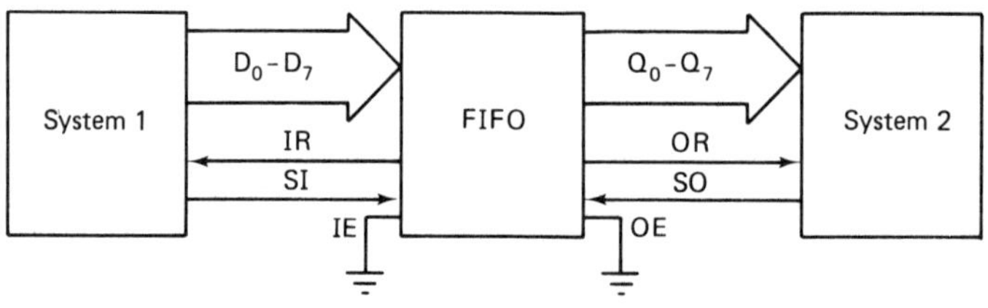

Fig. 7.2 Connection of the FIFO as a data-rate buffer between two systems.

In the same way, additional words can be loaded one after the other into the stack. If all storage locations in the stack become full, *IR* goes to logic 0 and locks out transfer of additional data words from system 1.

Whenever a valid data word is held in the output stage, the FIFO sets control signal *OR* to the 1 logic level. This logic 1 level tells system 2 that a valid word is available at Q_0 through Q_7. The system must read the word and then issue a pulse at the *SO* clock input to bring the next word down the stack into the output stage.

At the leading edge of *SO*, the data at the outputs become invalid. The FIFO output is not ready; therefore, *OR* is automatically switched to logic 0. System 2 is instructed not to read data from Q_0 through Q_7. Next, a new word is shifted into the output stage of the FIFO after which *OR* returns to logic 0. At the trailing edge of *SO*, the circuitry within the FIFO causes all words held in the stack to shift one stage toward the output.

If clocking *SO* makes all stages of the FIFO empty, *OR* stays at logic 0 until another word has been loaded at the input and propagates through the stack to the output.

Although the write-in and readout of data words for the FIFO are synchronous with respect to clock pulses at *SI* and *SO*, its input/output operation is asynchronous. This is because the input clock *SI* and output clock *SO* are independent. Actually, the FIFO is capable of performing read and write operations independently, or at the same time.

7.3 INTERNAL ARCHITECTURE OF THE FIFO[1]

Having introduced the FIFO memory and its input/output operation, let us turn our interest to its internal circuitry and operation. For this purpose, a block diagram showing the internal architecture of a FIFO is provided in Fig. 7.3. Looking at this drawing, we find that there are six basic parts of a FIFO. They are the *input buffer*, *information register array*, *output buffer*, *control register*, *input control logic*, and *output control logic*.

Input Buffer

The input buffer circuit is used to buffer the data inputs of the FIFO. It limits loading of the circuits driving the data inputs.

A simplified input buffer circuit is shown in Fig. 7.4. Here we see that the inputs of the circuit are data bits D_0 through D_3. These inputs are inverted by gates 1 through 4, respectively, to produce reset outputs R_0 through R_3. The inverter outputs are inverted one more time with gates 5 through 8 to give set outputs S_0 through S_3.

The set and reset outputs of the input buffer are supplied to the inputs of the first stage in the information register array. The logic levels of S_0

[1] Doug Farrer, "Understanding the FIFO," APP-332 (Mountain View, CA: Fairchild Camera and Instrument Corp., June 1975). (Courtesy of Fairchild Camera and Instrument Corp.)

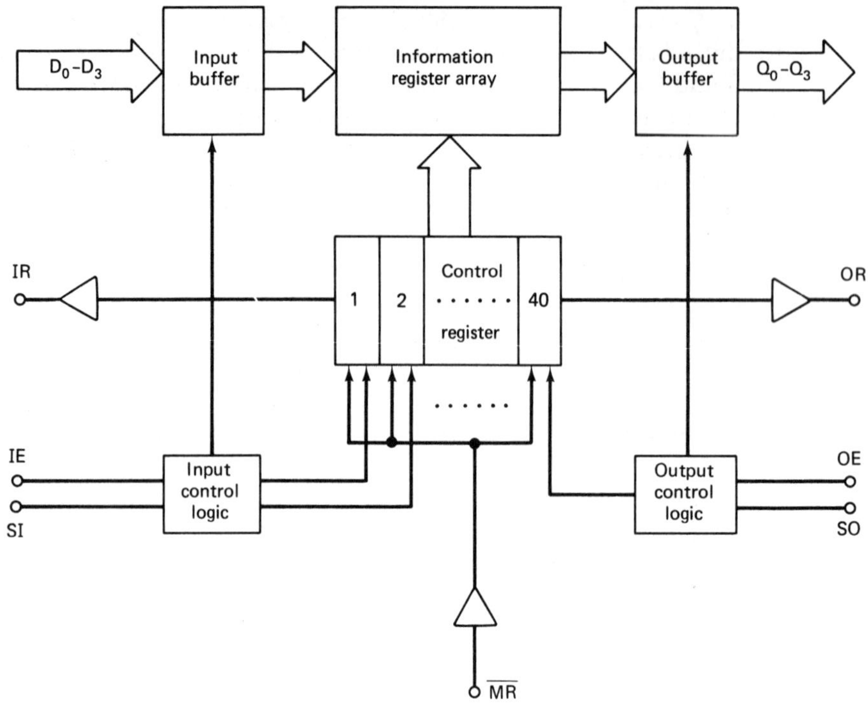

Fig. 7.3 Internal architecture of a FIFO (Fairchild Camera and Instrument Corp.).

through S_3 are equal to that of their corresponding input. On the other hand, the levels of reset signals R_0 through R_3 are the complements of the data inputs.

> *EXAMPLE 7.1* What are the outputs of the input buffer circuit in Fig. 7.4 when the input data word is $D_3D_2D_1D_0$=0110?
>
> *SOLUTION* The data inputs are first inverted to give the reset signals.
>
> $$R_3R_2R_1R_0=\overline{D}_3\overline{D}_2\overline{D}_1\overline{D}_0=1001$$
>
> The reset signals are inverted to give the set outputs.
>
> $$S_3S_2S_1S_0=\overline{R}_3\overline{R}_2\overline{R}_1\overline{R}_0=0110$$

Information Register Array

The memory array in the FIFO, called the information register array, is used to temporarily store the data words. Figure 7.5 represents a simplified information register array circuit. This circuit has the ability to store four 4-bit data words.

Notice that the information register array contains four register stages connected in cascade. Each of these registers is constructed from four set-

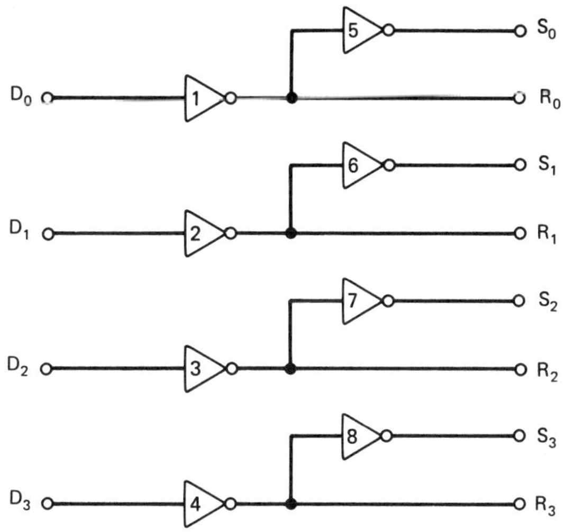

Fig. 7.4 Input buffer.

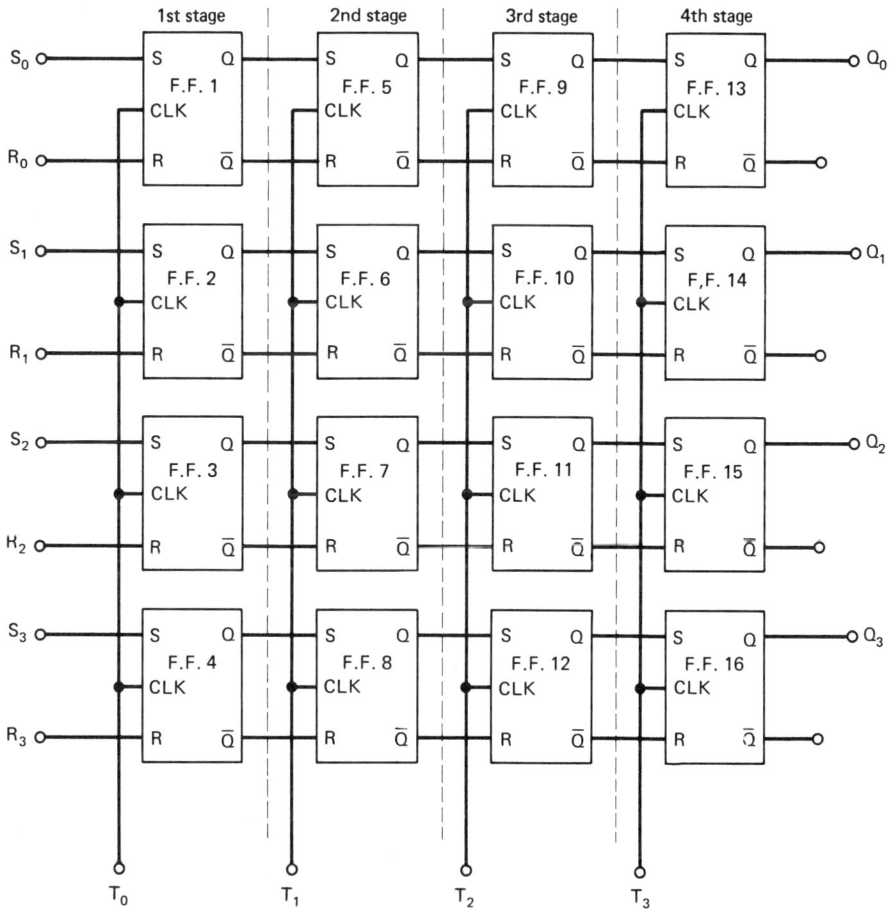

Fig. 7.5 Information register array (Fairchild Camera and Instrument Corp.).

reset flip-flops, one to store each bit of the data word. For example, the first stage, which represents the input register, is formed from flip-flops 1 through 4. Its inputs are the set and reset signals produced by the input buffer. The Q and $\bar{Q}$ outputs of the input register supply set and reset inputs, respectively, to the second stage. The other two stages are connected in the same way. The outputs Q_0 through Q_3 of the information register array are taken from the Q outputs of the flip-flops in the fourth stage. This stage is the output register.

The four registers are separately clocked over control lines T_0 through T_3. By sequentially pulsing these lines, a data word is written into the input register and then shifted up through the stages of the information register array toward the output stage. These clock signals are generated by the control register section of the FIFO.

When a pulse is applied at T_0, the logic levels of set inputs S_0 through S_3 and reset inputs R_0 through R_3 cause the outputs of the flip-flops in the input register to switch to the logic levels defined by the input data word. That is, the Q outputs of the first stage become equal to the data inputs.

As the data word appears at the Q and $\bar{Q}$ outputs, they are directly applied to the inputs of the SR flip-flops in the second stage. If this register does not already store a valid data word, the control register produces a pulse on the T_1 line which causes the data word to be written into the second stage.

Actually, the data word is now held in both stage 1 and stage 2 of the information register array. However, the control register retains the fact that only the word in stage 2 is valid.

Under the influence of the control register, the word continues to shift through the stages of the information register array. It will eventually reach the output stage.

If the array already holds data words, the word only shifts through the stack until it reaches the register holding the lowest valid data word. It is not written into this stage; instead, it is left as a valid word in the stage below this register. Notice that valid data words are automatically stacked toward the output of the information register.

Data words are retained in the stages of the information register array until a word is read out. After a word is read, the control register pulses T_2, T_1, and T_0 in that order to shift all words one stage toward the output.

Output Buffer

Outputs Q_0 through Q_3 of the information register array are normally buffered to produce FIFO outputs O_0 through O_3. This permits the manufacturing of devices with open-collector or three-state outputs. A typical output buffer circuit is shown in Fig. 7.6. Here we find that four noninverting buffers are used to produce three-state outputs.

Making control signal output enable $\overline{OE}$ logic 0 enables the outputs of

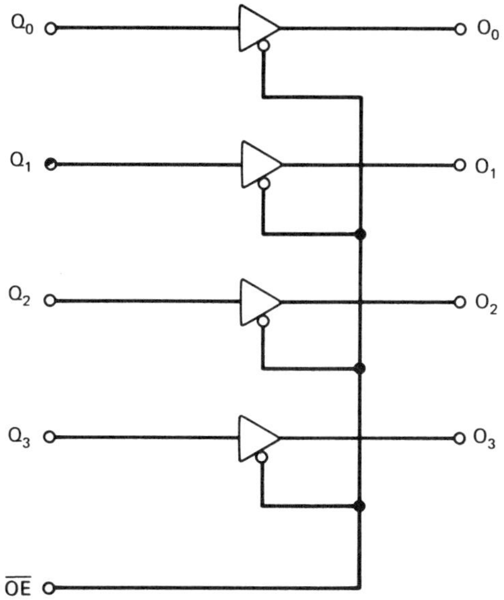

Fig. 7.6 Output buffer.

the FIFO for operation. In this case, outputs O_0 through O_3 follow the logic levels of inputs Q_0 through Q_3.

As $\overline{OE}$ is switched to logic 1, the outputs are disabled. O_0 through O_3 are now in the hi-Z state and electrically act as open circuits.

EXAMPLE 7.2 The word input to the output buffer in Fig. 7.6 is $Q_3Q_2Q_1Q_0$ =0110. What are the logic levels at the outputs when $\overline{OE}$ is logic 1?

SOLUTION Even though the inputs to the buffer are $Q_3Q_2Q_1Q_0$=0110, logic 1 at $\overline{OE}$ disables the outputs and puts O_0 through O_3 in the hi-Z state.

Control Register and Input/Output Control Logic

The control register directs the shifting of data through the information register array of the FIFO. A typical control register is shown in Fig. 7.7. From the diagram, we find that it contains one *control flip-flop* for each register in the information array. The logic states held in these flip-flops indicate whether the corresponding stage of the information register holds a valid or invalid data word. If the flip-flop is set, it stores a 1, which indicates a stage that contains a valid word. On the other hand, a logic 0 in the flip-flop identifies a stage holding an invalid word.

The control register produces pulses at its T_0 through T_3 outputs to control the shifting of data words up through the stages in the information register array. During a write operation, a pulse is first produced at T_0. This loads the data word into the input register stage. After this, pulses are generated at T_1, T_2, and T_3 to transfer the word through stages 2, 3, and 4 to the output of the FIFO.

During a read operation of the word in the output stage of the information register array, the control register generates a pulse at T_4 to bring the

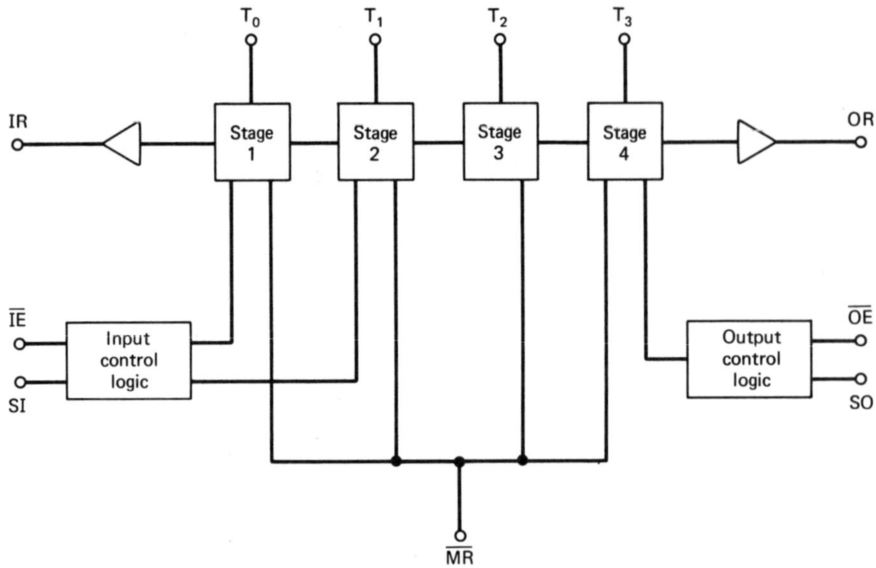

Fig. 7.7 Control registers and input/output control logic.

next word to the output. This pulse is followed by pulses at T_3, T_2, and T_1 —in that order—to shift all data words one stage toward the output.

The operation of stages 1 and 2 of the control register depends on the logic state of the *shift-in* (*SI*) and *input enable* ($\overline{IE}$) inputs. When *input ready* (*IR*) is logic 1 and $\overline{IE}$ logic 0, the input of the FIFO is ready to accept a data word.

On the 0-to-1 transition of *SI*, the outputs of the input control logic circuit enable the first stage of the control register and at the same time disable the second stage. Enabling the first control flip-flop generates a pulse at T_0. This pulse causes the word at FIFO inputs D_0 through D_3 to be loaded into the input register stage.

At the same instant, the first-stage flip-flop in the control register sets. This indicates that a valid word is held in the input register. *IR* switches to logic 0 indicating that the input register is full, and that the FIFO cannot yet accept additional words at its input.

Since the second stage of the control register is disabled, the data word stays at the outputs of the first information register. Let us assume that the second information register is empty; therefore, its flip-flop in the control register is reset. As *SI* switches from 1 back to 0, the first control register stage is disabled and the second stage enabled. A pulse is automatically generated at T_1 and the word at the outputs of the first stage is written into the second-stage register.

As this happens, the flip-flop in the second stage of the control register sets, and the flip-flop in the first stage resets. Now the second stage holds a valid data word, and the first stage an invalid word. *IR* switches back to logic 1 and indicates that the input is ready to accept the next word.

When a valid data word is available at outputs O_0 through O_3 of the FIFO, OR is logic 1. The 1 at OR tells the circuits reading the outputs of the FIFO to initiate a read operation. Of course, $\overline{OE}$ must be logic 0 for a read operation to be performed. After reading the output, SO must be pulsed to bring the next word to the output stage of the information array.

When SO switches to logic 1, the control flip-flop for the output stage is reset to 0. At the same instant, OR switches to logic 0, indicating that the output is no longer ready. This is because a new data word is being transferred into the output stage of the information register array.

Let us assume that the third information array also holds a valid data word. As SO returns to logic 0, the fourth stage of the control register generates a pulse at T_3. This causes the word at the output of the third stage to shift into the fourth stage. Once the word is stable at the outputs, OR returns to logic 1. This means that the next word is available at the outputs of the FIFO.

The *master reset input* ($\overline{MR}$) of the FIFO is used to initialize the control register. Applying a pulse to logic 0 at $\overline{MR}$ automatically resets all flip-flops in the control register to logic 0. This causes IR to switch to logic 1 and OR to logic 0. The FIFO is now signaling that its input is ready to accept a data word, but its output is not ready to be read.

Notice that pulsing $\overline{MR}$ does not clear the words in the information register array; instead, it clears the control register so that it indicates that all words in the information register array are invalid.

Control Register Circuit Operation

The type of circuitry used to make the control register stages is shown in Fig. 7.8. Let us look more closely at the operation of the circuit.

We begin by assuming that all stages are reset. This makes the Q output of all flip-flops logic 0. Looking at stage N-1, we find that $Q_{N\text{-}1}$=0 makes one input on the NOR-gate logic 0. The other three inputs of the gate are also logic 0; therefore, its output switches to logic 1. Line $T_{N\text{-}1}$ has now switched to logic 1, producing the leading edge of the transfer pulse.

At the same time that $T_{N\text{-}1}$ goes to logic 1, the $S_{N\text{-}1}$ input of the SR flip-flop is made logic 1. This causes the control flip-flop to set. Its $Q_{N\text{-}1}$ output is latched at logic 1 and $\bar{Q}_{N\text{-}1}$ at logic 0. The 1 at $Q_{N\text{-}1}$ is returned to the NOR gate, where it forces the output back to logic 0. This produces the trailing edge of $T_{N\text{-}1}$ and the pulse is complete. This sequence of events corresponds to the loading of a word into the N-1 stage of the information register array. The 1 held at $Q_{N\text{-}1}$ indicates that the stage holds a valid data word.

Earlier, we stated that if the next stage in the information register array does not already contain a valid data word, the word from the previous stage will be automatically transferred into the stage.

As $T_{N\text{-}1}$ switches back to logic 0, it makes the corresponding input on the NOR gate in stage N logic 0. The other three inputs are already at the 0 logic level. Therefore, its output switches to logic 1, starting a pulse at

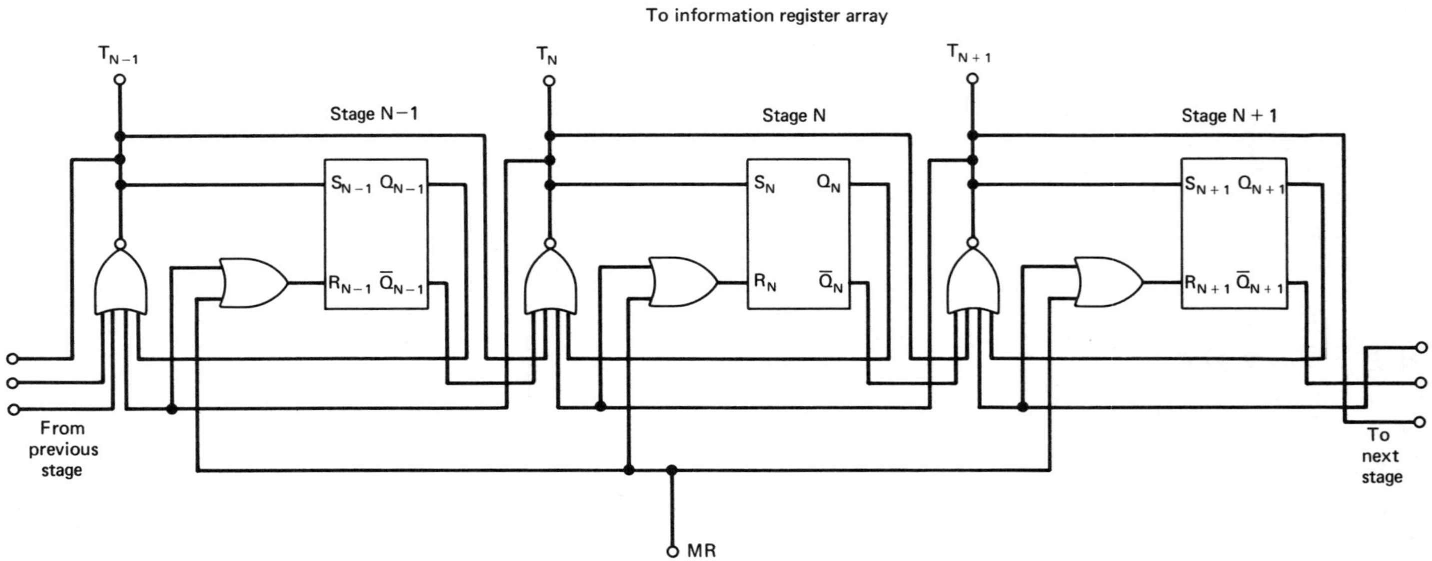

Fig. 7.8 Stages of the control register (Fairchild Camera and Instrument Corp.).

T_N. The logic 1 at T_N sets output Q_N of the flip-flop to logic 1. Q_N is returned to one input on the NOR gate, where it causes T_N to switch back to the 0 level. The pulse just generated at T_N shifts the word into stage N of the information register array.

Notice that T_N is also returned to the OR gate at the reset input of the flip-flop in stage N-1. When T_N is pulsed, the flip-flop in stage N-1 is reset. It now indicates that the N-1 stage of the information register array holds an invalid data word.

This shows how data words automatically move up through the stages of the information array.

Now let us look at the case where stage N of the information register array is already full and a word is written into the register of stage N-1. The control flip-flop for stage N is set so that the Q_N output equals logic 1 and $\bar{Q}_N$ equals logic 0. Going back to the N-1 stage, we are assuming that it is empty and has a data word available at its inputs. All inputs on its NOR gate are logic 0; therefore, a pulse is generated at the $T_{N\text{-}1}$ output. This pulse loads the data word into the N-1 stage of the information register array.

The data word held in stage N-1 is applied to the inputs of stage N in the array. Normally, a pulse would be automatically initiated to shift the word up through the registers. However, we said that stage N of the array is already full. The 1 at output Q_N of its control flip-flop is returned to one input of the NOR gate and the output is held at logic 0. A pulse cannot be generated at T_N. Therefore, the word stops in the $T_{N\text{-}1}$ stage of the information register array. The flip-flop for this stage is not reset and retains the set status of a valid data word. In this way, we see that a word entered at the input only shifts through the registers in the array until it enters the stage just before the one holding the lowest valid data word in the stack.

There is one more type of operation that is performed by the control register. It is the automatic shifting of words up through the register stack after a word is read out. To demonstrate this type of operation, let us assume that information registers N and N+1 already contain valid data words. The control flip-flops for these two stages are set giving logic 1 at the Q_N and Q_{N+1} outputs. These outputs are returned to their respective NOR gate, where they hold the T_N and T_{N+1} outputs at logic 0.

As the data are read out of stage N+1 of the information register array, the output control logic resets the stage N+1 control flip-flop. Now all inputs on its NOR gate are logic 0 and a pulse is generated at T_{N+1}. The data word at the output of stage N in the information array is shifted into stage N+1, and its control flip-flop is again set to indicate a valid data word.

At the same time, the pulse at T_{N+1} is returned to the OR gate at the reset input of the control flip-flop for stage N. The flip-flop resets and now indicates that stage N holds an invalid word. Stage N is now ready to accept a data word. This sequence repeats until all valid words have shifted one register toward the output.

7.4 WRITE AND READ OPERATIONS OF THE FIFO[2]

Now that we have covered the internal architecture and operation of the FIFO, we trace the sequence of events that occurs within it during a write operation and a read operation.

Write Operation

Let us begin by assuming that all stages in the information register array are empty. Therefore, all flip-flops in the control register are reset and the first stage of the control register produces a logic 1 at *IR*. This initial stage is shown in frame 1 of Fig. 7.9.

During a write operation, the 0-to-1 transition of *SI* initiates a pulse at the T_0 output of the control register. This pulse causes the 4-bit word $A_3A_2A_1A_0$ to be loaded into the first stage of the information register array. The pulse at T_0 also sets the Q_0 output of the flip-flop in the first stage of the control register. The logic 1 at Q_0 indicates that a valid word is held in the input register stage. Frame 2 in Fig. 7.9 shows this state.

The second stage of the control register is always examining the output state of the first control flip-flop. When this output is logic 1, it signals that a valid data word is held in the first information register. This word is applied to the inputs of the second information register. As *SI* returns from 1 to 0, the second control flip-flop generates a pulse at T_1. This pulse causes the data word held in the first register to be written into the second stage of the information register array. At the same moment, the second control register flip-flop is set to identify a valid data word. As the flip-flop output sets, it causes the flip-flop in the first stage of the control register to reset.

As shown in frame 3 of Fig. 7.9, the first and second stages of the information register array now hold the same data word. However, only the second stage of the control register is set to logic 1. This indicates that the word in information register 2 is valid but that the one in stage 1 is invalid.

In the same way, the data word is shifted up through the remaining stages of the information register array until it resides in the output stage. Frame 4 in Fig. 7.9 shows the word at the output.

Actually, the FIFO is ready to accept another data word as soon as *IR* returns to logic 1. Therefore, the next word can be entered as soon as the previous word is shifted into the second stage, instead of waiting until it propagates down to the output register.

If a second word $B_3B_2B_1B_0$ is loaded into the FIFO, the word propagates through the FIFO in the same way, except that the word stops in the next-to-last information register stage. It is not written into the output stage because its control flip-flop is already logic 1. This operation is given

[2] John Springer, *Application of First-in, First-out Memories* (Sunnyvale, CA: Advanced Micro Devices, 1974), p. 8-67. (Copyright © 1974 Advanced Micro Devices, Inc. reproduced with permission of copyright owner)

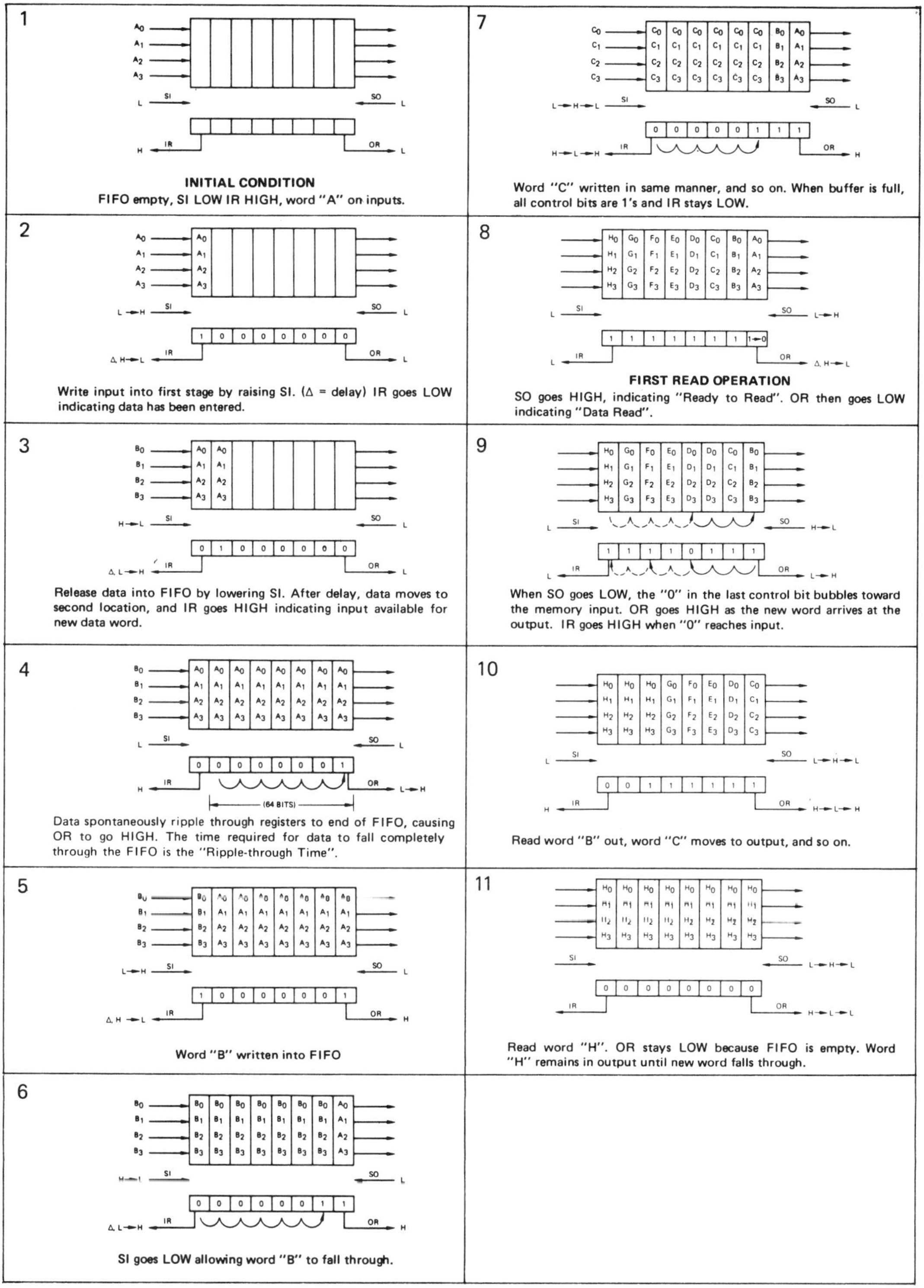

Fig. 7.9 FIFO operations (copyright © 1974 Advanced Micro Devices, Inc. Reproduced with permission of copyright owner.).

in frames 5 and 6 of Fig. 7.9. Notice that the FIFO stack now contains two valid words.

The status of the information register array and control register for the loading of a third word $C_3C_2C_1C_0$ is shown in frame 7 of Fig. 7.9.

Once the FIFO stack is full, the *IR* lead switches to logic 0. When in this state, no new words can be written into the FIFO.

Read Operation

Let us see what happens in the information register array and control register when a word is read out. We begin by assuming that the FIFO is originally full.

The 4-bit word $A_3A_2A_1A_0$ in the output stage of the information register array causes *OR* to be logic 1. The word is read from the outputs of the FIFO and then *SO*-pulsed to bring the next word down the stack to the output stage.

As *SO* switches from logic 0 to 1, the control flip-flop for the output register stage is reset to logic 0. Now the word in the output stage is invalid. Therefore, the words in the lower stages of the stack must all shift one stage toward the output. Notice that in frame 8 of Fig. 7.9 the next-to-last stage flip-flop in the control register holds logic 1, and the last stage has just changed to logic 0. This condition makes the control register generate a pulse on the *T* line for the output stage. In turn, the word $B_3B_2B_1B_0$ from the next lower stage is written into the output stage, the control flip-flop of the output stage sets to logic 1, and the flip-flop in the next lower stage of the control register is reset to logic 0. The *OR* output switches back to 1, indicating that the output is ready to be read.

Now the invalid word is one stage lower in the FIFO, but it does not stay there. As shown in frame 9 of Fig. 7.9, the sequence of events just described automatically repeats. In this way, the invalid information register and its corresponding 0 in the control register continue to bubble back through the FIFO until it reaches the input stage.

With the FIFO in the state shown in frame 9, either a write or another read operation can be performed. Frame 10 in Fig. 7.9 shows the result of reading the next word $B_3B_2B_1B_0$ out of the FIFO. Here a second invalid state is shown to have bubbled back to the input.

If the remaining valid words in the stack are read out in the same way, the information array eventually contains all invalid words. As shown in frame 11, the control register is reset with all flip-flops holding logic 0. In this state, *IR* is logic 1 telling that the input is ready to accept a data word, and *OR* is logic 0, telling that the output is not ready to be read.

7.5 STANDARD FIFO ICS

Up to this point in the chapter, we have studied the input/output operation of the FIFO, its internal architecture, and internal circuit operation. Here we continue by introducing some of the standard FIFO ICs available in the electronic marketplace.

3351-1 40-Word by 9-Bit FIFO

The 3351-1 integrated circuit is one of the popular FIFO memories. This device contains a 40-word by 9-bit stack made with PMOS circuitry. Figure 7.10(a) is a block diagram of its internal circuitry. Looking at this diagram, we see that the internal architecture of the 3351-1 is identical to that described in Section 7.3.

For this reason, we will not repeat the description of its operation here. Instead, we will look into its important timing characteristics. Input switching characteristics for the device are shown in Fig. 7.11(a). In these waveforms, we find the first two key switching characteristics: the *data setup time* t_{DS} and the *data hold time* t_{DH}. For the 3351-1, t_{DS} equals 0 ns. This

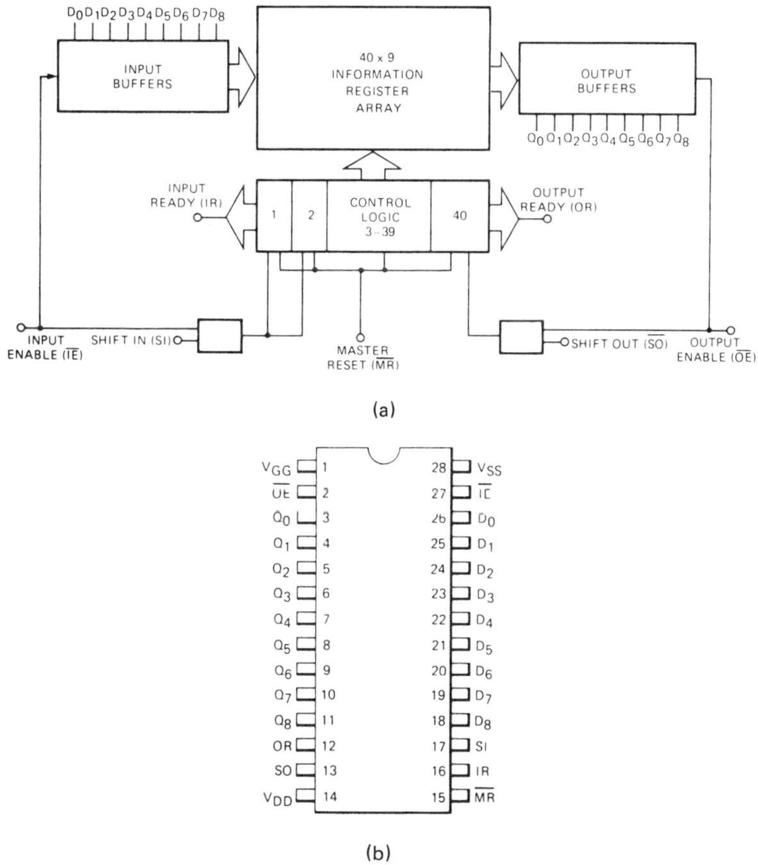

Fig. 7.10 (a) 3351-1 block diagram (Fairchild Camera and Instrument Corp.); (b) 3351-1 pin layout (Fairchild Camera and Instrument Corp.).

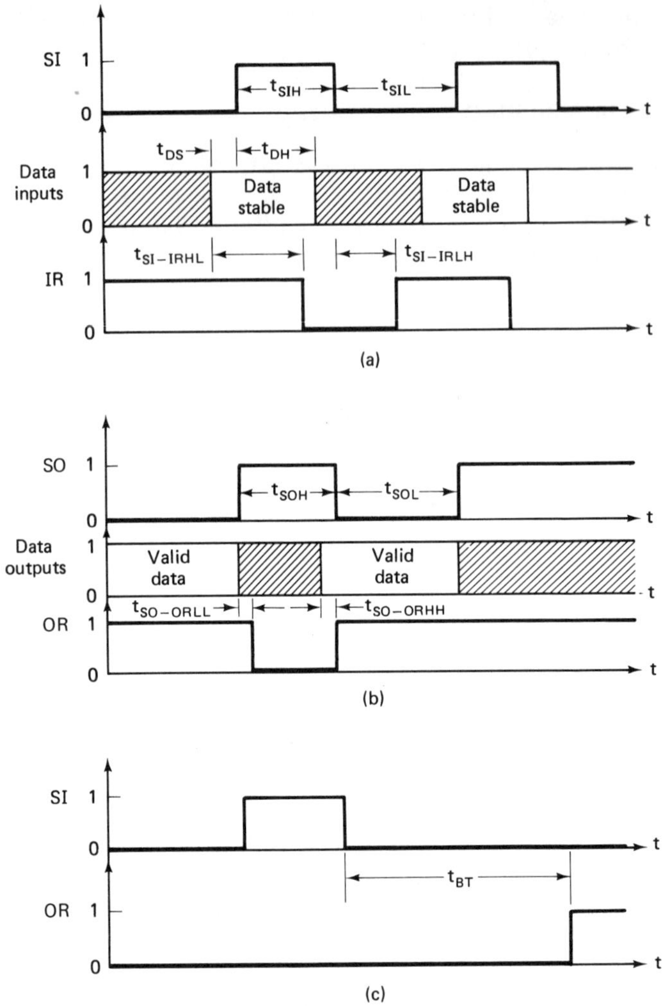

Fig. 7.11 (a) Input switching characteristics; (b) output switching characteristics; (c) bubble-through time.

means that data do not have to be available at the inputs for an interval of time before the 0-to-1 edge of the clock pulse at *SI*.

On the other hand, hold time t_{DH} is rated at 220 ns. Therefore, the input data must be held at the inputs for a minimum of 220 ns after the positive edge of *SI*.

Two other important timing characteristics are the *minimum shift-in pulse width* t_{SIH} and *pulse interval* t_{SIL}. To perform a write into the 3351-1 correctly, the device must be clocked with a signal having a minimum pulse width of 220 ns and a minimum pulse interval of 280 ns.

In Fig. 7.11(a), we find two more input switching characteristics: $t_{SI\text{-}IRHL}$ and $t_{SI\text{-}IRLH}$. These times represent the delay between the corresponding shift-in edge and transition of *IR*. After the 0-to-1 edge of *SI*, there is a 220-ns delay called $t_{SI\text{-}IRHL}$ before the *IR* line switches to logic 0 to indicate that the input is busy. The delay before *IR* returns to logic 1 after the negative edge of *SI* is labeled $t_{SI\text{-}IRLH}$ and equals 280 ns.

The output switching characteristics of the 3351-1 are shown in Fig. 7.11(b). For reading, a pulse must be applied to the *SO* input of the FIFO. This pulse must have a *minimum pulse width* t_{SOH} = 300 ns and *minimum pulse interval* t_{SOL} = 200 ns. Notice that there is also a delay between the 0-to-1 clock edge and the transition of *OR* to logic 0. This delay is denoted $t_{SO\text{-}ORLL}$ and has a maximum value of 200 ns. A similar delay $t_{SO\text{-}ORHH}$ is defined for the return of *OR* to logic 1 when the output becomes valid. This delay has a maximum value of 300 ns.

The last timing characteristic we will consider is called *bubble-through time*. This interval is marked t_{BT} in Fig. 7.11(c). It represents the amount of time it takes a word to propagate from input register through to the output register. For the 3351-1, t_{BT} is equal to 9 μs.

From the pin layout in Fig. 7.10(b), we see that like other PMOS devices, the 3351-1 requires two supply voltages. These voltages are V_{SS} = +5 V ± 5% and V_{GG} = −12 V ± 5%. Both supplies are measured with respect to V_{DD}. When operating, the IC uses a maximum of 520 mW of power.

All inputs and outputs of the 3351-1 are TTL-compatible. Its input logic levels are rated at V_{IHmin} = 4 V and V_{ILmax} = 0.8 V. The outputs are rated at V_{OHmin} = 2.4 V and V_{OLmax} = 0.4 V.

AM3341 64-Word by 4-Bit FIFO

Another PMOS FIFO device is the AM3341. This IC has the ability to stack 64 4-bit words. Its internal architecture is given in Fig. 7.12(a). Here we see that the circuitry differs slightly from that of the 3351-1 IC. Notice that there is no data input or data output buffer circuit. Therefore, there are no input enable and output enable control inputs.

On the other hand, the information register array, control register, and input/output control logic are essentially the same as those of the 3351-1.

The input/output operation of the AM3341 is identical to that described earlier. When stage 0 of its information register array is empty, *IR* is at logic 1. This signals the circuits supplying data inputs D_0 through D_3 that the information array is ready to accept a 4-bit data word. The word is written into the stack synchronously with a pulse to logic 1 at *SI*. After loading, the word automatically bubbles up through the stack toward the output stage.

If a valid data word is available in stage 63 of the stack, logic 1 is produced at *OR*. This signals circuits at the data outputs to read the word. After the word has been read, *SO* must be pulsed to shift a new word into stage 63. All other words automatically shift up through the stack toward the output.

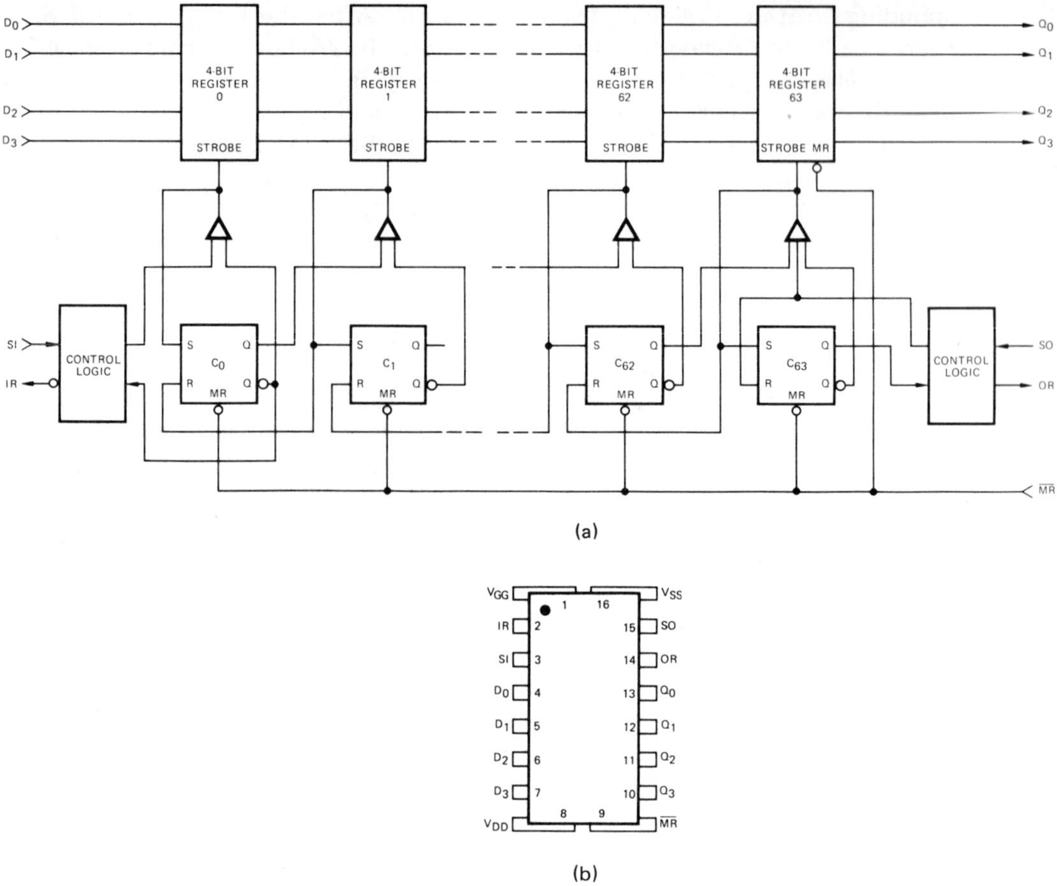

Fig. 7.12 (a) AM3341 block diagram (copyright © 1974 Advanced Micro Devices, Inc. Reproduced with permission of copyright owner.); (b) AM3341 pin layout (copyright © 1974 Advanced Micro Devices, Inc. Reproduced with permission of copyright owner.).

Although the AM3341 is made with PMOS circuitry, internal pull-up circuitry is included to make the inputs and outputs TTL-compatible.

The AM3341 is a slower operating device than the 3351-1. We define the same basic switching characteristics as introduced for the 3351-1. Here we will just give values for its data setup time, data hold time, and bubble time. They are t_{DDmin} = 25 ns, t_{DSImax} = 400 ns, and t_{PTmax} = 32 μs, respectively.

A pin layout of the IC is illustrated in Fig. 7.12(b).

CD40105B 16-Word by 4-Bit FIFO

The CD40105B FIFO device differs from the two devices just introduced in that it is made with low-power CMOS circuitry. This device has a 16-word by 4-bit storage capacity. A block diagram of the device is shown in Fig.

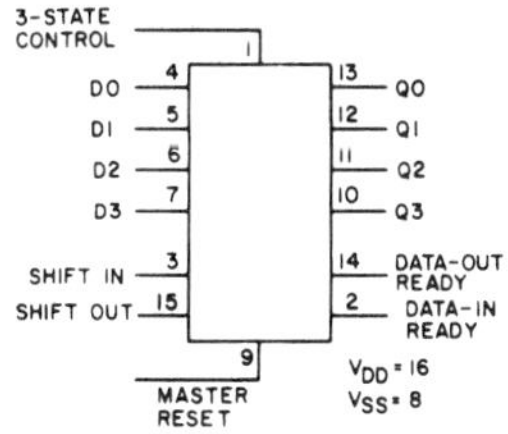

Fig. 7.13 CD40105B block diagram (RCA Solid State Division).

7.13. In this drawing, the leads are numbered with their pin locations on the IC package. Even though the names of the control leads have been changed, operation is the same as for the 3351-1 and AM3341 FIFOs.

The logic level of *DATA-IN READY* indicates that the input stage of the information register is full or empty. When this lead is logic 1, the first stage is empty. The parallel data word at inputs $D_3 D_2 D_1 D_0$ can now be written into the FIFO synchronously with a pulse at *SHIFT IN*. The word automatically propagates up through the information register array toward the output. On the other hand, logic 0 at *DATA-IN READY* says that the first stage is full, and the FIFO is not yet ready to accept another word.

At the output of the CD40105B, control signal *DATA-OUT READY* indicates that a valid output word is available or that the outputs are changing states. Logic 1 at this output indicates that a valid word exists at parallel outputs $Q_3 Q_2 Q_1 Q_0$. When the *SHIFT OUT* lead is pulsed to bring a new word to the output, *DATA-OUT READY* switches to logic 0 while the outputs are changing logic levels. This 0 level indicates that the output states are invalid. When the outputs have stabilized to their new logic levels, *DATA-OUT READY* returns to logic 1.

In addition to the *DATA-OUT READY* lead, there is one additional lead provided to control the output circuitry. This lead is called *3-STATE CONTROL*. Logic 0 at this input enables the output circuitry, and logic 1 puts all outputs in the hi-Z third state.

Since CMOS circuitry is in use, the IC can be operated with any supply voltage V_{DD} between 3 and 18 V. The supply voltage is connected between V_{DD} at pin 16 and V_{SS} at pin 8. With the supply set to 5 V, the input and output logic levels produced by the device are $V_{OLmax} = 0.05$ V, $V_{OHmin} = 4.95$ V, $V_{ILmax} = 1.5$ V, and $V_{IHmin} = 3.5$ V.

The bubble-through time of the CD40105B is 2 μs.

AM2812 32-Word by 8-Bit FIFO

The AM2812 is another PMOS FIFO device. This IC contains a 32-word by 8-bit storage array. A block diagram of the device with pin numbers is shown in Fig. 7.14. It differs from all the earlier mentioned devices in that it has the ability to input and output data in either serial or parallel form.

Parallel input/output operation of the AM2812 is identical to that of the other FIFO devices. Data are synchronously entered from data inputs

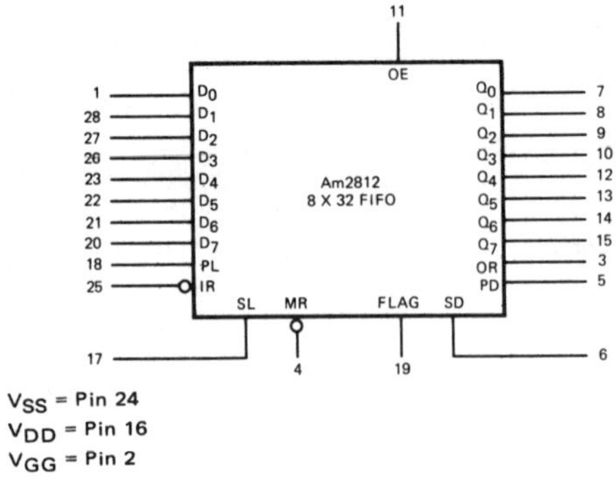

Fig. 7.14 AM2812 block diagram (copyright © 1974 Advanced Micro Devices, Inc. Reproduced with permission of copyright owner.).

D_0 through D_7 with pulses at the *parallel load* (PL) input and synchronously shifted out at Q_0 through Q_7 with pulses at the *parallel dump* (PD) input. When the device is set up to work in the parallel mode, serial clock leads SL and SD must be grounded.

If the AM2812 is set up for serial-in, serial-out operation, bit serial data words are written in at data inputs D_0 and read out from output Q_7. The bits of the serial data word applied at D_0 are synchronously loaded with pulses at the *serial clock* (SL) input. The input is ready to accept bits of the data word when IR is at the 1 logic level. With each pulse, a new bit of the 8-bit word enters from D_0, and previously entered bits shift through the first information register stage. As each bit is loaded, IR momentarily switches to logic 0, indicating to the circuitry supplying the inputs that the bit has entered. Then the next bit of the word is supplied at D_0 and SL again clocked. At the eighth pulse, the input information register is filled with an 8-bit word, and the word automatically shifts through the registers in the information array as a parallel word.

When a valid data word is available in the output stage of the information register array, OR is logic 1. For each pulse applied to the *serial dump* (SD) input, a new bit of the data word appears at Q_7. During the interval when the output data are changing, OR switches to logic 0 to indicate that the output is not ready. As the output stabilizes, OR returns to logic 1.

After the complete 8-bit word has been output in bit-serial form, the FIFO automatically shifts the next word into the thirty-second register and all other words move one stage up the stack.

When the AM2812 is connected for serial-in, serial-out operation, its *parallel load* (PL), *parallel dump* (PD), and unused data inputs D_1 through D_7 must be grounded.

One additional control lead, labeled $FLAG$, is found on the AM2812 IC. The logic level at this output indicates that the FIFO is more than or less than half full. $FLAG$ switches to logic 1 when a fourteenth, fifteenth, or sixteenth word is written into the stack. It remains at logic 1 as long as the stack contains 16 or more words.

7.6 EXPANDING FIFO STORAGE CAPACITY

Earlier, we indicated that the capacity of a FIFO memory is defined in terms of the number of words that can be stored in its stack and their word length. In many applications, the storage capacity provided by a single IC may not be sufficient. For instance, possibly, the word length must be 16 bits, but the largest word length available in standard devices is 9 bits. This limitation can be overcome by connecting two FIFO ICs in parallel. In this section, we demonstrate how to expand both FIFO word length and word capacity.

Word-Capacity Expansion[3]

In our study of standard FIFOs, we found that ICs were manufactured with word capacities such as 16, 32, 40, and 64 words. However, many applications require a stack that can store more than these numbers of words. For instance, a stack could require a minimum of 100 words of storage. This requirement can be satisfied by connecting two 64-word FIFOs in cascade.

Figure 7.15 illustrates how two 3351-1 ICs are cascaded to expand word capacity beyond the single-device limit of 40 9-bit words. Notice in the diagram that 9-bit words are input to FIFO 1 at D_0 through D_8. Outputs O_0 through O_8 of the first FIFO are directly applied to inputs D_0 through D_8 of FIFO 2. Moreover, the parallel outputs of the circuit are produced at O_0 through O_8 of FIFO 2.

As part of the cascade connection, the inputs and outputs of both FIFO devices are permanently enabled. This is done by wiring the *IE* and *OE* leads to ground. This makes these inputs logic 0.

Let us begin by assuming that the control registers in both devices have been reset; therefore, their stacks are empty. This is done by pulsing the *MR* input on FIFO 1 and FIFO 2 to logic 0. In this initial state, we find that *IR* on FIFO 1 is logic 1. This indicates that the input register is ready to accept a data word. At the same moment, *OR* on FIFO 1 is logic 0. This tells that its output stage is empty. Since FIFO 2 is also empty, its *IR* output is logic 1 and *OR* is logic 0.

Now the 9-bit data word applied to D_0 through D_8 of FIFO 1 can be written into the circuit synchronously with a clock pulse at *SI*. At the positive edge of the pulse, the word is loaded into the first information register stage. As the negative edge of *SI* occurs, the word shifts into the second stage. Under the influence of the control register, the word bubbles up through the registers in FIFO 1 toward its fortieth stage. When the word is loaded into the output stage of FIFO 1, it appears at data outputs O_0 through O_8. These outputs are directly applied to data inputs D_0 through D_8 of FIFO 2.

[3] Farrer, "Understanding the FIFO," p. 4. (Courtesy of Fairchild Camera and Instrument Corp.)

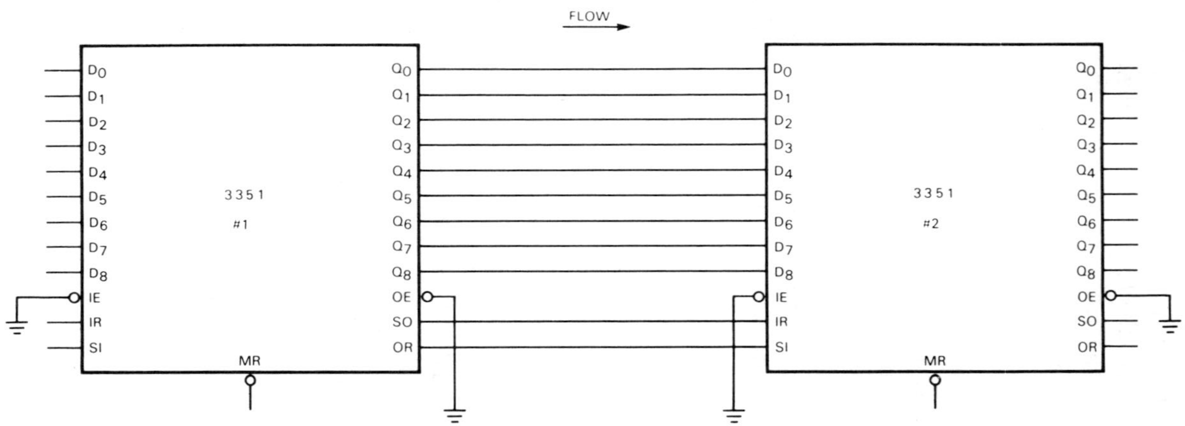

Fig. 7.15 Expanding word capacity (Fairchild Camera and Instrument Corp.).

A valid data word in the output stage causes *OR* to switch from logic 0 to the 1 level. This transition produces the positive edge of a clock pulse at *SI* of FIFO 2. On this edge, the data word is written into FIFO 2 from data inputs D_0 through D_8.

The data word is now held in the first stage of FIFO 2 and causes its *IR* output to switch to logic 0. This produces the negative edge of the clock pulse at *SO* of FIFO 1. The control flip-flop in the fortieth stage of the control register in FIFO 1 is reset. FIFO 1 is again empty; therefore, *OR* switches back to logic 0.

As *OR* goes back to 0, the pulse at *SI* of FIFO 2 is finished. This negative edge causes the data word to shift from stage 1 into stage 2, and *OR* on FIFO 2 returns to the 1 logic level.

The data word automatically propagates up through the stages of FIFO 2 until it appears as a 9-bit parallel word at outputs O_0 through O_8. When the word is stable at the output, *OR* from FIFO 2 switches to the 1 level. This signals that the word is ready to be output.

Additional words are written into the FIFO stack in the same way. When the fortieth word is stacked into FIFO 2, its first stage stays filled. Output *IR* cannot return to logic 1 and the positive edge of *SO* is not produced for FIFO 1. Because *SO* is not clocked, a duplicate word is held in the fortieth stage of FIFO 1 and the first stage of FIFO 2. The rest of the stages in FIFO 1 can then be filled. In this way, we see that the circuit in Fig. 7.15 has the ability to store 79 9-bit words, not 80 as we would expect.

The circuit remains in this state until a word is read out of FIFO 2. With both devices full, we find that FIFO 1 has its *IR* output at logic 0 and *OR* at logic 1. *IR* of FIFO 2 is also logic 0 and *OR* logic 1.

The word at outputs O_0 through O_8 of FIFO 2 is ready to be read out of the stack. After reading, *SO* must be pulsed to bring the next word to the output stage. *OR* switches to logic 0 as the data change, and when the outputs stabilize to their new logic levels, *OR* returns to the 1 level.

The control register shifts all valid words one stage toward the outputs of the circuit. As this happens, the empty register status propagates down toward stage 1 of the control register in FIFO 2. As the word in the first stage is transferred into the second stage, *IR* of FIFO 2 switches to logic 1. This change at *IR* produces the positive edge of the *SO* clock pulse for FIFO 1. The fortieth stage of the control register resets, the word from the thirty-ninth stage is written into the fortieth stage, and the duplicate word previously held in the fortieth stage is dumped. The empty register status continues to propagate down toward the first stage of FIFO 1.

When the new word becomes stable at O_0 through O_8 of FIFO 1, *OR* switches to the 1 level. This initiates a shift in operation to FIFO 2 and the word is written into the first information register. FIFO 2 is again full, and *IR* cannot return to logic 1. The word is again duplicated in the output stage of FIFO 1 and input stage of FIFO 2.

The circuit waits in this state for another read or write operation to be initiated.

Expanding Word Length[4]

In other applications, the word capacity of a standard IC is satisfactory, but a larger word length is required. Word length can be increased by connecting FIFO devices as illustrated in Fig. 7.16. Here two 3351-1 ICs have been connected in parallel to form a 40-word by 18-bit FIFO memory. Notice that the *SI* leads of the two devices are wired together to make a single shift-in clock input called *INPUT CLOCK*. The *SO* leads are connected in the same way to provide a single shift-out clock input marked *OUTPUT CLOCK*.

For the input of the circuit to be ready to accept an 18-bit data word, the *IR* leads of both devices must be logic 1. Moreover, for the inputs to be busy, *IR* of both devices must be logic 0. Owing to the differences in shift-in switching characteristics of the two devices, the *IR* outputs will not become ready or busy at the same instant of time. For this reason, the *IR* leads of the two FIFOs are combined with a 9309 4 line-to-1 line multiplexer circuit to produce a single input ready lead labeled *INPUT READY FLAG*.

The *IR* leads of the two FIFOs are used as select inputs for the 9309 input multiplexer. *IR* from the upper FIFO goes to S_0 and *IR* from the lower FIFO goes to S_1. When both S_0 and S_1 are logic 1, the 1 level at input I_{3a} is multiplexed to the Z_a output. This produces the 1 level at *INPUT READY FLAG* and indicates that both FIFOs are ready to accept a data word.

If one of the *IR* leads switches to logic 0 faster than the other, the multiplexer maintains *INPUT READY FLAG* at its previous logic level by switching the output level from I_{1a} or I_{2a} to Z_a. This state is held until the other *IR* lead goes to the 0 level. When both S_0 and S_1 reach logic 0, the multiplexer passes the logic 0 from I_{0a} to output Z_a. *INPUT READY FLAG* now indicates that the FIFO is busy.

The *OR* leads of the two FIFOs are combined with the same circuit to provide a single output ready signal called *OUTPUT READY FLAG*.

When *INPUT READY FLAG* is at the 1 level, the circuit is ready to accept an 18-bit word at its input. Pulsing *INPUT CLOCK*, 9 bits of the word are written into each FIFO. While the word is still held in the first stage, both *IR* outputs switch to logic 0 and produce logic 0 at *INPUT READY FLAG*. In this way, the circuit signals that it cannot yet accept another input word.

As the control register shifts the word into the second stage of the two FIFOs, the *IR* lead returns to logic 1. The multiplexer output switches to the 1 level and *INPUT READY FLAG* indicates that the circuit is ready to accept another word.

The word automatically bubbles through the stack toward the output stage. When the word stabilizes into the fortieth stage of the two FIFOs, their *OR* signals switch to logic 1. This makes control inputs S_0 and S_1 of

[4] Ibid., p. 6.

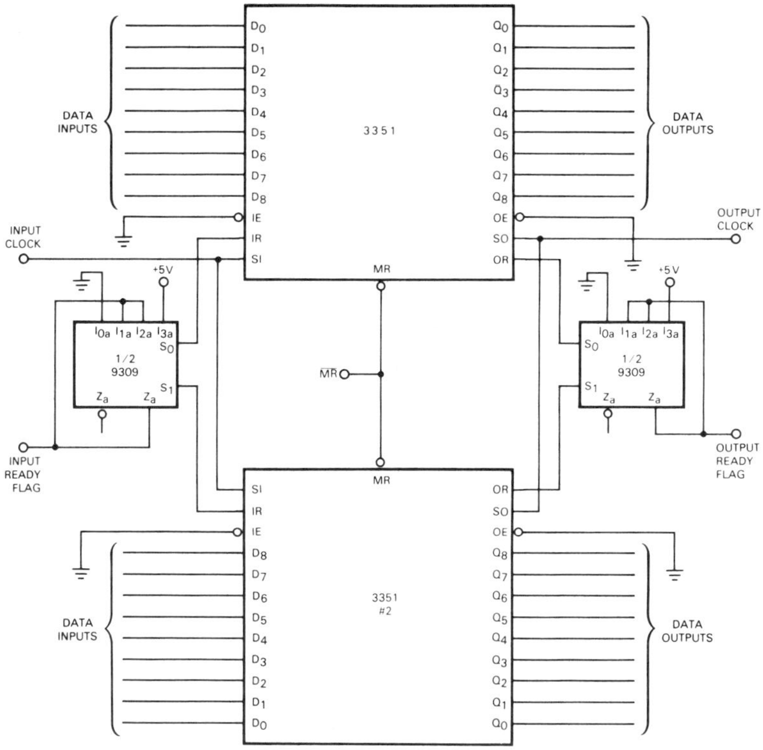

Fig. 7.16 Expanding word length (Fairchild Camera and Instrument Corp.).

the 9309 output multiplexer logic 1 and switches I_{3a} to output Z_a. *OUTPUT READY FLAG* now indicates that a data word is available at the outputs.

After the word is read out, *OUTPUT CLOCK* must be pulsed to shift the next word in each FIFO into their output stage. As the outputs change states, the *OR* leads of the FIFOs momentarily switch to logic 0. This switches the logic 0 at I_{0a} of the multiplexer to *OUTPUT READY FLAG*. The circuit is signaling that the data at its outputs are invalid. After a short delay, the data stabilize at the outputs, and the *OR* leads return to logic 1. The 1 level at the I_{3a} multiplexer input is passed to *OUTPUT READY FLAG*. A new word is available at the data output.

Expanding Word Capacity and Word Length[5]

We have just seen separate circuit configurations that can be used to expand word capacity and word length of a FIFO memory. However, the cascade and parallel FIFO connections can be used together in the same circuit. In this way, we can expand both word capacity and word length at the same time.

[5] Springer, *Application of First-in, First-out Memories*, p. 8-67. (Copyright © 1974 Advanced Micro Devices, Inc. reproduced with permission of copyright owner)

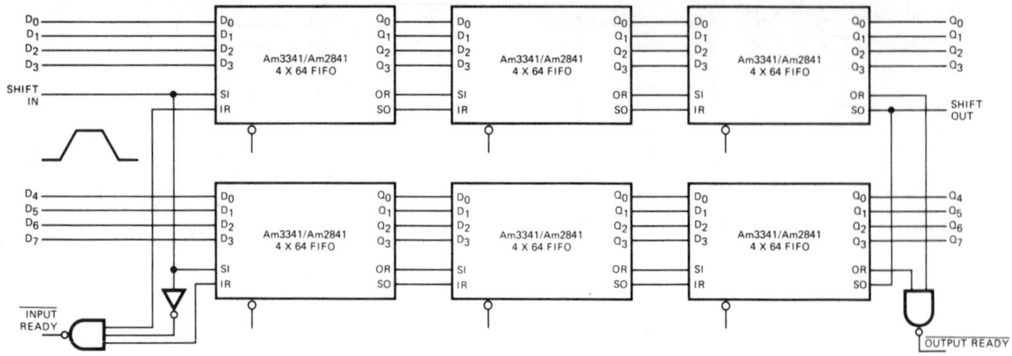

Fig. 7.17 Expanding word capacity and word length (copyright © 1974 Advanced Micro Devices, Inc. Reproduced with permission of copyright owner.).

Figure 7.17 shows such a circuit. Here we find six AM3341 ICs interconnected to form a 190-word by 8-bit FIFO memory.

7.7 FIFO APPLICATIONS

The most common use of the FIFO in digital equipment is as a data-rate buffer. In this application, it is used to interface the data transfer between slow-speed and high-speed circuits or systems. However, FIFOs are also employed in other applications such as an input buffer for storage of data from an input device, or as an output buffer for storage of data so that it can be output synchronously to the operation of an output device. In this section, we see how the FIFO works as a data-rate buffer and as a keyboard code buffer.

Data-Rate Buffer[6]

The circuit in Fig. 7.18 is a data-rate buffer that can be used to interface the transfer of data between two systems. It is capable of storing 40 9-bit data words in the 3351-1 FIFO. Data words are synchronously written into the FIFO from its data inputs D_0 through D_8 with clock pulses at the *INPUT CLOCK* line. Data words are shifted to outputs O_0 through O_8 synchronously with clock pulses at the *OUTPUT CLOCK* line. This circuit is unique in that control logic has been included so that it can interface with systems that produce free-running clock signals.

Notice that the data inputs and data outputs of the FIFO are permanently enabled. This is done by wiring *IE* and *OE* to ground. On the other hand, *INPUT CLOCK* and *OUTPUT CLOCK* are enabled through NAND gates to the *SI* and *SO* inputs of the FIFO, respectively. In this way, pulses

[6] Farrer, "Understanding the FIFO," p. 6. (Courtesy of Fairchild Camera and Instrument Corp.)

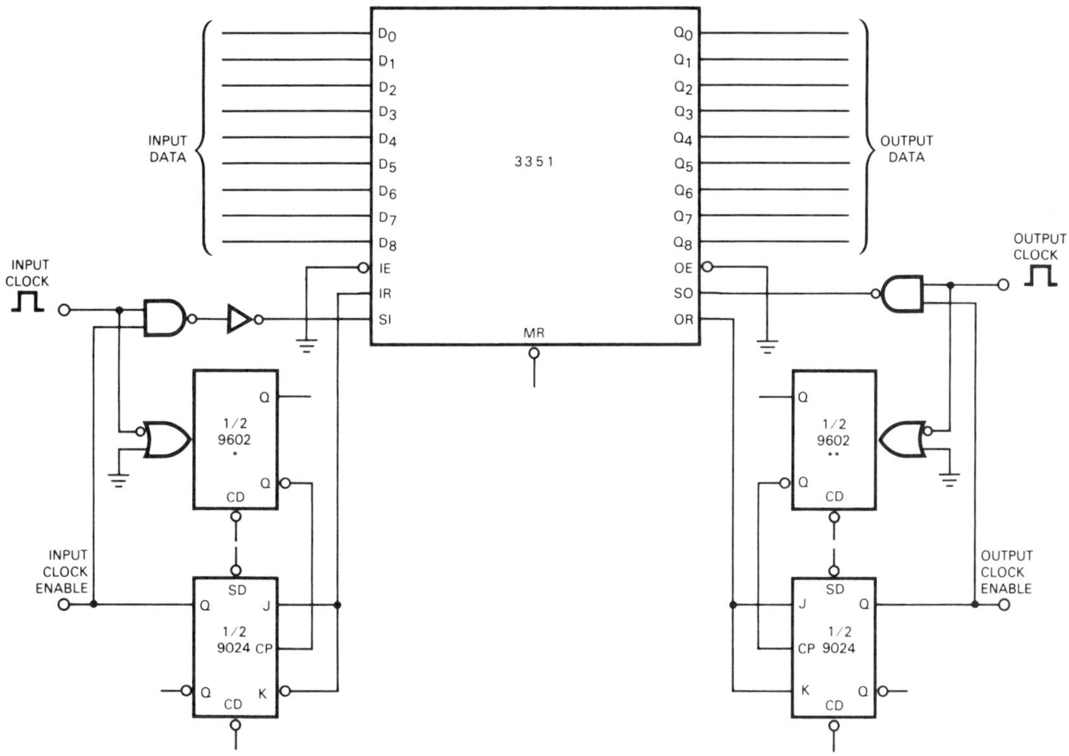

Fig. 7.18 Data-rate buffer (Fairchild Camera and Instrument Corp.).

at *INPUT CLOCK* and *OUTPUT CLOCK* are locked out unless *IR* or *OR*, respectively, is at logic 1.

Let us assume that *IR* has just returned to the 1 level. This indicates that the FIFO is ready to accept a word at its inputs. *IR* goes to the *J* and $\overline{K}$ inputs of the 9024 flip-flop and makes both logic 1. The flip-flop is ready to be set. On the negative edge of the next clock pulse, the 9602 monostable multivibrator is triggered. It generates a short-duration pulse to logic 0 at its *Q* complement output. This pulse goes to the *CP* input of the flip-flop and the outputs set. The *Q* output which is *INPUT CLOCK ENABLE* is logic 1.

The 1 at *INPUT CLOCK ENABLE* signals to the system driving the inputs that the data-rate buffer is ready to accept a data word. In response, the system must output a word to input lines D_0 through D_8.

As *INPUT CLOCK ENABLE* switches to logic 1, it also enables the NAND gate that controls *INPUT CLOCK*. On the 0-to-1 transition of the next pulse at *INPUT CLOCK*, the NAND gate output switches to logic 0, and the inverter output that goes to *SI* is 1. The data word at D_0 through D_8 is written into the first stage of the FIFO. This causes *IR* to switch to logic 0, signaling that the FIFO is busy.

On the trailing edge of *INPUT CLOCK*, *SI* returns to logic 0. At the same time, the 9602 monostable is triggered once more. This time the *J* and

$\bar{K}$ inputs of the flip-flop are logic 0, and it is ready to be reset. The pulse output by the monostable to *CP* resets the *Q* output to logic 0. *INPUT CLOCK ENABLE* is now logic 0. It signals that the input of the circuit is busy.

Under the influence of the control register, the word shifts out of the first stage of the FIFO and bubbles up through the stack. As the word moves from the first stage to the second stage, *IR* returns to logic 1. The negative edge of the next clock pulse triggers the monostable and the pulse produced at *CP* sets the *JK* flip-flop. *INPUT CLOCK ENABLE* is once more logic 1 and indicates that the data-rate buffer is ready to accept another data word.

The outputs of the FIFO are controlled by the identical circuit as the input. Before a word can be read out, *OUTPUT ENABLE CLOCK* must be logic 1. In this way, it enables the NAND gate, which passes pulses from *OUTPUT CLOCK* to *SO* of the FIFO. With each pulse at *SO*, the FIFO brings a new word to the outputs.

Keyboard Buffer[7]

The circuit in Fig. 7.19 shows another type of FIFO application. This circuit is used to identify switch closures in a keyboard. When a closed switch is detected, a code representing the key is stored in the FIFO.

Looking at the diagram, we see that the keyboard matrix consists of 16 column lines and 8 row lines. The junction of each row and column represents a switch location. This gives a total of 128 switches in the matrix. The AM93L16 binary counter on the left drives the AM93L11 binary decoder. These devices are used to generate scan pulses for the columns of the key matrix. A scan pulse is produced at one decoder output after the other in time and applied to the column inputs of the matrix. The other AM93L16 counter in conjunction with the AM93L12 multiplexer is used to test one row output after the other looking for a closed switch in the matrix. The binary count held in these two counters represents the row and column location of the key switch being scanned. For this reason, it is used as the key code and applied to the data inputs of the FIFO.

When a key is depressed, its switch contacts in the matrix close. The scan pulse applied to its column by the decoder is passed through the closed switch contacts to the row output and multiplexer input. When the multiplexer selects the row line, the pulse is sent to the multiplexer output and is loaded into the *D*-type flip-flop. The pulse appears at the flip-flop output and causes the key code to be written into the FIFO. The code automatically propagates up through the stack toward the output.

Now that we have overviewed the operation of the circuit, let us look more closely into its operation. We begin by assuming that both counters are initially reset. Therefore, the output of the column counter is $Q_3 Q_2 Q_1 Q_0$ =0000. This count is input to the binary decoder, where it makes the first

[7] Springer, *Application of First-in, First-out Memories*, p. 8-73. (Copyright © 1974 Advanced Micro Devices, Inc. reproduced with permission of copyright owner)

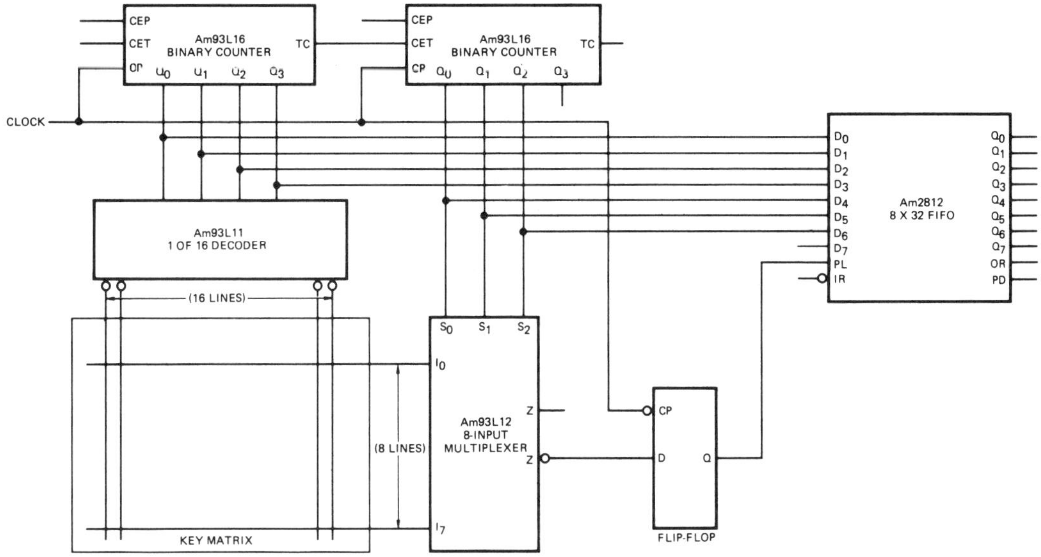

Fig. 7.19 Keyboard buffer (copyright © 1974 Advanced Micro Devices, Inc. Reproduced with permission of copyright owner.).

column output switch to logic 0. At the same instant, the three least significant bits of the row counter output are applied to select inputs S_0 through S_2 of the multiplexer. They are all initially 0 and select the logic level of the first row I_0 to be output at the $\bar{Z}$ output. This corresponds to the scanning of the switch located at column 0 of row 0. If this switch is closed, the logic 0 at the column 0 decoder output is passed to the row 0 input of the multiplexer. The 0 is inverted as it passes through the multiplexer to the $\bar{Z}$ output. The 1 from $\bar{Z}$ is applied to the D input of the flip-flop. On the trailing edge of the clock pulse, the Q output of the flip-flop switches to logic 1. This output goes to the PL lead of the FIFO, where it causes the count 0000000 at inputs D_0 through D_6 to be written into the FIFO as the key code.

On the next clock pulse, the column counter increments to $Q_3 Q_2 Q_1 Q_0$ =0001 while the row counter output remains at 0000. Now the switch between column 1 and row 0 is being scanned. The counters hold the key code 0000001.

The scan of row 0 continues for the next 15 clock pulses as the column counter increments up through 1111. This completes the scan of all 16 switches in row 0. The seventeenth clock pulse causes the column counter to reset to 0000. At this instant, the trickle count TC output pulses the row counter and increments its output to 0001. Now the first column decoder output is again logic 0, but the row counter selects the second row output. The switch in column 0 of row 1 is being scanned. Clock pulses that follow increment the column counter to scan the rest of the switches in row 1.

The column and row counter continue to work in this way until the switches in all eight rows of the key matrix are tested. This completes one full scan of the matrix. After this, the scan sequence starts over with column 0 of row 0.

EXAMPLE 7.3 The switch at which column and row in the matrix of Fig. 7.19 is being scanned when the counter on the left holds $Q_3Q_2Q_1Q_0$=0010 and the counter on the right holds $Q_3Q_2Q_1Q_0$=1001?

SOLUTION The counter on the left holds the count that selects the column of the key matrix. This count is

$$Q_3Q_2Q_1Q_0=0010=2$$

This makes the column 2 output of the binary decoder switch to logic 0. The row counter, which is on the right, holds

$$Q_3Q_2Q_1Q_0=1001$$

However, only the three least significant bits are used to select the row.

$$Q_2Q_1Q_0=001=1$$

This selects the row 1 input of the multiplexer. Therefore, the switch at column 2 of row 1 is being scanned.

ASSIGNMENTS

Section 7.2

1. What does "FIFO" stand for?
2. Is the FIFO a serial-access or random-access storage device?
3. How is the storage capacity of a FIFO defined?
4. What are the four groups of leads provided on the FIFO?

Section 7.3

5. What are the six main parts of the internal architecture of the FIFO?
6. What is the function of the input buffer part of the FIFO?
7. Describe the operation of the information register array in Fig. 7.5 as a data word is input.
8. Describe the operation of the control register and input/output control logic in Fig. 7.7 as a data word is clocked into the FIFO.

Section 7.4

9. Assume that a FIFO is empty, as shown in frame 1 of Fig. 7.9. Describe a write operation of the word $A_3A_2A_1A_0$ into the FIFO and the reading of the word from its output.

Section 7.5

10. Define the data setup time, data hold time, pulse width, pulse interval, and bubble-through time characteristics of a FIFO.
11. What are the storage capacities of the 3351-1, AM3341, and CD40105B FIFOs?
12. How does the AM2812 FIFO differ from the 3351-1, AM3341, and CD40105B devices?

Section 7.6

13. Show how to cascade two CD40105B devices to obtain a low-power 31-word by 4-bit FIFO memory.
14. Show how four CD40105B FIFOs can be interconnected to give a storage capacity of 31 8-bit words.

Section 7.7

15. In the keyboard buffer circuit of Fig. 7.19, what key code is loaded into the FIFO when a switch closure is detected at column 1 of row 7 in the key matrix?

8

CONTENT ADDRESSABLE MEMORY

8.1 INTRODUCTION

Content addressable memory is another type of special-purpose memory. Unlike the FIFO, the content addressable memory is a random-access device. In this chapter, we study its operation, architecture, IC devices, and applications. The following topics are introduced for this purpose.

1. Content addressable memory
2. Internal architecture of the CAM
3. Standard CAM ICs
4. Expanding CAM storage capacity
5. CAM as a learning memory

8.2 CONTENT ADDRESSABLE MEMORY

Content addressable memory (CAM) provides read and write functions just like RAM. However, it also has the ability to perform a new function called *association.*

For use in association, part of each word stored in the memory array is a code that is used as a key. During an association operation, the CAM automatically compares an input code to the key of each word. For each word where the key matches, an output signal is produced to identify that a match condition has occurred. After we have found out which storage locations contain words that match the key, read or write operations can be performed to these addresses. In some applications, the complete word represents the key, instead of a few bits.

CAMs are high-speed memory devices. For this reason they are made with the bipolar technology. A number of commercially available CAM ICs are constructed with emitter-coupled logic (ECL) circuitry.

Block Diagram of a CAM

Figure 8.1 shows a block diagram of a typical CAM. Let us assume that this CAM has a 16-bit storage capacity and is organized into eight 2-bit words. Since the memory is organized into 2-bit words, the block has two input leads and two output leads. The *input leads* are marked I_0 and I_1. They are used to input data for write and associate operations. Data are read out of the CAM at its *output leads* D_0 and D_1.

During a read or write operation, the Y_0 through Y_7 lines are used to select the storage location. Notice that there is one address input for each word in the CAM. These leads are called the *linear select address inputs.* By linear select, we mean that the logic level at each of these inputs selects one of the eight storage locations in the CAM. It does not employ a binary address code like the random-access devices introduced in earlier chapters.

On the other hand, when an association operation is performed, the Y lines serve a second function. In this case, they are outputs instead of inputs. Again, one corresponds to each word in the memory. If during an association operation a stored word matches the input key, the logic level produced at its Y output indicates the match condition.

As mentioned earlier, the CAM can perform three basic operations:

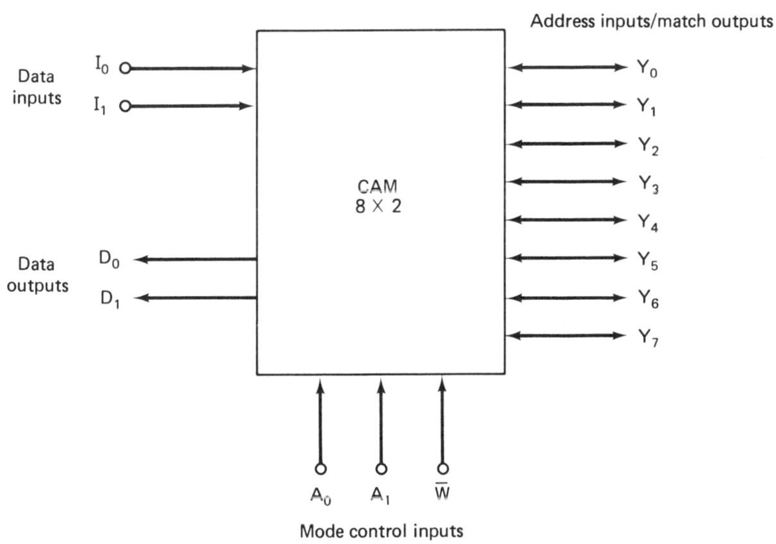

Fig. 8.1 Block diagram of a CAM.

read, *write*, and *associate*. These modes of operation are selected by the code at *control inputs* A_0 and A_1 together with the logic level of *write control input* $\overline{W}$.

Read Mode

The read operation permits access to the data stored at the address locations within the CAM. Figure 8.2(a) shows how the CAM is set up to perform a read. Notice that the code at the mode control inputs is $A_1 A_0 = 00$. Moreover, $\overline{W}$ is set to logic 1 to tell the CAM that a read is to occur.

Now the CAM is ready to be read. To do this, the Y input corresponding to the address of the word to be read is switched to logic 0. The CAM responds by outputting the word held at this location on the $D_1 D_0$ lines. The data inputs I_0 and I_1 are don't-care states during the read operation and can be at the 0 or 1 logic level.

Actually, it is possible to read more than one address location at a time.

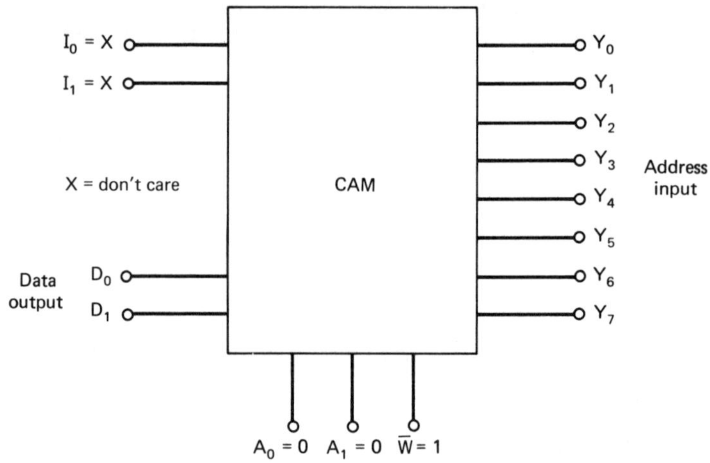

(a)

Word location	Content
0	0 1
1	0 0
2	1 1
3	0 1
4	1 0
5	1 0
6	1 1
7	0 0

(b)

Fig. 8.2 (a) CAM set for read operation; (b) CAM data content.

This happens if more than one address input is switched to logic 0. The CAM outputs the content of each address selected; however, the words are ORed together to produce a single output word. The readout of data words from CAM is nondestructive.

EXAMPLE 8.1 The CAM in Fig. 8.2(a) contains the table of data given in Fig. 8.2(b). What is the word at data outputs $D_1 D_0$ when the address input is $Y_7 Y_6 Y_5 Y_4 Y_3 Y_2 Y_1 Y_0$=11111011?

SOLUTION Bit Y_2 of the address is logic 0. Therefore, the data word held at this address is read out of the CAM. This is word 2 in the table.

$$D_1 D_0 = 11$$

Write Mode

The write operation performed by a CAM differs from that studied earlier for RAM. Just as for RAM, a data word is stored in the addressed location of the memory array. However, unlike RAM, write data also appear at the data outputs of the CAM.

The CAM connection in Fig. 8.3(a) is required to perform a write operation. Here we see that mode control inputs $A_1 A_0$ are again both logic 0, but this time $\overline{W}$ is switched to logic 0. $\overline{W}$ now signals that a write operation is to be performed.

We apply the data word to be written into the CAM at data inputs $I_1 I_0$. As the appropriate address input Y_0 through Y_7 is switched to the 0 level, the word at $I_1 I_0$ is loaded into this memory location. At the same instant, the word appears at data outputs $D_1 D_0$. The CAM has destructive write-in.

EXAMPLE 8.2 The data inputs of the CAM in Fig. 8.3(a) are $I_1 I_0$=00 and the Y_4 address input is made logic 0 to select the storage location. If the CAM initially holds the data shown earlier in Fig. 8.2(b), what is the content of the memory array after the write operation?

SOLUTION When Y_4 switches to logic 0, $I_1 I_0$=00 is written into the storage location that holds word 4. The data in all other locations remain unchanged. The new data content of the CAM is given in the table of Fig. 8.3(b).

Association Mode

The special operation that the CAM is designed to perform is called an association. During an association operation, the CAM searches through the content of its memory array looking for the storage locations of words that match the key applied to the data inputs. For all locations where a match occurs, the CAM produces a match output signal.

The CAM is connected as in Fig. 8.4 for association operation. Notice that $A_1 A_0$=11 selects association mode. Also notice that the logic level at $\overline{W}$ is a don't-care state. Moreover, data outputs D_0 and D_1 are not in use. The 2-bit data word searched for is applied at $I_1 I_0$. The CAM searches through

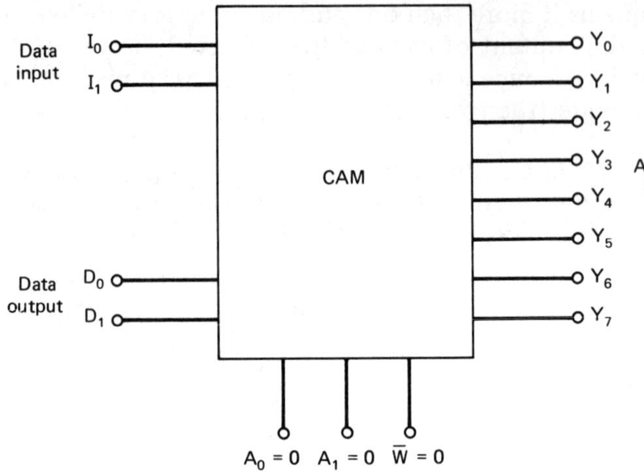

(a)

Word location	Content
0	0 1
1	0 0
2	1 1
3	0 1
4	0 0
5	1 0
6	1 1
7	0 0

(b)

Fig. 8.3 (a) CAM set for write operation; (b) new CAM data content.

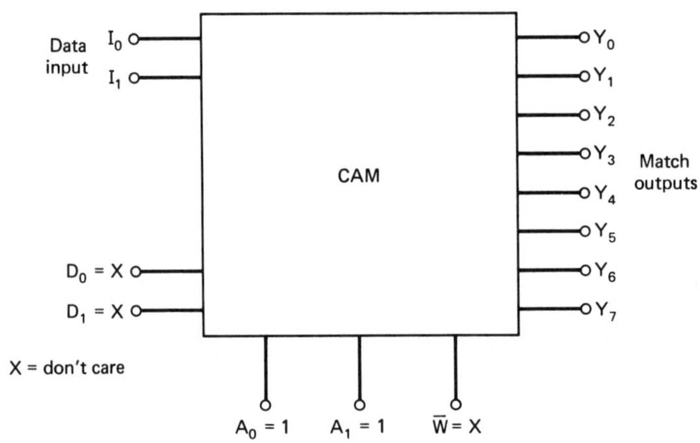

Fig. 8.4 CAM set for association operation.

the words held in its memory array and sets the Y output to logic 0 for those addresses that contain the input word.

Using the addresses corresponding to the match outputs produced by the CAM, read or write operations can be performed at these storage locations.

EXAMPLE 8.3 The CAM in Fig. 8.4 holds the data shown in Fig. 8.3(b). If the word applied to data inputs $I_1 I_0$ equals 00, which Y outputs signal with a match condition?

SOLUTION Comparing input $I_1 I_0$=00 to the words in the table of Fig. 8.3(b), we find that three matches occur. These words make Y_1, Y_4, and Y_7 switch to logic 0.

$$Y_1 = 0$$

$$Y_4 = 0$$

$$Y_7 = 0$$

8.3 INTERNAL ARCHITECTURE OF THE CAM[1]

Now that we have introduced the block diagram of the CAM and its three basic modes of operation, the internal architecture and operation of the CAM will be studied.

Figure 8.5 is a diagram of the circuitry within a CAM IC. Notice that the circuit has 16 storage cells, one group of eight on the left labeled M_{00} through M_{70} and another group of eight on the right labeled M_{01} through M_{71}. For storage purposes, cells are arranged into eight 2-bit words. The first word is stored in the upper two cells, M_{00} and M_{01}. Figure 8.6 shows these two cells in detail. Here we see that each cell contains a D-type flip-flop which acts as the storage element. Furthermore, logic gates are included to control operation of the cells during read, write, and associate operation.

Let us look more closely at the circuit. First we see that the two cells share a common linear select line which is marked Y_0. In addition, there are three input leads on the M_{00} cell: data input I_0, write control $\overline{W}$, and mode control A_0. The output of the cell is gated to the D_0 data output. The same inputs and outputs are supplied on cell M_{01}, except here they are labeled I_1, $\overline{W}$, A_1, and D_1.

The rest of the cells in Fig. 8.5 are paired in the same way. For instance, M_{10} and M_{11} provide storage for the second word. This gives a total of eight 2-bit words. A separate Y line is provided for each group of cells. On the other hand, the I_0, $\overline{W}$, and input line A_0 of all cells in the left group are wired in parallel. Moreover, the data output of all cells in the left group are

[1] Signetics Corp., "10155 Content Addressable Memory (CAM)," AN-004 (Sunnyvale, CA: Signetics Corp., March 1979). (Permission to reprint granted by Signetics Corp., a subsidiary of U.S. Philips Corp., 811 E. Arques Avenue, Sunnyvale, CA 94086)

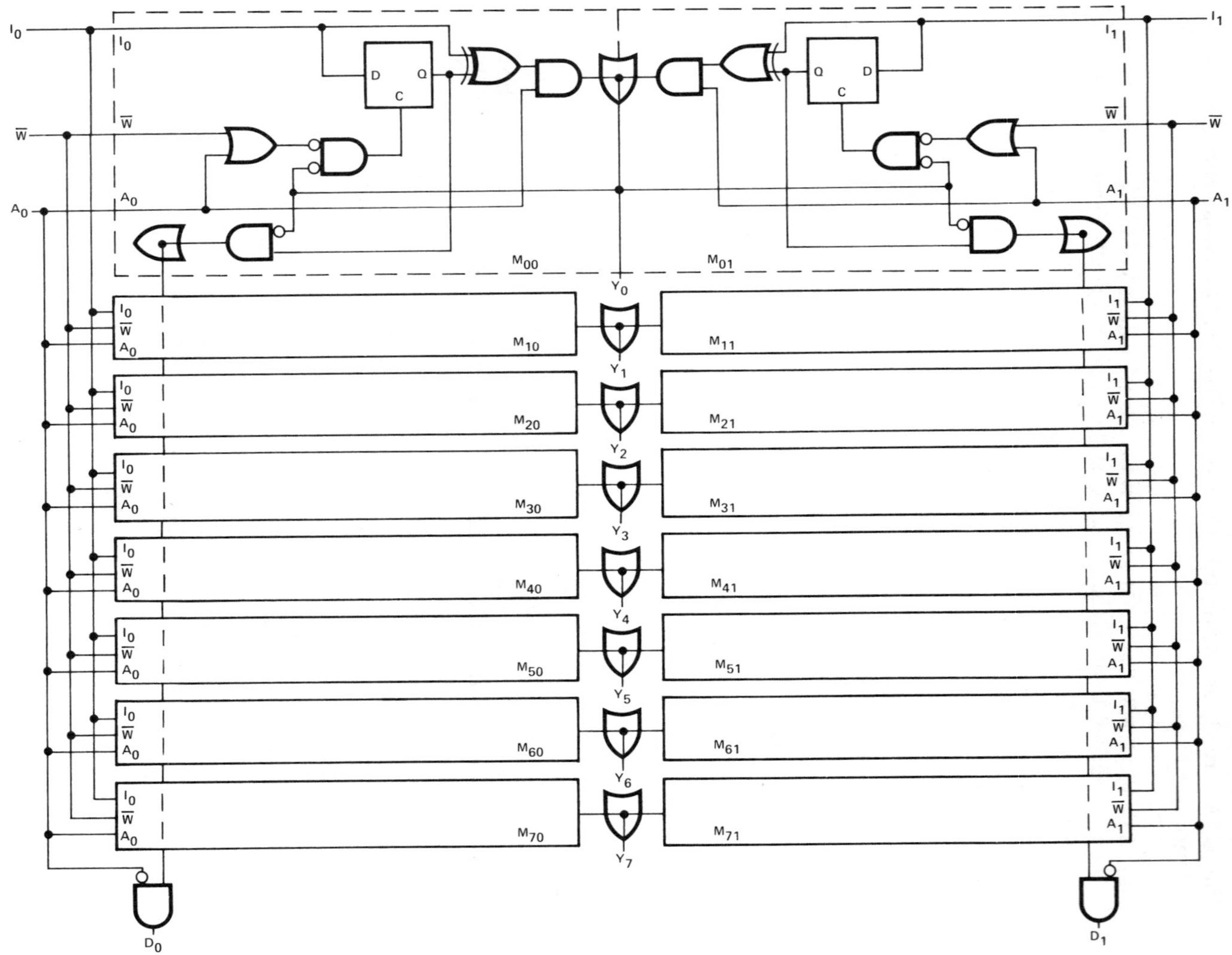

Fig. 8.5 CAM architecture (Permission to reprint granted by Signetics Corporation, a subsidiary of U.S. Philips Corp., 811 East Arques Avenue, Sunnyvale, CA 94806).

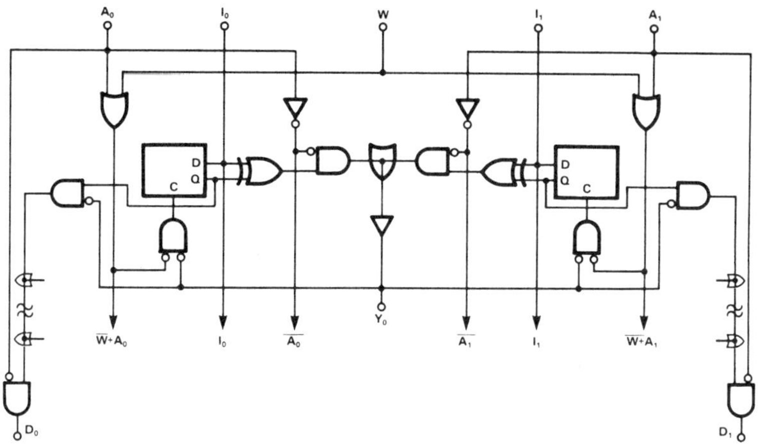

Fig. 8.6 CAM cell circuit (Permission to reprint granted by Signetics Corporation, a subsidiary of U.S. Philips Corp., 811 East Arques Avenue, Sunnyvale, CA 94806).

wire-ORed together at one input of the gate that produces output D_0. The inputs and outputs in the right group of cells are connected in the same way.

Association Operation

Having looked over the internal architecture of the CAM and the structure of its cell circuit, we continue by tracing the function of the circuit in Fig. 8.5 while an association operation is performed.

Let us begin by setting A_0 and A_1 to logic 1. This input condition selects the association mode of operation. Remember that for this mode the $\overline{W}$ input is a don't-care state and can be logic 0 or 1. The CAM is now ready to perform an association operation.

The word at data inputs $I_1 I_0$ is associated with the content of the CAM. Assume these inputs are both logic 0; therefore, we are associating the word $I_1 I_0$=00 with each of the eight data words held in the CAM.

At this point, we know all inputs of the circuit. Next we must find out what happens to the data stored in the D-type flip-flops and what outputs are produced by the CAM. The logic 0 at I_0 is directly applied to the D input of the flip-flop in cell M_{00}. Over the same path, it goes to one input on the exclusive-OR gate. Notice that the other input of this gate is supplied by the Q output of the flip-flop. If the logic level of Q matches that of I_0, the output $I_0 \oplus Q$ is logic 0. However, if they are the opposite logic levels, the gate output is logic 1. In this way, we see that input I_0 is compared to the data held in cell M_{00}. That is, they are associated.

From the output of the exclusive-OR gate, the match signal is connected to one input of a 2-input AND gate. Its other input is supplied by mode control input A_0. Recall that A_0 was set to logic 1 to select association mode. The AND gate output follows the logic level of the match output of the exclusive-OR gate.

At the same time that I_0 is being associated with the content of the flip-flop in the M_{00} cell, the logic level at I_1 is compared to the Q output of the flip-flop in the M_{01} cell. When they match, the output of the exclusive-OR gate, which is $I_1 \oplus Q$, switches to logic 0. This signal is combined with A_1=1 by an AND gate to give $A_1 \cdot I_1 \oplus Q$=0.

The outputs of these two AND gates are wire-ORed together to produce the Y_0 match output. When the bits of the word are the same logic level as those held in the corresponding cells, the AND-gate outputs switch to logic 0. This condition signals that the word held in cells $M_{01}\,M_{00}$ is identical to that applied to the $I_1\,I_0$ inputs.

If the content of either cell does not match its data input, the corresponding AND-gate output stays at logic 1. This pulls the Y_0 output to the 1 logic level. In this way, the CAM indicates that the word held in $M_{01}\,M_{00}$ does not match that applied at $I_1\,I_0$.

As the association operation just described occurs for the word in cells $M_{01}\,M_{00}$, the identical sequence of events are occurring at the cells for the other seven words. The Y outputs for all other words that are equal to $I_1\,I_0$=00 also switch to the 0 logic level.

Actually, we have already traced completely through the sequence of events that occur during an association operation. However, let us look into three other things that happen within the CAM: what happens to the $\overline{W}$ input, what happens at the clock input C of the flip-flop, and what happens at the data outputs. To do this, let us look just at cell M_{00}. This can be done because we have found that the two cells for each word work identically.

From cell M_{00} of the circuit in Fig. 8.5, we find that A_0 goes to one input of an OR gate while the other input of the gate is $\overline{W}$. During an association operation, A_0 must be logic 1. With A_0=1, the output of the OR gate is held at logic 1, independent of the logic level at $\overline{W}$. This confirms that the logic level of $\overline{W}$ is a don't care state during association operation.

Moreover, the 1 at the OR-gate output holds the clock input C of the D-type flip-flop at logic 0. Therefore, the data applied at I_0 are not written into the flip-flop. The logic states held in the cells of the CAM do not change during an association operation.

Now let us go to the output circuitry of the M_{00} cell in Fig. 8.5. Here we see that data at the Q output of the flip-flop goes to one input of a two-input AND gate. The other input of this gate is supplied by Y_0. When Y_0 is logic 0, the data at Q are passed through the AND gate. This occurs if a match condition results from an association. The AND gate output is wire-ORed together with the outputs from all other cells in the left group and applied to one input of the output control AND gate. The second input of this gate comes from mode control input A_0. For data to be output at D_0, A_0 must be logic 0. However, during an association operation A_0 is at the 1 logic level and data are not passed to D_0.

8.4 STANDARD CAM ICS

In previous sections of this chapter, we covered the input/output operation, internal architecture, and internal operation of the content addressable memory. Let us now continue our study of the CAM with some of the standard ICs that are presently available.

10155 Eight-Word by 2-Bit CAM

The 10155 IC contains a bipolar CAM circuit. This circuit is made with high-speed ECL circuitry. It has a total storage capacity of 16 bits and is organized to form eight words, each with 2 bits.

A block diagram of the 10155 is given in Fig. 8.7(a). Here we see the device is identical to that introduced in Section 8.3. Pin numbering for the leads of the device are given in this diagram. Power-supply leads are not shown in this diagram. They are V_{CC1} at pin 1, V_{CC2} at pin 18, and V_{EE} at pin 9. The voltages required at these inputs are V_{CC1} = 0 V, V_{CC2} = 0 V, and V_{EE} = -5.2 V ± 5%. The ECL technology produces a circuit that requires a large amount of power to operate. For example, the typical current drawn from the V_{EE} supply is 115 mA. This results in close to 600 mW of power per IC.

Modes of operation for the 10155 are shown in the chart of Fig. 8.7(b). From this chart, we find that $A_1 A_0$=00 with $\overline{W}$=1 selects the read mode of operation. During a read, one of the eight Y_0 lines is set to logic 0 to select its address location in the memory array. The word held at this location is output at $D_1 D_0$. Notice that inputs I_0 and I_1 are don't-care states during a read operation.

The timing of a read operation is illustrated in Fig. 8.8(a). After the mode and address are set up, there is a *read access time* labeled T_{A5}. This access time is typically 6 ns. When the Y line returns to logic 1, another delay occurs before the output data become invalid. This *delay time* is labeled T_{D3} and has a typical value of 9 ns.

If more than one Y input is switched to logic 0, the data words at the selected locations are ORed together to produce the $D_1 D_0$ output data word.

The write mode of operation is also shown in the chart of Fig. 8.7(b). Again the mode select inputs are $A_1 A_0$=00; however, in this case $\overline{W}$ is switched to the 0 logic level. The storage location is selected by making the appropriate Y line logic 0. When this is done, the data word at input $I_1 I_0$ is written into the location. Notice that in the chart the states of flip-flop outputs Q_{n1} and Q_{n0} become equal to the I_1 and I_0 data inputs, respectively. One feature that is unique to the write operation of the CAM is that input data also appear at data outputs $D_1 D_0$.

The timing of a write operation is shown in Fig. 8.8(b). In this diagram, T_{A3} represents the *$\overline{W}$ to data output write access time.* This interval has a

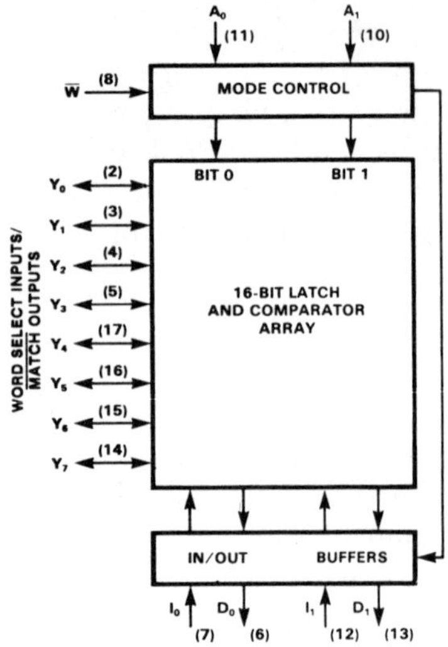

(a)

MODE	A_0	A_1	I_0	I_1	$\overline{W}$	D_0	D_1	Q_{n0}	Q_{n1}	Y_n
Associate[1]	1	1	1/0	1/0	X	0	0	Q_{n0}	Q_{n1}	$Q_{n0} \oplus I_0 + Q_{n1} \oplus I_1$
Associate[1,2] (masked)	1	0	1/0	X	1	0	D_1	Q_{n0}	Q_{n1}	$Q_{n0} \oplus I_0$
Associate[1,2] (masked)	0	1	X	1/0	1	D_0	0	Q_{n0}	Q_{n1}	$Q_{n1} \oplus I_1$
Read[3]	0	0	X	X	1	D_0[2]	D_1[2]	Q_{n0}	Q_{n1}	0 (Selected address)
Write[3,4]	0	0	1/0	1/0	0	I_0	I_1	I_0	I_1	0 (Selected address)
Hybrid[5]	1	0	1/0	1/0	0	0	I_1	Q_{n0}	$I_1 \bullet \overline{Y_n}$	$Q_{n0} \oplus I_0$
Hybrid[5]	0	1	1/0	1/0	0	I_1	0	$I_0 \bullet \overline{Y_n}$	Q_{n1}	$Q_{n1} \oplus I_1$

X = Don't care
Q_{n0} = Contents of address n, Bit 0 (n = 0 to 7)
Q_{n1} = Contents of address n, Bit 1

NOTES

1. 1 (high) = Mismatch, 0 (low) = Match
2. Read mode: $D_0 = Q_{00} \bullet \overline{Y_0} + Q_{10} \bullet \overline{Y_1} + \bullet \bullet \bullet + Q_{70} \bullet \overline{Y_7}$
   $D_1 = Q_{01} \bullet \overline{Y_0} + Q_{11} \bullet \overline{Y_1} \bullet \bullet \bullet + Q_{71} \bullet \overline{Y_7}$
3. In normal operation a single Y address is selected for read or write
4. Write is transparent
5. Simultaneous Associate and Write at all "Match" addresses.

(b)

Fig. 8.7 (a) 10155 block diagram (Permission to reprint granted by Signetics Corporation, a subsidiary of U.S. Philips Corp., 811 East Arques Avenue, Sunnyvale, CA 94806); (b) modes of operation (Permission to reprint granted by Signetics Corporation, a subsidiary of U.S. Philips Corp., 811 East Arques Avenue, Sunnyvale, CA 94806).

typical value of 13 ns. The interval marked T_W represents the write pulse width and it has a minimum value of 10 ns.

By changing the mode control inputs to $A_1 A_0$=11, the 10155 is put into the associate mode. In this mode, $\overline{W}$ is a don't-care state, and can be logic 0 or logic 1. The data word applied to $I_1 I_0$ is compared to each data

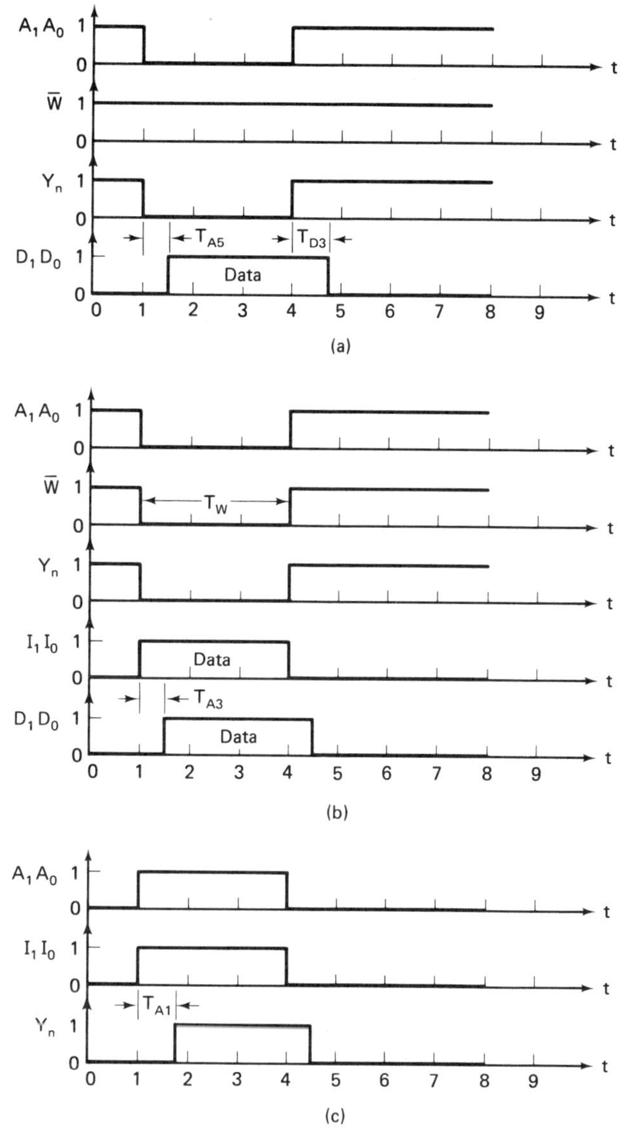

Fig. 8.8 (a) Read timing; (b) write timing; (c) associate timing.

word held in the CAM. The *Y* leads are now used as match outputs, those corresponding to the locations where the stored word matches the input switch to logic 0. During association operation, data outputs D_0 and D_1 stay at logic 0. Moreover, the data held in the flip-flops remain in their previous logic states.

Timing for the association operation is shown in Fig. 8.8(c). T_{A1} represents the *data input to match output access time*, which has a typical value of 8 ns.

By switching either A_0 or A_1 from logic 1 to 0, the CAM operates in a *masked association mode.* As shown in Fig. 8.7(b), $\overline{W}$ must be logic 1 for these modes of operation. In masked association, the storage cell corresponding to the A input that is 1 is masked out of the association operation. That is, the association is decided on a comparison of one bit of the input data word instead of both. For example, when A_0=1 and A_1=0, the I_1 input is a don't-care state and data at I_0 are compared to its corresponding bit in each word. For each word where a match occurs, the Y output switches to logic 0.

The 10155 is capable of performing one other type of operation, identified as a *hybrid operation* in Fig. 8.7(b). Notice that the A_0 and A_1 inputs are set up the same way as for a masked association except that $\overline{W}$ is switched to logic 0. With the CAM set up like this, associations are performed for the cells corresponding to the A input that is logic 0. If match conditions occur, a write operation is automatically performed on the cells which have as their A input logic 1 and Y line logic 0.

An example is when A_0=0 and A_1=1 with $\overline{W}$=0. This causes I_1 to be associated with Q_{n1}. If the logic level of I_1 matches the corresponding bit in any of the cells, their outputs switch to logic 0 to indicate the match condition. The logic 0 on the Y line initiates a write of the data at input I_0 into the cell of the other half of the word. In Fig. 8.7(b), this is indicated by Q_{n0} equals $I_0 \cdot \overline{Y}_n$.

F100142 Four-Word by 4-Bit CAM

The F100142 is another standard CAM device. It also contains a 16-bit bipolar memory array made with ECL circuitry. However, the F100142 is organized into four words, each with 4 bits.

Figure 8.9(a) is a block diagram of the CAM. Notice that its leads are different than those for the 10155. Here we find four data inputs, D_0 through D_3. During write and associate operations, a 4-bit word is applied to these leads. Moreover, 4-bit data words are output at Q_0 through Q_3 during both read and write operations. The leads marked A_0 through A_3 are linear select address inputs. A storage location is selected for a read or write operation by switching its A input to logic 0.

The logic level of the write select control input $\overline{WS}$ tells the CAM that a read or write operation is to be performed. When $\overline{WS}$ is logic 0, a write operation is to be performed, and 1 at $\overline{WS}$ identifies a read operation. The write select control must be logic 1 during association operations.

There are two other sets of leads on the F100142. They are its match outputs M_0 through M_3 and mask inputs MK_0 through MK_3. When an association operation is performed, match conditions are signaled with logic 0 on the corresponding M lines. On the other hand, by applying logic 1 to an MK input, a match condition is forced for that bit of the word and the storage of data is blocked from the corresponding D input. The addition of these lines make it possible to perform an association operation on less than a complete 4-bit word. The internal circuitry of the F100142 is shown in Fig. 8.10.

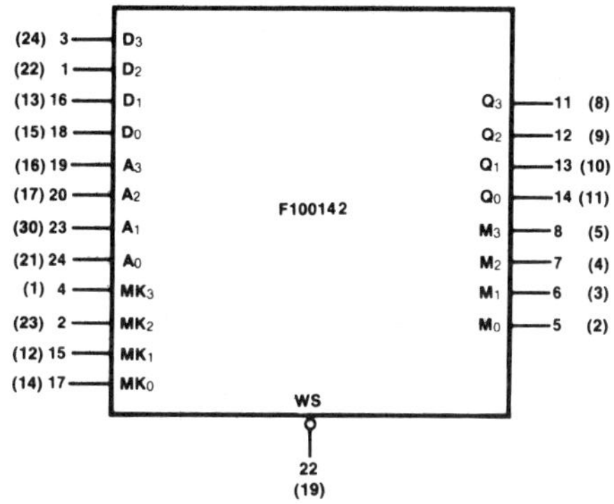

(a)

OPERATION	INPUTS				FLIP-FLOP	OUTPUTS	
	$\overline{WS}$	A_i*	D_j	MK_j	Q_{ij}	M_i**	Q_j
	$\overline{WS}$	A_0 A_1 A_2 A_3	D_0 D_1 D_2 D_3	MK_0 MK_1 MK_2 MK_3		M_0 M_1 M_2 M_3	Q_0 Q_1 Q_2 Q_3
Write Disabled	X	H	X	X	NC	X	L
	X	L	X	H	NC	L	$Q_{ij}n-1$
	H	L	X	X	NC	X	$Q_{ij}n-1$
Write	L	L	H	L	H	L	H
	L	L	L	L	L	L	L
Read	H	L	X	X	H	X	H
	H	L	X	X	L	X	L
Match Masked	H	X	X	H	NC	L	X
Match Not Satisfied	H	L	H	L	L	H	L
	H	H	H	L	L	H	L
	H	H	L	L	H	H	L
	H	L	L	L	H	H	H
Match Satisfied	H	L	H	L	H	L	H
	H	H	H	L	H	L	L
	H	H	L	L	L	L	L
	H	L	L	L	L	L	L

H = High Voltage Level (Most Positive)
L = Low Voltage Level (Most Negative)
X = Don't Care (May be either HIGH or LOW)
NC = No Change from Previous State
$\overline{WS}$ = Write Strobe
A_i = Address for ith Word

D_j = Data for jth Bit
MK_j = Data mask for jth Bit (H = Mask)
Q_{ij} = Cell State for ith Word, jth Bit
M_i = Match Output of ith Word (L = True)
Q_j = Data Output of jth Bit
Qn-1 = Previous Cell State

(b)

Fig. 8.9 (a) F100142 block diagram (Fairchild Camera and Instrument Corp.); (b) modes of operation (Fairchild Camera and Instrument Corp.).

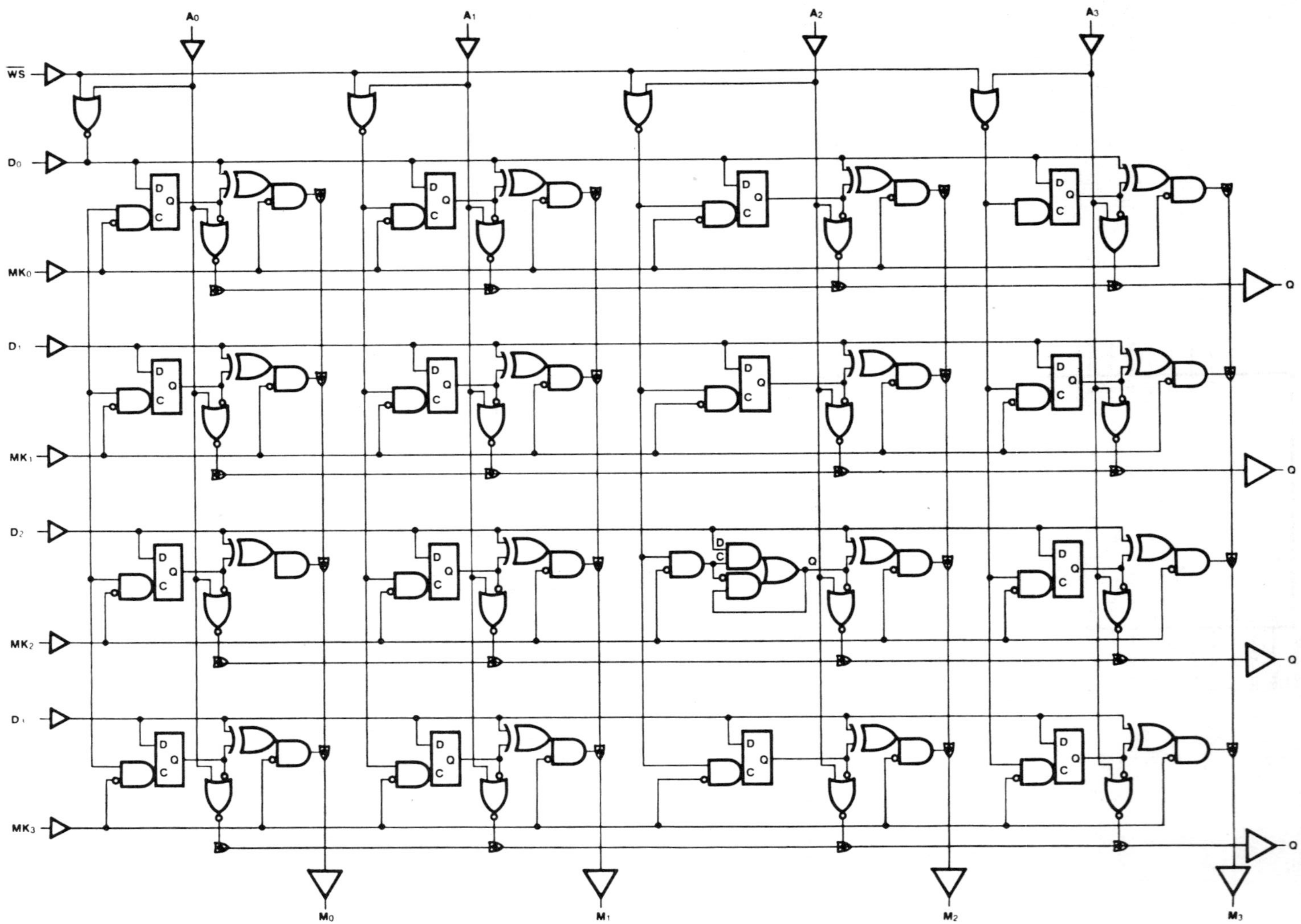

Fig. 8.10 F100142 circuitry (Fairchild Camera and Instrument Corp.).

The table in Fig. 8.9(b) describes the operation of the F100142. From this table, we find that the ability to write into the CAM can be inhibited three different ways. They are to make all address inputs logic 1, to make all mask inputs logic 1, or to switch $\overline{WS}$ to logic 1.

To set up the CAM to perform a write operation, three things must be done: $\overline{WS}$ is set to logic 0, the address input of the storage location is switched to logic 0, and the data are applied to the D inputs. Just as for the 10155 CAM, the data are written into the cell and also appear at the Q data outputs. The *write to data output delay* has a typical access time t_{WD} = 5 ns and the typical *write select pulse width* t_w is 2 ns.

In the chart of Fig. 8.9(b), we also see that to read a word held in the CAM $\overline{WS}$ is set to logic 1 and the address input for the storage location is set to logic 0. The data word held at this address is read out at the Q outputs. The *address to output delay* of the F100142 is denoted t_{AD} and has a typical value of 2.7 ns.

The operation in Fig. 8.9(b), called *match masked*, represents masking out of all data inputs. This is done by setting all MK_j inputs to logic 1. In this case, the match outputs are all forced to the 1 logic level.

The last two modes of operation listed in the table represent association. The first group of states, identified as match not satisfied, corresponds to an association operation during which no match is found between the input data D_j and the content of the flip-flops Q_{jk}. Notice that in the first case D_j is 1 and Q_{ij} is 0. Since no match occurs, the M outputs are logic 1.

On the other hand, the last group represents match satisfied. We see that the data at input D_j and the state of the flip-flop Q_{jk} are the same. Therefore, the match output switches to the 0 logic level. The *data input to match output delay time* is called t_{DM} and equals 3.3 ns.

8.5 EXPANDING CAM STORAGE CAPACITY[2]

For practical applications, the 16-bit storage capacity of a single CAM IC is not normally sufficient. However, as with other memory devices, word length and word capacity can be increased by simply interconnecting devices.

An example of an expanded CAM memory is illustrated in Fig. 8.11. Here are eight 10155 ICs connected to give 16 words by 8 bits of storage. In this circuit, the ICs are grouped into four pairs. The two devices vertically aligned on the left are parallel-connected and together produce 16 2-bit words. The output of these two CAMs are D_7 and D_6 which represent the two most significant bits of the 8-bit word. The other three pairs of CAM ICs are connected in the same way and produce the lower-order bits, D_5 through D_0, of the output. There are eight data inputs and eight mode control inputs to the circuit. They are labeled I_0 through I_7 and A_0 through A_7, respectively. Moreover, there is a single write control input $\overline{W}$.

Notice that the Y lines of the upper four devices are connected in

[2] Ibid., p. 5.

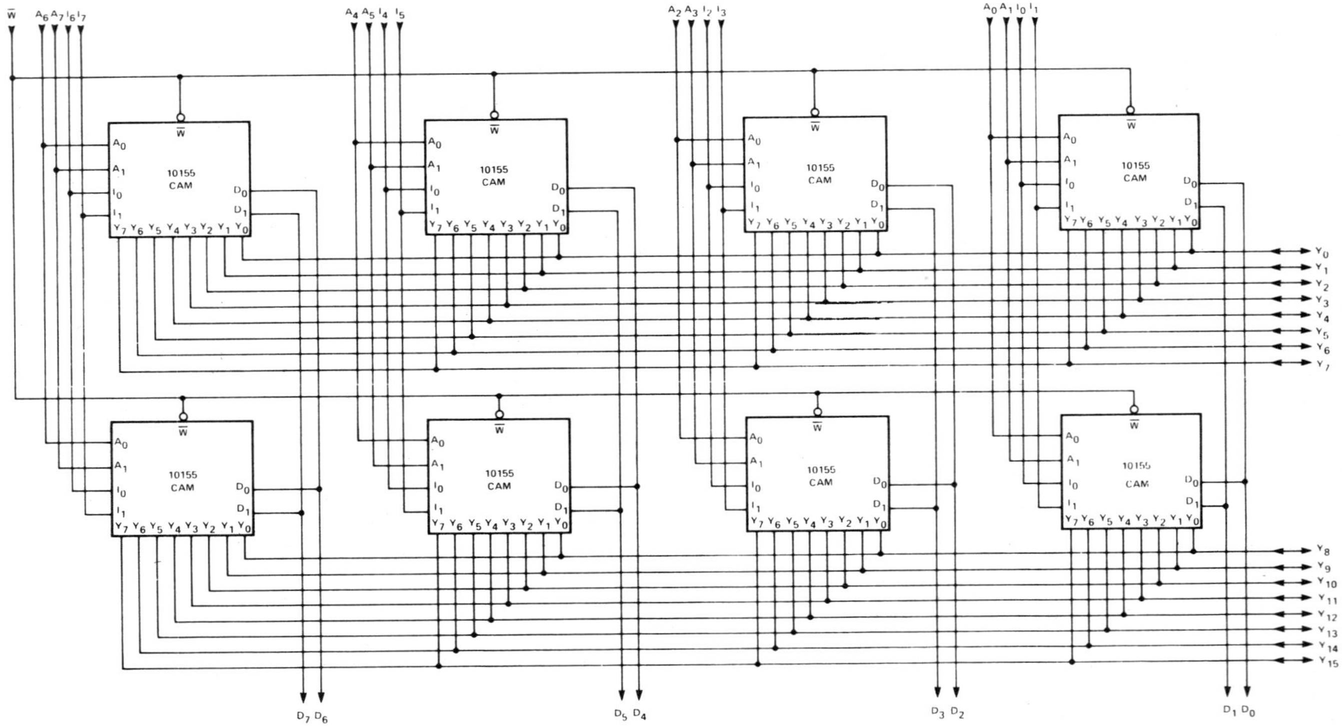

Fig. 8.11 Expanding word length and word capacity (Permission to reprint granted by Signetics Corporation, a subsidiary of U. S. Philips Corp., 811 East Arques Avenue, Sunnyvale, CA 94806).

parallel. They provide address/match lines Y_0 through Y_7 from the first eight storage locations. The lower four ICs are connected in the same way and correspond to address/match lines Y_8 through Y_{15}. These lines represent the second eight storage locations.

EXAMPLE 8.4 The inputs to the CAM circuit in Fig. 8.11 are

$$A_7A_6A_5A_4A_3A_2A_1A_0=00000000$$

$$I_7I_6I_5I_4I_3I_2I_1I_0=01001100$$

$$\overline{W}=0$$

$$Y_1=0,\ Y_0=Y_2=\cdots Y_{15}=1$$

What type of operation is performed? To which address and group of devices is it performed? What are the data outputs?

SOLUTION The mode control inputs on each of the four groups of CAM ICs are $A_1A_0=00$ and the $\overline{W}$ input on all ICs are logic 0. Therefore, the circuit is set up for a write operation.

Logic 0 at Y_1 selects the second storage location in the upper group of four devices. The bits of data at I_0 through I_7 are written into these four devices.

When a write is performed, the input data also appear at the data outputs of the circuit.

$$D_7D_6D_5D_4D_3D_2D_1D_0=01001100$$

8.6 CAM AS A LEARNING MEMORY[3]

Up to this point in the chapter, we have introduced the operation of the CAM, covered several standard ICs, and showed how they can be interconnected to expand word length and word capacity. Now we demonstrate how the CAM can be applied in a circuit application.

Earlier we pointed out that the CAM is used in applications where a part of the input word or the whole word is used as a key during the association operation. The *learning memory* shown in Fig. 8.12(a) is such a circuit. This type of circuit has the ability to decide if it already stores the data word that is applied to its inputs. If the word is held in the memory, it is ignored. On the other hand, if the word is not already stored, a write operation is initiated and the word is loaded into the next available address location. In this way, we see that the circuit learns new words that are applied at its input.

At the top of the circuit in Fig. 8.12(a), we find four 10155 ICs. Together they form an eight-word by 8-bit CAM. Words to be learned are applied to inputs IN_0 through IN_7 of these devices. The sequence of operations performed by the circuit are defined by the program in the ECL PROM controller. The outputs of the PROM are latched into a hex D-type flip-flop.

[3] Ibid., p. 6.

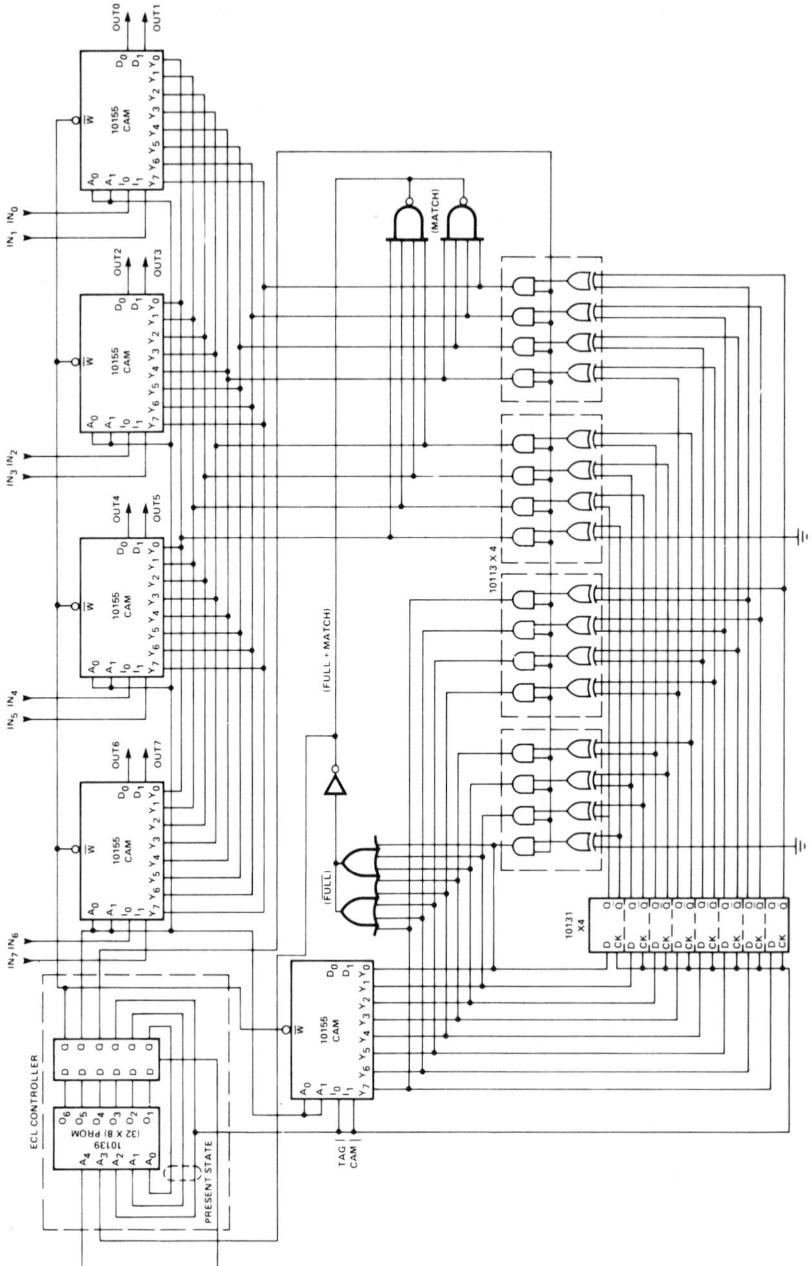

OUT0
OUT1
OUT2
OUT3
OUT4
OUT5
OUT6
OUT7
IN1 IN0
IN3 IN2
IN5 IN4
IN7 IN6
10155 CAM
10155 CAM
10155 CAM
10155 CAM
10155 CAM
(MATCH)
(FULL + MATCH)
(FULL)
10113 X 4
10131 X4
ECL CONTROLLER
10139 (32 X 8) PROM
PRESENT STATE
TAG CAM
INPUT
SYSTEM CLOCK

(a)

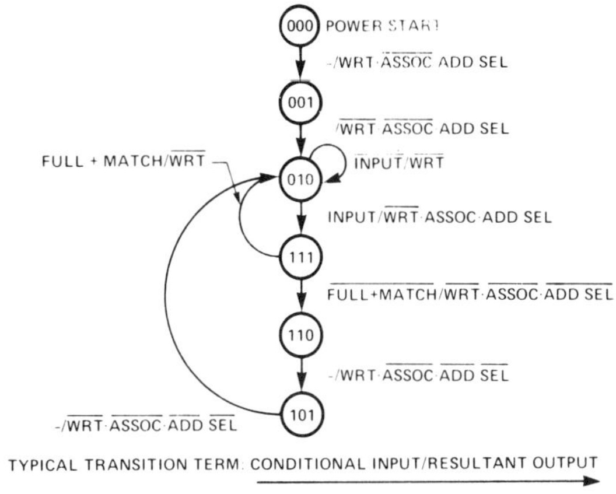

(b)

Fig. 8.12 (a) Learning memory (Permission to reprint granted by Signetics Corporation, a subsidiary of U.S. Philips Corp., 811 East Arques Avenue, Sunnyvale, CA 94806); (b) state diagram (Permission to reprint granted by Signetics Corporation, a subsidiary of U.S. Philips Corp., 811 East Arques Avenue, Sunnyvale, CA 94806).

The program sequence starts when logic 1 is applied to the *INPUT* lead. This causes the control word at the first location to be output at Q_6 through Q_1. On the next pulse of the *SYSTEM CLOCK* input, the control code is loaded into the Q outputs of the latch.

The upper three bits of this code are applied to $\overline{W}$, A_0, A_1, and the address control logic. It is these outputs that determine the operation of the circuit. The three lower bits are returned to inputs of the PROM. Here they are used together with the signal called *FULL+MATCH* to form the address that determines which word will be output next.

Just below the PROM controller is another 10155 CAM. This device functions as a *tag CAM*. That is, it keeps track of which address locations are full. This CAM is initially cleared. After an address location in the learning memory array is written into, the location in the tag CAM corresponding to the address location is filled with 11. By associating the logic 1 applied at its $I_1 I_0$ inputs with data in the CAM, all Y outputs up to the one that is empty stay at logic 0. This is because used addresses hold 11, which matches the input. Match outputs of the empty addresses are logic 0. This code is latched into the D-type flip-flops. Its outputs are decoded to generate the address for loading new words into the learning memory array during write operations and also addressing the tag CAM to write 11 into the same address location.

If the learning memory array is full, all outputs of the tag CAM switch to logic 0. This condition is sensed off by the OR gate wired to its Y outputs. $\overline{FULL}$ switches to logic 0 and *FULL+MATCH* to logic 1. This changes the PROM address and switches the control sequence. The PROM sets the CAMs up to perform an association operation on the complete word applied at inputs IN_0 through IN_7. If the word is already in the memory array, the corresponding match line switches to logic 0. This match condition is sensed by the NAND gates and makes $FULL{+}MATCH$ switch to the 0 logic level. This changes the PROM address and control sequence so that the word is not written into the CAM.

On the other hand, if no match occurs and the tag CAM does not signal full, all Y outputs of the learning memory array are logic 1. $MATCH$ switches to logic 0 and $\overline{FULL}$ to logic 1. This makes $FULL{+}MATCH$ equal logic 0. The PROM controller initiates a write operation. The code at the tag CAM output is latched into the D-type flip-flops and decoded to produce an address code. This address is applied to the Y_0 through Y_7 inputs of the tag CAM and learning memory array. The data word is written into the learning memory array, and at the same instant, the storage location in the tag CAM corresponding to this address location is loaded with 11. After this, the program returns to initiate another association operation for the next data word.

A state diagram for the circuit is given in Fig. 8.12(b).

ASSIGNMENTS

Section 8.2

1. What does "CAM" stand for?
2. What is the name of the unique operation performed by a CAM?
3. What data are read out of the CAM in Fig. 8.2 when the address input is $Y_7Y_6Y_5Y_4Y_3Y_2Y_1Y_0$=01111111?
4. The address inputs to the CAM in Fig. 8.3 is $Y_7Y_6Y_5Y_4Y_3Y_2Y_1Y_0$=11111110 and data inputs I_1I_0=11. What is the new data content of the memory?
5. If the CAM in Fig. 8.4 contains the data shown in Fig. 8.2(b) and the data inputs are I_1I_0=11, which Y outputs signal a match condition?

Section 8.3

6. Describe the operation of the CAM circuit in Fig. 8.5 during a read operation.

Section 8.4

7. Describe the operation of the 10155 CAM when its control inputs are A_0=1, A_1=0, and $\overline{W}$=0. The data inputs are I_1I_0=11.
8. A F100142 CAM is set up with $\overline{WS}$=0, $A_3A_2A_1A_0$=1110, and $D_3D_2D_1D_0$=1111. What type of operation is performed? Which storage location is accessed? What is the output data word?

Section 8.5

9. The inputs to the CAM circuit in Fig. 8.11 are $A_7A_6A_5A_4A_3A_2A_1A_0$=11111111, $I_7I_6I_5I_4I_3I_2I_1I_0$=10010110, and $\overline{W}$=1. What type of operation is performed?

10. Show how F100142 CAMs can be connected to expand storage capacity to eight words by 4 bits.

Section 8.6

11. Describe the operation of the learning memory circuit in Fig. 8.12(a).

9

CHARGE-COUPLED-DEVICE MEMORY

9.1 INTRODUCTION

The preceding four chapters introduced additional devices that fall into the category of semiconductor memories. These devices are the shift register, PLA, FIFO, and CAM. Here we introduce a more modern technology used for the manufacture of memories. It is called the *charge-coupled-device* (CCD) *technology*. When CCDs are used as memory devices, they are called CCD memories.

In this chapter we introduce the charge-coupled-device technology and present the charge-coupled-device memory. Then we turn our attention to the architecture of CCD memory, methods of reading and writing, and an actual charge-coupled memory IC. This chapter closes with an introduction to the application of CCD memories. The following topics are covered:

1. The charge-coupled device
2. Architecture of the CCD memory
3. Methods of reading and writing
4. Standard CCD memory IC
5. Expanding word length and word capacity
6. CCD memory system

9.2 THE CHARGE-COUPLED DEVICE

The charge-coupled device utilizes a different technique from devices described so far to store and maintain data. As with the dynamic RAM and dynamic shift register, data in the charge-coupled device are stored as a charge in a capacitor. For instance, a small amount of charge can represent the 0 logic level, and a large amount logic 1. Actually, the CCD memory was developed in an effort to find a semiconductor equivalent to the magnetic bubble memory.

Charge-Coupled-Device Technology

The manner in which the charge is maintained in a CCD is unique. Recall that in the dynamic RAM there were MOSFETs connected to each capacitor. The capacitor MOSFET combination formed a dynamic RAM cell. These cells were organized into orderly arrays. In contrast, a CCD memory is made up of long rows of semiconductor material capacitors. These rows are called *CCD channels*, or simply *channels.* Figure 9.1 demonstrates the concept of a channel. One plate of each capacitor is a gate, and the other plate, which is common to all capacitors, is the semiconductor substrate. Data are entered into these channels in serial form. Here each bit of data is represented by a large or small packet of charge. The shift of charge through the channels is accomplished by the clocks. Clock pulses are sequentially applied to push or pull the packets from capacitor to capacitor along the channel. To conserve space, the CCD channels on the chip are arranged into *loops*, *parallel channels*, and *other area-saving configurations.*

In this way, we see that the CCD memory differs from RAM in that its data are stored in serial form in channels, while in dynamic RAMs the data are stored in an array of randomly accessible cells. The operation of the CCD memory also differs from that of a dynamic shift register. In a dynamic shift register, data are shifted from flip-flop to flip-flop; in a CCD, the charge is simply shifted from capacitor to capacitor down the channel.

The CCD memory is volatile. That is, when power is removed, its data will be lost. In addition to power, however, the CCD memory shift clocks must also be maintained. This is because the charges in the CCD channels must be periodically restored (refreshed). Refreshing the CCD charge level is accomplished by using internal *refresh amplifiers.* The refresh circuitry restores the proper level of charge for each particular charge packet. If the charge is not reestablished within a certain amount of time, data will be lost. The refresh circuitry is located at one point in a CCD loop. Each charge

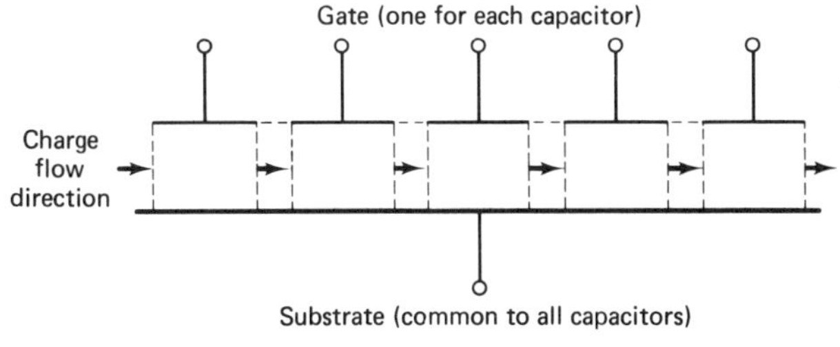

Fig. 9.1 Charge-coupled-device channel.

packet must be shifted through the refresh area before too much charge is lost. The process of shifting the charges and passing them through the refresh circuitry when a write or a read operation is not in progress is frequently called *recirculation.*

Storage Capacity

Because of their simple structure CCD memory cells can be made very small. In fact, the CCD has a higher bit packing density than even dynamic RAMs made with single-transistor-cell circuits.

Although CCD memories initially promised the use of a well-known technology, semiconductor technology, practical CCDs have been slow in development. After initially leading dynamic MOS RAMs in storage capacity with 64*k* bits of storage per device, the MOS RAM has now reached the same maximum storage capacity as the CCD. At the same time, the magnetic bubble memory, its direct competitor, far exceeded this capacity.

Use of the Charge-Coupled-Device Memory

Charge-coupled-device memory is a serial-accessed memory. It competes for application with other serial memory devices, such as the shift register, bubble memory, disks, and drums. Because of their small size, lack of moving parts, ruggedness, and relatively fast access, they could compete well against magnetic drums, disks, and tapes for use in low-capacity mass storage applications. However, a disadvantage of employing the CCD in these types of applications is that it is volatile.

General CCD Memory Block Diagram

A block diagram of a general CCD memory is shown in Fig. 9.2. Looking at this illustration, we find that the device has five sets of signal leads: *address inputs*, *data inputs*, *control inputs*, *clocks*, and *data outputs*.

As in ROM and RAM, the address word is used to select the storage locations within the CCD memory. However, addresses of the CCD differ from those of ROM and RAM. For a CCD, the address applied at $A_1 A_0$

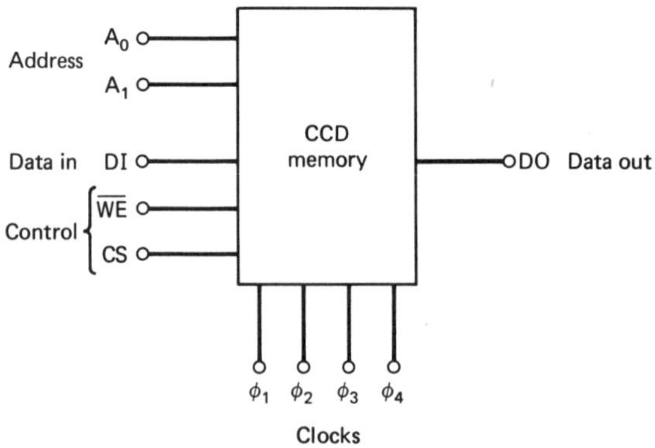

Fig. 9.2 CCD memory block diagram.

represents only part of the total address required to identify a storage location. Here, some of the clock inputs also play a role in determining which location is to be accessed. The two address bits specify a block of storage locations, and the clocks indicate the individual storage positions within that block.

The *data input* lead (*DI*) is used to input data to the CCD memory. While a write operation is in progress, the bits of data are applied one after the other at *DI* and clocked into consecutive storage locations within the selected block. On the other hand, during a read operation, data held in the bit positions of its block are output one bit at a time at *data output* (*DO*). Each bit appears synchronously with the respective clock inputs. In this way, we see that the CCD memory is a serial-in, serial-out storage device.

The input/output operation of the CCD memory is performed under the control of the signals *chip select* (*CS*) and *write enable* ($\overline{WE}$). The logic level of *CS* can be set to enable or disable the output buffer and *write enable input*. When enabled, the level at $\overline{WE}$ controls input of data from *DI*.

A CCD memory has a group of *clock inputs* (ϕ_1 through ϕ_4). They are involved in the shifting of data through the channels, timing of input data, and latching of output data. Within the device, the clock signals are further divided to generate additional clocks.

Modes of Operation

There are three basic modes of operation for the CCD memory. They are *write data in*, *recirculate data*, and *read data out*. In general, the sequence of events that occur during each operation will be described.

The write-data-in operation represents the input of data to the CCD for storage. The write cycle begins by applying the address of the storage block at inputs A_1A_0. At the same time, *CS* is set to logic 1. The device is now enabled for operation. Next, the bit of data to be written into the device is applied at *DI*. After it has stabilized, $\overline{WE}$ is switched to logic 0. The data are synchronously entered into the location selected within the block by the clocks.

With the device set this way, additional bits of a serial stream of data can be written into consecutive locations of the block. This is done by simply changing the data at *DI*, and after the new bit of data stabilizes, activating the clock inputs. The actual location that is accessed is determined by external circuitry that counts the clock inputs.

The sequence of events that occur during a read cycle is similar to that found in the write cycle. Again we start with the input of the *block address* at A_1A_0 and switch *CS* to logic 1. But at this point in the cycle, instead of setting $\overline{WE}$ to logic 0, it is left at the 1 level. This sets the device for a read operation. Synchronously with the clock inputs, the bit of data is latched at the output. Again, consecutive storage positions in the block are accessed on the clock inputs that follow. In this way, a bit-serial stream of data is read out of the CCD memory at *DO*.

When a read or write operation is not in progress, the data must still be recirculated around the channels within the CCD memory. This operation is called recirculation, and is required to refresh the data stored within the device. Otherwise, the data would be lost.

During recirculation, the CCD memory chip is not selected; therefore, the data output buffer is disabled, and the output lead is in the high-impedance state. Moreover, in this state the address, write enable, and data input signals are ignored. However, the clocks are continuously supplied to the CCD memory device. They cause the data within the device to continuously circulate around their loops. In this way, the charge packets that represent the bits of data pass through the refresh circuit located in their loops, and are restored to their original charge levels.

During all read and write operations, data are also passed through these refresh areas, and refresh is automatically achieved.

9.3 ARCHITECTURE OF CCD MEMORY[1]

We have already introduced CCD memory, its block diagram, and input/output operation. We next turn our interest to the internal structure of the device.

In Fig. 9.3 we have shown a typical block diagram of the internal architecture of a CCD memory. Looking at the diagram, we find seven fundamental parts. They are the *address buffer/latch*, *address decoder*, *CCD storage array*, *control gates*, *internal clock generator*, *chip select latch*, and the *output latch/buffer*. All these functional blocks are built into the CCD integrated circuit.

In this section, we consider the function of each of these parts with respect to overall CCD memory operation. Moreover, the basic circuitry used in each part is introduced.

The Memory Array

The memory array is the portion of the CCD memory in which data are stored. As shown in Fig. 9.3, the storage array is subdivided into a number of smaller storage sections called *blocks*. During a read or write operation, an address is input to the CCD to select one of these blocks. Only locations within the selected block can be accessed. But regardless of which block is selected, data are always being synchronously clocked around the loops in all blocks.

The blocks can employ a variety of different loop configurations. The simplest is the *single serial loop* shown in Fig. 9.4(a). This configuration is effectively a CCD recirculating shift register. New data at serial input *DI* can

[1] Fairchild Charge Coupled Device, "F464: 65,536 × 1 Dynamic Serial Memory" (Mountain View, CA: Fairchild Semiconductor, Inc., August 1978). (Courtesy of Fairchild Camera and Instrument Corp.)

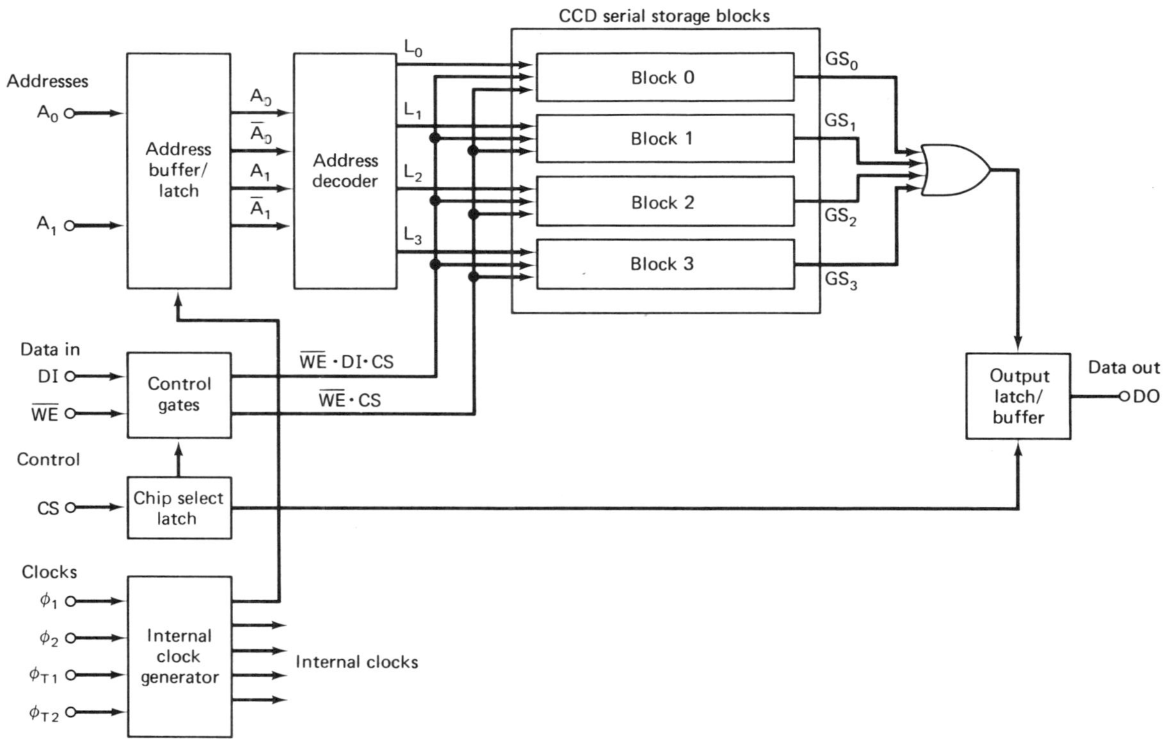

Fig. 9.3 Typical block diagram of a CCD memory.

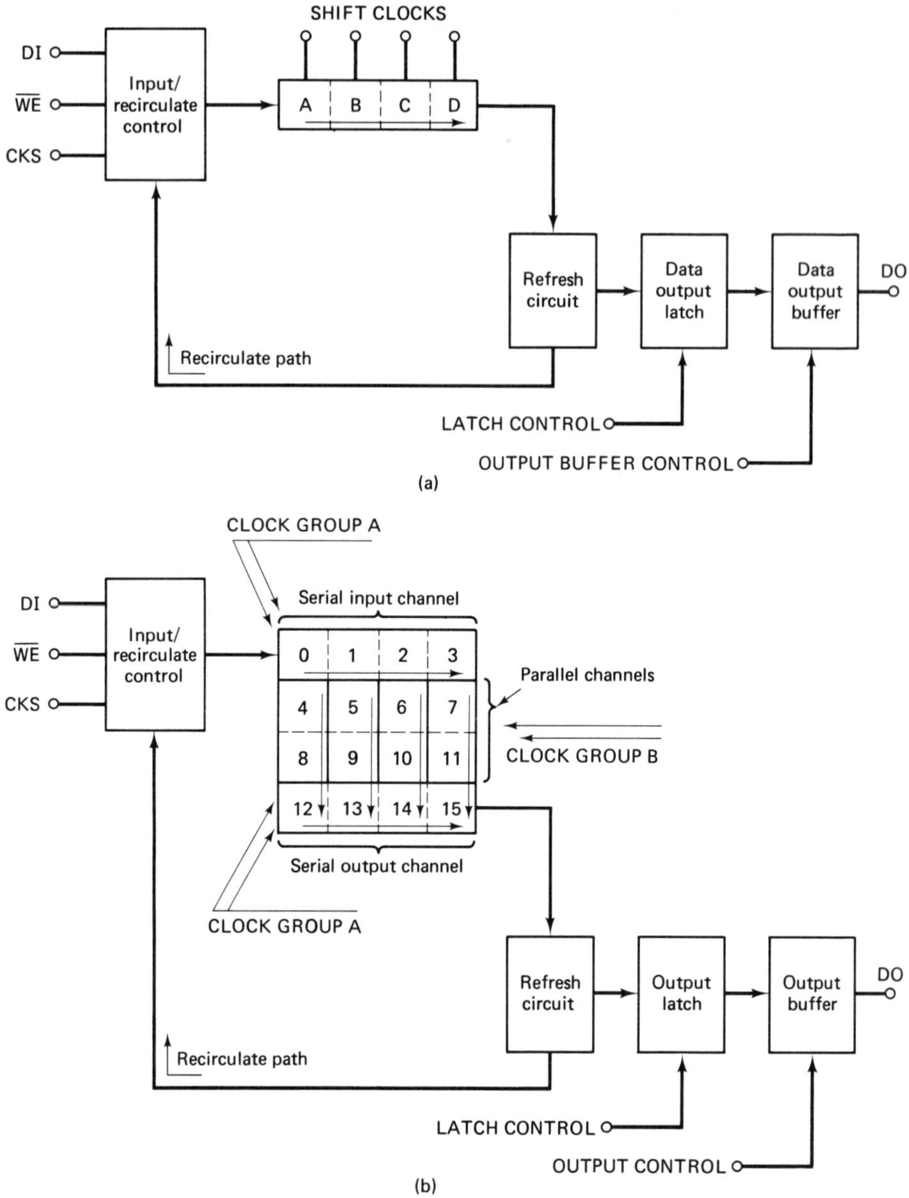

Fig. 9.4 (a) Serial CCD memory loop; (b) twelve bit serial-parallel-serial CCD memory loop.

be written into storage position A of the channel. In the case of a recirculation operation, the data from the last position in the channel (D), instead of data from DI, are returned to A. During a read operation, serial data are output at DO.

Before going to a second block configuration, let us look more closely at the write, recirculate, and read operations of the single CCD loop. The write sequence begins by setting up control input *CS*, applying the data at *DI*, and setting $\overline{WE}$ for a write operation. In this case, the input/recirculate control circuit stops the refreshed data bit from *D*, but passes that at *DI*. The bit is shifted into the *A* position of the channel with the next pulse at *shift clock CKS*.

If a block is not selected, it is automatically in the recirculate mode of operation. Now the data bit from the *D* position is refreshed and then gated through the input/recirculate control circuit to the *A* position. Here it is reloaded with *CKS*. At the same time, all other bits within the channel move one position farther.

When a read operation is required, *CS* and $\overline{WE}$ must first be set for this mode. Then the data at position *D* in the channel are refreshed and stored in the output latch and at the same time recirculated to the *A* position of the channel. The output is then buffered and passed to *DO*.

To output a specific bit or group of bits from the loop, we must wait for the appropriate bit to be shifted around to the output of the channel. The time that it takes from the moment a request is made to access the bit until it is available at the output is sometimes called the *latency time*. This can be as long as several milliseconds. However, once the bit is in place by the output, the bits that follow are available just one clock shift away. For this reason, access of the first bit of a data stream can be relatively slow, but the remaining bits of the stream are accessed relatively fast.

The single serial loop just described was used in some earlier lower-capacity devices. However, because of its poor use of the chip area and its resulting lower packing density, the single serial loop is not practical for the newer high-capacity CCDs. By switching to a *serial-parallel-serial* (SPS) loop configuration, area is conserved, and devices with higher storage capacities have been achieved. Figure 9.4(b) shows a simplified SPS block configuration.

Let us now trace the operation of the SPS CCD block for a write cycle. With *CS* and $\overline{WE}$ set up for write mode, bits of serial data from *DI* are shifted through the input/recirculate control circuit to the serial input channel. In this way, the first four bits of data are serially shifted into bit positions 0 through 3. This is done at a rate set by *clock group A*. At the same time that serial input is happening, the data bits in positions 12 through 15 of the serial output channel are passed through the refresh circuit.

When four bits have been written into positions 0 through 3, they are ready for parallel transfer into the first bit position of the parallel channels. After transfer, the data bits previously in positions 0 through 3 reside in positions 4 through 7, respectively. This parallel transfer occurs at the rate set by *clock group B*. This rate is one-fourth that used to shift data through the serial channels. Therefore, after every four bits of data are serially input and output, a *parallel transfer* occurs. As this parallel transfer occurs, the data that were in locations 4 through 7 and 8 through 11 are also shifted down the parallel channels. They now reside in locations 8 through 11, and 12 through 15, respectively. Notice that during the write operation of four consecutive bits, the old data originally held in locations 12 through 15 are lost.

The read operation is similar; however, this time the data bits held at 12 through 15 are passed to data output *DO*. At the same time, these data are refreshed and reloaded into positions 0 through 3 of the serial input channel.

In practice, it is not uncommon to find a SPS block such as that just mentioned with a capacity of 4096 bits. The memory array in a 64*k*-bit CCD memory will require 16 of these blocks.

To gain additional packing density, the serial bit positions of the input and output channels are shared with two of the parallel channels as shown in Fig. 9.5. When the serial input channel is full, the bits of data can be multiplexed into either of the two groups of parallel channels. Therefore, it takes two serial load operations, one for each group of channels, to fill the first bit position in all the parallel channels. This shared structure is called *interlaced serial-parallel-serial architecture.* A typical interlaced SPS block would consist of two serial channels, each with 32 bit locations. One serial channel is used for input of data, and the other for output of data. These serial channels service two groups of 32 parallel channels, each with 64 bit positions. This gives a total storage capacity of 4096 bits.

The Address Buffer/Latch, Chip Select Latch, and Address Decoder

The signals applied at address inputs A_1A_0 and chip select input *CS* are latched within the CCD memory. This is done by the address buffer/latch circuit and chip select latch circuit, respectively. Figure 9.6 shows the type of circuits used in this section of the CCD.

From the circuit diagram, we see that the logic levels at A_1A_0 and *CS* are latched into flip-flops 1 through 3, respectively. Notice that these flip-flops are edge-triggered. Therefore, noise on the input lines at times other

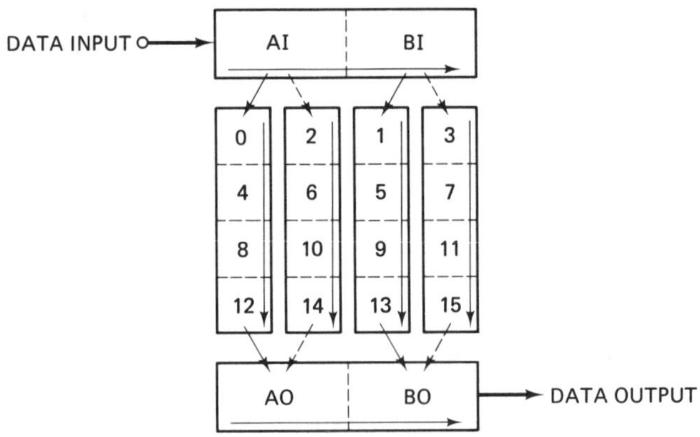

Fig. 9.5 Interlaced serial-parallel-serial structure.

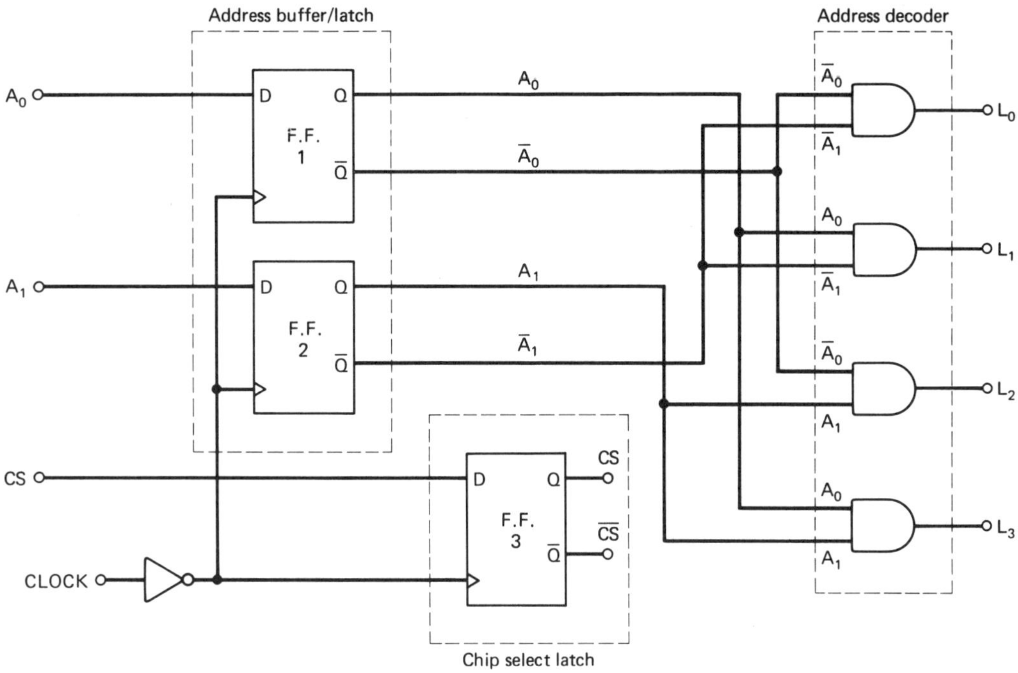

Fig. 9.6 Address buffer/latch, chip select latch, and address decoder circuits.

than the clock edge will have no effect on the memory operation. All three output signals are provided in their normal and complemented forms.

At the same time, the flip-flops provide a buffer action. They assure that the logic levels supplied to the internal circuits are correct and also limit loading of circuits driving the inputs.

Earlier in this section, we mentioned that the storage array in the CCD memory contains more than one storage block. During a read or write operation, data can only be accessed from one of the blocks. The selection of this block is performed by the address decoder. Figure 9.6 shows how the two address bits A_1A_0 and their complements $\overline{A}_1\overline{A}_0$ are decoded to select one of four blocks. The block enable outputs of the decoder are L_0 through L_3. For instance, if the input to the circuit in Fig. 9.6 is $A_1A_0 = 00$ when *CLOCK* is pulsed, the outputs of the flip-flops become $A_0 = 0$, $\overline{A}_0 = 1$, $A_1 = 0$, and $\overline{A}_1 = 1$. This input to the decoder makes output L_0 switch to logic 1, and block 0 of the storage array is selected.

The Input/Output Control and Refresh Circuit

Figure 9.7 shows the data input/output control and its relationship to the refresh circuit. The input/output control gates can be divided into two categories: those that are shared by all the storage blocks in the memory array, and those that are not shared with other blocks. Looking at the

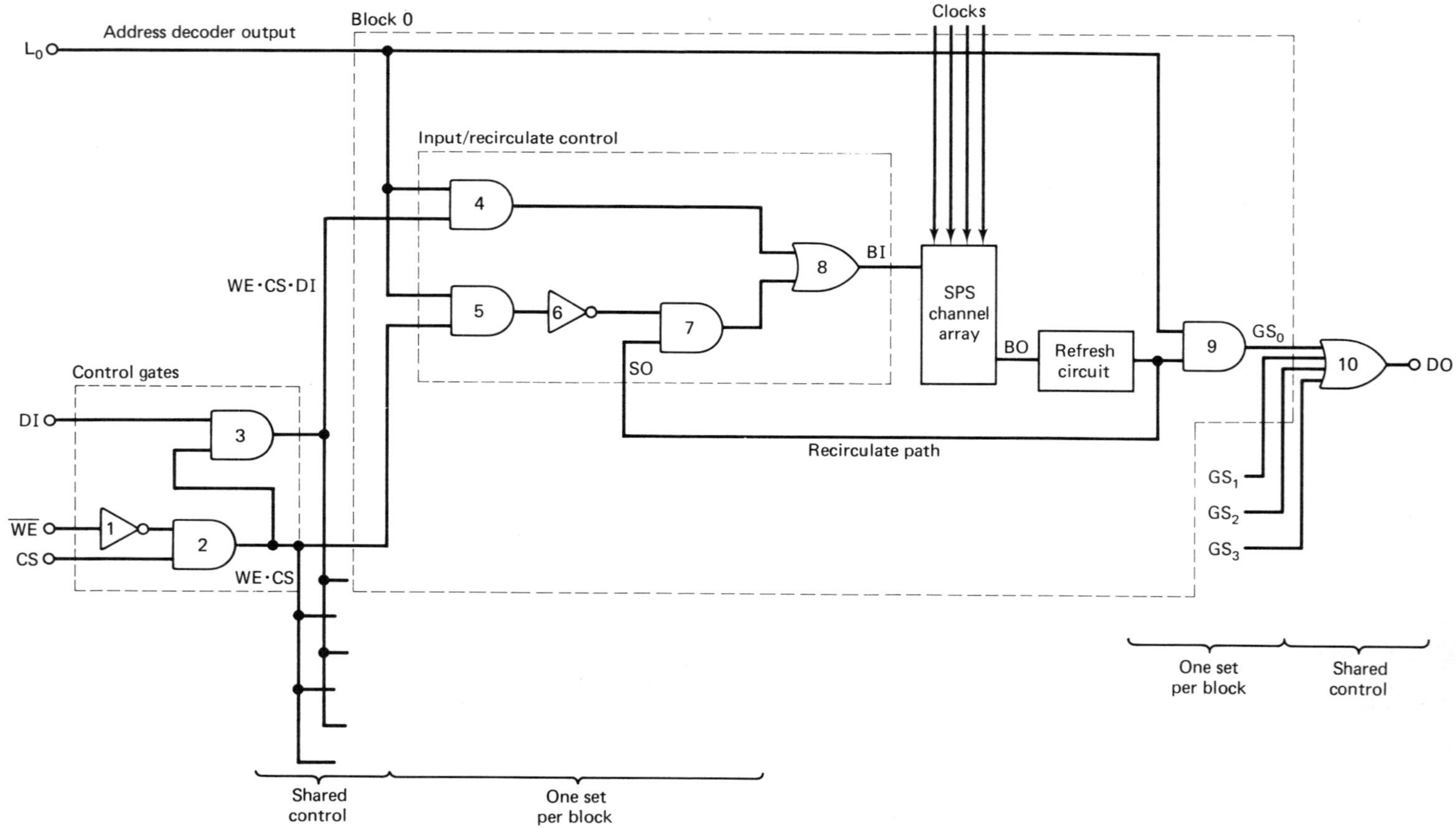

Fig. 9.7 Input/output control logic and refresh circuit.

diagram, we see that the input control gates which are labeled 1 through 3 as well as OR gate 10 at the output are shared by all blocks in the storage array. On the other hand, gates 4 through 8 of the input/recirculate control and gate 9 of the output are provided separately for each storage block.

Let us assume that the CCD chip is selected and a write operation is to be performed to the storage block corresponding to decoder output L_0. For this to be the case, CS must be logic 1, $\overline{WE}$ logic 0, and L_0 logic 1. The inputs to gate 2 are both 1; therefore, its output switches to the 1 level. This enables gate 3, and its output $WE \cdot CS \cdot DI$ follows the logic level of the data at DI.

The address decoder output L_0 is used to enable the input gates of the input/recirculate control. Since L_0 is 1, gates 4 and 5 are enabled, and the data from $WE \cdot CS \cdot DI$ are passed through gate 8 to the input of the SPS array. Here the bits of data are loaded and shifted through the serial input channel and eventually transferred into the parallel channels.

As each new bit is written into the serial input channel, a bit from the output channel appears at BO. The charge level of this bit is restored by the refresh circuit before it is output through gates 9 and 10. At the same time, the bit is passed around the recirculate loop to gate 7. Both inputs of gate 5 are logic 1, and its output switches to logic 1. However, this output is inverted and turns off gate 7. Therefore, the recirculate path is disabled, and data at SO are not passed to the input of gate 8. The data are not recirculated.

If a recirculate operation is to be executed, the output of gate 2 is logic 0. This disables gate 3, and data at DI is not input to the input/recirculate control. Instead, the output of gate 5 is switched to logic 0, and the output of gate 6 to logic 1. This enables gate 7. Recirculated data from the refresh circuit output are now passed through gates 7 and 8 for entry into the serial input channel. Bits of data continuously recirculate in this way.

During a read operation, the data available at the output of the refresh circuit are passed through gates 9 and 10. Notice that gate 9 is also enabled by address decoder output L_0. Gate 10 ORs the outputs of all blocks together and supplies them to the input of the output latch. But remember that only one block can be read at a time. Therefore, data will be present only on one of the GS lines. Recirculation occurs during all read operations.

Output Latch and Buffer

The bits of serial data read from the output channel of the storage block are latched and buffered for output at DO. The circuit in Fig. 9.8 shows the output latch and buffer. Data from one of the blocks enter through OR gate 1 synchronously with pulses at $CLOCK$. With the chip selected, the output of gate 2 follows the clock input. For each pulse at $CLOCK$, a new bit of data is latched into flip-flop 3. $CLOCK$ is timed to allow the data

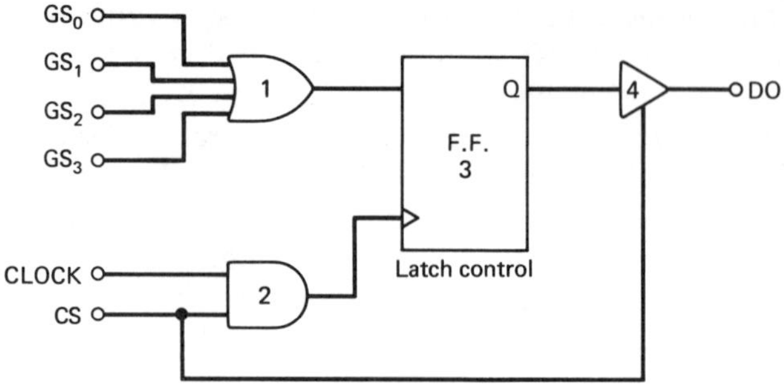

Fig. 9.8 Output latch and buffer.

output from the block to propagate through the refresh circuit and output control gates.

The output buffer, gate 4, is also controlled by *CS*. If the chip is selected, data at the output of flip-flop 3 are buffered, and appear at *DO*. On the other hand, if the chip is not selected, *DO* is in its hi-Z state.

The Memory Map

Before going further, let us first clarify addressing methods of the CCD storage array. Figure 9.9(a) shows the address decoder connection to a CCD storage array that consists of four serial-parallel-serial blocks. The address at input A_1A_0 is decoded to select one of these blocks. It does this by setting the logic level of the appropriate L line. Notice that just a block has been selected, not the actual storage location within the block. After the block address is fixed, its 16 storage locations are sequentially accessed on consecutive clock counts. This clock count is kept in external circuitry.

Let us trace the address sequence for writing data into the complete storage array. The address input starts at A_1A_0=00. This makes the L_0 output switch to logic 1, selecting block 0. On the first four clock pulses, bits of data are written into the input channel of block 0, and then shifted down into the parallel channels. On the clock pulses that follow, additional bits of data continue to enter and move down through the block. After the sixteenth pulse, block 0 is full with bits B_0 through B_{15}.

Before additional data can be stored in the CCD array, the input address must be incremented. Changing A_1A_0 to 01 enables block 1. For the next 16 clocks, data are written into cells 0 through 15 of block 1. It is now full with data bits B_{16} through B_{31}. In the same way, data are written to the remaining two blocks. When full, they contain B_{32} through B_{63}.

The diagram in Fig. 9.9(b) represents a *memory map* of this CCD. Here, the locations of the data bits are illustrated relative to their block and clock count. One way of viewing this storage array is as 64 consecutive, sequentially accessible storage locations. However, the blocks do not necessarily have to be addressed sequentially. We can read from or write to the blocks randomly.

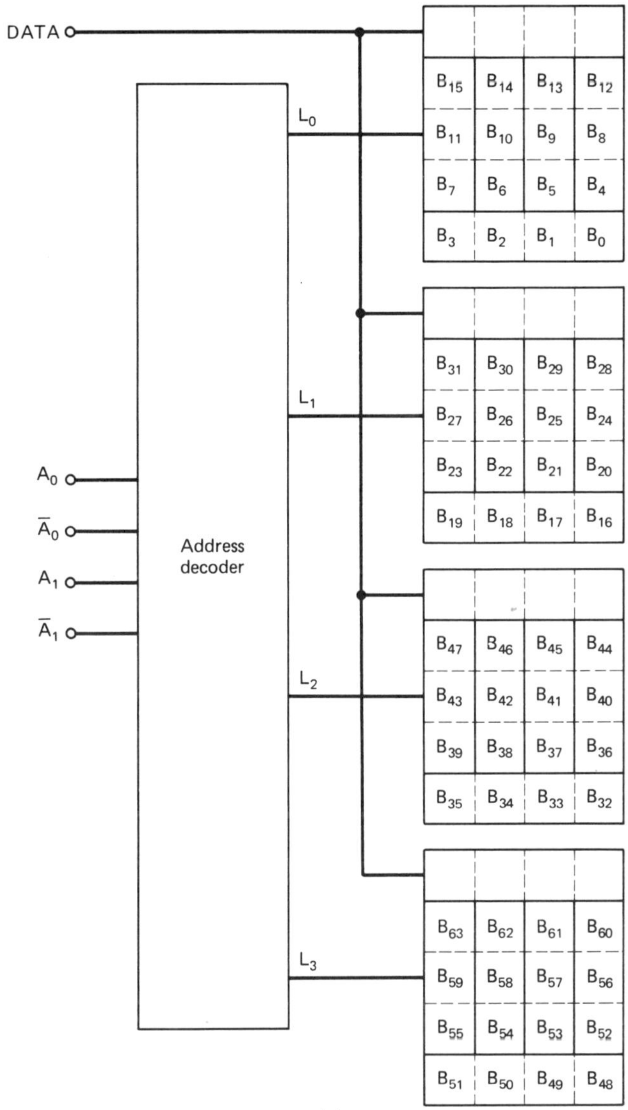

(a)

Block address \ Clock count	0	1	2	3	4	5	6	7	8	9	10	11	12	13	14	15
0	B_0	B_1	B_2	B_3	B_4	B_5	B_6	B_7	B_8	B_9	B_{10}	B_{11}	B_{12}	B_{13}	B_{14}	B_{15}
1	B_{16}	B_{17}	B_{18}	B_{19}	B_{20}	B_{21}	B_{22}	B_{23}	B_{24}	B_{25}	B_{26}	B_{27}	B_{28}	B_{29}	B_{30}	B_{31}
2	B_{32}	B_{33}	B_{34}	B_{35}	B_{36}	B_{37}	B_{38}	B_{39}	B_{40}	B_{41}	B_{42}	B_{43}	B_{44}	B_{45}	B_{46}	B_{47}
3	B_{48}	B_{49}	B_{50}	B_{51}	B_{52}	B_{53}	B_{54}	B_{55}	B_{56}	B_{57}	B_{58}	B_{59}	B_{60}	B_{61}	B_{62}	B_{63}

(b)

Fig. 9.9 (a) Addressing the storage array; (b) memory map.

9.4 F464 CHARGE-COUPLED-DEVICE MEMORY

Up to this point in the chapter, we have introduced the basic concepts of the CCD memory, its internal architecture, and circuitry. We are now ready to turn our attention to a standard CCD, the F464. It has a storage capacity of 65,536 (64k) bits organized as 65,536 1-bit words. Figure 9.10(a) and (b) show the logic symbol and block diagram of the F464, respectively.

Looking at Fig. 9.10(b), we see that the internal architecture of the F464 is identical to that introduced in Section 9.3. Notice that it contains 16 storage blocks labeled 0 through 15. Each block has a serial-parallel-serial configuration that utilizes the interlaced data input/output scheme. The serial input and output channels are 32 bits long, and the 64 parallel channels that they service can each store 64 bits of data. Therefore, each block in the CCD is capable of storing 4096 bits.

One of the 16 blocks is selected for access by the 4-bit address word applied at inputs A_0 through A_3. This address is latched into the decoder section synchronously with the ϕ_1 clock. It is then decoded to switch one of the decoder outputs, 0 through 15, to the 1 logic level. The block corresponding to this output is selected for read/write operation.

Serial data are input to or output from the CCD at the D_{IN} and D_{OUT} leads, respectively. Read and write operations are performed under control of the chip select (CS) and write enable ($\overline{WE}$) signals. For either operation to occur, CS must be logic 1. On the other hand, the logic level of $\overline{WE}$ selects the read or write mode of operation. When $\overline{WE}$ is 0, a write cycle is performed, and when 1, a read cycle.

Four clocks must be supplied to the CCD memory. They are ϕ_1, ϕ_2, ϕ_{T1}, and ϕ_{T2}. Clocks ϕ_1 and ϕ_2 control the movement of data in the serial input and output registers. Both ϕ_1 and ϕ_2 are the same frequency and this value can be a maximum of 2 MHz, 4 MHz, or 5MHz, depending upon whether the F464-4, F464-3, or F464-2 device is employed.

The other two clocks, ϕ_{T1} and ϕ_{T2}, are provided to control the movement of data down through the parallel registers. These signals must have a frequency equal to 1/32 of the serial shift clock rate. Within the device, ϕ_{T1} and ϕ_{T2} are converted to additional clock signals. It is these internal clocks that actually cause the data to shift down the parallel registers.

Except for the clocks, all inputs and the output are TTL-compatible. The clock inputs are at MOS levels; therefore, they must switch between 0-V and +12-V levels.

To perform a write operation with the F464, we begin by setting CS to logic 1 and applying the address to A_0 through A_3. The chip select and address setup times are illustrated in Fig. 9.11(a). Here we find that chip select and address signals must be stable for intervals t_{CSS} and t_{AS}, respectively, before the leading edge of clock ϕ_1. Both values are rated as a minimum of 5 ns. Next, the $\overline{WE}$ control is switched to logic 0, and data are applied to input D_{IN}. The *setup times* for these two signals are identified

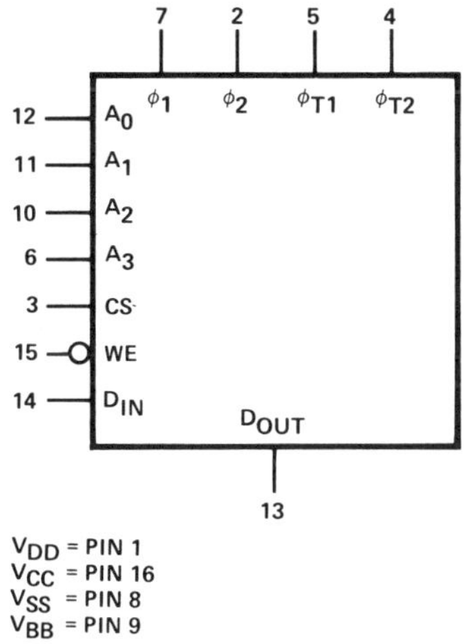

(a)

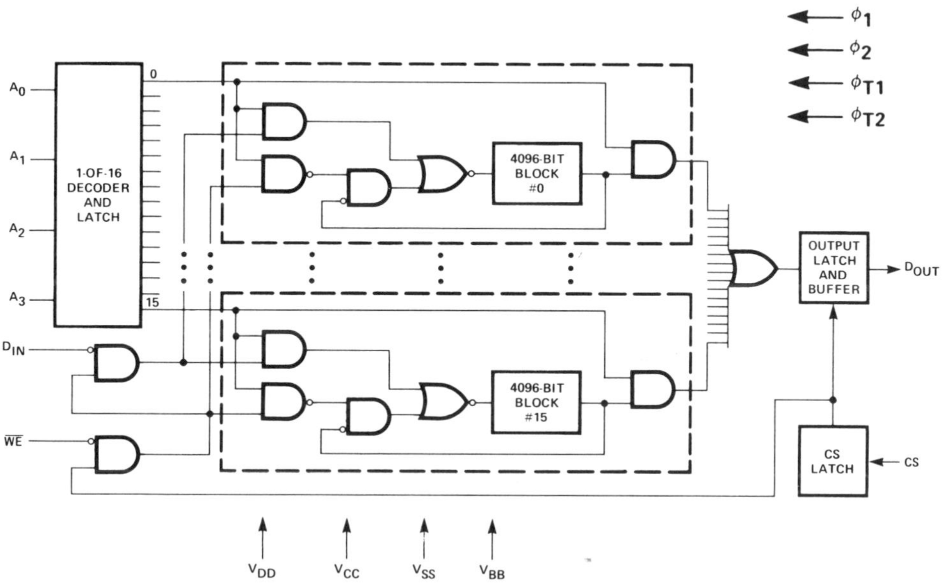

(b)

Fig. 9.10 (a) F464 CCD logic symbol (Fairchild Camera and Instrument Corp.); (b) F464 CCD block diagram (Fairchild Camera and Instrument Corp.).

as t_{WCS} and t_{DS}, respectively, and are shown in Fig. 9.11(b). Both times are rated 0 ns with respect to the falling edge of ϕ_1. This says that the inputs could occur at any time before this edge or even as ϕ_1 falls to the logic 0 level.

To assure that the write operation occurs correctly, A_0 through A_3 and *CS* must be held after the falling edge of ϕ_1. In Fig. 9.11(c) these *hold times* are labeled t_{AH} and t_{CSH}, respectively. Their values are also both the

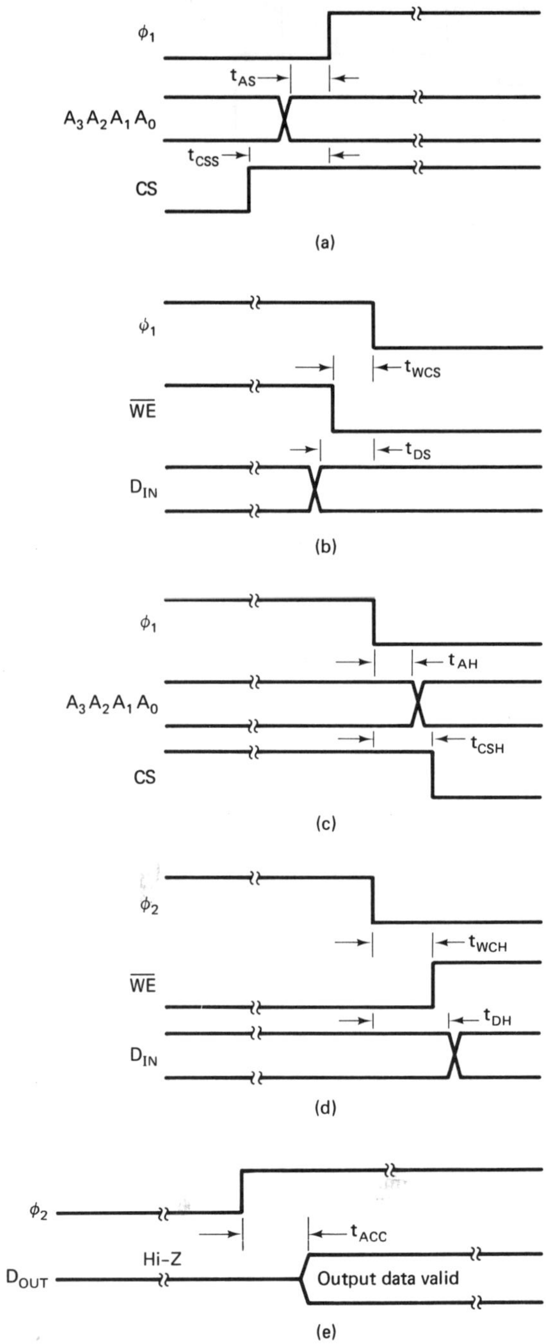

Fig. 9.11 (a) Address and chip select setup times; (b) write enable and data-in setup times; (c) address and chip select hold times; (d) write enable and data-in hold times; (e) data-out access time.

same and equal to 5 ns. The hold times of $\overline{WE}$ and D_{IN} are defined with respect to the trailing edge of ϕ_2 instead of ϕ_1. In Fig. 9.11(d) we find that they are labeled t_{WCH} and t_{DH}, respectively. These two hold times are rated as 25 ns.

Timing of the input signals during a read cycle are similar. The differences are that $\overline{WE}$ is left at the 1 level and data applied at D_{IN} are not gated into the IC. The *access time* of the data output for a read operation is referenced from the rising edge of ϕ_2. This time is marked t_{ACC} and has a value of 70 ns, 60 ns, and 50 ns for the F464-4, F464-3, and F464-2 devices, respectively. Output switching characteristics are drawn in Fig. 9.11(e).

The F464-2, F464-3, and F464-4 all have a *minimum operating frequency* of 1 MHz. This means that when the F464 is operating at its slowest access rate, the device can have 1,000,000 memory operations performed on it per second.

However, this access rate does not take into account the time required to shift the storage location into position for input or output of data. Depending upon the location of the position within the serial-parallel-serial array, it could require as many as 4096 clock cycles to bring that location into place. This corresponds to a *maximum latency time* of 4.1 ms at the minimum clock rate. Once the position is in place, consecutive bit locations can be accessed in 1 μs.

The F464 requires three power supplies: V_{CC} = +5 V, V_{BB} = -5 V, and V_{DD} = +12 V. The maximum power consumption during normal operation is 109 mW. However, when not chip-selected, this device is in a low-power, standby mode. Now it consumes just 66 mW. These values are determined for the 1-MHz minimum clock rate.

9.5 EXPANSION OF CCD MEMORY CAPACITY

The CCD memory finds applications in replacing other serial memory devices such as magnetic disks and tapes. To use the CCD in such a system, more storage capacity is required than that available with a single device. For this reason, a number of devices must be interconnected to expand bit storage capacity. Another type of application is as a secondary storage memory for a microcomputer. In this case, its word length and possibly its bit capacity would need to be increased. In this section, we describe the concepts of the circuitry required to expand both bit capacity and word length.

Expanding Bit Capacity

Let us turn our attention to the circuit configuration in Fig. 9.12. This shows the connections made to expand bit capacity. Here, we see that all input and output leads on the four devices other than chip select are tied in parallel. Moreover, we find that two new address bits, A_4 and A_5, have

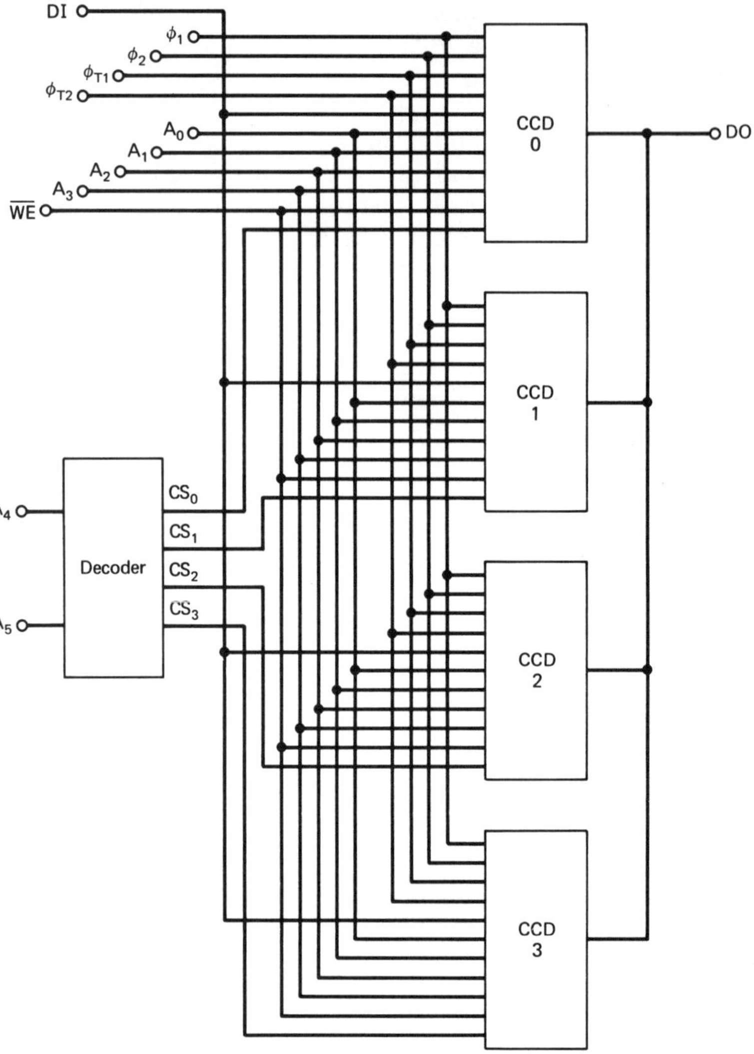

Fig. 9.12 Expanding bit capacity.

been introduced. The 2-bit code $A_5 A_4$ determines which of the four CCDs is selected for read/write operation.

For instance, making $A_5 A_4 = 00$ switches CS_0 to logic 1, enabling CCD 0 for operation. Assuming that $\overline{WE}$ is set for a write operation, data at *DI* are written into the storage position defined by the lower-order address bits, $A_3 A_2 A_1 A_0$, and the shift clock count.

If this circuit is constructed with F464 devices, we have expanded storage capacity to 262,144 bits, which is called 256*k*. But we have not changed the single-bit serial input/output organization.

Expanding Word Length

A microcomputer requires a multibit word for input or output on its data bus. To use CCD memory in this case, we must expand its word length. Figure 9.13 shows the type of connection we can use. Here, the address, chip select, write enable, and clock inputs, of the four devices are all tied in parallel. On the other hand, this time the data input and output leads

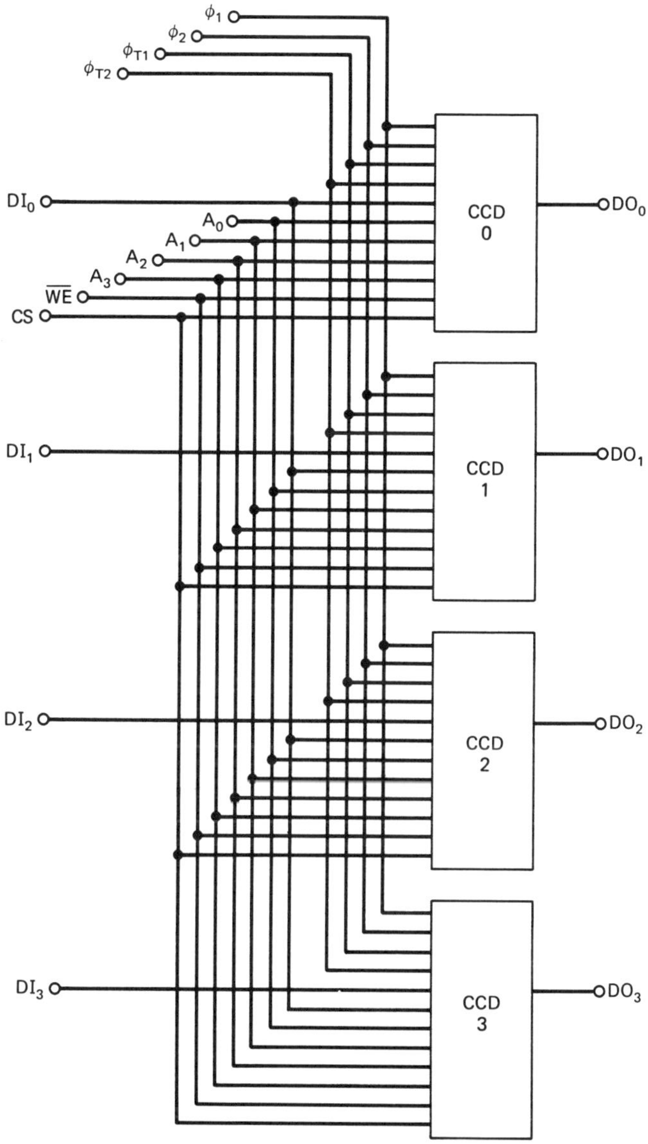

Fig. 9.13 Expanding word length.

of the devices are not connected. Therefore, we have four independent data inputs, DI_0 through DI_3, and four independent data outputs, DO_0 through DO_3. The result is 4-bit input/output words where each memory device holds one bit of the word.

In this manner, we have increased the number of bits per word that respond to a specific address. If F464 devices are in use, the circuit produces 64*k* of 4-bit words.

Expanding Both Bit Capacity and Word Length

For some microcomputer applications, the circuit in Fig. 9.13 would not be able to store enough words. To satisfy this requirement, we must expand both bit capacity and word capacity. The circuit in Fig. 9.14 shows how this

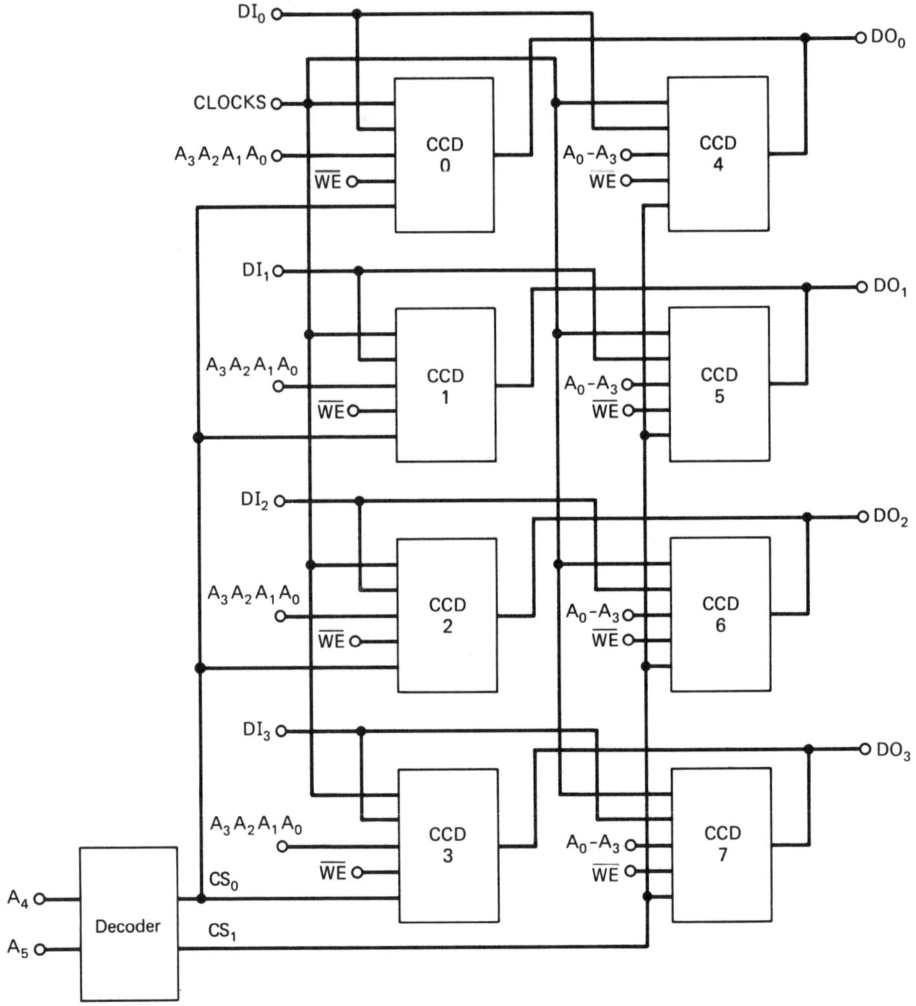

Fig. 9.14 Expanding bit capacity and word length.

is done. If F464 devices are employed in this configuration, the total capacity is 128*k* 4-bit words.

9.6 THE CCD MEMORY SUBSYSTEM

In practical applications CCD memory devices are connected with external circuitry to form a large memory subsystem. Figure 9.15 shows a typical *CCD memory subsystem.* Here the CCD memory array part of the system has the ability to store a large amount of data. For processing purposes, data are broken down into serial strings with a fixed number of bits. Each string is called a block of data. The bits of the block are stored at successive locations within the memory array.

External circuitry is included in the subsystem to provide tracking of the data as they shift through the storage locations within the CCD memory array. This circuitry is also used to determine when the starting position of the block to be accessed is in place for input/output.

All read and write operations begin with the CPU putting an address on lines A_0 through A_{17}. This 18-bit address is loaded into the address latch with a pulse at *CLOCK*. Its two MSBs, A_{17} and A_{16}, are a device select code. They are input to the chip select decoder. When enabled by the data cycle generator, the decoder outputs a chip select signal to the appropriate CCDs in the memory array. The next four bits, A_{15} through A_{12}, are applied directly to address inputs on all CCDs. This 4-bit code selects for operation one of the serial-parallel-serial blocks within the chip selected CCDs. The 12 LSBs, A_{11} through A_0, are input to the address compare circuit. The code on these lines identifies the starting location of the block of data to be accessed.

The CCD system clock generator is continuously producing pulses at its five outputs: *CLK*, ϕ_1, ϕ_2, ϕ_{T1}, and ϕ_{T2}. The ϕ clock signals cause the shift of data through the channels of all CCDs. At the same time, the signal *CLK* increments the index counter as each new data position comes into place. Its count C_0 through C_{11} identifies the storage location within the serial-parallel-serial block of the CCD.

The address compare circuit has as its inputs address bits A_0 through A_{11} and the index count C_0 through C_{11}. A_0 through A_{11} represent the starting point of the block of locations to be accessed, while C_0 through C_{11} represent the position presently available for access. If the address and count do not match, the clock generator continues to pulse the CCD. Data shifts through the serial-parallel-serial blocks while the index counter is incremented.

When A_0 through A_{11} equal C_0 through C_{11}, the starting position of the block of locations to be accessed is in place, and a memory operation is to be performed. In response, the address compare circuit produces its output signal *IMC*. This stands for *initiate memory cycle*, and indicates to the data cycle generator that the system is ready to perform a read/write operation.

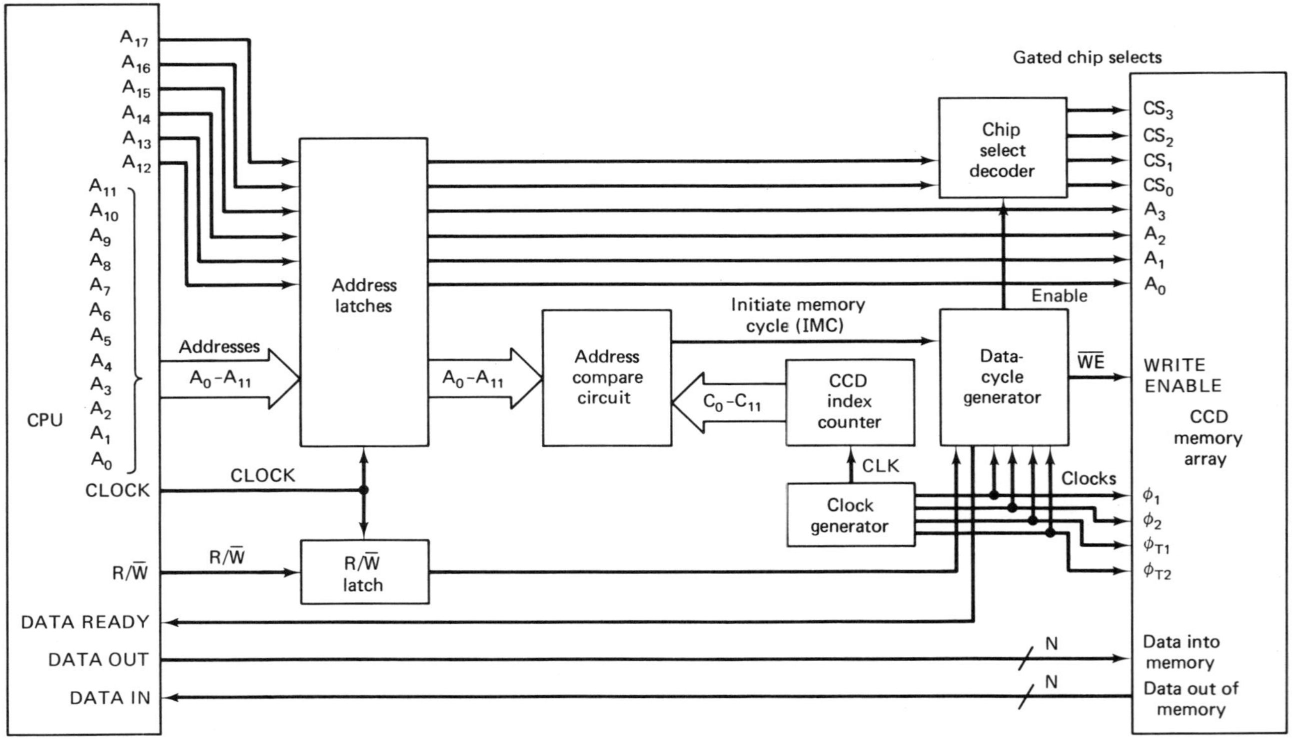

Fig. 9.15 Typical CCD memory subsystem.

The data cycle generator begins by enabling the chip select decoder. In turn, the *CS* line picked by $A_{17}A_{16}$ switches to logic 1 and selects the appropriate CCDs. The latched logic level of *WE* is now passed to the CCD array. It indicates whether a read or write operation is to occur. Finally, the data cycle generator signals the CPU over the *DATA READY* line to input or output data.

Data are carried over *DATA OUT* or *DATA IN* and can be a single-bit or multibit word. The output organization depends on the CCD expansion configuration needed to interface with the data bus at the CPU.

After the starting address of the block has been accessed, read or write operations can be rapidly performed to the locations that follow. This is accomplished by just loading the successive addresses into the address latch, while simultaneously inputting or outputting data.

ASSIGNMENTS

Section 9.2

1. What is the storage element in a CCD memory?
2. Is the CCD memory volatile or nonvolatile?
3. Is the CCD a serial-accessed or random-accessed memory?
4. Describe the write data in, recirculate data, and read data out modes of operation.

Section 9.3

5. What are the seven fundamental parts of the CCD memory?
6. Describe the read operation of the SPS CCD memory loop in Fig. 9.4(b).
7. If the inputs to the circuit of Fig. 9.6 are A_1A_0=11 and *CS*=1, what are the outputs after the *CLOCK* input is pulsed?
8. If the inputs to the circuit in Fig. 9.7 are L_0=1, *DI*=1, $\overline{WE}$=1, and *CS*=1, describe the input/output operation of the circuit.
9. For the storage array in Fig. 9.9(a), if A_1A_0=00, show the location of bits B_0 through B_7 after the eighth group A clock pulse. Assume that the CCD is set for read mode of operation.

Section 9.4

10. What is the total storage capacity and organization of the F464 CCD memory?
11. What is the configuration of the serial-parallel-serial blocks in the F464 device?
12. What is the minimum operating frequency of the F464?

Section 9.5

13. The inputs to the circuit in Fig. 9.12 are $A_5A_4A_3A_2A_1A_0$=110000 and $\overline{WE}$=0. What type of operation is performed, and to which device and storage block?
14. The inputs to the circuit in Fig. 9.14 are $A_5A_4A_3A_2A_1A_0$=011111 and $\overline{WE}$=1. Which devices are selected, and what type of operation is performed?

Section 9.6

15. Describe the operation of the CCD memory subsystem in Fig. 9.15 for a read operation.

10

MAGNETIC BUBBLE MEMORIES

10.1 INTRODUCTION

The preceding chapters were devoted to the many different types of semiconductor memory devices. However, one of the most important recent developments in the memory industry is a magnetic device, magnetic bubble memory. In this chapter, we conclude our study of electronic memories with this new device.

The chapter begins with an introduction to the magnetic bubble memory technology. The sections that follow introduce the popular architectures used to design magnetic bubble memories, standard devices presently available in the marketplace, and the magnetic bubble memory system. Following are the topics covered:

1. Magnetic bubble memory
2. Major/minor loop architecture
3. Read and write operating cycles
4. Block replicate architecture
5. Standard magnetic bubble memory devices
6. The magnetic bubble memory system

10.2 MAGNETIC BUBBLE MEMORY

The *magnetic bubble memory* (MBM) is a solid-state magnetic memory device. It is the newest type of memory device to become available in production quantities. Magnetic bubble memories differ from the semiconductor

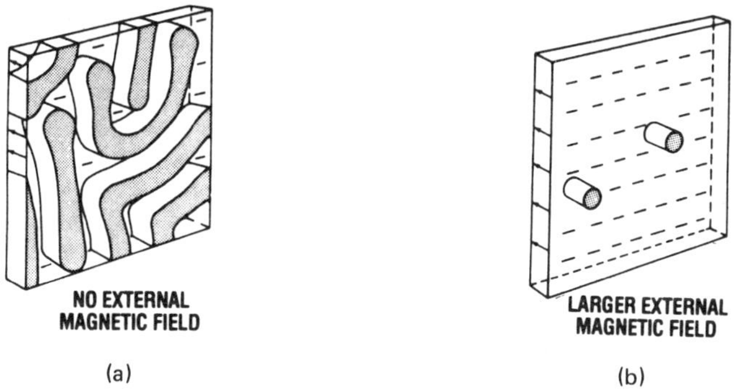

Fig. 10.1 (a) Random serpentine pattern (Texas Instruments Incorporated); (b) cylindrical magnetic domains (Texas Instruments, Incorporated).

devices introduced in earlier chapters in that the logic states of digital data are represented by tiny cylindrical magnetic domains instead of by electrical voltages, currents, or charges. These magnetic domains are called *bubbles* and exist within the MBM in storage locations called *bit periods* or *bit positions.* Presence of a bubble in a bit period represents logic 1, and absence of a bubble represents logic 0.

Magnetic Bubble Technology[1]

Now that we have introduced the bubble and bit period as the storage mechanism of the MBM, questions rise as to how bubbles are created and moved within the MBM.

The bubble chip of the magnetic bubble memory is formed on a *nonmagnetic synthetic garnet substrate.* The bit periods that represent the storage cells of a MBM are formed in a thin film of synthetic garnet that is deposited on the substrate. In practical MBM devices, *gandolinium–gallium garnet* is widely used for the thin film.

With no external magnetic field applied to the bubble chip, the magnetic domains in the thin film would form random patterns with equal area. They are known as *serpentine domains.* Figure 10.1(a) shows this serpentine pattern.

By applying an external magnetic field perpendicular to the thin-film surface, domains that are polarized opposite of the field are shaped into tiny cylinders. Several domains that have been concentrated into cylinders are shown in Fig. 10.1(b). Looking at these cylinders from the end, they appear to be circular. It is from this that the magnetic bubble gets its name.

In the MBM, this fixed field is produced by *permanent magnets.* They provide the static bias needed to maintain stable bubbles within the film.

[1] Texas Instruments, Incorporated, *TIB0203 Magnetic Bubble Memory and Associated Circuits* (Dallas, TX: Texas Instruments, Incorporated, 1978). (Courtesy of Texas Instruments, Incorporated)

Now that we have stable bubbles, we are still faced with the problem of moving them in an orderly fashion through the film. It is found that by applying a varying magnetic field parallel to the film, the bubbles move laterally through the film. To control the direction of movement, magnetic material is deposited on the surface of the thin film in the shape of a path. The path is actually constructed from a large number of magnetic areas. These areas have the shape of what is known as an *asymmetrical chevron*. An example of an asymmetrical chevron pattern is given in Fig. 10.2.

By sequentially magnetizing the chevrons along the path with a rotating magnetic field, the magnetic polarity of the chevrons are changed in such a way as to pull bubbles through the chevron areas and down the path. This field is provided by the *drive coils (orthogonal coils)* of the MBM.

Figure 10.2 also shows the propagation of bubbles through the chevron path. Notice that the polarity of the chevron and position of the bubble are given for each of four 90° changes of the drive coil field.

Storage Capacity

At present, a magnetic bubble is as small as 2 to 3 μm. For this reason, magnetic bubble memory devices have the ability to store a large amount of

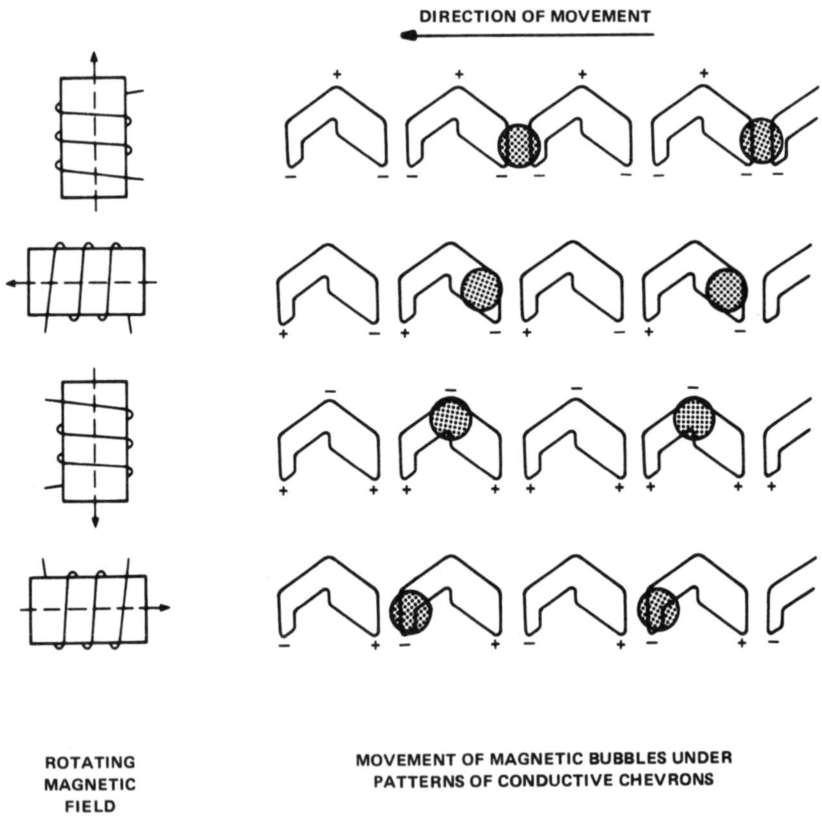

Fig. 10.2 Magnetic bubble propagation (Texas Instruments, Incorporated).

data. Presently, standard devices are available with maximum storage capacities of 92k, 250k, 500k, and 1M bits. Furthermore, we can interconnect a number of these devices in a memory system configuration to obtain even higher storage capacity. Newer devices are being developed based on 1 μm bubbles.

Use of Magnetic Bubble Memories

The MBM competes for memory applications with both semiconductor memories and magnetic media memory systems. In microcomputer systems, the MBM competes directly against dynamic RAM and CCD memory. For these applications, the MBM offers important advantages over semiconductor devices. For instance, it has higher storage capacity and is nonvolatile. In many applications, nonvolatility is the deciding factor in choosing MBM. The primary disadvantage of MBMs compared to semiconductor memory is their slower access times.

MBMs are also finding a place in the mass-storage market. This type of application has been traditionally implemented with magnetic-media systems such as disks, drums, and cassette tapes. For some mass-storage applications, specifically those that do not require extremely large storage capacity and removable storage media, MBM systems can be used to replace the mechanical system.

In this case, the MBM offers faster access time, smaller size, lower maintenance, and higher reliability. A further advantage of the MBM is that it provides storage capacity in smaller increments. For this reason, the design can more closely meet the specified storage requirements of the digital system.

10.3 STRUCTURE OF THE MAGNETIC BUBBLE MEMORY[2]

The physical structure of a magnetic bubble memory is shown in Fig. 10.3. Here we see that it is made from a number of independent parts. The four key parts are the *bubble memory chip*, *orthogonal coils*, *permanent magnets*, and *magnetic shield assembly*. The shield assembly is not shown in the diagram.

Each of these parts serve a function in overall MBM operation. The bubble memory chip is the heart of the MBM. It contains the pattern of magnetic paths and control elements required to input, store, and output data.

The orthogonal coils, permanent magnets, and magnetic shield assembly provide auxiliary functions that are essential to the MBM device's correct operation. For example, the two orthogonal coils (drive coils) are activated with currents that produce rotating magnetic fields. It is these fields that cause bubbles to propagate through the chevron paths within

[2] Ibid.

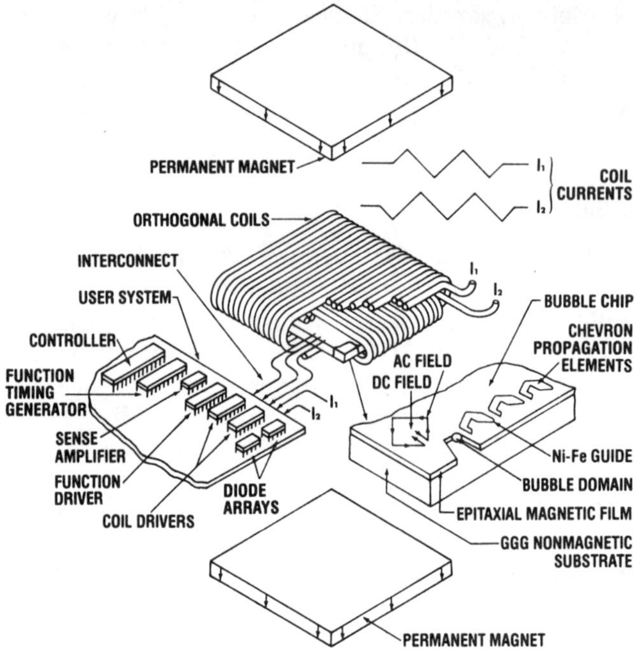

Fig. 10.3 Structure of the magnetic bubble memory (Texas Instruments, Incorporated).

the bubble chip. At the same time, the permanent magnets produce the static magnetic fields that keep the bubbles within the chip stable.

The shield assembly partially surrounds the chip. It protects the bubble memory chip from stray magnetic fields. If the MBM is exposed to an external magnetic field in excess of its maximum rating, the device is not guaranteed to operate correctly.

10.4 MAJOR/MINOR LOOP ARCHITECTURE[3]

The configuration of the magnetic storage section in a standard 92*k* MBM device is known as a *major/minor loop architecture.* Figure 10.4 shows a simplified diagram of this type of architecture.

Looking closely at this diagram, we see that it is actually a serial-parallel-serial configuration. That is, it contains a serial loop for input and output of data. This is identified as the *major loop*. The control elements found in this loop are the *generator*, *replicator*, and *detector.* The replicator is also known as the *replicator/annihilator element.* Serial data are written into the major loop at the generator. Data are also read out of the major loop in serial form. This occurs at the replicator and detector elements. In this way, we see that the MBM is a serial-in, serial-out storage device.

[3] Ibid.

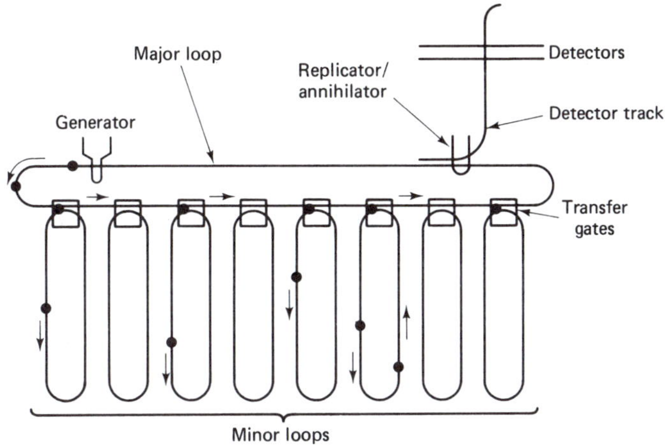

Fig. 10.4 Major/minor loop architecture (Texas Instruments, Incorporated).

The second arrangement of loops is called the *minor loops.* This parallel arrangement of loops is positioned perpendicular to the major loops and interfaced to it with a set of *transfer gates.* It is in these minor loops that data are stored.

Storage Capacity and Redundant Loops

A typical MBM device using this architecture contains 157 minor loops, each with 641 bit periods. This gives a *gross storage capacity* of 100,637 bits. However, all MBM devices are designed to include a number of *redundant loops.* Extra loops are made because there may be defective loops. These defective loops are made into the redundant loops and cannot be used to store data. Since extra loops are provided, all loops do not have to be good, and improved production yield is obtained.

For instance, the MBM just mentioned has 157 minor loops. However, of these loops, 13 are redundant. This leaves 144 for storage of data and a total capacity of 92,304 (92*k*) bits.

The purchaser of the device is provided with a map of the defective loops. This map is either marked on the case of the device, or in some cases is built within the device as bubbles in a special *redundancy loop.* These redundant loops must not be used for data storage.

Circulation of Data in the MBM

Bubbles within the MBM propagate around the loops following the direction indicated by arrows in Fig. 10.4. This propagation of bubbles is caused by the rotating fields provided by the orthogonal coils. These two coils are driven by triangular-shaped currents and produce rotating magnetic fields that are 90° out of phase. It is these fields that cause the bubbles to continuously circulate through the chevron paths of the major and minor loops.

For each 360° of the coil drive signal, all bubbles move one bit period around their respective loop.

Pages of Data and Multipaging

Data are input to and output from the major loop in a block of bits called a *page*. A page consists of a number of bits equal to the number of usable minor loops. For example, the MBM mentioned earlier has a page length of 144 bits. It is also possible to access consecutive pages for input or output of data. This is known as *multipaging*.

Control Operations of the MBM

Six control operations are involved in the read and write cycles of the MBM: *generation*, *transfer in*, *transfer out*, *replication*, *annihilation*, and *detection*. Before going into detailed descriptions of the read and write cycles of the MBM, let us first look at what happens when each of these operations is initiated.

In a MBM, bubbles must be created in accordance with the logic level of input data. This is done by a process known as generation. A one-turn metalized loop known as the generator element is provided in the major loop for this purpose. When the bit period to be written into is in place by the generator element, a current is applied to the loop. This causes a magnetic field in the vicinity of the loop and creates the bubble.

The transfer control is also initiated by supplying a current to a metalized loop. When a complete page of data has been input and shifted through the major loop to a position where it is aligned with the minor loops, a transfer-in operation must be initiated. As the appropriate storage location in the minor loops comes into place, the transfer gates are enabled. The bubbles pass through the transfer gates into the minor loops.

The transfer-out operation is similar to transfer in. However, this time the current pulse causes the page of data held in the minor loops to go into the major loop. This function must happen when data are read out of the MBM.

Replication is also involved in the output process. During read cycles, the bubbles in the major loop are shifted toward the replicator element. As each bit period arrives at the replicator, a current is injected into the replicator element. The fields produced by this current cause the bubble to elongate and then divide into two identical bubbles. That is, a replica of the bubble has been formed. One bubble is left in the major loop and the other is passed into the detector track. The bubble that has been retained in the major loop is the key to the nondestructive readout characteristic of the MBM.

During read operations, the existence or absence of a bubble in a bit period is determined by the detector. The detector is a *magnetoresistive element*. Bubbles replicated into the detector track propagate into the detector element. Here the magnetism of the bubble causes a resistance change.

In turn, a low-amplitude current signal is produced at the detector output. It is this current that is sensed to produce the logic level of the output data.

On the other hand, when we want to write new data into the MBM, the old data held in the minor loops at the location to be accessed must first be removed. This is done by an annihilation operation. At the replicator element, the bubbles are transferred into the detector track, but not replicated. The bubbles are then destroyed in the detector track.

10.5 READ AND WRITE CYCLES

Up to this point in the chapter, we have introduced magnetic bubble technology, the use of the magnetic bubble memory, the structure of the bubble memory device, and the major/minor loop architecture of the bubble chip. Before introducing a second bubble chip architecture, let us first trace the read and write operating cycles of a MBM that employs the major/minor loop architecture.

Read Cycle

The pages of data in a MBM are continuously circulating around the minor loops under control of the drive coil clocks. When a page of data already stored in the minor loops is to be accessed, we must perform a read operation.

Let us assume that we want to read out the word highlighted in Fig. 10.5(a). This page has three bubbles and represents binary 1011. Before the page can be retrieved, it must first rotate to the top position in the minor loops as shown in Fig. 10.5(b). Notice that the bits of the page are lined up with the transfer gates to the major loop. We must now pulse the transfer control with a current. The magnetic field produced by this current makes the page move out of the minor loops and pass through the transfer gates. The page is now located in the major loop as shown in Fig. 10.5(c).

After the word has been transferred to the major loop, it must be shifted, in serial form, in the direction of the replicator/annihilator element. As the first bit of the page comes into place, the replicator/annihilator loop is pulsed and the field that is produced causes the bubble to elongate and then split into two separate bubbles. As shown in Fig. 10.5(d), one bubble is transferred into the detector track while the other stays in the major loop.

The bubble that is now in the detector track is read by the detector element. The magnetism of the bubble causes the resistance of the detector to change. In response to this change, a pulse of current is produced in the detector output. The voltage produced by this current is read by a sense amplifier to produce the 1 logic level. After detection, the bubble is destroyed.

As the next bit period moves into place, we see in Fig. 10.5(e) that there is no bubble in this location. Since a bubble does not exist, the detector track remains empty and the detector does not produce a current pulse.

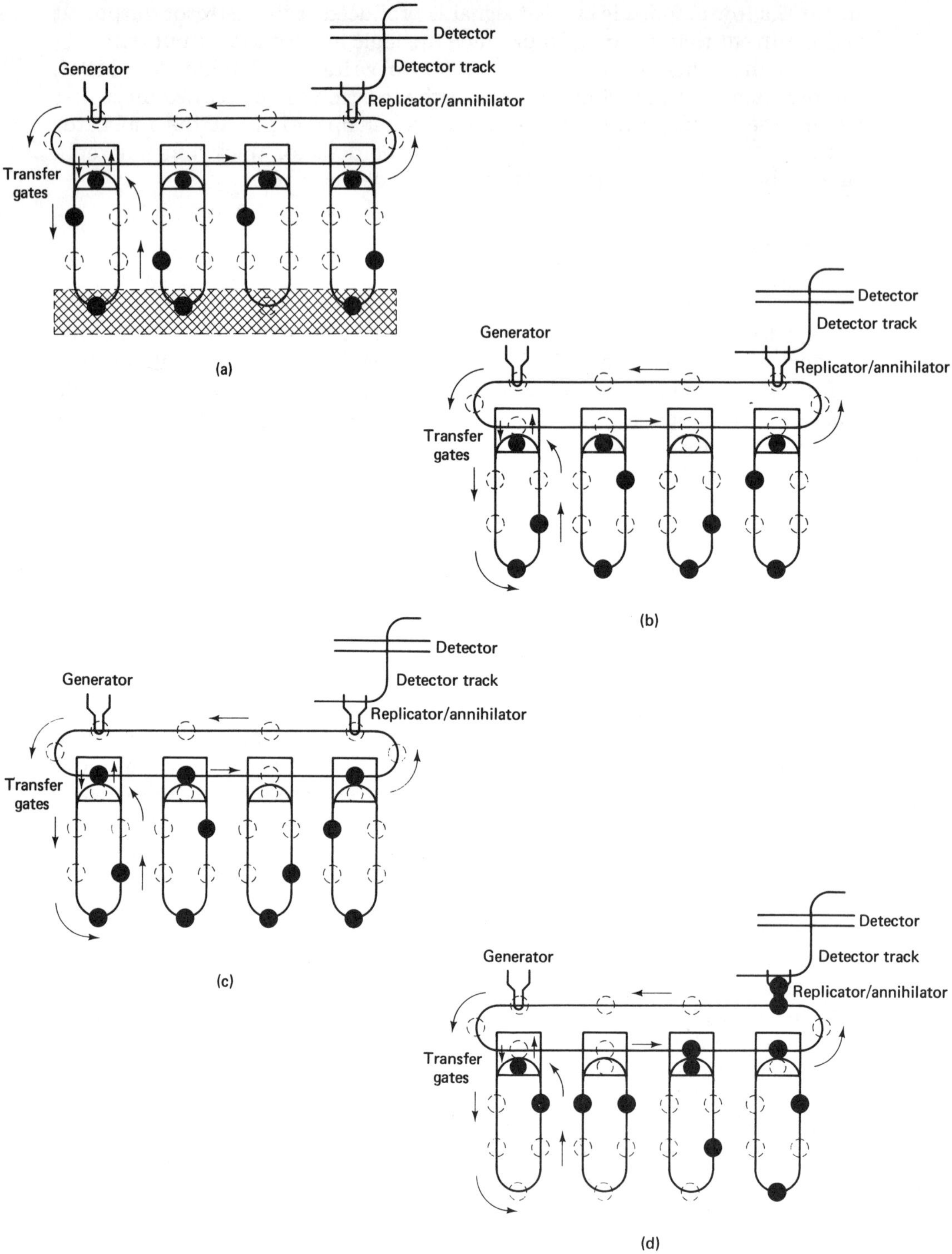

Fig. 10.5 Read cycle.

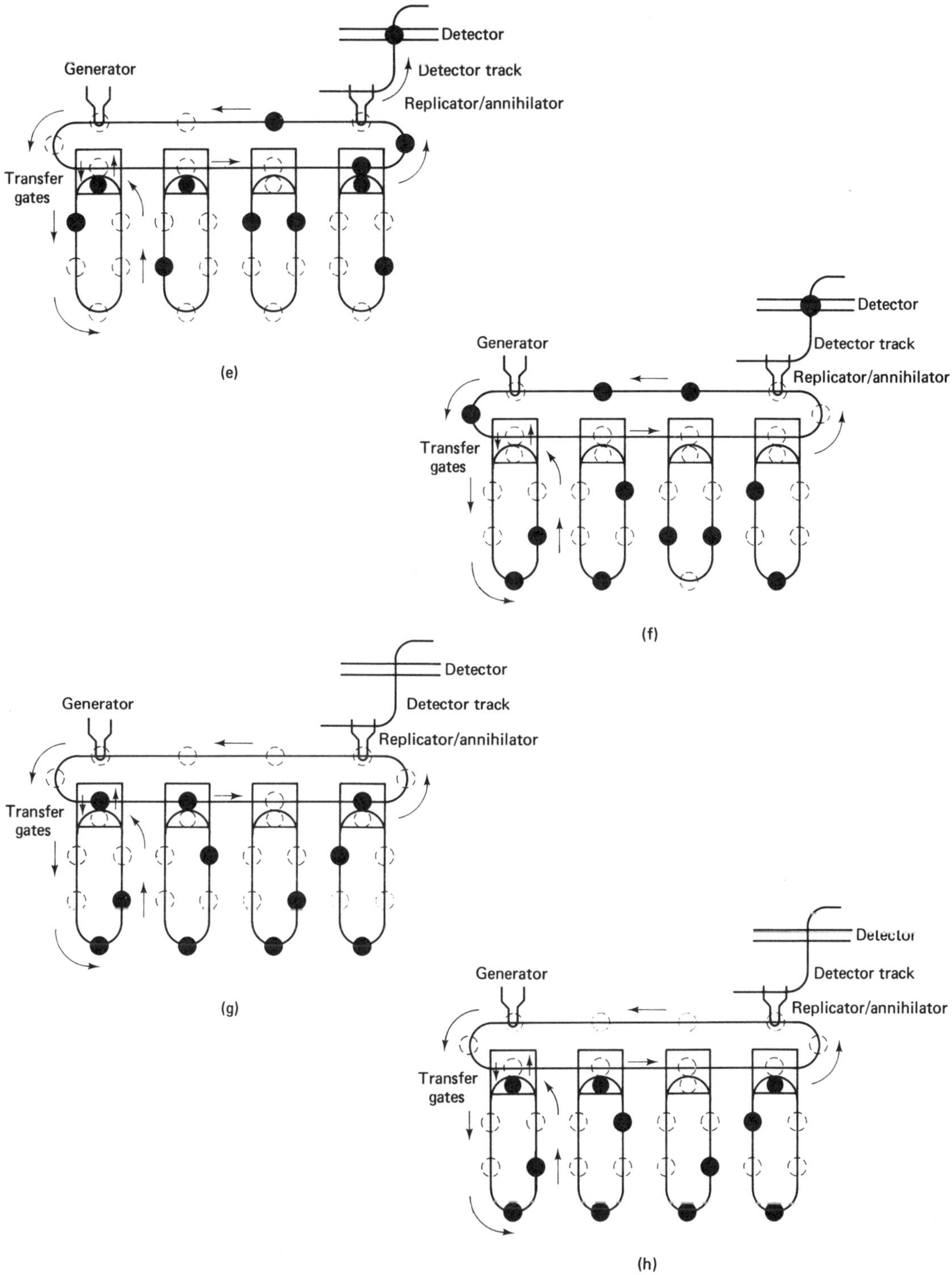

Fig. 10.5 Continued

The same replication and detection operations occur as the remaining two bit periods move into place. This produces two more current pulses in the serial bit stream at the detector output. This stream of pulses represents the bits of the page of data.

Notice in Fig. 10.5(f) that the complete page has been retained in the major loop. These data continue to circulate around the major loop until they are again aligned with the transfer gates, as shown in Fig. 10.5(g). As the storage location comes into place at the top of the minor loops, the transfer gates are again enabled. But this time a transfer in occurs and the page is returned to its storage location, as shown in Fig. 10.5(h). The read cycle is now complete. In this way, we see why the MBM has nondestructive readout characteristics.

Write Cycle

Before a new page of data can be written into the MBM, the existing page of data at the location to be accessed must be cleared out. This is done with what is known as an annihilation operation. The sequence of events that occurs during an annihilation is similar to that in a read operation. However, it is a destructive read.

Figure 10.6(a) shows the location into which we want to write the data word 1101. As this storage location reaches the top of the minor loops, the transfer gates are activated. All bits of the old page of data transfer into the major loop, as shown in Fig. 10.6(b).

Now the page moves toward the replicator/annihilator element at a rate set by the drive coil clock signals. Figure 10.6(c) illustrates the page just as the first bit reaches the element. It is at this point that the read and write operations differ. This time the current pulse applied to the replicator/annihilator does not split the bubble. Instead, the whole bubble is transferred out of the major loop into the detector track. This state is shown in Fig. 10.6(d). From here the bubble propagates through the detector track to the guard rail and off the device. As the page continues to circulate through the major loop, the rest of its bits are annihilated. The major loop is now empty, as shown in Fig. 10.6(e).

As the annihilation operation is completed, the new page of data begins to be generated in the major loop. The first bit of our page is logic 1. For this reason, the generator loop is pulsed with a current. This produces a magnetic field in the vicinity of the generator element, and a bubble appears in the bit period. Figure 10.6(f) shows the first bit of the new page entered.

After this, the bubble moves away from the generator and the next bit period comes into place. The data bit is again logic 1; therefore, the generator element is again pulsed, and a second bubble appears. This sequence of events repeats for bits three and four of the page. These bits are 0 and 1, respectively. The complete word generated in the major loop appears in Fig. 10.6(g). Notice that the third bit period remains empty. This is because it holds a logic 0.

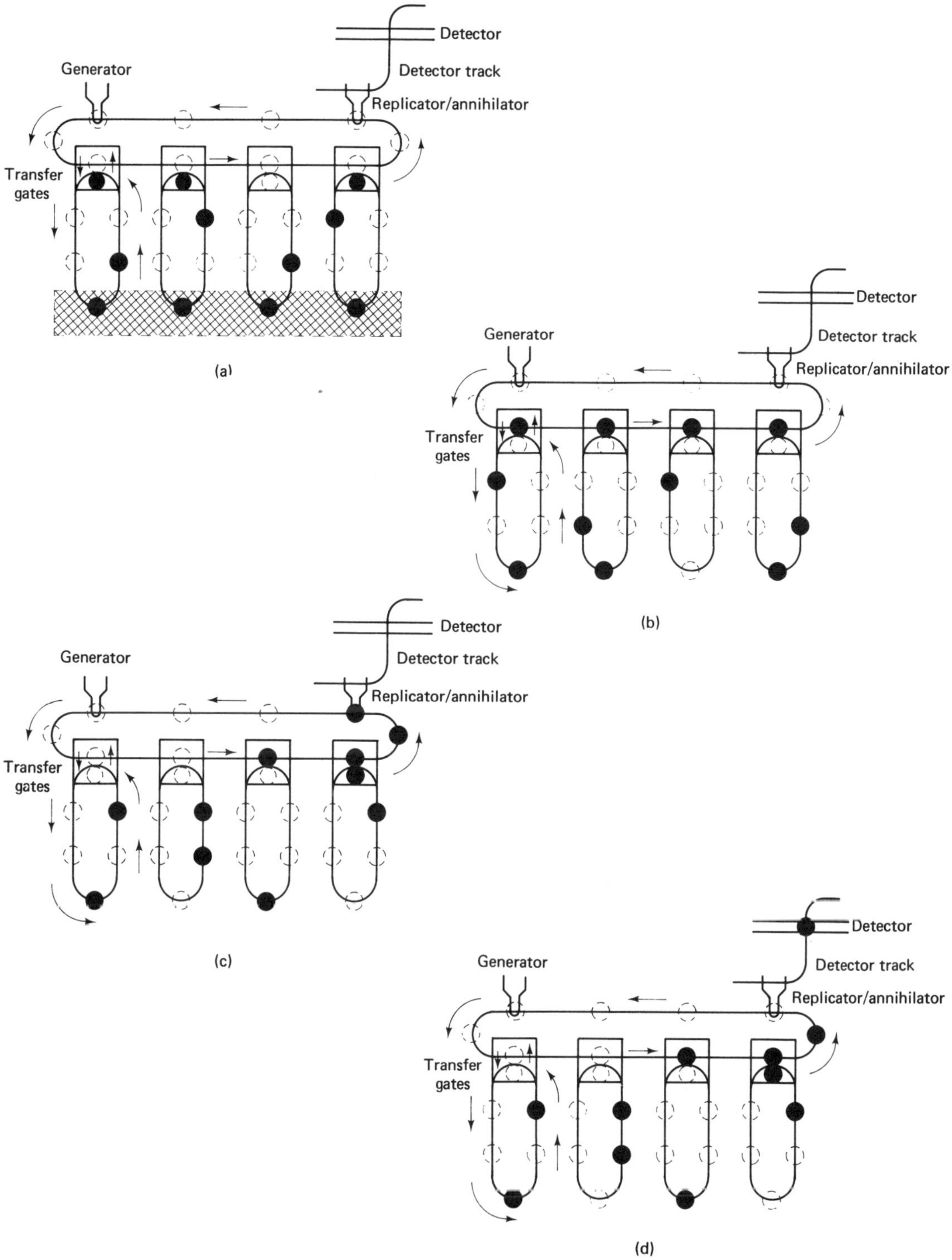

Fig. 10.6 Write cycle.

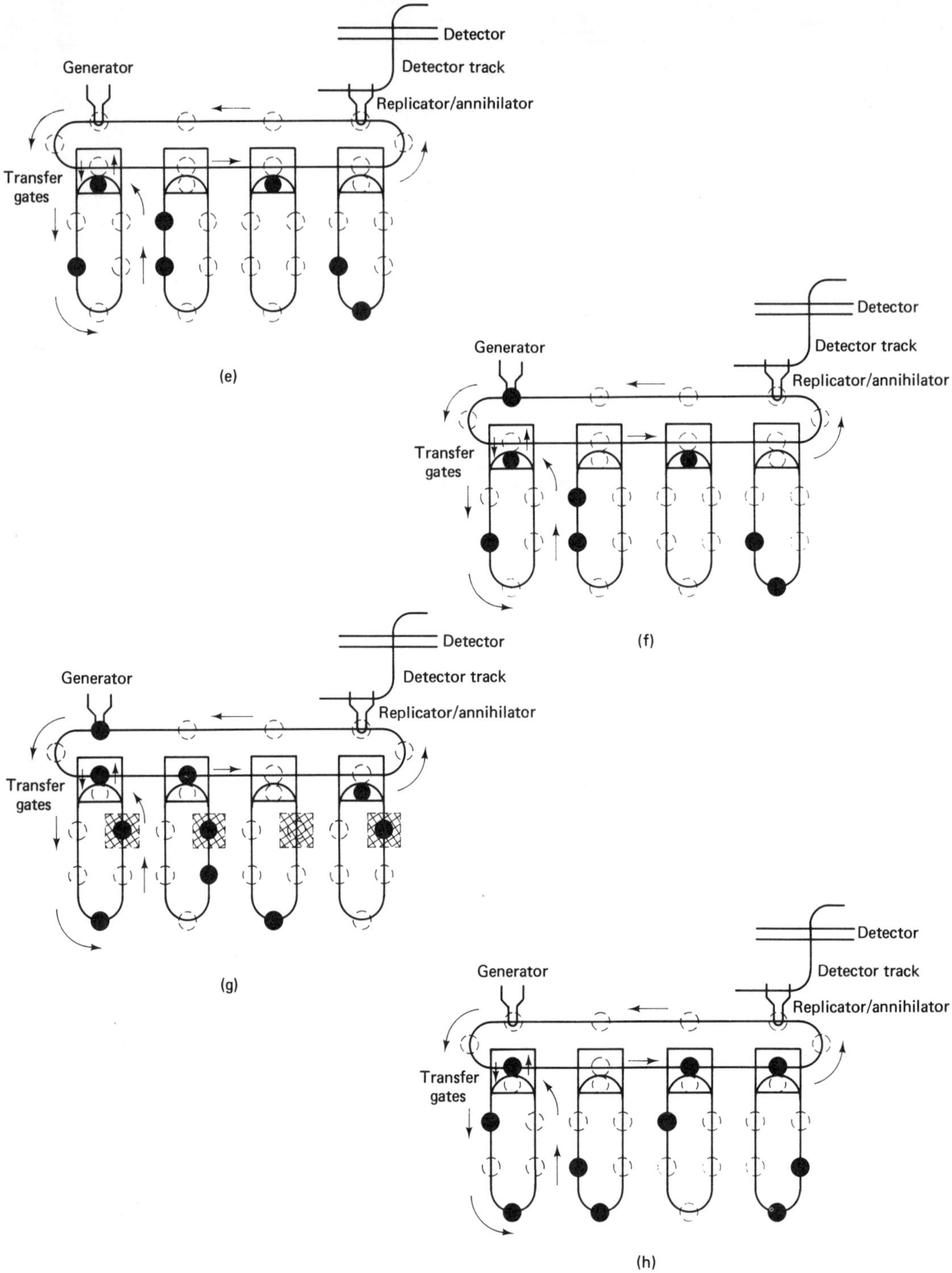

Fig. 10.6 Continued

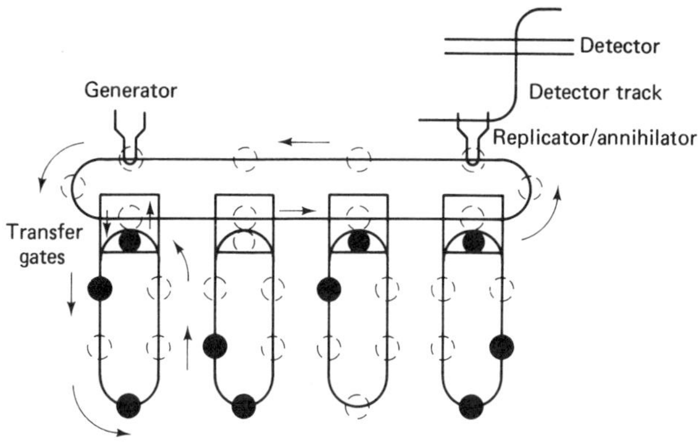

(i)

Fig. 10.6 Continued

The page continues to shift around the major loop until the leading bit is in position at the transfer gate of the rightmost minor loop and the last bit is at the entrance to the leftmost minor loop. This state is given in Fig. 10.6(h).

In this position, the page is ready to be transferred into the minor loops. The proper storage location simultaneously appears at the top of the minor loops. Therefore, the transfer gates are once more enabled and the page passes through the gates into the minor loops. As shown in Fig. 10.6(i), one bit of the page is stored in each of the four minor loops. The data circulate away from the top of the minor loops.

10.6 BLOCK REPLICATE ARCHITECTURE

Higher-capacity MBM devices use another bubble chip architecture. The drawing in Fig. 10.7 is a simplified example of this configuration. It is known as the *block replicate architecture.* Changes have been made to improve operating speed. From the illustration, we see that the primary change is that the major loop has been removed and replaced with separate *input* and *output tracks.*

The minor loops remain essentially the same, but the way in which data are input and output from these loops has been changed. Here *swap gates* are provided at the input side instead of transfer gates. These swap gates have the ability to pass bubbles in both directions at the same time.

At the other side of the minor loops, each loop is interfaced to the output track with a separate replicator gate. In this way, the bits of the page are directly replicated out of the minor loops. This is known as *block replication.*

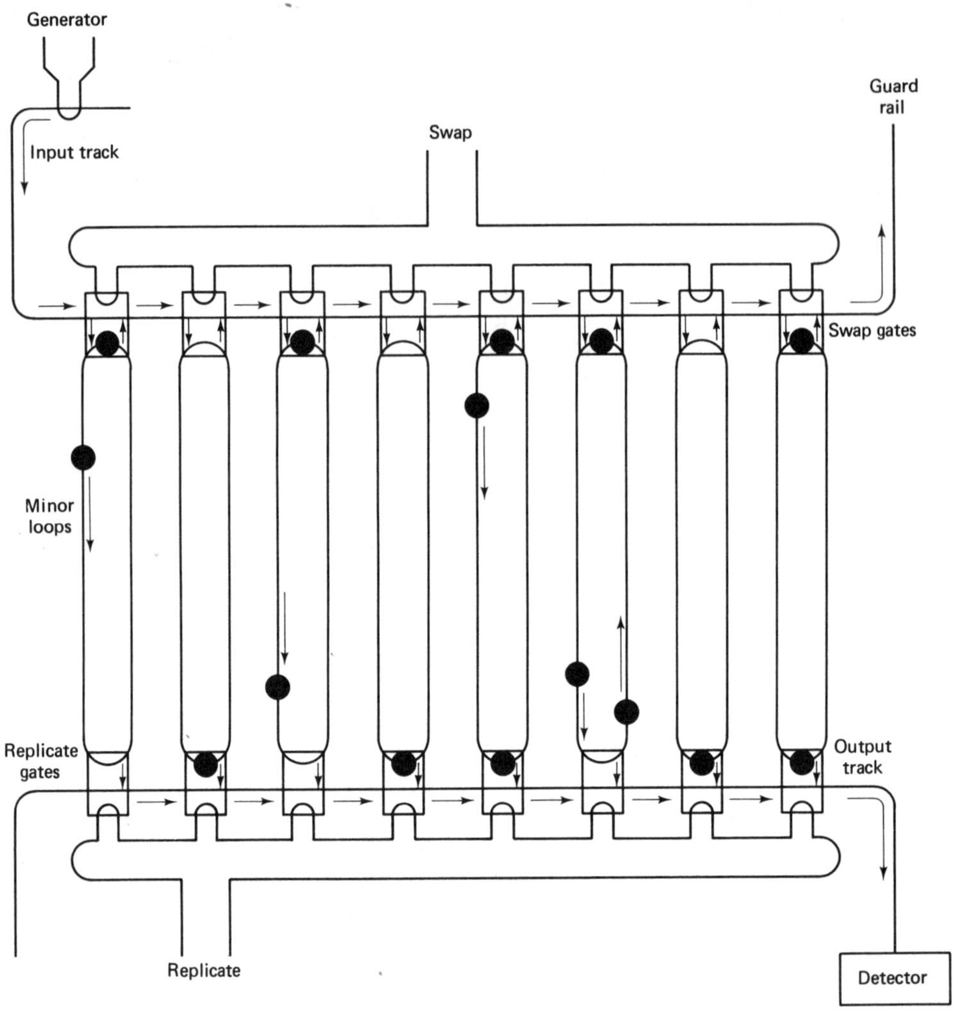

Fig. 10.7 Page swap/replicate architecture.

Write Cycle

To write a page of data into the bubble chip, we begin by generating the bits of the new page in the input track. The page is then shifted until the bits are positioned for entry into the minor loops. As the storage location at which the page is to be stored arrives at the top of the minor loops, the swap gates are activated with a current pulse. The bits of the new page pass in parallel through the swap gates into the minor loops, and at the same time the old page is transferred into the input track. After this, the old page is shifted to the *guard rail*, where it is destroyed.

By replacing the transfer gates with swap gates, we have eliminated the need for two separate transfer operations during a write cycle. With the major/minor loop architecture, we had to first transfer the old word out of the minor loops for annihilation. Later, a second transfer is performed to put the new word in the minor loops for storage. By using the block replicate architecture, both transfers occur simultaneously. This results in improved write access time.

Read Cycle

Improved operation is also experienced for the block replicator architecture during read operations. For a read operation to occur, the page of data to be output must first be circulated to the bottom of the minor loops. When it is in place by the replicator elements, a current pulse is applied at the replicator input. Each bubble is split into two. One stays in the minor loops giving nondestructive read, and the other is transferred into the output track. The page in the output track now shifts toward the detector element, where it is read out. After reading, the bubbles are destroyed.

Notice that we have saved the time required by the major/minor loop architecture to recirculate the page from the replicator element and reload it into the minor loops. This decreases the read-cycle access time.

10.7 STANDARD MAGNETIC BUBBLE MEMORY DEVICES

The bubble technology is a new emerging memory technology. At this time, a number of manufacturers have released MBM products. Here we introduce a few of the more important devices.

TIB0203 MBM[4]

The TIB0203 magnetic bubble memory is one of the earlier MBM devices. It has a usable storage capacity of 92,304 (92*k*) bits. Figure 10.8(a) is a pin layout of its 14-pin package.

This device employs a major/minor loop architecture similar to that introduced in an earlier section of the chapter. Figure 10.8(b) shows the internal structure of its bubble chip. Notice that the major loop serves as a serial input/output loop. It contains the generator element, replicator/annihilator element, and provides the path by which bubbles travel to the detector element. There are a total of 640 bit positions in this loop. Moreover, we find that the bubble chip contains 157 minor loops, each with 641 bit positions. The minor loops are interfaced to the major loop with transfer gates. These gates can be set to work in the input or output mode.

Let us determine the gross storage capacity of the TIB0203. This is found by multiplying the total number of minor loops by the number of bit positions per loop. This gives 100,637 bits. However, not all of these loops can be used for data storage. Thirteen are redundant loops that are not guaranteed by the manufacturer to work correctly. They are not to be used for data storage. This leaves 144 loops and results in a total usable

[4] Ibid.

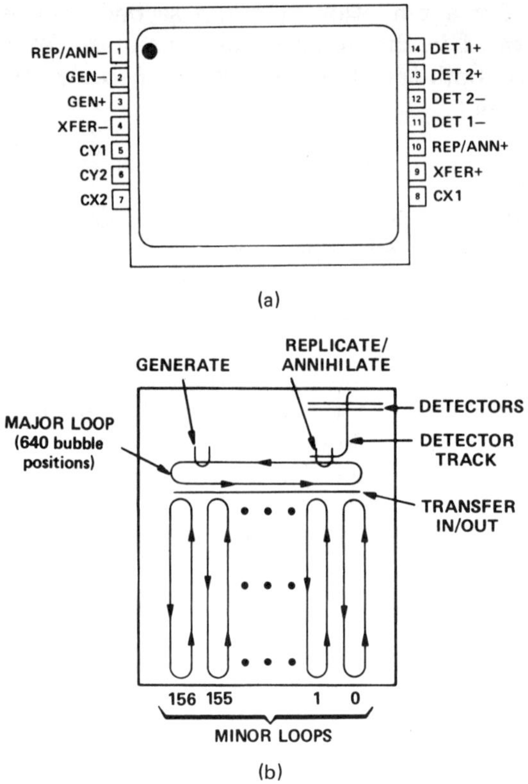

Fig. 10.8 (a) Pin layout of the TIB0203 MBM (Texas Instruments, Incorporated), (b) architecture of the TIB0203 (Texas Instruments, Incorporated).

storage capacity of 92,304 (92*k*) bits. Addresses for the redundant loops are printed on the case in hexadecimal form.

Data in the minor loops are circulated under control of the coil drive signals. There are two coil drive loops on the TIB0203. There inputs are at the CX_1, CX_2 and CY_1, CY_2 leads and are driven by two 100-kHz triangular-shaped currents that are 90° out of phase. This frequency gives a clock period of 10 μs. All bubbles in the loops move one bubble position during each clock period.

The bits of data are organized in the loops with an empty bit position between data bits. This is done so that consecutive bubbles do not magnetically interact. Because of this spacing, minor loops are actually arranged two bit periods apart. Therefore, the data transfer rate is one-half the clock rate, or 50 kHz.

During a write operation, the old page is first transferred into the major loop. This is done by first waiting until the word is positioned at the top of the major loops and then pulsing the *transfer loop* (*XFER+*, *XFER–*). The page is circulated toward the replicator/annihilator element. As each bit enters this element, the *REP/ANN+*, *REP/ANN– loop* is pulsed in such a way as to not replicate the bubble, but instead to transfer the bubble intact into the detector track. Here the bubble is circulated to the guard rail, where it is destroyed.

A serial bit stream of data is generated into the major loop by pulsing the *GEN+*, *GEN– loop* each time a bubble is to be produced. The bits of the page are shifted around the loop until the leading bit is positioned by its corresponding minor loop. When the empty page is at the top of the minor loops, the transfer loop is again pulsed, but this time in such a way as to enter the new page into the storage location.

The read operation begins when the page location to be accessed appears at the top of the minor loops. The *XFER+*, *XFER–* loop is pulsed, causing the page to be transferred into the major loop. From here the page circulates toward the detector. This time the *REP/ANN+*, *REP/ANN–* loop is pulsed in such a way as to produce replication. The bubble splits, leaving the data in the major loop as well as transferring a replica of the bubble to the detector track. The bubble is read by the detector element and corresponding current pulses are produced at outputs *DET1+*, *DET1–* and *DET2+*, *DET2–* of the MBM. These outputs are supplied to inputs of sense amplifiers for conversion to readable logic levels.

The data retained in the major loop are circulated back to the entry position of the minor loops. Then the *XFER+*, *XFER–* loop is pulsed once again and the page reloaded into the minor loops.

The TIB0203 can operate in environments with an external magnetic field of up to 20 oersteds (Oe) and over a temperature range from 0 to 50° C.

TIB1000, TIB0500, and TIB0250 MBMs[5]

The TIB1000, TIB0500, and TIB0250 devices represent a family of electrically and pin-for-pin equivalent devices. They offer storage capacities of 1M, 512*k*, and 256*k* bits, respectively. These devices permit upgrading of system storage capacity by simply replacing the devices with a higher-capacity member of the family. The devices are packaged in a common 24-pin DIP case. Figure 10.9(a) shows the pin layout of the TIB1000.

All three devices use the block replicate architecture introduced in Section 10.6. A drawing of this basic bubble chip configuration is shown in Fig. 10.9(b). Looking at this diagram, we find separate input and output tracks. The input track is interfaced with the minor loops with an array of swap gates. On the other hand, the minor loops connect to the output track through separate replicate elements.

The TIB1000 is organized as two separate 512*k*-bit storage arrays. Each array is identical in architecture to that illustrated in Fig. 10.9(b). These arrays both contain 300 minor loops, each with 2049 bit positions. Two such sections give a gross storage capacity of 1,229,400 bits. Of these 300 loops, 26 are redundant and are permitted to be defective during manufacturing. This gives a total of 274 good loops. Two of these loops are

[5] Texas Instruments, Incorporated, *Users Manual TBB5005 and TBB5010 Bubble Memory Systems* (Dallas, TX: Texas Instruments, Incorporated, 1980). (Courtesy of Texas Instruments, Incorporated)

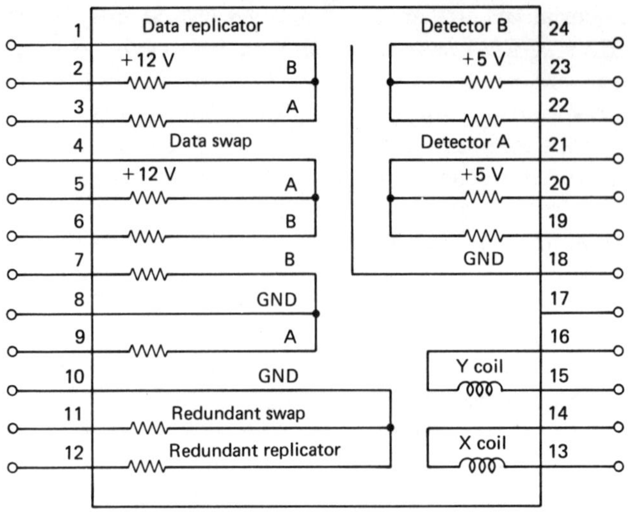

(a)

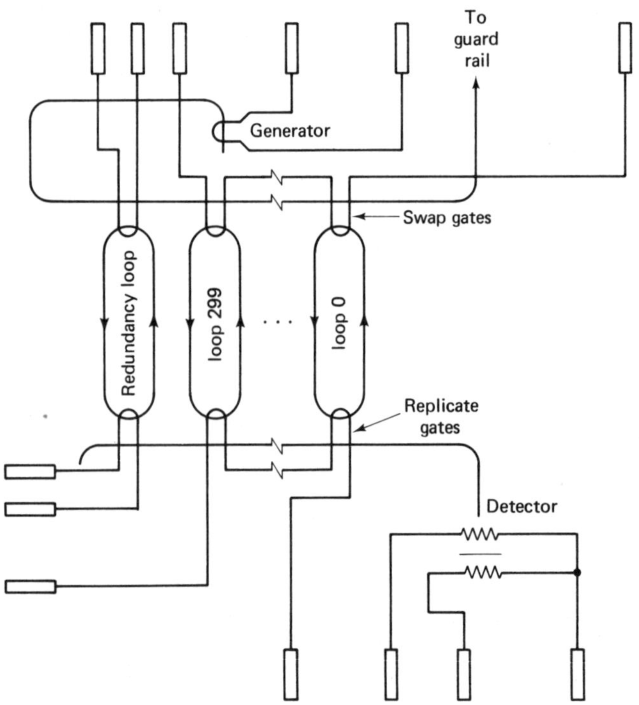

(b)

Fig. 10.9 (a) Pin layout of the TIB1000 MBM (Texas Instruments, Incorporated); (b) architecture of the TIB1000 (Texas Instruments, Incorporated).

normally allotted for maintaining parity bits for the pages of data. This leaves 272 loops for storage of data.

In the TIB1000, the length of each of the 2049 pages is 272 bits or 34 bytes. For this reason, the data storage capacity of each of the two arrays is 557,328 bits or 69,666 bytes. In this way, we find that the total usable storage capacity is 1,114,656 bits or 139,332 bytes.

When error correction is in use, 18 of the minor loops are allocated for this purpose. This leaves only 256 loops for storage of data. In this case, the total storage capacity is reduced to 1,049,088 bits or 131,136 bytes.

A separate loop is provided for storage of a map of the redundant minor loops. The map stored in this loop can be read to provide transparent handling of the redundant loops during read/write operation.

The internal architecture of the TIB0500 and TIB0250 are essentially the same as that of the TIB1000. However, in the TIB0500 a single 512*k*-bit storage array is used. This array also has 300 2049-bit minor loops, of which 274 are good for storage of data. On the other hand, the 300 minor loops in the TIB0250 are shortened to 1025 bits.

Data in both sections of the TIB1000 are circulated together under control of the 100-kHz drive clocks. A new type of gate, known as a *double-period gate*, is used in the tracks and loops of the device. This name comes from their causing data to be circulated two bit periods per cycle. In this way, a bit of data is generated or detected during each clock cycle instead of every other cycle as with the TIB0203. This results in higher operating speed.

We can read or write independently to either of the two 512*k*-bit sections of the TIB1000. Notice in Fig. 10.9(b) that separate replicate, swap, and generate control inputs as well as data outputs are provided for each section of the storage array. One section is called *A* and the other *B*.

Let us trace a write operation for section *A* of the TIB1000 MBM. The write cycle begins with generation of a page of 256 bits at the *generate inputs* (*GA*–, *GA*+). The page shifts through the input track until it is positioned for entry into the minor loops. When the correct storage location comes into place by the swap gates, the swap gates are enabled with a pulse at inputs *SA*–, *SA*+. This transfers the new page into the minor loops, where it is stored and the old page passes into the input track. From here, the old page is shifted to the guard rail, where it is destroyed.

Now that we have described how a page of data can be written into the MBM for storage, we shall now see how a page can be read out of section *A*. The read cycle begins with the storage location to be accessed, shifting toward the replicator gates. As the page comes into place, the data replicator input for section *A* (*RA*–, *RA*+) is pulsed and a replica of the page is put into the output track. After this, the page shifts toward the detector, where its bits produce signals at data outputs *DA*+, *DAD* and *DA*+, *DAL*.

With the 100-kHz drive clocks CX_1, CX_2 and CY_1, CY_2, the *average access time* of the TIB1000 for a read or write cycle is 11.2 ms. This delay represents the amount of time it takes for a page to circulate through the input or output track and halfway around the minor loop array. On the other hand, *maximum access time* represents the amount of time it would take a page to circulate through the input or output track and around the complete minor loop array. Its value is 21.5 ms.

Average data rate is another important characteristic of a MBM. This represents the rate at which consecutive pages of data can be written in or read out during a multipage operation. For the TIB1000, the average value of this characteristic is 85*k* bits per second per channel.

7110 MBM[6]

Another 1M-bit MBM is the 7110 device. It is housed within a 40-pin solderless DIP package. The pin layout of the device is shown in Fig. 10.10(a).

The structure of a channel of the 7110 is given in Fig. 10.10(b). It contains two such channels. This serial-parallel-serial structure is similar to the block replicate architecture already introduced. Notice that the storage array is divided into two parts: one stores odd-numbered pages and the other even-numbered pages. Moreover, we find not only a single input track, but also two separate output tracks that are combined at the detector.

The storage array contains 320 minor loops, each with 4096 storage locations. This corresponds to a gross storage capacity of 1,310,720 bits. However, 48 loops are redundant and 16 are reserved for error correction. This leaves 256 minor loops for storage of data and a total storage capacity of 1,048,576 bits.

An extra loop is provided to hold a map of the locations of the redundant minor loops. In the 7110, this is known as the *boot loop*. The on-chip map can be read out of the boot loop and serves as a guide for transparent handling of redundant loops.

For read/write operation, data are organized into 2048 pages, each with 512 bits. This corresponds to 64 bytes per page and a total storage of 128*k* bytes. Data can be read in single-page or multipage mode with an average read/write access time of 40 ms and an average data rate of 78 kHz.

The 7110 requires +12-V and +5-V dc supplies and consumes 1.3 W of standby power. Moreover, it can operate in an environment with external magnetic fields having a typical value as high as 40 Oe.

[6] Intel Magnetics, "A Total System Solution to Magnetic Bubble Memory Applications," *Preview Magazine*, July/August 1979 (Santa Clara, CA: Intel Corp.). (Courtesy of Intel Corp.)

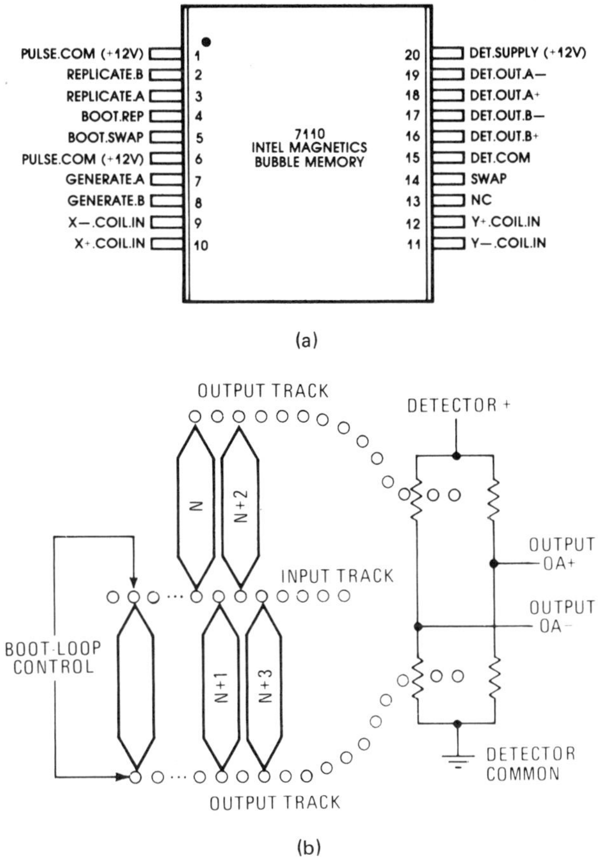

Fig. 10.10 (a) Pin layout of the 7110 MBM (Intel Corp.); (b) architecture of the 7110 (Reprinted from Electronics (April 26, 1979), Copyright © McGraw-Hill, Inc. (1979). All rights reserved).

RBM256 MBM[7]

The RBM256 is a 256k-bit magnetic bubble memory device. Figure 10.11 shows its internal architecture and numbering of its pins. This architecture is also similar to the block replicate configuration. Here we find that it has a separate input port and two separate output ports.

The storage array consists of 282 loops, each with 1025 bit positions. This represents a gross storage capacity of 289,250 bits. Only 260 of these loops are guaranteed to be usable. For this reason, read/write data are organized into 1025 260-bit pages. However, for byte operation, we can only

[7] Rockwell International Corp., "256k-bit Bubble Memory Device," Document No. D-RBM 256, Rev. 1 (Anaheim, CA: Rockwell International Corp., February 1979). (Courtesy of Rockwell International Corp.)

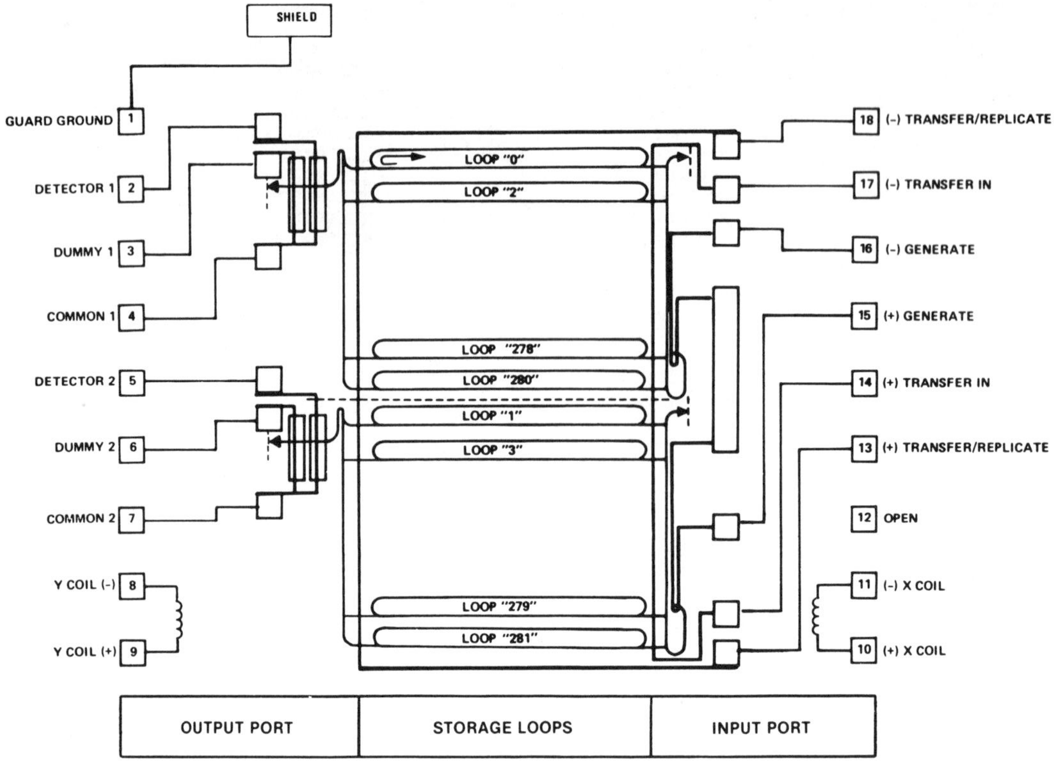

Fig. 10.11 Architecture of the RBM256 MBM (Rockwell International Corp.).

use 256 of the loops for data storage which gives 32 bytes per page. When used in a binary configuration, the total storage capacity is 262,400 bits or 32,800 bytes. Data are circulated through the loops at a 150-kHz clock rate.

The RBM 256 consumes 820 mW of power and can work in an environment with an external magnetic field as high as 50 Oe.

NBM 2256 MBM[8]

Figure 10.12 shows the internal architecture of another 256*k*-bit magnetic bubble memory device, the NBM 2256. This device uses the block replicate architecture to produce a storage array with 282 loops, each with 1024 storage positions. Notice that the storage array is arranged into separate even loop and odd loop sections. Of the 282 loops, 256 are available for storage of data. This gives a storage capacity of 262,144 bits (32,768 bytes) of data. Of the remaining loops, six are used for storage of error correction code; two are for the redundant loop map; and 18 are redundant loops.

[8] National Semiconductor Corp., "National's NBM 2256 Bubble Memory," (Santa Clara, CA: National Semiconductor Corp., 1980). (Courtesy of National Semiconductor Corp.)

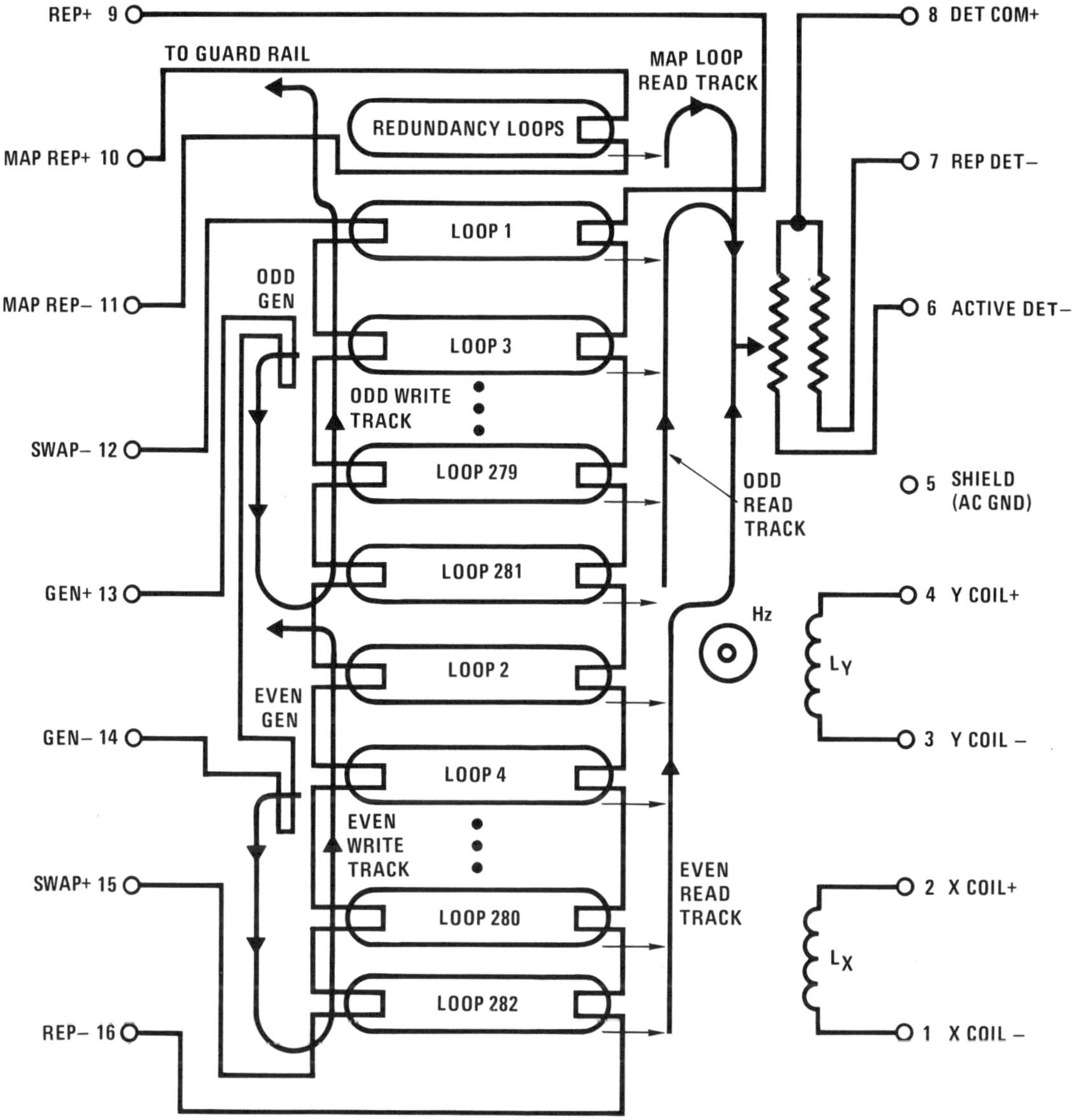

Fig. 10.12 Architecture of the NBM 2256 MBM (National Semiconductor Corp.).

10.8 THE MAGNETIC BUBBLE MEMORY SYSTEM

Up to now, we have concentrated on the MBM device. But this device alone is not capable of effectively operating as a memory system. It needs a number of support circuits to produce the current pulses and timing for control of the read and write operations, clocks for circulation of data around the loops, conversion of the output to usable logic levels, and to map out redundant loops.

The TIB0203 MBM System[9, 10]

Figure 10.13 is a MBM system that employs the TIB0203 MBM device. From this diagram, we see that the system contains five key elements: *controller*, *function timing generator*, *function driver*, *coil drivers*, and *sense amplifier*. The controller and function timing generator implement a *MBM controller* section. On the other hand, the coil drivers, function driver, and sense amplifier together with the magnetic bubble memory device represent the *memory module.*

Notice that just one TIB0203 device is employed in this circuit. This provides a total system storage capacity of 92*k* bits or 11.5*k* bytes. However, the controller section is capable of driving 17 of these memory modules. In this way, storage capacity can be expanded to about 1.5M bits or 195*k* bytes.

A controller device is required to interface the MBM system with the microcomputer. The TMS 9916/5502 is designed to interface the TIB0203 MBM to a TMS 9900 CPU. Figure 10.14 is a block diagram of the internal architecture of the TMS 9916/5502 IC. From this drawing, we see that it contains a *decoder*, *control registers* and *counters*, *comparator*, *FIFO*, *clock distributor*, and *microsequencer.*

This device operates in a *memory-mapped method.* That is, the CPU selects and commands it into operation over the address bus. Bits A_4 through A_{14} of the address are externally decoded to chip select the controller. The remaining four bits, A_0 through A_3, represent a *command code.* A list of the command codes available for the TMS 9916/5502 is given in Fig. 10.15 (a). By using these commands, the CPU sets the controller to perform operations.

For example, address codes 0 and 1 are decoded to initiate loading of a 16-bit page select address into the page select register of the controller. Applying $A_0A_1A_2A_3$=0000, we load a parallel byte from data bus lines D_0 through D_7 into the least significant byte part of the register. By now making $A_0A_1A_2A_3$=0001, a second byte is loaded into the register but this time into the most significant byte location. The register now holds the 16-bit address of the page to be accessed.

Before the controller can function with the MBM system, it must be initialized with the number of pages in the MBM device and the number of bytes in each page. The number of pages that can be stored in the TIB0203 device is 641, and it is loaded into the minor loop size register with address command 8. On the other hand, the number of bytes per page must be written into the page size register. This is achieved with address command 9.

Assume that we now want to perform a multibit read operation of data

[9]Texas Instruments Incorporated, *TIB0203 Magnetic Bubble Memory and Associated Circuits.* (Courtesy of Texas Instruments, Incorporated)

[10]Texas Instruments, Incorporated, *TIB0203 Magnetic Bubble Memory System Application Manual* (Dallas, TX: Texas Instruments, Incorporated, March 1979). (Courtesy of Texas Instruments, Incorporated)

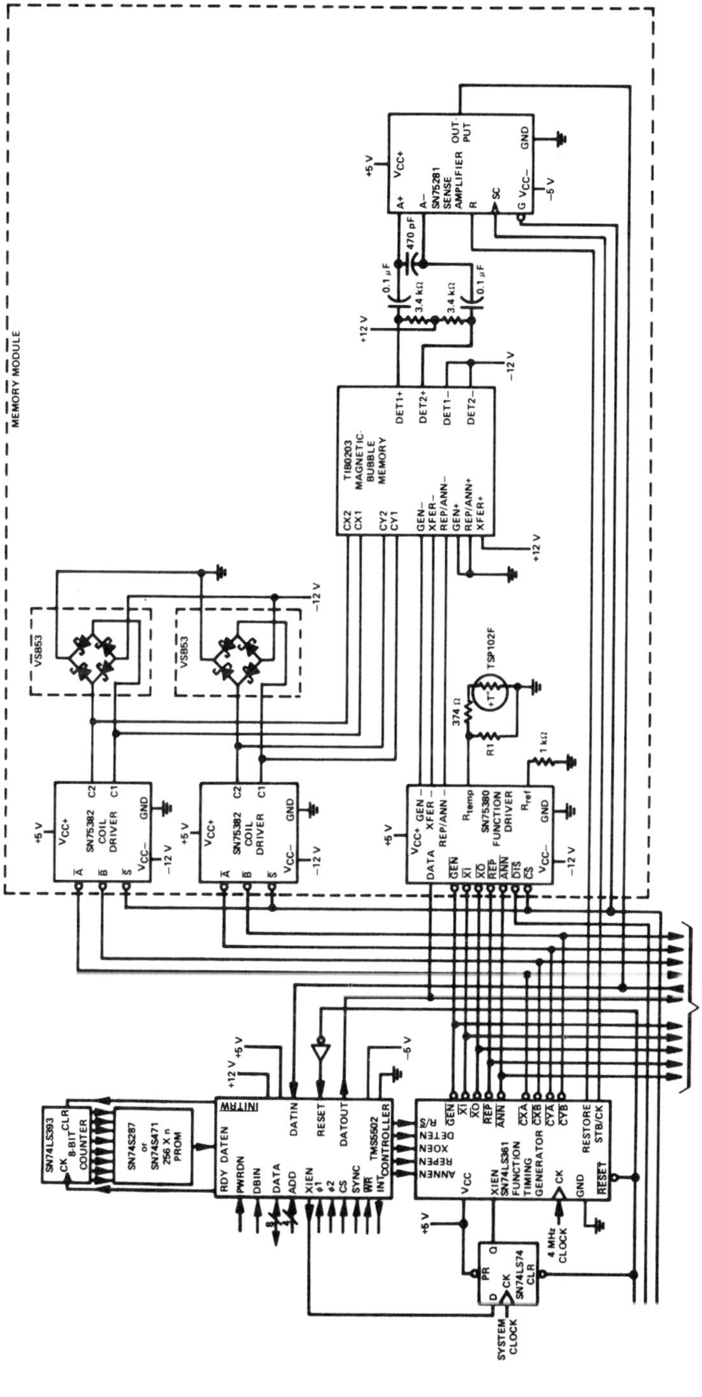

Fig. 10.13 TIB0203 MBM system (Texas Instruments, Incorporated).

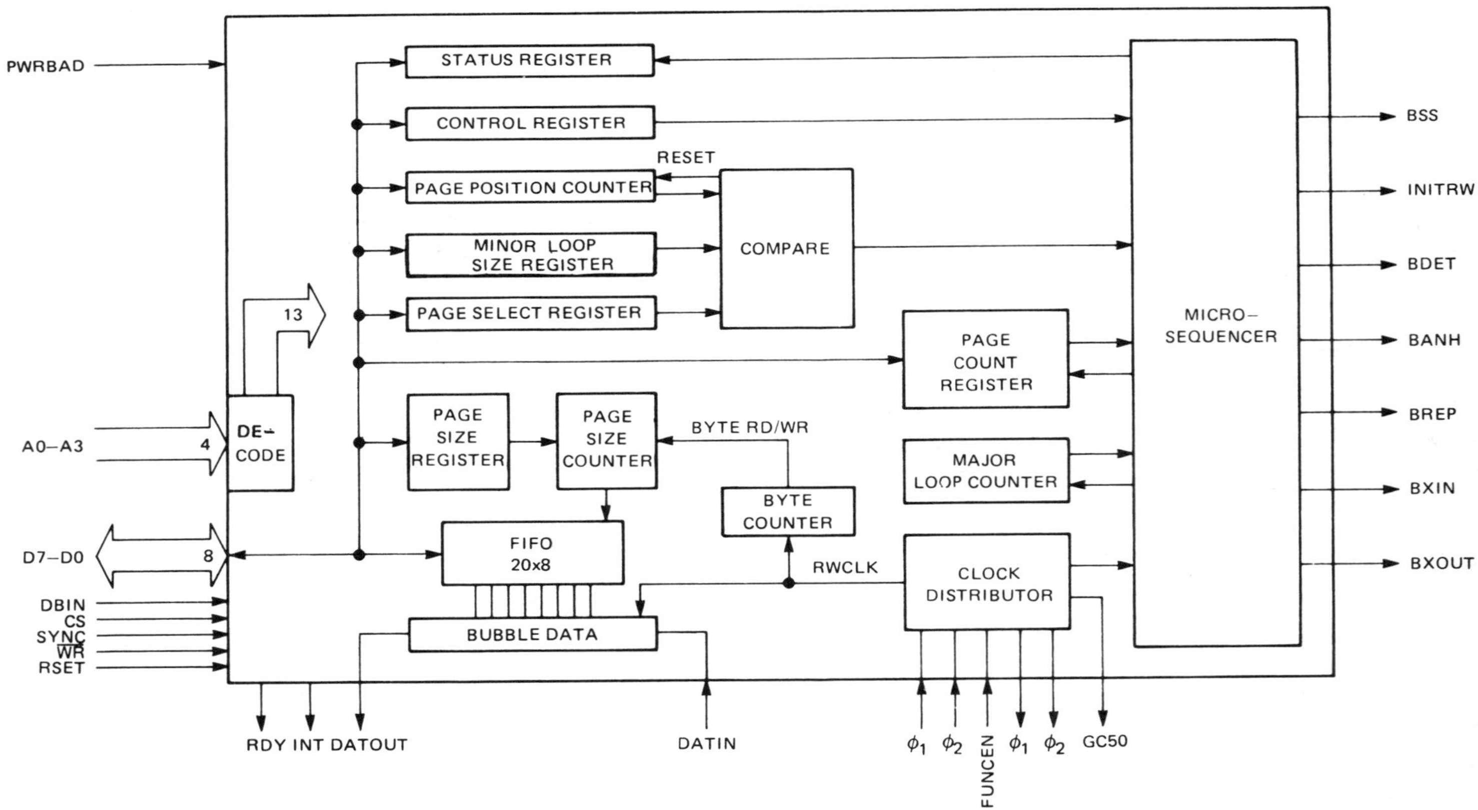

Fig. 10.14 TMS9916/5502 MBM controller (Texas Instruments, Incorporated).

ADDRESSES (A0-A3)	DATA COMMANDS	OPERATION
0	Load Page Select Reg 1	Write LSB
1	Load Page Select Reg 2	Write MSB
2	Load Control Command Register	Write (see Table 2)
3	Read Byte	Read FIFO
4	Write Byte	Write FIFO
5	Read Status	Read
6	Page Counter 1	Read/Write LSB
7	Page Counter 2	Read/Write MSB
8	Load Minor Loop Size Reg 1	Write LSB
9	Load Minor Loop Size Reg 2	Write MSB
A	Page Position Counter 1	Read/Write LSB
B	Page Position Counter 2	Read/Write MSB
C	Load Page Size Reg	Write
D	Read ROM Byte (for testing only)	Read & Incr. Pointer
E	Read/Write State Address (for testing)	Read ROM ADDR Reg

(a)

BIT NO.	CONTROL COMMAND	RESET FUNCTION	FUNCTION
0	Initialize	System* + CRRST**	"Cold Start" initilization
1	Read Page	System + CRRST	Read page from bubble memory into FIFO page buffer
2	Write Page	System + CRRST	Write page from FIFO page buffer into bubble memory
3	Single Page Mode	Bit 4 = "1"	Sets up controller for single page transfers
4	Multi-Page Mode	System + Bit 3 = "1"	Sets up controller for multi-page transfers
5	Test Mode	System + Bit 5 = "0"	Enables control ROM verification
6	Reset		Software System Reset (Pulse)
7	Interrupt Mask	System + Bit 5 = "0"	Resets Interrupt Level (Pulse)

(b)

Fig. 10.15 (a) MBM address functions (Texas Instruments, Incorporated); (b) MBM control commands (Texas Instruments, Incorporated).

from the MBM. We begin by loading the controller with the address of the starting page of the group to be accessed. The CPU does this with 2-byte write operations to the page select register. After this, the number of consecutive pages to be accessed are written into the page count register with commands 6 and 7. The controller is now ready to have the read operation initiated.

The read operation is initiated by loading a control command into the control register. This is done with address command 2. The possible control commands are listed in Fig. 10.15(b). Each bit of the command byte is used to select one operation. For our example, bits 1 and 4 are set to logic 1 to select read page and multipage mode.

The MBM controller is now ready to perform a read operation; however, the read cannot yet occur. First the page of data must shift into place by the transfer gates for entrance to the major loops. As the pages of data circulate around the minor loops, the page position counter increments as each new page comes into place. In this way, it tracks the page positions within the MBM. This count is continually compared to that of the starting page. When they are equal, the comparator output signals the microsequencer. After this, the microsequencer produces the accurately timed sequence of function signals at its *BANH*, *BREP*, *BXIN*, *BXOUT*, and *BDET* outputs to control the transfer out, replicate, detection, and transfer-in operations required during the read cycle.

Serial data are read in and written out of the controller at the *DATIN* and *DATOUT* leads, respectively. Input and output of data are synchronous to the *RWCLK* signal that is produced by the clock distributor. The byte counter section tracks the bytes of data as they are input and output at the bubble data register. For each byte transferred, the page size counter is decremented by 1 and a byte of data is transferred into or out of the 20-word by 8-bit FIFO. When the count reaches zero, the page transfer is complete.

Movement of bubbles through the major loop is tracked by the major loop counter. As this happens, redundant bit locations are identified to the controller by the signal *FUNCEN*. In the memory system of Fig. 10.13, this signal is produced by an SN74S287 PROM. This device holds a map of the redundant loop locations. As data circulates through the MBM, the SN74LS383 counter is incremented. Its output addresses consecutive memory locations, and the logic level output indicates whether the corresponding minor loop is good or bad. If it indicates a bad loop at *FUNCEN*, shifting of data in the data register is inhibited, and no data are input or output.

Once the page of data is held in the FIFO, it must be read by the CPU. Looking at Fig. 10.15(a), we find that address command 3 is used to read a byte of data out of the FIFO. This command must be repeated for each byte in the page.

Now that we have introduced the operation of the controller IC, let us continue with the other part of the MBM controller the TIB0951/SN74LS361 function timing generator. In Fig. 10.13, we see that the

TIB0951/SN74LS361 interfaces the controller with the following parts of the memory module: the coil drivers, the function driver, and the sense amplifier.

The function timing generator has four primary functions: to generate coil drive signals, to start and stop coil drive clocks, to sense power failures and control power down, and to develop the precisely timed function signals that are required during the read and write cycles.

A 4-MHz clock signal is input at the *CLK* lead. This signal is used to derive the 100-kHz clock signals $\overline{CXA}$, $\overline{CXB}$ and $\overline{CYA}$, $\overline{CYB}$. The signals output at these leads are the pulse waveforms labeled X_1, X_2 and Y_1, Y_2 in Fig. 10.16(a).

The logic level at control input $R/\overline{S}$ is used to control the clocks. When $R/\overline{S}$ is logic 1, the device is in the run state and the clock signals are output to the coil driver circuits. On the other hand, setting $R/\overline{S}$ to 0 signals the function timing generator to stop the clock. In response, it puts the MBM in a known state with all data stored in the minor loops and then turns the clock OFF. Now the MBM is in a low-power state in which data are not circulated. The function timing generator signals that the system is in this state by setting the $\overline{CYCCMP}$ line to logic 0. The $\overline{CYCCMP}$ line is not shown in Fig. 10.13. When $R/\overline{S}$ returns to logic 1, the MBM clock restarts.

A power fail circuit is also provided within the SN74LS361 device. If V_{CC} drops below approximately 3.5 V, the coil drive outputs are switched into the hi-Z state. This protects the MBM system during power failures.

Within the function timing generator, a counter divides the 10-μs period of the drive coil clocks into 40 equal intervals. The clock counts are identified in Fig. 10.16(b). The outputs of the counter are inputs to a decoder matrix which produces the accurately timed signals required to perform the generate, transfer, replicate, and annihilate operations as well as control operation of the sense amplifiers. Notice that the signal for transfer out ($\overline{X}_0$) begins at clock pulse 14 and ends with clock pulse 38. On the other hand, the transfer in pulse is timed differently. It starts at pulse 3 and continues through 27.

In Fig. 10.13, we see that control signals *ANNEN*, *REPEN*, *XOEN*, and *DETEN* are inputs to the function timing generator. It is these signals that control the gating of control signals produced by the decoder to outputs $\overline{GEN}$, $\overline{XI}$, $\overline{XO}$, $\overline{REP}$, and $\overline{ANN}$. These signals are applied to inputs of the TIB0861/SN75380 function driver. On the other hand, the signals *RESTORE* and *STB/CK* are enabled by *DETEN* and passed to inputs of the sense amplifier. Here they control reading of the MBM output.

The reset input ($\overline{RESET}$) is used to initialize the function timing generator IC. Setting this input to logic 0 causes the flip-flops within the device to be initialized.

Looking at Fig. 10.13, we find that two coil drivers and diode bridges interface the clock outputs of the function timing generator to the orthogonal coil drive inputs of the MBM. The function timing generator produces the clock pulse signals labeled *X* and *Y* in Fig. 10.16(a). These signals are at

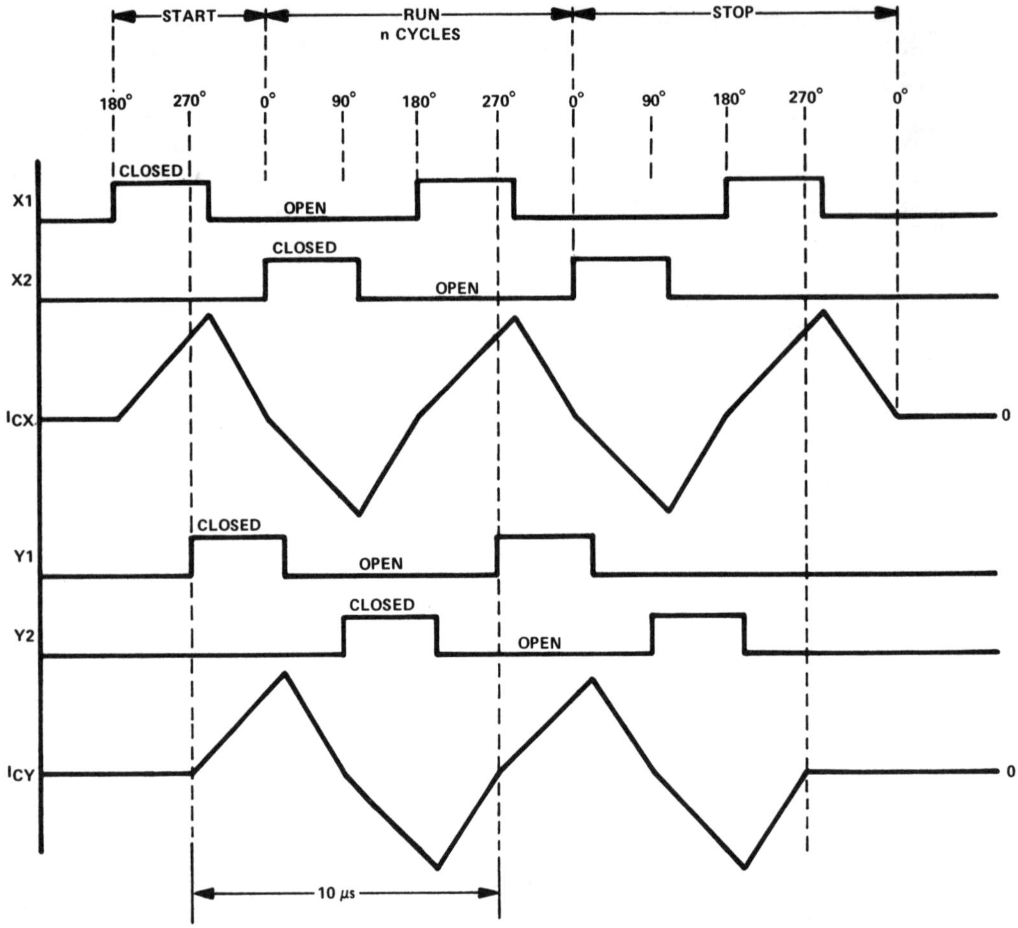

(a)

Fig. 10.16 (a) Coil drive signals (Texas Instruments, Incorporated); (b) function timing signals (Texas Instruments, Incorporated).

100 kHz; therefore, it takes 10 μs to go through one complete 360° cycle. Notice that the output of the coil drivers are triangular-shaped currents I_{CX} and I_{CY}. These two signals are 180° out of phase.

Figure 10.17(a) shows the internal circuitry of the TIB0801A/SN75382 coil drivers. Inputs to the circuit are drive signals $\overline{A}$ and $\overline{B}$ and chip select $\overline{S}$. The coil drive outputs are labeled C_1 and C_2. The table in Fig. 10.17(b) represents input/output operation of the device.

From the clock waveform in Fig. 10.16(a), we see that during the first 180° to 270° quarter cycle $X_1 = \overline{A}$ is logic 1 and $X_2 = \overline{B}$ is logic 0. This input condition switches outputs C_2 to $-V_{CC}$ and C_1 to GND. The output voltage is integrated by the inductance of the orthogonal coil and current I_{CX} ramps in the positive direction.

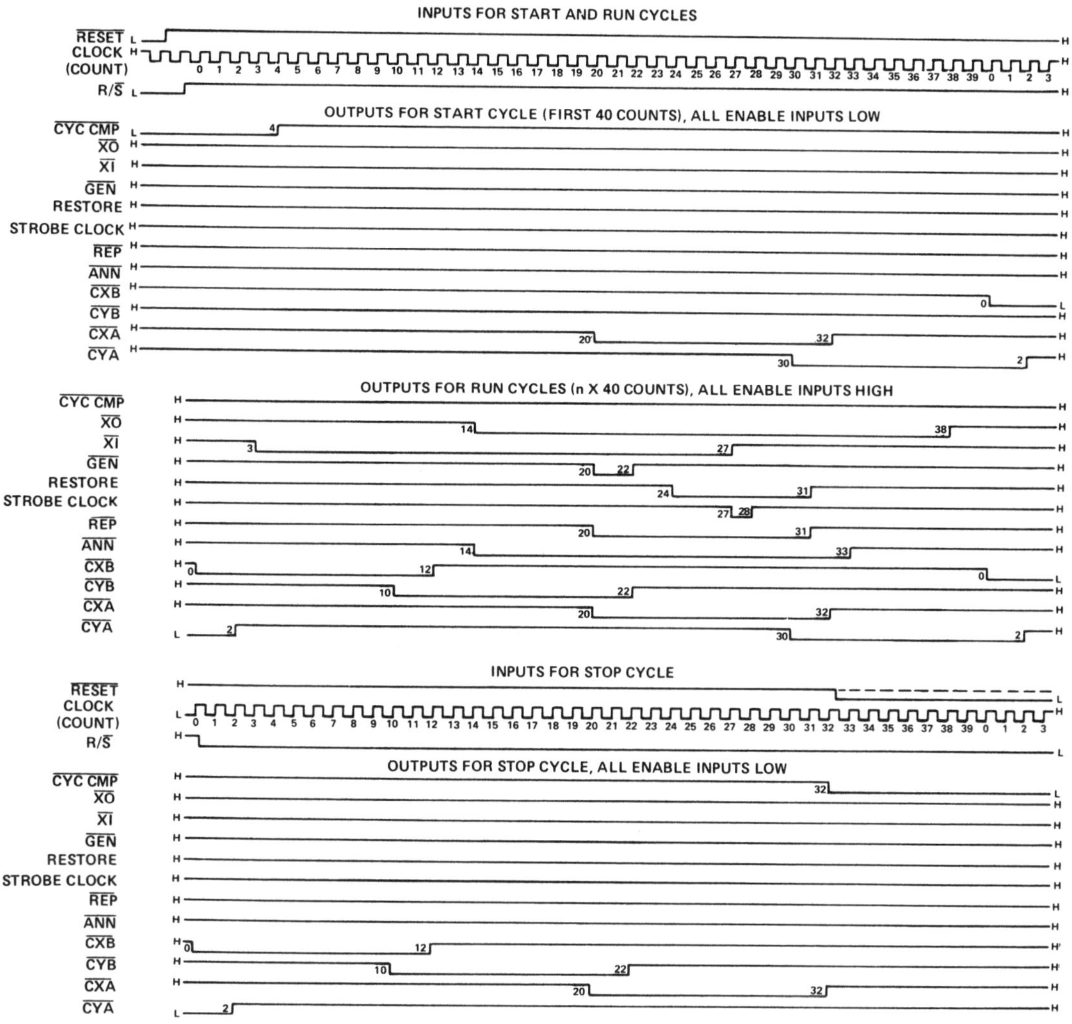

(b)

Fig. 10.16 Continued

During the 270° to 0° quarter cycle, both $X_1 = \overline{A}$ and $X_2 = \overline{B}$ are logic 0. Therefore, the output of the coil driver switches to the hi-Z state. Now the field in the drive coil collapses through the commutating bridge and current ramps downward.

As the next quarter-cycle begins, $X_2 = \overline{B}$ is switched to logic 1 while $X_1 = \overline{A}$ is held at logic 0. Output C_1 is at $-V_{CC}$ and C_2 at *GND*. Coil current I_{CX} now begins to increase in the opposite direction. From 90° to 180°, the coil drive signals are again both logic 0. This puts the outputs in the third state and current ramps back toward zero.

The outputs of the coil driver can be turned OFF by switching $\overline{S}$

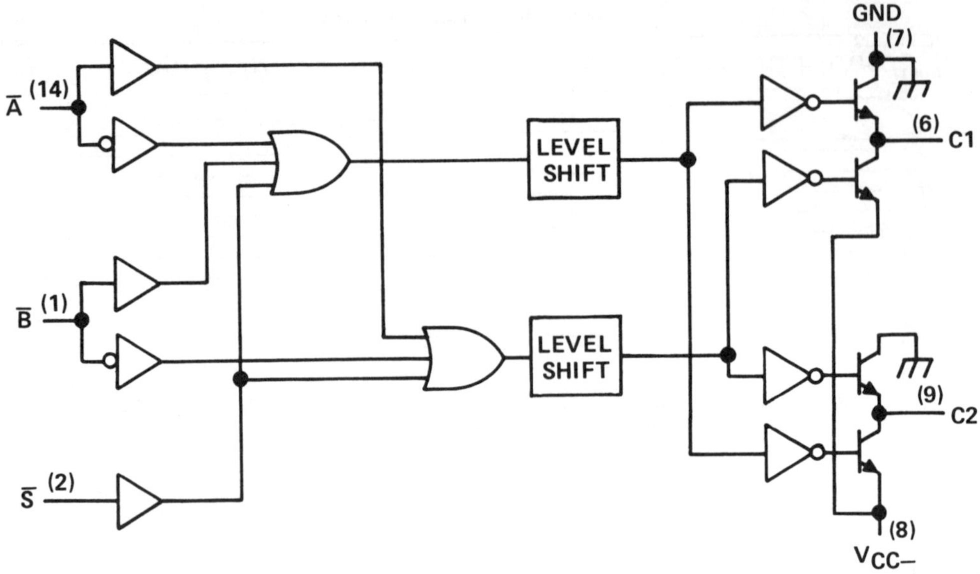

(a)

INPUTS			OUTPUTS	
$\overline{A}$	$\overline{B}$	$\overline{S}$	C1	C2
X	X	H	Z	Z
L	L	L	Z	Z
L	H	L	≈ V_{CC-}	≈ Gnd
H	L	L	≈ Gnd	≈ V_{CC-}
H	H	L	Z	Z

(b)

Fig. 10.17 (a) Coil driver circuit (Texas Instruments, Incorporated); (b) operating truth table (Texas Instruments, Incorporated).

to logic 1. This puts the C_1 and C_2 outputs in the hi-Z state. When power is turned ON or OFF, the start or stop sequence is critical. Start-cycle and stop-cycle timing are shown in Fig. 10.16(b). Stop must occur with the positive decay of current at C_2 and start must occur with the positive rise of current at C_2. If these conditions are not met, data may be lost.

Just as the coil drivers interface the clock signals to the MBM, the TIB0861/SN75380 function driver interfaces the function drive outputs of the function timing generator to the MBM. In the MBM system of Fig. 10.13 we see that the function driver accepts inputs at $\overline{GEN}$, $\overline{XI}$, $\overline{XO}$, $\overline{REP}$, and $\overline{ANN}$ from the function timing generator as well as serial data from the controller at input *DATA*. The inputs are used to derive control currents for input to the *GEN–*, *XFER–*, and *REP/ANN–* function loops of the MBM.

A diagram of the internal circuitry of the TIB0861/SN75380 is given in Fig. 10.18. Here we find five constant current sources. Moreover, each current source is supplied by a control gate. Inputs $\overline{DIS}$ and $\overline{CS}$ must both be

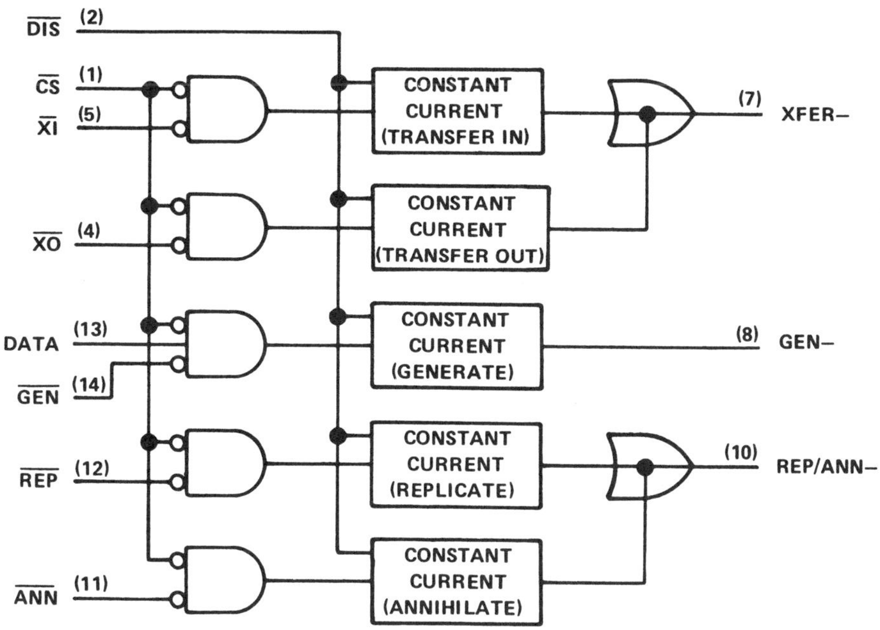

Fig. 10.18 Function driver circuit (Texas Instruments, Incorporated).

logic 0 to enable the circuit for operation. After this, the function timing generator applies appropriately timed voltage pulses to the inputs of the function driver. In response, the corresponding current generators produce currents at their outputs.

For instance, when $\overline{X}_0$ is switched to logic 0, the output of its gate switches to logic 1. A transfer-out current pulse is produced at *XFER*–. This current flows through the transfer loop of the MBM and causes a page of bits to be transferred out of the minor loops and into the major loop.

The generate section operates in a similar way. But here the logic level of *DATA* is gated with $\overline{GEN}$. If *DATA* equals 1, a generate output is produced. This current is supplied to the *GEN*– loop of the MBM, where it causes generation of a bubble in the major loop. However, if *DATA* equals 0 instead of 1, the gate output stays at the 0 level. In this case, no current pulse is produced at *GEN*– and a bubble is not generated.

Notice in Fig. 10.13 that a thermistor is connected from the R_{temp} output of the function driver to ground. This device is required to maintain the level of the *GEN*– output current over a wide temperature range. If this temperature compensation were not included, the generate current level would increase with increasing temperature. This could lead to multiple bubble generation.

There is another resistor connected to the function driver in Fig. 10.13. It is tied from the R_{ref} lead to ground. The value of this resistor sets the current levels of the *XFER*– and *REP/ANN*– outputs. A 1% precision resistor is required in this location.

The last part of the MBM system in Fig. 10.13 to be considered is the sense amplifier. This device, TIB0833/SN75281, is designed to read the bubble detector output of the MBM and convert it to TTL-compatible logic levels.

Looking at Fig. 10.13, we find that the MBM outputs *DET1+* and *DET2+* are coupled through an RC circuit to the *A+* and *A–* differential inputs of the sense amplifier. Moreover, the output of the sense amplifier is returned to *DATIN* of the MBM controller for input to the CPU.

As a bubble moves through the magnetoresistive element in the MBM, it produces a current in the detector loop. This results in the voltage signal shown in Fig. 10.19(a) across the input of the sense amplifier.

The second pulse in this signal represents the existence of a bubble. It is this pulse that must be read by the sense amplifier. Notice that the

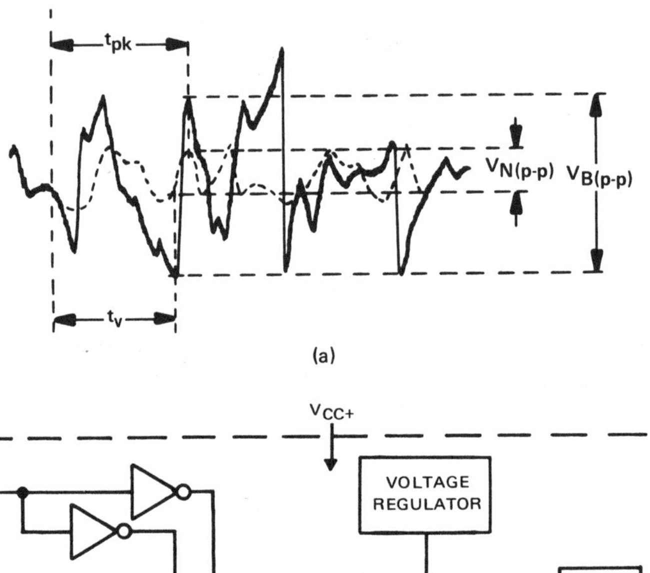

(a)

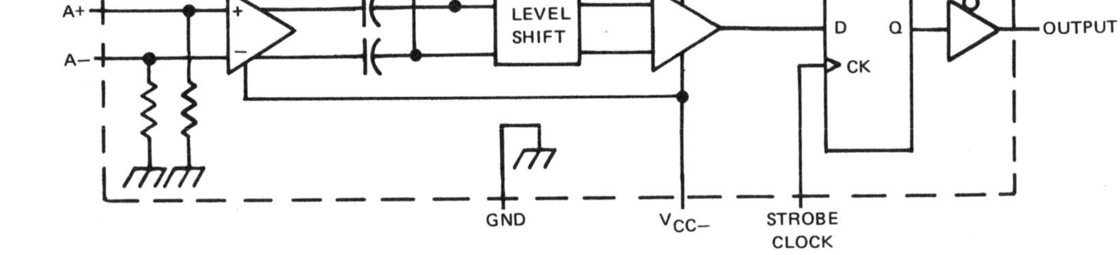

(b)

Fig. 10.19 (a) MBM output voltage (Texas Instruments, Incorporated); (b) sense amplifier circuit (Texas Instruments, Incorporated).

peak occurs at time t_{PK}, which has a typical value of 7 μs. The peak-to-peak value of this bubble voltage is labeled $V_{B(P\text{-}P)}$ and has a typical value of 3.5 mV. Time t_v represents the valley before the bubble pulse and $V_{N(P\text{-}P)}$ is the peak-to-peak noise level of the output. In this way, we see that the timing for sensing of the bubble is critical. For this reason, it is precisely controlled by the *RESTORE* and *STB/CK* signals from the function timing generator.

Figure 10.19(b) shows internal circuitry of the TIB0833/SN75281 sense amplifier. When the function timing generator pulses the *RESTORE* input, a dc voltage level is set on the internal coupling capacitor of the device. The device is now enabled to sample data a short time later. As the peak bubble voltage $V_{B(P\text{-}P)}$ is reached, the function timing generator applies a pulse to the *STROBE CLOCK* input. With this pulse, the logic level sensed by the amplifier is latched into the *D*-type flip-flop and the data bit is available at *OUTPUT*. The output of the TIB0833/SN75281 is three-state and is enabled with logic 0 at *OUTPUT CONTROL*.

The TIB1000 MBM System[11]

A magnetic bubble memory system that employs the TIB1000 1M-bit device is shown in Fig. 10.20. Just like the TIB0203 system, this circuit has two functional parts, the MBM controller and memory module. Here the controller section again contains the bubble memory controller device and function timing generator. Its function is to interface the bubble module to the microcomputer.

The memory module section contains the MBM device and support circuits required to control its operation. This section has changed slightly from that in the TIB0203 system. Notice that the single function driver has been replaced with separate read and write function drivers. Moreover, two sense amplifiers are required, one for each output of the MBM.

A single MBM module is connected to the controller in Fig. 10.20; however, the outputs of the function timing generator have the ability to drive up to 10 such modules. This permits storage capacities in the range 139*k* to 1.39M bytes. In fact, by adding buffers at the outputs of the function timing generator, it is given the ability to drive more than 10 bubble modules and further expands storage capacity.

The TIB0903 bubble memory controller is used to interface the MBM system to the TMS 9900 microprocessor. It contains a command register and a status register, as well as registers that represent the starting page and number of pages to be involved in read or write operations. The TMS 9900 writes into or reads from these registers in a memory-mapped fashion. The content of these registers determines if a read or write operation is to

[11] Texas Instruments, Incorporated, *Users Manual TBB5005 and TBB5010 Bubble Memory Systems.* (Courtesy of Texas Instruments, Incorporated)

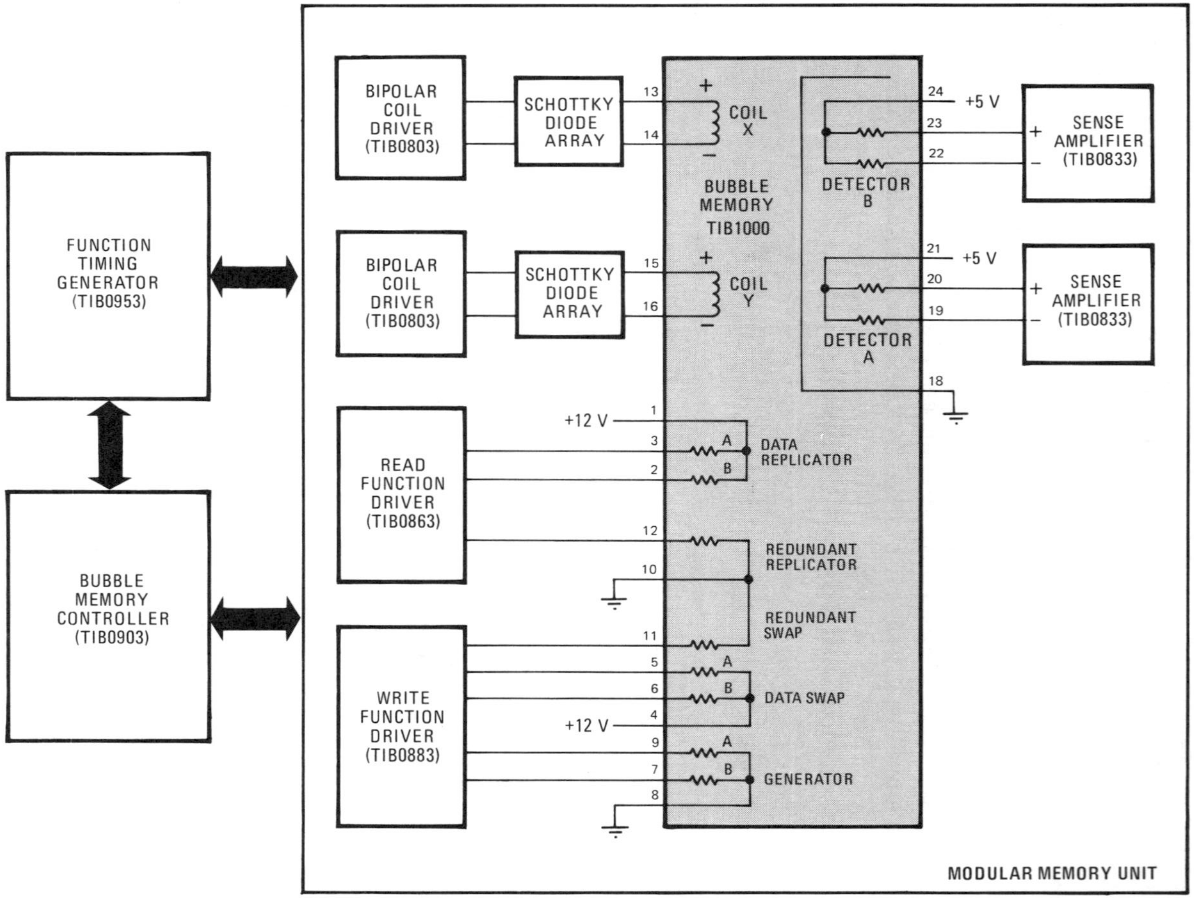

Fig. 10.20 TIB1000 MBM system (Reprinted from Electronics (Nov. 8, 1979), copyright © McGraw-Hill, Inc. (1979). All rights reserved).

be performed for which pages, and whether it will be a single-page or multi-page operation. The controller also contains a data buffer and circuits to convert between serial and parallel data organizations. The data interface to the microprocessor is in parallel byte form and that to the bubble memory is in serial page form.

The TIB0953 function timing generator receives control signals from the MBM controller and produces the precisely timed signals that are required to synchronize the operation of the devices in the bubble memory module. Remember that the TIB1000 device uses the block replicate architecture instead of the major/minor loop architecture. For this reason, the function timing generator has outputs for coil drive, generation, swap, replication, and detection operations. This device also monitors the power-supply voltage. If a power failure occurs, the function timing generator shuts the coil drive signals off, and MBM operation is stopped.

The windings of the X and Y orthogonal coils within the MBM are driven by the TIB0803 coil drivers. Pulses input from the function timing generator are converted to higher voltages which are integrated by the coils to give triangular-shaped currents. It is these currents that cause the bubbles to move through the input track, output track, and storage loops. The Schottky diode arrays act as commutating diode when the coil driver outputs are turned off.

Current pulses, not voltage pulses, are needed to initiate the generate, swap, and replicate operations of the MBM. These current pulses are produced by the TIB0863 read function driver and TIB0883 write function driver. For instance, as the proper page of data comes into place by the replicator element, a current pulse is produced at the data replicate output of the read function driver. This causes a block replication of the page of data into the output track. After this, the data circulate toward the detector element, where its bits produce signals at the detector outputs.

On the other hand, the write function driver controls the generation of a page of data in the input track. After a page has been generated and circulated into place by the swap gates, the swap output of the driver is activated. This current pulse causes the page to be swapped with that in the storage loops. The old page, now in the input track, is driven to the guard rail, where it is annihilated.

The TIB0833 sense amplifiers are used to detect the existence or absence of a bubble at the detector element. The function timing generator sets a clamp signal to the amplifier, indicating that a page of data is to be read and at the appropriate instant clocks the amplifier to latch the logic level of the data at the output.

The outputs of the coil drivers, read function driver, and write function driver are controlled by time-out circuits. In this way, it is assured that their output signals will not remain active too long and damage the elements within the MBM.

The 7110 MBM System[12]

The circuit diagram in Fig. 10.21 represents a magnetic bubble memory system based on the 7110 1M-bit bubble memory. This circuit includes a 7220 *bubble memory controller* (BMC) and a single bubble memory module made with the 7242 *formatter/sense amplifier* (FSA), 7230 *current pulse generator* (CPG), and 7250 *coil predriver* (CPD) together with its associated 7254 *drive transistors.* This system has a storage capacity of 128*k* bytes; however, the 7220 controller has the ability to control up to eight memory modules. This permits systems with up to a maximum of 1M bytes of storage.

The 7220 bubble memory controller provides an interface between the 8080/8085 microprocessors and 7110 MBM module. Communications of data and commands between the microprocessor and controller occur over the data bus D_0 through D_7. The controller contains command and status registers, as well as registers that represent the address of the location in MBM to be accessed and the number of pages for multipage operations. The microsequencer within the controller interprets the command and initiates the sequence of control signals required to execute the read or write data transfer operation. Pages of data are temporarily stored in the 40×8 FIFO. Transfer of data between microprocessor and controller is performed over parallel data lines D_0 through D_7. A ninth line, D_8, is provided for use as a parity bit. On the other hand, data transfers between controller and MBM are performed in serial form over the bidirectional data line *DIO.* In multipage mode, up to 2048 consecutive pages can be accessed.

The 7242 formatter/sense amplifier device serves several functions in the MBM system. First, it contains two sense amplifiers for detection of bubble signals produced at the detector outputs of the 7110 MBM. Data levels are latched into the sense amplifier outputs.

Second, the 7242 has the ability to perform transparent handling of redundant loops. As the MBM system is initialized, the 7220 controller causes the map of the redundant loops that is held in the boot loop of the MBM to be read into a boot loop register within the 7242 device. Once loaded, this register identifies to the sense amplifiers which bits at the detector outputs are to be sampled.

The third feature of the 7242 is its *burst error detection and correction* capability. It contains a 14-bit *fire code* which can be added to the 256-bit pages of data before being written into the MBM, or in the case of a read operation, the page of data can be temporarily stored in a buffer within the 7242, tested for errors, and corrected before it is transferred to the FIFO in the controller. Errors are signaled to the controller over the $\overline{ERR.FLG}$ line.

During read and write operations, correctly timed enable signals for the generation, swap, and replication operations are produced by the micro-

[12] Intel Magnetics, "A Total System Solution to Magnetic Bubble Memory Applications." (Courtesy of Intel Corp.)

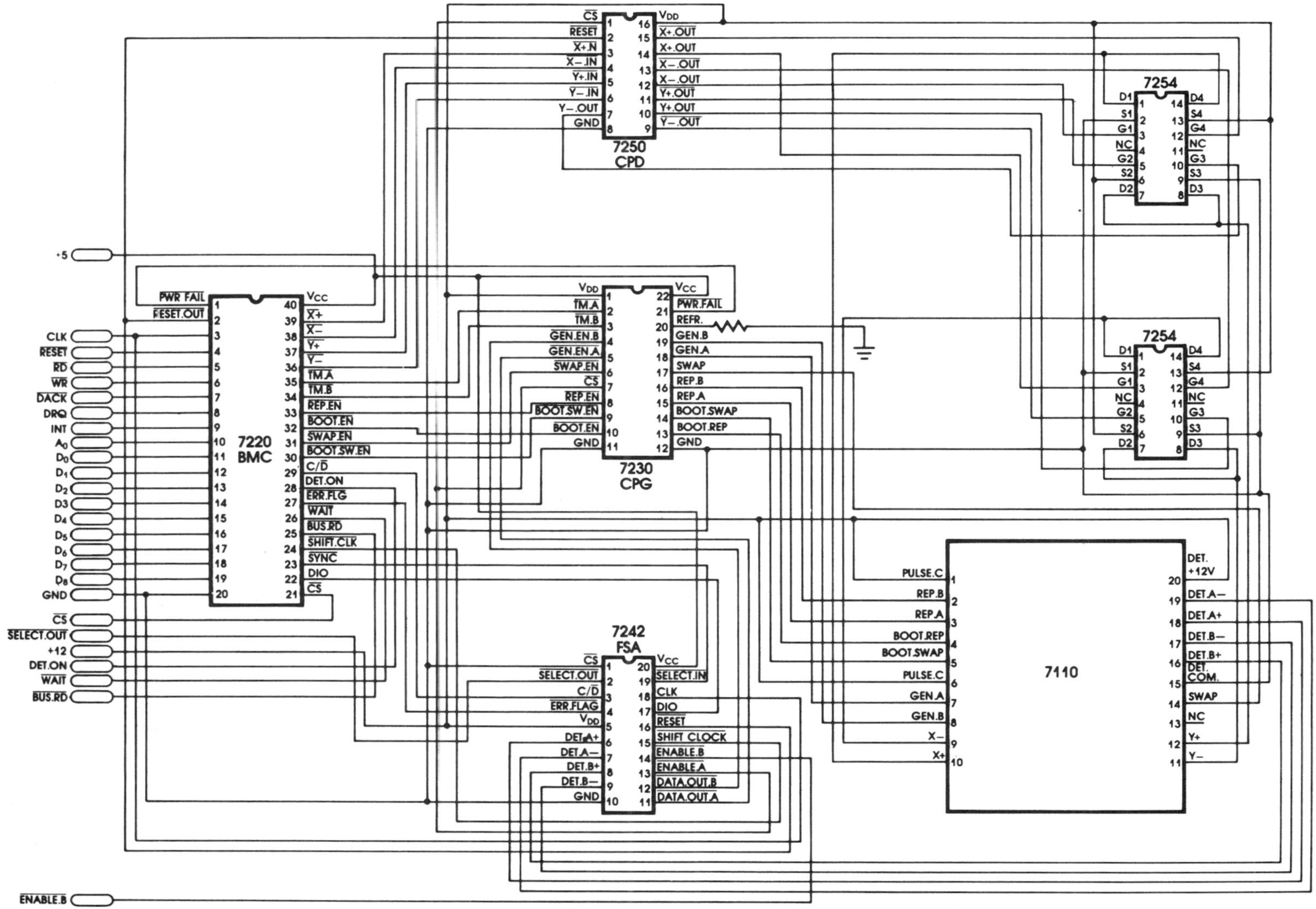

Fig. 10.21 7110 MBM system (Intel Corp.).

sequencer inside the 7220 controller. These signals are output to the 7230 current pulse generator. Here they enable current sources that produce the appropriate value current pulses to initiate the operations within the 7110 MBM.

The 7230 also contains power-fail circuitry. If a power failure occurs, the current pulse generator switches $\overline{PWR.FAIL}$ to logic 0. This signal is input to the 7220 controller, where it initiates an orderly power-down sequence. The controller waits until the MBM is in the stop position and then sets $\overline{RESET.OUT}$ to logic 0. This signal tells the coil predriver to shut off its coil drive outputs. As long as the supply voltage is maintained for 100 μs after the power-failure condition is sensed, the shutdown will be correctly completed and the integrity of data retained.

The X and Y field coils of the 7110 MBM require high-value triangular-shaped currents. It is the magnetic fields produced by these coils that cause movement of the bubbles within the MBM. These drive currents are produced by the 7250 coil predrivers and 7254 quad VMOS FET drive transistors.

ASSIGNMENTS

Section 10.2

1. What is used to represent the 0 or 1 logic level in a MBM?
2. Give two basic types of applications for MBM.

Section 10.3

3. Describe the function of the bubble memory chip, orthogonal coils, permanent magnets, and magnetic shield assembly.

Section 10.4

4. What is the data input/output configuration of the MBM?
5. What is meant by "redundant loops"?
6. What term is used to refer to the unit of data input or output from a MBM?
7. Define the following MBM operations: generation, transfer in, transfer out, replication, annihilation, and detection.

Section 10.5

8. Describe the read cycle of the major/minor loop MBM.
9. Describe the write cycle of the major/minor loop MBM.

Section 10.6

10. How does the block replicate architecture differ from the major/minor loop architecture?
11. Describe the write cycle of a block replicate MBM.
12. Describe the read cycle of the block replicate MBM.

Section 10.7

13. What is the usable data storage capacity of the TIB0203?
14. What is the data page length of the TIB0203?
15. What type of architecture is used in the TIB0203?
16. What are the ratings of the TIB0203 for external magnetic fields and temperature?
17. What type of architecture is employed in the TIB1000?
18. How much data storage capacity is available in each of the following devices: TIB-1000, TIB0500, and TIB0250?
19. What are the average access time and maximum access time of the TIB1000?
20. What is the total usable storage capacity of the 7110 MBM?
21. What are the average read/write access time and average data rate of the 7110?
22. What is the total usable storage capacity of the RBM256?

Section 10.8

23. What are the key elements of the TIB0203 MBM system?
24. How high can the storage capacity of the TIB0203 system be expanded?
25. Describe how a page of data is written from the TMS 9900 CPU into the FIFO within the controller of the TIB0203 MBM.
26. Describe how a page of data held in the controller of the TIB0203 system is written into the MBM device.
27. What are the primary functions of the function timing generator part of the TIB0203 MBM system?
28. What is the primary function of the coil drivers and diode bridges in the TIB0203 MBM system?
29. What is the primary function of the function driver in the TIB0203 MBM system?
30. What is the primary function of the sense amplifier in the TIB0203 MBM system?

BIBLIOGRAPHY

Advanced Micro Devices, *Data Book*. Sunnyvale, CA: Advanced Micro Devices, 1974.

Alfke, Peter and Ib Larsen, eds., *The TTL Applications Handbook*. Mountain View, CA: Fairchild Camera and Instrument Corp., August 1973.

Bobeck, Andrew H., and H. E. D. Scovil, "Magnetic Bubbles," *Scientific American*, June 1971, pp. 78-90.

Boyce, Jefferson C., *Digital Logic and Switching Circuits: Operation and Analysis*. Englewood Cliffs, NJ: Prentice-Hall, Inc., 1975.

Bryson, Don, Dick Clover, and Dave Lee, "Megabit Bubble—Memory Chip Gets Support from LSI Family," *Electronics*, April 26, 1979 (Intel Magnetics, AR-92).

Davies, John E., "The 7110, A One Megabit Magnetic Bubble Memory," Intel Magnetics RR-22. Santa Clara, CA: Intel Corp., September 1979.

Deem, Bill R., Kenneth Muchow, and Anthony Zeppa, *Digital Computer Circuits and Concepts*, 3rd ed. Reston, VA: Reston Publishing Co., Inc., 1980.

EDN Staff Report, "Memory Devices," *EDN*, May 5, 1979.

Eimbinder, Jerry, ed., *Semiconductor Memories*. New York: John Wiley & Sons, Inc. (A Wiley-Interscience Publication) 1971.

Eugent, Bruce, and Stuart Rasenberg, "HMOS Reliability", Intel RR-18. Santa Clara, CA: Intel Corp., May 1978.

Fairchild Camera and Instrument Corp., *TTL Data Book*. Mountain View, CA: Fairchild Camera and Instrument Corp., 1978.

Fairchild Semiconductor, Inc., *MOS/CCD Data Book, 1975*. Mountain View, CA: Fairchild Camera and Instrument Corp., 1975.

Farrer, Doug, "Understanding the FIFO," APP-332. Mountain View, CA: Fairchild Camera and Instrument Corp., 1975.

Geusic, Joseph E., "Magnetic Bubble Devices: Moving from Lab to Factory," *Bell Laboratories Record*, Western Electric and Bell Labs [date not known].

Heuner, R., J. Litus, Jr., and A. Havasy, "COS/MOS MSI Counter and Register Design and Applications," ICAN-6166. Somerville, NJ: RCA Solid State Division, June 1978.

Hnatek, Eugene R., *User's Handbook of Semiconductor Memories.* New York: John Wiley & Sons, Inc. (A Wiley—Interscience Publication), 1977.

Howe, M. J., and D. V. Morgan, eds., *Charge Coupled Devices and Systems.* New York: John Wiley & Sons, Inc., 1979.

Intel Corp., *2141, 4096 × 1 Bit Static RAM.* Santa Clara, CA: Intel Corp., August 1978.

Intel Corp., *M2147, 4096 × 1 Bit Static RAM.* Santa Clara, CA: Intel Corp., August 1978.

Intel Corp., *Data Catalog 1977.* Santa Clara, CA: Intel Corp., 1979.

Intel Corp., *Memory Handbook.* Santa Clara, CA: Intel Corp., 1977, 1978.

Intel Magnetics, Inc., *Bubble Memory Design Handbook, One Megabit.* Santa Clara, CA: Intel Corp., 1979.

Intel Magnetics, "A Total System Solution to Magnetic Bubble Memory Applications," *Preview Magazine,* July/August 1979. Santa Clara, CA: Intel Corp., 1979.

Luecke, Gerald, Jack P. Mize, and William N. Carr, *Semiconductor Memory Design and Application,* Texas Instruments Electronics Series. New York: McGraw-Hill Book Company, 1973.

Malvino, Albert P., and Donald Leach, *Digital Principles and Applications,* 2nd ed. New York: McGraw-Hill Book Company, 1975.

Mostek Corp., *1979 Memory Data Book and Designers Guide.* Carrollton, TX; Mostek Corp., August 1979.

Motorola Semiconductor Products, Inc., *Semiconductor Data Library, MOS Memories,* Vol. 7, Series A. Austin, TX: Motorola, Inc., 1975.

National Semiconductor Corp., *Memory Data Book.* Santa Clara, CA: National Semiconductor Corp., January 1976.

Prioste, Jerry E., "Replacing Sequential Logic with ROMs," AN-722. Austin, TX: Motorola, Inc., 1974.

RCA Solid State Division, *COS/MOS Integrated Circuits.* Somerville, NJ: RCA Corp., 1978.

Rockwell International Corp., Bubble Memory Products Data Sheet, "256K- Bit Bubble Memory Device" Document No. D-RBM256, Rev. 1. Anaheim, CA: Rockwell International Corp., Microelectronics Devices Division, February 1979.

Signetics Corp., *Bipolar and MOS Memory Data Manual.* Sunnyvale, CA: Signetics Corp., June 1977.

Signetics Corp., *ECL 10000.* Sunnyvale, CA: Signetics Corp., August 1979.

Signetics Corp., *Field Programmable Logic Arrays—An Applications Manual.* Sunnyvale, CA: Signetics Corp., July 1978.

Signetics Corp., *Logic—TTL—Specification Military Summary Data Manual.* Sunnyvale, CA: Signetics Corp., May 1978.

Signetics Corp., "10155 Content Addressable Memory (CAM)," *Note,* AN-004. Sunnyvale, CA: Signetics Corp., March 1979.

Texas Instruments, Incorporated, *The Bipolar Microcomputer Components Data Book for Design Engineers,* 2nd ed. Dallas, TX: Texas Instruments, Incorporated, 1979.

Texas Instruments, Incorporated, *The MOS Memory Data Book for Design Engineers.* Dallas, TX: Texas Instruments, Incorporated, 1980.

Texas Instruments, Incorporated, *The Semiconductor Memory Data Book for Design Engineers.* Dallas, TX: Texas Instruments, Incorporated, 1975.

Texas Instruments Incorporated, "A Texas Instruments Application Report—32K EPROM Decision TMS2532 or Intel 2732?" Dallas, TX: Texas Instruments Incorporated, August 1979.

Texas Instruments, Incorporated, *TIB0203 Magnetic Bubble Memory and Associated Circuits.* Dallas, TX: Texas Instruments, Incorporated, 1978.

Texas Instruments, Incorporated, *TIB0203 Magnetic Bubble Memory System Application Manual.* Dallas, TX: Texas Instruments, Incorporated, March 1979.

Texas Instruments, Incorporated, *The TTL Data Book for Design Engineers*, 2nd ed. Dallas, TX: Texas Instruments, Incorporated, 1976.

Texas Instruments Incorporated, *User's Manual TBB5005 and TBB5010 Bubble Memory Systems from Texas Instruments.* Dallas, TX: Texas Instruments, Incorporated, 1980.

Triebel, Walter A., *Integrated Digital Electronics.* Englewood Cliffs, NJ: Prentice-Hall, Inc., 1979.

Young, Sam, "64K RAM with Single Supply Could be the Standard for Future Design," *Electronic Design 13*, June 21, 1979.

ANSWERS TO SELECTED ODD-NUMBERED PROBLEMS

CHAPTER 1

Section 1.2 1. Input of data, processing of data, and storage or output of results. 3. Integrated circuit.

Section 1.3 7. Input unit, central processing unit, memory unit, and output unit. 9. Input unit.

Section 1.4 13. Read-only memory, random access read/write memory, and shift register. 15. Smaller size, higher operating speed, and lower power requirement.

Section 1.5 17. Density, speed, power consumption, cost, noise immunity, and reliability. 19. Standard TTL and Schottky TTL.

Section 1.6 25. Magnetic domain called a bubble.

Section 1.7 27. High-speed operation.

CHAPTER 2

Section 2.2 3. $11111111_2 = FF_{16}$. 5. 16,384 (16*k*) bits. 7. $D_3D_2D_1D_0 = 0001$, $A_3A_2A_1A_0 = 2_{16}$, and $D_3D_2D_1D_0 = 1_{16}$.

Section 2.3 9. $B_3B_2B_1B_0 = 1000$. 13. C_3.

Section 2.4 15. Nonvolatile.

Section 2.5 17. Access time (t_{ACC}) indicates the amount of time that elapses between the instant the address is applied at the inputs of the ROM and the moment that valid data are available at the output; chip select time (t_S) represents the amount of time that elapses before data appear at the outputs if the ROM is already addressed and then the chip select input is switched to enable the output; and chip deselect time (t_D) gives the time that elapses before the outputs of an addressed ROM turn OFF after the *CS* lead is disabled.

Section 2.6 19. The 74S271 is organized into 32 rows by 64 columns instead of 32 rows by 32 columns, to give a total bit capacity of 2048 bits.

Section 2.7 25. The fuse link process is the most popular method for programming bipolar PROMs. A Nichrome or other type of fuse link is built into each cell in the memory array. In an unprogrammed device, all links are in place. During programming, the data pattern is set up by electrically injecting a current through those fuses that are to be opened.

Section 2.8 27. 1024 bits, 256 4-bit words, tungsten-titanium fuse links, and t_{ACC} = 42 ns.

Section 2.9 31. The FAMOS cells of the EPROM are discharged by exposing the device to ultraviolet light.

Section 2.10 35. The 1702AL operates in a low-power dynamic mode by pulsing its V_{GG} power supply.

CHAPTER 3

Section 3.2 3. Binary to XS-3.

Section 3.3 5.

$A_3A_2A_1A_0$	$D_3D_2D_1D_0$
0 0 0 0	0 0 1 1
0 0 1 1	0 1 0 0
0 1 0 0	0 1 0 1
0 1 0 1	0 1 1 0
0 1 1 0	0 1 1 1
0 1 1 1	1 0 0 0
1 0 0 0	1 0 0 1
1 0 0 1	1 0 1 0
1 0 1 0	1 0 1 1
1 0 1 1	1 1 0 0
1 1 0 0	0 0 0 0

Section 3.4 7. In a microcomputer system, ROM is used to store the instructions of the program that controls overall system operation.

Section 3.5 9.

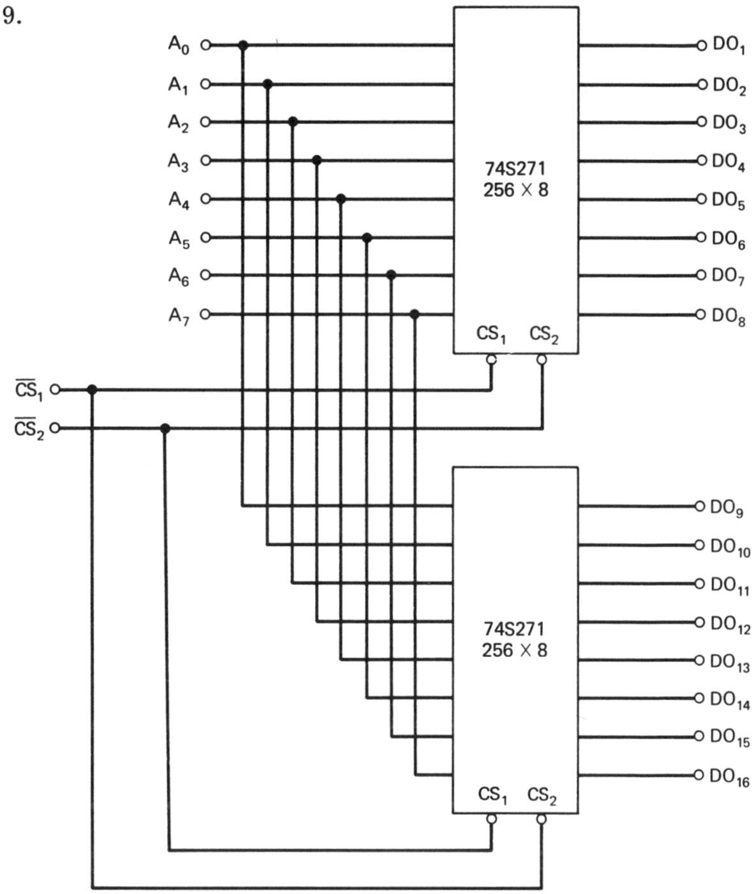

Section 3.6 13. $A_7A_6A_5A_4A_3A_2A_1$=1011010, $B_1B_2B_3B_4B_5B_6B_7B_8$=0.11000111, and $\theta = 35°$.

Section 3.7 17. $b_7b_5b_4b_3b_2b_1$=000100 and $BA8421$=101011.

Section 3.8 19. $b_6b_5b_4b_3b_2b_1L_2L_1L_0=300_8=011000000_2$ through $b_6b_5b_4b_3b_2b_1$ $L_2L_1L_0=307_8=011000111_2$.

CHAPTER 4

Section 4.2 3. Static and dynamic. 5. The RAM block diagram differs from that of the ROM in that it has data input leads DI_0 through DI_3 and a read/write control $R/\overline{W}$.

Section 4.3 7. Address buffer, row decoder, memory array, column decoder, write and sense amplifiers, control buffer, data input buffer, and data output buffer. 9. $\overline{R}_0$=1, $\overline{R}_1$=1, $\overline{R}_2$=1, and $\overline{R}_3$=0. 11. C_2 .

Section 4.4 13. Cell 3.

Section 4.5 15. 64 bits and 16 words by 4 bits. 17. 74S289.

Section 4.6 21. Capacitor. 23. Refreshing.

Section 4.7 27. 2 ms. 29. 64*k* and 65,536 1-bit words.

Section 4.8 31.

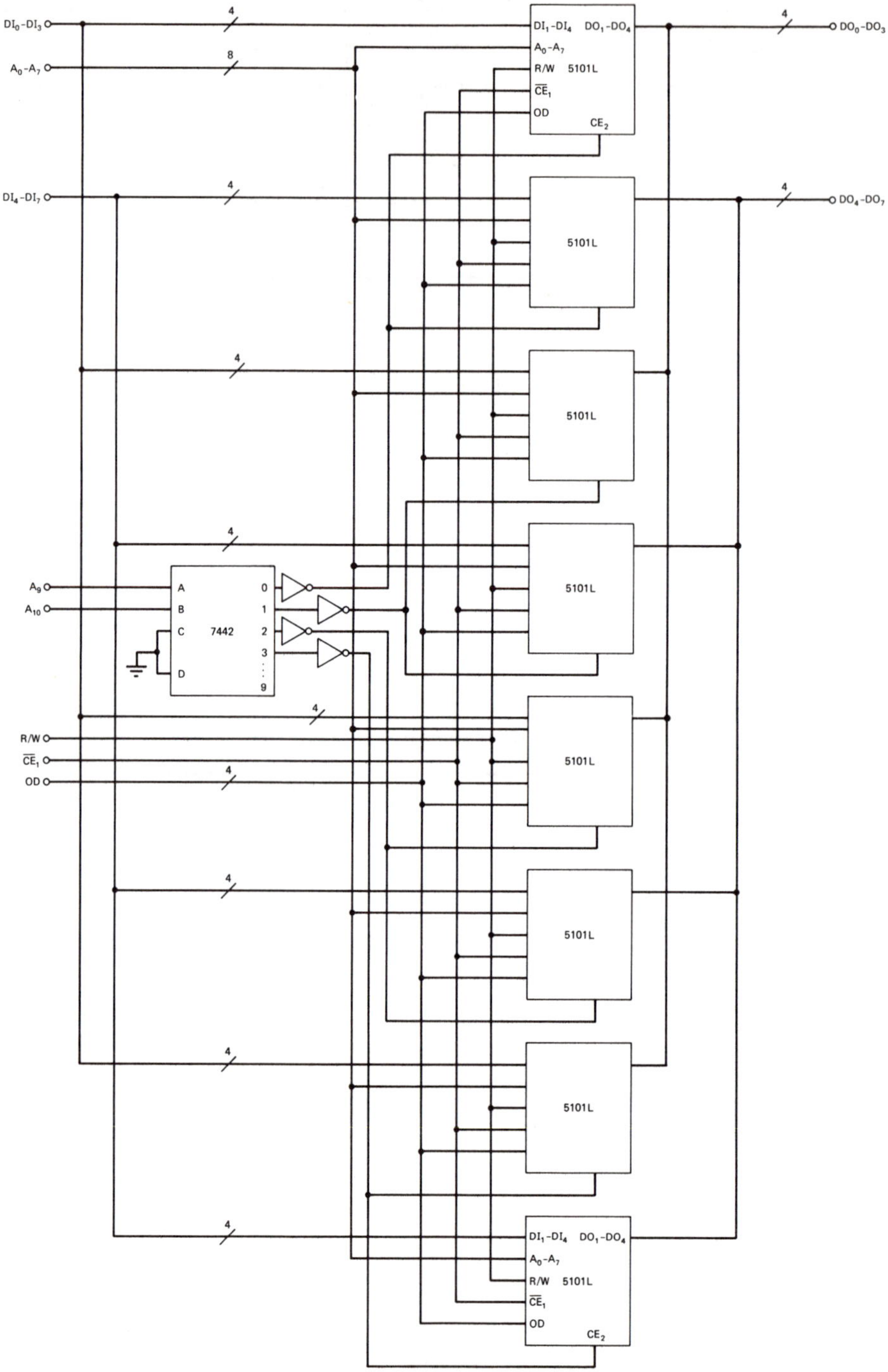

Section 4.9 33. 8*k* bytes.

CHAPTER 5

Section 5.2 3. On the 0-to-1 edge of the clock pulse, the inputs to the master flip-flop are $S_1=1$ and $R_1=0$. The 1 at *CLK* makes the common input on gates 3 and 4 logic 1. Therefore, the output of gate 3 switches to logic 0 and the output of gate 4 stays at logic 1. This input to the master set-reset flip-flop causes its output to set, giving $Q_1=1$ and $\overline{Q}_1=0$. As the 1-to-0 edge of the clock pulse occurs, the control gates of the slave flip-flop are enabled. The output of gate 7 switches to logic 0 and the output of gate 8 to logic 1. The slave outputs now set to $Q_2=1$ and $\overline{Q}_2=0$.

Section 5.3 7. The 9328 is a faster-operating device than the 7491.

Characteristic	9328	7491
t_p	35 ns	40 ns
t_s	20 ns	25 ns
f_{MAX}	20 MHz	10 MHz

Section 5.4 9.

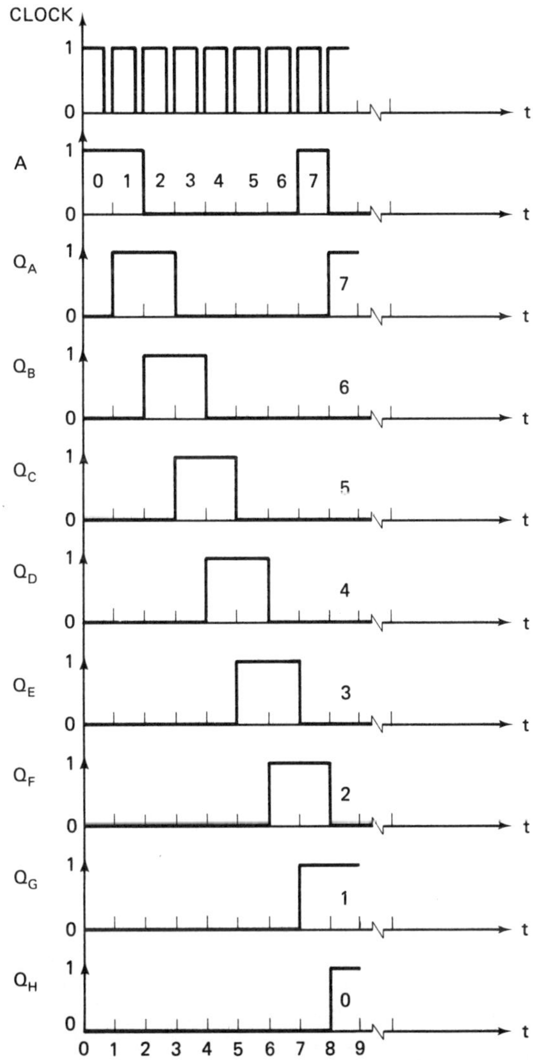

Section 5.5 11.

$$DCBA = 1101$$

$$f = 100 \text{ kHz}$$

$$T = \frac{1}{100 \text{ kHz}} = 10\ \mu s$$

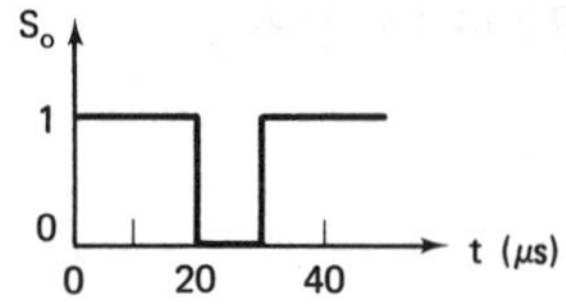

Section 5.6 15.

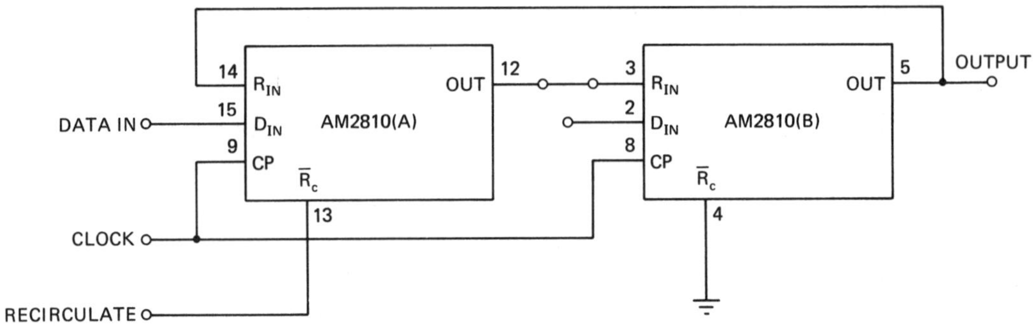

Section 5.7 17. $D_OC_OB_OA_O$=0111, $D_OC_OB_OA_O$=0011, and $D_OC_OB_OA_O$=0001.

Section 5.8 19.

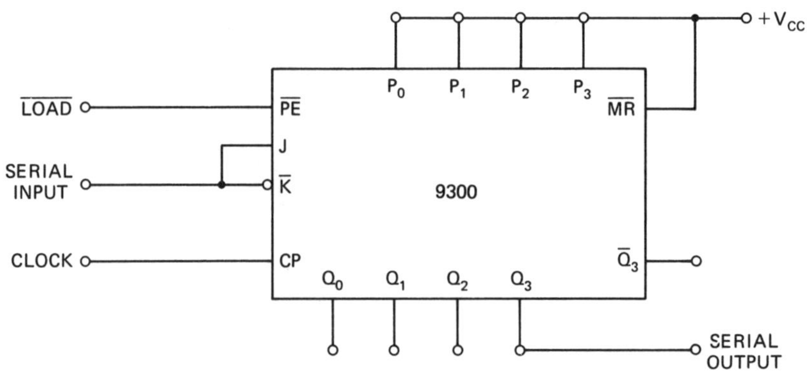

Section 5.9 21. Data are stored in a dynamic shift register as charge on capacitive nodes instead of as voltage levels in flip-flops. For this reason, they cannot be dc-operated like static devices. The data must be refreshed by continuously recirculating them through the register.

Section 5.10 23. Read operation and upper most pair of registers.

CHAPTER 6

Section 6.2 1. PLAs have more inputs, faster access time, and different internal architecture. 3. Nonvolatile.

Section 6.3 7. $P_0=P_1=P_2=P_3=0$. 9. $S_3=P_1+P_2=I_3\,I_2\,\overline{I}_1\,\overline{I}_0+I_2\,I_1\,I_0$, $I_3I_2I_1I_0=1100$, $I_3I_2I_1I_0=0111$, and $I_3I_2I_1I_0=1111$.

Section 6.5 11. $F_1=I_3\overline{I}_2\overline{I}_1\overline{I}_0+I_3I_2I_1I_0$.

Section 6.6 13. 16 inputs, 8 outputs, and 48 product terms. 15. 82S201.

Section 6.7 17.

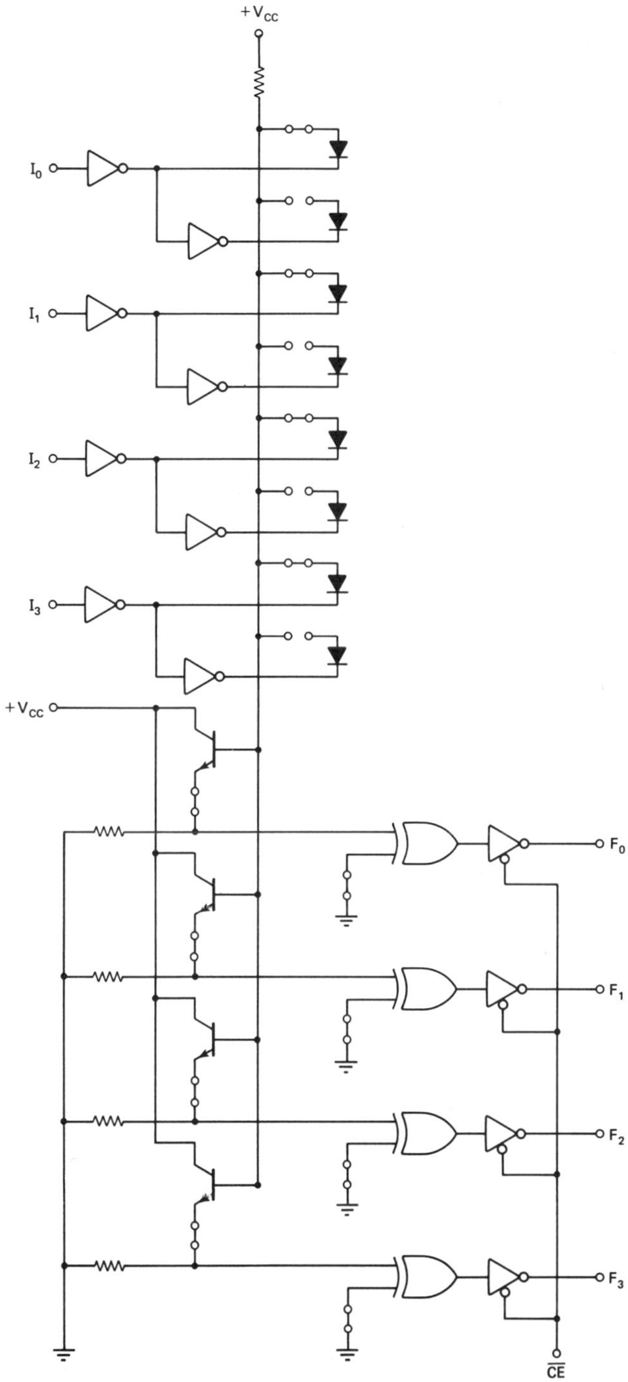

Section 6.8 19. PLA 10 and the word at address 0000_{16}.

CHAPTER 7

Section 7.2 3. Number of words that can be stored in its stack and their word length.

Section 7.3 7. The input buffer produces the set and reset input for the first stage of the information register array. When the *SI* input of the FIFO is clocked, the control register supplies a pulse to the T_0 input of the information register array. This causes the input data word to be loaded into the first register stage. The word appears at the Q and $\overline{Q}$ outputs of the flip-flops, where they are input to the set and reset inputs, respectively, of the second register stage. The control register automatically produces a pulse at T_1 and the word is loaded into the second stage. It is now held in both stages. After this, the control register produces pulses at T_2 and T_3, causing the word to shift through stages 3 and 4. The word is now held in all stages of the information register array.

Section 7.4 9. Initially, *IR* is logic 1, signaling that the FIFO is ready to accept write data at its inputs. On the 0-to-1 transition of *SI*, the word $A_3A_2A_1A_0$ is loaded into the input stage of the information register. The first flip-flop stage of the control register is set to logic 1, indicating a valid data word. *IR* switches from logic 1 to 0, signaling that the FIFO is busy. On the 1-to-0 transition of *SI*, the control register shifts the word into the second stage of the information register array. After this happens, the first flip-flop stage of the control register is reset. This causes *IR* to return to logic 1, indicating that the input stage is empty. The word propagates through the information register array until it reaches the output stage. Now the control register stage remains set and *OR* switches to logic 1 to indicate that the word is available to be read out.

A read operation is performed by the circuitry at the output of the FIFO. Then the *SO* input is pulsed to bring the next word to the output stage. However, in this case, the rest of the stages in the FIFO are empty. Therefore, the flip-flop in the output stage of the control register is reset to 0. *OR* switches to logic 0, indicating that valid data are not available at the output and the FIFO waits for new data to be written in.

Section 7.5 11.

Device	Word length	Word capacity
3351-1	9 bits	40 words
AM3341	4 bits	64 words
CD40105B	4 bits	16 words

Section 7.6 13.

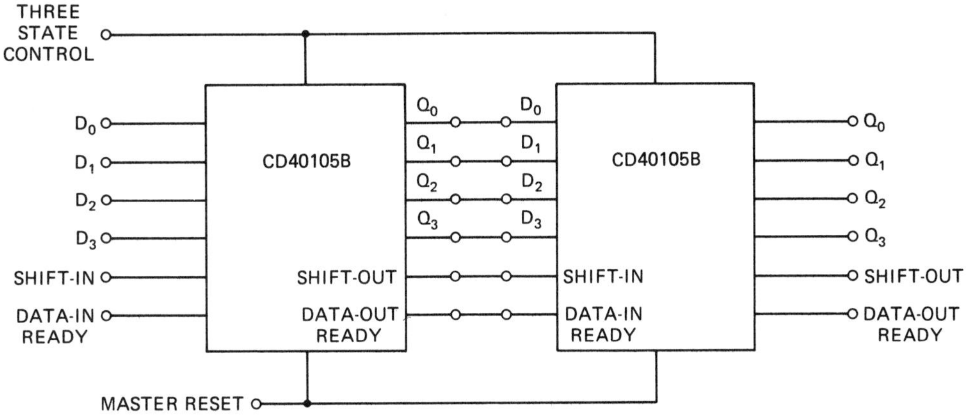

Section 7.7 15. $D_6D_5D_4D_3D_2D_1D_0$=1110001.

CHAPTER 8

Section 8.2 3. D_1D_0=00. 5. $Y_7Y_6Y_5Y_4Y_3Y_2Y_1Y_0$=10111011.

Section 8.4 7. Input I_0=1 is associated with the corresponding bit in all cells. If the 1 matches the content of any cell, the corresponding Y output switches to logic 0. The 0 on the Y line causes I_1=1 to be written into the flip-flop of the other half of the cell.

Section 8.5 9. Association.

CHAPTER 9

Section 9.2 1. Capacitor. 3. Serial-accessed.

Section 9.3 7. L_0=0, L_1=0, L_2=0, and L_3=1. 9.

B_7	B_6	B_5	B_4
B_3	B_2	B_1	B_0
B_{15}	B_{14}	B_{13}	B_{12}
B_{11}	B_{10}	B_9	B_8

Section 9.4 11. 16 blocks, each organized as 64 parallel 64-bit channels.

Section 9.5 13. Write mode, CCD 3, and block 0.

Section 9.6 15. The read cycle begins with the CPU putting an 18-bit address on the address bus. This address is latched for application to the CCD memory system. Bits A_{17} and A_{18} are input to a decoder circuit and when this circuit is enabled, its output selects one of the groups of CCDs in the memory array for operation. Bits A_{15} through A_{12} of the word are applied to all four CCDs in parallel and define the block location. The remaining bits A_{11} through A_0 are input to an address compare circuit. These bits define the starting location of the block of data to be read out. The clock generator is continuously producing pulses and its outputs are *CLK*, ϕ_1, ϕ_2, ϕ_{T1}, and ϕ_{T2}. The ϕ signals cause the data to circulate through the channels of all CCDs. At the same time, *CLK* increments the index counter. Its count, C_0 through C_{11}, identifies the storage location within the serial-parallel-serial blocks. When this count is the same as the address A_0 through A_{11}, the memory-cycle initiate signal *IMC* is output by the compare circuit. In response, the data-cycle generate circuit enables the decoder circuit output ($CS_3 CS_2 CS_1 CS_0$), read operation ($\overline{WE}$), and signals the CPU that data are ready (*DATA READY*). Data are read out of the CCD and carried to the CPU over the *DATA IN* line.

CHAPTER 10

Section 10.2 1. Magnetic domain called a bubble.

Section 10.3 3. A bubble memory chip contains the pattern of magnetic paths and control elements required for input, storage, and output of data. The orthogonal coils produce the rotating magnetic fields that cause the bubbles to propagate through the chevron paths of the bubble chip. Permanent magnets are provided to produce the static magnetic field required to keep the bubbles in a stable state. The magnetic shield protects the bubble memory chip from stray magnetic fields that could affect stored data or operation.

Section 10.4 5. Extra loops that are permitted to be defective during manufacturing. They are provided to improve production yield and cannot be used for storage of data.

Section 10.5 9. As the page in the minor loops that is to be written to comes into place by the transfer gates to the major loop, a transfer out operation is performed. The page is passed through the gates into the major loop. After this, the page is circulated toward the replicator/annihilator element. At the replicator/annihilator, the bubbles are transferred into the output track, where they are destroyed. A new page of data is generated in the major loop and circulated toward the entry point to the minor loops. When in place and the correct minor loop position is located adjacent to the major loops, a transfer in operation is performed to enter data into the minor loops.

Section 10.6 11. The write cycle begins with the generation of a page of data in the input track. The page is then shifted through the input track until it is positioned by the minor loops. As the page location of the minor loops where the word is to be stored comes into place, the swap gates are activated and the old page is passed into the input track while the new page is passed into the minor loops. After this, the old page is shifted to the guard rail, where it is destroyed.

Section 10.7 15. Major/minor loop architecture. 17. Block replicate architecture. 19. Average access time = 11.2 ms; maximum access time = 21.5 ms.

Section 10.8 23. Controller, function timing generator, function driver, coil driver, and sense amplifier. 27. Generate coil drive signals, start and stop the coil drive clocks, sense power failures and control power down, and develop the precisely timed function signals required during read and write operations.

INDEX

INDEX

D

E

F

G

H

I

K

L

M

N

O

P

Q

R

S